DIESEL EQUIPMENT I
Lubrication, Hydraulics, Brakes, Wheels, Tires

ERICH J. SCHULZ

Former Director of Training Programs
Pacific Vocational Institute, Burnaby Campus
Burnaby, British Columbia

Gregg Division
McGraw-Hill Book Company
New York • Atlanta • Dallas • St. Louis • San Francisco • Auckland
Bogotá • Guatemala • Hamburg • Johannesburg • Lisbon • London
Madrid • Mexico • Montreal • New Delhi • Panama • Paris • San Juan
São Paulo • Singapore • Sydney • Tokyo • Toronto

Library of Congress Cataloging in Publication Data

Schulz, Erich J
  Diesel equipment.

  Includes index.
    CONTENTS: v. 1. Lubrication, hydraulics, brakes,
  wheels, tires.—v. 2. Design, electronic controls,
  frames, suspensions, steering, transmissions, drive
  lines, air conditioning.
    1. Motor vehicles. 2. Construction equipment.
  I. Title.
  TL145.S33   629.2'25   80-15383
  ISBN 0-07-055716-0 (v. 1)
  ISBN 0-07-055708-x (v. 2)

DIESEL EQUIPMENT I: Lubrication, Hydraulics, Brakes,
Wheels, Tires

1 2 3 4 5 6 7 8 9 0   SMSM   8 9 8 7 6 5 4 3 2 1

Editors: D. Eugene Gilmore, Paul Berk
Design Supervisor: Nancy Axelrod
Production Supervisor: Priscilla Taguer
Art Supervisor: George T. Resch

Manuscript Editor: Galen Fleck
Cover Designer: Infield D'Astolfo Associates
Technical Studio: Burmar Technical Corp.

ISBN 0-07-055716-0

Contents

Foreword

Today's changing economy and technology require improved efficiency, additional power, and extended service life in modern on- and off-highway equipment. Because the supply of suitably trained diesel technicians has not kept pace with the demand, more must be trained, and the skills of those already trained must be upgraded. Experienced technicians often have difficulty coping with the technological advancements in their field, because innovations occur so rapidly and new material becomes available in such huge quantities that there is not enough time to properly assimilate it before having to use it.

There has long been a need for a comprehensive approach to the organization of information used in the diagnosis, maintenance, and repair of today's on- and off-highway diesel equipment. This material must also be in a form that both novice and experienced technician will find useful.

The author has written these textbooks with this goal in mind. His many years of experience as a diesel technician, instructor, and author in the area of diesel mechanics and the related fields of on- and off-highway equipment are evident in his systematic approach. His extensive training experience is evident to the users of the workbooks and instructor's guides that accompany the text. His experience has provided him with the background necessary to write a textbook whose philosophy keeps the student foremost while presenting the realities of work in the industry and stressing the instructor's role in the learning process. These texts, along with the author's previous book, *Diesel Mechanics*, fill a vacuum that existed for materials for use in training diesel service technicians.

Thomas L. Lownie
Campus Principal
Burnaby Campus
Pacific Vocational Institute

Preface

Mechanical engineering technology has greatly advanced since the appearance of the first engine-powered motor vehicle and track machine. This progress is particularly apparent when we look at modern motor buses, on-highway motortrucks, truck-tractor trailers, huge off-highway motortrucks, and modern farm and industrial tractors. This equipment has become significantly more efficient, rugged, and customized to its end use. But at the same time it has become so sophisticated that 4.5 million mechanics are employed to keep diesel equipment operating. Moreover, as production continues and new technology makes more equipment obsolete each year, a shortage of trained mechanics is developing. Fifty thousand more mechanics are needed now, and the projected figures for 1990 call for 100,000 more.

Industrial consumers expect a motortruck, truck-tractor, or motor bus to travel at least 300,000 miles [482,700 kilometers] before requiring a major overhaul. Users of off-highway motor vehicles expect the equipment to operate at least 10,000 hours before a major overhaul is necessary. Although these expectations are usually met, improved work performance and durability cannot be credited to a single component, part, or system; it is the combined improvement of all these areas that has resulted in the overall technological success of modern on- and off-highway equipment. Nevertheless, if one area were to be seen as improving the productivity and handling performance of the equipment, it would be the various hydraulic systems. Power plants, transmissions, tires, and tracks have progressed almost simultaneously to improve performance and to decrease fuel consumption, thereby helping to lower operating costs.

Extending the service life of on- and off-highway equipment does not rest entirely with improved engineering design. Credit must also be extended to those responsible for maintaining and servicing the equipment. While it is true that vast sums of money have been spent and will continue to be spent on research to develop equipment that will meet the constantly increasing demands placed upon it, the problem of getting good mechanics, that is, those trained to the degree of competence required to service this sophisticated equipment, must also be solved.

It is the objective of Diesel Equipment I and II to help solve this problem by expanding the knowledge of all student mechanics so that they will eventually be able to diagnose, repair, and service much of today's on- and off-highway equipment.

Each of these textbooks can be used by the novice or the experienced mechanic, since each unit comprehensively covers the design and purpose of a particular system and its components and concludes with troubleshooting and servicing.

With the exception of the unit entitled "Shop Safety," which is in both textbooks, the units are not repeated. Diesel Equipment I covers lubrication, seals, gaskets, filters, bearings, hydraulics, tires, wheel hubs, and the various brake systems. Diesel Equipment II covers electricity and electronics, on- and off-highway equipment design, frames and suspensions, steering systems, track-type undercarriages, final drives and steering mechanisms, mechanical clutches, standard transmissions, fluid couplings, torque converters, drive lines, front and rear carriers, winches, wire ropes, and air-conditioning and refrigeration.

The time needed to cover both of these books would be about 30 weeks, with about 40 percent classroom lecture and assignment time, and 60 percent "hands on" shop work projects. The student must first know how to use hand and power tools and measuring instruments and understand the fundamentals of electricity and electronics. It would be helpful, although not essential, to know something of the design, operation, and servicing of the power plant. However, the latter may be taught before or after completing the Diesel Equipment program.

The author's engine textbook, Diesel Mechanics, may be used along with its accompanying workbook and instructor's guide for instruction in the design, operation, and servicing of diesel engines.

Workbooks have been prepared to complement these texts. They contain questions directly related to the textbook contents and also suggest hands on assignments for shop practice. The textbooks and workbooks have been organized so that the instructor can begin with any unit and then select units thereafter according to the course outline.

Instructor's guides, which give answers to the workbook questions, are available.

Dual dimensioning has been used throughout Diesel Equipment I and II. Metric measurements are given in brackets following the U.S. Customary measurement, and metric conversion tables and a glossary are included at the back of the book.

It is hoped that through this program students will achieve sufficient knowledge and practical experience to make them employable in today's ever-growing diesel equipment field.

Erich J. Schulz

Acknowledgments

Many of the illustrations in this textbook were provided by the companies listed below. To these companies, I wish to express my thanks for their cooperation and generosity.

Bear Applied Power Inc.
Terex Division of General Motors Corporation
J I Case Company Agricultural Equipment
  Division
Caterpillar Tractor Co.
Mack Canada Inc.
Eaton Corporation
Cummins Engine Co. Inc.
Federal-Mogul, Worldwide Marketing Group
International Harvester Co.
Sperry Vickers Division of Sperry Inc.

WABCO, An American-Standard Company
The Weatherhead Co. of Canada Ltd.
Stratoflex Canada Ltd.
Fiat-Allis
Firestone Tire and Rubber Company of Canada,
  Limited
Motor Wheel Corporation—Goodyear
The Budd Company
Chrysler Corporation
Schrader Automotive Products Division Scovill
FMC Corporation

To my wife, I gratefully acknowledge the never ending hours when she placed her personal projects second in priority to the typing of this manuscript.
                                    Erich J. Schulz

Introduction

The Design and Purpose of On and Off-Highway Equipment

Diesel Equipment I and *II* were originally intended to be a single book. However, a single volume could not provide the space for a thorough study of the subject without being inconveniently large; nor could any of the subject matter be cast aside. For these reasons, the material has been published as two volumes and arranged so that the units are logically organized and not repeated. Each unit is complete in itself, so that the texts can be studied in whatever sequence is most suitable.

Diesel Equipment II contains units on electricity, electronics, electric circuit testing, frames, suspensions, steering, transmissions, drive lines, front and rear carriers, winches, air conditioning, and transport refrigeration. It also includes two units on the design and purpose of on- and off-highway equipment. Because it would be helpful for users of this first volume to be familiar with basic information on the design and purpose of on- and off-highway equipment, this brief introduction is included.

There are many on- and off-highway equipment manufacturers—some in competition with one another, some who manufacture specialized, unique equipment, and some who manufacture only parts and components but do not do the final assembly of the motor vehicle. This industrial equipment is designed to transport goods or perform mechanical work. Motor buses and recreational vehicles are included in this group. Diesel equipment is classified into two broad categories:

1. *On-highway equipment,* designed to transport either objects and property or groups of people. This equipment group includes motortrucks, truck-tractors and trailers, semitrailers, dumpers, and motorbuses and recreational vehicles. This is by far the largest group. It also is subject to the most innovation in design and size in order to improve efficiency and durability.

2. *Off-highway equipment,* used to perform work such as earthmoving, excavating, digging, pushing or towing, logging, and raising and lowering heavy objects. This equipment group includes tractors, cranes, loaders, backhoes, log-skidders, and manlifts.

All these machines have certain things in common. Each has a frame to which the suspension, axles, wheels, and body are fastened. Self-propelled equipment requires an engine, transmission, steering controls, and a driver or operator compartment.

These components are also fastened to the frame. The design of the motor vehicle is influenced by such factors as the conditions under which it will operate and its intended use. Accordingly, the horsepower will vary considerably and the engine may be either diesel or gasoline, whichever is most suitable. Engine manufacturers produce engines that range from 70 to 1400 horsepower [52 to 1044 kilowatts]. The manufacturers must design transmissions, drive lines, front and rear carriers, axles, wheels, and tires that can meet the same wide range of needs.

The following descriptions refer to on-highway vehicles:

- A *motortruck* is propelled by an engine or motor and carries the load weight over its own wheels.

These motor vehicles will be found in off-highway use as well.

- A *truck-tractor* is designed to pull a *semitrailer,* and at the same time carry part of the load and

weight of the semitrailer. The semitrailer has one or more dead axles, and its front end is connected to the truck-tractor through the fifth wheel.

- A *full trailer* is a vehicle which is pulled by another, but which has at least two axles that support the weight of the entire load.

- A *dumper* could be a motortruck, semitrailer, or full trailer, designed to dump its own load (which is carried within the body).

- *Motor buses* and *recreational vehicles* have bodies and interior designs that fulfill particular or unique requirements.

The overall length, height, width, and load-carrying capacity of on-highway motor vehicles are governed by law. Motor buses and recreational vehicles must meet as well the special safety laws that apply to vehicles that carry passengers.

Off-highway equipment includes those vehicles "designed to perform work." These are the workhorses of the roadbuilding, construction, and mining industries. There are no legal or theoretical limitations on the overall size or load-carrying capacity of this type of equipment, but in practice the tires determine the load limitations of these vehicles. This category includes:

- backhoes and excavators
- tractor scrapers
- shovels
- drag lines
- tractors
- motor graders
- cranes
- log loaders
- manlifts

A *backhoe* and an *excavator* are similar, except that the backhoe's excavating mechanism and its

frame are attached to the tractor or machine, whereas the excavator's mechanism and its frame form part of the tractor or machine. Both the backhoe and the excavator are classified by their digging depth and bucket capacity and not by their overall size or engine horsepower.

Tractor scrapers are designed to scoop up (load) dirt, gravel, or whatever, and to transport and unload

it. They are classified by (1) their load-carrying capacity, measured in yards or in cubic meters; (2) the method by which the bowl is loaded and unloaded; and (3) the mechanism by which the tractor scraper is steered.

A *shovel* used to be thought of as a mechanical excavator which had a fixed boom and a movable dipper stick, and a dipper (bucket) whose opening pointed forward. However, this classification now includes shovels that are designed to move the boom hydraulically. Shovels are classified by (1) the method by which the shovel operates (mechanically

or hydraulically); (2) the dipping reach; and (3) the bucket capacity.

A *drag line* is designed to scoop up terrain with its drag-line bucket, and to move and unload the bucket by using winches and wire ropes. When a clamshell is attached to the wire rope, it can be manipulated by the winch control to excavate and load. Drag lines may be powered by gasoline or diesel engines, or by electric motors. Engine power is usually between 70 and 250 horsepower [52 and 187 kilowatts]. Shovels and drag lines are classified according to: (1) reach, (2) digging capacity, (3) power supply, and (4) type of undercarriage to which they are attached, that is, to a motortruck or track-type carrier.

Tractors, both wheel- and track-type, make up the largest off-highway equipment group. A wheel-type tractor has rubber tires. A track-type tractor has

metal tracks that carry the weight and pull the tractor in a forward or reverse direction. Both types of tractors are used mainly for pulling and are generally found in farming and in the construction industries. They are classified by (1) their pulling power, (2) by the method of steering, and (3) by the number of drive axles.

Attached to the basic wheel- or track-type tractor may be a loader, dozer, or backhoe. The basic tractor can also be modified with special attachments fastened to its frame so that it may serve as a pipe layer, log skidder, log grapple, or roller.

- A *loader* is a tractor attachment used to load, transport, and unload material.
- A *dozer* is a tractor attachment used to push, dig, and level ground.
- A *pipe layer* is a tractor having an attachment that can transport, raise, and lower large cumbersome pipes.
- A *log skidder* is a tractor having an attachment that can raise the log end off the ground and then skid it from the felling site to the loading site.
- A *log grapple* serves the same purpose as the log skidder, however, it has an attachment like a jaw

clamp which holds one end of the log up off the ground during the skidding operation.

These last four types of tractors are classified by their performance ability rather than by their pulling or pushing power.

A motor grader is a modified wheel-type tractor with attachments fastened to its frame. These attachments are used for leveling ground, grading road surfaces, cutting ditches, and dressing and cutting embankments. Motor graders are classified according to their work performance and steering method.

A *crane* is a hoisting device which can move its load in a horizontal or lateral direction and may be

attached to a motortruck or carrier. There are two types of cranes: (1) those having a nontelescoping

boom, that is, the boom consists of individual sections bolted together to make up a desired fixed boom length and (2) cranes having telescoping booms. Telescoping booms have three major sections: two boom sections that can be hydraulically extended from or retracted into one main boom section in order to vary the overall boom length. Winches and wire ropes are used to raise and lower the load. Cranes are classified by their maximum boom length, maximum lifting power, type (telescoping or nontelescoping), and the type of carrier to which the crane is attached.

A *log loader* is designed for one purpose only—to move logs from one place to another. It may be operated hydraulically, or through winches and wire ropes.

Manlifts, regardless of classification, are designed to raise, to lower, and/or to move a worker horizontally into a work position. They are classified by (1) the method by which they move the worker into position, (2) by their lift height and reach, (3) and according to the type of tractor, motortruck, or carrier to which they are attached.

Unit 1
Shop Safety

Employers and employees alike know the meaning of the word "safety," and each has some concept of the responsibility it conveys. The most basic rule of safety can be summed up in three words—use common sense! A number of applications of this elementary rule are as follows:

- Never take chances or shortcuts.
- Always block the vehicle or equipment before removing a wheel or hydraulic cylinder.
- Carefully select the blocking material or tool to conform to the weight, size, and other specifications of the vehicle.
- Check the service manual for specifications, torque, etc. (do not guess).
- On completion of the job, recheck to make certain that you have not forgotten to tighten a cap screw, nut, fitting, etc., and that, when necessary, they have been secured with a cotter pin, lockwire, or lockplate.

Sometimes the urgency of a job causes you to consider dispensing with one or more safety rules, but stop and *think*—what profit is there in a few minutes when time is balanced against the life or limb of the operator, or your fellow worker, or perhaps yourself? And in financial terms a lawsuit could be filed against you and/or your employer if, for instance, a tire were incorrectly inflated or installed and the operator, as a result, were maimed in an accident.

To protect the worker, the federal government has enacted safety rules, but the onus is on the individual to practice good work habits even where governmental laws do not apply. Although today's workshops and equipment have built-in safety devices, their value is limited if tools are unclean, inflammables are left uncovered, and so forth. In the final analysis, it is up to each individual manufacturer, shop owner, service mechanic, operator, and worker to obey all safety rules, use common sense, and practice good work habits whether the job is complicated or simple. And finally, maintain your tools at peak efficiency and conform to the relevant service manual with regard to specifications and other recommendations. **NOTE** There are no such things as fail-safe tools, machines, vehicles, or equipment in the hands of the careless. Accidents do not happen, they are caused, primarily from unsafe working conditions or careless work habits, including negligence due to haste. See Fig. 1-1.

Safety Rules for the Mechanic
- Keep your mind on your work. If you daydream or allow your personal problems to divide your attention you become an easy mark for an accident.
- Keep fit, and do not continue to work when you are overtired.
- Do not wear an open jacket or shirt when coveralls should be worn. Either one could get caught in a machine or vehicle and cause injury to the wearer.
- Do not wear unclean coveralls. They should be free of oil, grease, or fuel to prevent skin irritation or severe burns if a spark should ignite them.
- Wear safety shoes and make certain they are in good condition.
- Do not wear any type of jewelry (not even a wedding ring). Neck jewelry can get caught in machinery, and rings can get hooked on a corner, ledge, bolt, etc.
- When working on electrical equipment, batteries, starters, etc., use a leather watch band rather than a metal one, but preferably remove the watch temporarily. For instance, in removing a cable connection, a metal watch band or jewelry could cause the connection to ground, resulting in severe skin burning or the loss of a hand or finger.
- Wear a hard hat when this is recommended. Failure to do so may result in a severe head injury or even cost your life.

An endless set of accident prevention rules would be required to cover servicing and operating the myriad of vehicles, machines, and equipment used in the on- and off-highway industry. The precautions you would take, for instance, to lift a tire manually from a light-duty truck would be considerably different from those to lift a tire of a 300-ton dump truck, a task that would require a 10-ton lifting device. Nevertheless a number of common precautions, warnings, and safety rules are listed that will prevent minor and/or major accidents and personal injury. See Fig. 1-2.

Fig. 1-1 Accidents do not happen; they are caused.

4

Fig. 1-2 Accidents do not pay. Ask the person who had one.

Safety Rules—Explosion and Fire Inflammable materials, when heated to their kindling temperature in the presence of oxygen, will ignite. However, these materials do not have the same atomic structure, and therefore their thresholds for ignition differ and the methods by which the fire can be extinguished differ correspondingly. Fires may be classified into three categories (A, B, and C). Fire extinguishers may be classified into six categories (Numbers 1 to 6). See Fig. 1-3.

Class A fires are those in which the combustible material is wood, fiber, paper, fabric, rubber, etc. Subdue these fires by cooling and quenching, using a fire hose or No. 1 to No. 3 fire extinguishers.

Class B fires are those in which the combustible material is a liquid, such as gasoline, fuel, or paint. Subdue these fires by smothering, using No. 2 to No. 6 fire extinguishers.

Class C fires are those in which the combustible materials are electrical components, such as motors, generators, or switch panels. Subdue these by smothering or by using No. 4 to No. 6 fire extinguishers, which have a nonconducting extinguisher agent.

You can prevent most explosions and fires from spreading by activating the fire alarm before attempting to extinguish the fire. It is therefore important that you do the following:

- Know where the fire alarm switches are located.
- Know where the different fire extinguishers are located.
- Know where the fire hoses are located.
- Know which type of fire extinguisher to use.
- Know how to operate the different types of fire extinguishers.
- Regularly check that all fire-fighting equipment is in operating condition and in its proper place and that the fire extinguishers are full.
- Keep all inflammable fluid and material in a safe container and whenever possible store them in a separate area.
- Keep your workshop clean and immediately discard all rubbish and combustibles. Dispose of oily rags as soon as you are finished with them by placing them in a covered steel container.
- Keep all solvent tanks tightly covered when they are not being used.

- Use solvent as a cleaning fluid; do not use gasoline or carbon tetrachloride.
- Make certain that all electrical equipment is properly connected and grounded.
- Avoid using an octopus connection when employing power tools, for this could overload the extension cable.
- Make certain that the lamp guard is in place when using an extension light. Lamp breakage near accumulated oil or fuel may cause a fire.
- Make certain that you have a fire extinguisher within reach when using a torch of any kind and always keep your attention on the flame.
- Never point the flame toward yourself or others and never rest a flaming torch on an object. Shut the torch off immediately after using it.
- Do not enter a room marked "No Smoking" with an open flame or even a smoldering cigarette.
- Do not flip a match or cigarette in any direction before you are certain it is extinguished. Do use an ashtray.
- Do not block fire doors with any object whatsoever.
- Do not approach a battery that is being charged with an open flame or lighted cigarette, since the charging gases are highly explosive.
- Do not connect the charger cables to the battery when the charger is switched on, or an explosion may result.
- Disconnect the battery ground cable first when removing batteries; when reconnecting the batteries, connect the ground cable last.
- Connect the ground cable of the booster battery to the engine and not to the vehicle battery when boost-starting an engine.
- Do not leave a soldering iron or heating device plugged in after you have finished with it. Left unattended, these devices could overheat and cause a fire.

Safety Rules—Starting and Stopping the Engine and Moving the Vehicle Many accidents occur when a mechanic is starting an engine or moving a vehicle into a shop area or into a safe working area, usually because the mechanic is not familiar with the machine or vehicle or is in a hurry and therefore neglects to follow basic safety rules (see Fig. 1-4).

Because of the endless variety of equipment, it is impractical to categorize every safety rule; however, some basic safety steps and dos and don'ts are listed here.

Before attempting to start an engine to move equipment to a work area, make certain that (1) no one is working on the machine; (2) no parts or components are removed or missing that would affect the operation of the engine or the brakes or the movement of the vehicle or the working attachments; (3) you know the nature of the intended service so that you do not start the engine or move the vehicle if this would cause further damage to the vehicle or to those nearby; (4) you familiarize yourself with the location of the instruments, brake control, steering system, the starting and stopping control of the engine, etc., and the operation and shift

	CAPACITY	PROTECT FROM FREEZING	EXTINGUISHING EFFECT	APPROXIMATE STREAM RANGE	METHOD OF DISCHARGE
1	**Soda-Acid**				
	2½ gal			45-55 ft	Chemically generated gas pressure
	20 gal	Yes	Cooling	65-75 ft	
	40 gal			65-75 ft	
	Clear Water, Pressurized Type				
	2½ gal	Yes	Cooling	40-45 ft	Stored air pressure
2	**Clear Water, Cartridge Type**				
	2½ gal	Yes	Cooling	40-45 ft	Gas pressure from carbon dioxide cartridge
	Antifreeze, Cartridge Type				
	2½ gal	No	Cooling	40-45 ft	Gas pressure from carbon dioxide cartridge
3	**Pump Tank (Antifreeze or Plain Water)**				
	2½ gal	Where clear water is used — Yes Antifreeze Solution — No	Cooling	45–50 ft	Hand pump action
	5 gal				
	Loaded Stream, Pressurized Type				
	2½ gal	No	Cooling	45-60 ft	Stored air pressure
	Foam				
	2½ gal			30-40 ft	Chemically generated gas pressure
	20 gal	Yes	Blanketing	55-65 ft	
	40 gal			55-65 ft	
4	**VL Pressurized Type**				
	1 qt			25-30 ft	Internally stored air pressure
	2 qt	No	Smothering	25-30 ft	
	1 gal			25-30 ft	
	VL Hand Pump Type				
	1 qt	No	Smothering	25-30 ft	Hand pump action
	1½ qt			25-30 ft	
	Dry Chemical				
	2½ lb			10-12 ft	Stored air pressure
	5 lb			10-12 ft	
	10 lb			10-12 ft	
	10 lb	No	Smothering	10-12 ft	Gas pressure from carbon dioxide cartridge
	20 lb			15-20 ft	
5	30 lb			15-20 ft	
	75 lb			18 ft	Gas pressure from nitrogen cylinder
	150 lb			18 ft	
	Carbon Dioxide				
	2½ lb				
	5 lb				
	10 lb				
6	15 lb	No	Smothering	Approx. 8 ft	Carbon dioxide under pressure in extinguisher
	20 lb				
	50 lb				
	75 lb				
	100 lb				

Fig. 1-3   Fire extinguishers.

Fig. 1-4 Operate that vehicle as if it were your own—with your family in it! Think first!

control of the transmission, hydraulics, and winches if the machine is one that you have not previously started, operated, or driven.

If you have not been informed about the engine's or machine's present condition, promptly check the coolant, the oil level of the engine and of the machine, the hydraulics, and the transmission.

NOTE When checking the engine coolant level after the engine has been operating, turn the pressure cap slightly before removing it completely. Check or close the air reservoirs.

Next, place the transmission in neutral or in the safety position or disengage the master clutch. If it is necessary to use a preheater (glow plug), turn it on and, after about 15 s, engage the electric, hydraulic, or air starter. The engine should start after about three full revolutions. **NOTE** Do not run the engine in an enclosed area without proper exhaust piping and ventilation. The lack of oxygen or the carbon monoxide could asphyxiate you before you are aware of the danger.

Once the engine is running, check the lubricating oil pressure and closely watch the coolant temperature and the rise in the air pressure. If the air pressure is not rising but you have closed the reservoirs, stop the engine and check the air compressor and the drive belts for broken or leaking air hoses. Repair if necessary. Do not move the vehicle on its own power unless you know the brakes are adequate.

Operate the engine at about 1000 rpm until the engine temperature gauge shows about 180°F [82°C]. When the engine reaches this temperature, the air pressure is at the cutoff pressure; the vehicle is then ready to be moved into the work area.

Depending on the type of machine and the location of your work area, you may require an assistant to guide you into the shop or to drive the machine into servicing position. If an assistant is not available, recheck the entire travel area and make certain that there are no obstructions and that the shop doors are fully open. Then raise the working attachment off the ground and position it to a level that gives you good vision and good maneuverability. Release the parking brakes, place the transmission into the lowest gear, and then drive the vehicle into

the shop or to the desired location. If you use an assistant to guide you into position, follow the hand signals implicitly, for the assistant is responsible for your safe maneuvering.

NOTE Operate the vehicle as though it were your own. (Think before taking action.)

After the machine is in position, apply the parking brakes or block the wheels. This depends, of course, on the type of machine, as well as on the service you have to perform. Next, position the attached equipment, for example, the loader, excavator, shovel, crane, etc., in such a way that it will not impede your work and then block the equipment securely. Reduce the engine temperature by placing the throttle in low idle, and when it declines to about 160°F [71°C], turn off the ignition switch or pull the fuel stop. **NOTE** Each manufacturer provides special instructions for moving its equipment or machine. As an example here are a few safety steps one manufacturer recommends for a crane mounted on a crawler carrier: Do not travel with the swing brakes released. Do not engage the engine clutch until you are sure that everything is clear and in neutral. Do not maintain less than 5 ft [1.525 m] of clearance around high-voltage lines. Do not travel on a steep slope without the use of blocking (in case a drive chain fails).

Safety Rules for Lifting, Blocking, and Cleaning
Before starting any type of service work, with the exception of engine tuneup, disconnect the batteries, remove the hydraulic pressure from the system and from the cylinders, and drain the air reservoir.

NOTE Use extreme care if it is necessary to make adjustments on the engine or equipment while the engine is running. Keep your hands away from moving parts.

Clear away any parts from your work area that would obstruct your work. It is statistically proved that a high percentage of injuries and accidents occur while someone is removing, cleaning, or installing parts or components. When selecting a lifting device, a chain block, a come-along, a crane, a loader, a fork lift, etc., make certain that the lifting capacity of the unit is higher than the load to be lifted. Use, when possible, an adjustable lifting beam, chains, and eyebolts in such fashion that the chains are parallel to each other and as near to perpendicular as possible to the top of the object to be lifted. This will ensure that each eyebolt and chain carries only half the load. Place the sling eyes or chain rings on the lift hook only when the slings or chains are vertical; do not lay one eye over the other. Both should lie on the bottom of the hook. When it is necessary to remove components and the slings or chains have to be fastened at an angle to the object to be lifted, note that with an increase in angle the force on the slings or chains increases and may exceed the load capacity (see Fig. 1-5). Therefore, shackle both sling eyes or chain rings together and then place the shackle on the hook. Bottom the eyebolts against the object to be lifted or support them as

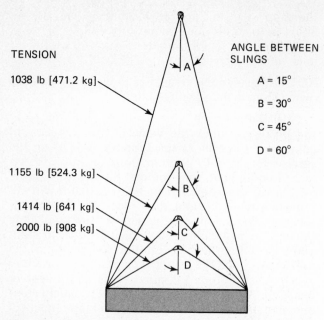

TENSION

1038 lb [471.2 kg]

1155 lb [524.3 kg]

1414 lb [641 kg]

2000 lb [908 kg]

ANGLE BETWEEN
SLINGS

A = 15°

B = 30°

C = 45°

D = 60°

Fig. 1-5 The greater the angle between the slings, chains, or ropes used when lifting a piece of equipment, the greater the strain on them and the stronger they must be.

shown in Fig. 1-6; otherwise the eyebolts could bend and break.

When selecting a wire rope sling, make certain the eyes are spliced properly and that there are no wire breaks or sharp kinks. Fiber or synthetic ropes or slings are not as often used to lift an object but are used as tag lines (guidelines).

When using a rope, make certain that it is properly hitched or knotted to the object. Use the common timber hitch, half hitch, the square or reef knot, or the bowline knot, all of which are easy to remove (see Figs. 1-7 to 1-10).

When lifting, stay clear of the load and lift it only as high as required, then swing it free and lower it to the minimum height. Do not leave the load suspended in the air or travel with the load highly suspended, for the lifting device could tip when the load pendulates back and forth. If it is necessary to

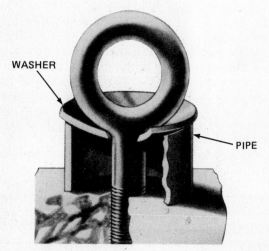

WASHER

PIPE

Fig. 1-6 Lifting eye.

have the load highly suspended, use tag lines to prevent it from swinging.

When placing the object on the bench, jack, or floor, make certain it is supported by wooden blocks so that it cannot tip over.

When lifting a vehicle with a hydraulic jack or screw jack, block the wheels and/or apply the parking brakes. Select a jack with adequate lifting capacity and make sure that its footing holds firm and is on level ground. If necessary, use wood blocking to increase the area on which the jack rests. Place the jack square to the components to be lifted and use a suitable saddle, head, or wooden block to ensure safe lifting.

After the object is raised, support it with rigid stands or axle stands or through cross blocking, in case the hydraulic jack should bleed off and gradually lower the vehicle.   **NOTE** Whenever working beneath a vehicle, wear safety glasses to prevent any fuel, oil, acid, or dirt from dropping into your eyes; even a drop of acid can cause blindness. When placing a load or a component on a fork lift or lift truck, use a pallet if possible. If a pallet is not available, secure the object to the mast with a rope so that it cannot fall off the forks. When operating a fork lift or lift truck, be alert for other floor traffic and obstructions, especially when passing through doors or beyond blind openings.

Have respect for weight as it applies to your own strength and bear in mind that you may lift or place an object of a particular weight in position when standing upright, but when lying on your back you can maneuver less than half that weight. Never attempt to lift heavy parts—use a lifting device.

Your hands are the most important tools you possess—protect them! Never try to use them as a vise or a hammer, etc., and do not place them or your arm between objects to be engaged or moved into mesh. Use a rope, a wire, a pair of pliers, or a pry bar, etc.

If you must manually lift an object, lift it from a squat position. Avoid pushing objects—pull them and always make sure you have a firm grip, in each case to prevent muscle and back strain (Fig. 1-11).

Safety Rules—Tools   To avoid injury to yourself or to others, always use the tool designed for the job. Do not use a pair of pliers as a jumper cable, or your hands will be burned. Do not use a pair of pliers to tighten a nut or fitting. They are inadequate and will cause a leak or a loose fastener, which will eventually lead to an accident. Do not use screwdrivers in place of a chisel or pry bar. In such circumstances these have been known to break and cause injury to the user or helper. Do not use blunt chisels or chisels or punches having mushroom heads. Dress them properly to prevent cuts. Do not jump or reach awkwardly for a tool you have inadvertently dropped or you may find yourself in a precarious and dangerous position. Perform your work carefully without undue haste and make certain that all bolts, nuts, and fittings are tightened properly and, if applicable, locked. Do not use oily or dirty tools, for they could slip from your hands and cause injury to yourself or

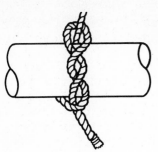

Fig. 1-7 Timber hitch.

Fig. 1-8 Half hitch.

Fig. 1-9 Square or reef knot.

Fig. 1-10 Bowline knot.

to others. Do not use wrenches that have spread jaws or are defective. They will slip. Do not use a file without a handle, for it may pierce your hands. Do not use a hammer on a hardened surface, for knife-like slivers could fly off the hammer or surface and cut you or others. Do not use a drill until the object to be drilled is properly secured. Never use any type of electrical equipment, electric machine, or tool that is not properly grounded or cables or tools that are not in good working condition. You could be electrocuted. If you are inexperienced in welding, grinding, chiseling, or any other task that has an element of danger to it, leave it to those who are qualified. If you are doing any of these jobs, place a shield around your work area and wear the correct face shield or goggles. It is a good habit to write "hot" on parts just welded, cut, or grounded to warn others against the possibility of burns.

When filling the battery with electrolyte, wear a face shield and rubber gloves as protection against skin blisters in case you accidentally spill the acid. If any is spilled, use a lot of water and wash it away. If electrolyte is spilled on the vehicle, sprinkle baking soda onto the contacted area and then wash the area thoroughly with water.

Safety Rules for Cleaning   A great percentage of eye injury and cuts result from a disregard for the simplest of rules in cleaning components. For instance, you should never use compressed air to clean your clothes, hands, or body. The pressure could cause the cleaning fluid or dirt particles to penetrate your skin, resulting in infection and/or blood poisoning. You should never spin a bearing (fool

around) using compressed air. It could explode. Do not use compressed air unless you are wearing a face shield—this could cause eye injury. Do not use compressed air to clean an object immediately after it has been removed from a hot cleaning tank. First rinse the cleaning solution away with water. Do not use carbon tetrachloride as a cleaning solution. The fumes, when inhaled, can cause serious internal injury and possibly result in death. Wear a face shield and rubber gloves when inserting or removing components or parts from a hot tank. If the acid solution spills or splashes on you, it can cause skin infection and burns. Lower the object slowly

Fig. 1-11   Always bend at the knees when lifting a heavy object.

Fig. 1-12 Never be careless with compressed air! Never aim the air stream at yourself or another person.

into the hot tank to prevent splashing. When using a power wire wheel, always wear a face shield and also place a shield around the object to protect others from flying wire and particles. When using a putty knife or scraper, keep your free hand behind the tool so that it won't be pierced in the event the scraper should slip. When steam-cleaning, place the object to be cleaned on a pallet and wear a face shield and rubber gloves for protection against loose debris (see Fig. 1-12).

If a job or cleaning task requires the use of gloves, use the appropriate gloves. Do not, for instance, use welding gloves when removing an object from a hot tank, or rubber gloves when welding. If you have cut, nicked, or burned yourself, or something has got

into your eyes, report immediately to the first-aid person. Procrastination could cause blood poisoning, even from a slight cut, or could place your eyesight in jeopardy.

Review Questions

1. Describe acceptable working clothes for a diesel mechanic.

2. Why is it extremely important to ground all electric power tools and motors?

3. Explain why an overloaded electric circuit can cause a fire.

4. Sketch the outside work area of your shop, indicating: (a) the location of the fire alarm; (b) the location of the fire hose outlet, and the hose length; (c) the type of fire extinguisher.

5. What precaution must you take before checking the cooling system when the engine temperature is about 158°F [70°C]?

6. If you are required to drive an unfamiliar tractor, machine, or other vehicle to the work area, which controls or instruments would you first learn to use?

7. Why is it imperative that the driver follow the hand signal of the assistant when driving the machine or vehicle into position?

8. What checks should you make before using: (a) a wire rope sling? (b) a fiber rope sling?

9. Practice knotting and hitching, using a lumber hitch, the half hitch, the square or reef knot, and the bowline knot.

10. Define the term *cross blocking*.

11. What precautionary measures must you take when lifting or transporting an object with a forklift or lift truck?

12. Why should you use a shackle rather than place both sling eyes onto the lift hook?

Unit 2
Lubrication

It is easy to select the right bolt for a nut simply by threading the bolt into the nut or by measuring the diameter and determining the number of threads per inch. However, in the selection of a lubricant for the engine, hydraulic system, bearings, transmissions, carriers, etc., no such simple yardstick exists. Selection of the correct lubricant becomes an even greater challenge when one considers that it must, under all working conditions, (1) lubricate the moving components or parts to reduce harmful wear and friction, (2) seal clearances between components or parts to prevent efficiency loss and oil leakage, (3) dissipate heat from the stress areas, (4) transmit power easily without power loss, (5) be uncompressible [that is, to not more than 1 percent per 1000 psi (6890 kPa)], (6) prevent oxidation, corrosion, and foaming.

HYDRAULIC AND POWER SHIFT TRANSMISSION OIL

Selection   Selection of the appropriate hydraulic and transmission oil and maintenance of the oil are of great importance to the life of the components, as well as to the efficient performance of the hydraulic system and the transmission. While it is simple to keep the oil clean by regularly changing it and by maintaining a good filtering system, it is not so easy to determine the oil characteristics most suitable to the system. In selecting oil, consider the variables under which the oil must perform, as well as the oil's tendency to undergo chemical breakdown. This breakdown results in the formation of sludge, carbon, gum, acid, and other deposits which adversely affect lubrication (increase wear), reduce openings, and inhibit proper functioning of valves and actuators.

Many farm and industrial machines have one common oil reservoir which serves the hydraulic equipment, the power shift transmission, the power steering, and, in some cases, the brakes. Therefore many equipment manufacturers use a special-purpose fluid, referred to as a four-way oil, because of the many services it can provide.

Among the sources of information available to help you select the proper oil for your hydraulic system and transmission are (1) the manufacturers of the equipment, (2) the oil marketing companies, (3) the performance data, and (4) your own previous experience. In determining the appropriate oil to be used, among the first things to consider are the properties and characteristics relating to its performance. Under all operating conditions an adequate oil film must be present between the components or parts, so that there is very little, or preferably no, metal-to-

metal contact. Also of prime importance are the viscosity and the viscosity index of the oil.

Viscosity   Viscosity is the physical property of an oil with which the mechanic is most concerned. It is a measurement of fluidity or resistance to flow. If the viscosity is low, the fluidity is high (the oil has thinned out). If the viscosity is high, the fluidity is low (the oil has thickened). Fluidity, or resistance to flow, changes with the temperature, and therefore its measurement is always related to temperature.

Of the many instruments developed to measure viscosity, the most popular among technicians and engineers is the Saybolt Universal viscosimeter, which consists of a calibrated reservoir (in which the test oil is placed) with a fixed (universal) orifice at the bottom. The reservoir is surrounded by a bath, which is heated by heating coils to bring the test oil to the temperature at which the viscosity of the oil is to be measured. A container marked at the 60-cm^3 (0.180-ft^3) level is placed under the orifice. When the test oil reaches the desired temperature, the orifice is opened. The number of seconds it takes for the oil to reach the 60-cm^3 level is expressed in Saybolt Universal Seconds (SUS), also referred to as Seconds Saybolt Universal (SSU).

Another device for testing the viscosity of an oil is the kinematic viscosimeter tube. A measured amount of test oil is drawn into a viscosimeter tube and placed into a bath heated to 210°F [98.8°C]. The time required for the measured amount of oil to flow through the small-diameter tube (called a capillary tube) is then recorded. The pressure causing the flow in this instrument comes from the height of the column of oil above the tube plus the density or gravity of the oil. The viscosity determined in this way is called *kinematic viscosity*. It is expressed in SUS and is converted into engineering units, that is, centistokes (cSt). Centistoke viscosity is calculated by multiplying the SUS by the correction factor of the viscosimeter.

A newer method of testing the viscosity of an oil at 0°F [−18°C] to simulate cold starting is by measuring the strength of a film of the oil under precise conditions. The measurement is taken at 0°F in centimeters, grams, and seconds. The unit is called a *poise* (P) or *centipoise* (cP).

NOTE   Viscosity is the fluidity of a liquid and is not a classification of the quality of an oil.

VISCOSITY INDEX   The viscosity index (VI) is a numerical method of indicating the extent to which an oil changes viscosity with changing temperature. The higher the viscosity index, the more stable the

11

oil viscosity as the temperature changes. For example, an oil with a VI of 100 will thin out less than an oil with a VI of 50 when each is heated.

Pour Point The pour point is the point at which an oil solidifies from the formation of wax crystals. This can happen through a gradual increase in viscosity because of operating conditions, or as the ambient temperature drops. Pour point is of serious concern only when the equipment must be started while the ambient temperature is lower than the pour point of the oil. Under this condition the hydraulic pump will not receive oil and could therefore destroy itself.

Flash Point The flash point is the temperature at which an oil vaporizes and ignites from a source of ignition. The flash point of oil varies with the viscosity and quality of the oil. It can range from 380 to 500°F [190 to 260°C] or more. When the flash point falls below 320°F [160°C] owing to contamination, an explosion could occur.

Oil Additives The success of today's hydraulic oil depends very much on the complex chemicals (additives) which are blended into the oil-base stock. Many of the additives affect more than one of the oil's characteristics.

One purpose of additives is to prevent deterioration of metallic surfaces; however, a discussion of this deterioration must make some distinction between the words *oxidation*, *corrosion*, and *rust*. As you know, when a once bright and shiny steel surface is exposed to the atmosphere, it loses its brightness, becomes spotted, and eventually becomes fully coated with a reddish-brown deposit called *rust*. To the chemist this is an oxide—a product formed during a reaction called *oxidation*. Corrosion is a term used in reference to the deterioration of a metallic surface by chemical action. Rusting is but one type of corrosion. During the process of corrosion, metal dissolves and is washed away, and the metal surface is left pitted. During the process of rusting, oxygen fuses with the metal and it gains dimension.

- *Oxidation inhibitors* prevent varnish and sludge formation. To prevent corrosion, organic compounds containing sulfur, phosphorus, or nitrogen (such as organic amines, sulfides, or phenols) are used. Metals such as tin, zinc, or barium are often incorporated.
- *Anticorrosion (rust)* additives prevent failure of alloy bearings. To prevent corrosion of other metal surfaces, metal salts of thiophosphoric acid and sulfurized waxes are added in addition to the organic compounds already mentioned.
- *Detergent additives* keep metal surfaces clean. To prevent any type of deposit formation, metalloorganic compounds such as phosphates, phenolates, sulfonates, alcoholates, and soaps of magnesium, barium, calcium, and tin are added. These additives are used basically to prevent corrosive acids or sludge particles from forming deposits and to hold such particles in suspension.

- *Antiscuff and antiwear additives* reduce friction and prevent galling, scoring, and seizure and also give the oil extreme pressure properties. Organic compounds of chlorine, phosphorus, and sulfur, such as chlorinated waxes and organic phosphates, are used. Phosphates such as tricresyl phosphate and zinc dithiophosphates are used.
- *Foam inhibitors,* as the term implies, prevent foaming. Most commercial oil solutions contain about 10 percent air by volume. When under pressure, the oil solution absorbs a much larger amount of air; however, no harmful effects are produced as long as this air is in the solution. If the air dissolves into the oil when under pressure, it tends, once the pressure is released, to produce foam as it comes out of the solution. To lower the amount of aeration (foaming), the manufacturer puts additives (silicone polymers) into the oil solution. The additives cause the small air bubbles to combine and become larger, and this results in a quicker air separation. When the air is not separated, the components receive less lubrication. This increases wear and may cause tiny explosions, which cause pitting of components.
- To prevent *seal swell*—shrinkage or hardening which would cause a fluid leak—organic phosphates, aromatics, and halogenated hydrocarbon are added.

Storing and Handling Hydraulic Oils To reduce the risk of contaminating a hydraulic oil, store it indoors, in drums placed in an oil-drum rack, in a designated area. Always keep the drumheads, taps, measuring cans, dispensers, and surrounding area clean. Never use empty antifreeze cans for dispensing any oil. Identify each oil clearly to reduce the possibility of dispensing the wrong oil. Use a power dispenser or a separate measuring can for each product. When possible, use taps for each drum to prevent damage to the bungs or contamination of the lubricant. Bungs and drumheads must be replaced and tightened immediately after each use. To prevent damage from frequent opening and closing, use only a bung wrench.

Use only lint-free rags when cleaning the dispensers, since lint can accumulate and stop oil circulation. If you must store the drums outside, tilt them slightly with the bungs at 3 o'clock and 9 o'clock or lay them on their sides so that water cannot enter. Always wipe up any spilled oil around the drums. Do not use sand or a chemical to soak up the oil. A chemical is not only a fire hazard but may also get into the oil.

GREASE

Grease is a semifluid lubricant containing a mixture of mineral oil or a synthetic fluid with a thickening agent. The thickener may be a soap compound, or a nonsoap substance such as calcium, sodium, aluminum, lithium, barium, or bentone. To improve its performance characteristics and its properties, add supplements. The quality of the grease is governed by the fluid used, the ratio between the fluid and thickener, the chemical structure of the thickener, and its additives.

A grease is used instead of an oil under the following circumstances: (1) when it is required to cling to the mechanism to be lubricated, (2) when the lubricant is partly responsible for sealing out contaminants, (3) when the bearing or bushing is required to carry an extremely high load, (4) when the opportunity to lubricate the mechanism hourly or daily is limited, and (5) when an oil would run to one side, leaving the other side without lubricant.

Because the following characteristics are peculiar to grease, it cannot be used as a cooling or cleaning agent:

1. The fluid and the thickener attract each other and are very difficult to separate. However, bleeding, that is, slight separation of the liquid lubricant from the grease, does not detract from it.
2. Grease is electrically attracted by the metallic bushing, shaft, rollers, balls, raceways, and/or gear teeth, and so there is always a thin layer of grease on the surfaces.
3. Grease has directional fluidity. In other words, when the shaft or the inner or outer race or the gears rotate, the grease tends to shear into thin layers and follows the direction of the movable components. Even when it becomes very fluid owing to excessive operating temperature, grease does not alter direction, or run, or squeeze out from between the shaft and bushing; between the rollers, balls, and races; or between the gears.

Properties, Grades, and Types To be effective, grease must be selected according to its inherent properties. It is therefore graded according to its chemical structure and its particular properties and included additives. When you can anticipate the performance required of the grease, you should then be able to select the appropriate grease for your equipment.

Consistency Number (Grade) In selecting an engine oil, in contrast to grease, your first concern is the appropriate viscosity. Grease, is, however, graded by its hardness, and the hardness is not graded by its viscosity; it is expressed in terms of American Society for Testing and Material (ASTM) penetration or National Lubricating Grease Institute (NLGI) consistency number.

ASTM penetration is a numerical representation of an actual test of an object as it sinks into grease under specific test conditions. It is measured in tenths of a millimeter. NLGI uses consistency numbers 000 to 6 to classify the grease, with use of ASTM penetration test results. For example, a grease having the consistency number 000 is soft, like ice cream at a room temperature of 77°F [25°C], whereas a grease having the consistency number 6 is hard, like butter just removed from a refrigerator. NLGI 2 grease is suitable for most ambient temperatures for either light or heavy applications. However, for extremely low ambient temperatures, NLGI 0 or 1 is

Table 2-1 GREASES

NLGI consistency grades	ASTM worked penetration, mm/10	Description and use
000	445—475	Semifluid
00	400—430	Very soft
0	355—385	Soft—grease gun
1	310—340	Grease gun
2	265—295	Grease gun
3	220—250	Grease cup
4	175—205	Grease cup
5	130—160	Grease cup—brick type
6	85—115	Brick grease

recommended. The consistency grades and their uses are listed in Table 2-1.

Grease Characteristics The terms used to describe greases, and their definitions, are as follows.

- *Structural stability* is the capacity of a grease to maintain its original texture and consistency, after the movement has stopped, regardless of operating temperature, operating condition, or age of the grease.
- *Mechanical stability* is the capacity of a grease to retain its consistency under various operating conditions or to provide adequate lubrication and sealing.
- *Dropping point* is the temperature, in degrees Celsius, when a grease changes to a liquid state under standard test conditions.
- *Texture and structure* are smoothness, stickiness, and stringiness (like chewing gum). They have no bearing on the quality or grade of a grease. Nevertheless, they are factors to be considered in applying or transporting greases.

Consistency number, structural and mechanical stability, and dropping point contribute equally to the performance of the grease. However, such properties as oxidation resistance, capacity to protect against corrosion, friction, and wear are also important.

Types of Grease There are seven types of grease available, each manufactured for a special purpose: (1) wheel bearing grease, (2) universal joint grease, (3) chassis grease, (4) extended lubrication interval (ELI), (5) multipurpose grease, (6) extreme-pressure grease (EP), and (7) spindle grease. The one commonly recommended for most applications is the multipurpose grease, which contains at least 3 percent of molybdenum disulfide, MoS_2. Multipurpose grease has a high structural and mechanical stability, a high dropping point, and high oxidation resistance. With the addition of the MoS_2, protection against friction, wear, corrosion, and washout is increased; resistance to oxidation is greater; and a heavier load-carrying capacity is possible. A special lubricant growing fast in usage because of its versatility and performance is the MoS_2 paste. It has a 40:70 ratio MoS_2 content in an oil-soap solution of semifluid consistency.

14

Grease Application One of the present objectives of the equipment designers is to design equipment that can be initially lubricated for life. The automotive manufacturers are close to realizing this objective, and the day may come when on- and off-highway equipment is initially lubricated for the life of the machine.

Grease for friction bearings is applied by hand packing, by a bearing packing device, by a hand- or power-operated grease gun, or by a centralized lubrication system.

CENTRALIZED LUBRICATION

Centralized lubrication systems are becoming increasingly popular on on- and off-highway equipment because they reduce downtime and maintenance costs.

From a central storage point lubricant is pumped in a precalculated quantity to individual lubrication points. This system consists of an oil or grease reservoir, a pump, a master feeder, secondary feeders, and the lines that connect the components to the lubrication points.

The network of feed lines and secondary feeders is shown in Fig. 2-1.

System Operation Each time the pump is operated (manually or automatically), lubricant is delivered to the master feeder. Here it is divided into three, four, or five lines leading to the secondary feeders. Each individual line receives the proportionate amount of lubricant required to supply the secondary feeders so that each lubrication point receives its precalculated amount of lubricant. The shovel shown in Fig. 2-1, for example, has more than 180 lubrication points; all receive the precalculated amount of lubricant, so that the pump develops the pressure needed.

Because a centralized lubrication system works on the principle of progressive piston displacement, each feeder piston must complete its stroke before the next piston can start its stroke. When one piston fails to complete its stroke because of a plugged or bent feedline or because of excessive restriction at the lubrication point, the pressure rises within the system, warning the operator that there is no lubrication action. An indicator on the feeder assembly shows which lubrication point caused the pressure buildup, so that a quick diagnosis and repair can be made.

TRANSMISSION AND AXLE LUBRICANT

The correct selection of transmission or axle lubricant is of vital importance for today's modern transmissions and axles because of the increased gear-tooth and bearing pressure and the high rotating speed of shafts and gears. Despite the fact that manufacturers of transmissions and axles provide service manuals and service bulletins which fully outline service procedures, show how and when to change the oil, and specify the type of oil to be used and the lubricant capacity, a large number of transmission and axle failures are, nevertheless, caused by improper lubrication and poor maintenance.

Transmission and axle lubricant is a refined petroleum product of straight mineral oil to which additives and inhibitors are added to meet the various operating requirements. A thickener (filler) which produces an untrue viscosity is not recommended.

NOTE In addition to its designed function, lubricant also dissipates heat and has a flushing action on bearing and gearteeth surfaces to wash off abrasive material.

Properties, Performance, Characteristics, and Grades Transmission and axle lubricant is classified by the American Petroleum Institute (API) into six major groups (API-GL-1 to API-GL-6) which des-

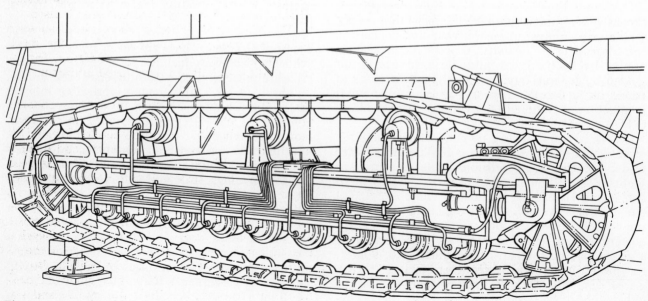

Fig. 2-1 Centralized lubrication system.

ignate the intended service application. In addition, each group is again divided according to its viscosity grade and load-carrying capacity.

One of the most important characteristics of a transmission or axle lubricant, also referred to as extreme-pressure (EP) lubricant, is its load-carrying capacity. A lubricant with EP additives has a heavier load-carrying capacity than a straight mineral oil product. To make known the load-carrying capacity of a lubricant, API and the Coordinating Research Council (CRC) have arrived at a numbering classification, reference gear oil (RGO) 100 to RGO 115.

Whereas RGO 100 is a straight mineral oil with a very low load-carrying capacity, RGO 115 may be the same type oil but contain 15 percent, by weight, of EP additives.

Viscosity The selection of a lubricant having the right viscosity grade to perform most effectively at certain temperature ranges is extremely important, since the lubricant must not only flow freely to all components or parts that require lubrication but must also have a viscosity grade high enough to lubricate and protect them.

The viscosity grade of a transmission and axle lubricant is not the same as that of an engine oil, because engine oil is graded by its viscosity and viscosity index, whereas a transmission and axle lubricant has a viscosity calculated from the high- and low-temperature test value. Therefore axle and transmission lubricant having a viscosity of, say, SAE 90 could have the same viscosity as an SAE 50 engine oil. You must therefore read your service manual carefully when selecting the lubricant. If, for instance, the service manual directs that engine lubricant be used, you must never use axle lubricant or vice versa. For the SAE viscosity grade of transmission and axle lubricant, see Table 2-2.

Channeling Channeling means that the rotating parts cut a channel into the solidified lubricant, reducing the flow to the part to be lubricated. Therefore when the machine is to be started and stopped at very high ambient temperature variations, channeling temperature is important.

Channeling has nothing to do with pour point. A lubricant may have a low pour point but may, at this temperature, flow between the rotating parts with ease.

Flash and Fire Point Flash and fire points are of concern only when the operating condition of the lubricant could exceed a given temperature.

NOTE A lubricant with a high flash point suffers little (quantity) loss during operation.

Oxidation, Corrosion, and Foaming Any lubricant that has to operate at high and low temperatures and under light and heavy load conditions and is continuously in motion must have some inhibitor additive to protect the gear or bearing surfaces from oxidation and corrosion and to prevent foaming. (Foaming reduces lubrication.)

Lubrication Oil Designation API-GL-1 lubrication oil is recommended for use in spiral bevel gears, axles, worm gear axles, and manual transmissions because the sliding velocity and the load pressure are low in these applications. This lubricant may have oxidation, corrosion, and defoamer additives or inhibitors added to improve the operating characteristics.

API-GL-2 lubrication oil is similar to GL-1 but has very mild antiwear and extreme-pressure additives. It is therefore suitable for worm gear applications and worm gear axles, where a GL-1 lubricant cannot perform satisfactorily.

API-GL-3 lubrication oil is similar to GL-1 lubricant but has a higher load-carrying capacity (about RGO 104).

API-GL-4, 5, and 6 are lubricants with higher EP additives and are therefore more suitable for service in a hypoid gear axle having an antiscore protection from RGO 105 to RGO 115. The API-GL-6 lubricant is recommended for service in hypoid gears when the gear set operates under high-speed–low-torque, low-speed–high-torque, or shock-load conditions or when a special high-offset hypoid gear is used.

NOTE Many manufacturers recommend an even higher performance characteristic from the lubricant, suggesting a military specification; for instance, MIL-L-2105B is a much-used lubricant.

Oil Change Recommendations It is the mechanic's or operator's responsibility to see that the oil level is checked regularly, that the magnetic plug and filters are clean or are changed regularly, and that the oil has not thickened or discolored. This is good maintenance procedure and will extend the service life of the vehicle. **NOTE** Before checking the oil level, make certain that the temperature of the lubricant is as specified in the service manual. Some manufacturers recommend checking the oil level at operating temperature, whereas others check the oil level at ambient temperature. **CAUTION** Do not add lubricant unless it is of the same grade and classification—you could degrade the quality and viscosity of the oil. If you are not certain what lubricant

Table 2-2 AXLE AND MANUAL TRANSMISSION LUBRICANT VISCOSITY CLASSIFICATION

SAE viscosity number	Maximum temperature for viscosity of 150,000 cP (150 Pa·s) °F	°C	Viscosity at 210°F [99°C] Minimum cSt	SUS	mm²/s	Maximum cSt	SUS	mm²/s
75W	−40	−40	4.2	40	4.2	—	—	—
80W	−15	−26	7.0	49	7.0	—	—	—
85W	+10	−12	11.0	63	11.0	—	—	—
90	—	—	14.0	74	14.0	<25	120	25
140	—	—	25.0	120	25.0	<43	200	43
250	—	—	43.0	200	43.0	—	—	—

is being used, drain and refill. Always follow the service manual instructions in regard to the grade and classification of oil and the oil level.

Oil Change   The general procedure when changing oil is first to drive the equipment onto a level surface. Lower the hydraulic equipment if so equipped, apply the parking brakes, and/or block the wheels. Hang a warning sign on the steering wheel reading "Do not start the engine." Clean the surrounding area and remove all drain and filler plugs, the filter, and the breather. Allow sufficient time for proper drainage so that the accumulated contamination can run out. Examine the magnetic plugs and filter and the drained oil for abrasive wear, sludge, or gum. Always clean the magnetic plug, filters, and breathers. Check the effectiveness of the magnetic plug. (It usually has a 2-lb [907.18-g]-pickup capacity.) If it cannot pass this test, then the abrasive wear particles will not be removed from the lubricant. Such particles circulating in the lubricant will pass through the gears and bearings and reduce the service life of the transmission or axle. This is also true when the transmission filter is not cleaned or changed at regular intervals.

Do not overlook cleaning or replacing the breather. When the transmission or axle cannot breathe, there may be a pressure buildup that could cause seal failure. Furthermore, accumulated moisture may not vaporize, and oxidation, corrosion, and acid formation could result.

If the lubricant is contaminated, clean (flush) the housing with the flushing oil recommended in the service manual. If flushing oil is not available, use diesel fuel. After the flushing oil has drained, correctly reinstall the drain plugs (use new gaskets), filter, and breather. Fill the housing with the gear lubricant to the level of the filler hole or as specified in the service manual. Reinstall the filler plug and torque all plugs and bolts to specification.

Review Questions

1. Why is it very important that you use only the type of lubricant recommended by the manufacturer for a particular application?

2. List four main purposes of an oil lubricant.

3. Of the many properties and characteristics of an oil, which two are most important to its performance?

4. List all the precautions you would take to prevent oil contamination (a) during storage, (b) during handling, (c) during filling of the reservoir, crankcase, transmission, etc.

5. What is the main composition difference between an oil and a grease?

6. Give three reasons why grease will not, under normal operating conditions, run out or squeeze from the components.

7. Which property of an oil or grease (other than its consistency number) is, in your opinion, the most important?

8. Why do service shops so often use multipurpose grease?

9. Standard-transmission and axle oils are divided into six major groups and each group is subdivided. Identify the six major groups.

10. Why does the viscosity of an engine oil having SAE 30 differ from a transmission or axle having a viscosity of SAE 30?

11. List two conditions which commonly occur in checking oil that would result in an incorrect oil level reading.

12. From a service manual among your training aids, copy the steps recommended to flush a particular transmission or rear axle.

Unit 3
Seals and Gaskets

Many different types of seals and gaskets are designed for use on hydraulic systems, engines, power shift transmissions, etc. Their function is to confine oil, fuel, or coolant within a given area; prevent unwanted air, dust, dirt, or foreign material from entering the system; and avoid a vacuum buildup within the system. Manufacturers have made great efforts to combat sealing problems created by high and low temperatures, expansion and contraction, vibration, pressure or vacuum, corrosion, and oxidation. However, even with today's large selection of seal and gasket designs and available materials, it is difficult to find a seal which is 100 percent leak-free under all operating conditions.

Engine manufacturers specify the type of seal or gasket to be used on their equipment, and their instructions should be followed for best results. If the specified seal or gasket is not available, care must be taken in deciding on a suitable substitute. Remember that inadequate sealing reduces the life and efficiency of the components and results in higher costs owing to the downtime.

Although seals and gaskets do sometimes cease to function properly, they should not be instantaneously regarded as the source of trouble. Quite often what appears to be the result of a leaking seal or gasket is in fact the result of a mechanic's inadequate preparation of the seal surfaces, improper alignment of the mating surfaces, improper installation, or incorrect torque.

Classification of Seals   There are two kinds of seals: static and dynamic. A seal used between two stationary components is called a *static seal*. If it can also seal two components moving in relation to each other, it is called a *dynamic seal*.

Mechanical Seals   Mechanical seals are found in hydraulic systems, pumps, and on-track machines. The most efficient seals are metal-to-metal, metal-to-carbon, and metal-to-synthetic material. In each case the two lapped mating surfaces are forced against each other by a hold-down device in the form of a spring or an O ring (see Fig. 3-1).

O-Ring Seals   All O rings are used to seal passages or openings by crushing or compressing together the two surfaces to be sealed. The construction material of today's O rings is such that they can be used as either static or dynamic seals or can be used to seal at high or low temperatures or at high or low pressures. The O rings of a shape similar to that shown in Fig. 3-2 are of an elastic material that may be of buna, neoprene, Teflon, butyl, Viton, silicone, polyacrylic, or nitrile rubber. To identify the various

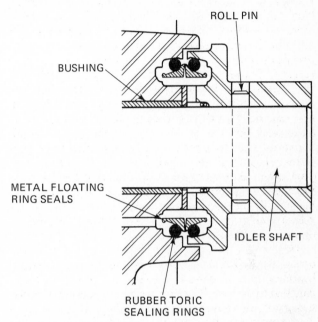

Fig. 3-1   Seal assembly.

synthetic materials from which an O ring is made, a lettering system is used. The color code has no bearing on the correct selection.

Each material used has advantages and disadvantages. Viton material, for instance, is especially appropriate where high heat and chemicals are present. Manufacturers test and select the material to be used for a particular application, and therefore, when a replacement is necessary, you should use the relevant manufacturer's replacement seals. If none are available, analyze the conditions under which the seal must perform before making your selection.

The O rings are molded to close tolerances in the

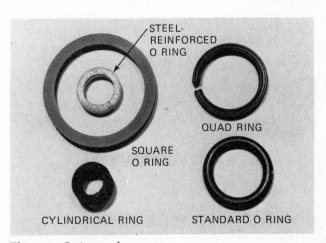

Fig. 3-2   O-ring seals.

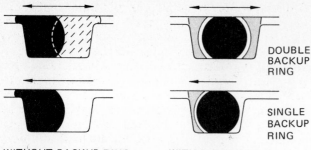

WITHOUT BACKUP RING   WITH BACKUP RING

DOUBLE
BACKUP
RING

SINGLE
BACKUP
RING

Fig. 3-3 O-ring reaction, with and without backup ring.

cross-sectional area and to the inside and outside diameters. When an O ring is applied statically or dynamically, it is fitted into a right-angular groove machined into the mechanism to be sealed. When installed, the mating surfaces compress the O ring about 10 percent.

When used dynamically, the groove is about 30 percent wider than the diameter of the O ring. This permits the O ring to roll slightly during the reciprocation of the moving components and allows for deformation when the oil pressure acts on the O ring surface.

To improve the sealing efficiency when a high pressure is applied, extrusion rings (backup washers) are used. The extrusion rings prevent O ring extrusion, act as a wiper seal, prevent a wider clearance between the parts to be sealed, and form a seal across the clearance gap. The illustration (see Fig. 3-3) shows the reaction of the O ring, with and without an extrusion ring, under various pressures.

Removal and Installation of O Rings When removing an O ring, take care not to damage the grooves or corners. A suitable O-ring-removing tool should be used. Check the O-ring groove and mating surface for nicks and burrs and make certain that the replacement O ring is of the recommended type and size. To determine if an oil leak is caused by a defective O ring, roll the O ring inside out and stretch it slightly to reveal any small cracks or any other irregularities.   **NOTE** Never reuse an O ring.

During installation make certain that the O ring is well lubricated, that it is not twisted, and that it fits properly into its groove. When only one backup washer is used, install it toward the lower pressure side and lubricate it and the O ring after the installation.

Gaskets The most common static seal is the gasket. Gaskets are carefully designed to suit particular needs and are therefore manufactured from many different materials. When selecting a gasket, remember that its composition is of prime importance, since you must consider the flexibility and smoothness required for the mating surfaces and the pressure and temperature under which it will be used. Other important features to be considered are what the conditions are under which it must seal off oil, water, dirt, and air, and whether or not it must be relied on to prevent vacuum buildup.

Gasket Materials Copper, aluminum, steel, fiber, asbestos, synthetic rubber, paper, and various combinations of these materials are used to make gaskets. (See Fig. 3-4.) Copper, aluminum, steel, or fibers are frequently used as gasket material under bolt-adjusting caps or between components.

NOTE Copper gaskets can be reused in an emergency by annealing (softening) them. The gasket is heated until the material changes color slightly, and it is then cooled in water. This process makes copper more pliable.

CORK GASKETS Cork is another material from which gaskets are made. The physical properties of cork make it the most versatile material where vibration, expansion, or uneven surfaces are to be found. The cork gasket is further improved by coating its surface with synthetic rubber or combining synthetic rubber with the cork. Cork gaskets require frequent retorquing if they are to maintain a leak-free seal.

SYNTHETIC RUBBER Although wide ranges of synthetic rubber gaskets are available, varying in density, tensile strength, and capacity to withstand extreme variations in temperature, they are seldom used on off- or on-highway equipment or on diesel engines.

PAPER (CHLOROPRENE) Chloroprene is a synthetic rubber and fiber composition that comes in sheet form, and is a widely used gasket material. It is water- and oil-resistant, varies in strength and softness, and is adaptable to low and high temperatures and high pressures. To increase chloroprene's ability to withstand the latter two conditions, rubber, asbestos, or other fibers are added to the original chloroprene composition.

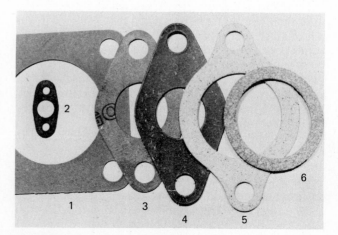

1. Paper
2. Synthetic rubber
3. Asbestos and paper combination
4. Chloroprene and asbestos
5. Asbestos
6. Cork

Fig. 3-4 Gaskets of different materials.

Gasket Construction   On the whole, the majority of gaskets are simple in construction. A single layer of gasket material is cut to fit the opening and surface contour to be sealed, without reinforcement.

When heavy stress, high pressure, or temperature is to be encountered, the common gasket is not used. Under these circumstances, special gaskets are designed, usually of a multilayer of materials. The layers may be of similar materials or of different types of alloys. In some cases the openings are reinforced by a grommet.

Rules for Preventing Sealing Failure

- Never reuse a seal or gasket. The elasticity deteriorates, and small nicks and cracks (invisible to the naked eye) reduce their sealing capacity.
- Make certain that the mating surfaces are smooth before reassembling and that the grooves or shafts are free of any foreign material. Inspect the gasket for cracks, nicks, burrs, or dents before installing it.
- Check that the O ring is not twisted and that the backup washer is placed on the correct side.
- Always check the seal or gasket for correct fit. The opening that holds the seal should not be enlarged, and the openings of the gasket must not restrict the flow.
- Before installing cork or paper gaskets, which could have shrunk due to long or improper storage, soak them for a few minutes in lukewarm water. Because wet cork or paper gaskets have the tendency to enlarge, place the wet gasket in a warm place before use. However, remember that temperatures over 100°F [38°C] will cause the gasket to curl.
- Do not remove seals or gaskets from their packing kits until ready to use them. Inspect fittings and clean off any foreign contaminants before installation.
- Follow installation instructions carefully.
- Torque the bolts or nuts in the correct sequence, taking care not to overtorque.

Liquid and Adhesive Sealants   Liquid sealing compound is commonly used to hold a gasket in place and, in emergency situations, to repair an oil gasket. It can also be used to improve a gasket seal that has an oxidized or uneven surface or to seal a hose connection.

To ensure effectiveness, you must be able to select the compound best suited to your particular purpose and to apply it correctly. You should therefore be thoroughly familiar with all the different types of sealers, their applications, their individual capacities to withstand different temperatures and high pressure, and their reaction to various liquids. A self-explanatory chart of the most common sealants is provided in Table 3-1.

Liquid sealants should be used sparingly. Too thick a coat will plug small oil, water, or air passages. It is also very important to follow the manufacturer's directions implicitly to ensure an effective seal.

Antiseizure Compounds   As the name indicates, the function of an antiseizure compound is to prevent seizure of bolts, nuts, or shafts. It also prevents corrosion, oxidation, galling, and chemical reaction between two elements and reduces friction. This compound should be applied to exhaust manifold bolts and to pipes where a corrosive condition or chemical reaction is likely to occur. Where precise torquing is important, a light coat of antiseizure compound should be applied on the bolts and nuts to reduce friction.

Lock Compounds   A liquid lock compound is used to prevent bolts, nuts, seals, bearings, cones, and other components from becoming loose or moving out of position. This compound fills the space between the components, making them inflexible. It should be used only in cases of emergency, since its application leaves the component to which it has been applied difficult to remove without damage once the compound has set. If it does become necessary to loosen the grip of the compound, use moderate heat. Fuel oil or lubricating oil will also help dissolve this compound.

Making a Gasket   Sometimes it becomes necessary to make a gasket. If a gasket made from cork, polyacrylic, or asbestos is required, the procedure is fairly simple. Two different methods of making gaskets are open to you:

METHOD 1
1.   Lay the gasket material over the components to be sealed.
2.   Secure the material so that, while you are tracing the outline of the component, the gasket material will remain in place.
3.   Cut the inner and outer circumferences with tin snips or scissors and use a gasket punch to cut any openings.

METHOD 2   This method is recommended only when the edges of the component are sharp. If the edges are not sharp, the material will not cut properly and damage will result.

1.   Lay the gasket over the component and use a ball peen hammer to gently tap out one bolt hole. **CAUTION** If the hole is threaded, take care not to damage the threads.
2.   Insert a bolt in the tapped-out hole.
3.   At first, tap out only a minimum number of holes to secure the gasket material to the component.
4.   Finally, tap out the remaining bolt holes and openings.
5.   Tap gently around the edges of the material so that it is cut to the contour of the component.

Lip-type Seals   Lip-type seals are found in large numbers on off-highway and on-highway equipment. Their designs vary according to the use to which they will be put, that is, for sealing off oil or water or dirt or low pressure. They may even be required to seal in two directions.

Table 3-1 PERMATEX SEALANT CHART

Product	Method of application	Temperature range and pressure	Uses	Resists	Drys/sets/ solvent
Permatex High Tack Spray-A-Gasket® Adhesive-Sealant No. 99	Aerosol spray can	−65 to +500°F [−53.8 to +260°C] 5000 psi [351.5 kg/cm²]	All engine gaskets, transmission and rear-end housing gaskets. All threaded connections, radiator and heater hose connections, antislip agent for fan belts, adhesive for general use. Tubeless-tire beads, battery terminal protector and wire waterproofer. Can be used on any type of gasket, felt, cork, metal, paper, asbestos, etc.	Gasoline, oil, kerosene, lube oils, water, steam, antifreeze solutions	Sets up fast . . . super tacky . . . yet allows gasket movement. Under engine operating temperatures, it converts to super sealant Lacquer thinner
Permatex High Tack Brushable Adhesive-Sealant No. 98	Brush in can	−65 to +500°F 5000 psi	All engine gaskets, transmission and rear-end housing gaskets. All threaded connections, radiator and heater hose connections, antislip agent for fan belts, adhesive for general use. Tubeless-tire beads, battery terminal protector and wire waterproofer. Can be used on any type of gasket, felt, cork, metal, paper, asbestos, etc.	Gasoline, oil, kerosene, lube oils, propane, butane gases, water, steam, antifreeze solutions	Sets up fast . . . super tacky . . . yet allows gasket movement. Under engine operating temperatures, it converts to super sealant Lacquer thinner
Permatex High Tack Super Adhesive No. 97	Tube has applicator tip or use spatula or putty knife	−60 to +450°F [−51.1 to +232.2°C] 5000 psi	All-purpose adhesive-sealant for bonding weatherstrip, trim, feathering sanding disks, leather, vinyl, cloth, rubber, glass, metal, wood, silencer pads, mats, cork, asbestos, paper, insulation, repairing arm rests, holding engine gaskets, fastening headers and padded dash. Sealant for drip rail, car seams, convertible tops, water-proofing cracks, etc.	Gasoline, oil, kerosene, glycol, transmission fluid, brake fluid, antifreeze solutions, grease, glycerin, lube oil, propane or butane gases, or water	Fast Firm, nonbrittle stage Lacquer thinner
Form-A-Gasket® No. 1 Mil Spec. Type I MIL-S-45180B (Ord.)	Spatula, putty knife, etc.	−65 to +400°F [−53.8 to +204.4°C] 5000 psi	Permanent assemblies, repair gaskets, fittings, uneven surfaces, thread connections, cracked batteries	Water, steam, kerosene, gasoline, oil grease, mild acid, alkali and salt solutions, aliphatic hydrocarbons, antifreeze mixtures	Fast Hard Alcohol
Form-A-Gasket® No. 2 Mil Spec. Type II MIL-S-45180B (Ord.)	Spatula, putty knife, etc.	−65 to +400°F 5000 psi	Semipermanent reassembly work. Cover plates, threaded and hose connections	Water, steam, kerosene, gasoline, oil, grease, mild acid, alkali and salt solutions, aliphatic hydrocarbons, antifreeze mixtures	Slow Flexible Alcohol
Aviation Form-A-Gasket® No. 3 Mil Spec. Type III MIL-S-45180B (Ord.)	Brush	−65 to +400°F 5000 psi	Sealing of close-fitting parts. Easy to apply on irregular surfaces	Water, steam, kerosene, gasoline, oil, grease, mild acid, alkali and salt solutions, aliphatic hydrocarbons, antifreeze mixtures	Slow Flexible Alcohol
All-Purpose Cement No. 50	Spatula, putty knife, etc.	−40 to 225°F [−40 to +100°C]	Glass to glass, glass to metal, glass to rubber	Water, polishes, and cleaners.	Fast Hard Toluene
Pipe Joint Compound No. 51 New, improved formula. U.L. approved	Brushable, viscous liquid	−65 to +400°F 5000 psi	Threaded fittings, flanges. Can be applied over oil and grease film	Hot and cold water, steam, natural gas, propane, butane, fuel oils, kerosene, lubricating oils, petroleum-base hydraulic fluids, antifreeze mixtures	Slow Flexible Alcohol
Super "300" Form-A-Gasket® No. 83	Brush	−65 to +425°F [−53.8 to +218.3°C] 5000 psi	Assembly work on high-compression engines, diesel heads, cover plates, high-speed turbine superchargers, automatic transmissions, gaskets	High-detergent oils and lubricants, jet fuels, heat-transfer oils, glycols 100%, mild salt solutions, water, steam, aliphatic hydrocarbons, diester, lubricants, antifreeze mixtures, petroleum-base hydraulic fluids, aviation fuels	Slow Flexible Alcohol
Indian Head Gasket Shellac No. 5.	Brush	−65 to +350°F [−53.8 to +176.4°C] Variable	General assembly work and on gaskets of paper, felt, cardboard, rubber and metal	Gasoline, kerosene, greases, oils, water, antifreeze mixtures	Slow Hard Alcohol

Types and Designs of Lip Seals The most common lip-type seal designs are illustrated in Fig. 3-5. Upon examining these seals, you will notice two common facts: a sealing element is angled and bonded to a steel or synthetic case, and one side is open and faces toward the side having a higher pressure.

There are several variable factors in the design of a lip-type seal. Some seals use a garter spring to increase lip contact, and some have a rubber coating over the outer circumference of the seal case (to improve housing sealing). Regardless of design or location, when the lip seal is properly installed, the elasticity of the seal material and, if used, of the

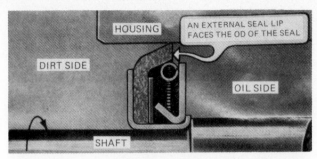

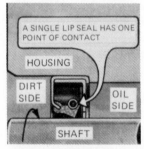 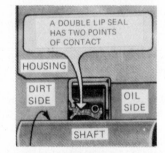

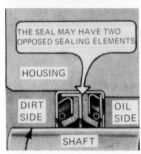 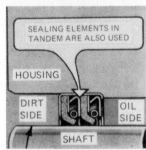

Fig. 3-5 Various lip-type seals (*Caterpillar Tractor Co.*)

and location. Silicones, polyacrylics, and Viton, for instance, are heat-resistant and the least vulnerable to chemicals. However, these products are not as effective against very high temperatures or abrasives. Moreover, certain chemicals used in oils could cause them to deteriorate. In such applications, a seal from nitrile rubber compounds would be more suitable.

The most suitable replacement seal is, of course, the one specified by the manufacturer. The replacement should be made as soon as possible after the seal has failed, to safeguard other components. Needless to say, proper storage, careful handling, and correct installation procedures are factors that affect the service life of the seal.

Removal and Installation of Lip Seals
1. Before cleaning the components, inspect them to determine the cause of seal leakage. After locating the leakage area, check for accumulation of oil, carbon, or rust.
2. Check the alignment of the seal on the shaft and in the bore.
3. Look for the presence of tool marks.
4. Check the shaft and the seal cage housing for the origin of the leakage.

Almost any method is acceptable for the removal of a seal, provided no damage occurs to the shaft or the housing bore. The most common ways to remove a seal with a punch and hammer, with a slide hammer, with a drive and hammer or a press, or as shown in Fig. 3-6.

After the seal has been removed, examine the components to determine the cause of the oil leakage.

1. Measure the shaft and housing for roundness.
2. Check the shaft for roughness, misalignment, or grooves.
3. Check the shaft for runout or bearing wear.
4. Check the seal wear pattern, giving regard to problems of misalignment.

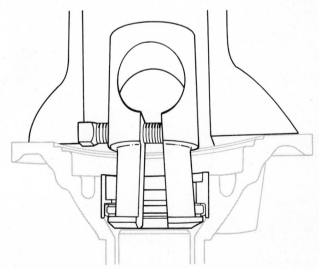

Fig. 3-6 Using jaw gripper tool to remove seal. (*Mack Canada Inc.*)

garter spring, forces the lip face at a predetermined angle against the surface to be sealed. Any additional force placed behind the lip of the seal aids in sealing but may also lead to additional shaft wear.

A lip-type seal is used to seal internally (to keep oil in) or externally (to keep air out). Its composition is important and is determined by its intended use

5. Check for evidence of abrasive wear. The type of abrasive indicates which components you should check for excessive wear.
6. Check for previous installation damage.
7. Check inside the bore and seal for evidence of foreign material.

Pointers for Installing a Lip-type Seal Before installation, recheck that you have selected the seal specified in the service manual and that it has the correct inside and outside diameters and the correct dimensions. Clean the bore opening or recess and remove any nicks or burrs present. Polish the shaft with 600-grit oil paper or crocus cloth. When the shaft is grooved, use either a spacer or a sleeve to make a new lip contact. When using this method, however, you must first check that the lip has a sealing surface and that the seal case does not rub on the rotating surface.

If you are using a seal case without rubber coating, before installing, apply a thin coat of nonhardening sealing compound to the counter bore. This ensures easy installation and improves the sealing

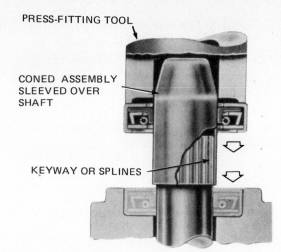

Fig. 3-9 Installing seal over shaft. (*Mack Canada Inc.*)

quality. Next, lubricate the shaft and the seal lip. See Figs. 3-7 and 3-8 for appearance of a correctly installed seal. Finally, place the open side of the seal with its face toward the oil side and drive or push the seal into place. **NOTE** A seal that is installed backward will cause sealing failure because the oil, the air, or atmospheric pressure will lift the seal lip off the surface to be sealed.

When the shaft is in place, take care not to cut the lip or to damage the seal element as you slide the seal over the shaft. When the shaft end and counter bore are at the same height or when the shaft is splined or has a keyway, use a sleeve guide provided by the manufacturer. If this is not available, follow the procedure shown in Fig. 3-9. If it is at all possible, you should solder the seams and then smooth the surface. This will help prevent lip damage during installation.

If the seal must be driven below the face, select a seal driver which fits loosely in the counter bore. Under all circumstances the force on the seal case must be exerted on its strongest point, that is, the outer circumference. In the event that a seal driver is not available, use a socket or pipe close to the outside dimension of the seal. Never use a punch to install a seal and do not drive the seal in place with a hammer, for this will deform the seal housing, as well as the sealing element. (See Fig. 3-9.)

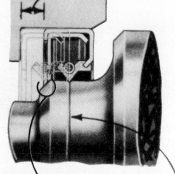

Fig. 3-7 Making new lip contact. (*Caterpillar Tractor Co.*)

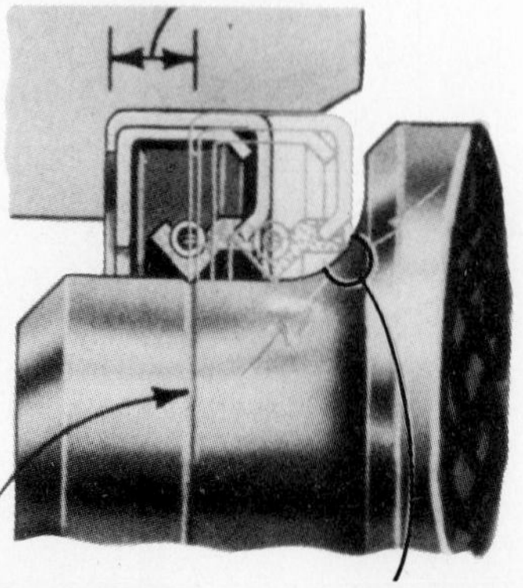

Fig. 3-8 Making new lip contact. (*Caterpillar Tractor Co.*)

Review Questions

1. Approximately 90 percent of gasket and seal failure can be traced back to the mechanic's improper handling rather than to manufacturing frailties. In this regard, list at least eight things you should do (or not do) to prevent early seal or gasket failure.

2. List eight major types of gasket materials and state where these gaskets are primarily used.

3. List at least five reasons why, in a static application, an O ring has a better sealing effect than a gasket.

4. Give three reasons why some gaskets have internal and/or external grommets.

5. When or for what reason would you use: (a) a sealant compound, (b) an antiseizure compound, (c) a lock compound?

6. What additional precautions or measurements would you take when a cover spans over two components?

7. List three major differences among various lip-type seals.

8. Why should you examine the lip-type seal and the seal area before actually removing the seal?

9. Even if a seal is properly installed and positioned, an oil, fuel, or coolant leak may still occur because of some other factors. List three reasons why a lip-type seal could fail to seal (other than improper installation, incorrect positioning, or normal wear on the seal lip).

10. Why is it important to use only the lip-type seal recommended by the manufacturer?

11. When you install a lip-type seal that must have its opening side facing outward, what precaution must you take when pressing the seal into its bore?

12. When must you use a seal protection sleeve when installing a lip-type seal?

Unit 4
Filters

The most efficient way to maintain a fully effective hydraulic system and prolong its life is to keep the system clean. The hydraulic system includes the lubricant, coolant, power steering, transmission, and rear and front axles.

Contaminants are the most frequent cause of any systems failure. Foreign matter can enter the system because of a mechanic's carelessness or through ineffective components. If the service life of the components is to be extended and the downtime reduced, component contamination must be prevented. Since the manufacturer originally installs the filters, screens, strainers, and breathers, and provides detailed service manuals, it is up to the mechanic or service worker to maintain the system.

Although no single definition appears to be applicable to screens, strainers, and filters, all three have the same purpose—to remove impurities or solids from liquids and to hold them in suspension.

Commonsense Rules
- Change or clean filters, screens, and breathers at regular intervals or when indicated by gauge testing.
- When changing filters or strainers, also clean the filter housing and bowl thoroughly.
- Cut the filter open to determine the condition of the system.
- Check for corrosion.
- Do not reuse seals.
- Repair faulty components as soon as possible.
- Make certain that serviced or exchanged components are clean before they are installed.
- Maintain proper oil and coolant levels.
- Drain fuel tank and fuel filter traps weekly, or even daily if necessary.

Filter Element Material   There are three general classes of filter materials: mechanical, inactive absorbent, and active absorbent.

The mechanical filter is composed of closely woven metal wire screens called a sieve. Mechanical filters are primarily intended to prevent only fairly coarse, insoluble particles from passing through the system.

Inactive absorbent filters are composed of materials such as cotton, yarn, cloth, impregnated cellulose paper, or porous metal. This type of filter material traps quite small particles. Some even stop water and water-soluble contaminants from passing into the system. The filter elements are often treated to give an affinity to the contaminants likely to be found in the system.

Active absorbent filter materials, such as charcoal or fuller's earth, remove particles by absorption as well as by filtering. Other than for the exhaust system, they are not used as filter material on hydraulic systems.

Nearly all hydraulic systems use a full-flow filtering system. The location of the filter varies. The fluid may be filtered before it enters the system and/or as it returns from the system. Sometimes the filter is part of the engine or equipment, or it may be connected with lines to the system.

A bypass filtering system (used for the coolant and lubrication systems) is additional to the full-flow filtering system. The bypass filter is connected in shunt to the main fluid flow. That is, the inlet of the filter is connected to the main fluid flow, and the fluid return line is connected from the filter to the low-pressure side of the system. The bypass filtering system filters only part of the fluid, but eventually all the fluid finds its way through the filters.

An exception to the bypass filter is the transmission filter assembly, which has no line connection (see Fig. 4-1). It is bolted to the standard power takeoff opening. When the transmission is operating, transmission oil is forced into the large opening of the filter assembly, passes through the filter material, drains, and then reenters the transmission through the small opening. About 80 percent of the abrasive material that may be in the oil, in the form of road dirt, metal particles, and grit, is removed.

Screens and Strainers   Screens or strainers are surface filters and are occasionally referred to as mechanical filters. They are commonly used as inlet filters to prevent large particles from entering the hydraulic pump. Alternately, they are used as inlet

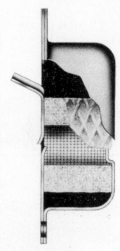

Fig. 4-1   Cross-section of a transmission oil filter assembly. (*Eaton Corporation*)

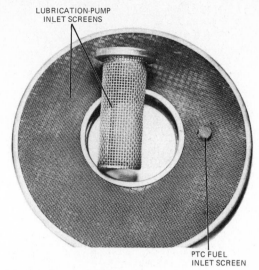

LUBRICATION-PUMP
INLET SCREENS

PTC FUEL
INLET SCREEN

Fig. 4-2 Mechanical filter.

strainers to prevent large particles from entering the hydraulic reservoir or the fuel tank.

Upon examining Fig. 4-2, you will see that the various screens are constructed of a wire-mesh screening element. The wire is especially processed to improve its durability; by varying the density of the screen mesh, one can vary the quality of the filtering.

Filter, Screen, and Strainer Ratings The unit of measurement to determine the effectiveness of a filter is the micron (μm). A micron is equal to 0.000001 m (0.000039 in). When new, a filter prevents a large percentage of particles of a specific minimum size (measured according to the filter's micron rating) from passing through it. If the filter was rated to be 25 μm, for instance, particles of up to 25-μm size would pass through and into the system. It is therefore important that you use the replacement filters from the original manufacturer to screen out undesirable contaminants.

Strainers and screens are rated by sieve or by a mesh number that relates to the micron rating; see Table 4-1.

Filters Because the hydraulic systems on the various types of diesel engines and equipment are numerous, filters are manufactured in a multitude of sizes, micron ratings, designs, and materials. The appropriate size of the filter is dictated by the flow volume; the type and micron rating of the filter ele-

ment is governed by the hydraulic system in which it is used. Its location will depend on whether it is to be used as an inlet or an outlet filter.

There are three basic types of filter elements: surface filters, deep filters, and edge filters (see Figs. 4-3, 4-4, and 4-5).

SURFACE FILTERS Surface filters (Fig. 4-3) are designed as cartridge and spin-on types. Their filter elements are identically composed of specially treated micronic cellulose paper. The paper is formed in vertical convolutions (wrinkles) fashioned in a cylindrical pattern to increase filter area. The cartridge element is reinforced with perforated sheet metal, both inside and out, to give the filter element strength. A seal on the top and bottom prevents the filtered fluid from passing into the unfiltered fluid.

The spin-on (surface) filter also uses a multipaper element, which is placed in an internally reinforced housing. The open side of the housing is male- or female-threaded, so that the filter can be screwed to the filter base. A seal, fastened to the open end of the housing, seals the inlet fluid from the outlet fluid.

DEEP FILTER From the outside this type of filter (see Fig. 4-4) looks similar to the surface filter. However, because of its depth, the filter material used is more efficient and also has a longer service life. Some deep filters are made up of two or three different types of filter materials, increasing their efficiency even more.

Porous metal filters This type of deep filter is used on fuel systems having a low flow volume. The porous metal filter element of fine woven copper or steel material is pressed to a shape suitable for the filter housing.

The porous metal filter element is also effective when made by the sintered process. Here the porous metal element consists of minute metal balls joined together as one inflexible piece. The metal used for this element is usually bronze or stainless steel. This element filters particles greater than 2 μm (approximately 0.00078 in [0.000002 m]).

Fig. 4-3 Surface filter.

Table 4-1 STRAINER AND SCREEN RATINGS

Mesh number	U.S. sieve number	In microns (μm)
30	555	550
50	297	292
60	251	246
70	210	215
80	195	190
90	171	166
100	149	151

Fig. 4-4 Deep filter material. (*a*) Cotton. (*b*) Spin-on element, short cotton filter. (*c*) V-type paper element.

EDGE FILTERS Edge filters (see Fig. 4-5) are used as primary filters in the lubrication and fuel injection systems. The filter element is designed of many copper, bronze, or stainless steel disk plates which are bolted or otherwise held together as an assembly at a predetermined pressure. The assembly is then placed over a tube. The tube acts as a fluid line and directs it to the outlet port. The inlet port is the outer housing of the filter. Some edge filters have the added convenience of an automatic or hand-operated scraper device for cleaning the outside of the disk. This helps, of course, to extend the life of the filter.

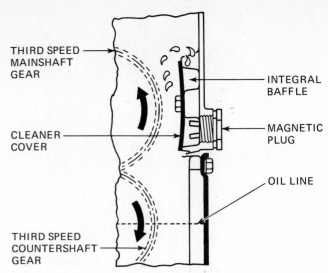

Fig. 4-6 Sectional view of magnetic plug installation. (*Mack Canada Inc.*)

Magnetic Oil Cleaner The magnetic oil cleaner, in the form of a magnetic plug or disk fastened to the drain plug, is a natural magnet (amber). It is positioned in a precise place within a hydraulic system so that it can catch and hold metal particles deposited in the oil as they pass by (see Fig. 4-6).

Liquid Flow through a Filter Filter elements are sealed to a housing or are in a sealed housing. O rings (or sealing rings) separate the filtered oil from the unfiltered oil. Liquid enters near the top of the filter housing (see Fig. 4-7), or, in the case of spin-

Fig. 4-5 Edge filter with hand-operated scraper.

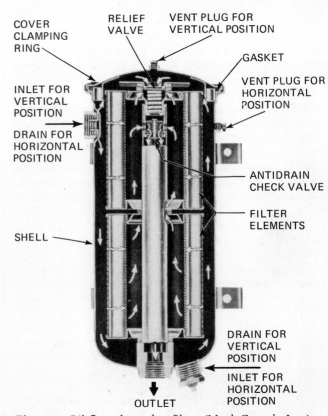

Fig. 4-7 Oil flow through a filter. (*Mack Canada Inc.*)

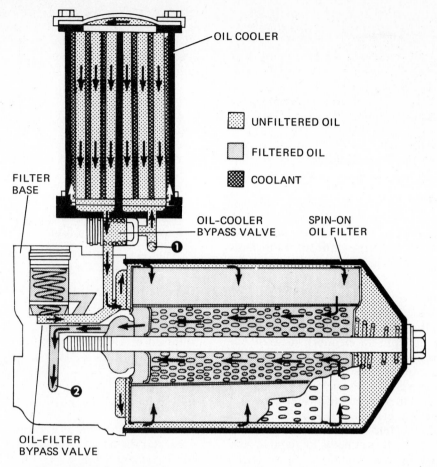

OIL COOLER

UNFILTERED OIL

FILTERED OIL

COOLANT

FILTER BASE

OIL-COOLER BYPASS VALVE

SPIN-ON OIL FILTER

①

②

OIL–FILTER BYPASS VALVE

1. From the hydraulic system
2. Return to sump or to the lubrication system

Fig. 4-8 Air flow through the filter and oil cover. (*J I Case Company Agricultural Equipment*)

on oil filters, it enters via the adapter plate into the outer area of the filter element (see Fig. 4-8). The system pressure forces the liquid through the filter element into the center area. Regardless of the micron rating, the pressure on the center area is always lower than that on the outside area. As a result, filtered fluid then passes through the center of the outlet port tube. Some filters are designed with an antidrain check valve to prevent fluid from draining from the filter bowl when the fluid flow is stopped. This ensures instant oil pressure when the engine is being restarted.

Full-flow oil filters have either a built-in relief valve or a relief valve which is separately mounted, except for fuel filters which have no bypass valves. If the filter element becomes clogged, the function of the relief valves is to allow the fluid to bypass the filter and to flow on to the system, thereby assuring lubrication or oil supply. Depending on which system the filter is used in, the relief valve will unseat when the pressure drop is greater than the energy of the valve spring. The opening range is between 5 and 30 psi [34.47 and 206.7 kPa].

Servicing an Oil Filter In order to replace an externally mounted filter element, first clean the sur-

rounding area. Remove the drain plug to drain the filter housing. Remove the cover and filter element. Clean and inspect the bowl and cover. Clean and examine the relief valve. Make sure that the return outlet holes and orifices are free of any foreign materials.

Replace the drain plug and install a new filter element. Fill the filter. When replacing lubricant, choose the correct type and grade. Place a new gasket on the cover and make sure that the cover is positioned correctly.

Check the oil level. Start the engine and run it at low idle. Loosen the vent plug, but close it as soon as the oil appears.

Run the engine at least 4 to 5 min to determine if there are any oil leaks.

Stop the engine and check the oil level. (Add more oil if it is required.)

Spin-on or Fuel Filters When changing a spin-on oil or fuel filter, clean the surrounding area, and with a strap wrench or box-end wrench, loosen and remove the filter.

Clean the filter base and make certain the base is not nicked or burred.

When the relief valve is part of the filter base,

remove and clean the valve assembly. Make certain the spring tension is not changed and that the valve slides freely within its bore.

Apply oil to the filter base end seal ring and then screw the filter in place. Pay special attention to the torque recommendations. (An overtorqued filter could cause distortion of the filter and/or dislodgement or splitting of the O ring.)

Servicing a Coolant Filter   The procedure for changing a coolant filter element conforms to that for a cartridge or spin-on oil or fuel filter, but you must, in addition, close off the inlet and/or outlet valves to prevent coolant loss. If there is no shutoff valve, the coolant must be drained to below the filter housing. With the engine running, you must then check (by means of the condition indicator) the coolant flow and the coolant color. Also check for the presence of air.

Servicing Fuel Filter Elements   The procedure for changing a fuel filter element is similar to that for changing a cartridge, spin-on, or lubrication oil filter. The exceptions are: (1) Any air present in the filter housing must be removed by using the hand primer or a low-pressure source or by allowing the gravity force on the fuel to create a fuel flow. (2) When an edge element is used, the filter element must be washed in solvent and blown (with shop air) from the inside to the outside to remove any particles. If necessary, this procedure must be repeated to ensure element cleanliness. (3) Never blow air from the outside to the inside. This may damage the element because it would force foreign material into the metal shell or disk.

Review Questions

1. Which two classes of filter materials are used for filters on on- and off-highway equipment?

2. List the four basic types of filter designs.

3. Describe the basic difference between a surface filter and an edge filter.

4. What is the functional difference between a full-flow filter and a bypass filter?

5. Explain why a full-flow filter requires a bypass valve.

6. A factor common to all filters is that they filter liquid or air from the outside to the inside. Explain why this method of flow is used.

7. Outline each of the steps you would follow to service or replace a (a) spin-on oil filter, (b) replacement-element oil filter.

8. What service would you perform to maintain or extend the service life of a fuel or oil filter?

Unit 5
Bearings

Everything that turns requires a bearing (or bearings) to reduce friction between the moving and stationary parts, to lessen power loss, and to decrease wear. Many types of bearings have been designed in an effort to overcome friction and frictional heat.

Friction is defined as the resistance to movement between any two surfaces in contact. It is classified as sliding, rolling, or fluid friction.

Bearings may be divided into two main types: friction and antifriction bearings. Both are used on on- and off-highway equipment to support shafts, gears, or pullies.

Friction Bearings   The simplest type of friction bearing is a hole drilled into a support plate to guide a shaft. When the shaft or support plate moves lengthwise or in rotary motion, the contact areas of the shaft and support plate slide against each other (sliding friction). The friction bearings used on diesel engines, transmissions, etc., are called *insert bearings,* and those used specifically with camshafts, crankshafts, or connecting rods are referred to as *precision insert bearings* because they are manufactured to a precision fit and dimension.

Bushings   Bushings are a type of friction bearing and are made in three varieties: those rolled to form a cylinder with the ends butting against each other, clinch bushings (usually precision finished), and those of a solid structure. Some bushings are completely finished to specified dimensions, while others come with a specified outside diameter, leaving the inside to be reamed to the desired specification. Depending on the intended use, the bushing may be manufactured from solid metal or alloy, or of a synthetic material such as nylon. Some applications require bushings with a special inner contact surface thinly layered with babbitt, copper, or nickel alloy (see Fig. 5-1).

Function of Friction Bearings   Friction bearings must be held firmly in place and in full contact with the supporting bore if they are to withstand extreme force and dissipate heat. The most common method of ensuring that a friction bearing is held in position involves simply pressing it into its supporting bore. If there is a chance that the bearing may become loose or dislodged, locating lugs or dowel pins are used to hold it in position.

A friction bearing must also have the ability to maintain a film of lubricant between the moving and stationary parts to reduce wear. To achieve this, one of various types of groove patterns is cut inside the bearing.

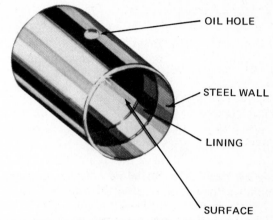

Fig. 5-1   Clinch bushing. (*Cummins Engine Co. Inc.*)

Friction Bearing Action   When a mechanism is in motion, the drive or driven shaft rotates, and oil or grease slides through the clearance between the shaft and bearing. The wedge formed by the oil or grease lifts the shaft away from the bearing contact (load) area (see Fig. 5-2). Some lubricant molecules tend to stick to the shaft and bearing. The molecules on the shaft rotate with the shaft, while those on the bearing are somewhat stationary. The slippage of the lubricant molecules past each other is known as fluid friction. The film thickness of the lubricant is not always the same, because of the load variation during operation. Under extreme load conditions only the lubricant which is stuck to the shaft and

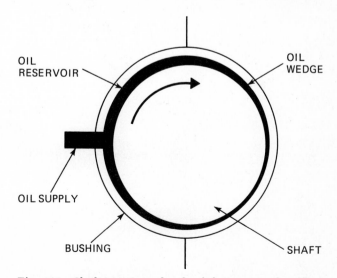

Fig. 5-2   Shaft rotation plus load forms an oil wedge. (*Federal-Mogul. Worldwide Marketing Group*)

bearing area remains, and this circumstance permits a metal-to-metal contact which could lead to excessive wear of shaft and bearing.

Antifriction Bearings All antifriction bearings use a rolling element (balls, rollers, or needles) between the inner and outer ring (race) to convert sliding friction into rolling motion. Either the inner or the outer ring remains stationary.

Because of the small contact area between the rolling elements and the inner and outer rings (races) and because of the need to withstand the high compression stress, the material used for ball bearings is usually of heat-treated chromium-alloy steel, and the material for most roller bearings is usually carbonized steel alloy.

The load placed on the bearing can be perpendicular to the shaft and axis of the bearing (radial load), parallel with the axis of the shaft and bearing (thrust load), or a combination of radial and thrust loads.

The radial load is carried by only half of the rolling elements by compressing the inner ring against the rolling element, to the outer ring or vice versa. However, the thrust load is carried equally by all the rolling elements (see Fig. 5-3).

ACTION The operating action of an antifriction bearing is similar to that previously outlined for friction bearings. However, owing to the antifriction bearing's triple-unit construction, each roller or ball represents a shaft, and therefore an oil wedge is formed on each side of the rolling elements. This not only improves lubrication, but also reduces friction and increases the bearing support.

TYPES Antifriction bearings may be classified into six types: (1) ball bearings, (2) cylindrical roller bearings, (3) needle bearings, (4) tapered roller bearings, (5) self-aligning roller bearings, and (6) thrust bearings. However, each type is further coded according to its intended application.

IDENTIFICATION CODE Ball bearings and roller bearings are identified by a numerical code indicating the bore in millimeters or in sixteenths of an inch. Letter codes indicate the type of bearing, the outside diameter (OD), the width, the cage, the seal or shield, the modification, and the required lubrication. The internal fit, the tolerance, and any special characteristics are coded by number.

Ball Bearings A single-row deep-groove (no loading) ball bearing is shown in Fig. 5-4. The balls roll in a single deep groove, one in each race. The high supporting grooves and the close fit allow the bearings to take a very high radial load. Because the load is through the axis of the ball, it can also withstand a substantial thrust load.

NOTE Since little or no movement exists between the inner and outer races, careful installation and alignment between the shaft and the housing is necessary.

A single-row, loading-groove ball bearing is shown in Fig. 5-5. It is so named because the balls are inserted through a filling groove or loading groove. This type of bearing has a higher radial load capacity than the bearing shown in Fig. 5-3, because more balls are inserted.

NOTE Where thrust load may be a factor, this type of bearing should be installed with the loading groove facing toward the thrust side.

Ring Bearings A snap ring placed in the groove of the outer ring is used to provide a shoulder for the axial location of the bearing in the bore.

Shield Bearings A shield or plate on one or both sides of a shield bearing (see Fig. 5-6) limits the entrance of small particles between races and balls and at the same time reduces the pressure and flow of oil through the balls.

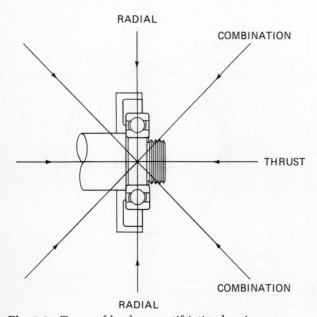

Fig. 5-3 Types of loads on antifriction bearings.

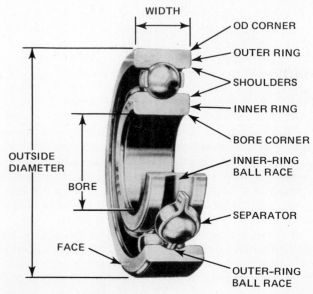

Fig. 5-4 Single-row, deep-groove ball bearing. (*International Harvester Co.*)

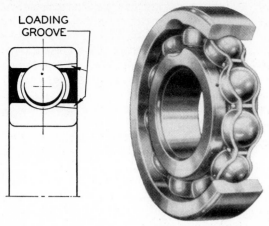

LOADING
GROOVE

Fig. 5-5 Single-row, loading-groove ball bearing. (*International Harvester Co.*)

NOTE Extreme care and cleanliness must be exercised during the handling and cleaning of this type of bearing. Do not damage the shield during removal or installation; it may contact the bearing separator and cause wear or increased friction.

Sealed Bearings Sealed bearings have a permanent seal either on one side or on both sides (see Fig. 5-7). Bearings having a seal on both sides are prelubricated and cannot be cleaned. When their seals are damaged or the bearings feel rough during rotation, they must be replaced.

NOTE When you install or remove these bearings, be extremely careful not to damage the seals.

Where only one seal is used, take care that no dirt enters the bearings during installation. It is difficult to remove dirt once it has worked its way between the balls, separator, and races and has reached the seal.

Single-Row, Angular-Contact Bearings Single-row, angular-contact bearings are used where radial load and thrust loads are combined. However, the thrust can be applied in only one direction. Single-row, angular-contact bearings are usually used in pairs, with one bearing on each side of the shaft.

NOTE When you install these bearings in pairs, make certain that the thrust faces point in directions

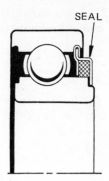

SEAL

Fig. 5-7 Sealed bearing. (*International Harvester Co.*)

opposite to each other. When they are used for one-sided heavy-thrust loads, install them as shown in Fig. 5-8.

Double-Row, Deep-Groove Bearings The design of double-row, deep-groove bearings does not differ from that of the single-row, deep-groove ball bearings, but the load capacity in any application is, of course, higher because of the two rows of balls.

Double-Row, Angular-Contact Bearings The design of double-row, angular-contact bearings is similar to that of single-row, angular-contact bearings. However, they are usually constructed with a predetermined internal preload. They are used where a shaft must be held tightly, radially as well as axially.

Cylindrical (Straight) Roller Bearings Cylindrical bearings use straight rollers as their rolling elements and have a very high radial capacity since the roller axis and the inner and outer race (or the contact surface) are parallel (see Fig. 5-9). They are manufactured in single or double rows and in various designs.

Needle Bearings Initially, needle bearings were considered cageless roller bearings because they use rollers as their rolling element. They are classified as needle bearings when their length is at least six times the diameter of the rollers. This type has high radial capacity but no thrust-carrying capacity.

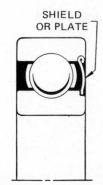

SHIELD
OR PLATE

Fig. 5-6 Shield bearing. (*International Harvester Co.*)

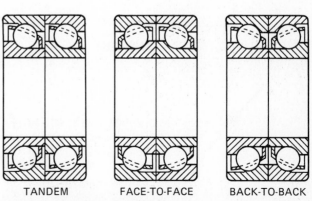

TANDEM   FACE-TO-FACE   BACK-TO-BACK

Fig. 5-8 Installing single-row, angular-contact bearings. (*International Harvester Co.*)

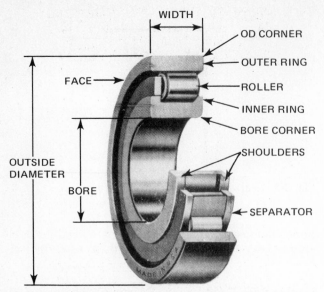

Fig. 5-9 Cylindrical (straight) roller bearing. (*International Harvester Co.*)

A needle bearing may be any one of the designs shown in Fig. 5-10, that is, with or without a separator, without inner ring or outer ring or cage, or without an outer ring or cage.

NOTE When you install a needle bearing which has an outer cage, exert the force on the side bearing the identification mark.

Self-aligning Roller Bearings One type of self-aligning roller bearing has single- or double-row spherical rollers and an outer spherical raceway (see Fig. 5-11). The contour of the inner raceway has the shape of the roller. The second type of self-aligning roller bearing has an inner spherical raceway and the rollers have an hourglass shape (see Fig. 5-12). The contour of the outer raceway has the shape of the rollers.

Tapered Roller Bearings Tapered roller bearings have tapered rollers as the rolling element between the cone and the cup (see Fig. 5-13). The lines of contact between the rollers, cones, and cup, when extended, intersect in the center of the shaft. The cage and the high shoulder on the cone keep the

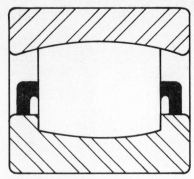

Fig. 5-11 Self-aligning roller bearing. Single-row, spherical roller with outer spherical raceway. (*International Harvester Co.*)

rollers aligned. These bearings are designed to carry high combined radial and thrust loads. As a general rule, tapered bearings are used in pairs with one bearing on each side of the shaft.

NOTE Tapered roller bearings need periodic adjustment to take up any looseness which may have developed owing to wear or stress.

Thrust Bearings Thrust bearings are designed for axial thrust load application only; their radial load-carrying capacity is only incidental. They use balls, tapered rollers, or cylindrical rollers as their rolling element (see Fig. 5-14). The tapered or cylindrical thrust bearings generally use short rollers to compensate for the variation in speed between the outer and the inner diameters.

Cleaning Antifriction Bearings Let the bearings soak in a basket for some time in a recommended cleaning solution, in a high-grade kerosene, or in Varsol.

CAUTION All solvents are highly inflammable. Handle them with care to prevent a fire.

After a period of time, agitate the basket several times. Air can also be used to agitate the cleaning fluid. This will remove the particles (contaminants) from the bearings.

Remove and inspect one bearing at a time. If fur-

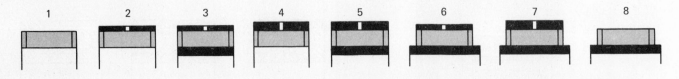

1) ROLLER ONLY
2) ROLLER ASSEMBLY WITH OUTER RING
3) ROLLER ASSEMBLY WITH OUTER AND INNER RINGS
4) ROLLER ASSEMBLY WITH OUTER RING AND SEPARATOR
5) ROLLER ASSEMBLY WITH OUTER AND INNER RINGS AND SEPARATOR
6) ROLLER ASSEMBLY WITH OUTER RING AND WIDE INNER RING
7) ROLLER ASSEMBLY WITH OUTER RING, WIDE INNER RING, AND SEPARATOR
8) ROLLER ASSEMBLY WITH WIDE INNER RING

Fig. 5-10 Needle bearing designs. (*International Harvester Co.*)

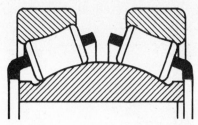

Fig. 5-12 Self-aligning roller bearing. Double-row, hour-glass roller with inner spherical raceway. (*International Harvester Co.*)

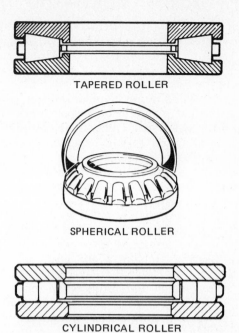

TAPERED ROLLER

SPHERICAL ROLLER

CYLINDRICAL ROLLER

Fig. 5-14 Types of thrust bearings.

ther cleaning is necessary, use a durable brush (the bristles must not come out or break off during cleaning) to loosen the remaining dirt particles, and other contaminants.

After stubborn dirt has been loosened, complete the cleaning by moving the bearings back and forth in the solvent and then repeat this procedure in a clean solvent bath. Use forced air to dislodge any remaining particles and to remove the solvent, but hold both races stationary. Never allow a race to spin by the force of the air; the ring may explode. Always use caution when employing forced air (see Fig. 5-15).

When you clean bearings which have removable shields, dismantle the shields and then clean the bearings and the shields separately. When you clean bearings with fixed single- or double-sided shields or with a single seal, use only an oil spray cleaner. Otherwise continuously rinse them with clean solvent to wash out the particles.

CAUTION If compressed air is used, take care not to damage the seal or the shields.

Never attempt to clean cage needle bearings. It is much more convenient to replace them.

Inspecting Antifriction Bearings After the bearings are clean, dip them in light engine oil, gently rotate them a few times, and place them on clean paper to drain off the excess oil.

To determine the serviceability of a bearing, hold it by inserting your fingertips in the center bore and then check it for discoloration, cracked or damaged races, damaged shield (or shields) or seals, damaged separator, broken or damaged balls or rollers, and brinelled, flaked, or spalled areas on balls, rollers, or races. Any of the above defects will necessitate bearing replacement.

If, on inspection, the bearing appears satisfactory and during inspection does not feel rough or have a tendency to stick, it should be dipped in clean oil and stored in greaseproof paper until it is to be reinstalled.

If bearings are to be stored for a longer period, coat them thoroughly with grease so that no air can come in contact with their surfaces and then wrap

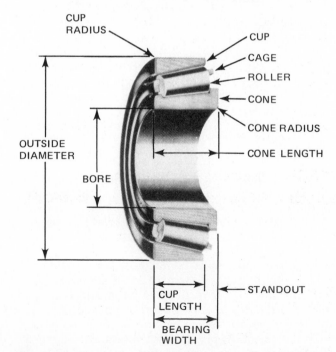

Fig. 5-13 Tapered roller bearing. (*International Harvester Co.*)

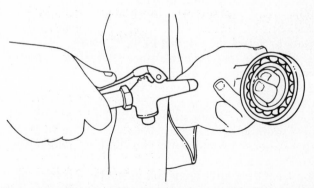

Fig. 5-15 Bearing correctly held during cleaning procedure.

them in greaseproof paper. Identify the wrapping paper with the bearing part number or indicate on it the location from which the bearing was removed.

Removing or Installing Press-Fitted Parts Your first concern when removing or installing bearings, bushings, or gears should be the cleanness of the tools and the work area. Once the job is underway, meticulous attention should be given to even the smallest detail, since careless work habits promote early bearings, bushing, or gear failure.

All service shops possess a hydraulic floor portable press, some type of puller set with attachments, and a bushing insert and removal set. The hydraulic press and the puller set or bushing removal set are essential to any service shop to ensure proper removal of bearings, bushings, and gears, and in addition they are profitable timesavers.

One of the major difficulties when removing or installing press-fitted parts such as the aforementioned is that of getting a firm enough grip on the parts themselves to pull them out of position. Tool manufacturers have designed a great variety of pullers and attachments to take care of the three basic pulling and pushing problems. These are (1) pulling or pushing gears, bearings, pulleys, etc., from a shaft and reinstalling them; (2) pulling or pushing press-fitted internal bearing cups or retainers, or removing seals from a housing and reinstalling them; (3) pulling or pushing shafts from or into a housing.

Remember that precision gears, bearings, races, etc., whether small or very large, are delicately machined parts. They must be gripped in a manner that will not damage them, but the grip must be firm enough to prevent the puller from slipping off, and the support must not give way when force is applied. Unfortunately gears and bearings, etc., are often located in places which are extremely difficult to reach and are often frozen to the supporting components.

The proper grip and support are not the only aspects of pulling or pushing components from or into position. *Force* is equally important. As well as being sufficient to remove press-fitted parts that may be frozen or rusted into place, the force must be properly applied. In other words, it must be evenly distributed on all bore surfaces. If a gear, bearing, or bearing cup, etc., is cocked by an improperly applied force, it will be damaged during installation or removal—if it can be removed at all!

Some basic methods of gripping and pulling bearings, gears, pulleys, etc., are shown in Fig. 5-16.

How to Select the Correct Puller
1. Analyze the area of resistance. It can vary greatly between seemingly similar jobs.
2. Select a pulling screw which is at least one-quarter larger in diameter than the shaft of the object to be pulled. When using a hydraulic puller, the maximum (ton) force exerted should be 7 to 10 times the diameter (in inches) of the shaft, to reduce friction.
3. Check for alignment and grip after the slack has been taken up.
4. For rusted parts, or when the area of resistance

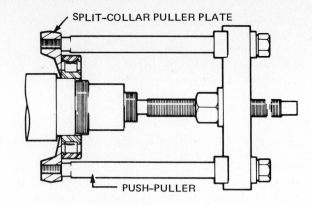

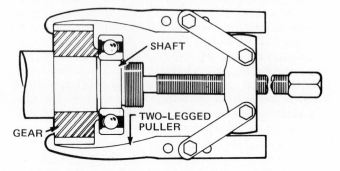

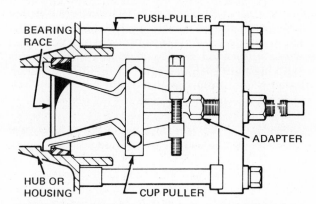

Fig. 5-16 The three basic puller arrangements. (*International Harvester Co.*)

is large, use, if necessary, penetrating oil or moderate heat.
5. Be prepared in the event that the object to be pulled ejects with a great force from the shaft or bearing.

Pointers When Using a Hydraulic Press
1. Before using a hydraulic press, clear the surrounding area of any obstructions.
2. Adjust the table to a suitable working height. Secure it firmly and then make certain there is slack in the winch cables.
3. Support the object being pulled or pushed by using a pulling attachment or other accessory. Ensure that the center of the hydraulic ram is in the center of the object to be pulled or pushed.
4. Screw out the extension and bring it in contact with the object. Apply moderate pressure and check the alignment.
5. Bearings, gears, or any other objects which can

break during press action should be wrapped with a cloth to protect you and others against injury.

6. To prevent damage to the pressed-out object (which may eject with great force), have a pail of sawdust or a slab of wood on which they may fall.

Dos and Don'ts When Removing a Bearing The following rules are applicable whether the bearing is to be discarded or reused:

- Never use a hammer, a hammer and punch, or an impact wrench in conjunction with a puller arrangement when removing bearings. This could brinell the races and the contact surfaces of the rolling elements and lead to spalling and premature failure.
- Never heat a bearing with a cutting torch. Use a heating tip and a temperature stick to determine the temperature.
- When possible, press or pull the bearing or the race from the shaft or housing. Use the correct puller and attachments or, alternatively, drive them out of the bore or off the shaft as illustrated in Fig. 5-17.
- When using a press to remove a bearing or race, support the bearing or the housing correctly (see Fig. 5-18).
- When using a tube tool, take care not to cock the bearing. Drive it alternately, first one side and then the other.
- When using heat to remove an inner ring that is equal to the diameter of the shaft, wear asbestos gloves to prevent your hands from being burned. Alternatively, heat only one part of the ring, or cut off part of the ring, and then remove it. When it still cannot be removed, drive the cutting edge of a cold chisel into the heated area to enlarge the ring or to crack the ring open (see Fig. 5-19).
- After the bearings have been removed, handle them as carefully as you would if they were new. Wrap them in clean wax paper or promptly place them in a basket and immerse it in clean solvent.

Fig. 5-18 Supporting a bearing when pressing it from the shaft (partial cutaway view). (*International Harvester Co.*)

CAUTION Never "rotate" a removed bearing—it could be damaged by such practice.

- To prevent shield damage, do not place shielded bearings in the same container.
- Do not place a two-sided shield or a sealed bearing in solvent for cleaning. Wipe the surface clean and wrap it in clean wax paper for future inspection.
- Do not place too many bearings in one basket for cleaning. This reduces the cleaning effectiveness because the dirt from one bearing washes into the others.

Bearing, Gear, and Shaft Installation Bearings, gears, and shafts are installed in an order precisely reverse to that in which they were removed. However, before you press, pull, or drive them into place, clean the shaft, the bore, gear, or bearing seat and check them for nicks and burrs. If either is present, remove them by using an oil stone or a fine-cut file.

When installing a bearing, apply a moderate amount of oil to the bearing seat and bore, and at

Fig. 5-17 Driving a bearing off the shaft (partial cutaway view). (*International Harvester Co.*)

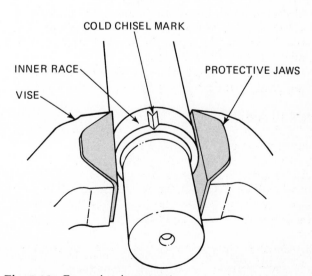

Fig. 5-19 Removing inner race.

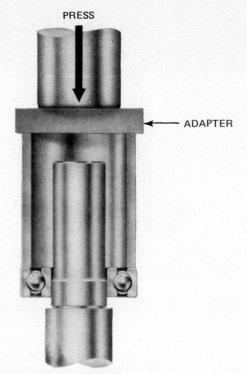

PRESS

ADAPTER

Fig. 5-20 Installing a bearing using a press (partial cutaway view). (*International Harvester Co.*)

this time remove the bearing from its package. Your hands and your tools must be spotlessly clean.

Align the bearing on the press bed, align the shaft with the bore (see Fig. 5-20), and then press or pull the bearing until it seats firmly against the shoulder.

If it is necessary to install the bearing with the shaft in place and no puller or press is available, tap the bearing lightly with a makeshift tool similar to that shown in Fig. 5-21. This will start it square into

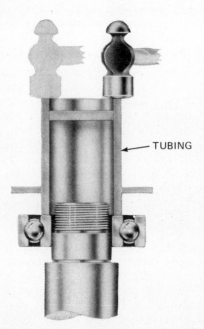

TUBING

Fig. 5-21 Installing a bearing using a piece of tubing and a hammer (partial cutaway view). (*International Harvester Co.*)

the bore or into the shaft. Be certain it is not cocked; otherwise it will scrape or burr the shaft and/or the bore.

To prevent the balls or rollers from being damaged while driving a bearing against the seat, you should place a lint-free cloth around the assembly.

CAUTION Under no circumstances should you use an impact wrench to turn the puller spindle, the puller nut, or the shaft nut when pulling the bearing into place. Such practice could damage the rolling elements and the races.

The safest way to install a bearing to a shaft is to heat the bearing to 250°F [121°C] in an oven or a heat plate, or as shown in Fig. 5-22. This will expand the bearing so that the inner race slides freely onto the shaft. Work as speedily as possible when positioning the bearing, for it cools very quickly.

Another safe method of installing a bearing is to cool the shaft or the bearing, depending on bearing installation, using dry ice to shrink the shaft or the bearing.

CAUTION Always use protective asbestos gloves when using dry ice.

When installing a press-fitted gear to a shaft, properly support the gear or shaft which is most suitable onto the press bed. Lubricate the gear or shaft with a good-grade oil, align the gear bore with the shaft, and bring the press ram in contact with the shaft or gear. Now start to apply force and check the alignment. When the gear or shaft has started to protrude into the bore, press the gear into position.

A safe way to install a gear and also to prevent damage to the bore or shaft is to heat the gear in an oven to about 350°F [177°C]. Before placing the gear onto the shaft, lubricate the shaft and the gear with high-pressure grease. Then, using asbestos gloves, quickly place the gear onto the shaft. It may be necessary to drive the gear into position with a piece of tubing.

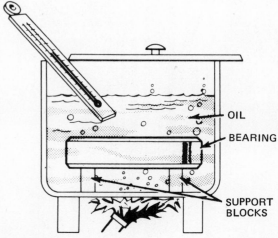

OIL

BEARING

SUPPORT BLOCKS

Fig. 5-22 Heating a bearing for assembly on the shaft. (*International Harvester Co.*)

Bushing and Bearing Failure The cause or causes of premature bushing or bearing failure or of excessive bushing or bearing wear may be one or more of the following: (1) dirt, abrasives, coarse particles, moisture, or acid (a lubricant by-product) in the lubricant; (2) insufficient, wrong, or excessive lubricant, and high temperature; (3) vibration, shockloads (or shock-loading); (4) damage due to improper removing, installation, or adjustment.

The most prevalent cause of bushing or bearing failure is the passage of foreign matter, dirt, and/or abrasives between the shaft and the bushing or between the balls or rollers and the races. The type of foreign matter in the lubricant determines the extent to which the bushing and bushing journals, the balls or rollers, and races become scratched, scored, or pitted.

If the particles in the oil are 30 μm or less, they will act as a lapping compound and increase the assembly tolerances. The surface of the bushings, shaft, or balls, etc., will change to a grayish color, the shaft will lose its support, and the bearings will become noisy.

If the particles in the lubricant are smaller than 0.001 in [0.025 mm], they could lodge between the shaft and bushing or between the balls or rollers and races. They may cause the bushing or bearing to score, scratch, pit, or lock. As a result the bearing's outer race would rotate with the shaft and spin in the bore, or the inner race would rotate on the shaft. The shaft, roller, or races would become scored, scratched, or pitted and could prevent the rolling element from rotating (see Figs. 5-23 and 5-24).

How to Keep Dirt from Contaminating the Lubricant
- Thoroughly clean your work area and tools.
- Before installing a bushing or bearing, make sure that all components, shafts, and bores are clean.
- Keep fine dust out of transmissions, rear axles, etc., by covering them with a plastic sheet.
- Keep the bearings or bushings in their packing material until used.
- Use only clean grease storage containers; clean dispensers, measuring equipment, and grease guns; and clean oil.

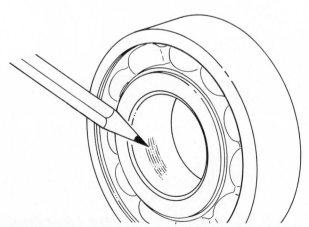

Fig. 5-23 Evidence of inner race rotation. (*International Harvester Co.*)

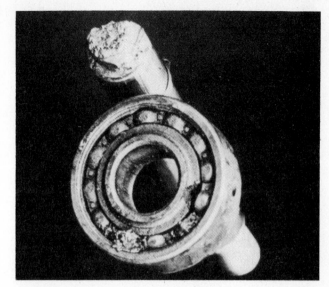

Fig. 5-24 Result of a bearing lockup.

- Always follow the manufacturer's recommendations in regard to type of oil, number of filter changes, type of grease, and intervals of greasing.
- When adding or changing oil or when greasing, first wipe clean the area around the filler hole or grease nipple and always clean up the spilled oil or remove the excessive grease.

Always bear in mind that the entry of even a small amount of dirt into the lubricant will cause damage at a later date.

Origin of Coarse Particles in the Lubricants The coarse particles that can cause bearing or bushing failure when they contaminate the lubricant may originate as residue from moving components such as shaft, gears, clutches, etc., from improper handling of lubricant; from careless work habits; or from inadequate cleaning of components or housing.

Bearing Failure Due to Improper Installation The second most prevalent cause of bearing failure is improper installation by using a punch and hammer instead of the recommended tool and thus damaging the inner and outer race, the cage, or the rolling elements or brinelling the bearing (see Fig. 5-25). Brinelling occurs when the balls or rollers are forced into the inner or outer raceways, creating a detent and causing metal displacement in the raceways and flat spots on the rollers or balls. When rotating, a brinelled bearing is noisy, and it has an effect similar to that of dirt lodged between the rolling element and raceways.

Brinelling also takes place when the radial load on the bearing exceeds the hardness of the bearing. This could occur (1) when the machine is vibrating excessively during transport, (2) when the machine is too securely tightened down, (3) when the bearing preload exceeds the torque specification, or (4) when one is using an impact wrench to turn the puller screw or adjusting nut. In all cases the damage done will increase friction, reduce lubrication, increase

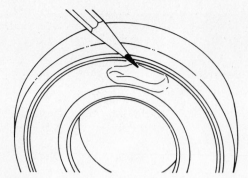

Fig. 5-25 Bearing seal damaged when improperly installed or when removed with a punch. (*International Harvester Co.*)

Fig. 5-26 Bearing destroyed by water and acid.

the operating temperature, and at a later date may cause spalling or chipping.

Improper Bushing or Bearing Contact Bushing or bearing failure due to improper contact between the inner race and shaft, the outer face and bore, or the bushing and bore is uncommon. However, if some small foreign particles or nicks and burrs are within the bushing or bearing bore, they may deform the bushing or bearing and may decrease the clearance. This is also true if the bore is out-of-round. In the latter case it may decrease the clearance at one point and increase it at another.

If the shaft is oversize or if the bore is undersize, the outer or inner race or bushing will be forced to the size of the bearing bore or shaft, decreasing the clearance. In all cases rolling friction will increase, lubrication will decrease, and operating temperature will increase.

A bearing which is loose on its shaft or in its bore will cause vibration, resulting in reduced lubrication and false brinelling. False brinelling occurs when the balls or rollers have metal-to-metal contact with the raceways, causing localized wear of the rolling elements and raceways.

Bearing failure due to lack of lubrication, overlubrication, or low-quality lubricant will cause increased friction, temperature, and wear. The resultant damage may vary from light wear to total destruction. This damage can be prevented by a good maintenance program that includes repairing oil leaks promptly, changing oil regularly, greasing moving parts regularly, and using only the specified lubricant.

Although bearing failure due to high bearing temperature is not common, it could, if it occurs, destroy the bearing completely because the heat reduces the lubricant between the balls, rollers, and raceways, resulting in excessive friction. Increased temperature could arise from insufficient lubrication, overlubrication, or contaminated lubricant. It would also occur if the bearing were overloaded or not positioned properly. However, most high bearing temperature occurs from radial distortion, that is, when the inner raceway expands or the outer raceway retracts owing to the following: oversize diameter of shaft, nicks or burrs on the shaft, undersized bore, or dirt, nicks, and burrs in the bore.

Bearings exposed to water or acid oxidize, corrode, and pit. The corrosion further increases contamination of the lubricant and starts a chain reaction which will eventually destroy the bearing completely (see Fig. 5-26).

Bearing or bushing damage from electric current shows small pits in a defined pattern. The extent of the pitting depends on the amount of current flow. The origin of the electric current may be welding or a short circuit in a motor or switch. What occurs is that the current uses the bearing or bushing as a conductor from or to the electric source. This causes electric arcing, which creates pitting and small weld spots on the roller and hardened spots on the raceway. The hard spots eventually separate and contaminate the lubricant. To prevent bearing or bushing damage from electric current, make certain that all electric components are properly grounded, and when welding on the machine, make certain the ground cable is attached to the object to be welded.

Review Questions

1. List the three main purposes of a bearing.

2. How is the lubrication (film) maintained between the bearing surface and shaft?

3. When a ball bearing has 27 balls, how many balls carry: (*a*) the radial load? (*b*) the thrust load?

4. Name five common antifriction bearings used on on- and off-highway equipment.

5. List the main differences between a ball bearing and a roller bearing.

6. Needle bearings and roller bearings both use cylindrical elements. What are the main differences between needle bearings and roller bearings?

7. Explain why tapered roller bearings are used when high radial and thrust load must be carried by the bearing.

8. Explain the procedure for removing a roller bearing from an exposed shaft (using a heating tip).

9. What precautions must you take when cleaning a shield bearing?

10. Briefly outline four conditions you might find while inspecting a bearing for its serviceability that would call for mandatory bearing replacement.

11. List three considerations to be taken when selecting a puller arrangement.

12. What precautionary measure should you take if you believe the bearing could explode during the press operation?

Unit 6
Introduction to Hydraulics

An adequate knowledge of the fundamental principles of hydraulics is essential to the individual beginning a career in the field of diesel mechanics who will specialize in on- and off-highway equipment. The flourishing application of hydraulics over the past 10 years has resulted in more and more sophisticated systems, even though they are built on the same principle. By learning the basic principle of each hydraulic component and its working in relation to others, by learning how to analyze the percentage of component wear by the use of test instruments, and by learning how to diagnose problems to determine the cause of system failure, you will be able to maintain equipment at its peak efficiency level.

Among the obvious reasons for the accelerating acceptance by industry of hydraulics over the mechanical or electric power transmitter and multiplier are (1) mobility, (2) simplicity (in general), (3) simplicity of control, (4) extreme flexibility of location with respect to actuators, (5) wide variety of speed and force, (6) reduction of wear of moving components by controlling acceleration and deceleration, (7) automatic release of pressure at overload, (8) limited vibration, and (9) automatic lubrication.

The word *hydraulics* is derived from the Greek words *hydros,* which means water, and *aulis,* which means tube or pipe. Originally the study of hydraulics constituted only the physical behavior of water at rest and in motion. Use has broadened its meaning to include the physical behavior of all liquids, including gases under pressure.

The science of hydraulics may be divided into two areas—hydrodynamics and hydrostatics. Hydrodynamics is the science of moving liquids; hydrostatics is the science of liquid under pressure. A hydrodynamic device is one which uses kinetic energy—potential energy that a substance or a body can ultimately use, by virtue of its mass (weight) and velocity—rather than pressure to perform work. Examples would be the fluid coupling, the torque converter, or the water wheel (see Fig. 6-1). A hydrostatic device, on the other hand, uses power generated by exerting pressure on a confined liquid.

The study of fluid behavior is an ancient science. The early Egyptians, Asians, and ancient peoples of Persia, India, and China had only a crude appreciation of the physics of fluid flow, and yet they dug wells, constructed canals, and operated water wheels and pumping devices. Historians say that the water wheel dates back 5000 years. The Greek mathematician Archimedes (287–212 B.C.), in his study of the law of floating and submerged bodies, invented a device known as the Archimedes screw that would pump water. (This type of water pump is used today in cement pumps.) Hero of Alexandria actually built a crude turbine.

After the fall of the Roman Empire no progress is recorded in fluid mechanics until the time of Leonardo da Vinci. He designed and built, near Milan, Italy, the first chambered canal lock. He was also responsible for other hydraulically designed machinery based on fluid flow rather than pressure. At the end of the seventeenth and the beginning of the eighteenth century, physical science flourished because of the interest and research of men such as Pascal, Bernoulli, and Newton. More serious thought was given to the use of water as a source and generator of power. It was in this period that the rules relating to pressure, fluid flow, resistance, and motion were laid down.

Pascal's Law Through discoveries of the French philosopher and mathematician Blaise Pascal it became possible to use fluid (water) to generate power. Pascal's fundamental law of physics may be stated as follows:

Pressure exerted anywhere upon the surface of a liquid enclosed in a vessel is transmitted undiminished in all directions and acts with equal force on equal surfaces, and at right angles to the surfaces [see Fig. 6-2].

To apply this fundamental law of hydraulics, it is important to understand and interpret in the mechanical concept terms such as force, pressure, specific gravity, atmospheric pressure, work, and power.

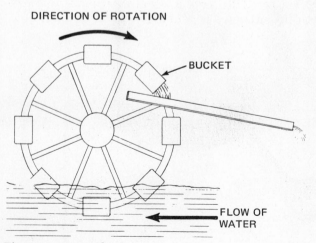

DIRECTION OF ROTATION

BUCKET

FLOW OF WATER

Fig. 6-1 Water wheel.

40

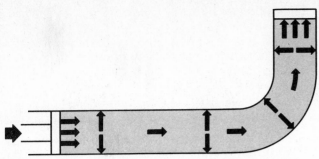

Fig. 6-2 Pascal's law describes the pressure exerted by a fluid upon the surfaces of a vessel in which it is contained.

Fig. 6-4 Illustration of Newton's third law.

Force Although the role of force in everyday life is familiar, its effects should nevertheless be interpreted in the mechanical concept. For instance, when you are using muscles to push or pull things, you are "using force." However, force is not always correlated with motion; for example, if two equal and opposite forces act on a body, there is no movement. If there is no resistance, there is no force.

It is the gravitational force on an object that affects its weight. If an object were weighed on a scale at sea level, for example, the scale would register more than it would if the same object were weighed on the same scale at the top of a mountain.

Force is one of the three standard units of measurement from which all other units of measurement are derived. The standard units of measurement for force are pounds (lb) or ounces (oz) and the metric unit of measurement is the newton (N). (See the metric conversion tables.)

The concept of force may be summed up in three simple laws:

1. Law 1: A body remains at rest, or if in motion, it remains in uniform motion with constant speed in a straight line, unless it is acted on by an unbalanced external force.
2. Law 2: The acceleration produced by an unbalanced force acting on a body is proportional to the magnitude of the net force, in the same direction as the force, and inversely proportional to the mass of the body (see Fig. 6-3).
3. Law 3: Whenever one body exerts a force on a second body, the second body exerts a force on the first body. This force is equal in magnitude but oppositely directed (see Fig. 6-4).

Specific Gravity In the case of hydraulics, the specific gravity is the ratio of the weight of a body to the weight of an equal volume of water.

Specific gravity of body
$$= \frac{\text{weight of body}}{\text{weight of water equal in volume to body}}$$

Atmospheric Pressure Torricelli, an Italian physicist, observed that, when he inverted a tube full of mercury in a bowl of mercury, the column of mercury in the tube would fall to a height of 29.92 in [76 cm]. This was because at this point the atmospheric pressure on the surface of the bowl balanced the gravitational pressure of the mercury in the tube. In addition he proved that the barometric pressure changed with weather conditions and also that an increase in altitude, say, at the top of a mountain, would decrease the height of mercury in a tube. Specifically then, at sea level the weight of the air on an average day is equal to 1 atmosphere (atm), which is equal to 14.7 psi [101.32 kPa], or 29.92 in [76 cm] of mercury. (See the metric conversion tables.)

Pressure (P) is force per unit area. For example, it is easy to balance a crowbar on your hand, but if you try to balance it with the point resting on the palm of your hand, the experience will be painful. The force on your hand is the same in both cases, but the difference is in the pressure. **NOTE** When calculating the force on a unit area, you are calculating the pressure, or, in other words, the pounds per square inch (psi) or newtons per square meter (pascals):

$$P = F/A$$
$$= \text{lb/in}^2 \text{ (psi) } [\text{N/m}^2(\text{Pa})]$$

AREA The standard English measure of a surface area (A) is expressed in square yards (yd²), square feet (ft²), or square inches (in²). In the metric standard unit of measure it is expressed in square meters (m²), square centimeters (cm²), or square millimeters (mm²). (See the metric conversion tables.)

The formula to calculate the area of a round surface is as follows: area is equal to the square of the diameter times 3.1416 divided by 4, or the square of the radius times 3.1416.

$$A = 3.1416 \times D^2/4 \qquad A = 3.1416 \times R^2$$

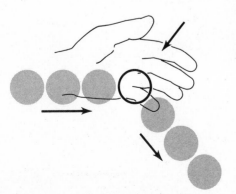

Fig. 6-3 Illustration of Newton's second law.

Work (Energy)   Work has a technical meaning as well as the common meaning of expenditure of effort. Both meanings suggest that a force is exerted on an object to produce change. But physicists interpret work strictly to be "force acting through distance," in other words, a force that produces motion.

$$Work = Force (F) \times Distance (D)$$

The work done is expressed in foot-pounds (ft·lb) or inch-pounds (in·lb). In the metric system it is expressed in joules (J):

$$1 \text{ joule (J)} = 1 \text{ newton (N)} \times 1 \text{ meter (m)}$$

$$1 \text{ J} = 1 \text{ N} \cdot \text{m}$$

(See the metric conversion tables.)

Torque   Torque is the twisting effort applied to a crank at a 90° angle. The twisting effort on the shaft is equal to the distance from the center of the shaft to the point at which the force is applied. The standard units of measure for torque are the pound-foot and pound-inch (lb·ft, lb·in). The metric unit is the newton-meter (N·m). (See the metric conversion tables.)

EXAMPLE   (See Fig. 6-5.) If the distance is 12 in [0.3 m] and the force is 100 lb [444 N], then the torque will equal (12 × 100) ÷ 12 = 100 lb·ft [133.2 N·m]. If the distance is 6 in [0.15 m] and the applied force is 100 lb, then the torque will equal 6 × 100 = 600 lb·in, or (6 × 100) ÷ 12 = 50 lb·ft [66.6 N·m].

Torque can produce work only when the applied torque is greater than the resistance. Torque can be increased by increasing the distance, force, or both.

Power   Power is the time rate at which energy is transferred or converted into work. In English units of measure it is expressed in horsepower (hp). This term was first used by James Watt as he tried to compare the power of a steam engine with the rate of work maintained by an average dray horse, which amounted to 33,000 ft·lb/min. Hence, in mechanics, 1 hp is equal to 33,000 ft·lb/min. In metric units of measure the equivalent is 745.7 watts (W).

Volume   The English units of measure for volume are cubic feet (ft³) or cubic inches (in³), and in the metric units of measure cubic centimeters (cm³) and cubic millimeters (mm³), or liters (l). (See the metric conversion tables.)

To calculate the volume of a cylinder, you must multiply the area times the height or length.

$$V = R^2 \times 3.14 \times H$$

EXAMPLE   When the cylinder has a diameter of 10 in [25.4 cm] and a height of 10 in, the volume is:

$$V = (5 \text{ in})^2 \times 3.14 \times 10 \text{ in} = 785 \text{ in}^3 \text{ [12,866 cm}^3]$$

Mechanical Levers   A mechanical lever may be defined as "an inflexible rod or beam capable of motion about a fixed point called a fulcrum which is used to transmit and modify motion." It is one of the oldest devices known to transmit and modify motion and force. With regard to directing its applied force to work, the mechanical lever's uses are limitless.

You may have used the principle of a first-, second-, or third-class lever to perform work, without concerning yourself about the amount of force required to complete the work. In hydraulic systems and certain other applications, however, the maximum force and the maximum work performance are fixed factors. The lever used, therefore, is dependent on the use to which it will be put.   **EXAMPLE** A small child, using a first- or second-class lever, can balance a much heavier adult by the simple law of the lever. To quote Newton, this law or principle is: "the applied force multiplied by the perpendicular distance between the line of force and fulcrum always equals the delivery force multiplied by the perpendicular distance between the fulcrum and the line of force." In other words (using the first-class lever), when the adult weight is 200 lb [888.0 N] and the applied force of the small child is 50 lb [222.0 N], then the child must have a lever arm of 4 ft [1.22 m] and the adult must be 1 ft [0.305 m] from the fulcrum to achieve a balance. To prove this, you can multiply the adult's distance from the fulcrum by the weight of the adult: 1 × 200 = 200 lb·ft [0.305 × 888 = 270.84 N·m] and the child's distance from the fulcrum by his weight, 4 × 50 = 200 lb·ft [1.22 × 222 = 270.84 N·m]. See Fig. 6-6.

When using a second-class lever, and the lever arms remain the same in length, the child must apply a force of 50 lb [222.0 N] to lift the adult off the ground (see Fig. 6-7).

When using a third-class lever, the child could never lift the adult, because of the lever's disadvan-

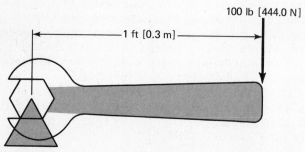

Fig. 6-5   Torque equals 100 lb·ft [135 N·m].

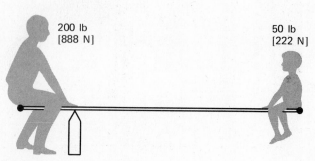

Fig. 6-6   First-class lever.

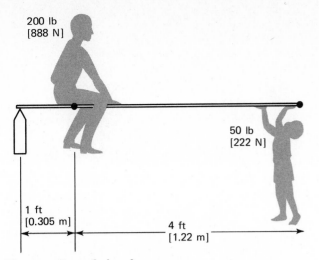

Fig. 6-7 Second-class lever.

tage. The child does not have the force necessary to lift the adult.

It is apparent that in the examples given a 200-lb [880.0-N] force must be applied to balance the adult if the ratio of the lever arm lengths is 1:1. As the boy moves closer toward the fulcrum, more force is required to achieve a balance.

EXAMPLE If the lever arm is 4 ft [1.22 m] long and the weight at the end is 200 lb [888.0 N], and the lifting force is applied 3 ft [0.913 m] from the fulcrum, a force of 266.66 lb [1186.59 N] is required, since the lever has a 3-to-4 disadvantage (see Fig. 6-8).

$$4 \text{ ft} \times 200 \text{ lb} = 800 \text{ lb·ft}$$
$$800 \text{ lb·ft}/3 \text{ ft} = 266.66 \text{ lb}$$

Hydraulic Levers Pascal observed that a smaller weight on a smaller piston will balance a larger weight on a larger piston, provided the piston area is in proportion to the weight. For example, when a force of 1 lb [4.44 N] acts on an area of 1 in²

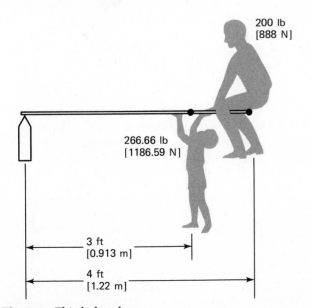

Fig. 6-8 Third-class lever.

[0.000645 m²], the applied pressure (P) equals

1/1 = 1 psi [6.89 kPa].

When the area of the larger piston is 10 in² [0.00645 m²] the force equals the pressure multiplied by the area of the larger piston. $F = P \times A = 1 \text{ psi} \times 10 \text{ in}^2 = 10 \text{ lb } [44.4 \text{ N}]$. (The ratio is 10:1.)

Unfortunately Pascal never put this law to any practical use. It was not until 1795 that Joseph Braem applied this principle in developing the first hydraulic press. This invention combined the effort of mechanical/hydraulic levers and may have been similar in appearance to that shown in Fig. 6-9.

If the hydraulic lever is left at the same measurements mentioned and a mechanical lever is added with a ratio of 10:1, the lifting force would be 10 times greater, or 100 lb [444 N].

Ratio Ratio is the relationship or proportion that one number bears to another. When one lever arm is 10 m, or 10 in, or 10 ft, and the other lever arm is 1 m, or 1 in, or 1 ft—or when the area of one piston is 10 cm² or 10 in², and the other piston is 1 cm² or 1 in²—or when one gear has 100 teeth and the other gear has 10 teeth, the ratio is 10:1 or 1:10 (depending on which gear, lever, or piston the force or torque is applied to).

In the examples just given, when force is applied to the longer lever or to the smaller piston, or when the torque is applied to the smaller gear, the ratio is said to be a 10:1 advantage.

When the ratio has an advantage, the applied force or torque is multiplied by the ratio.

EXAMPLE When a mechanical or hydraulic lever having a ratio of 10:1 and a force of 100 lb [444 N] is applied, the lifting force would be 100 × 10 = 1000 lb [4444 N]. If a torque of 10 lb·ft [13.55 N·m] is applied to the smaller gear, the larger gear will have a torque of 10 × 10 = 100 lb·ft [13.55 × 10 = 135.5 N·m].

When the ratio has a disadvantage of 1:10, the ratio is divided into the applied force or torque.

EXAMPLE If the same figures are used again, the mechanical or hydraulic lever will have a lifting force of 10 lb [44.4 N] (100/10 = 10 lb [444.0/10 =

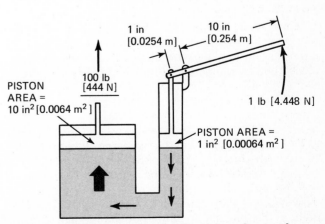

Fig. 6-9 Combination of hydraulic and mechanical lever.

44

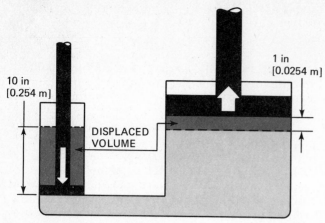

Fig. 6-10 Displacement of fluid by small piston moves the large piston.

44.4 N]) and the small gear will have a torque of 10 lb·ft [13.55 N·m] (100/10 = 10 lb·ft [135.5/10 = 13.5 N·m]).

From personal experience you are aware that, to gain equal advantage, you must move a lever or a smaller piston or turn a smaller gear a distance in proportion to the ratio. Again, with the same figures and with a ratio of 10:1, the lever must travel 10 times the distance to lift the load to the height of the fulcrum. The smaller gear must turn 10 times before the larger gear has completed one revolution, and the smaller piston must displace 10 times its volume to raise the larger piston the distance traveled by the smaller piston (see Fig. 6-10).

EXAMPLE When the area of the small piston is 1 in² [6.45 cm²] and the piston has a stroke (travel) of 1 in [2.54 cm], with each stroke it will displace 1 in³ [16.4 cm³] into the larger piston. If the larger piston's area is 10 in² [64.5 cm²], then we can find the distance it will be moved by using the formula:

Stroke = displacement/area
= 1 in³/10 in² = 0.1 in [0.254 cm]

Pressure Gauges Manometers are generally used to measure pressure up to 30 psi [206.7 kPa] and vacuum as high as absolute, that is, 29.9 inHg [76.2 cmHg]. When higher pressures are to be tested, pressure gauges of the Bourdon tube or coil spring design are used. The Bourdon tube design most commonly used in the mechanical field consists of a curved hollow tube in the shape of a half moon. The closed end is connected through linkage to a gearset, and the indicator needle is fastened to the pinion gear. The dial is properly calibrated in pounds per square inch (psi) or kilopascals (kPa) so that the needle points to the number corresponding to the exact pressure exerted at the open end (which is fastened to the housing) of the Bourdon tube. As pressure is applied into the tube, the tube straightens because the inside area of the outer half circle of the tube is larger than the inner half circle. The movement of the tube is transmitted by the linkage to gear and then to the pointer (see Fig. 6-11).

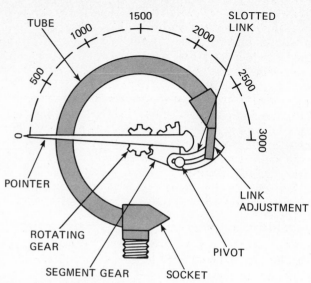

Fig. 6-11 Bourdon tube pressure gauge.

Gauge Snubber Every hydraulic system has pressure oscillation. In some systems it is extensive and in others it is small. This oscillation, caused by the pump or the operating conditions, can damage the gauge and create incorrect pressure readings. To prevent oscillation, the oil flow to the test gauge is restricted; that is, the oil must go through a small orifice (gauge snubber) of about 1/32 in [0.79 mm] before it can enter the tube.

Absolute Gauge Pressure Any pressure test instrument used by you, the mechanic, indicates gauge pressure. This could be in units of pounds per square inch, kilopascals, or inches or centimeters of mercury (inHg [cmHg]). Note, however, that the gauges mentioned are exposed to atmospheric pressure, and, therefore, to achieve an absolute pressure reading, the atmospheric pressure must be added to the gauge pressure reading.

Fluid Flow To understand the action in a hydraulic system, it is essential to become acquainted with the characteristics of fluid and fluid flow. Do not forget that Pascal's law pertains only to the function of static fluid in a closed vessel. In hydraulics, however, we are concerned with velocity, pressure, and friction.

As you know, all work requires energy, and energy produces work. Energy, insofar as hydraulics is concerned, has three classifications: (1) potential energy, (2) kinetic energy, and (3) heat energy.

Before defining these three terms, let us look at the word *energy*. Energy is a quantity that cannot be used up. It can be neither created nor destroyed, but it may be converted from one form to another.

Potential energy may be described as stored energy, capable of work when released. It is always in static form.

Kinetic energy is energy in motion. The greater the velocity, the greater the kinetic energy.

Heat energy is a result of kinetic energy and, in a hydraulic system, results in energy loss.

Matter Matter consists of solids, liquids, or gases. The molecules of solids are rigid and resist change in shape, and when any force is exerted on them, the force is carried directly to the opposite end. Gas molecules repel each other and therefore possess the quality of expansion. Liquid molecules possess balance in characteristics of both solids and gases. The liquid molecules are flexible yet rigid enough to maintain a change in the fluid distance between one another; in other words, they can change shape, divide into parts, and unite as a whole and are therefore infinitely flexible.

Where only the forces of gravity and atmospheric pressure are present, that is, when the fluid is not subject to differences in pressure, liquid seeks its own level, regardless of the shape of the container. If there is a difference in pressure at any point in the system, a fluid flows until it finds its balance or pressure equilibrium.

When fluid-motion velocity becomes a factor, three dynamic factors resist this motion. They are friction, viscosity, and inertia. There is no simple law governing the relationship among them and the three static factors (atmospheric pressure, gravity, and applied force).

Bernoulli's Principle The relationship among the three static factors—atmospheric pressure, gravity, and applied force—and the three dynamic factors—inertia, friction, and velocity—was solved by Daniel Bernoulli (1700–1782), a Swiss mathematician and physicist. Bernoulli's principle states:

Static pressure of a moving liquid varies inversely with velocity, or, as velocity increases, pressure decreases, or, as velocity decreases, pressure increases. (See Fig. 6-12.)

Bernoulli proved the law of Newton, that inertia, a fundamental property of all matter, offers resistance to any change in the state of motion. Therefore any increase or decrease in velocity increases or decreases the inertia and opposes resistance. He also proved that the friction caused by a liquid moving through a tube causes the kinetic energy to be converted to heat energy; therefore, the farther the liquid moves, the greater will be the energy loss due to friction.

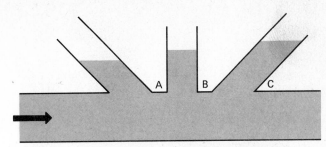

Fig. 6-13 Pressure due to change in flow direction.

Another factor which could cause an increase in friction is the flow of liquid in a hydraulic system. When liquid flow is streamlined, the friction is low. If the flow is turbulent, the friction is high.

From the illustration in Fig. 6-13, you will see that, when the liquid flow has to change direction or when the hydraulic lines are too small or too large in relation to the flow rate, the turbulence increases and therefore the resistance increases. The viscosity of liquids also plays an important part in the total efficiency of the hydraulic system. This is covered in Unit 2.

The relationship between velocity and pressure must be fully understood if one is to appreciate any hydraulic system as a whole.

Velocity Velocity is the rate of liquid flow. It is normally expressed in feet per second (ft/s), or in metric units of measure as meters per second (m/s). The rate of flow is determined by the average speed at which the moving liquid molecules pass a given point.

Refer to Figs. 6-14 and 6-15, showing the effects of friction and velocity on pressure. Bernoulli proved that pressure at B (Fig. 6-14) must be less than at A because velocity at B means an increase in kinetic energy. At A the extra kinetic energy has been converted back to pressure. If there were no friction loss (heat energy), the pressure at B and C would be equal.

Most people have themselves, at one time or another, applied this principle or have seen it applied. For example, let us imagine a gardener attempting to water flowers in a far corner of his or her yard. It may at first appear that the water from the hose can-

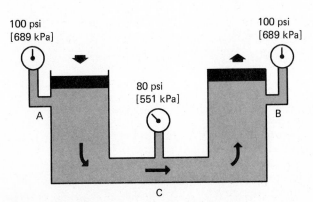

Fig. 6-12 Relation of velocity and pressure.

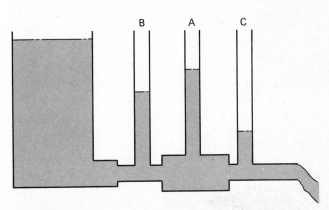

Fig. 6-14 Effects of friction and velocity on pressure. (*Sperry Vickers Division of Sperry Inc.*)

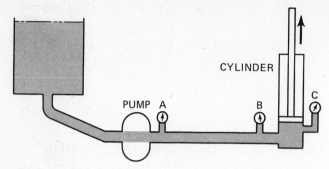

Fig. 6-15 Pressure change within hydraulic lines due to change in velocity.

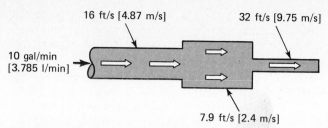

16 ft/s [4.87 m/s]   32 ft/s [9.75 m/s]

10 gal/min [3.785 l/min]

7.9 ft/s [2.4 m/s]

Fig. 6-16 Flow rate (volume) and rate of flow (velocity) in hydraulic lines of different sizes.

not reach the flowers. However, when the gardener closes the opening of the spray nozzle, the water sprays farther because the reduced opening of the nozzle has increased the velocity and has therefore decreased the pressure. As previously mentioned, Bernoulli's principle applies only to liquid in motion.

The combined effort of friction, velocity, and pressure is illustrated in Fig. 6-15. When the hydraulic pump is operating, the potential energy (which was static pressure in the line leading to the cylinder) is converted into velocity pressure (kinetic energy). The conversion from static pressure to velocity pressure results in a pressure drop in the fluid line. This is indicated by the lower psi reading on gauges A and B. As the liquid moves into the cylinder, velocity decreases, resulting in a higher reading on pressure gauge C. Since pressure gauges A and B are located in the same line, it may appear that they should possess identical pressure readings. However, the actual pressure on gauge B is less than on A. The lower pressure on gauge B is caused by heat loss due to friction created by the high velocity pressure in the hydraulic line between pressure gauge A and B.

In reference to the illustration (Fig. 6-15), when the piston comes to the end of its stroke, the three pressure gauges will read the same because liquid motion ceases and the velocity pressure is converted to static pressure. This is a direct application of Pascal's law.

From the foregoing, you can see that the three dynamic factors of inertia, friction, and velocity apply only to liquids in motion, whereas the three static factors of atmospheric pressure, gravity, and applied force apply equally to liquids in motion or at rest. The three static forces apply force at any point in a liquid at any time in addition to the force of any dynamic factors which may be present at the same point in the system.

Flow Rate   Liquids flow if there is a pressure differential. The pressure differential could be the result of atmospheric pressure, the weight of the liquid, or the pumping action of the pump against a resistance. The flow rate, or quantity of flow, is measured in gallons per minute (gal/min) or liters per minute (l/min), and is determined by the number

of moving (liquid) molecules that pass a given point in a given time interval.

With regard to liquid measures, in North America you are confronted with two different gallon measurements, the U.S. gallon, which contains 231 in², and the British Imperial gallon, which contains 277.4 in³. (See the metric conversion tables.)

Following are some illustrations to show how flow rate (volume) and rate of flow (velocity) behave when different sizes of hydraulic lines are used (see Fig. 6-16). Suppose you pump 10 gal/min [137.85 l/min] into a hydraulic system which uses a ½-in [1.27-cm] tube, hose, or pipe. The flow rate would be 10 gal/min [137.85 l/min] anywhere in the system as long as the velocity (rate of flow) and pressure remain the same. The rate of flow in this case would be 16 ft/s [4.87 m/s] because the area of the tube is 0.2 in² [1.27 cm²], and the formula for finding velocity is:

$$\text{Velocity (ft/s)} = \frac{\text{flow rate (gal/min)} \times 0.3208}{\text{area (in}^2)}$$

$$= \frac{10 \times 0.3208}{0.2}$$

$$= 16 \text{ ft/s} \quad [4.87 \text{ m/s}]$$

(Note that the 0.3208 value is used only when calculating in the units shown. It would not be used if the initial measurements were given in liters per minute and square centimeters.)

Whenever the area of the hydraulic line is changed, the velocity also changes. Since the area of a ¾-in [1.91-cm] tube is a little more than twice the area of a ½-in [1.27-cm] tube, or 0.44 in² [2.8 cm²], then the velocity will also reduce by half.

Conversely, when the area is reduced from a ½-in [1.27-cm] tube with an area of 0.2 in² [1.29 cm²] to a ¼-in [0.63-cm] tube which has an area of 0.11 in² [0.7 cm²], the velocity will increase to twice the velocity of the ½-in [1.27-cm] tube, that is, to 32 ft/s [9.75 m/s].

Remember that, when the velocity is increased, pressure drops in relation to the applied pressure and velocity.

To measure flow (the number of moving molecules that pass a given point) in a hydraulic system and thereby determine the efficiency of the system, a flowmeter is used, calibrated in gallons per minute or liters per minute. (A nutating piston disk, propeller, or turbine-type or electric flowmeter is used when high volume and high pressures are to be measured.) In most cases the flowmeter is incorporated into a hydraulic test unit which has a pressure gauge, a thermometer, and a load valve.   **NOTE** The use of a flowmeter and the testing procedure are covered in later units.

Review Questions

1. List seven major advantages of a hydraulic-power transmitter over a mechanical device.

2. Name the fundamental law of physics governing pressure.

3. Calculate the pressure: (a) in psi and (b) in kPa when a force of 1150 lb is exerted on an area of 6 in².

4. How much work is performed when a force of 1000 lb moves an object 18 in? (Give answer in J.)

5. Why is it that a small force acting on a small piston can balance a greater force acting on a larger piston?

6. What is the purpose of each of the following gauges: (a) pressure, (b) manometer, (c) vacuum?

7. What is the purpose of a gauge snubber?

8. In regard to Bernoulli's principle, what two facts are most relevant to the mechanic?

9. List the four main causes of energy loss in a hydraulic system.

10. Define *velocity*.

11. How is the rate of flow measured?

12. With what instrument is the flow rate measured?

Unit 7 Hydraulic System Reservoirs, Lines, and Fittings

A hydraulic system consists of one or more independent circuits. The components which make up any hydraulic system are (1) the reservoir (for the hydraulic system, the power steering, or the transmission), (2) hydraulic lines (which may be pipes, tubing, or hoses), (3) hydraulic filters and screens, (4) hydraulic pumps (positive or nonpositive in design), (5) hydraulic control valves, (6) actuators, and (7) seals and gaskets. Finally, and extremely important, of course, is fluid, which may be oil, water, gasoline, or diesel fuel.

A basic hydraulic system is shown in Fig. 7-1. (Not all the listed components are shown in this illustration.)

RESERVOIR

Functions   The reservoir (see Fig. 7-2), whether in the form of the side frames of the loader or in the form of a square tank, has many functions in addition to that of supplying storage space. It must (1)

dissipate heat by way of convection, conduction, and radiation; (2) trap foreign matter (filters and/or strainers within the reservoir are common, but at times the sediment is simply allowed to settle on the bottom of the reservoir); (3) separate air from the system (accomplished through baffles which reduce the velocity of the oil within the reservoir and allow the air bubbles more opportunity to escape to the surface); (4) have three times the oil capacity of the actuators (when no cooling devices are used) to ensure that the hydraulic oil will not exceed 100°F [37.8°C] of ambient temperature.

Fittings   To perform adequately and to fulfill its designed purpose, the reservoir must have (1) a filling device and a cap (sealed or atmospherically vented), (2) a filter screen, (3) a device which checks the fluid level (high and low), (4) a fluid drain plug or drain cock to drain the oil, (5) strength sufficient to withstand vibration, (6) a pump outlet connection to connect the reservoir with the hydraulic pump, (7) a screen or filter to clean the oil before it enters

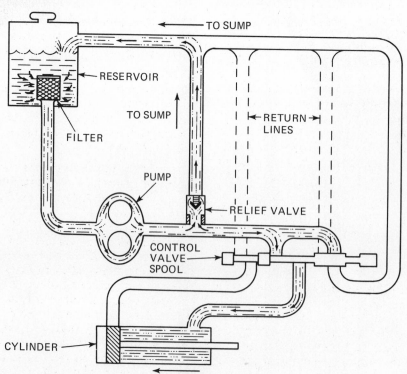

Fig. 7-1   A basic hydraulic system. (*J I Case Company Agricultural Equipment Division*)

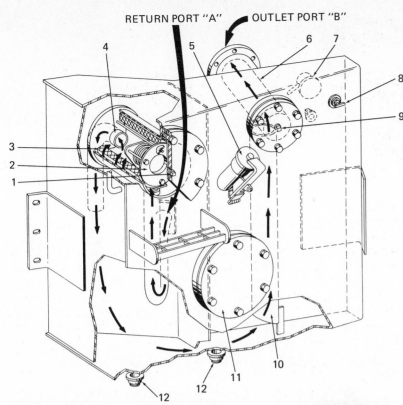

RETURN PORT "A"   OUTLET PORT "B"

1. Antisyphon plug
2. Bypass relief valve assembly
3. Filter element
4. Tube
5. Filler cap and security latch
6. Screen
7. Pressure relief valve
8. Pet cock
9. Antisyphon plug
10. Tube
11. Cover plate
12. Drain plugs

Fig. 7-2 A hydraulic system reservoir. (*Terex Division of General Motors Corporation*)

the pump, (8) a return oil inlet to ensure that the return oil enters below the low oil level (otherwise the oil would create aeration), (9) separators and/or baffles to ensure that the return oil has time to cool adequately before mixing with the pump inlet oil.

Pump Location The location of the reservoir in relation to the hydraulic pump is particularly important since a continuous supply of fluid to the hydraulic pump inlet is needed to promote (pump) efficiency and to prolong life of the hydraulic pump and the system as a whole. To accomplish these objectives, any one of five designs may be used: (1) the hydraulic pump may be in the reservoir, (2) the hydraulic pump may be below the reservoir, (3) the hydraulic pump may be above the reservoir, (4) the main pump may be supercharged from a second pump, (5) designs (1), (2), and (3) may use a pressurized reservoir.

It is general knowledge that our atmosphere exerts a pressure on the earth's surface relative to the height above sea level and that oil has weight (specific gravity), and this weight produces pressure.

Head of Liquid; Fluid Weight If the radiator of a truck has a hole near the bottom, the coolant will run out faster than it would if the hole were halfway up the side of the radiator, because the weight of the water (the *pressure head*) at the two holes differs. Once the distance between the coolant level and the holes is known, it is easy to determine the head pressure.

For example, suppose the height of the coolant

above one hole level is 1 ft [0.304 m]. One cubic foot of water weighs 62.4 lb [277 N] at 32°F [0°C]. Since 1 ft² = 144 in² [0.929 m²], the pressure is 0.433 psi [2.98 kPa] because 62.4 lb of water resting on a surface of 144 in² exerts a force over each square inch of 62.4/144 = 0.433 psi [2.98 kPa] according to the formula $P = F/A$. (See Fig. 7-3.) However, if the fluid is hydraulic oil having a specific gravity of 0.8790, the head pressure would be less because 1 ft³ of hydraulic oil weighs 54.84 lb [24.89 kg].

EXAMPLE The weight of 1 ft³ of hydraulic oil is found by multiplying the weight of the water by the specific gravity of oil: 0.8790 × 62.4 = 54.84 lb [24.89 kg]. Therefore, an oil column 4 ft [1.22 m] high would have a head pressure of: 0.38 × 4 = 1.52 psi [10.47 kPa].

Applying this knowledge, you can understand why the location of the reservoir in relation to the pump is sufficiently important to prove one design superior to another.

Assume, for example, that a hydraulic pump is located within the reservoir and the fluid level to the pump inlet is 4 ft [1.22 m]. Assume also that the reservoir is atmospherically vented, which means it has an air filter which allows clean atmospheric air to enter the reservoir while the fumes reenter the atmosphere. In this case there would be a static pressure of 1.52 psi [10.47 kPa] at the pump inlet. A loose pump inlet connection would not affect the system, since air cannot enter the system and furthermore there are no energy losses.

If the hydraulic pump were located 8 ft [2.44 m] below the fluid level, there would be a static pres-

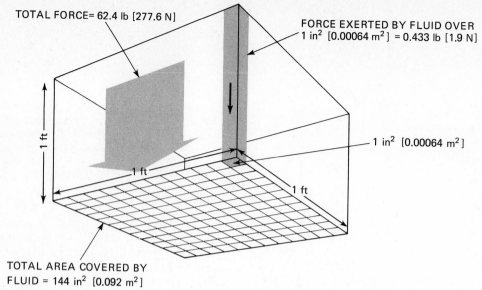

TOTAL FORCE= 62.4 lb [277.6 N]

FORCE EXERTED BY FLUID OVER
1 in^2 [0.00064 m^2] = 0.433 lb [1.9 N]

1 ft

1 ft

1 ft

1 in^2 [0.00064 m^2]

TOTAL AREA COVERED BY
FLUID = 144 in^2 [0.092 m^2]

Fig. 7-3 Fluid weight versus pressure.

sure of 3.03 psi [20.94 kPa] at the pump inlet with a resultant gain in the hydraulic pump's efficiency.

When the hydraulic pump is located above the fluid level, it has to rotate to create a pressure lower than the atmospheric pressure in order to cause a fluid flow into the pump. There would be a loss in hydraulic pump efficiency which, in this example, would be about 5 percent. The efficiency would decrease as the distance from the reservoir to the pump increased, and at about 38 to 39 ft [11.59 to 11.89 m] only vapor would enter the hydraulic pump. The reason for this is that the (perfect) vacuum created by the pump of 29.9 inHg [75.94 cmHg] can raise an oil column about 39½ ft, at which point the weight of the oil column balances atmospheric pressure. If the pump is located above this level, no oil will reach it.

Another method of pressurizing the reservoir, a method employed on larger hydraulic systems, is to use air from the vehicle's air brake system. Advantages of this method are that the oil level in the reservoir is not so critical, the reservoir pressure is constant, and it is present as soon as the air brake system

has pressure. However, an air pressure regulator is required to reduce the pressure to that desired (see Fig. 7-4).

When the main hydraulic pump is supercharged, an even higher efficiency is achieved, but the cost and maintenance of the hydraulic system are correspondingly higher.

Pressurized Reservoirs   The simplest way to gain pump efficiency is to pressurize the reservoir through the oil expansion (see Fig. 7-5). The pressurized reservoir is actually a sealed unit which is protected against excessive pressure buildup by a relief valve and against low pressure by a vacuum valve. The relief valve exhausts the air into the atmosphere at a predetermined pressure. A vacuum valve is used to prevent the pressure from receding below atmospheric pressure and to protect the tank from damage. When a pressurized reservoir is used, it is essential to follow the manufacturer's instructions with regard to checking the hydraulic oil level; otherwise the reservoir may not build up pressure. For instance, when checking the oil level of a loader

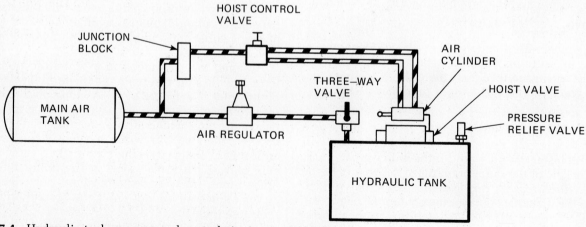

Fig. 7-4 Hydraulic tank pressure and control air circuit. (*WABCO, An American-Standard Company*)

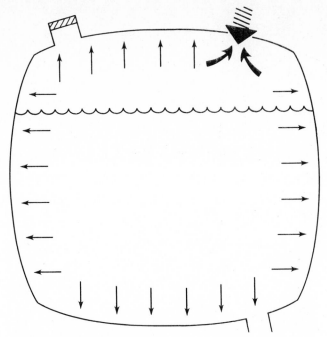

Fig. 7-5 Pressurized reservoir. (*J I Case Company Agricultural Equipment Division*)

backhoe, the manufacturers instruct that the loader must be on the ground and the bucket in the rollback position. The backhoe dipper stick must be brought toward the boom and the boom must be in the fully raised position, with the stabilizer up. The oil should be near ambient temperature.

When each of these conditions has been met, the oil level can then be checked.

When the equipment is operating, the temperature of the oil increases and expands, causing the pressure within the reservoir to rise. The relief valve pressure setting is between 20 and 30 psi [137.8 and 206.7 kPa], depending on the equipment used. After the equipment is shut down, the oil cools, and the pressure gradually diminishes. When the pressure decreases to less than atmospheric pressure, the vacuum valve opens, preventing damage to the reservoir.

Draining Oil from the Reservoir   First check the appropriate service manual to determine the reservoir's fluid capacity and then make certain you have enough clean barrels available to store the hydraulic fluid.

Through the filler neck or pipe, insert a hand- or motor-driven pump and pump the fluid from the reservoir. If this is not possible, remove the pressure from the tank and then securely close it again. When an atmospheric tank is used, remove the filter and install a pipe plug or a suitable fitting to seal off the reservoir.

Next, remove the pump inlet hose and hold the hose end into the container or barrel.   **NOTE** Only a small amount of oil can come from the hose, since there is no atmospheric pressure acting on the reservoir fluid surface. Slowly open the vent screw to control the oil flow from the reservoir. When the oil is drained, remove all hydraulic lines from the

reservoir and instantly plug their openings to prevent contaminants from entering the system. Next, bring your lifting device into position and use a rope sling (or use the existing lifting fixture) to hold the reservoir while removing its mounting bolts or screws.

Servicing the Reservoir   When servicing a reservoir, regardless of its design, location, or the service to be performed, you must always proceed with care and follow the recommended precautionary steps outlined in the service manual. In most cases, service is confined to replacing leaking gaskets, cleaning or replacing inlet and outlet screens, filter and relief valves, or cleaning the magnetic plug or the reservoir itself. Since reservoirs vary greatly in regard to size and design, only those steps and precautions which are generally applicable are given.

Servicing should commence with a thorough steam-cleaning of the area surrounding the reservoir. If the circumstances warrant, remove the floor board, a fender, or a shield, etc., to allow the steam to penetrate to the reservoir and surrounding area.

When a large reservoir is to be removed, drive the equipment to a location where you can use the appropriate facilities of your workshop to lift, slide, or lower it from the loader, truck, crane, tractor, or other vehicle. Make sure you position the hydraulic equipment so that you have unrestricted access to the reservoir and, when necessary, block the hydraulic equipment. Stop the engine, apply the brakes, and block the wheels. Operate the control valves back and forth to remove the pressure from the cylinders. This also removes the pressure from the reservoir when it is not atmospherically vented. Otherwise close the air valve prior to operating the control valve.   **CAUTION** Remove the ground battery cable to prevent accidental starting of the engine and on the steering wheel hang a warning sign, "SERVICE WORK BEING PERFORMED."

The next step, when applicable, is to loosen, slowly, the vent screw or the special filler cap to remove the remaining pressure from the reservoir and then drain it. After removing the reservoir from the equipment, remove all its covers, screens, filters, and plugs. Thoroughly steam-clean the reservoir and dry it with compressed air. Check all threaded holes for damage or wear. Make certain the baffles have not broken loose and that the return pipe is rigid. Remove all nicks and burrs from the mounting flanges to ensure good sealing. If you have welded any part of the reservoir, make certain that no contaminants or particles are left inside.   **NOTE** Follow all recommended safety precautions when welding.

Clean the screens in solvent. If the sealing surface or the screens are damaged, replace them. Do not forget to clean the filters, the screen, and the relief valve. Make certain the valve is free and in its bore and that the spring is not damaged.

Torque the inspection cover bolts to the specified torque; otherwise you may damage the cork gasket, and this would result in a leaking cover. Use Teflon tape on all pipe fittings to improve the seal.

NOTE If the reservoir is not installed immediately, apply a coat of oil to all unpainted surfaces to prevent oxidation. (It is also good practice to pressure-test a reservoir before installation.)

When installing the reservoir, make certain the mounting bolts are torqued to specification and that the return and inlet hose connections are not twisted, bent, or rubbing on the frame.

HYDRAULIC LINES AND FITTINGS

The hydraulic lines and fittings are as important as any component in the hydraulic system. In transporting the fluid, they become an integral part of the system. Poor or inadequate piping, regardless of the type of hydraulic line used, reduces not only the efficiency of the system, but also the service life. Various hydraulic lines and fittings are available, and it is essential that the mechanic know about the advantages and shortcomings of each type.

The three most common types of hydraulic lines used are pipes, tubing, and hose. In selecting the appropriate hydraulic line, a mechanic should know where and how the line is located, at what temperature and pressure the line will operate, what volume of liquid the line will carry, and what type of liquid will be used.

The location, temperature, and pressure determine the type of material to be used for the hydraulic line. The volume of the fluid flow determines the size of the line.

NOTE Manufacturers recommend a maximum velocity of 15 ft/s [4.57 m/s] on pressure lines, and 5 ft/s [1.52 m/s] on inlet lines. Supply charts and data tables, obtainable from most manufacturers, can be used as a further aid in selecting the most suitable line.

Regardless of the type of line used, the length of the line and the number and radii of the bends must be kept to a minimum. Every section of the line must be fastened securely. This reduces vibration and moves the weight from the fittings or joints. Some correct and incorrect methods of tubing installations are shown in Fig. 7-6. When making your selection, remember that bends are preferable to elbows, for

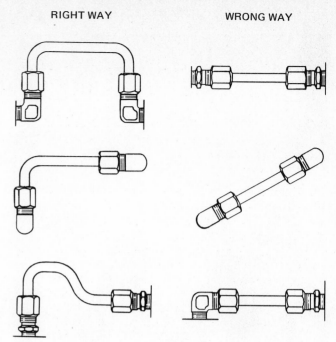

RIGHT WAY   WRONG WAY

Fig. 7-6 Proper and improper tube installation. (*Sperry Vickers Division of Sperry Inc.*)

they reduce friction and turbulence. The ideal bend radius is $2\frac{1}{2}$ to 3 times that of the inside diameter of the pipe or tubing. When a hose is used instead of tubing, you must consider the applied pressure and the movement of the hose due to the actuator, as well as the reduction of the bend radius. Pressure can cause the hose to expand and contract. Try to keep to the maximum bend radius in order to have the minimum amount of friction and turbulence.

Pipes Many manufacturers classify piping and tubing indiscriminately, whereas, in actual fact, there are a number of differences between them. When ordering or selecting supplies, you should first check the individual manufacturer's terminology to avoid misunderstandings.

To the mechanic, the words *pipe* and *tubing* have many meanings. Distinctions lie, not in the material or the design, but in the dimensions, that is, the outside diameter, the inside diameter, and the wall thickness. Nominal dimensions are used to simplify

Nominal size, in	Pipe OD, in	Inside diameter, in									
		Schedule 10	Schedule 20	Schedule 30	Schedule 40	Schedule 60	Schedule 80	Schedule 100	Schedule 120	Schedule 140	Schedule 160
⅛	0.405				0.269		0.215				
¼	0.540				0.364		0.302				
⅜	0.675				0.493		0.423				
½	0.840				0.622		0.546				0.466
¾	1.050				0.824		0.742				0.614
1	1.315				1.049		0.957				0.815
1¼	1.660				1.380		1.278				1.160
1½	1.900				1.610		1.500				1.338
2	2.375				2.067		1.939				1.689
2½	2.875				2.469		2.323				2.125
3	3.500				3.068		2.900				2.624

Fig. 7-7 Nominal pipe size and wall thickness.

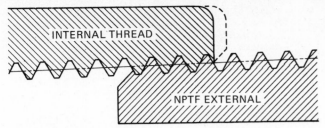

Fig. 7-8 Dryseal pipe thread. (*J I Case Company Agricultural Equipment Division*)

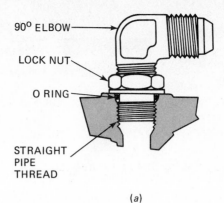

the standardization of pipes. The wall thickness is identified by a schedule number.

Fig. 7-7 shows the old and new pipe identification, the nominal pipe size, and wall thickness. Review the schedule recommendation for pressure up to 2500 psi [17,225 kPa], remembering that the pressure recommendation is for standard steel only.

Although manufacturer classifications of pipe and tubing overlap, you should know when to use one as opposed to the other. Tubing is used much more frequently for hydraulic lines because of the difficulty in bending and sealing pipes. The sealing problem, however, has been improved as a result of the cooperation of industry with the Society of Automotive Engineers (SAE) in setting up improved standards for pipe thread. The result has been the "dryseal pipe thread" (see Fig. 7-8). Dryseal threads form a tighter, safer seal because they can be tightened to make a leakproof joint without excessive torque.

Pipe Fittings A great variety of pipe connectors (fittings) is manufactured to meet the needs of industry. Most common are the threaded pipe connectors of the tapered and straight dryseal design. Standard fittings are adequate to accommodate an operating pressure up to 3000 psi [20,670 kPa], a proof test rating of 15,000 psi [103,350 kPa], and a temperature range of −65 to 400°F [−54 to 204°C].

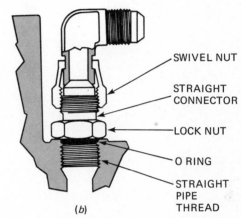

Fig. 7-9 (a) Adjustable 90° elbow JIC flare. (b) Adjustable straight connector JIC flare. (*Weatherhead Co. of Canada Ltd.*)

All tapered pipe threads should be tightened to a minimum of two and one-half full turns past hand-tight. The straight pipe threads, on the other hand, can be positioned and then sealed with a lock nut and O ring. Some straight and tapered pipe fittings are shown in Figs. 7-9 and 7-10, respectively. Less common are the flange connectors and the welded connectors shown in Figure 7-11.

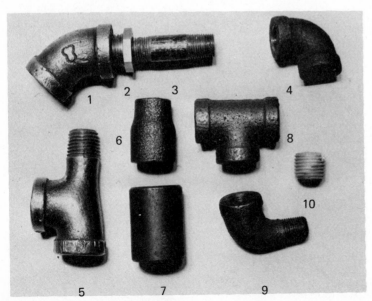

1. 45° elbow
2. Bushing
3. Nipple
4. 90° elbow
5. Street tee
6. Reducer
7. Coupling
8. Tee
9. Street elbow
10. Slotted plug

Fig. 7-10 Tapered pipe fittings.

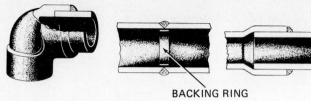

BACKING RING

Fig. 7-11 Welded connectors.

Table 7-2 STANDARD TUBING DASH NUMBERS

Actual outside diameter, inches	Standard dash number
$\frac{3}{16}$	-3
$\frac{1}{4}$	-4
$\frac{5}{16}$	-5
$\frac{3}{8}$	-6
$\frac{13}{32}$	-7
$\frac{1}{2}$	-8
$\frac{5}{8}$	-10
$\frac{3}{4}$	-12
$\frac{7}{8}$	-14
1	-16
$1\frac{1}{8}$	-18
$1\frac{1}{4}$	-20

Tubing Tubing made from steel, copper, nylon, polyethylene, or other synthetic material is most commonly used for hydraulic lines on off- and on-highway equipment.

A tubular product is referred to as a "tube" if its nominal size is the actual measurement of the outside diameter (OD). Standard tubing varies in size from $\frac{1}{8}$ to 3 in [0.31 to 7.62 cm].

When examining the tubing size designations in Table 7-1, note that the tube sizes increase in $\frac{1}{16}$-in increments to $\frac{3}{8}$ in, and in $\frac{1}{8}$-in increments (from $\frac{3}{8}$ to $\frac{3}{4}$ in). Within each tube size there is a selection of wall thicknesses to fill the various pressure demands.

To identify a standard rigid tube size, a dash number system is used. This dash number system relates to the outside diameter (OD) of the tube size, in sixteenths of an inch. Standard tube size increments by dash numbers are given in Table 7-2.

Tube Cutting Tube cutting should never be considered so routine that it is done carelessly. Avoid, under all conditions, bending tubing more than is necessary.

Table 7-1 TUBING SIZE DESIGNATION

Tube OD	Wall thickness	Tube ID	Tube OD	Wall thickness	Tube ID	Tube OD	Wall thickness	Tube ID
$\frac{1}{8}$	0.028	0.069		0.035	0.555		0.049	1.152
	.032	.061		.042	.541		.058	1.134
	.035	.055		.049	.527		.065	1.120
			$\frac{5}{8}$	.058	.509	$1\frac{1}{4}$	.072	1.106
$\frac{3}{16}$	0.032	0.1235		.065	.495		.083	1.084
	.035	.1175		.072	.481		.095	1.060
				.083	.459		.109	1.032
				.095	.435		.120	1.010
$\frac{1}{4}$	0.035	0.180						
	.042	.166		0.049	0.652		0.065	1.370
	.049	.152		.058	.634		.072	1.356
	.058	.134		.065	.620		.083	1.334
	.065	.120	$\frac{3}{4}$	.072	.606	$1\frac{1}{2}$	.095	1.310
				.083	.584		.109	1.282
$\frac{5}{16}$	0.035	0.2425		.095	.560		.120	1.260
	.042	.2285		.109	.532		.134	1.232
	.049	.2145						
	.058	.1965		0.049	0.777		0.065	1.620
	.065	.1825		.058	.759		.072	1.606
				.065	.745		.083	1.584
$\frac{3}{8}$	0.035	0.305	$\frac{7}{8}$	.072	.731	$1\frac{3}{4}$	.095	1.560
	.042	.291		.083	.709		.109	1.532
	.049	.277		.095	.685		.120	1.510
	.058	.259		.109	.657		.134	1.482
	.065	.245						
				0.049	0.902		0.065	1.870
$\frac{1}{2}$	0.035	0.430		.058	.884		.072	1.856
	.042	.416		.065	.870		.083	1.834
	.049	.402		.072	.856	2	.095	1.810
	.058	.384	1	.083	.834		.109	1.782
	.065	.370		.095	.810		.120	1.760
	.072	.356		.109	.782		.134	1.732
	.083	.334		.120	.760			
	.095	.310						

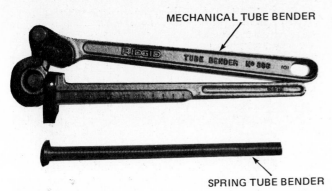

MECHANICAL TUBE BENDER

SPRING TUBE BENDER

Fig. 7-12 Spring tube bender and mechanical tube bender.

Hold the tube roll in an upright position on a clean and straight surface. The tube end is held firmly against the surface while the tube coil is rolled out to the desired length. Never pull the tube end from the tube roll, and remember to keep the open end closed off to avoid the entry of foreign material.

In cutting the tube, use a tube cutter to ensure a clean, square cut on the edges. Do not force the cutting wheel into the tube. Instead, let the wheel cut into the tube by rotating the tube cutter 360° and gently increasing wheel pressure after each revolution.

While cutting, support the waste section of the tube so that its weight does not interfere with the final cut.

Do not let your cut become too harsh, for it will burr both the inside and outside of the tube. If this occurs, use a reamer blade to remove the inside burrs. (The reamer blade is mounted on the tube cutter and can be folded away when not in use.) The outside burrs can be removed with a file or an outside burr remover. In all cases strive to achieve smooth, square edges. Above all, make sure that all debris from the cutting operation is removed from the tube.

Tube Bending Steel or copper tubing that is small and has thin walls is easy to bend if a spring tube bender is used (see Fig. 7-12). After the correct spring size is selected, slide the spring over the tubing and gently shape the tubing to the desired bend. A slight overbending will facilitate spring removal.

Larger tube sizes and thicker walls are bent much more easily with a mechanical tube bender. Here also, select the proper size mechanical tube bender

to avoid impairment of the tube. It is recommended that the bend be made prior to the flaring or to the cutting of the final length.

TUBE BENDING POINTERS Mark the start of the bend on the tube. (For example, you might be bending a $\frac{1}{2}$-in steel tube to a 90° angle.) Note that, if the bend must be located immediately after the flare or compression nut, it should be started a distance of two to three times the length of the nut from the nut. This ensures easy installation.

Position the tube so that your mark coincides with the center line mark of the tube bender. Then hook the hold-down foot over the tube.

Gently move the handles together until the desired angle (for example, 90°) is reached. Always overbend a little. This is to compensate for the tube's tendency to straighten out slightly after removal.

Tube Fittings and Adapters A tube may be connected to a component, hose, pipe, or to another tube by one of several kinds of tube connectors. Quite often, a welded tube connector similar to the one shown in Fig. 7-13 is used. The most common tube connectors, however, are those of the threaded design, and so these are the ones you should be most familiar with.

In general, threaded tube fittings and adapters are divided into two types: flare fitting and compression fitting.

Flare fittings and adapters are connected and sealed by spreading (flaring) the ends of the tube to an angle of 37° or 45°. The fitting nut and adapter, when properly torqued, will make a secure, leakproof seal.

Compression fittings and adapters are connected and sealed by screwing the fitting nut to the adapter and thus compressing the sleeve or sleeve nut onto the tube. The six threaded connectors are as follows: (1) SAE 37° (JIC) flared twin, (2) SAE 45° flare, (3) 45° flare inverted, (4) compression fitting, (5) self-aligning, and (6) threaded sleeve.

Because of the numerous types of fittings and adapters, various thread sizes are used. Tube fitting thread size comparisons of the six threaded fittings (in each classification of tube size) are given in Table 7-3.

By examining this chart, you will recognize the ambiguity arising from the countless number of fittings, adapters, and thread designs. All six types of fittings have good sealing results when the tube is properly flared, installed, and torqued.

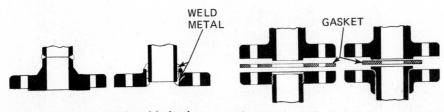

WELD METAL

GASKET

Fig. 7-13 Flange and welded tube connectors.

Table 7-3 THREADED CONNECTORS

Tube size	37° Flare flare-twin	45° Flare SAE	Inverted flare	Compression, self-aligning	Threaded sleeve
$\frac{1}{8}$-2	$\frac{5}{16}$-24	$\frac{5}{16}$-24	$\frac{5}{16}$-28	$\frac{5}{16}$-24	$\frac{5}{16}$-24
$\frac{3}{16}$-3	$\frac{3}{8}$-24	$\frac{3}{8}$-24	$\frac{3}{8}$-24	$\frac{3}{8}$-24	$\frac{3}{8}$-24
$\frac{1}{4}$-4	$\frac{7}{16}$-20	$\frac{7}{16}$-20	$\frac{7}{16}$-24	$\frac{7}{16}$-24	$\frac{7}{16}$-24
$\frac{5}{16}$-5	$\frac{1}{2}$-20	$\frac{1}{2}$-20	$\frac{1}{2}$-20	$\frac{1}{2}$-24	$\frac{1}{2}$-20
$\frac{3}{8}$-6	$\frac{9}{16}$-18	$\frac{5}{8}$-18	$\frac{5}{8}$-18	$\frac{9}{16}$-24	$\frac{9}{16}$-20
$\frac{7}{16}$-7	—	$\frac{11}{16}$-16	$\frac{11}{16}$-18	$\frac{5}{8}$-24	$\frac{5}{8}$-18
$\frac{1}{2}$-8	$\frac{3}{4}$-16	$\frac{3}{4}$-16	$\frac{3}{4}$-18	$\frac{11}{16}$-20	$\frac{11}{16}$-16
$\frac{5}{8}$-10	$\frac{7}{8}$-14	$\frac{7}{8}$-14	$\frac{7}{8}$-18	$\frac{13}{16}$-18	—
$\frac{3}{4}$-12	$1\frac{1}{16}$-12	$1\frac{1}{16}$-14	$1\frac{1}{16}$-16	1-18	—
$\frac{7}{8}$-14	$1\frac{3}{16}$-12	—	—	—	—
1-16	$1\frac{5}{16}$-12	—	—	$1\frac{1}{4}$-18	—

Inverted Flares Inverted flare fittings are used on hydraulic brakes and on fuel and lubrication lines but are uncommon on other applications because the short nut is unable to support the hydraulic line adequately (see Fig. 7-14).

Forming a Double Flare To form a good flare, you must keep the tube straight. Moreover, the procedures outlined in the section on tube cutting should be strictly adhered to.

1. Select the proper adapter and hole size in your tube-holding fixture.
2. Slide the nut on the tube.
3. Insert the tube and clamp securely when the tube extends to the height of the adapter.
4. Lubricate the tube slightly and insert the adapter.
5. Locate the cone of the yoke over the center of the adapter and run it down until it bottoms against the tube-holding fixture. This action causes the tube to bell out or flare and is the first step in forming a double flare (see Fig. 7-15).
6. Remove the adapter and run the cone tightly against the belled tube to form the finished flare.
7. Remove the tube, check the flare diameter, and examine the flare for excessive thinning out of material (see Fig. 7-16b).

Installation of Flare Tubing Before beginning the installation, check that all foreign materials have been removed from the nut, the adapter, and the inside of the tube. Lubricate the threads before aligning the tube to the adapter. No excessive force should be used in alignment, for this can cause a cross-threaded fitting and stress on the tubing. Hand-tighten the tube nut and then use a flare

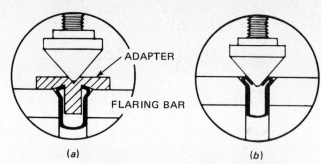

Fig. 7-15 (a) First step in making a double flare. (b) Finishing the flare. (*The Weatherhead Co. of Canada, Ltd.*)

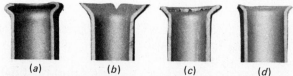

Fig. 7-16 Improper flares and their causes. (a) Tubing cut at an angle. (b) Improper flare length. (c) Burrs not removed. (d) Improper flare length.

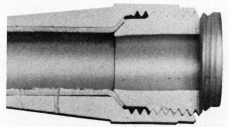

Fig. 7-17 Cutaway view of an SAE 45° flare fitting.

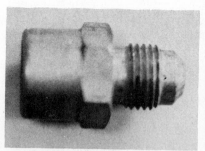

FEMALE CONNECTOR MALE CONNECTOR

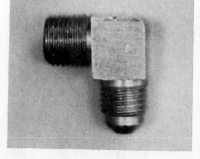

MALE ELBOW UNION

Fig. 7-18 SAE 45° flare fitting adapters.

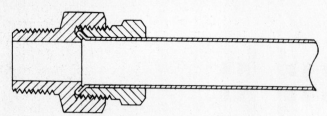

Fig. 7-14 Inverted flare.

wrench until a solid feeling is encountered (about one-sixth of a turn).

SAE 45° FLARES   A single SAE 45° flare (using a long nut) is shown in Fig. 7-17. Various adapters are shown in Fig. 7-18. For on- and off-highway equipment it is recommended that only long nuts and a double flare be used. This helps decrease connection failure.

Flaring and installation procedures are the same as those suggested for an inverted flare fitting.

SAE 37° (JIC) FLARED TWINS   A two-piece and a three-piece SAE 37° (JIC) flared twin fitting assembly is shown in Fig. 7-19. Various adapters are shown in Fig. 7-20. From the illustrations you will recognize how these types of fittings give greater tube support and why, therefore, they are recommended.

Flaring and installation procedures are the same for the SAE 37° (JIC) flared twin as those suggested for the inverted flare and the SAE 45° flare. The flaring angle for the (JIC) flared twin is, of course, 37° instead of 45°.

Flareless Connectors   Threaded sleeve, self-aligning, and compression fittings are not recommended, in that the connectors cannot withstand vibration. By using a long nut on self-aligning and compression fittings, improved vibration resistance is achieved. A correctly assembled threaded sleeve is shown in Fig. 7-21. Note that when you are installing a tube with this type of fitting, the tube must rest on the adapter shoulder, not over the tight nut. Also, after the nut is hand-tightened, an additional one and one-half turn with a wrench is recommended. A self-aligning fitting is shown in Fig. 7-22, and a compression fitting, in Fig. 7-23. Note that the assembly and torque procedure is identical to that outlined for a threaded sleeve.

Flexible Tubing   Tubes made from nylon, neoprene, or other synthetic materials are used to connect fuel, oil, and lubrication lines to instrumentation panels. This type of tubing has gained wide acceptance because of its adaptability, durability, and high vibration resistance. Nylon tubing is preferred in the diesel field because of its resistance to petroleum products.

Table 7-4 outlines the required data for proper selection of tube size, wall thickness, bend radius, working pressure, and fitting size.

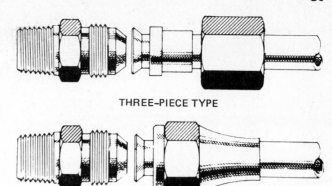

THREE-PIECE TYPE

TWO-PIECE TYPE

Fig. 7-19   SAE 37° JIC flared twin fitting assemblies. (*The Weatherhead Co. of Canada, Ltd.*)

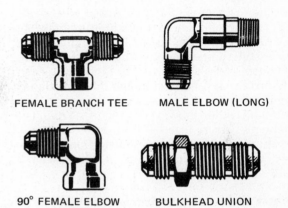

FEMALE BRANCH TEE   **MALE ELBOW (LONG)**

90° FEMALE ELBOW   **BULKHEAD UNION**

Fig. 7-20   Hydraulic tube fitting adapters. (*The Weatherhead Co. of Canada, Ltd.*)

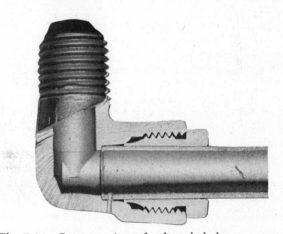

Fig. 7-21   Cutaway view of a threaded sleeve.

Table 7-4   NYLON TUBING

For fittings size (dash numbers)	Size	OD, in	ID, in	Wall thickness, in	Max working pressure, psi at 70°F	Min burst pressure, psi at 70°F	Min bend radius, in
-2	$\frac{1}{8}$	$\frac{1}{8}$	0.096	0.015	333	1000	$\frac{3}{4}$
-3	$\frac{3}{16}$	$\frac{3}{16}$	0.138	0.025	333	1000	$1\frac{1}{2}$
-4	$\frac{1}{4}$	$\frac{1}{4}$	0.190	0.030	333	1000	$2\frac{1}{2}$
-5	$\frac{5}{16}$	$\frac{5}{16}$	0.242	0.035	333	1000	3
-6	$\frac{3}{8}$	$\frac{3}{8}$	0.295	0.040	333	1000	$3\frac{1}{2}$
-8	$\frac{1}{2}$	$\frac{1}{2}$	0.375	0.062	333	1000	4

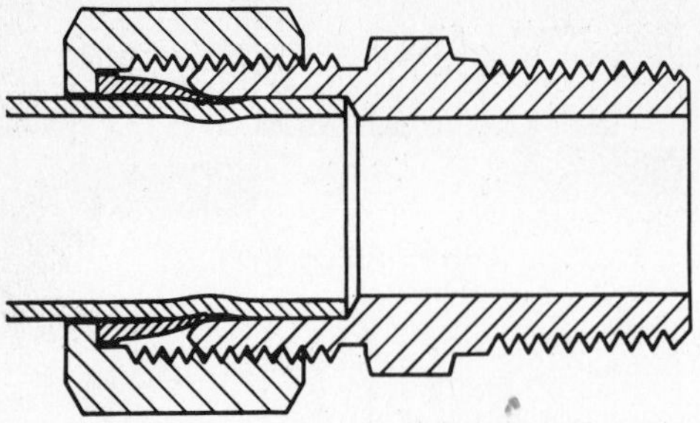

Fig. 7-22 Schematic view of a self-aligning fitting. (*The Weatherhead Co. of Canada, Ltd.*)

Fig. 7-24 Cutaway view of a synthetic grommet compression fitting.

The compression, self-aligning fitting shown in Fig. 7-22 is seldom used. The synthetic grommet fitting shown in Fig. 7-24 is quite common. Having flexible connections, it can be used with steel, copper, or synthetic tubing. The nut is bottomed against the adapter, and this makes overtorquing of the nut impossible. Consequently, there is no distortion of the tube or restriction to the fluid flow. For these reasons the synthetic grommet fitting is highly recommended.

It is advisable, however, when using nylon or synthetic tubings, to insert a sleeve in order to maintain a good seal and avoid tube distortion. This should be done regardless of the type of compression fitting used (see Fig. 7-25).

Heater and Cooling System Hoses Cooling system hoses and heater hoses differ in design, construction, and composition. They and all standard hose styles use a dash number system to identify the inside dimension (ID).

Today's diesel engine cooling systems operate at a maximum pressure of 26 psi [179.14 kPa]. The burst pressure of 2-in [5.08-cm] cooling system hose is about 70 psi [482.3 kPa], and the hose must be flexible to a point of 40°F [4.44°C] and must not expand more than 2 percent at 212°F [100°C].

The inner hose is usually made from Buna, Teflon, or silicone because these materials are oil-resistant and do not swell or peel. They are reinforced with a single or double fiber or coarse steel braid. The outer cover is usually neoprene, silicone, or synthetic rubber. Some radiator hoses, especially on the inlet side of the water pump, are susceptible to collapse. To compensate for this, spiral steel wires are molded into the hose or inserted over the inner cover, giving the hose more nearly uniform strength.

Hydraulic Hoses Hose styles and sizes are as numerous and varied as those of pipes and tubings. To accommodate the numerous hydraulic applications, manufacturers have included in their hose style products four or five groups classified according to working pressure. Each individual group includes different hose compositions to suit different types of liquids. The hose group styles are as follows: Group 1: low pressure with a maximum working pressure up to 400 psi [2756 kPa]; Group 2: medium working pressure up to 2000 psi [13,780 kPa]; Group 3: high working pressure up to 3000 psi [20,670 kPa]; Group 4: very high working pressure up to 5000 psi [34,450 kPa]. Some companies have special groups for special products.

To distinguish hydraulic hoses by quality (style) and size, a lettering and numbering system is used. No doubt you are familiar with the names *Weatherhead, Aeroquip,* and *Stratoflex.* All three companies use a numbering system. The letter stamped on the hose identifies the manufacturer, and the first digit describes the basic hose style. Obviously, the numbers vary from company to company. The number stenciled on the side of the hose is the dash number, which is used on both tubing and hoses. Note, however, where the dash number indicates the inside diameter (ID) of a hose, it indicates the outside diameter (OD) of tubing. With respect to the odd size hose, these dash numbers refer to the equivalent ID of the tube. To determine the proper size when connecting a hose with a tube, the dash number of the hose is matched with the number of the tubing.

Fig. 7-23 Cutaway view of a compression fitting.

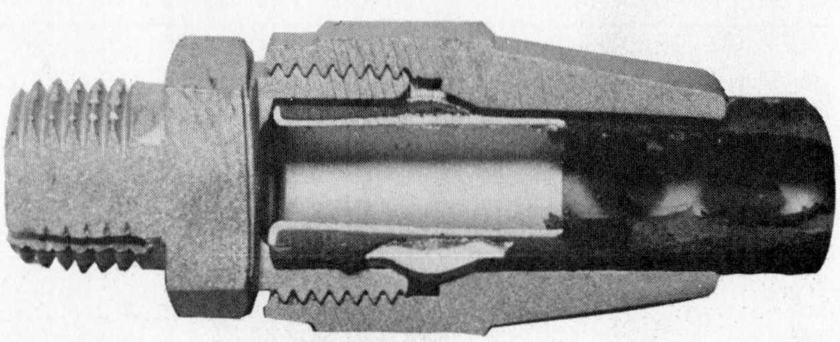

Fig. 7-25 Cutaway view of a compression fitting using nylon tubing with an insert.

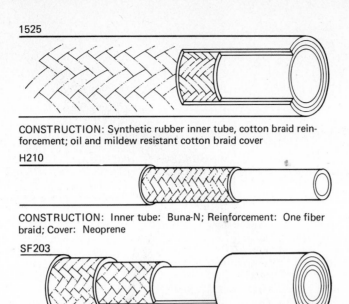

1525

CONSTRUCTION: Synthetic rubber inner tube, cotton braid reinforcement; oil and mildew resistant cotton braid cover

H210

CONSTRUCTION: Inner tube: Buna-N; Reinforcement: One fiber braid; Cover: Neoprene

SF203

CONSTRUCTION: Seamless synthetic rubber inner tube reinforced with two layers of fabric, and with cover of synthetic rubber

| PART NO. | DASH NO. | SIZE | | PRESSURE | | | MINIMUM BEND RADII, in | VACUUM, in Hg |
		HOSE ID, in	HOSE OD, in	MAXIMUM WORKING PRESSURE, psi	PROOF TEST PRESSURE, psi	MINIMUM BURST PRESSURE, psi		
1525	-8	0.500	0.750	250		1000	5	28
H210	-8	1/2	13/16	200	400	800	5	5
SF203	-8	1/2	3/4	250		1000	5	

Fig. 7-26 Group 1 hose construction and specifications.

EXAMPLE Three low-pressure hose products from the three companies previously named are shown in Fig. 7-26. All three hoses have about the same working pressure—200 to 250 psi [1378 to 1722.5 kPa]—and about the same burst pressure—800 to 1000 psi [5512.0 to 6890.0 kPa]. The only difference between the companies' products lies in the materials from which the hoses are manufactured.

Figures 7-27, 7-28, and 7-29 illustrate hose styles classified as Group 2, Group 3, and Group 4, respectively. When examining the hoses and charts, you notice the following differences among companies: (1) material and construction, (2) outside diameter of the hose size, (3) working and burst pressure, and (4) bend radius. (This change correlates with the variation in pressure.)

Hose Ends and Adapters Because of the great variety in hose styles and connections a large assortment of hose ends and adapters is needed. The hose end serves only one purpose—to connect a hose (trouble-free) to an adapter or component. Each hose style uses the same socket; the nipple is the only variable factor in connecting with the different types of adapters.

To classify hose ends and adapters, all manufac-

turers use a numbering system. As with most reference systems, the numbering varies from manufacturer to manufacturer. Examples of hose ends are given in Fig. 7-30, and adapters, in Fig. 7-31. The hose end basic fitting style for the male pipe is No. 348-12-125 and is used with a double wire hose No. 12 and has a 1/2-in pipe thread. The adapter style No. 1020-12-12B is a 45° elbow. The thread and flare design are JIC on one side and pipe thread on the other. The thread size and the hose size are each 1/2 in.

Hose Service A hydraulic hose very seldom causes a shutdown of the equipment. Any failure that does arise owing to a hose will be because of improper assembly, incorrect hose length, improper installation, or unsuitable application.

A number of improper hose installations are shown in Fig. 7-32. Before reading further, try to ascertain the various inadequacies shown in the illustrations.

- A hose will change slightly in length (from 2 to 4 percent) when pressurized. Slack in the hose should be provided to compensate for any change in length which may occur (Fig. 7-32a).
- Hose line or tubing passing close to a hot exhaust

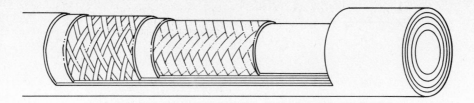

PART NO.	HOSE SIZE	HOSE ID, in	HOSE OD, in	MINIMUM BURST PRESSURE, psi	MAXIMUM WORKING PRESSURE, psi	MINIMUM BEND RADIUS, in	APPROXIMATE WEIGHT PER FOOT, lb
213-4-L	-4	3/16	31/64	6000	1500	2	0.109
213-5-L	-5	1/4	35/64	6000	1500	2 1/4	0.115
213-6-L	-6	5/16	39/64	4000	1000	2 3/4	0.159
213-8-L	-8	13/32	47/64	4000	1000	4 5/8	0.205
213-10-L	-10	1/2	53/64	3500	875	5 1/2	0.310
213-12-L	-12	5/8	61/64	3000	750	6 1/2	0.357
213-16-L	-16	7/8	1 13/64	1500	250	7 3/8	0.347
213-20-L	-20	1 1/8	1 31/64	1250	250	9	0.442
213-24-L	-24	1 3/8	1 23/32	1000	250	11	0.530
213-32-L	-32	1 13/16	2 9/64	750	250	17	0.674

HOSE CONSTRUCTION: Seamless synthetic rubber inner tube, reinforced with one fabric braid, one braid of high tensile steel wire, and covered with a synthetic-rubber-impregnated, oil-resistant fabric braid

Fig. 7-27 Group 2 hose construction and specifications. (*Stratoflex Canada Ltd.*)

manifold will deteriorate. It should be protected with a fireproof baffle (Fig. 7-32b).
- For neater appearance and easier maintenance, use elbows and adapters if the flow volume is low. Remember, however, that, where flow volume is high, the use of elbows should be kept to a minimum (Fig. 7-32c).
- Any vibration or external force here could cause failure owing to the insufficient support of the hose or tubing. If rubber-coated clamps were used, external damage and excessive vibration would be prevented (Fig. 7-32d).
- The bend radius on this hose (Fig. 7-32e) does not allow sufficient flow volume, and it thereby reduces pressure. Any high pressure here might cause line failure. To ensure maximum connection security, the bend radius should be increased.

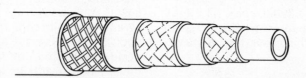

DASH NO.	SIZE		PRESSURE			MINIMUM BEND RADIUS, in	VACUUM, in Hg
	HOSE ID, in	HOSE OD, in	MAXIMUM WORKING PRESSURE, psi	PROOF TEST PRESSURE, psi	MINIMUM BURST PRESSURE, psi		
5	1/4	19/32	5 000	10 000	20 000	4	30
6	3/8	3/4	4 000	8 000	16 000	5	30
8	1/2	7/8	3 500	7 000	14 000	7	30
12	3/4	1 5/32	2 250	4 500	9 000	9 1/2	—
16	1	1 1/2	2 000	4 000	8 000	11	—
20	1 1/4	1 7/8	1 625	3 250	6 500	16	—
24	1 1/2	2 5/32	1 250	2 500	5 000	20	—
32	2	2 21/32	1 125	2 250	4 500	22	—

HOSE CONSTRUCTION: INNER TUBE: Buna-N; REINFORCEMENT: two-wire braid, one cotton braid; COVER: Neoprene

Fig. 7-28 Group 3 hose construction and specifications. (*The Weatherhead Co. of Canada Ltd.*)

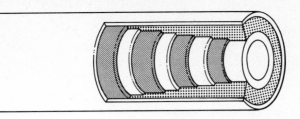

PART NO.	HOSE ID, in	HOSE OD, in	RECOMMENDED WORKING PRESSURE, psi	MINIMUM BURST PRESSURE, psi	MINIMUM BEND RADIUS, in
FC136-06	0.375	0.844	5 500	22 000	5.00
FC136-08	0.500	0.969	5 000	20 000	7.00
FC136-12	0.750	1.266	4 000	16 000	11.00
FC136-16	1.000	1.562	3 500	14 000	14.00
FC136-20	1.250	2.000	2 500	10 000	18.00
FC136-24	1.500	2.250	2 250	9 000	22.00
FC136-32	2.000	2.750	2 000	8 000	28.00

HOSE CONSTRUCTION: Synthetic rubber inner tube, multiple spiral wire wrap reinforcement, synthetic rubber outer cover

Fig. 7-29 Group 4 hose construction. (*Aeroquip Corporation*)

- A twisted hose will reduce flow volume. Moreover, the socket could become loose under high pressure (Fig. 7-32*f*).

Servicing Hydraulic Hoses The assembly of a hose end to a hose need not be difficult if the correct assembly procedure is followed. However, owing to the numerous varieties of hose sizes, fittings, and styles, small but sometimes very costly mistakes can be made. Another problem that contributes to hose failure is the lack of uniformity among manufacturers in the numbering system for the outside dimension. It is essential, therefore, in assembling hose and hose ends, to make all purchases from the same manufacturer.

Perhaps the next greatest factor contributing toward hose failure is the mechanic's disregard for the recommended assembly procedure. The following points may seem obvious, but they are the key if accuracy and perfection are desired.

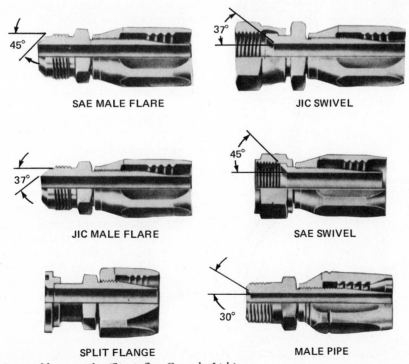

Fig. 7-30 Cutaway views of hose ends. (*Stratoflex Canada Ltd.*)

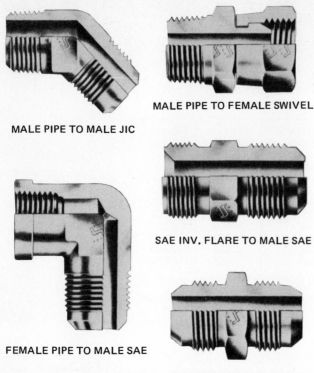

MALE PIPE TO MALE JIC

MALE PIPE TO FEMALE SWIVEL

SAE INV. FLARE TO MALE SAE

FEMALE PIPE TO MALE SAE

MALE SAE TO MALE SAE

Fig. 7-31 Cutaway views of hose-end adapters. (*Stratoflex Canada Ltd.*)

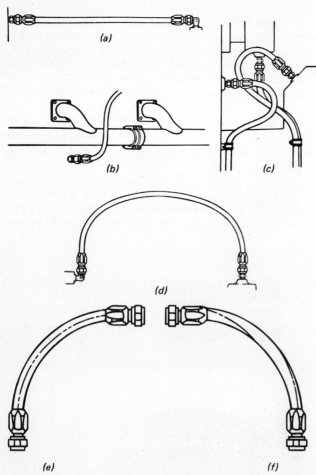

(a)

(b)

(c)

(d)

(e)

(f)

Fig. 7-32 Improper hose installations. (*Sperry Vickers Division of Sperry Inc.*)

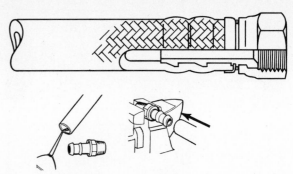

Fig. 7-33 Socketless hose assembly procedure. (*Stratoflex Canada Ltd.*)

Assembly Procedure   The correct assembly procedures for the four most popular hose styles, illustrated in Figs. 7-33 to 7-35, are:

A. Socketless assembly (see Fig. 7-33).

1. Cut the hose square to the required length. Oil the inside of the hose and the outside of the nipple.
2. Push the hose on the fitting underneath the protective cap.

B. Medium-pressure assembly (see Fig. 7-34).

1. Cut the hose square to the length required with a fine-tooth hacksaw or a cutoff wheel. Put the socket in the vise and screw the hose counterclockwise into the socket until it bottoms, then back off one quarter turn.   **NOTE** An assembly tool is required for all single-wire braid hoses in sizes of $\frac{1}{4}$ in through $\frac{3}{4}$ in.
2. Liberally oil the nipple threads, the assembly tool mandrel, and the inside of the hose.
3. Male ends: Push the assembly tool into the nipple. Oil the nipple and then screw it clockwise into the socket and hose. Tighten the nipple until it is snug against the socket.
4. Swivel ends: Tighten the nipple and the nut on the assembly tool. Oil the nipple and then screw it clockwise into the socket and hose. Leave $\frac{1}{32}$- to $\frac{1}{16}$-in clearance between the nut and the socket so that the nut will swivel.

C. High pressure.

1. Cut the hose to the length required.
2. Some double-wire braid hose must be stripped of its rubber cover before it is inserted in the socket (whereas others do not require this). To do this, locate the stripping point by putting the hose end next to the high-pressure fitting (as shown in Fig. 7-35) from the hose end of the socket to the notch on the socket. To strip the hose, cut around down to the wire braid, slit it lengthwise, raise the flap, and pull it off with pliers. Clean the wire braid with a wire brush or soft wire wheel, being careful not to fray or flare it.
3. Put the socket in the vise and screw the hose into the socket counterclockwise until it bottoms.
4. Oil the nipple threads and the inside of the hose liberally. No assembly mandrel is needed for a dou-

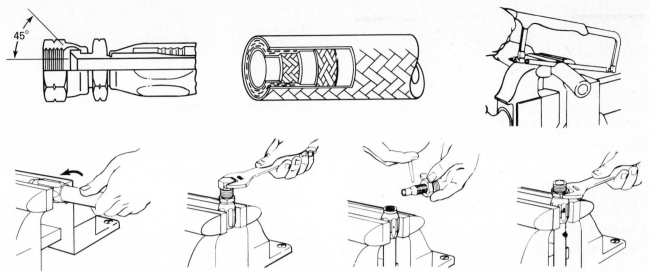

Fig. 7-34 Medium-pressure hose assembly procedure. (*Stratoflex Canada Ltd.*)

ble-wire braid hose. Use grease instead of oil for larger sizes.

5. Screw the nipple into the socket and hose. Leave $\frac{1}{32}$- to $\frac{1}{16}$-in clearance for takeup.

D. Teflon.

1. Cut the hose to the correct length. Trim any loose wires flush with the tube stock; remove any burrs on the tube end with a knife. Slip two sockets back to back over the "necked down" end of the hose, positioning them 3 in from each end.

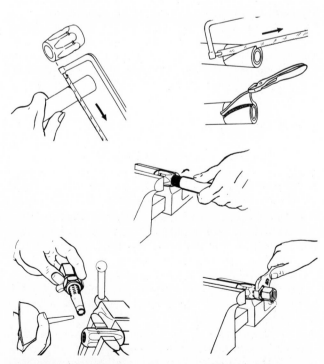

Fig. 7-35 High-pressure hose assembly procedure. (*Stratoflex Canada Ltd.*)

2. Mount the nipple hex in a vise. Work the hose bore over the nipple to size the tube and aid in separating the braid prior to fitting the sleeve. Then remove the hose from the nipple.

3. (a) Start the sleeve over the tube and under the wire braid by hand. Complete the positioning of the sleeve by pushing the hose squarely against a hard surface. Make sure that the tube butts against the shoulder of the sleeve. (b) Lubricate the nipple and socket threads. For stainless steel fittings, use molybdenum disulfide lubricant, and for other material combinations use standard petroleum lubricants. (c) Push the hose over the nipple with a twisting motion until it is seated against the nipple chamber. Push the socket forward and hand-start the threading of the socket to the nipple. Wrench-tighten the nipple hex until the clearance with the socket hex is $\frac{1}{32}$ in or less. Then tighten a little further in order to align the corners of the nipple and socket hexes.

4. To disassemble, unscrew and remove the nipple, slide the socket back on the hose by tapping against a flat surface, and then remove the sleeve with pliers.

AIR BRAKE (LOW PRESSURE)

1. Cut the hose square to the required length.
2. Slide the nut and sleeve onto the hose, making sure the bevel edge of the sleeve faces out toward the fitting.
3. Push the hose into the fitting until it bottoms.
4. Tighten the nut down all the way (see Fig. 7-36).

Fig. 7-36 Air brake fitting.

Review Questions

1. Name the major components or parts which make up a simple hydraulic system.

2. By what two methods is the reservoir pressurized?

3. Explain why a pressurized reservoir requires: (a) a relief valve, (b) a vacuum valve.

4. Why should you avoid, as much as possible, using (a) a 90° elbow? (b) restrictors?

5. If, when installing a hose or tube, you are required to go around an object or component, how small can you make the bend radius if a No. 16 hose is to be used?

6. Does the dash number system identify (a) the inside or outside diameter of a tube? (b) the inside or the outside diameter of a hose?

7. What two factors determine the type of hydraulic line (hose, pipe, or tubing) to be used?

8. List two reasons why you should use a mechanical tube bender when bending a tube to a bend-angle greater than 20°.

9. Explain how you can avoid making an oversize flare end.

10. Explain why a hydraulic hose is more reliable for connecting components than a tube.

11. What problems could arise if the hose stripping point is too long or too short?

12. When installing a hose fitting, why is it necessary to back off one quarter turn after bottoming?

Unit 8 Hydraulic Pumps, Accumulators, and Oil Coolers

The power source is the heart of the hydraulic system; it is responsible for the flow of liquid and the movement of the fluid against resistance. The resistance referred to is what it will encounter from the friction within the system's passages, as well as the resistance at the actuator(s). The usual power sources of a hydraulic system are a hydraulic pump, a volume of fluid stored at a specific height, and an accumulator. (See discussion of reservoirs in Unit 7.) Bear in mind that a power source does not create pressure—it provides flow, and "pressure" is the result of resistance to flow.

The objective of this unit is to familiarize you with the "moving fluid" within a hydraulic system so that you can better understand how it reacts to move a load or transmit mechanical energy from one point to another. Various hydraulic pump designs are therefore discussed with regard to the manner in which they operate to move fluid, to the way in which they are classified and rated, and to the methods whereby they are serviced.

PUMPS

Pump Classification   Although the types and designs of hydraulic pumps are numerous, they are easily categorized by simply determining their ability to displace fluid. (This also determines whether the pump is of the positive or nonpositive displacement design.) Nonpositive displacement pumps are those which supply a continuous flow until the resistance in the discharge line equals the designed capacity of the pump.

Whether a pump is positive or nonpositive, it pumps fluid by means of rotating or reciprocating motion of the pumping elements, which create low pressure on the inlet side of the pump. This traps the fluid, and as the pump elements are rotated or reciprocated, fluid is forced out of the outlet side. The rotating or reciprocating parts may be loosely or closely fitted between the stationary parts, but their function nonetheless is to minimize fluid slippage from the higher to the lower pressure side of the pump.

Pump Rating   Again, whether the pump is of the positive or nonpositive design, it is nevertheless rated according to its performance, which is based on three factors:

- The amount of oil the pump can deliver to the system, measured in gallons or liters per minute (gal/min [l/min]);
- The speed at which the pump operates (rpm);
- The pressure, measured in psi or kilopascals (kPa), at which the pump must operate to supply the specified flow rate.

The performance data are recorded on the pump by the manufacturer (for example: 2100 rpm, 150 l/min, 1200 kPa). It is shown alongside the manufacturer's name and the pump serial number.

Impeller Pumps   Nonpositive displacement pumps of the centrifugal (impeller) design are used as coolant pumps or, in larger applications, as irrigation pumps. Basically they are designed with an impeller which has straight, curved, or cone-shaped blades. The impeller is positioned on a shaft in a spiral or volute-shaped housing. The clearance between the impeller and end-plate housing is about 0.020 in [0.50 mm]. The fluid inlet is at or near the center of the housing, and the fluid outlet is at the enlarged opening in the housing.

OPERATION   When the impeller is driven, it creates a low pressure, and the atmospheric pressure forces fluid into the inlet port. As the fluid starts to revolve, the centrifugal force moves the fluid out (between the blades) to a greater and greater radius. This increases the tangential velocity and centrifugal force. The liquid thrown off the tip of the blades follows the contour of the housing. From Fig. 8-1 you will see that the pump chamber (in which the impeller rotates) gradually increases in area toward the outlet port. Owing to its design, the velocity head is gradually converted into pressure head. When the pump

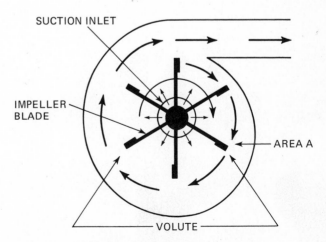

Fig. 8-1   Schematic view of an impeller pump. (*J I Case Company Agricultural Equipment Division*)

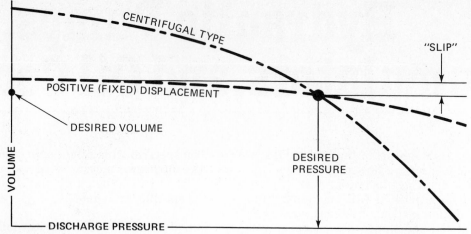

Fig. 8-2 Discharge pressure versus volume.

approaches its designed pressure and volume, say, 100 psi [689.0 kPa] and 100 gal/min [378.5 l/min], it is working at its highest efficiency. When the discharge line resistance increases until there is no more increase in flow, the flow rate gradually decreases but the pressure remains at its maximum. However, since the impeller still moves the liquid within the housing, it causes a high slippage within the pump and produces heat. The design and the rpm determine the maximum pressure and volume. No pressure relief valve is needed.

Positive Displacement Pumps   All positive displacement pumps produce a pulsating fluid flow while revolving or reciprocating, some more than others. (A multipiston pump has the lowest pulsation.) A valve is required to relieve displacement once maximum opening pressure has been obtained, to prevent damaging the hydraulic pump, the drive coupling, or the engine.

All positive displacement pumps are designed to effectively seal between the pumping element and housing. As a result they have very little volumetric slip when the system pressure increases to its designed maximum. The efficiency of any hydraulic pump depends on the design of its rotating or reciprocating members and its ability to maintain its seal at various pressures and temperatures.

A comparative chart, shown in Fig. 8-2, displays the characteristics of a nonpositive and a positive displacement pump in relation to pressure and volume (on the assumption that the rpm is constant).

Positive displacement pumps are divided into two types: fixed and variable displacement. The term *fixed displacement* identifies a type of pump capable of delivering a specific volume of fluid for each revolution or stroke. The term *variable displacement* identifies a type of pump capable of changing its specific volume of fluid for each revolution or stroke. For example, consider a water wheel operating at a constant speed to which eight 1-gal (3.785-l) buckets are attached. When the wheel makes one revolution, it will deliver 8 gal [30.68 l] of water. Since the wheel delivers the same volume for each revolution, it is the equivalent of a fixed displacement pump.

However, if, while the wheel was in motion, you were able to change the capacity of the buckets from 1 gal to $\frac{1}{2}$ gal [1.892 l], you would then have the equivalent of a variable displacement pump.

To calculate the displacement for a given pump, use the following formula:

gal/min [l/min] = rotating pump speed (rpm)
$\times$ displacement in in³ [cm³]
per revolution divided by
231 U.S. gal, 277 Imperial gal,
or liters.
gal/min = rpm $\times$ displacement/231
(or 277) gal
l/min = rpm $\times$ displacement/liters

Rotary Pump Classification   The various rotary pumps are generally classified by the rotating members, as well as by construction. The four most common types used for on- and off-highway hydraulic equipment are (1) the external gear pump, (2) the unbalanced and balanced vane pump, (3) the internal gear pump, and (4) the gerotor pump.

The External Gear Pump   Of the hydraulic pumps the external gear type is the most popular. It has a

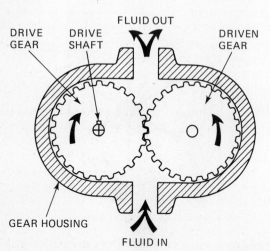

Fig. 8-3 Schematic view of an external gear pump.

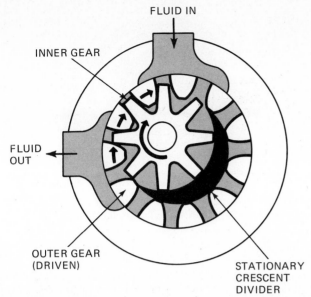

FLUID IN

INNER GEAR

FLUID OUT

OUTER GEAR (DRIVEN)

STATIONARY CRESCENT DIVIDER

Fig. 8-4 Schematic view of an internal gear pump. (*J I Case Company Agricultural Equipment Division*)

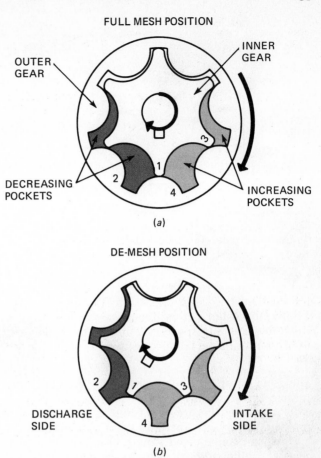

FULL MESH POSITION

OUTER GEAR

INNER GEAR

DECREASING POCKETS

INCREASING POCKETS

(a)

DE-MESH POSITION

DISCHARGE SIDE

INTAKE SIDE

(b)

Fig. 8-5 Schematic view of a gerotor pump. (*J I Case Company Agricultural Equipment Division*)

lengthy service life and is reasonably efficient and economical to operate.

An external gear pump (see Fig. 8-3) is composed of two mesh gears that revolve in a housing. The clearance is very small between the gear teeth and the gear housing, between the gear sides and wear plates, and between the gears as they mesh. The inlet and outlet ports are opposite one another. One gear is turned by the drive shaft, which is connected to the power source. As the drive shaft turns, the attached (drive) gear must obviously turn in the same direction while the meshing (driven) gear is forced in the opposite direction. As the power rotates the drive shaft, the drive and driven gear teeth unmesh, and a low pressure (vacuum) is created at the inlet side of the pump and oil flows into the pockets formed between the gear teeth, the wear plates, and the housing. The oil is carried around in the gear pockets of the drive and driven gear. The fluid is prevented from returning to the inlet side of the pump because of the close tolerance between the components. As the teeth mesh (on the outlet side), the fluid from both pockets is forced out against the system pressure.

The Internal Gear Pump Internal gear pumps are used in automatic transmissions or where space is limited. The drive gear of an internal gear pump may be described as the inner gear, which has teeth projecting outward. The teeth of the drive gear (outer gear) project inward and are in mesh with the inner gear between the outlet and inlet side of the pump (see Fig. 8-4).

The drive shaft of the pump is set off-center in a circular chamber. This chamber is the bearing and support of the outer gear. Opposite to the inlet and outlet port there is a crescent-shaped seal which is machined into the pump housing. This seal is positioned between the gears to seal between the inlet and outlet port.

OPERATION The pumping principle of the internal gear pump should be familiar to you since it is patterned after all other gear pumps. The drive shaft rotates the inner gear, which, in turn, causes the outer gear to rotate. This motion traps the fluid in the gear space as it passes the crescent. As the fluid is carried away from the intake side of the pump, a low pressure is created, allowing more fluid to enter. The fluid is carried by the gear pockets from the inlet to the outlet side. As the gear teeth pass the crescent, they gradually begin to mesh, and the fluid is then forced out against the system pressure.

The Gerotor Pump The gerotor type of hydraulic pump is used in power steering or as a lubrication pump. The gerotor pumping elements consist of a pair of strange looking gears, one within the other, in a housing. The inner gear, which has always one tooth less than the outer gear, is the drive gear. Five teeth are, at all times, in sliding mesh with the outer gear ring. One pair of teeth is always in full mesh position and one set is in demesh position. In Fig. 8-5 the full mesh position is shown in part a. Note that, when the inner gear is driven, the inlet pockets increase in size while the discharge pockets decrease.

By observing the diagrams, you will notice that the pockets formed between 1 and 3 and 4 increase to the maximum size while the pockets formed between 1 and 2 decrease. From this you can determine

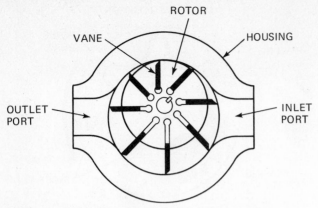

Fig. 8-6 Schematic view of an unbalanced vane pump. (*J I Case Company Agricultural Equipment Division*)

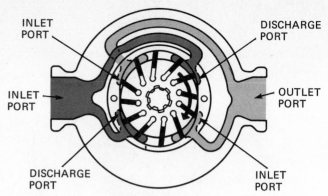

Fig. 8-7 Schematic view of a balanced vane pump. (*J I Case Company Agricultural Equipment Division*)

that the intake side of the pump is on the right side, and the discharge side, on the left. The advantage of this pump design is that the outer gear rotates at a much lower rate of speed than that of the drive gear and this minimizes component wear.

The Vane Pump Vane pumps are applicable to any system whether the volume is high or low or whether or not the pressure range is variable. They compensate for self-wear and are highly efficient.

However, unbalanced vane pumps (see Fig. 8-6), because of the side pressure on the drive shaft, are more commonly used as variable displacement pumps or where a medium pressure is required.

A vane pump of the unbalanced design has the rotor positioned on the drive shaft. The rotor has numerous slots into which movable vanes are fitted. The rotor is placed off-center in a circular chamber with the inlet and outlet ports located 180° from each other. Depending on the size of the pump, the vanes are forced out against the center ring by a spring(s), centrifugal force, and system pressure.

OPERATION As the rotor revolves, pumping chambers are formed between the vanes, rotor, cam ring, and the two side plates (wear plates). As the space between the vanes, rotor, and cam ring increases, a low pressure is created and fluid under atmospheric pressure moves in to fill the space. When a vane passes the inlet port, it traps the fluid and conveys it to the outlet side. As the cam ring forces the vanes inward, it decreases the volume. This action discharges the fluid out of the outlet port and into the system.

Balanced Vane Pumps The balanced vane pump design is most prevalent on hydraulic systems because it has two pumping sides within one pump housing (see Fig. 8-7). This is achieved by replacing the circular cam ring with an elliptical one. As a result the output volume is double that of an unbalanced vane pump of the same size. Furthermore there is no side thrust on the drive shaft, because there are two outlets (180° apart) which equalize the force. The bearing life is therefore increased.

On smaller balanced and unbalanced vane pumps, the vanes are forced outward through centrifugal force and through system pressure, which increases wear on the vanes and cam ring. Larger types of balanced vane pumps, or high-speed pumps, are modified to reduce the wear on the vane and cam ring. This is achieved by placing a small, loosely fitted piston (intravane) into the cutout portion of each vane. The rotor has vertically and diagonally drilled passages. The diagonal passages end at the bottom of each vane and are in line with either the outlet or inlet port.

The vertical passages leading to the intravane are in line with ports in the pressure plate, and they direct system pressure at all times into the intravane area. As a result the vanes are forced out against the cam ring by system pressure when discharging and by inlet pressure plus intravane pressure when charging, minimizing wear on the vanes and cam ring.

Piston Pumps (Reciprocating Pumps) A piston pump is one which, through the back-and-forth movement (reciprocation) of a piston within a cylinder, transmits fluid (with the assistance of an outlet and inlet valve) from the inlet to the outlet port.

Similar to rotary pumps, the reciprocating pumps are of the positive displacement design. With each stroke of the piston a definite volume of fluid is displaced into the system. If the pumping stroke is shortened by means of some kind of device, the volume is then reduced and a variable displacement pump is created.

Piston Pump Classification Piston pumps are classified in the same manner as rotary pumps—according to their design. The types of piston pumps most widely used for various hydraulic systems are single-acting, double-acting, axial, and radial. The radial piston pumps are also referred to as rotary piston pumps because the pistons are moved into reciprocating motion (within the cylinder) through rotary motion.

Single- or double-acting piston pumps are an extremely popular power source for hydraulic jacks or shop cranes and are used to pump fuel or oil into or

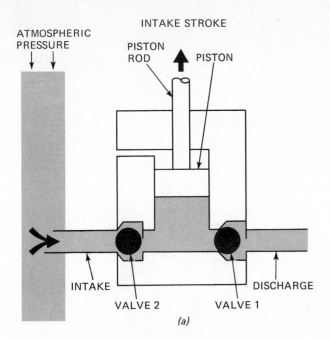

INTAKE STROKE

ATMOSPHERIC PRESSURE

PISTON ROD — PISTON

INTAKE — DISCHARGE

VALVE 2 — VALVE 1

(a)

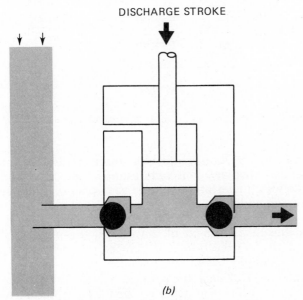

DISCHARGE STROKE

(b)

Fig. 8-8 Schematic view of a single-acting piston pump. (*J I Case Company Agricultural Equipment Division*)

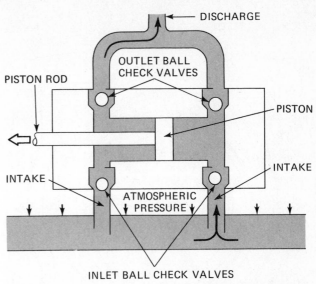

DISCHARGE

PISTON ROD

OUTLET BALL CHECK VALVES

PISTON

INTAKE

INTAKE — ATMOSPHERIC PRESSURE

INLET BALL CHECK VALVES

Fig. 8-9 Schematic view of double-acting piston pump.

out of a reservoir or to apply pressure to a brake system.

Axial or radial piston pumps are generally used where the system pressure exceeds 3000 psi [20,670 kPa]. They are also used where fluid direction or volume changes are desired, because the direction of the fluid flow can be changed simply by altering the drive direction without requiring any changes within the pump itself. The axial and radial pumps have a lesser pulsation (fluid) flow than any other type of positive displacement pump.

NOTE All piston pumps require a good filtering system (to reduce wear occasioned by the very close tolerance between the cylinder and piston) and a good static pressure at the pump inlet (to prevent pump cavitation).

Single-Acting Piston Pumps A simplified single-acting piston pump is shown in Fig. 8-8. The check valves used are simple ball checks held on the valve seat by a light spring force. The piston of the pump is loosely fitted in the bore and is equipped with a cup or O-ring seal to increase its sealing effectiveness. The reservoir is connected to the inlet port of the piston pump, and the lift cylinder is connected to the outlet port.

OPERATION As the piston is moved upward, low pressure is created below, which allows the oil at atmospheric pressure to open the inlet check valve and to enter the void space. When the oil pressures in the cylinder area and the reservoir have equalized, the spring closes the inlet check valve, trapping the oil. On the down stroke of the piston, the pressure rises. When this pressure is greater than that in the lift cylinder, the outlet valve opens. This allows fluid to enter the chamber below the lift cylinder. As the pressure equalizes, the check valve closes through its spring. To lower the lift piston (that is, lower the load), the shutoff valve is opened (not shown). The pressure in the lift cylinder is then reduced because the fluid returns via the return line to the reservoir.

Double-Acting Piston Pumps When a greater pump volume is required, a double-acting piston pump is used to gain a higher oil flow. Portable presses and engines using a hydrostatic starting system, for instance, use this design.

A double-acting piston pump requires two additional check valves. Its piston rod must be sealed to prevent oil losses and the entrance of air. It is designed to allow oil to be pumped with every movement of the piston (see Fig. 8-9).

Note that the existence of the piston rod lowers the stroke volume but creates a higher pressure when the applied forces (left or right) are equal because of the reduced piston area. For example, assume the following: (1) that the area of the piston is

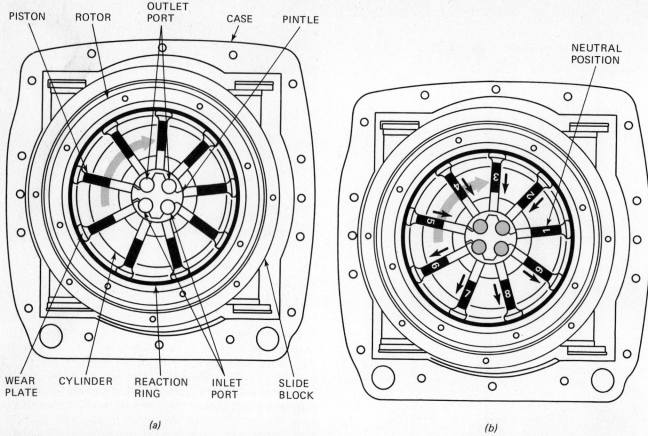

PISTON   ROTOR   OUTLET PORT   CASE   PINTLE

NEUTRAL POSITION

WEAR PLATE   CYLINDER   REACTION RING   INLET PORT   SLIDE BLOCK

(a)

(b)

Fig. 8-10 *(a)* Nine-piston radial piston pump. *(b)* Operation.

2 in² [12.9 cm²], (2) that the area of the rod is 1 in² [6.45 cm²], (3) that the applied force on the piston in both directions is 100 lb [444 N], and (4) that the stroke is 3 in [7.62 cm].

The pressure, therefore, when the piston is forced to the right, equals

$$F/A = 100/2 = 50 \text{ psi } [344.5 \text{ kPa}]$$

When the force is to the left, the pressure equals

$$F/A = 100/1 = 100 \text{ psi } [689 \text{ kPa}]$$

The volume displaced when the piston moves to the right equals 6 in³: area × stroke = 2 × 3 = 6 in³ [98.34 cm³]

The volume displaced when the piston moves to the left equals 3 in³: area × stroke = 1 × 3 = 3 in³ [49.17 cm³].

Radial Piston Pumps   Although a radial piston pump is somewhat similar in design to an unbalanced vane pump, a cylinder is used rather than the rotor (see Fig. 8-10a). In this cylinder, an uneven number of bores are machined, into which pistons are fitted. The cylinder is also off-center from the centerline of the housing and rotates on the stationary pintle, which also serves as the oil inlet and outlet valve. The fixed circular ring of the vane pump is replaced with a reaction ring. When the pump is of the variable displacement design, the reaction

ring is adjustable in a fashion similar to that of the variable displacement vane pump. There are shoe-like wear plates on the end of each piston to reduce friction and wear.

The flow rate of any type of piston pump depends on the displacement of the piston, the number of pistons, and the rpm at which the pump is driven. For example, when the diameter of the piston is 0.500 in [1.27 cm], the stroke is 1 in [2.54 cm], and the pump has nine pistons, then the displacement of one cycle is 1.766 in³:

$$R^2 \times \pi \times \text{stroke} \times \text{number of pistons}$$
$$0.250 \times 0.250 \times 3.14 \times 1 \times 9 = 1.766 \text{ in}^3$$
$$[28.94 \text{ cm}^3 \ (0.0289 \text{ l})]$$

Assume that the operating speed of the pump is 3000 rpm, then the flow rate is

$$1.766 \times 3000/231 = 22.93 \text{ gal/min (U.S.)}$$
$$= [86.8 \text{ l/min}]$$
$$1.766 \times 3000/277 = 19.12 \text{ gal/min (Imp.)}$$
$$= [72.4 \text{ l/min}]$$

OPERATION   Whether or not the cylinder is rotating, four pistons are always open to the pump inlet port and four to the pump outlet port. See Fig. 8-10b. The one piston between the inlet and the outlet port is in the neutral position and is on the bottom of its stroke. All the other eight pistons are at different distances from the center of the pintle. When the

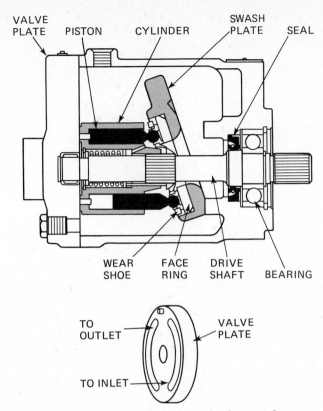

Fig. 8-11 Fixed displacement, swash plate axial pump.

cylinder rotates in a clockwise rotation, pistons 2, 3, 4, and 5 are forced inward and pump fluid into the system via the outlet ports. Pistons 9, 8, 7, and 6 are forced outward and are charged via the inlet ports. The rotation moves piston 2 into the neutral position. Piston 1 begins to charge and piston 6 begins to discharge. This sequence continues until the cylinder stops rotating.

Axial Piston Pumps A fixed displacement, swash plate axial pump is shown in Fig. 8-11. Nine pistons are evenly spaced and closely fitted within the cylinder block, which is splined to the drive shaft and is supported by bearings in both housing ends. Each piston has a wear shoe, which rests against a fixed plate called the *swash plate*; this is angled about 20° from the centerline of the drive shaft. It has a thrust-bearing face ring called the retraction ring. The left side of the cylinder bores is closed off by the valve plate. The valve plate has two slots—the inlet slot, which covers four cylinder bores, and the outlet slot, which also stretches over four cylinder bores. One cylinder bore is covered by the valve plate. The piston of this cylinder bore is on the bottom of its stroke and is in neutral position. The remaining eight pistons are at various distances from the valve plate. Four pistons are always in the discharging stage and four in the charging stage.

OPERATION When the drive shaft rotates, it rotates the cylinder. Four pistons then discharge fluid into the system as four pistons receive fluid from the reservoir or from a charging pump. The rotation of the cylinder causes the piston shoe to slide on the tilted

reaction ring, which forces four of the pistons inward and allows four to move outward. The ninth piston's cylinder bore opening (which was in neutral) moves over the charging slot. The adjacent cylinder opening, which has just completed its stroke, moves into the neutral position. The piston that has completed its charging stroke moves its cylinder bore opening over the discharge slot.

The construction of some swash plate pumps varies, but the variances are not externally visible. Nevertheless, it is because of these changes that some swash plate pumps are referred to as *wobble plate piston pumps*. The construction changes referred to are the following: (1) the cylinder block (including the piston) is fixed to the pump housing, (2) the swash plate is splined to the drive shaft (which rotate together), and (3) individual cylinder inlet and outlet valves are used with inlet and outlet slots, instead of a valve plate.

The swash plate (or wobble plate) pumps oil into the system in the same manner as the axial piston pump.

Variable Displacement Axial Piston Pumps The major difference between a variable and fixed displacement axial piston pump is that the swash plate is fastened to a yoke and the yoke can pivot. A servocontrol fastened to the yoke in the form of a mechanical or hydraulic device can change the swash plate angle from the "maximum" to the "no-stroke" angle. When the swash plate angle is at its maximum, the piston stroke is also at its maximum and therefore the maximum designed output flow is achieved. Any reduction in the stroke (by changing the swash plate angle) reduces the displacement of the piston. When the swash plate is at a 90° angle to the cylinder, the piston stops reciprocating and there is no fluid output (see Fig. 8-12).

Bent Axis Piston Pumps The bent axis piston pumps of either the fixed or variable displacement type are used less frequently than the axial piston pumps. The main reason may be that the bent axis

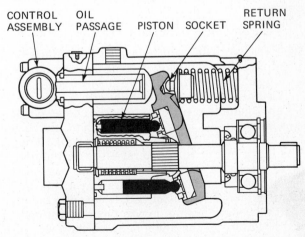

Fig. 8-12 Variable displacement, swash plate axial pump. (*J I Case Company Agricultural Equipment Division*)

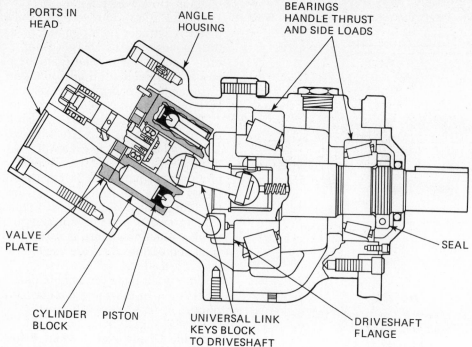

Fig. 8-13 A bent axis piston pump. (*Sperry Vickers Division of Sperry Inc.*)

type has more movable components and therefore lends to more wear.

A fixed displacement bent axis piston pump is shown in Fig. 8-13. Note that the drive shaft is supported by tapered roller bearings in the drive housing. The bearings take the force and the side thrust from the piston when the pump is operating. One end of the piston rod is fastened to the drive shaft flange to allow it to pivot with minimum friction. The cylinder block and its pistons are supported (and rotate) on roller bearings in the angled housing, which is bolted to the drive housing. A valve plate of similar design to that of the axial piston pump is bolted to the angled housing. The other end of the piston rod is fastened to the piston by means of a ball socket. The drive shaft and cylinder block are connected by the universal link, which is a constant-velocity joint that ensures an even rotating speed from the drive shaft to the cylinder block.

OPERATION The bent axis and the axial piston pump operate identically except that the pumping action (reciprocation of the pistons) varies.

Assume that you are dealing with a nine-piston pump. Again, four pistons are in the charge position at various stroke lengths and four are in the discharge stroke position, also at various stroke lengths. The ninth piston is in neutral—it is on the bottom of its stroke. When the drive shaft is rotated, the motion is transmitted by the universal link to the cylinder block. The piston rod, fastened to the drive shaft flange and piston, moves the four pistons outward because of the angle between the drive shaft flange and the cylinder block. Oil is allowed to enter the cylinder via the inlet slot. The four pistons move inward, and fluid displaced by the four pistons is

forced into the outlet slot and into the system. The rotation causes the neutral cylinder's bore opening to pass over the inlet slot. The adjacent cylinder bore (the piston of which has just reached the bottom of the stroke) comes to the neutral position, and the piston that had just completed its charging stroke positions itself over the outlet slot.

To make this type of piston pump of the variable design, a yoke is fastened to the cylinder block. The

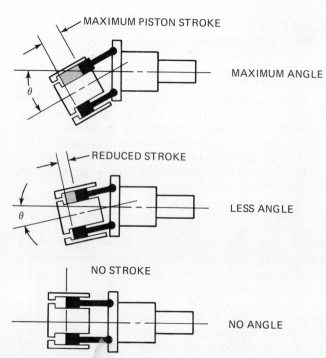

Fig. 8-14 Varying the angle changes the effective stroke. (*Sperry Vickers Division of Sperry Inc.*)

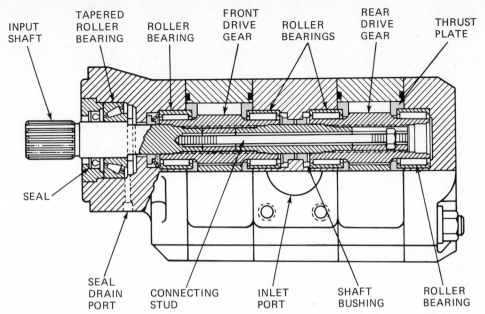

INPUT SHAFT — TAPERED ROLLER BEARING — ROLLER BEARING — FRONT DRIVE GEAR — ROLLER BEARINGS — REAR DRIVE GEAR — THRUST PLATE

SEAL

SEAL DRAIN PORT — CONNECTING STUD — INLET PORT — SHAFT BUSHING — ROLLER BEARING

Fig. 8-15 Sectional view of a multistage gear pump. (*J I Case Company Agricultural Equipment Division*)

methods used on axial pumps are also used on axis pumps to vary the angle between the drive shaft flange and the cylinder block. Varying the angle changes the effective stroke of the pistons and therefore reduces the fluid displacement (see Fig. 8-14).

Multistage Hydraulic Pumps Most large hydraulic systems use multistage pumps, of either an external gear type or a balanced vane pump design. This is to increase the fluid flow into the system or to accommodate two independent systems with two different pressures. More important, however, it increases the service life of the pumps. When two smaller pumps are used rather than one large pump, the circumference speed of the gears or vanes is less. Wear is thereby minimized and less heat develops within the pump.

The multistage gear type pump design in Fig. 8-15 shows two pumps, side by side. These pumps may be of equal output and operate against the same pressure setting, or one of them may be of a lower output and may operate against a higher or lower pressure setting. The main relief valve may be built into the pump housing, but more commonly it is within the first directional valve. Hydraulic systems using pumps of this type are outlined later in this text.

A different type of multistage pump arrangement is used whenever the application requires a fast actuator piston speed, that is, a high volume at low pressure, and whenever the pressure rises, to switch to the low-volume pump at a higher pressure setting. In Fig. 8-16 the outlet of the high-volume pump is closed off and an unloading valve, rather than a main relief valve, is placed in the pump housing. In some cases the outlet is connected to a remotely mounted unloading valve. A check valve is placed between the low- and high-volume outlets and faces toward the high-volume outlet side.

OPERATION When the drive shaft is rotated, both pumping elements pump fluid into the system. The output of the higher volume pump passes through the unloading valve and then passes by the check valve because the system pressure has not reached the set pressure of the unloading valve. As the system pressure reaches the set pressure (of the unloading valve), for example, 1500 psi [10,335 kPa], the pump volume (of the high-volume pump) is redirected to the reservoir. This results in a pressure drop, say, to 200 psi [1378 kPa], which in turn causes the check valve between the high- and low-volume pump to seat. Only then does the low-volume pump supply a flow to the system. This reduces the actuator piston speed but at a higher pressure.

Hydraulic Pump Failure Premature hydraulic pump failure is not as common as it used to be. This may be attributable to good preventive maintenance programs, improved engineering in the hydraulic

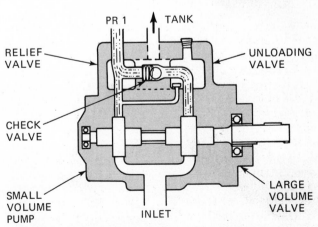

Fig. 8-16 Schematic view of a multistage gear pump using unloading valve.

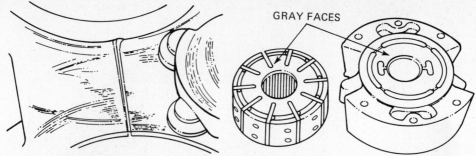

Fig. 8-17 Results of fine dirt contamination of oil. (*Caterpillar Tractor Co.*)

system and components, and additional refinements in hydraulic oils. This does not mean, however, that hydraulic pumps are immune to failure.

Pump failure is evidenced by excessive noise, drive shaft seal leakages, or a drop in pumping capacity. Since any of these malfunctions may be due to one or several causes, it is important to find and correct any such failure before installing a new or serviced pump. Clues to pump failure may be found in the disassembled hydraulic pump. Other indicative sources are the condition of the hydraulic oil and the condition of the filters and the screen. The cause of pump failure may also be ascertained from the conditions under which the system operated. For instance, when worked under extreme conditions (at main relief valve setting), a pump will show accelerated wear because of the continuous high pressure and temperature. The condition of the piston and piston rod packings should also be included in your diagnosis. If they are worn or damaged, the oil may be contaminated with dust or may be allowing air into the system. These components and the hydraulic oil are also adversely affected when the wiper seal does not perform satisfactorily. The service records of the hydraulic system may also provide some information. They will give you, for instance, the operating hours of the pump, filters, reservoir screen or filters, cylinders, control valves, and hydraulic lines and the date of the last oil change. Each piece of information should be evaluated if the pump has failed, including the recently recorded service or inspection records.

The five major causes of hydraulic pump failure are fine particles in the oil, aeration, cavitation, large particles in the oil, and insufficient lubrication.

CONTAMINATED OIL Fine dirt, not visible to the naked eye, causes precision-machined components to develop a dull finish and then gradually show wear. This increases the tolerances between components and increases wear on packings and seals (see Fig. 8-17).

Fine dirt can enter the system owing to (1) careless storage and handling of hydraulic oil; (2) inadequate servicing of components; (3) failure to cap the openings when the service work is being performed; (4) use of improper procedures in refilling the reservoir, such as failure to employ clean containers or to clean the surrounding area; (5) use of a damaged air filter through which contaminated air can enter the system when a reservoir vented to the atmosphere is employed; or (6) use of a damaged or worn wiper seal, a worn rod bushing, a bent piston rod, or a damaged piston or piston packing. In any of these circumstances the wiper seal does not wipe off the dirt as the piston retracts, and consequently, dirt is drawn past the rod packing and into the system. **NOTE** To check the effectiveness of the wiper seal, extend the piston (obeying all safety rules), wipe off the extended rods, and generously coat the piston rod with oil. Then retract the rods and extend them again. If the wiper seal is performing effectively, a thin, even layer of oil should be noticeable 360° around the piston rod. If the oil on the rod is streaky, the wiper seal is not performing satisfactorily.

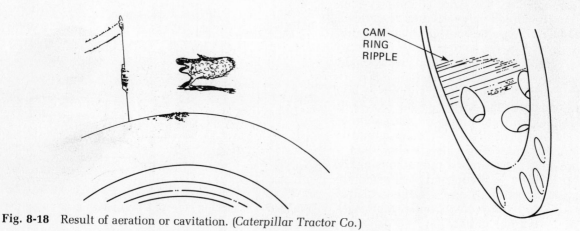

Fig. 8-18 Result of aeration or cavitation. (*Caterpillar Tractor Co.*)

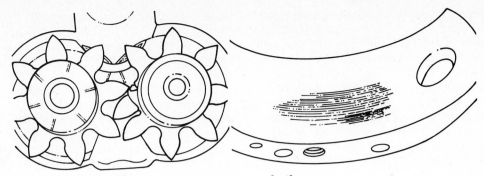

Fig. 8-19 Result of wear from large-particle contamination of oil. (*Caterpillar Tractor Co.*)

AERATION Aeration is the result of air's mixing with oil. The aerated oil, when under pressure, creates tiny implosions which cause pitting and eroding. The fine eroded metal particles sweep into the system to wear away the surfaces they contact (see Fig. 8-18).

Aerated oil can also reduce pump lubrication and result in a squealing or rattling pump noise. In addition the cylinder action is spongy and/or jerky because the air in the oil is compressed and released as the piston rod retracts and extends.

Air can enter the system through (1) a loose or perforated inlet line; (2) a pump seal damaged because of improper installation, misalignment of the pump, or wear on the pump bearing(s); (3) incorrect or improper seal installation; (4) the system return oil's entering above the oil level; (5) improper action of the wiper seal or piston rod packing.

CAVITATION Cavitation occurs when the static pressure drops to the liquid's vapor pressure, causing vapor bubbles to form within the oil and then collapse when under pressure. Cavitation is as damaging to a hydraulic pump or system as aeration. It could arise from (1) a restricted inlet filter, screen, or hydraulic line (which would reduce the static inlet pressure); (2) the oil viscosity's being too low; (3) too high an oil temperature; (4) malfunction of the anticavitation valve (regeneration valve or makeup valve).

CONTAMINATION BY LARGE PARTICLES Pump failure resulting from large metallic or nonmetallic parti-

cles' contaminating the oil could occur instantly or gradually, depending on the circumstances. Large particles come from components that have been damaged (see Fig. 8-19). These components would include (1) the piston or piston packing, (2) the control valve, (3) the hydraulic pump, or (4) any other component, if the system is not flushed thoroughly after the damage occurs.

Pump failure and control valve or cylinder damage arise when the larger particles are forced between the closely fitted rotating or reciprocating components. Very noticeable surface damage is created in the form of scratches, grooved scores, or total destruction of the pump, control valve, or cylinder.

INSUFFICIENT LUBRICATION Hydraulic pump failure due to insufficient lubrication is uncommon, but when it does occur, the pump overheats and becomes increasingly noisy (see Fig. 8-20). A pump may be insufficiently lubricated because (1) the operator did not check the oil level; (2) the oil level was checked when the loader, backhoe, etc., was not in the recommended position; (3) the hydraulic system contains numerous small oil leaks (by the end of the working shift, or during the shift, the temperature of the oil would then rise to, say, 250°F [121°C] or more); (4) the terrain on which the equipment is being operated is extremely steep and the pump inlet (in the reservoir) would therefore be deprived of oil when it flowed to the end of the reservoir; (5) the pump inlet is restricted owing to a collapsed inlet hose, plugged inlet screen, or filter; (6) the newly installed pump was not primed properly; (7) the

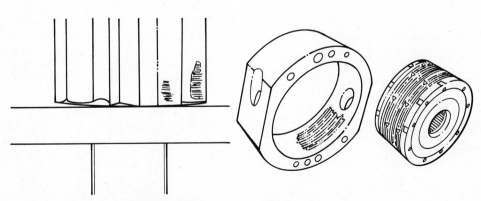

Fig. 8-20 Result of wear from insufficient lubrication. (*Caterpillar Tractor Co.*)

equipment is being operated at an ambient temperature above 110°F [43°C] or below −10°F [−23°C], and the viscosity of the oil is not appropriate to it; (8) the hydraulic oil is of poor quality or of a low viscosity index.

The symptoms of pump failure caused by insufficient lubrication are similar to those of failure caused by metal particles. However, in some cases you may also see some discoloration on the components and, in extreme cases, total destruction of the pumping elements or breakage of the coupling or drive shaft.

Servicing Rotary Hydraulic Pumps Let us assume you have, through testing, determined that the hydraulic pump has lost 40 percent of its efficiency and you are therefore forced to either replace or service it. If you are going to remove it, the procedure can vary according to the location and size of the pump, and the task may be a simple one or a job occupying many hours. Nevertheless, if you have to remove a pump from a tractor or machine that you have not previously removed, *you must first refer to the service manual.*

There are general rules applicable under most circumstances to the servicing of rotary hydraulic pumps. In the first instance, you should prepare and clean your work area, the tools, and the needed components thoroughly. When possible, steam-clean the area around the hydraulic tank and hydraulic pump. Make certain that the equipment is parked safely, that the wheels or tracks are blocked, and that the

battery ground cable is removed. Position the hydraulic equipment (and block it) to allow the pumps to be removed with ease. **NOTE** See discussion of reservoirs, in Unit 7, in regard to draining the hydraulic fluid.

Use suitable drain pans under the pump and the hydraulic lines to take up the oil that leaks from the components. Remove and identify the hydraulic lines in regard to their position and cap all openings to prevent the entry of contaminants. Attach a lifting device such as a rope sling or eyebolt to the pump before removing the mounting bolts. **NOTE** It requires double the effort to lift a device which is in an awkward place. Do not overestimate your strength!

To determine if the pump was properly aligned, check (immediately after the pump is removed) the drive coupling and drive shaft for worn splines. A misaligned pump can cause excessive side thrust, vibration, and noise, which result in increased wear on the pump bearing, drive shaft, and coupling.

External Gear Pumps There are many types of external gear pumps. The multistage gear pump (shown, reduced to components, in Fig. 8-21) is used by several companies. This pump has a rating of 77 gal/min [291.4 l/min] at 1825 rpm, at 2000 psi [13,780 kPa]. The pumping action is comparable with that explained previously in this unit, but it has additional components which increase the efficiency of the pump.

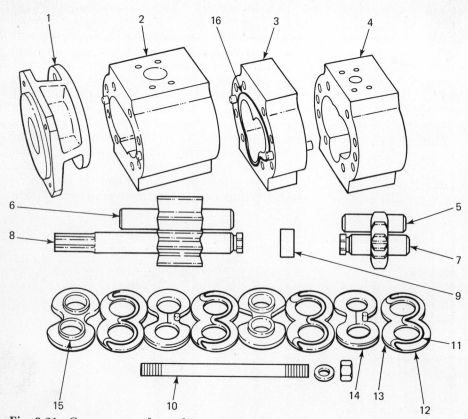

1. Flange end
2. Front gear housing
3. Bearing carrier
4. Rear gear housing
5. Driven gear (rear pump)
6. Driven gear (front pump)
7. Drive gear (rear pump)
8. Drive gear (front pump)
9. Splined coupling
10. Studs
11. O-ring retainer
12. Backup ring
13. Isolation plate
14. Pressure plate
15. Guide ring
16. O ring

Fig. 8-21 Components of a multistage gear pump. (*Caterpillar Tractor Co.*)

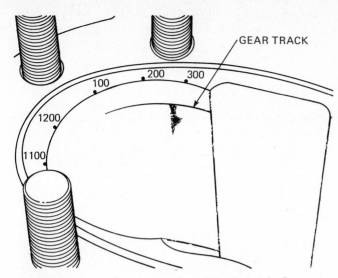

GEAR TRACK

100 200 300

1200

1100

Fig. 8-22 Gear wear pattern has passed 3 o'clock.

DESIGN Bronze pressure plates are used to increase the sealing efficiency between the wear plates and the gear ends and to lengthen the service life of the pump. The rubber ring, backup ring, and retainer are placed below the wear plates on the outlet side. Outlet oil pressure is fed into the space between them, and this pressure holds the wear plate against the gears and thus prevents pressure loss to the inlet side of the pump. The isolation plate is placed under the wear plate toward the inlet side to counterbalance the applied pressure holding the wear plates parallel to the gears. When the pump is operating, outlet pressure forces the oil into the oil grooves of the bushings. The continuous oil flow attained ensures good lubrication and cooling and prevents a hydraulic lock. To achieve a continuous flow, the bushing ends are connected by passages and rerouted through the center of the idler gear, through the check valve, and to the low-pressure side.

SERVICING Mount the cleaned pump to a holding fixture or in a vise having protected jaws. Mark the relative positions of the small gear housing, bearing carrier, large gear housing, and flange end to ensure proper reassembly. Remove the sharp edges and burrs from the drive shaft spline to allow the shaft, on removal, to pass through the bushing without causing any damage. Loosen and remove the eight stud nuts and flat washers. Gently tap the flange, using a soft-faced hammer, to loosen it from the dowels of the large gear body.

NOTE Do not use a screwdriver or a chisel to pry apart the components. This would damage the mating surfaces. Then, remove, in order, the parts 10, 1, and 11 to 15. Before removing the drive and the driven gear shafts, mark the gear in such a manner that, if the parts are reusable, they can be reassembled in the same meshing position. This precaution will reduce gear noise and wear.

Using both hands, lift out the drive and the driven shafts with a quick motion. Usually this also lifts out the lower pressure plate. If the pressure plate re-

mains in position, do not attempt to remove it at this time. Tap the large gear body loose from the dowels of the spacer plate and lift it, as well as the coupling and the parts from 11 to 15, from the small gear body. Again, using the same method, lift out the small drive and the driven gear.

To remove a wear plate which is stuck in the gear body, first remove any internal visible wear marks or burrs which could interfere with the removal. Use compressed air to clean the interior of the gear body and generously lubricate it. Now, with several quick actions (taps), tap the gear body against a well-supported piece of wood to spring the wear plate loose.

INSPECTION Start your inspection by examining the gear body. Check whether the gear wear pattern on the low-pressure side has passed the two-o'clock mark (see Fig. 8-22). This indicates that the shaft or bushings are worn because the gears have milled out the gear body to such an extent (beyond specification) that a replacement is necessary. If the gear bodies are reusable, replace the bushings (see the discussion of bearings in Unit 5). In some cases the bushings are not reusable, and so you must replace the pump bodies.

The next step is to determine the extent of the wear on the shafts at the bushing locations and on the overall length and diameter of the gears. Use a micrometer to measure the height of the gears and the diameter of the shafts and then compare the results with the service manual specification (see Fig. 8-23). In most cases the gear diameter will not have decreased, because of the wearability of the aluminum alloy from which the gear body is made. The gear shafts are within specification when the gears show no pitting, galling, or score marks, and the splines are not worn. If the gears or the shafts have sharp edges, nicks, or burrs, remove them by using an oil stone.

You should replace the gear bodies, spacer plate, or flange if they are twisted, or if the dowel holes or

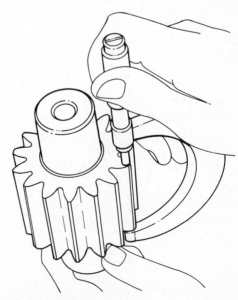

Fig. 8-23 Measuring gear wear.

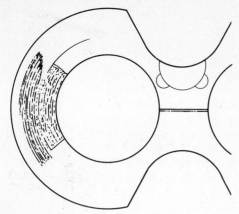

Fig. 8-24 Pressure plate worn due to lack of lubrication. (*Caterpillar Tractor Co.*)

bores are elongated or the threaded holes damaged. If this is not the case, then simply lap all flat surfaces to ensure good alignment and sealing.

To determine if the coupling splines are worn, place the coupling on a new gear shaft and check its fit.

Replace all O rings, rubber rings, backup rings, retainers, and the shaft oil seal. If the pressure plates show erosion, pitting, or excessive one-side wear—lubrication problems that could be caused by cavitation, aeration, or bushing wear (see Fig. 8-24)—the plates must be replaced. Minor pitting, nicks, burrs, or scratches can be removed by lapping the pressure plate. **NOTE** Do not remove the check valve plug when a leaking valve is suspected. Use a punch through the plugged hole opening and reseat the check valve.

REASSEMBLY External gear pump components are reassembled in precisely the reverse order of the disassembly. However, several precautions must be taken to ensure good reassembly and long pump service life.

Wash all components thoroughly in solvent. Dry with compressed air and lubricate them generously with oil. Position the small gear bodies so that the oil outlet side is at the left (see Fig. 8-25) and the body openings are facing you. Then, to the left side of the bushing, install the isolation plate with the

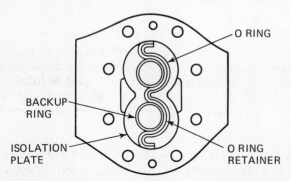

Fig. 8-25 Isolation plate, backup ring, O ring and retaining ring installed. (*J I Case Company Agricultural Equipment Division*)

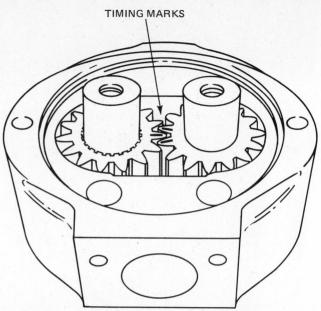

Fig. 8-26 Note timing mark on drive and driven gears. (*Terex Division of General Motors Corporation*)

rounded edges downward. To the right side of the bushing, install the rubber ring, the Teflon ring, and the nylon retainer. Locate the pressure plate with the relief pocket facing the pressure side (left) and then position it over the ring. Align the marks on the small gear shafts before placing the assembly into the bore and the shafts into the bushings.

Install the pressure plate with the relief pocket to the left. It must be flush with the housing. Place, on each shaft, a steel ring with the chamfered edges downward.

Place and position the sharp-edged isolation plate on the right side of the pressure plate and the rubber ring, backup ring, and retainer onto the left side. Locate the O ring in the spacing plate and position it on the small gear body. Recheck the aligning marks before tapping the plate over the dowels onto the gear body.

Install the components of the large gear pump in the same order as previously outlined and torque the stud nuts in three steps and in a diagonal sequence to their specified torque.

NOTE When the front and rear pumps of a dual hydraulic pump have equal volume, that is, when the diameter and the length of both pump gears are the same, the drive gears must be timed to prevent simultaneous remeshing of the gears (which would increase side thrust and decrease the service life of the pump).

When timing the drive gears, use a felt pen to mark the front drive gear shaft and the rear drive shaft across the root of the teeth (Fig. 8-26). When reassembling the pump, make certain that the felt pen lines on the drive shaft are precisely aligned.

Cessna and Dual-Stage Pumps For smaller hydraulic systems, a Cessna pump or one of similar design is used. The pump shown in Fig. 8-27 (a sin-

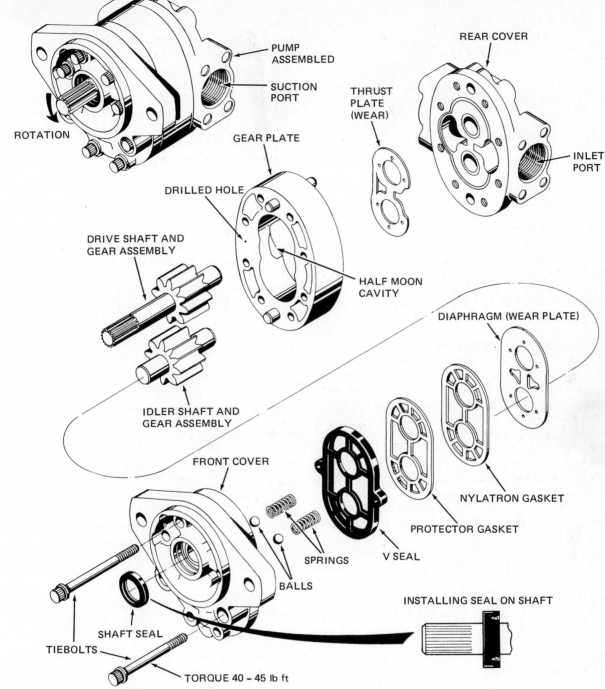

Fig. 8-27 Assembled and exploded views of Cessna hydraulic pump. (*J I Case Agricultural Equipment Division*)

gle-stage pump) is not fundamentally different from the dual-stage pump previously discussed. The major difference lies in the design of the wear plates (now termed "diaphragm"), diaphragm seal, protector, and gasket. However, the bushings are not replaceable. When the pump rotates, outlet oil pressure passes (through a hole in the gear plate) below the V-shaped diaphragm seal. The oil pressure forces the diaphragm seal, the gaskets, and the diaphragm (wear plate) against the gears and thus guarantees effective sealing. The six holes drilled into the diaphragm equalize the pressure on its sides. The port-

end cover uses only a thrust plate but also has six holes to equalize pressure on both sides of the plate. The two ball checks release the oil used to lubricate the bushings. One releases the oil pressure to the inlet side of the pump and the other releases it to the outlet side.

SERVICING The service procedures for a Cessna and a dual-stage pump are much the same. However, when the bushings of a Cessna are worn beyond the maximum wear limit, the drive-end cover and the port-end cover must be replaced. Be sure to place

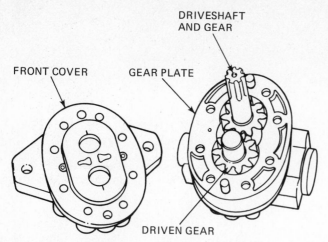

FRONT COVER GEAR PLATE DRIVESHAFT AND GEAR

DRIVEN GEAR

Fig. 8-28 Front cover (Cessna) removed; the pump is partly (and correctly) assembled. (*J I Case Company Agricultural Equipment Division*)

the diaphragm seal into the grooves of the drive-end cover first and then replace the protector gasket and the backup gasket. Place both check balls and springs into their bores before placing the diaphragm onto the drive-end cover. Be absolutely certain that you have not mixed up the diaphragm with the thrust plate, for this would cause a restricted oil flow into the pump. When placing the thrust plate onto the gear plate, make certain that the large cutout points toward the oil inlet passage (see Fig. 8-28).

Balanced Vane Pump To exemplify service procedure, a two-cartridge pump having a rating of 160 gal/min [606.0 l/min] at 2000 rpm and a pressure of 1800 psi [12,402 kPa] is used.

SERVICING Mount the pump to a holding fixture, or use a vise equipped with protected jaws to avoid damaging the body, or support the pump on two blocks. Mark the relative positions of the cover, inlet housing, and body to ensure correct reassembly. Remove the four through bolts and, in sequence, components 1 to 7 as shown in Fig. 8-29. If necessary use a puller to remove the first pump cartridge assembly from the shaft and body, then lift off the inlet housing. Turn the shaft and lift out the second cartridge assembly from the shaft and body. Remove the large lock ring and, using a soft-faced hammer, gently tap out the shaft assembly from the body. (See discussion of gasket and seals, Unit 3, for procedure for removing seals and wipers.)

If the shaft splines, the bearings, and seal surfaces are not damaged or worn, replace the bearings (see discussion of bearings, Unit 5). Remove and discard all seals, O rings, and backup washers. To check the serviceability of the cartridges, remove the two fillister head screws and disassemble, in the order shown, components 8 to 14, and 15 to 29. During the disassembly note the position of the ring, rotor, and vanes so that you can correctly reassemble the cartridge.

CLEANING AND INSPECTION Wash all parts in solvent and dry with compressed air. Inspect the body, inlet housing, cover, bores, surfaces, and threaded bores for damage. Remove nicks and burrs by lapping or by using fine emery cloth. Reclean to make sure that all abrasive material is removed. Inspect the surface of the pressure plates, rotors, vanes, rings, and wear plates. If the wear on the vanes or rotor slot is excessive (see Figs. 8-30 and 8-31), replace the vanes and the rotors. If the wear on the pressure plates and wear plates is also excessive, replace the cartridge.

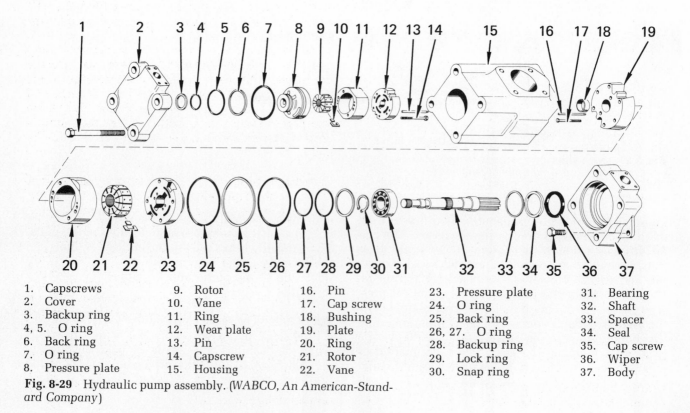

1. Capscrews
2. Cover
3. Backup ring
4, 5. O ring
6. Back ring
7. O ring
8. Pressure plate
9. Rotor
10. Vane
11. Ring
12. Wear plate
13. Pin
14. Capscrew
15. Housing
16. Pin
17. Cap screw
18. Bushing
19. Plate
20. Ring
21. Rotor
22. Vane
23. Pressure plate
24. O ring
25. Back ring
26, 27. O ring
28. Backup ring
29. Lock ring
30. Snap ring
31. Bearing
32. Shaft
33. Spacer
34. Seal
35. Cap screw
36. Wiper
37. Body

Fig. 8-29 Hydraulic pump assembly. (*WABCO, An American-Standard Company*)

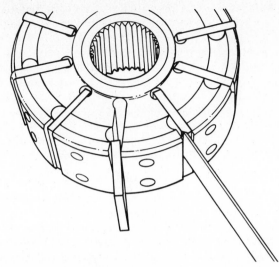

Fig. 8-30 Using a thickness gauge to measure vane wear. (*Caterpillar Tractor Co.*)

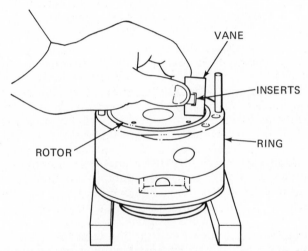

Fig. 8-31 Method used to measure insert wear. (*WABCO, An American-Standard Company*)

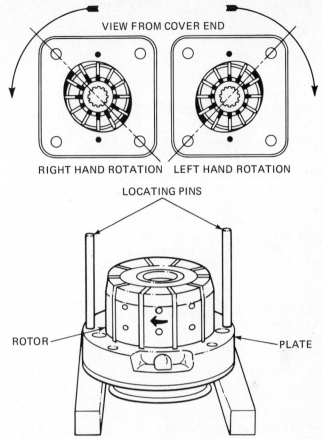

Fig. 8-32 Cartridge installation. (*WABCO, An American-Standard Company*)

Small score marks may be removed by lapping. Inspect the shaft for damaged splines and the seal and the bearing surface for wear. If the existing score marks cannot be removed with fine emery cloth or the rotor fits too loosely on the shaft, the shaft must be replaced.

NOTE Do not overlook checking the body for an eroded or pitted seal seating surface.

REASSEMBLY

NOTE Do not use any type of cleaning rags to clean components prior to assembly. Use compressed air and a generous amount of hydraulic oil during assembly.

Hold backup washers and O rings in place with a small amount of petroleum jelly. Start your assembly by pressing a new bearing onto the shaft (see discussion of bearings, Unit 5) and press a new seal and wiper into the body bore. Make certain that the bearing and the seal are placed exactly as specified in the related service manuals.

Reassemble the cartridge in the reverse order to disassembly. Make certain that the arrow on the rotor and the sharp edges of the vanes point in the correct rotation. When properly assembled, the end views for left and right rotating pumps should appear as shown in Fig. 8-32.

While inserting the vanes and inserts, make sure that they move freely within the rotor slot. During the insertion of the cartridges or installation of the inlet housing or cover, check that the O rings and backup washers are not dislocated or cut. Torque the four cap screws to specification. When the pump is properly assembled, the shaft should be turnable by hand.

Installation of a Pump First, assure yourself that the cause of pump failure was corrected, the oil filters were replaced, the screens were cleaned, and, if necessary, the system was flushed. Check the pump's mounting surface for nicks and burrs, and replace the O ring, seal, or gasket, when applicable. Examine the drive coupling for wear and then place it on the shaft. Remove the protection caps and prime the pump by rotating the pump shaft by hand until a good flow of oil leaves the outlet side of the pump. Recap the openings and install the pump to the drive components. Meticulously follow the service manual recommendations. **NOTE** Check that the drive coupling is movable or has sufficient play to ensure that the drive and the driven shaft are properly aligned.

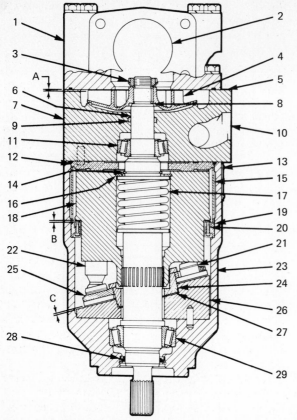

Fig. 8-33 Sectional view of axial piston pump. (*Caterpillar Tractor Co.*)

1. Inlet housing
2. Inlet port
3. Spanner nut and lock
4. Impeller
5. Arrow indicating direction of rotation
6. Drive shaft
7. Head
8. Impeller shims for dimension A
9. Teflon seal
10. Outlet port
11. Port plate
12. Seal
13. Pump housing
14. Spiral snap ring
15. Antitip bearing spacer
16. Snap ring
17. Spring
18. Barrel
19. Antitip bearing
20. Shims for dimension B
21. Slipper
22. Piston
23. Housing drain port
24. Retraction bearing
25. Slipper retraction plate
26. Cam
27. Retraction bearing shims for dimension C
28. Lip seal
29. Large tapered roller bearing
A- Impeller-to-inlet housing clearance
B- Anti-tip-bearing-to-barrel clearance
C- Slipper-to-cam-face clearance

Fill the reservoir with the recommended hydraulic oil. Before you start the engine, back out the main relief valve a couple of turns This is a safety precaution in that the valve may have been previously adjusted and consequently may be set too high for the new pump. Then start the engine and operate it at 1000 rpm. Position the loader, dozer, etc., as specified in the service manual and stop the engine. Check the oil level and reset the main relief valve.

NOTE If, in addition, the cylinders have been serviced, operate the system to remove the air from the cylinders. Check the oil level and refill it to the full level to prevent damaging the hydraulic pump.

Servicing an Axial Piston Pump The pump used here to exemplify service procedure is a nine-piston axial piston pump having a rating of 132 gal/min [499.7 l/min] at 2060 rpm with a test pressure of 1000 psi [6890 kPa].

The pump shown in Fig. 8-33 is of the fixed displacement design and is similar to a fixed displacement, swash plate pump. The pumping action is therefore the same, but the piston pump has its own centrifugal charging pump. As a result, when the drive shaft rotates, the impeller that is keyed to the drive shaft also rotates. Oil at static pressure is present at the inlet port (which is in the center of the impeller) and is present between the impeller blades. It supercharges the inlet slot and the four pistons. The centrifugal pump provides a maximum pressure of about 20 psi [137.8 kPa] to increase the efficiency and the service life of the pump.

DISASSEMBLY Before disassembling the piston pump, make certain that the pump, your tools, and the work area are clean. Remove the inlet housing bolts and then the inlet housing. Reinstall two bolts to hold the pump housing and head together as a unit. Bend the lock free from the impeller nut and remove the nut by using a hook wrench and by holding the drive shaft with a socket wrench. Lift off the lock, impeller, and spacer shims. Remove the key from the shaft. Then remove the remaining two bolts and lift the head and the port plate from the pump housing. With a puller arrangement remove the tapered roller bearing. Use a protecting plate so that you do not damage the barrel face. Compress the

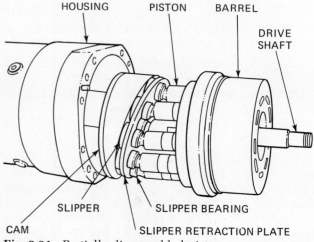

Fig. 8-34 Partially disassembled piston pump.

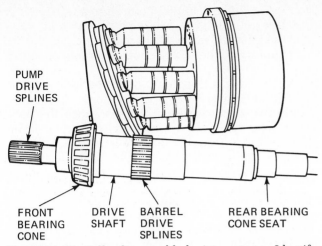

PUMP
DRIVE
SPLINES

FRONT
BEARING
CONE

DRIVE
SHAFT

BARREL
DRIVE
SPLINES

REAR BEARING
CONE SEAT

Fig. 8-35 Partially disassembled piston pump. Identify pistons and cylinder bores so that they will not be mixed up during reassembly.

large spring that holds the barrel at a determined force against the port plate. Remove the first snap ring by placing two wooden blocks on the barrel face and, with a plate and two bolts, retract the barrel slightly to allow removal of the first snap ring only. The second snap ring holds the spring under tension. **NOTE** Do not at this time pull the barrel from the piston (see Fig. 8-34).

To remove the drive shaft, cam, piston, barrel, and antitip ring as a unit, first remove the two bolts that hold the cam to the pump housing and then insert two guide rods into these holes. Hold the pump housing firmly and at the same time push on the rods. This will force the assembly out of the housing.

Although the pistons usually fit in any cylinder bore, it is helpful to identify all pistons with the bores from which they are removed. This ensures that each piston will be returned into the cylinder from which it was removed when the unit is reassembled (see Fig. 8-35).

Remove the drive shaft and then carefully slide the barrel from the piston. When you expect that the cam, slipper, or slipper retraction plate is worn or damaged, remove the four bolts that hold the retraction plate to the cam. Be careful not to damage the piston when removing or storing it.

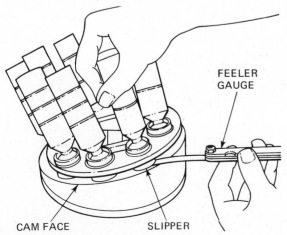

FEELER
GAUGE

CAM FACE   SLIPPER

Fig. 8-36 Measuring the clearance between the slipper and cam face.

NOTE A pump that has been operative will show some fine wear marks on the piston slippers, as well as on the cam face.

With the correct driver, remove the snap ring seal before driving the seal from the housing. Use a hammer puller to remove the bearing cups from the pump housing and head. If the spring that forces the barrel against the port plate must be removed, compress the spring and, with a press and adapter, remove the snap ring. **CAUTION** Slowly release the force on the spring and then remove the spacer, spring, and lower spacer. Always use a protection device on the barrel face during the removal and installation of the spring.

INSPECTION After each component part is cleaned and dried with compressed air, check the drive shaft for worn or damaged splines, the keyway and threads for damage, and the bearing surface for wear or damage. If, upon examining the piston or cylinder bores, you find that one piston or cylinder is scored or grooved, replace the assembly. If the cam, barrel face, or port plate is slightly scored, nicked, or burred, use an oil stone to remove the irregularities and then lap the surfaces.

Inspect the piston to see if the grooves around the piston are clean. If not clean, the piston will not receive adequate lubrication and the grooves will not trap dirt particles. Moreover, if there is dirt in the grooves, the oil cannot form a seal. Without this seal, the piston will not remain stably balanced, and hence, there will be metal-to-metal contact. The piston will then become scored.

Check that the small holes in the slipper are not restricted. If a hole is plugged, no lubricant is supplied to the slipper or cam and they will quickly deteriorate. Even more harmful, the counterforce of the applied piston force is removed and metal-to-metal contact results.

Examine the bores, threaded holes, and surfaces of the pump housing, head, and inlet housing for wear, nicks, and burrs. Remove the nicks and burrs with an oil stone and restore the surfaces through lapping.

REASSEMBLY Thoroughly clean all components and place them on clean toweling. Install the bearings and cups as outlined in the discussion of bearings in Unit 5. Then start the reassembly in an order that is precisely the reverse of that you used when disassembling the pump. Lubricate only those parts requiring lubrication, taking care not to contaminate other parts with lubricant. This precaution prevents dust and dirt from collecting on the clean components.

When you have assembled the pistons (in the correct order) to the cam, and when the cap screws are torqued to specification, measure the clearance between all slippers and the cam face (see Fig. 8-36) and compare your measurement with the service manual specification. If the clearance is too great, remove a shim, and if the clearance is too small, add a shim. Before installing the piston into the cylinder, you must measure and adjust the height difference between the pump housing's face and port plate. To

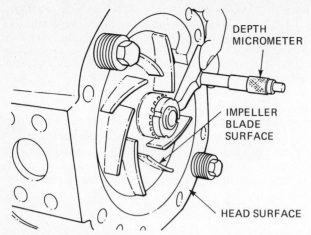

Fig. 8-37 Measuring distance between the top of the impeller blade and head surface.

do this, install the antitip bearing to the barrel and slide the barrel into the pump housing. Place the port plate onto the barrel. Now, using a dial gauge or depth micrometer, measure the distance between the surfaces. Compare it with the service manual specification. If the distance is not within specification, remove the barrel, disassemble the antitip bearing, and add shims or, alternately, remove the shims which were placed between the bearing and ring, to achieve the specified distance.

Align the cylinder and piston marks and start each piston into its bore.

When the head is bolted to the pump housing, the impeller installed, and the nut torqued to specification, measure the distance between the impeller face and head surface (see Fig. 8-37) and compare it with the service manual specification. If the distance is not correct, remove the impeller and add or remove shims to obtain the correct distance.

After the pump is reassembled, fill it (through the drain port) with oil. Using a socket placed onto the drive shaft spline, measure the rotating torque of the drive shaft (with a torque wrench).

If the rotating torque is too high, the pump must be disassembled, rechecked, reassembled, readjusted, and then retested to avoid pump failure.

Testing and Break-in Procedure To ensure that the service pump is broken in properly and that it

performs to specification, mount it to a test stand or install it to the engine. Fill the pump with oil. Connect the inlet and outlet hoses to the pump and, with a T connection, connect the flowmeter into the outlet line.

When using a test stand, open the load valve of the flowmeter tester fully. When the pump is tested (when installed to the engine), also open the flowmeter load valve fully but, in addition, remove the spring tension from the main relief valve so that no pressure buildup is possible. Next, operate the test stand or engine for about 5 min at 800 rpm with no load (pressure) on the pump. After 5 min, again operate the pump for about 5 min, this time at 1200 rpm, and gradually close the load valve to obtain a pressure of about 500 psi [3445 kPa]. Repeat this same procedure at 800 rpm against a pressure of about 800 psi [5512 kPa]. **NOTE** During this time do not allow the pump temperature or the oil temperature to exceed 180°F [82°C].

Finally, operate the pump for at least 10 min at rated speed (at 2000 rpm) and apply, with the load valve, a pressure of 1000 psi [6890 kPa]. After approximately 10 min readjust the pressure, check the temperature, and take a flowmeter reading.

NOTE Manufacturers of pumps allow a flow tolerance of 10 percent at specified operating pressure. In this example the pump was tested at less than half the specified pressure, and therefore the flow rate should not be less than 125.4 gal/min [474.4 l/min].

The last test, when a piston pump is being tested, is to measure the drain flow and thereby determine if the slipper and bearing are receiving adequate oil supply. If the pump is tested while on the engine, readjust the main relief valve to specification before removing the flowmeter from the outlet line. Then install the flowmeter (in series) to the drain line.

Next, operate the pump at rated speed. Close the load valve to obtain the rated pressure (or, when the pump is installed to the engine, retract one cylinder so that the pump has to develop main pressure and maintain the main pressure). Then read the flowmeter. The drain flow must be within specification. When the flow rate is more than specified, there is excessive leakage between the piston and cylinder or between the slipper and cam face.

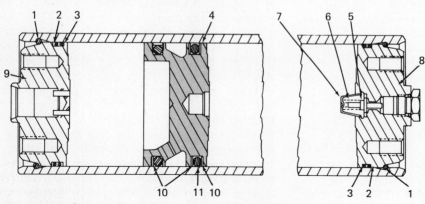

1. Retainer ring
2. Backup ring
3. O ring
4. Piston
5. Gas valve
6. Spring
7. Spring guide
8. Cylinder end
9. Cap
10. Backup ring
11. O ring

Fig. 8-38 Sectional view of an accumulator. (*Terex Division of General Motors Corporation*)

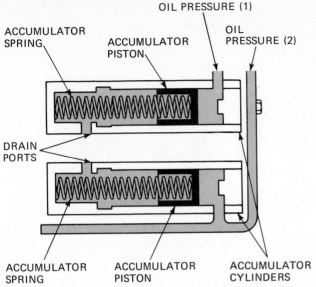

ACCUMULATOR SPRING

ACCUMULATOR PISTON

OIL PRESSURE (1)

OIL PRESSURE (2)

DRAIN PORTS

ACCUMULATOR SPRING

ACCUMULATOR PISTON

ACCUMULATOR CYLINDERS

Fig. 8-39 Schematic view of spring-type accumulator used in a power shift transmission.

ACCUMULATORS

You have now been familiarized with two hydraulic power sources, that is, the reservoir and the hydraulic pump. The third power source used on hydraulic systems is the accumulator (see Fig. 8-38).

It is obvious that a reservoir cannot supply fluid under pressure to the hydraulic pump when the reservoir is empty or is located below the hydraulic pump inlet or when there is no power to drive the pump. Similarly, an accumulator cannot be the power source before there is fluid under pressure within the accumulator.

Although accumulators vary considerably in regard to design and construction, they have one function in common, which is to store fluid under pressure. The purpose of an accumulator may vary, however, depending on its application. In hydraulic systems an accumulator is used mostly to maintain a nearly constant pressure between, say, 2000 and 2200 psi [13,780 and 15,158 kPa], or to maintain a fixed pressure in the power shift transmission, or to act as a shock absorber. With a few minor construction changes it can also become a Hydrair suspension.

Design and Operation The free-floating piston separates the cylinder into two sections. The seals used on the piston are commonly O rings with backup washers. One end cap is welded to the cylinder, whereas the other end cap is bolted or held to the cylinder with a snap ring. Small accumulators use a spring, inserted at one side, and when compressed by the fluid pressure on the other side, the spring becomes a source of potential energy (see Fig. 8-39).

Larger accumulators use a gas (nitrogen) instead of a spring. Nitrogen gas is used because it will not explode when mixed with oil.

The right side of the accumulator is charged from a nitrogen cylinder with nitrogen gas (through an air valve) to a predetermined pressure. The left side

of the cylinder is connected to the hydraulic system. Oil from the hydraulic system enters the accumulator, and, as the pressure rises, the piston moves to the right. This compresses the gas until its pressure is equal to the oil pressure, say, 2200 psi [15,158 kPa]. At this point the unloading valve opens, the check valve blocks the return oil flow and thereby maintains the system (including the accumulator) under pressure, and the unloading valve directs the pump output to the reservoir. When the system pressure drops about 10 percent, the unloading valve redirects oil into the system and thereby repressurizes the system and the accumulator (see Fig. 8-40).

In other applications the accumulator serves as a safety or emergency power source. In the event that the hydraulic pump fails to supply fluid flow, the accumulator has adequate stored energy to cause the brakes to function or to supply the steering system with oil under pressure and thus provide emergency brakes or power assist steering.

Servicing Generally speaking, accumulators (of any design) do not require much attention, since they have few moving parts and therefore seldom fail. If, however, the accumulator fails to operate, the cause in most cases is a leaking air valve, or worn piston seals, or damage incurred during installation, or improper installation.

When an accumulator has to be removed, stop the engine, block the equipment, and remove the battery's ground cable. Actuate the control valves to remove the system pressure and, when applicable, remove the pressure from the reservoir. Remove the nitrogen pressure by pressing the air valve core inward to allow the gas to escape. Disconnect the hydraulic line and cap the openings. Then remove the mounting bolts or clamps and lift the accumulator from the machine.

Remove the charging valve and the end cap and, by holding the cylinder upright against a piece of wood, tap to remove the piston. **CAUTION** Do not attempt to blow the piston from the cylinder with compressed air. The effect would be as dangerous as discharging a bullet from a gun.

Clean all components with solvent and dry with compressed air. Always replace O rings or seal rings. Check the piston, cylinder, and end cap for nicks and burrs. If present, remove by using a smooth file or emery cloth. If the cylinder is slightly worn or grooved, use a ridged hone to restore its bore surface. Replace the air valve and check the charging valve and the end cap for damaged threads.

REASSEMBLY Lubricate the piston O ring or sealing ring and install it to the piston. When backup washers are used, make certain that they are properly fitted. Lubricate the cylinders and insert the piston. Install the O ring to the end cap and the end cap to the cylinder.

Charging the Accumulator After the accumulator is reinstalled and the hydraulic line(s) connected, install the swivel nut to the charging valve (see Fig. 8-41). Then, if you have not previously done so, close the accumulator (gas) valve and tank valve.

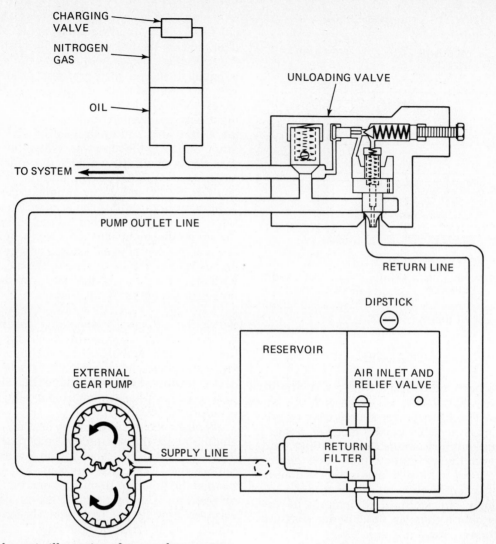

Fig. 8-40 Schematic illustration of accumulator system.

Next, connect the assembly to the nitrogen supply bottle by screwing the gland nut down. Open the valve of the nitrogen bottle fully and then open the tank valve until the gauge shows about 50 psi [344.5 kPa] above the desired accumulator pressure. Open the air valve on the accumulator to allow the nitrogen gas to enter the cylinder. Use the tank valve to maintain the required charging pressure.

To check the accumulator pressure, close the tank valve and open the bleed valve. The pressure gauge will show the accumulator pressure. If you have overcharged the accumulator, open the accumulator valve so that the excessive pressure can escape from the open bleed valve. When the desired pressure has been reached, close the nitrogen bottle valve, the tank valve, and the accumulator valve.

To check the accumulator valve for leakage, use the soapy water method. Bubbles will occur on the valve when there is a leak. If the air valve is leaking, you may be able to stop it by quickly depressing it once or twice. Then securely tighten the valve cap.

OIL COOLERS

When a hydraulic system operates at maximum capacity, the hydraulic oil temperature will rise. How-ever, if the hydraulic system is to be maintained at its maximum efficiency and the component wear kept to a minimum, the hydraulic oil temperature must be kept within 180 to 200°F [82 to 93°C]. A safe operating temperature can be achieved with the use of a larger reservoir to increase the oil capacity. Unfortunately this additional space is often not available. Oil coolers are the usual alternative to the larger reservoir; several types are manufactured because of the great variety of hydraulic systems.

Air-Oil Coolers   In the last few years, manufacturers have shown a preference toward air-oil coolers, especially on the smaller hydraulic systems. These coolers are mounted in front of the engine radiator and use the engine fan to draw or push air through the cooler. On some very small hydraulic systems the oil cooler is mounted in a place where natural air flow is present. On larger hydraulic systems the cooler is separately mounted and the fan is driven by an electric motor or through a drive arrangement from the engine.

Air-oil coolers are similar in design to radiators, although they have no filler cap and have only one oil inlet port and one oil outlet port. The oil flow is much the same in all cooler systems; that is, the

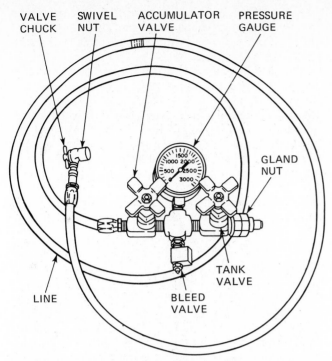

Fig. 8-41 Accumulator charging kit. (*Terex Division of General Motors Corporation*)

return oil from the system passes through the cooler and then back to the reservoir.

SERVICING An air-oil cooler requires minimal maintenance and service, but the cooler fins must be kept clean. Daily inspection and cleaning become necessary only when operating conditions are extreme, for instance, when one is working in the bush, in which case dust, leaves, insects, and other matter continuously become trapped between the cooler fins.

To dislodge alien matter, use an air hose and direct the compressed air over the total area of the cooler surface in a reverse direction to the normal air flow. It is sometimes necessary first to flush water through the fin area to loosen the sticky accumulation. When residual oil or grease causes dust to adhere to the fins of the core, a spray cleaning gun loaded with cleaning solvent may be required.

NOTE Never use a screwdriver or wire brush to dislodge grime from the fins, for this could damage the tubes and bend the fins.

Any repair to the cooler core should be done by a reputable radiator shop, because it carries the necessary equipment to make the required repairs and tests.

If it becomes necessary to remove the air-oil cooler, always follow the manufacturer's instructions and take all suggested precautionary measures in regard to safety.

Coolant Oil Coolers Coolant oil coolers may be either an inherent part of the radiator or a self-contained unit. They may also be of the coolant-to-oil or oil-to-coolant design. These coolers are not quite as efficient as the air-oil cooler design, because the

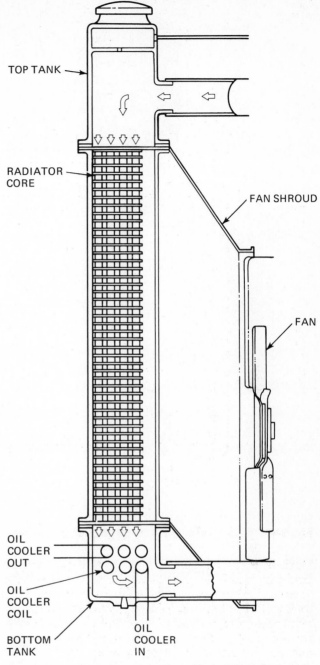

Fig. 8-42 Schematic view of a radiator oil cooler.

temperature of the engine coolant is always higher than the ambient temperature.

When the oil cooler is part of the radiator (see Fig. 8-42), the oil-cooling tube is wound to a coil and then placed in the lower section of the radiator. Oil from the hydraulic system passes through the tube and then back to the reservoir or, alternately, is first used to lubricate the power shift transmission and is then directed back to the reservoir. Engine coolant passes around the oil-cooling tube. In some applications an oil cooler relief valve is used to prevent the cooler from overpressurizing if it becomes plugged.

Any service to the radiator cooler should always be made by a radiator shop because it carries the required service and testing equipment.

When the oil cooler is of the self-contained de-

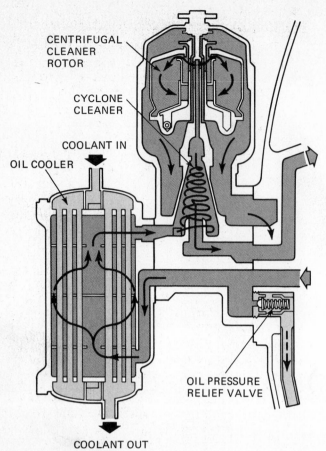

CENTRIFUGAL
CLEANER
ROTOR

CYCLONE
CLEANER

COOLANT IN

OIL COOLER

OIL PRESSURE
RELIEF VALVE

COOLANT OUT

Fig. 8-43 Oil flow through combination oil filter and cooler. (*Mack Canada Inc.*)

sign, it will have copper tubes welded or soldered to a seal ring located in a shell housing. Coolant enters from one side, passes through the copper tubes, and leaves by the other side. The oil, entering the shell at one end, surrounds the tubes and then leaves the shell at the other end. In some applications, it is the reverse, that is, the oil passes through the tubes, and the coolant surrounds the tubes (see Fig. 8-43).

The self-contained coolers also use a relief valve to avoid overpressurizing the cooler in the event that it becomes plugged. In this case, the valve opens and the return oil bypasses the cooler and goes directly to the reservoir.

Tube Oil Cooler Servicing   Service to a tube oil cooler can be done in your own shop. Broadly speaking, the procedure is as follows: Before disassembling the cooler for service, fill the cooler housing, through its ports, with mineral spirits (or a similar cleaning fluid) to loosen the oil residue and contaminants within the cooler. Otherwise, it may be difficult to remove the element.

After a period of time, say 1 h, remove the plug and drain the fluid. You could, in the meantime, clean the waterside (the inside) of the copper tubing. Because of the multitude of metals used, check your service manual for the proper solution strength and the recommended cleaning procedure.

Leave the oil cooler in the solution until the foaming and bubbling have stopped. Then remove the cooler and flush it with hot or warm water to remove the cleaning solution.

The general procedure for removing the cooler element is first to remove the cover, the gasket retainer, and the O ring. Then insert two stud bolts into the cooler element puller hole and secure a suitable puller bar to them. To prevent the residue from hardening, clean the cooler as soon as the element is removed. Flush trichloroethylene or an Oakite or alkaline solution (depending on the extent to which the cooler was clogged) around the cooler tubes or into the inlet of the cooler cores.   **CAUTION**   Use rubber gloves and eye protection and clean only in a well-ventilated room.

INSPECTION AND TESTING   Dry the cooler with compressed air and flush the tubes with light engine oil. Check for damaged tubes or core. Check the flared ends of the tubes for corrosion and for welding or soldering cracks. Check the housing and connections for damaged threads and the flanges for nicks, gouges, or cracks. Check the bypass valve spring for corrosion or a damaged surface.

To check for cooler tube or core leakage, seal both ends of the tubes and connect an air hose to the drilled and tapped hole. Using an air pressure regulator for control, pressurize the core to the recommended pressure.   **NOTE**   In view of the variety of oil coolers, be sure to refer to the appropriate service manual to determine the pressure to be applied. It varies from 20 to 150 psi [137 to 1033.5 kPa].

Immerse the core in water heated to 180°F [82°C]. When air bubbles rise, mark the location. In practice, a cooler which has a leak is either sent to a radiator shop for repair or replaced.

To repair damaged solder cracks, resolder the flared ends of the tubes. Take care not to melt the solder on the adjacent tubes.

To repair damaged tubes, insert a smaller tube into the damaged tube, flare both ends, and then solder the new and the old tube to the end plate.

REASSEMBLY AND INSTALLATION   Reassemble the oil cooler in a sequence precisely the reverse from the sequence in which it was disassembled. Make certain that the O rings are lubricated, are in their grooves, and are not twisted; that the gaskets are positioned properly; and that all hex bolts or nuts are torqued to specification. Install the bypass valve components in the correct sequence. When you mount the oil cooler onto the engine, make certain the mounting and sealing surfaces are clean and that the cooler faces in the correct direction in relation to the oil "in" and "out" and in relation to the coolant "in" and "out" connections.

When a multi-oil cooler is used, take care not to interchange the hydraulic oil lines with the engine oil lines. Make sure the nuts or bolts and plugs are torqued to specification and that the radiator and cylinder block hose connections or tubes are positioned correctly and clamped securely.

Review Questions

1. Into which two main groups are the hydraulic pumps classified?

2. Why is it said that "all positive displacement pumps have a pulsating flow?"

3. What is the purpose of the vane insert?

4. List the four basic types of piston pumps.

5. Why do swash plate, axial piston pumps find more applications than bent axial piston pumps?

6. List the two main purposes of multistage pumps.

7. What is the first indication of pump failure?

8. Explain why a worn, bent, or damaged piston rod or piston rod packing could reduce the service life of a hydraulic pump.

9. Outline the procedure to check the effectiveness of the piston rod wiper seal.

10. List four ways in which air could enter the hydraulic system.

11. List the precautions you must take before removing a hydraulic pump.

12. Why is it important to mark the pump gears after you have removed the rear cover from the gear plate (center section)?

13. What would cause (a) small cracks and wear of spline? (b) wear at shaft seal area? (c) rough spots and brinelling on bearing surfaces?

14. Why are there milled-out areas on the wear plates?

15. If the gear plate (center section) is worn or scored, where could you expect to find the wear or score marks?

16. List four causes of abnormal wear of the vanes and rotor.

17. List four major precautionary measures that must be taken before one installs a pump.

18. Why is it very important, if the pistons use slippers, to make certain the hole in the slipper is not blocked?

19. Give two reasons why it is vitally important to break in and test a new hydraulic pump.

20. Why is nitrogen gas used to precharge one side of the accumulator?

21. Briefly outline four mandatory precautionary steps to be taken before an accumulator is removed.

22. What is the purpose of a cooler relief valve?

Unit 9
Hydraulic Valves

Hydraulic valves are essential in any hydraulic system, for without them it would be impossible to control the flow or pressure.

A valve may be defined as a device having one or more movable parts which have the ability to open, restrict, or close off the fluid flow. The valve spool or piston can be actuated mechanically, electrically, hydraulically, by air, or by a combination of these methods.

Valves are rated by their size, pressure, capacity, and pressure drop within the valve. A valve may serve one precise purpose or may have several functions, as you will see when studying the various hydraulic systems.

Valves are classified into three groups: pressure control, flow control, and directional control. In addition they are classified according to their construction.

Pressure Control Valves
Pressure control valves are classified by name according to their purpose as follows: (1) main relief valve—used to control maximum system pressure; (2) secondary relief valve—used to control the maximum pressure in one application line of a circuit; (3) unloading valve—used to control maximum system pressure and, when the pressure within the system is reached, to direct the pump output to the reservoir (unloading the hydraulic pump); and (4) check valve—used either as a pressure control valve or as a directional valve.

Main Pressure Relief Valves
As previously stated, a positive displacement pump produces a fluid flow as long as the rotating or reciprocating pumping elements are in motion. Therefore, when the fluid flow is stopped through a valve or by the resistance of the actuator, the fluid from the pump must be redirected to prevent excessive pressure buildup which could damage the hydraulic pump, valves, lines, actuator, or the equipment itself. The valve that has the ability to perform these functions is called the main relief valve. It is always the first valve in the hydraulic system.

A main relief valve must have the capacity to redirect the full pump output to the low-pressure side of the system and to maintain the maximum system pressure. Depending on its design, the main relief valve can control the maximum pressure within 5 to 20 percent.

Main pressure relief valves are of the balance valve design and can be either simple or compound.

Simple Relief Valves
Simple relief valves are not commonly used, because by design they lend to great pressure fluctuations, which cause them to chatter. Although various designs may minimize their weakness, they are nevertheless unsatisfactory because of the great pressure override (see Fig. 9-1).

A simple relief valve can be of the piston, ball, or poppet design. By being forced on its seat by the pressure-regulating spring, it closes the return port to the reservoir. The energy of the spring can be increased or decreased through use of an adjusting device, by addition or removal of shims, or by a change in the spring rate to arrive at the desired system pressure.

OPERATION The system pressure is always exerted at the exposed valve surface; therefore, when the pressure increases, so does the force on the valve. As the oil force overcomes the spring force, the valve is lifted from its seat. This point is called the "cracking pressure." Through the lifting action, the oil can pass around the valve and into the outlet port and then return to the reservoir. The return oil flow causes a pressure on the back side of the valve which, added to the spring force, closes the valve. As a result the system pressure must increase above the cracking pressure to open the valve again. When the full oil flow passes through the relief valve, the system pressure is then at the relief valve setting. The pressure differential between the cracking pressure and the relief valve setting is the pressure override. For a simple relief valve this could be as high as 20 percent.

Compound Relief Valves
The compound relief valves used in hydraulic systems vary to some extent in their design; however, they all rely on the same operating principle. One simple (relief) valve (pilot poppet) is used as the triggering device and a main valve (dump valve or main poppet) is used to control

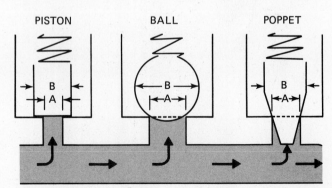

Fig. 9-1 Three types of simple relief valves. (*J I Case Company Agricultural Equipment Division*)

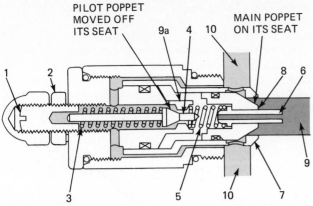

1. Adjusting screw
2. Locknut
3. Pressure spring
4. Pilot poppet seat
5. Balance spring
6. Orifice A
7. Main poppet seat
8. Main poppet seat
9. System pressure
9a. Chamber C
10. Return oil

Fig. 9-2 Sectional view of main relief valve in the cracking stage. (*J I Case Company Agricultural Equipment Division*)

the return flow. A light spring holds the dump valve on its seat, creating a pressure differential of about 20 psi [137.8 kPa]. The dump valve piston has a small orifice to allow the system pressure to pass into the chamber (C) (see Fig. 9-2) to balance the pressure when there is no relief flow and to act on the simple relief valve.

The main relief valve is commonly located at the inlet side of the directional control valve; therefore system pressure always acts on both the dump and the pilot valves.

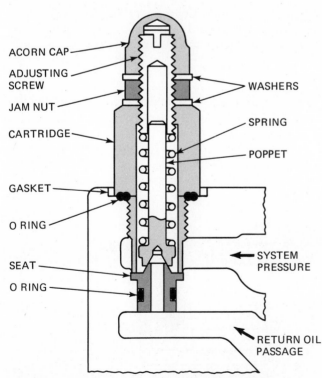

Fig. 9-3 Sectional view of secondary relief valve in the closed position. (*J I Case Company Agricultural Equipment Division*)

OPERATION When the system is under any pressure, this same pressure is found within the valve and against the pilot valve. When the system pressure reaches the cracking pressure of the simple relief valve, a small amount of oil, 10 drops for example, escapes from the area (C) via the pilot valve to the reservoir. When the pressure is reduced, it closes again, but a pressure differential between chamber C and the system pressure is created, causing the main poppet to open, resulting in a large dumping of oil to the reservoir. The pressure in chamber C and the system pressure cannot equalize instantly, because the orifice (A) restricts the oil flow into chamber C. When the pressure does equalize, the small spring of the dump valve closes this valve. The override of a compound relief valve is between 5 and 10 percent.

Secondary Relief Valves Secondary relief valves are of either a compound or a simple relief valve design and of either the cartridge (nonadjustable) or relief, and down-pressure circuit relief. These valves are either of a compound or a simple relief valve design and either of the cartridge (nonadjustable) or the adjustable type. To perform its duty, one simple relief valve is placed into one application line. This protects the hydraulic system, as well as the equipment, from becoming overloaded (see Fig. 9-3). The valve is screwed into the directional control valve body so that the circuit pressure is always exerted at the valve surface and the relief valve body is connected to the return line.

OPERATION Assume that the secondary relief valve is adjusted below the main pressure so that the operator cannot lift the equipment over a certain height from the ground. (Otherwise, the loader arms, the backhoe dipper, or the boom could be bent or twisted.) When the operator actuates the directional control valve, oil is directed to the hydraulic cylinder. As the circuit pressure reaches the cracking pressure of the secondary relief valve, this valve opens. Oil is then redirected into the return oil passage of the control valve and thereby maintains the lower application pressure.

When the relief valve is adjusted above the maximum relief valve setting, the main relief valve controls the maximum system pressure. The secondary relief valve has no effect on the maximum pressure. However, when the directional control valve is in neutral position, the main relief valve can no longer control the pressure, because it is isolated from the circuit. When, under these conditions, the line pressure increases to the secondary relief valve setting, the valve is forced off its seat. This in turn reduces the pressure in the application line and thus protects the system and the equipment. A pressure rise in the dipper application line could occur when one is rolling the bucket back while the dipper stick control valve is in the hold position, or when the loader circuit is in hold position and an additional load is dumped into the bucket, or when the bucket circuit is in neutral and the bucket is inadvertently forced backward.

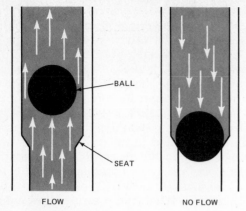

Fig. 9-4 Ball check valve.

Check Valves   As their name states, check valves check the oil flow. Check valves can be used as secondary relief valves, anticavitation valves, quick-dump valves, one-way directional valves, or sequence valves.

A check valve is simple in design (see Fig. 9-4). When used as a directional control valve, it is placed in series with the circuit and all oil must flow through it before reaching its destination. No oil, however, can flow in the reverse direction, because the light spring forces the valve closed as soon as the pressure on both sides of the valve is equal.

Pressure-Reducing Valves   Pressure-reducing valves could be of the simple relief valve design, or of the compound design, or of the compound and adjustable design as shown in Fig. 9-5.

When the valve is specially designed as a pressure-reducing valve, a spool is commonly used instead of the dump valve. The valves are able to reduce the main system pressure to a pressure desirable for a secondary circuit.

OPERATION   The pilot valve is held on the seat by the spring, which governs the system pressure. This spring is adjusted either by shims or by an adjusting

screw. The valve spool is also held on its seat by a light spring. The inlet port to the secondary circuit remains open until the inlet pressure approaches the valve setting. The reason the valve remains open is that the oil has passed through the orifice into the area of the spring and thus equalized the pressure below and above the spool, and the spring force on the spool causes the unbalanced condition. When the set (cracking) pressure is approached in the secondary circuit, the pilot valve opens, causing a reduced pressure above the valve spool. The higher primary pressure now forces the spool upward, reducing the port opening, which reduces the flow rate into the secondary circuit. This results in a pressure differential between the primary and secondary circuits.

The spool may never entirely close off the flow to the secondary circuit, because of the operating requirements of the circuit and the flow through the orifice, which maintains the spool in the control position.

Unloading Valves   Unloading valves can be of the simple or compound valve design. They are used to control the main system pressure and, when the pressure is reached, to direct the pump output to the reservoir. They are important for saving power, extending the life of the hydraulic pump, and maintaining a fixed pressure within the hydraulic system. This type of valve is also used in systems where two pumps supply oil to a system having one large-volume pump with low pressure and one small-volume pump with high pressure. When the lowest system pressure is reached, the large pump is unloaded and only the small pump supplies flow to the system.

OPERATION   The unloading valve (see Fig. 9-6) is basically a compound relief valve with the addition of a check valve. When the system pressure is below the unloading pressure, the pilot and dump valves are closed, and oil from the pump passes around the check valve and into the system. Under this condition, the pressure is equal above and below the dump valve piston, the pilot valve, plunger, and

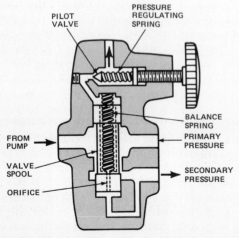

Fig. 9-5 Sectional view of an adjustable pressure-reducing valve in the reducing stage. (*Sperry Vickers Division of Sperry Inc.*)

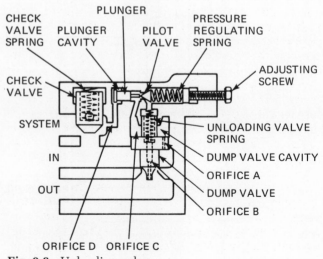

Fig. 9-6 Unloading valve.

check valve. When the pressure rises and overcomes the spring force of the pilot valve, the valve opens. This reduces the pressure in front of the plunger and above the dump valve (cavity A) by directing the oil through the center of the dump valve into the return line. The dump valve, however, remains on its seat because of the spring force. The system pressure rises slightly, in an amount equal to the force of the dump valve spring (about 20 psi [137.8 kPa]). This causes an increase in force on the plunger (orifice D), moving it to the right and thus mechanically forcing the pilot valve to an increased opening. This increases the pressure differential above and below the dump piston valve, causing the dump valve to open. The system pressure is reduced to the value of the dump valve spring, causing the check valve to close to maintain the system pressure and the pressure on the plunger to hold the pilot valve open. The affected plunger area determines when the plunger is forced to the left to allow the closure of the pilot valve. On the average the system pressure must drop about 10 percent before the pilot valve closes.

Servicing Pressure Control Valves   Although pressure control valves are not a cause of major system failure and need very little attention or maintenance, they are not entirely without malfunction. They should be readjusted at regular intervals and serviced after a major failure of one or more hydraulic components. Dirt or foreign particles clog small passages, cause the valve to stick and therefore operate erratically, and/or damage the spool, bore, or poppet seat and thus prevent the valve from maintaining the adjusted pressure.

If it is necessary to remove a pressure control valve, first steam-clean the area around the valve, park the machine securely, and block the hydraulic equipment. Remove the pressure from the system before loosening any hydraulic lines. Clean the valve again before disassembling it and after securing it so that the valve body, flanges, or surfaces cannot be damaged. Use the service manual as a guide when disassembling. Discard all seals and gaskets. Do not pry or drive the components apart or away from the bore. If they stick, reclean the valve, dry it with compressed air, and then relubricate it generously. The poppet, spool, piston, etc., must slide out from their bores without excessive force; otherwise the valve will be damaged. Wash all parts with solvent and dry them with compressed air so that a thorough inspection can be made. Inspect all parts and seats for excessive wear, nicks, and burrs. If, because of defects, some parts are not serviceable, replace the parts or the valve as a whole. Before reassembling, again clean the parts and generously oil them, including the seals and gaskets.

During the reassembly make certain that the parts are placed in the right order into their bores and slide freely within them; the seals and O rings are not cut during the assembly and the O rings are not twisted; the gasket is not mislocated; and the bolts or screws are torqued to specification.

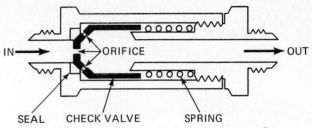

Fig. 9-7   Sectional view of a noncompensating flow control valve.

NOTE   Turn the pressure-adjusting screw inward just enough to hold the pilot valve components securely in their places, or insert a shim of the specified thickness. This prevents overpressurizing the system on start up.

Flow Control Valves   Flow control valves are used to reduce the actuating speed by limiting the flow rate of the fluid into a circuit or into one side of the actuator. For example, they could be used to reduce the lowering speed of a loader, the swing speed of a backhoe or crane, or the tilt speed of a dozer blade. Any orifice or valve could be used as a flow control valve because the underlying purpose of these valves is to restrict the flow. Flow control valves are divided into two distinct types—noncompensating and compensating.

Noncompensating Flow Control Valves   Noncompensating flow control valves (also called restricters or orifices) are of the fixed or adjustable orifice design. They are used where flow variation, due to pressure and temperature (viscosity), is considered not to be a critical factor. In some cases the restricter is spring-loaded to allow an unrestricted flow in the opposite flow direction.

OPERATION   The noncompensating flow control valve (see Fig. 9-7) is a check valve having several orifices to allow a calculated flow rate at a fixed viscosity. When the viscosity is too high, the oil cannot pass through the orifice at the calculated flow rate. This results in the oil pressure's lifting the check valve off its seat; this action increases the flow rate and thereby causes an uncontrolled flow. When the viscosity is low (as calculated for the valve), the flow rate through the orifice is high, the pressure on the piston is low, the check valve spring closes the valve, and the flow rate into the cylinder is as calculated.

Compensating Flow Control Valves   Some systems require a precise flow regardless of pressure or temperature, and this accuracy is ensured by using the specially designed compensating flow control valves. These valves react to pressure or temperature (viscosity) changes automatically by changing their setting to provide the desired flow rate (see Fig. 9-8).

The simplest temperature flow control valve is an orifice plug. This plug is made from a material which, with changes in temperature, has a high ex-

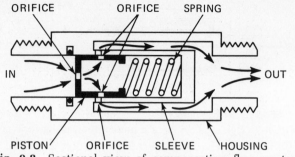

Fig. 9-8 Sectional view of compensating flow control valve.

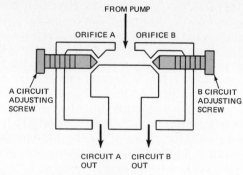

Fig. 9-9 Flow divider valve.

pansion and retraction rate. When the temperature is high, the orifice reduces in opening area, and when it is low, the orifice opening area increases.

Today, however, hydraulic oils are of low viscosity index and therefore temperature-compensating control valves are seldom used. Pressure-compensating control valves are more common. This type controls the flow rate to the actuating device or secondary system regardless of primary system pressure.

OPERATION When the inlet pressure is constant and the viscosity low, the combined force of the outlet pressure and the spring force holds the piston to the left. The calculated flow rate passes through the orifices in the piston and sleeve. These orifices create a calculated pressure drop on the right side of the piston. When the pressure increases, the piston is forced to the right because the orifices are not allowing an instant pressure rise at the right side of the piston. The piston's movement has reduced the orifice area (between the piston and the sleeve) to maintain the same flow rate at a higher pressure. When the inlet pressure is reduced, the outlet pressure, in conjunction with the spring force, moves the piston to the left. This increases the area of the orifices between the piston and sleeve and thereby increases the flow rate.

Flow control valves are placed in a circuit in either a "meter-in" or "meter-out" position. When placed in the meter-in position, the valve controls the flow rate to the circuit or actuator, and when placed in the meter-out position, it controls the flow rate by regulating the return flow from the circuit or actuator.

Flow Divider Valves Flow divider valves are not common in loader, dozer, crane, truck, or backhoe hydraulic systems, but if used, their task is to divide the fluid flow into equal or unequal streams of flow. In other words the oil flow from the pump is split in half or in unequal portions into two circuits. These valves, when used, are pressure-compensating flow dividers.

Simple Flow Dividers A simple flow divider has two fixed or adjustable orifices (see Fig. 9-9). When both orifices are equal in area and the pressure in both circuits is the same, the pump output is equally divided between both circuits. However, when the

resistance causes the pressure to rise in circuit A, say, by 100 percent to 2000 psi [13,780 kPa], this causes an increase of flow to circuit B and a reduced flow in circuit A until circuit B has (the same) 13,780 kPa pressure. The flow to circuits A and B is then equalized again.

Pressure-Compensating Flow Dividers One of the many pressure-compensating flow divider valves is shown in Fig. 9-10. The valve spool, with its two fixed orifices A and B, is placed in the valve bore so that the spool lands are positioned over the two outlet orifices C and D. The two orifices in the valve spool are sufficiently different in area that a higher pressure drop is created in area F than in area G, and this condition achieves a higher flow rate into circuit B than into circuit A. Say, for example, that circuit A will receive 25 percent of the flow and circuit B 75 percent. Regardless of the flow rate from the hydraulic pump or the pressure in circuit A or B, the flow rate into circuit A will be 25 percent and that into circuit B 75 percent.

OPERATION Assume that at idle speed the pump supplies 10 gal/min [37.85 l/min] to the divider valve and the pressure in circuits A and B is 100 psi [689 kPa]. The oil flow from the pump passes through both orifices A and B (in the valve spool),

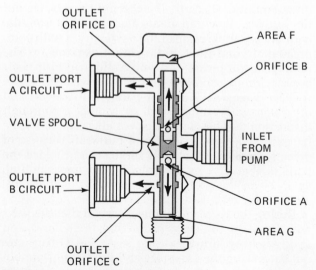

Fig. 9-10 Pressure-compensating flow divider. (*J I Case Company Agricultural Equipment Division*)

orifice B lowering the pressure by 75 percent in comparison to orifice A. The valve spool is moved so that both spool ends position themselves over the outlet orifices. This causes a flow rate of 7.5 gal/min [28.38 l/min] into circuit B because orifice C is increased and of 2.5 gal/min [9.46 l/min] to circuit A because orifice D is reduced. When the pump flow rate increases, say, to 100 gal/min [378.5 l/min], the proportion to the circuit (25 percent to 75 percent) remains the same. Consider, now, if the pressure between the A and B circuits were to vary; for example, that the pressure in circuit A were to rise 500 psi [3445 kPa] above circuit B owing to the resistance of the actuator. In such a case the pressure in area F would rise, causing the valve spool to move downward, increasing the orifice opening D, and this action would cause the flow rate into circuit B to increase. Until the pressures in both circuits equalize, the valve spool would float in either direction (according to the pressure exerted on the spool) to maintain an equal flow rate to circuits A and B.

SERVICING Both flow control and flow divider valves are simple valves and therefore contribute little to a system's failure. However, contaminated oil or large particles in the oil will cause orifices and passages to become clogged or the valve or bore to become scored, resulting in reduced efficiency.

When tests have proved that service is required, follow the same precautionary steps as outlined earlier in this unit in the discussion of pressure control valves. Follow the service manual precisely in regard to disassembly and reassembly procedures, because the valve, valve spool, and piston can be placed backward into the bore very easily. Remove nicks and burrs by using an oil stone and employ crocus cloth to ensure that the valve slides freely within its bore.

Directional Control Valves A directional control valve is any valve capable of controlling the direction of flow. From this statement you may deduce that almost any valve could be used as a directional control valve. For this reason and because of their great variation in physical design and operation it is difficult to classify them. In most cases the valve is classified by the method by which it controls the oil flow. Moreover, classification includes design and purpose. Some are not true directional valves but find great usage in hydraulic systems for other purposes. Examples of these valves are check; double check; shuttle; divider; anticavitation; counterbalance; quick-drop; sequence; two-way, two-position; and three-way, two- or three-position valves.

Double-Check Valves A double-check valve is used to hold the pressure within the hydraulic cylinder until the applied pressure overcomes the return line pressure. This ensures safe and controlled activation of the cylinder (fail safe) (see Fig. 9-11.) The valve consists of a spool having extended ends and check valves located in each end of the valve body. When used in conjunction with a power steering cylinder, one side of the spool has an orifice to

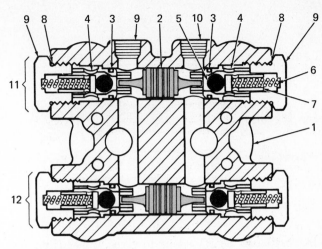

1. Valve body
2. Valve spool
3. Check valve body O ring
4. Check valve seat body
5. Ball check
6. Check valve spring
7. Check valve spring guide
8. Plug
9, 10. Inlet and outlet ports from steering control valve
11. Top double check valve for left steering cylinder
12. Lower check valve for right steering cylinder

Fig. 9-11 Schematic view of a double-check valve in neutral.

reduce the shift speed of the spool and to ensure that it is equal to the actuating speed of the steering cylinder. Without this orifice the initiation of retraction and extension of the cylinder rod would be difficult.

OPERATION When the directional control valve is in neutral, the double-check valve spools float between the ball checks. The check valve springs and system pressure hold the four ball checks on their seats.

NOTE The four ports leading to the two steering cylinders (not shown) are located above the ball checks. Consequently the cylinder ports are closed off, holding the steering, loader, the boom, or the outrigger piston rod(s) in a fixed position. When the directional control valve is moved to effect a left or right turn or to raise or lower the load, oil enters the double-check valve at either the left or right port. Assume at this point that oil enters at the right port, No. 10. This shifts the two check valve spools to the left but does not force the left ball checks off their seats. As the oil pressure increases and overcomes the force exerted on the ball checks, the two right ball checks are forced off their seats, the two valve spools are forced to the left, and the two left ball checks are mechanically forced off their seats. Oil now flows around the right ball checks into one end of the steering cylinders, and oil returns from the steering cylinders, passes around the left ball checks, and returns via line 9 to the control valve. The actions of the valve are in a precise sequence so that there is no pressure drop within the circuit and

96

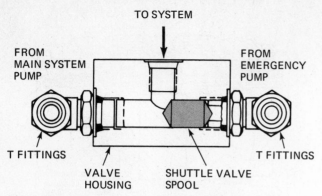

Fig. 9-12 Schematic view of a shuttle valve.

the load can be raised or lowered only when the pump pressure is higher than the pressure created by the load. When the turning, lifting, or lowering of the load is completed, the pressure at the right side of the double-check valve is quickly reduced. This causes the two valve spools to be shifted to neutral, closing all four checks and thereby holding the pressure within the cylinders.

Shuttle Valves   Shuttle valves are commonly used in hydraulic systems having an emergency supply system (see Fig. 9-12).

OPERATION   Within the shuttle valve is a free-floating spool. One valve end is connected to the main hydraulic pump and the other end is connected to the emergency pump. This valve has no neutral position. When the main hydraulic pump supplies oil to the system, the spool shifts to the right, allowing the oil to enter the system and at the same time closing the other port from the emergency supply system. If the main hydraulic pump fails to supply oil to the system, the electrically driven emergency pump switches on and supplies oil to the shuttle

valve's right port. The spool shifts to the left, closing off the main pump supply port. The emergency pump now supplies oil to the hydraulic system.

Sequence Valves   A sequence valve is used when the actuation of two cylinders or two circuits is required in sequence. The primary circuit is actuated first, and when the pressure from this circuit overcomes the spring force of the valve spool or piston of the sequence valve, the spool or piston is shifted and oil is directed into the second circuit or into the second cylinder (see Fig. 9-13).

OPERATION   When the primary circuit pressure is less than the energy of the spring, the valve spool is forced downward and thus closes off the opening to the secondary circuit. Flow is therefore available only to the primary circuit.

The primary circuit oil (pressure) has passed through the small passages, and the pressure is exerted onto the piston. When the primary oil pressure overcomes the spring force, the spool is forced upward and thus opens the secondary system port, allowing the oil to flow into the secondary circuit.

When the primary circuit pressure is reduced, the sequence valve loses its actuating pressure. The spring force is now greater than the applied pressure, and this condition forces the spool downward, opens the secondary circuit to the drain port, and allows the oil from the secondary circuit to drain out of this port.

Anticavitation Valves   Although anticavitation valves vary in design and nomenclature, they are, in most cases, simple check valves. Their purpose is to reduce cavitation by redirecting the higher return oil pressure to the lower pressure side of the system. The anticavitation valve is actuated when the piston rod is retracted or extended by the force of the load, not by the force of the hydraulic pressure from the

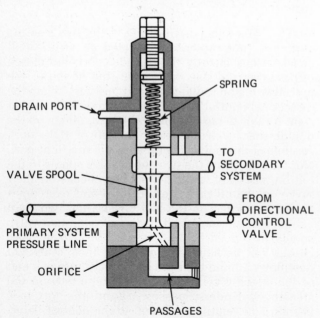

Fig. 9-13 Sectional view of a sequence valve. (*Sperry Vickers Division of Sperry Inc.*)

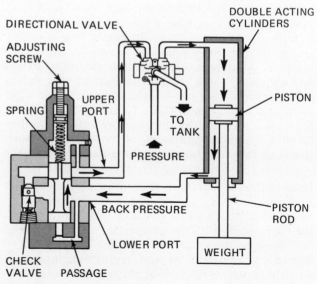

Fig. 9-14 Schematic view of counterbalance valve. (*Sperry Vickers Division of Sperry Inc.*)

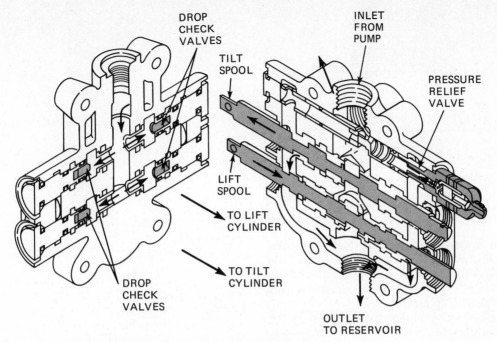

Fig. 9-15 View of loader directional control valve cut in half to show the components, passages, and ports. (*J I Case Company Agricultural Equipment Division*)

control valve. (See the discussion of sectional control valves later in this unit.)

Counterbalance Valves   Counterbalance valves restrict the oil flow from the return line while the load is forcing the piston rod to extend or retract. They can therefore control the speed of the rod extension or retraction.

OPERATION   When the system is under normal return pressure, about 15 psi [103.3 kPa], the spool is forced downward by its spring. The upper port is connected to the directional control valve and the lower port, in this example (see Fig. 9-14) to the rod end of the actuating cylinder. When the directional control valve directs oil to the rod end of the cylinder, the oil enters the upper port, forces the check valve open, and leaves via the lower port to the rod end of the cylinder. The oil flow is unrestricted within the counterbalance valve. When the directional control valve directs oil to the piston end of the cylinder, the pressure (or the load) forces the piston rod to extend. However, there is no oil flow through the counterbalance valve until the return pressure (acting on the spool) forces the spool upward against its spring force. The spool movement causes the upper port to open, allowing the piston rod to extend. The adjusting screw is used to increase or decrease the pressure required to open the port leading to the directional control valve.

Quick-Drop Valves   A quick-drop valve, when used, is installed in or on the actuating cylinder or control valve to allow the load to be dropped quickly. Because of its internal connection (to the system) the valve also reduces cavitation because the oil released from one side of the cylinder is redirected to the other side (see the discussion of actuators in Unit 10).

Sliding Spool Directional Control Valves   As you may know, 99 percent of all directional control valves use a sliding spool as their valve element. Very rarely is a rotary or poppet valve element used. Spool valves are preferable because (1) they have less flow restriction and therefore only a minimum pressure drop, (2) they are reasonably trouble-free in their operation, (3) they have a good service life, (4) they have greater versatility than other valves, (5) they have a simpler operating principle than that of other directional valves.

There are hundreds of different designs of directional control valve and valve spools to suit the various directional flow requirements. Manufacturers use a numbering system to codify the directional control valves and to enable the user to select one best suited for the hydraulic system. The model number indicates (1) the maximum flow rate, (2) the maximum operating pressure, (3) the pressure drop within the valve at maximum pressure, (4) the number of ports and spool positions, (5) the internal port connections when the spool is in neutral position, (6) the number of spools in one valve assembly, (7) the method by which the spool is centered, and (8) the method by which the spool is actuated.

Control Valve Design   The valve body or housing is cast with internal passages, lands, grooves, and openings to accommodate the spool, spool seal, and the various component parts required for a modern control valve. The valve housing is then machined, milled, and bored, and the spool bore positioned so that the presized machine spool slide-fits within the bore (see Fig. 9-15).

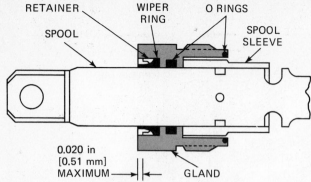

Fig. 9-16 Arrangement of spool-sealing parts. (*J I Case Company Agricultural Equipment Division*)

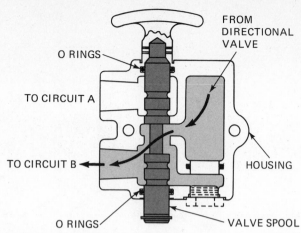

Fig. 9-18 Sectional view of a diversion valve showing oil flowing into circuit B.

Directional control valves that are internally mounted (that is, within the reservoir) have no need for spool seals, wiper seals, or wiper rings but in some cases require a vent to prevent the spool from becoming hydraulically locked.

A typical spool seal arrangement is shown in Fig. 9-16. The spool gland is fastened to the valve body and sealed by an O ring. A lip-type seal, quart ring, cup ring, or O-ring seal is placed into the gland to prevent oil leakage from the spool. Commonly, a lip-type wiper seal is used to clean the spool, to prevent the entry of dirt and/or air, and to increase the service life of the valve spool.

Two-way, Two-position Spool Valves   A spool valve often used is the two-way, two-position valve (see Fig. 9-17). It is used more or less as a shutoff valve to stop the flow into a circuit or to allow the oil to flow to the circuit. It is called a two-way, two-position valve because it has two ports (one inlet and one outlet port) and the spool has two positions (closed or open). The valve position, therefore, is of the finite design; that is, the valve is either fully open or fully closed. When the valve is of the infinite design, the spool can be moved or held in any place between the fully open and the fully closed positions. It then acts not only as a directional valve but also as a flow control valve.

Three-way, Two-position (Diversion) Valves   Because diversion valves have three ports and the valve spool has two positions, they are called three-way,

two-position valves. These valves are designed so as to render them capable of selecting the oil flow to port A or port B. However, they have no neutral position and cannot supply oil to both ports at the same time (see Fig. 9-18).

OPERATION   The spool has two lands and is sealed on both ends by O rings. The pump inlet port is at the right side and the two ports, A and B, on the left side. When the valve spool is pushed downward against its stop, oil from the inlet port passes around the reduced area of the spool and into the circuit B through port B. Port A is sealed off by the spool land. When the spool is lifted against its stop, port B is sealed off by the spool land and port A is open to circuit A.

Three-way, Three-position (Divider) Valves   As the name indicates, these have three ports and the spool has three positions. They can function as divider valves because they can direct the oil flow to port A or B or block both port openings when in neutral. However, they cannot supply oil to both ports at the same time.

When the spool valve is fully to the left or right position, oil is allowed to pass out either port A or B. When the spool is locked in the neutral position, both ports are closed off (see Fig. 9-19).

True Directional Control Valves   Up to now you have learned about directional control valves which can direct oil flow into the hydraulic system but cannot reverse the flow from the system. True directional control valves have the ability to reverse the oil flow from the system. The most common are four-way, three-position and four-way, four-position valves. These valves are all of the infinite design and are of either the open or closed center spool design. The spools are commonly spring-centered (neutral position).

A spool valve of the open center spool design is one which, when in neutral, allows the oil flow from the pump to pass unrestricted through the valve and has both ports to the actuator closed off. Open center spool valves which have one or both ports open to

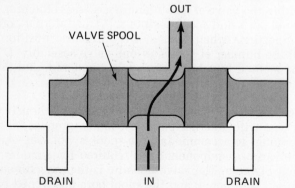

Fig. 9-17 Sectional view of a two-way, two-position spool valve.

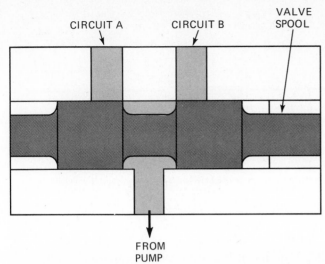

CIRCUIT A CIRCUIT B VALVE SPOOL

FROM PUMP

Fig. 9-19 A three-way, three-position directional valve in neutral position.

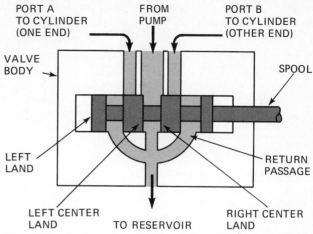

PORT A TO CYLINDER (ONE END) — FROM PUMP — PORT B TO CYLINDER (OTHER END)

VALVE BODY — SPOOL

LEFT LAND — RETURN PASSAGE

LEFT CENTER LAND — TO RESERVOIR — RIGHT CENTER LAND

Fig. 9-20 A four-way, three-position, open center directional valve.

the actuator are not used on loader or truck hydraulic systems.

A spool valve of the closed center spool design is one which, when in neutral, has both ports to the actuator closed off, and the spool blocks the oil flow from the pump. (There is no return flow to the reservoir.) Closed center valves having one or both ports open to the return side of the system are not used on hydraulic systems of loaders, trucks, etc.

Hydraulic systems using closed center spool valves (loaders, cranes, etc.) require an unloading valve and an accumulator to maintain the maximum system pressure.

Four-way Three-position (Open Center) Directional Valves All four-way, three-position spool valves, regardless whether or not they are of the open or closed center design, have four ports (see Fig. 9-24). The upper port is connected to the hydraulic pump side of the system, and the lower center port is connected to the reservoir side. The upper left or right port is connected to either the rod end or the piston end of the actuator.

When the spool is slowly moved to the left against its left spring force, the left center spool land gradually opens a passage and allows the pump oil to flow out of the left port. At the same time the right center land of the spool reduces the passage to the return port and opens the return passage from the actuator B port. The slow actuation of the spool to the left gradually increases the flow to port A and reduces the pump oil flow to the reservoir. It thereby acts as a flow control valve. However, the valve can be held in any position for the required actuating speed of the piston rod.

When the spool valve is in the fully open position (either left or right), the center land is blocking the return flow, and all pump flow is directed to the cylinder. When the cylinder comes to the end of its stroke, or the resistance to move the actuator is higher than the maximum pressure, the main relief valve unseats and directs the oil to the reservoir (to protect the hydraulic system).

When the spool is moved from the fully open position to the right, the oil passages to and from the actuator slowly reduce their openings, reducing the flow to and from the actuator until the spool land has blocked the pump and return flow. At the same time the right center land gradually opens the passage to allow the pump oil to flow to the reservoir.

A type of directional control valve commonly used is shown in Fig. 9-21. This valve is also of the open center, four-way, three-position design, but the major difference is that the valve spool is center-drilled and cross-drilled.

OIL FLOW WITHIN THE VALVE When the valve spool is in neutral position, oil from the pump enters the center port B and passes through the center cross-drilled holes. It then passes through the center-drilled passage in the spool and to the left and right cross-drilled holes. A passage within the valve body links both spool valve holes with the outlet port.

When the valve spool is moved to the left against the spring force, the centerhole of the spool comes over left port A and opens the return oil flow from the actuator to the return port. The position of the center land allows the pump oil to flow to port C. Oil from the pump that enters port B can now leave port C and flow to the actuator. Oil from the actuator

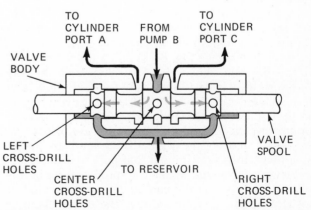

TO CYLINDER PORT A — FROM PUMP B — TO CYLINDER PORT C

VALVE BODY — VALVE SPOOL

LEFT CROSS-DRILL HOLES — CENTER CROSS-DRILL HOLES — TO RESERVOIR — RIGHT CROSS-DRILL HOLES

Fig. 9-21 An open center, four-way, three-position directional valve (neutral).

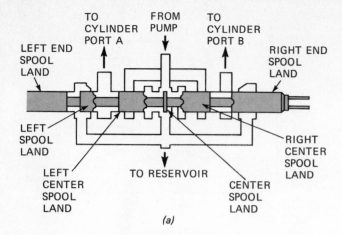

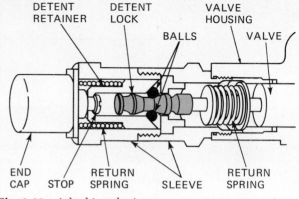

Fig. 9-23 A locking device.

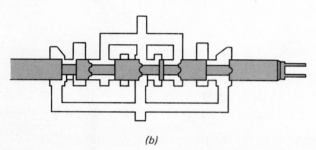

Fig. 9-22 A four-way, four-position spool valve in the (*a*) neutral and (*b*) float positions.

enters port A through the center cross-drilled hole in the spool and then flows into (and through) the center spool passage. It leaves at the left cross-drilled holes to enter into the return passage.

Four-way, Four-position Directional Valves When the application requires a spool position that will not apply a pressure to either side of the piston but will open both cylinder ports to the reservoir passage, a four-way, four-position directional control valve spool is used.

A four-way, four-position directional control valve is quite similar in design or operation to a four-way, three-position valve with the exception that the spool lands are relocated to accommodate an oil flow in the fourth position of the spool. The fourth position is usually a lock position and is called "float position" (see Fig. 9-22).

OIL FLOW IN FLOAT POSITION When the operator moves the valve spool all the way to the right, a locking device (see Fig. 9-23) holds the valve spool in this position. When the valve spool is all the way to the right, it puts the left spool end and left land in a position where port A is open to the return passage. The left center land then allows oil from the pump to pass through the valve and on to the reservoir. Moreover, the right center land and right spool end are so positioned that port B is also open to the return passage. When the spool valve is in this position, the piston rod can move in or out without restriction and therefore allows the dozer blade or bucket to follow the contour of the ground. In larger applications anticavitation valves are used to keep

the cylinder full of oil as the piston rod extends and retracts.

Four-way, Three-position, Closed Center Spool Valves The most significant difference between four-way, three-position open and closed center spool valves is the valve spool land's position as it relates to the port within the valve housing (see Fig. 9-24). The purpose of this position is to save engine power and to extend the life of the hydraulic pump; this position is used when instant pressure to the actuator is required.

OIL FLOW WITHIN THE VALVE When the spool valve is in the neutral position, the center spool land blocks the oil flow, and the left and right spool lands block the return port passages to the outlet ports. When the engine is operating, system pressure always exists on the inlet port B. When the spool is moved to the right, the center land opens a passage through which the oil flows to port A, and the right spool land opens the passage through which oil flows from the cylinder to the return port C. When the spool is moved from the fully open position to the hold position, the center land gradually reduces the oil flow to the cylinder until the flow ceases completely, and at the same time the right land reduces

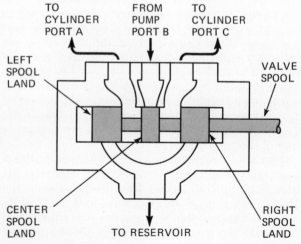

Fig. 9-24 A four-way, three-position closed center spool valve (neutral).

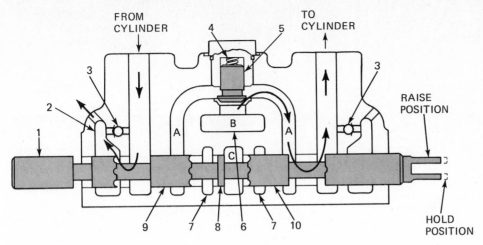

FROM CYLINDER   TO CYLINDER

RAISE POSITION

HOLD POSITION

1. Valve spool
2. Port B
3. Anticavitation valve
4. Load check valve spring
5. Load check valve
6. Parallel passage B
7. Parallel passage C
8. Center spool land
9. Left center spool land
10. Right center spool land

A – APPLIED PRESSURE
B, C – SYSTEM PRESSURE

Fig. 9-25 Sectional view of a four-way, three-position, open center spool valve into raised position. (*International Harvester Company*)

the return oil flow from the cylinder until the lands block the flow.

Load Check Valves The valve spool in a directional control valve must have clearance to slide within its bore. This clearance creates a minute internal oil leakage across the spool land and body land, which causes the loader or dozer blade, etc., to drift down (or prevents the stabilizer from holding the machine off the ground). Furthermore, when the loader, the boom, or the dozer is already raised; the valve spool is in the hold position; and the operator is required, under this condition, to lift the load an additional distance, the blade will drop down as soon as the directional control valve is moved to the raise position. The reason for this is that the pressure created by the load is higher than that from the pump. When a closed center spool valve is used, the load would not drop as far as it would if an open center spool valve were used, because of the existing high pressure at the spool valve. To prevent the load from falling or drifting and to take the applied load pressure from the spool, load check valves are used.

OPERATION A view of an open center directional control valve with load check valves is shown in Fig. 9-25. When the valve spool is in neutral position, the check valve is closed by the light spring force and by the hydraulic pressure existing in the actuator line. **NOTE** The pressure in the lines is held by the check valve and not by the spool or body lands. When the spool valve is moved to the left, oil from the parallel passage is directed to the load check valve because the center spool land stops the center passage oil flow, and the right spool land is open to the rod end of the cylinder. The left center spool land prevents the inlet oil from passing to the return oil passage. The load check valve is still on its seat. The pump pressure increases quickly because all the pump output is directed against the load check valve. The load check valve lifts off its seat as soon as the pump pressure is higher than the

pressure created by the load, and as a result the load cannot fall.

When the load check valve opens, the load rises, and oil, displaced by the piston, returns through port B back to the reservoir.

A design similar to that of an open center directional control valve having a load check valve, circuit relief valve, and anticavitation valve is shown in Fig. 9-26. This type of design is used when two or more valve spools are used in one valve body or when independent valve bodies are joined together to form a sectional valve bank. In both cases, when the valve spool is in neutral position, the load check valves and the circuit relief valves are seated. The anticavitation valve is forced onto its seat by the pressure in the actuator line and by a light spring force.

There are two oil supply passages within the directional control valve (see Fig. 9-27). One passage (1A) is unrestricted through the center of the valve spool, and the other passage (1B) is below the check valve and is blocked off at the end.

OIL FLOW WITHIN THE VALVE When the spool is moved to the left, the right center spool land gradually closes off the center oil flow from the pump to the reservoir. At the same time the right and left spool lands open their ports to circuits A and B. The pressure in the inlet passage below the load check valve increases and overcomes the force on the load check valve. Pump oil can then flow past the created opening into outlet A.

Return oil enters port B, passes the opening created by the left land, and returns via the passage to the outlet port. When the valve spool is moved fully to the left or right, there is no pump flow through the lower pump passage.

Sectional Directional Control Valves Sectional directional control valves are becoming very popular because they are less expensive to manufacture, are more easily serviced, and are more versatile than the

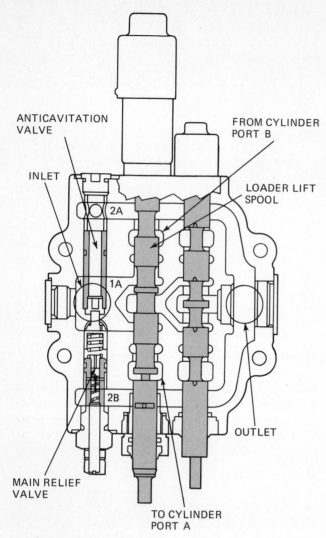

Fig. 9-26 Sectional view of an open center spool valve. The left spool is in the raised position. (NOTE The secondary relief valves are not shown.)

1A – SYSTEM PRESSURE
2A, 2B – RETURN OIL

single-body, multispool directional valve. When the latter fails to operate properly or is damaged, the entire valve must be discarded. Furthermore it is difficult to include the additional safety and anticavitation valve when one is using a single-body valve assembly.

An open center sectional control valve assembly is shown in Fig. 9-28. It is not apparent from an external view whether the assembly is of the open or closed center spool design. In any event, whether open or closed, the ends of the valve sections 1, 2, 3, 4, etc., are closed off by the inlet and outlet assembly ends. The cross passages from valve to valve and from the valve to assembly ends are sealed by O rings. Tie bolts hold the individual components together as a unit.

The sectional directional valves are very similar in design to single-spool directional valves of open or closed center, and the oil flows within the valve in a like manner. However, on most modern valve designs, regeneration (anticavitation) valves form part of the valve.

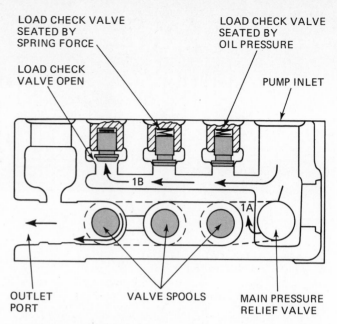

A – APPLIED PRESSURE
B – SYSTEM PRESSURE

Fig. 9-27 Sectional views of a directional control valve oil flow. (*J I Case Company Agricultural Equipment Division*)

OIL FLOW In an open center sectional control valve having a regeneration valve, oil from the loader control valve or hydraulic pump enters the inlet port at the inlet end and is directed through the open center passage of the spool valves to the outlet end and back to the reservoir and into the parallel passage. The latter passage, however, is blocked (dead-ended) by the regeneration valve (see Fig. 9-29). Load check valves are placed between the oil flow in the parallel passage and the ports leading to the actuator. Depending on the purpose of each directional valve, they may or may not have one or two secondary relief valves. The swing directional control valve may have, in addition to the two secondary relief valves, two anticavitation valves. Passages in the top and bottom of the valve section link the return oil from the actuator ports with the outlet end. The return oil can flow unrestricted to the reservoir because it can pass around the regeneration valve.

NOTE No main relief valve is used, because a power-beyond fitting is installed in the loader's directional control valve.

Regeneration Circuit Nearly all modern hydraulic systems use some kind of valves to reduce hesitation and/or cavitation of one or all hydraulic cylinders. A simplified form of regeneration circuit is shown in Fig. 9-29. To prevent cavitation or hesitation, a one-way check valve is placed between the return and supply line.

OIL FLOW IN THE CIRCUIT When the mechanical load causes the piston to move (extending the piston rod), oil is forced from the rod end of the cylinder through the directional control valve and back to the reservoir.

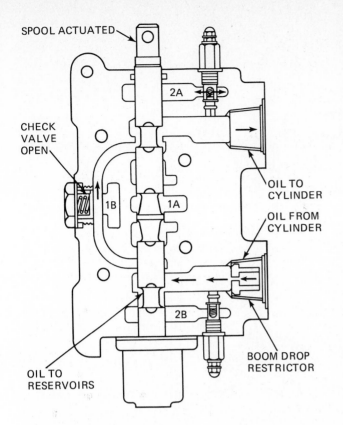

SPOOL ACTUATED

2A

CHECK
VALVE
OPEN

1B   1A

OIL TO
CYLINDER

OIL FROM
CYLINDER

2B

OIL TO
RESERVOIRS

BOOM DROP
RESTRICTOR

1A— SYSTEM PRESSURE

1B, 2A— APPLICATION PRESSURE

2B— RETURN LINE PRESSURE

Fig. 9-28 Sectional open center spool valve in the boom-lowering position. (*J I Case Company Agricultural Equipment Division*)

If the piston rod is forced out too fast, the pump is not able to keep the piston end of the cylinder filled and cavitation results. Because of the restriction in the return line, the pressure rises, and when the pressure is higher than the pump supply pressure, the regeneration check valve opens. This allows the return oil to pass through the regeneration check valve and join the supply line oil, adding to the pump oil to fill the piston end of the cylinder. It is not to be construed from this somewhat over-simplified circuit description that all regeneration circuits are this basic. Some are fairly sophisticated, but they function on the same general principle.

Closed Center Sectional Directional Control Valves
The main distinction between a sectional valve assembly having an open center spool design and one of a closed center spool design is that, in the latter, the oil flow from the pump or loader directional control valve is directed only through the center passage. When the spool valves are in neutral position, the oil flows from the pump into the port plate, into the center passage, and onto the end plate, where it is stopped (dead-ended). Passages in the top and bottom of the sectional valves link the return oil from the actuator ports with the port plate. These valve assemblies also use regeneration, anticavitation load check valves, as well as secondary relief valves.

Servicing of Directional Control Valves Directional control valves alone are rarely responsible for a major shutdown of the hydraulic system. However, they can be damaged when some other hydraulic components have failed or when the hydraulic system is not thoroughly flushed after a component failure. A directional control valve requires service when (1) the valve spool leaks oil; (2) the valve spool does not return to neutral or is sticky; (3) the spool will not stay in locked position; (4) the load drops when the spool is actuated; (5) the valve spool has excessive leakage across the land, causing pressure and volume loss; or (6) the secondary, main relief, anticavitation (regeneration) valves cause pressure and volume loss.

Service procedure is relatively the same for a directional control valve of the open or closed center design or for a single, tandem, or sectional control valve since each operates on the same general principle. Nevertheless the components of each make of valve are shaped and arranged differently within the assembly. It is also possible for a tandem or sectional control valve assembly to have one or two slightly different spool land locations or different secondary relief valve settings. Some also have an anticavitation valve in one section and none in the other.

Because of these variations, you should (if you have not had experience with these valves) refer to the appropriate service manual when reassembling them. Quite often, minor service, such as replacing spool valve seals and wipers, secondary or main relief valve components, or anticavitation valves, can be done while the valve is installed to the machine. Whether you are servicing valves on or off the machine, good work habits must be maintained.

First you should thoroughly clean the area where you will be working. Always position and block the equipment so that you can remove the valve assembly safely. Remove the pressure from all application lines and the air pressure from the reservoir.

NOTE When a closed center system is used, make certain that the oil pressure from the accumulator is also removed.

Before removing any hydraulic lines, tag them for identification to facilitate quick and correct installation. Use two wrenches when loosening the fittings to prevent damaging the fittings, the hose, the adapter, or the valve. Cap all openings promptly to prevent entrance of foreign matter. Once the mounting bolts are loose, attach a rope sling to the valve, then remove the bolts and lift the valve from the machine.

DISASSEMBLY AND INSPECTION Before starting the disassembly, clean the work area and your tools. Since the procedure to disassemble various directional valves is not always the same, you should use the appropriate service manual and follow the recommended steps implicitly.

There are procedures applicable to any directional valve, such as starting the disassembly by removing the main relief valve. The parts should come out of the bore without excessive force unless the

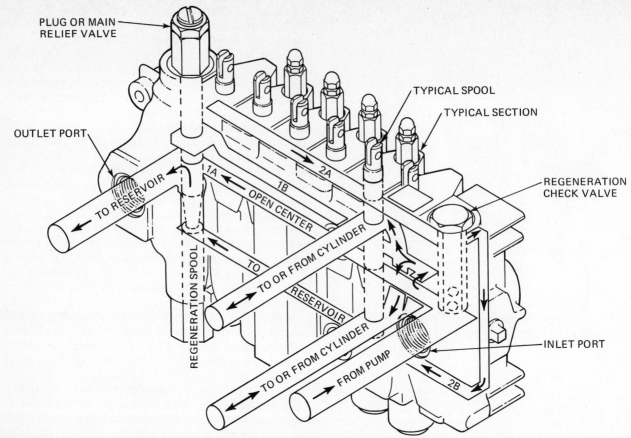

Fig. 9-29 Oil flow in a sectional control valve bank having a regeneration valve. (*J I Case Company Agricultural Equipment Division*)

poppet seat is press-fitted in the bore, in which case you should remove the valve only when the poppet or seat shows excessive wear. During the removal examine the parts to determine their serviceability but discard all seals, backup washers, and washers.

Next, remove the secondary relief valve and load check valve (see Fig. 9-30). These parts also should come out of the bores without excessive force, with the exception of the load check valve poppet seat (which is usually press-fitted in the housing).

Examine each part closely to determine its serviceability and lay the damaged parts or those showing excessive wear or nicks and burrs to one side for replacement.

Remove the lift spool components. Be very careful that you do not damage the bore or the spool when sliding the spool from the bore.

NOTE When tandem valves or sectional valves are serviced, mark the spool and valve body so that they are not interchanged when you are reassembling. You should also maintain the spool assembly as a unit for the same reason.

Remove the bucket spool and clam spool but do not remove the centering spring. This is necessary only when you must replace the spring or spring seats. **NOTE** Never force the spool out, for this will cause damage to the spool and/or bore. The spools should slide from their bores with ease; if

they do not, clean the assembly with new solvent, dry it with compressed air, and then lubricate the spool thoroughly through the openings in the valve body.

Examine the spool lands for scores, nicks, and burrs. If the lands are damaged in the valve body, the body must be replaced. If the body lands are in good condition but the spools are damaged, replace them with oversized spools. (All manufacturers provide oversized valve spools for this purpose.) They are identified in regard to size and type and by color code and a lettering system.

When examining the spool, pay special attention to the seal surface. This should not be pitted or show oxidation roughness. If the feathering edges or cutouts are damaged, the spool or the valve assembly must be replaced; otherwise you would have internal pressure losses.

Check that the small machined grooves around the valve spool are not damaged. If the valve spool eye bore is elongated, enlarge the bore and press a bushing into it to restore the bore. If this is not possible, the spool or valve must be replaced. Do not attempt to weld the spool eye bore to restore the bore, for this will damage the spool. When servicing a sectional directional control valve (as shown in Fig. 9-31), you must lap the sides of the valve body to ensure a 100 percent fit between the adjacent valve or end plate.

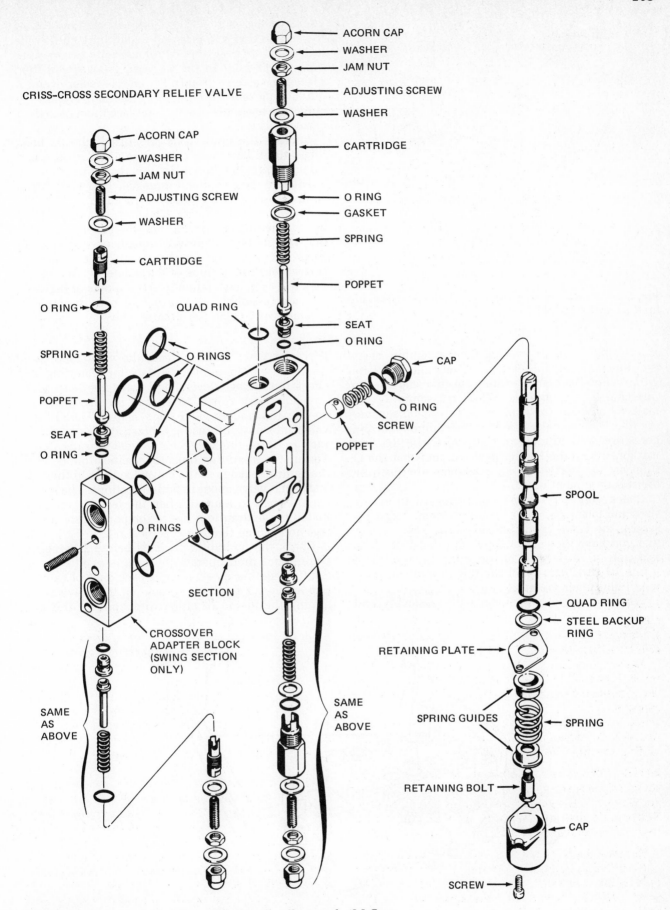

Fig. 9-30 Typical valve section schematically illustrated. (*J I Case Company Agricultural Equipment Division*)

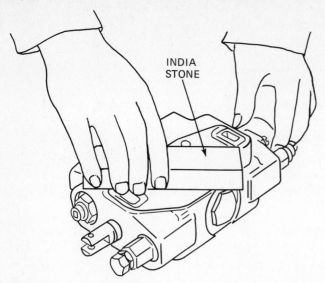

Fig. 9-31 Removing nicks. (*J I Case Company Agricultural Equipment Division*)

you have reassembled the individual sections, clamp the end section in a vise and install long guide rods to the end section. Use petroleum jelly or grease to hold the O rings in the recessed grooves and then place the valve section in the correct order over the guide rods onto the adjoining section. **NOTE** If shims are used, make sure you place them onto their correct positions.

Remove the guide rods and install the tie bolts finger-tight. Lay the assembly on a flat surface and then torque the bolts (in the recommended sequence) to the specified torque (see Fig. 9-32). Make certain, by forcing the valves in and out, that the spool valves do not stick. The valves should spring back to neutral. If they do not, the problem may be that the tie bolts are overtorqued, one or more O rings are dislocated, or the shims are not in their correct location. If none of these defects are present, then dirt may have fallen into the spools or between the valve assembly. It will then be necessary to disassemble and clean the sticking valve.

REASSEMBLY Before starting the reassembly, clean the valve body and all parts in solvent and dry them with compressed air. Be careful at this stage not to interchange components. When reassembling the main relief valve, the load check valve, and secondary relief valve, make sure that the components and bores are well lubricated, that the O-ring backup washers are in the correct position, and that the O rings are not twisted or cut while you are inserting the subcomponent parts.

Check your service manual in regard to spring sizes and locations before installing them. Before inserting the valve spool into its bore, make certain that you have the correct spool and that it is clean and well lubricated. Do not cock the spool or force it into its bore. The spool should slide in smoothly with light finger pressure.

When servicing a sectional valve assembly and

INSTALLATION Before lifting the valve into position, check the mounting surface for distortion and check the linkage, levers, and bores for wear. Make any necessary repair to ensure precise valve response and smooth valve spool action. Then lift the valve into position, using a hoist; it may be necessary to shim the valve to prevent misalignment. Torque the mounting bolts to specification, connect the control leakage to the valve spools, and then operate each valve spool in both directions. The spools should snap to neutral when the lever is released. Install the hydraulic hoses to the ports according to tags and torque them to specification.

Check the hydraulic oil level before starting the engine and then operate the engine at idle speed. Continuing this speed, operate each control valve to remove the air from the system but try to avoid bottoming the piston in either direction, for this will

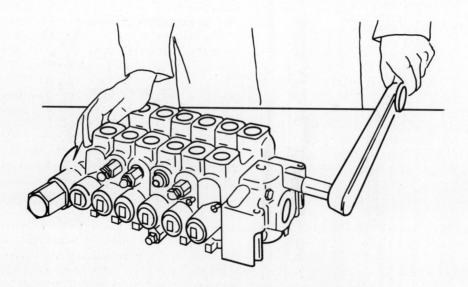

TORQUE EVENLY TO 30 lb·ft [41.6 N·m]

Fig. 9-32 Tightening tie bolts. (*J I Case Company Agricultural Equipment Division*)

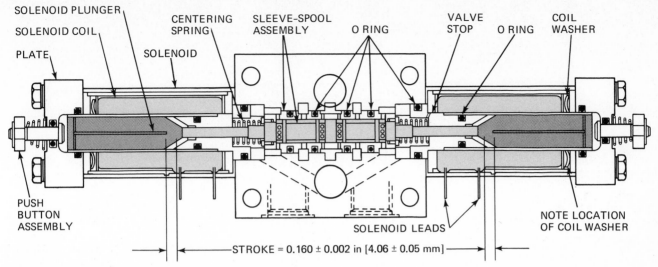

Fig. 9-33 Typical solenoid-operated valve. (*WABCO, An American-Standard Company*)

stall the engine. Check for oil leaks and recheck the oil level.

Install a flow meter to the system to check and adjust the main relief valve, low-pressure secondary relief valve, and the efficiency of the directional control valves.

Valve Spool Actuation An increasing number of huge hydraulically operated machines are using pilot-actuated directional control valves to increase the controlling speed of the valve spool.

You can move the valve spool into the actuating position by attaching a hydraulic or air cylinder to one or both sides of the valve spool and connecting the actuating cylinder with a hydraulic hose to an air or hydraulic control valve. When the valve spool is actuated through a solenoid, the solenoid housing is attached to one or both sides of the valve spool. One end of each solenoid coil is connected to a two-way toggle switch, and the other ends are connected to a ground (see Fig. 9-33).

AIR OR HYDRAULIC ACTUATION When air or hydraulic fluid is directed to one cylinder, the air or hydraulic pilot pressure forces the piston assembly to the right. This action moves the valve spool to the right or left, against the force of the centering spring, and the valve spool directs oil to the actuator. Return oil passes through the valve spool and back to the reservoir. When the air or hydraulic pilot pressure is reduced, the return spring forces the piston assembly to the left, and this allows the valve spool centering spring to force the valve spool to neutral.

ELECTRICAL ACTUATION When the toggle switch is placed into the raise or lowering position, it closes the electrical circuit, and the current flows from the battery over the switch contacts, through either the left or right solenoid coil, and then to ground. The magnetic force pulls or pushes the solenoid plunger directly, or the link forces the valve spool into the actuating position. When the toggle switch is placed

in the off position, the solenoid coil is deenergized, its spring force moves the plunger to neutral, and the valve spool centering spring positions the spools to neutral position.

Hydraulic and Air Swivels Hydraulic and air swivels have basically the same purpose and design. Their purpose is to direct oil or air from a nonrotating frame to a rotating structure. Their design allows an unrestricted flow of oil or air through the swivel whether there is a 360° rotation, or only partial rotation, or no rotation at all. A hydraulic or air swivel consists of a ported female housing, attached either to the rotating structure or to the nonrotating frame, and a male, ported, and grooved shaft, which is attached either to the nonrotating frame or to the rotating structure. The shaft is held to the housing through a cover and is sealed to the housing on both top and bottom with O rings. **NOTE** The swivel acts only as a directional valve. It has no side thrust, and no up-and-down force is exerted on it.

The number of ports in the female housing and male shaft can vary from one port to as many as seven. Each port in the housing has its corresponding port in the shaft, as well as a corresponding groove in the shaft. Each shaft groove is sealed by any of various types of seals. In the illustration, one synthetic rubber O ring and two Teflon backup rings are used to prevent the oil in one circuit from flowing into the adjacent circuit. The hydraulic swivel shown in Fig. 9-34 is used on a track excavator which requires seven ports to direct oil to and from the two hydraulic drive motors—one port for the low-pressure motor drain line, two ports each for the left and right leveler, and one port each for the left and right track brakes. In some cases the center of the shaft has additional tubes or passages which align with the same number of ports in the cover to direct oil from and to the left and right track brakes. Either the tubes or the passages carry the electrical wires for actuation of solenoid control, directional control valves.

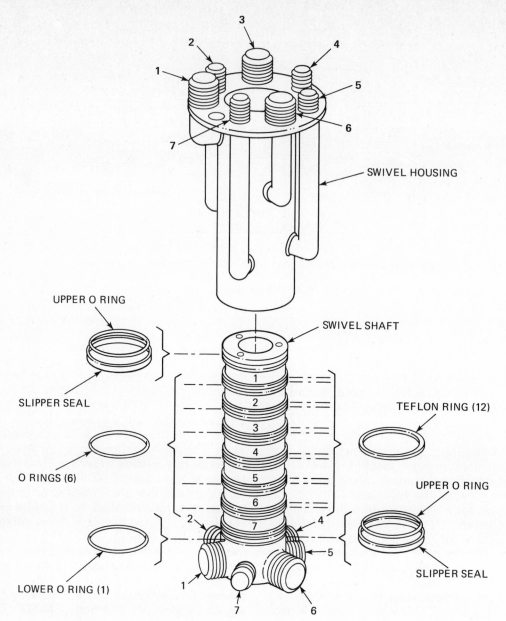

3
2
1
4
5
6
7

SWIVEL HOUSING

UPPER O RING

SWIVEL SHAFT

SLIPPER SEAL

TEFLON RING (12)

O RINGS (6)

UPPER O RING

2
4
5
1
7
6

SLIPPER SEAL

LOWER O RING (1)

Fig. 9-34 Hydraulic swivel. (*J I Case Company Agricultural Equipment Division*)

Review Questions

1. List three functions of a hydraulic valve.

2. Why are compound relief valves used in preference to simple relief valves?

3. Why is the first valve in any hydraulic system a relief valve?

4. A check valve is designed mainly to allow a one-directional flow. However, in hydraulic systems it can have four other applications. List them.

5. What is the major difference between a flow control valve and a flow divider valve, whether or not it is of the noncompensating or compensating valve design?

6. How would you define a directional control valve?

7. To which line or side does the quick-drop valve direct the oil flow, if the directional valve is in the quick-drop position?

8. List five advantages of a spool valve over any other directional control valve design.

9. Why are directional control valves classified by the number of ports and position?

10. When describing a valve spool as a three-way, two-position valve, what does *way* and *position* refer to?

11. Describe a valve spool of (*a*) finite position, (*b*) infinite positions.

12. All directional control valves use one- or two-load check valves (for one or more valve spools). What are the two main purposes of this valve?

13. Briefly outline the principle on which the regeneration or anticavitation valve operates.

14. Why should you identify every hydraulic line before (or immediately after) removing them from the valve or component?

15. Two common methods are used to achieve a smooth valve operation and oil flow. List two methods of achieving smooth raising, stopping, or lowering of the load.

16. Why are some directional control valves pilot-operated?

Unit 10
Actuators

The hydraulic components you have studied up to now function to supply, control, and direct the oil flow. As you know, the purpose of a hydraulic system is to perform work, which in this case is achieved by using an actuator.

Actuators are devices specially designed to convert an oil flow (hydraulic energy) into actuating motion. Although their design and application can vary, there are really only two basic designs, the hydraulic cylinder type and the hydraulic motor, and each is capable of converting hydraulic energy into motion. Only two basic designs are applicable because a flow of fluid can only push and cannot pull an object. Externally it may appear as though the fluid in a double-acting actuator pulls in the piston rod, but actually it pushes the piston in the opposite direction.

Basic Actuator Design   A hydraulic cylinder is a lineal actuator (see Fig. 10-1). It consists of a piston with seals to which a piston rod is fastened. A cylinder housing, commonly called a barrel or tube, is welded or capped closed at one end, the other end being closed by the cylinder head (sometimes called the head end or gland) through which the piston rod slides. A seal and wipers are installed in the cylinder head to confine the oil, to prevent air from entering the system, and to clean the rod during its retraction. A bushing (which may be composed of various materials) is used to extend the service life of the piston rod and the cylinder head. On each end of the cylinder barrel there is an oil supply port, one called the rod end port and the other the piston end port. To fasten the hydraulic cylinder to the machine, the piston end of the cylinder and the rod end have bores with bushings.

A hydraulic ram is also a lineal actuator; however, it differs in that the piston is also the piston rod, and furthermore it is a one-way actuator (see Fig. 10-2).

A hydraulic motor is a rotary actuator in that it converts hydraulic energy into rotary motion. Fluid under pressure is forced into the motor inlet and then into the chamber formed by the motor housing and the gears, or the vanes, or the piston. The oil under pressure is forced onto the gear teeth, or vane pockets, or the piston surface and thus causes the rotation or reciprocation.

Hydraulic Cylinder Actuators   About 98 percent of all hydraulic actuators are of the cylinder design because they can be easily modified to suit a multitude of applications. They are classified by their method of performing work and are too numerous to be covered individually in this textbook.

Single-Acting Cylinder Actuators   Single-acting cylinder actuators are illustrated in Fig. 10-2. Although a great number of components and parts are similar to those of a single and a double actuator, a dramatic difference is that single-acting actuators can perform work only in one direction, since their construction allows only the piston end to be pressurized. A three-way, three-position directional control valve is required to operate this actuator. The piston rod is only partly sealed to prevent dirt and water from entering the cylinder; therefore an air filter of some type is attached to the top side of the

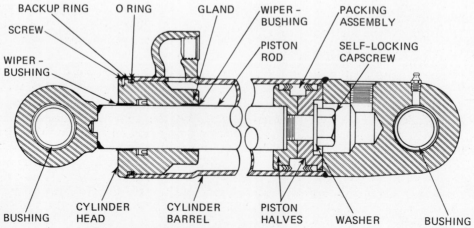

Fig. 10-1 Sectional view of a typical double-acting hydraulic cylinder. (*J I Case Company Agricultural Equipment Division*)

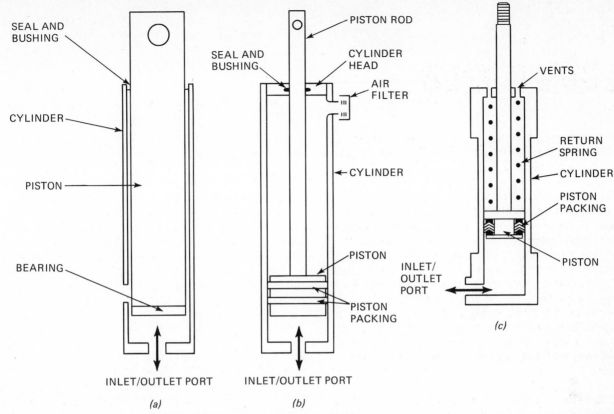

Fig. 10-2 Sectional view of single-acting actuators. (a) Hydraulic ram; (b) and (c) single-acting cylinder.

cylinder for the air to enter and to escape as the piston is forced upward (by the oil pressure) and downward (by the load or its own weight).

On some specially designed actuators a coil spring which rests against the piston and cylinder head is placed over the piston rod to ensure a positive return of the piston.

Cylinder Rams A typical cylinder ram, or displacement cylinder, is illustrated in Fig. 10-2. Although the actuator is single acting, it is designed and operates quite differently from any other type. The piston diameter is commonly about 0.125 in [3.17 mm] smaller than the cylinder bore, and the bore is sealed (to confine the oil) at the cylinder end opening. The piston on the lower end is supported through a bearing to stabilize the piston within the cylinder. No air filter is necessary, and the oil inlet port may be at any convenient place.

OPERATION When the piston is retracted, the oil may be fully drained from the cylinder, or it may partly surround the piston, or the cylinder may be full with oil. The quantity of the oil within the space between the cylinder barrel and piston depends entirely on the speed with which the operator positions the directional control valve to neutral. When the three-way, three-position directional control valve is moved to the raised position, oil enters the cylinder and fills the space between the cylinder barrel and piston. The oil pressure rises and acts on the circumference of the piston, the inner cylinder wall,

and the piston area. The load on the piston keeps it retracted until the oil pressure (acting on the piston area) increases, gains force, and lifts the piston and, correspondingly, the load. The pressure on the circumference of the piston area has no effect on the lifting force, but it stabilizes the piston during its extension and retraction.

NOTE The lifting force of the ram cylinder also depends on the piston area and the applied pressure.

Double-Acting Cylinder Actuators Double-acting cylinder actuators of the differential type are the most common. The term *differential* relates to the difference in piston area between the rod end and the piston end of the piston. Nondifferential and three-port double-acting cylinders are used for special applications only (see Fig. 10-3).

Actuator Operation When the oil from the directional control valve is directed to the rod end side of the cylinder, the piston is forced to the right, and the piston rod retracts. The piston then forces the oil out of the piston end port of the cylinder, where it is directed back to the directional control valve.

When the piston rod is indirectly attached to the bucket, or boom, etc., a first-, second-, or third-class lever can be used to gain force at the cost of speed or, on the other hand, to gain speed at the cost of force.

The construction and design of differential actuators can vary greatly. On the whole they differ in

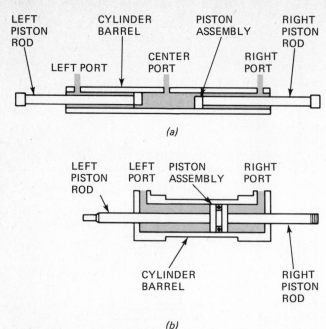

Fig. 10-3 Schematic vew of double-acting cylinders. (a) Three-port, double-acting hydraulic cylinder; (b) nondifferential double-acting cylinder.

regard to (1) the cylinder barrel (especially in length and diameter), (2) the cylinder head, (3) the piston, (4) the piston rod, (5) the piston seal, (6) the piston rod bearing, and (7) the piston rod seal. The positions of the cylinder ports and mounting facilities also vary to meet the application requirements. Some of the variations between the hydraulic cylinders are illustrated and discussed.

Pressure, Force, and Flow Rate You must now be aware that double-acting cylinders of the differential type develop different forces and flow rates because the piston area and the cylinder volume are less at the rod end than at the piston end of the cylinder by the difference of the rod area.

EXAMPLE (See Fig. 10-4.) When the cylinder diameter is 6 in [15.24 cm] and the piston rod is 2 in [5.08 cm] then the area at A is 28.62 in² [0.01823 m²], and at B, 25.12 in² [0.0162 m²] because the rod area is 3.14 in² [0.002 m²]:

Piston area at A = 3 in × 3 in × 3.14 =
28.26 in² [0.01823 m²]
Rod area = 1 in × 1 in × 3.14 =
3.14 in² [0.002 m²]
Piston area at B = 28.26 in² − 3.14 in² =
25.12 in² [0.0162 m²]

When the applied pressure is 1000 psi [6890 kPa], the force developed at the piston end (A) is 28,260 lb [125,700 N] and at the rod end (B), 25,120 lb [111,733 N], the difference in force being 3140 lb [13,967 N].

Force at A = 1000 psi × 28.26 in² =
28,260 lb [125,700 N]

Force at B = 1000 psi × 25.12 in² =
25,120 lb [111,733 N]

Difference = 28,260 lb − 25,120 lb =
3140 lb [13,967 N]

You may also be aware that a hydraulic system develops only as much pressure as it requires to lift the load or to perform the work. The pressure developed, therefore, is equal to the force of the load divided by the area on which the pressure acts.

Pressure (psi or Pa) =
Force (lb or N)/Area (in² or m²)

EXAMPLE Assume you have a loader having two hydraulic cylinders, each with an area of 28.26 in² [0.0182 m²] and a length of 5 ft [1.525 m] and the load to be lifted is 14,000 lb [62,272 N]. The pressure required to lift the load would be 233.3 psi [1607.4 kPa] because each hydraulic cylinder must lift half the load, that is, 7000 lb [31,136 N].

$P = F/A$
= 7000 lb/28.26 in² = 247.7 psi [1707 kPa]

However, the hydraulic cylinders are connected to the loader arms through a third-class lever. A typical example, a bowl lift mechanism, is shown in Fig. 10-5. The ratio of the lever is 1:3; therefore, the actual pressure required to lift the 14,000 lb [62,272 N] would be triple this calculation, that is, 699.9 psi [4822 kPa] because of the disadvantage.

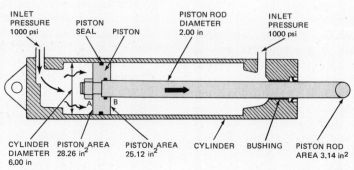

Fig. 10-4 Pressure, force, and flow rate.

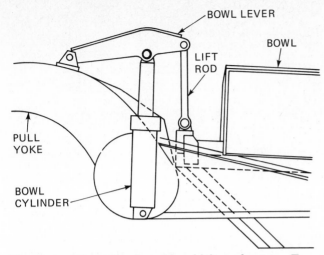

Fig. 10-5 Schematic view of bowl lift mechanism. (*Terex Division of General Motors Corporation*)

The speed with which a piston rod retracts or extends from the cylinder depends on the flow rate and the volume required to fill the space of one or two cylinders.

NOTE The load or working pressure has no bearing on the speed of the actuation.

As an example, the specifications used previously are used again, with the addition that the hydraulic pump supplies a flow of 100 gal/min [378.50 l/min] at the rated engine rpm.

To extend both cylinder rods fully to 5 ft [1.525 m], a volume of 3391.2 in³ [55,582 cm³] of oil is needed because volume is equal to the area times the length times the number of cylinders (which in this case is times 2).

$$V = A \times L \times 2$$
$$V = 28.26 \text{ in}^2 \times 60 \text{ in} \times 2 = 3391.2 \text{ in}^3 \text{ [55,582 cm}^3\text{]}$$

$$\frac{3391.2 \text{ in}^3}{231 \text{ in}^3/\text{gal}} = 14.68 \text{ gal [55.6 l]}$$

The time required to extend the rams fully is 8.8 s. To lower the load under power, only 13.1 gal [49.4 l] is required:

$$V = 25.12 \text{ in}^2 \times 60 \text{ in} \times 2 = 3014 \text{ in}^3 = 13.1 \text{ gal} \text{ [49.4 l]}$$

The time to retract the cylinder rod fully is 7.82 s.

Specially Designed Double-Acting Cylinders Specially designed double-acting cylinders are numerous. They can serve one or more special purposes, such as to reduce the speed and/or to cushion the end of the stroke. One method used to achieve either or both of those objectives is to drill a series of holes of various sizes in the end of the cylinder barrel and then connect the holes with the rod end port (see Fig. 10-6).

When the piston is forced upward, the return oil passes through all the holes in the barrel, into the

port and lines, and onto the directional control valve. As the piston approaches the end of its stroke, it closes one hole after the other, causing a restriction of the return oil flow and a pressure rise at the rod end side of the cylinder. As a result the piston speed is gradually reduced, and in addition, the piston is prevented from hammering on the cylinder head.

Another method of controlling speed and achieving cushioning action is through a spring-loaded restricter pin positioned within the piston (see Fig. 10-7). The end cap, which is welded to the cylinder barrel, has a bore into which the restricter pin can slide. As the piston and pin near the end of the stroke, the restricter pin comes in front of the bore and then slides into the bore. The oil's return flow is then gradually restricted, and the pressure begins to rise in the piston end of the cylinder. As the restricter pin bottoms in its bore, the pin is forced into the piston rod.

A third method of achieving the same results is through a stepup piston (see Fig. 10-8). This method has an additional feature—not only does it reduce the speed at the end of the stroke but it also increases the speed at the beginning of the stroke. When the piston is fully to the right, the stepup part of the piston is in its bore, reducing the piston area. When the oil is directed to the piston end port, the piston instantly moves to the left because of the oil volume from the pump's acting on the reduced cylinder volume. As soon as the stepup piston leaves its bore, the piston speed reduces because of the increased cylinder volume. **NOTE** In this case you have gained piston speed at the beginning of the stroke, but you have lost piston force.

Poppet or Limited Travel Valves Although low-pressure circuit relief valves are used in dozer circuits to protect the machines against damage, these valves also decrease the piston pressure and therefore reduce the piston force. To maintain the maximum pressure and the maximum force over the entire stroke while still protecting the machine, poppet valves, also called *limited-travel valves*, are used. These valves are simple one-way or two-way check valves within the piston (see Fig. 10-9). During the piston stroke the oil pressure acting on the valves causes them to close. The oil pressure exerted on the piston is controlled by the main or high-pressure secondary relief valve. However, when the piston comes within $\frac{3}{4}$ in [19.05 mm] of the end of its stroke, the extension of the one-way or two-way

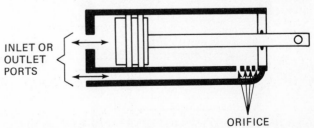

Fig. 10-6 Method used to control the piston speed by using orifices.

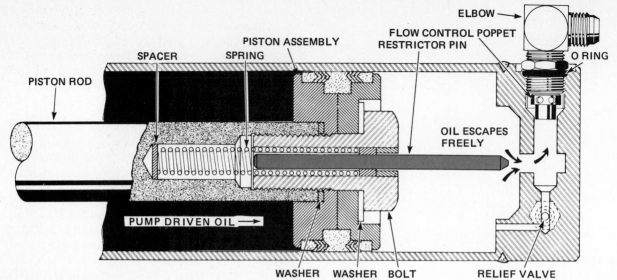

Fig. 10-7 Method used to control the speed at the end of the stroke by using a restricter pin. (*J I Case Company Agricultural Equipment Division*)

check valves bottoms against the cylinder head or the piston end cap of the barrel. This mechanical action opens the valves and allows the oil from the applied side to pass through the openings (made by the valves) to the oil return side and thus lowers the applied pressure. The pressure reduction achieved with these valves is about 800 psi [5512 kPa].

Poppet valves are especially important when the dozer has a tilt circuit. Assume that the tilt cylinder has tilted the blade and the dozer blade is now lifted up or forced down. As soon as one cylinder piston reaches the end of its travel, the applied pressure of both dozer cylinders is reduced and thereby prevents any extreme force on the dozer components and reduces the possibility of any distortion.

To equalize the applied speed of a differential cylinder so that a steering cylinder or a swing cylinder reacts with the same speed (and in both directions) in regard to the oil flow from the directional control valve, simple flow control valves, orifices, restricter plugs, or check valves are used. With all devices mentioned, the oil flow into one or both sides of the cylinder is controlled so that the piston speed is equal as it moves to the left or to the right.

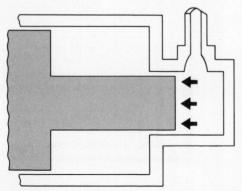

Fig. 10-8 Method used to control the speed at the end of the stroke by using a stepup piston. (*J I Case Company Agricultural Equipment Division*)

Quick-Drop Valves   To reduce the speed with which a loader, dozer, or boom falls when the directional control valve is moved to the down or float position, a flow control valve, in the form of a check valve, an orifice, or a restricter fitting, can be used. Since these devices also lower the speed with which the loader, boom, etc., is raised, quick-drop valves are used to prevent this problem (see Fig. 10-10).

OPERATION   When the directional control valve is in the hold or raised position, the springs hold valves 1 and 2 to the left, and the oil pressure cannot act on them to push them to the right. At this point, the directional control valve has closed the passage between the rod end and the piston end of the cylinder. Valve 3 is in the fully open position and does not restrict the oil flow.

When the directional control valve is moved into the down position, the weight of the dozer blade or loader pulls the piston down, causing the oil return pressure to increase above the applied pressure from the pump. The pressure differential causes valve 2 to move to the right against its spring force. The bore of valve 2 slides over valve 3, thus restricts the return flow to the directional control valve, and thereby increases the return pressure and aligns the opening of valve 2 with the passage that leads to valve 1. The return oil pressure now acts on valve 1 and moves it to the right, allowing the return oil to enter the pump oil passage and integrate with the pump oil. This valve action not only controls the drop speed but also fulfills the function of anticavitation valves.

Power Steering Cylinders   Another type of specially designed double-acting cylinder is used with linkage power steering. These cylinders have an outer shell to protect the inner cylinder barrel against external damage. The outer shell is fastened and sealed with an O ring to the cylinder head, and the piston end of the shell is welded to the end cap. The cylinder barrel is also fastened and sealed to the

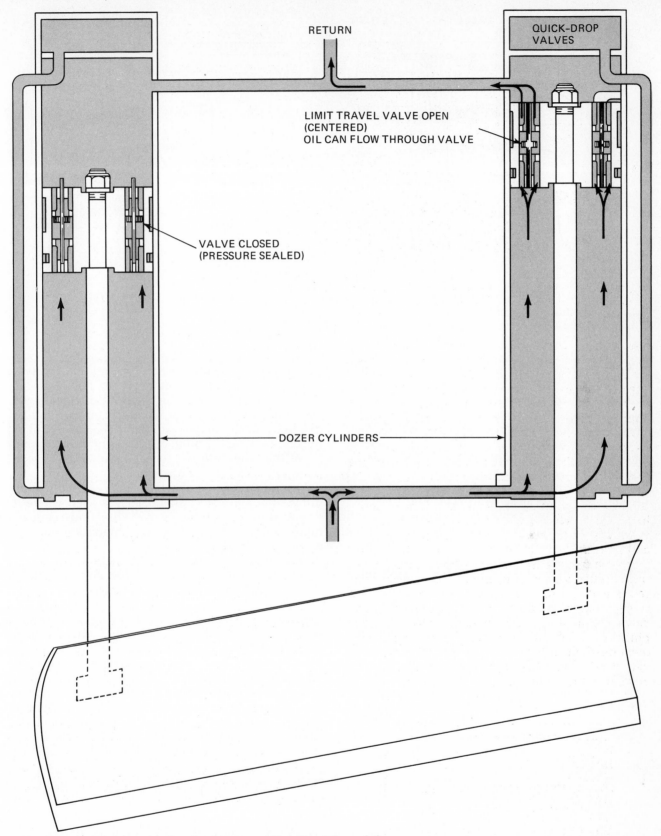

Fig. 10-9 Limited-travel valve function—moldboard raising while tilted. (*Fiat-Allis*)

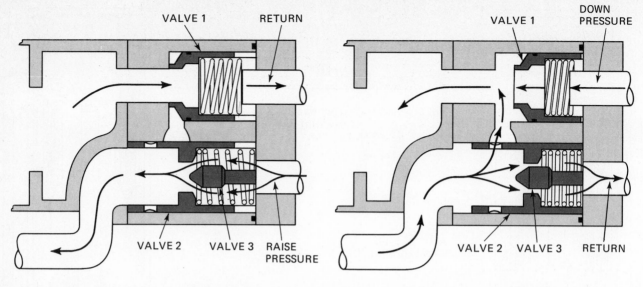

VALVE 1   RETURN

VALVE 1   DOWN PRESSURE

VALVE 2   VALVE 3   RAISE PRESSURE

VALVE 2   VALVE 3   RETURN

VALVES IN RAISE OR HOLD POSITION

VALVES IN QUICK-DROP POSITION

Fig. 10-10 Sectional view of the valve locations and positions when in the raised and quick-drop positions. (*Fiat-Allis*)

cylinder head, and its other end is open, and a small space is left between the cylinder barrel end and the cylinder end cap to allow the oil to pass from the outer shell to the piston end of the cylinder barrel. The cylinder head has the necessary seals and wiper to seal the piston rod but, in addition, has two ports, one leading to the cylinder barrel and the other located between the cylinder and the outer shell. This port arrangement ensures a good hose location and therefore minimizes hose failure (see Fig. 10-11).

When applications require that the cylinder barrel be the moving part of the cylinder or when safe hose connections are difficult to achieve, a differential double-acting cylinder of the design shown in Fig. 10-12 is used. In short the cylinder barrel is extended with a dummy barrel end to increase the distance between both cylinder mounting eyes. Nevertheless, the main differences between a standard double-acting cylinder and the one shown in Figure 10-12 are that the piston rod end is threaded to the piston rod, and an O ring is used to seal the area between the cylinder and the rod. The rod end has two supply ports. The piston rod is center-drilled, and into this bore a smaller tube is fastened. The tube is sealed to the piston with an O ring, and the other end of the tube is sealed to the piston end port, also with an O ring.

OPERATION When the piston rod end port receives oil from the directional control valve, the oil passes into the space between the tube and the piston rod and enters the rod side of the barrel through one or two holes in the piston rod. The piston is forced to the left, causing the oil to be forced through the center of the tube, into the rod end, out of the piston port, and back to the directional control valve.

Less common are the three-port, double-acting differential cylinders. This design is used where it is necessary to actuate in two directions concurrently (see Fig. 10-3). Also uncommon are the balance-type double-acting cylinders (see Fig. 10-3). Where the work requires two connections to the cylinder, and equal force and speed in both directions is mandatory, this cylinder type is used.

Telescoping Actuators Telescoping actuators of the one-way or double-acting cylinder type are used where space and stroke length are the important factors. This type of actuator finds primary application on dump trucks, spar trees in the lumber industry, and some scrapers. The one-way telescoping actuators are used on smaller rear dump trucks, whereas double-acting telescoping actuators are used on larger rear dump trucks. The two three-stage telescoping actuators shown in Figs. 10-13 and 10-14

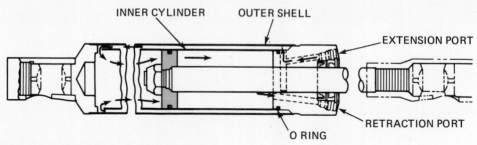

INNER CYLINDER   OUTER SHELL

EXTENSION PORT

RETRACTION PORT

O RING

Fig. 10-11 Sectional view of linkage steering cylinder.

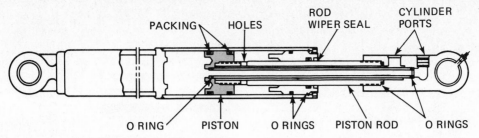

Fig. 10-12 Sectional view of a differential, double-acting, steering cylinder.

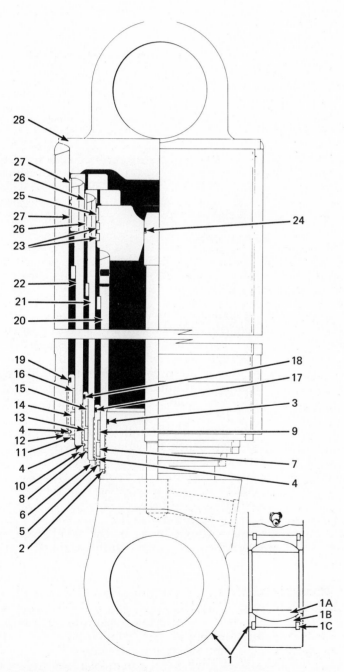

1. Rod end
2. Setscrew
3. O ring and backup ring
4. Nylon plug
5. Wiper
6. Gland
7. Seal
8. Wiper
9. Wear ring
10. Gland
11. Wiper
12. Gland
13. Seal
14. Seal
15. Wear ring
16. Wear ring
17. O ring and backup ring
18. O ring and backup ring
19. O ring and backup ring
20. 3rd stage cylinder
21. 2nd stage cylinder
22. 1st stage cylinder
23. Piston ring
24. O ring and backup ring
25. Wear ring
26. Wear ring
27. Wear ring
28. Housing
1A- Bearing
1B- Race
1C- Snap rings

Fig. 10-13 Sectional view of a three-stage telescoping-hoist cylinder. (*WABCO, An American-Standard Company*)

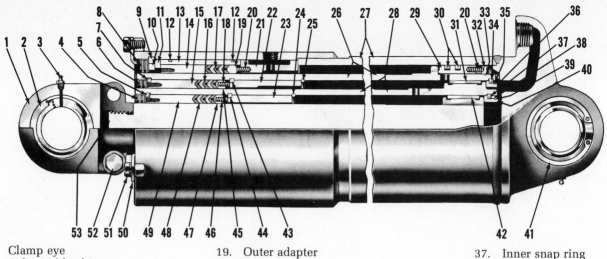

1. Clamp eye
2. Spherical bushing
3. Lube fitting
4. Inner wiper ring
5. Inner snap ring
6. Intermediate wiper ring
7. Intermediate snap ring
8. Outer wiper ring
9. Outer snap ring
10. Snap ring retainer
11. Retainer ring
12. O rings
13. Sleeve
14. Outer bushing
15. Intermediate bushing
16. Intermediate packing
17. Outer packing
18. Spring
19. Outer adapter
20. Spring
21. Outer spring retainer
22. Intermediate spring retainer
23. Inner spring retainer
24. Snap ring
25. Snap ring
26. Intermediate tube
27. Outer tube
28. Inner tube
29. Piston
30. Piston rings
31. Outer guide ring
32. Retainer ring
33. Snap ring
34. Intermediate snap ring
35. Snap ring
36. Intermediate thrust collar
37. Inner snap ring
38. Retainer ring
39. Snap ring
40. Inner thrust collar
41. Snap ring
42. Inner guide ring
43. Intermediate snap ring
44. Inner snap ring
45. Intermediate adapter
46. Springs
47. Inner adapter
48. Inner packing
49. Inner bushings
50. Outer seal clamps
51. Bolts and lockwashers
52. Bolts and nuts
53. Piston rod

Fig. 10-14 Three-stage, single-acting ejector cylinder (cutaway view). (*Terex Division of General Motors Corporation*)

are used on 120-ton rear dump trucks. The construction, as well as the seals, packings, and bearings, is different in design, but the general design and operation principle remain the same.

The three-stage actuator in Fig. 10-13 shows that the first-, second-, and third-stage cylinders are supported at the rod end by the cylinder glands and wear rings. The cylinder seals are special seals but could be V packings. The first-, second-, and third-stage cylinder heads are supported by wear rings, and the third-stage cylinder has additional piston rings. The rod end and cylinder head end bores use insert bearings consisting of a race and bearing, held in place by two snap rings. This type of bearing installation prevents damage to the cylinder due to misalignment in the event that the box or frame bends or twists when lifting a load.

When two telescoping cylinders are used, they could be mounted to the truck in either direction; that is, the rod ends of the cylinder could be fastened to the dump box body and the head end to the truck frame, or vice versa. When a single cylinder is used, it is sometimes swivel-mounted so that when it is fully retracted it lies nearly parallel with the truck frame.

OPERATION When the directional control valve of a three-stage, double-acting, cylinder-type, telescop-

ing actuator is moved to the raised position, oil is directed to and through a flow control valve or holding valve, and this allows an unrestricted flow to the hoist cylinder head ends. The oil pressure acts on the area of all three cylinders and so lifts or pushes them as a unit out of the housing or first-stage cylinder and housing is forced out as the first-stage cylinder extends through slots in the second-stage inder extends through slots in the second-stage cylinder. When the first-stage cylinder is fully extended, its stop ring has come to rest against the first-stage gland. However, the second- and first-stage cylinders are forced (as a unit) further outward. The oil trapped between the first- and second-stage space is forced out as the second-stage cylinder extends through holes in the third-stage cylinder. When the third stage is fully extended, its stop ring comes to rest against the third-stage gland.

Whenever the directional control valve is placed into the hold position, the oil flow to the cylinder stops, and the load check valve holds the pressure.

When the directional control valve is moved to the lowering position, the oil flow, to and from the cylinders, reverses its direction. However, the flow control valve or the holding valve restricts the return oil flow from the rod end side of the cylinder, reducing the lowering speed of the dump box and preventing a runaway.

The oil pressure acting on the head end area of all three cylinders is reduced, and (at the same time) the oil pressure acting on the rod end area of the third-stage cylinder increases, causing the third-stage cylinder to retract. When the third-stage cylinder is fully retracted, it comes to rest against the second-stage stop ring. The orifices in the third-stage cylinder align with the holes in the second-stage cylinder, allowing the pressure to build up in the area between the third- and second-stage cylinders. The pressure acting on the combined area of the third- and second-stage cylinders, along with the weight of the dump box, forces the second-stage cylinder to retract. When the second-stage cylinder is fully retracted, the pressure acting on the area of the third- and second-stage cylinders, and the weight of the dump box, force the first-stage cylinder to retract.

On some larger dump trucks, when the operator releases the directional control valve lever, the spring forces the valve spool into the float position, causing the valve spool to position in such a way that the oil is directed to retract the cylinders. The oil pressure is low because most of the pump oil returns to the reservoir, but it is sufficient to hold the dump body down (without floating upward).

Servicing Cylinder Actuators   A good maintenance program and good record keeping will indicate to you the operating condition of the entire hydraulic system, as well as a projected life span of the cylinder packing. However, over the span of a work shift, the cylinder barrel can become damaged or the piston rod bent. In either case, repair the damage immediately.

When you become aware, either through testing or through the operator's complaint, that the cylinders are losing their efficiency, they should be serviced instantly because, at this stage, only new packing may be required. To procrastinate may cause damage to the cylinder, the piston, or the rod and may cause the control valve to stick, or the filter to plug, or the pump to be damaged.

Because of the variations in cylinder mountings, a precise procedure for servicing cannot be outlined here. If, through testing, you find that a cylinder must be serviced, consult the appropriate service manual for the recommended steps to remove and service.

REMOVAL OF A CYLINDER   When possible, steam-clean the area you intend to work on to prevent the entry of dirt and to maintain working safety for yourself and others. A greasy cylinder, hose, frame, etc., could cause you to slip or to lose your grip.

Position and block the hydraulic equipment in such a way that you can remove the cylinder with ease. When the equipment is blocked, remove the pressure from all the cylinders by operating the directional control valve and then remove the pressure from the reservoir if so applicable. Use drip pans to prevent oil from dripping onto the floor. Use two wrenches to loosen the hose connections and disconnect them at a convenient place.

NOTE   When removing hydraulic lines, identify their positions to expedite reinstallation.

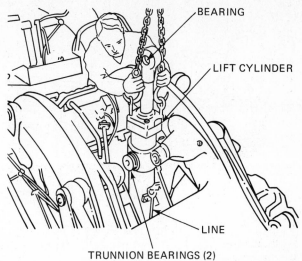

Fig. 10-15   Safe method to remove a hydraulic cylinder. (*Caterpillar Tractor Co.*)

Cap all openings instantly to prevent dirt from entering the system. Attach a suitable lifting device to the cylinder and then take the weight off the mounting pins. This action prevents exterior damage to the cylinder and facilitates removal of the mounting pins. Guide the cylinder when removing the pins and when lifting it from the machine to your work area (see Fig. 10-15).

DISASSEMBLY PROCEDURE   Again, the disassembly procedure varies somewhat, depending on the individual manufacturer's actuator design (with regard to size, cylinder barrel, cylinder head (gland), rod end, piston, and piston packing). In any case, care must always be taken not to damage the cylinder barrel or piston rod during the disassembly. Seek precise instructions from the service manual in regard to disassembly procedure and safety precautions.

Always hold the barrel end in a vise or in a special holding fixture rather than in the cylinder barrel itself, for this could cause damage to the barrel (see Fig. 10-16). Support the cylinder barrel by a suitable stand so that you can work freely at the rod end of the cylinder. Let the oil drain from the barrel into a suitable container. In some cases it is advisable to attach a short hose to each port for a safer draining procedure.

Remove the cylinder head by removing the bolts, or by unscrewing the cylinder head with a special wrench, or by forcing the head inward, and then remove the snap ring. You may have to loosen the rod's packing tension by unscrewing the piston nut or removing the bolts that hold the flange. When the cylinder head is loosened, support the piston rod and move it and the head from the barrel.

CAUTION   Do not allow the rod to cock, for this could damage the piston and barrel. Do not use shop air to blow out the piston, for this could damage the cylinder or cause an accident. When servicing a larger cylinder, it may be necessary to stand the cylinder upright, anchor it to the floor, and then use a

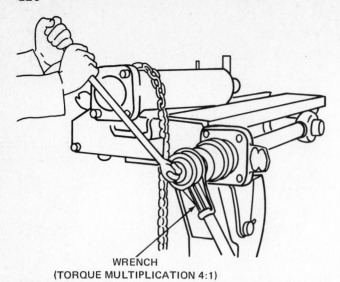

Fig. 10-16 Using a special holding fixture to disassemble the cylinder. (*Caterpillar Tractor Co.*)

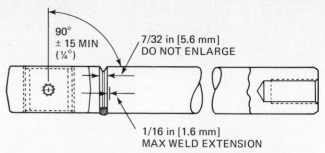

Fig. 10-17 Recommended preparation for welding the rod end to the piston rod. (*J I Case Company Agricultural Equipment Division*)

hoist to lift the rod assembly from the barrel. Such a large cylinder is not a job for one person—you will need help; otherwise you may get hurt or you may damage the components.

At this point of the disassembly it is advisable to examine the piston packing to determine the cause of failure. If the cylinder barrel is damaged, the packing will show a narrow wear mark over the total length of the packing, as well as on the wear ring. If the piston rod bearing is worn excessively, an excessive wear area will be prevalent over nearly half of the packing and wear ring. If the piston rod is bent, excessive wear will show on the upper and lower half of the packing assembly.

To remove the piston and cylinder head, hold the piston rod eye in a special holding fixture or device and support the rod so that no damage to it is possible.

CAUTION Use an impact wrench or a torque multiplier to ease loosening of the piston bolts or nuts and to prevent an accident (because the bolts or nuts are torqued up to 1500 lb·ft [2077.5 N·m]). Before removing the cylinder head, remove any nicks and burrs from the piston rod by using an oil stone.

INSPECTION AND SERVICING Discard all O rings, backup washers, packing and wiper seals, and the piston rod bearing. Wash all remaining parts in solvent and dry with compressed air. **NOTE** Use goggles.

Inspect the outer barrel area carefully; any dents may be transmitted to the inner side of the barrel. To restore the serviceability of the cylinder bore if the barrel shows a slight roughness or small high-spot, use a rigid cylinder hone and the same tool arrangement and setup as when honing the cylinder bore of an engine.

If the cylinder barrel is bell-mouthed or the threads are damaged, a replacement is necessary. Measure or check the barrel bushings for wear and fit. If a bushing is worn or loose within its bore, replace the bushing by using a portable or bench press. **CAUTION** Do not use a hammer to drive the bushing in place, for this could injure you or others nearby. Examine the cylinder head threads, grooves, and bore for excessive wear and for nicks and burrs. Restore the threads with a thread file. Check the piston rod for external damage and incorrect alignment. Your service manual will outline the conditions under which you can or cannot straighten the rod; the rod must be replaced (say, for instance, that it is damaged externally); a replacement eye can be welded to the rod if, say, the rod eye bore is elongated.

NOTE In the latter case, follow precisely the service manual instruction in regard to the removal of the old eye, the bevel of the rod edge, the welding rod, and the methods to be used to protect the rod during welding (see Fig. 10-17).

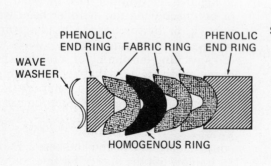
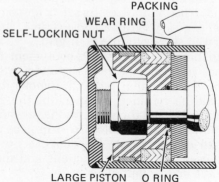

Fig. 10-18 Typical V packing, detailed and installed.

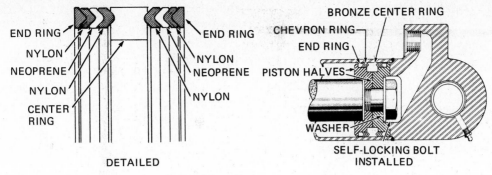

Fig. 10-19 Typical chevron packing, detailed and installed.

Remove any nicks and burrs by using an oil stone and then polish the rod with a 400-grit emery cloth, using rotary motion, not lengthwise motion. Check the piston or the two halves of the piston for damage on the grooves, bore, and surfaces. If the piston is not serviceable, replace it.

PISTON RODS, PISTON SEALS, AND PACKING Each manufacturer has its own seal design and packing arrangement, some of which are illustrated in this text. The most common piston rod and piston packings are the V type (Fig. 10-18) and the chevron type (Fig. 10-19), because their design and the material from which they are produced warrant a lengthy service life. These packings automatically increase their sealing effect with increased pressure, and they are self-wear compensating. Figure 10-19 illustrates the V seal's use where the application in a cylinder requires an effective seal in both directions. The assembly consists of two sets of triple V-lip-type seal rings, one of neoprene and two of nylon in each set. The center and end rings support the seal rings and act as bearings in order to prevent the seal rings from acting as bearings or carrying side thrust.

NOTE A packing should not serve as a bearing, and therefore the rate of compression is of great importance to the effectiveness and the service life of the seal rings.

When the application requires only one set of packings, a wear ring is used near the end of the piston to aid in piston stabilization.

The compression rate of a piston or rod packing is determined by the fixed distance (groove) of the two halves of the piston or by the length of the groove in the cylinder head. To achieve a good sealing effect, the chevron packing must have a clearance of about 0.005 to 0.015 in [0.127 to 0.381 mm], depending on the diameter of the piston or the piston rod.

When the rod packing is compressed by a retainer nut, tighten the nut only finger-tight during the reassembly procedure, and then, when it is installed to the machine, make the correct adjustment. When the packing is retained by a retainer plate, install the recommended shims between the cylinder head and retainer to ensure the specified clearance. To ensure that the seal does not act as a bearing, operate the cylinder and examine the extended piston rod. A light film of oil should be present on the rod when the adjustment of the rod packing is correct (see Fig. 10-20).

On large cylinders, seal rings and sometimes expanders are used as piston seals in addition to a wear ring or several wear rings. Some seal rings are Teflon, some are synthetic rubber, and some are a special alloy (see Fig. 10-21).

Cup or U seals are not commonly used as piston seals on today's hydraulic cylinders. Smaller hydraulic cylinders or cylinders that are not predominantly working cylinders use one or more O rings with a backup washer as the piston and piston rod seals. Some manufacturers use a nylon or Teflon U-cup piston rod seal which at the same time serves

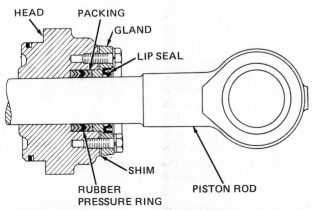

Fig. 10-20 Packing and shims installed. (*Caterpillar Tractor Co.*)

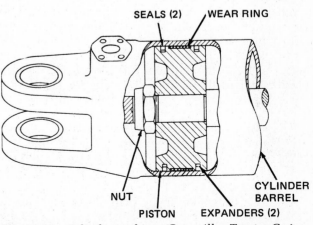

Fig. 10-21 Cylinder packing. (*Caterpillar Tractor Co.*)

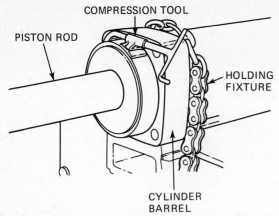

Fig. 10-22 Installing piston to cylinder. (*Caterpillar Tractor Co.*)

as the wiper seal, but in most cases the wiper seal is of the lip-type seal design.

REASSEMBLY OF CYLINDERS Clean all components thoroughly and lubricate all seals, packing, and O rings, but do not lubricate the backup washers. Install the cylinder head packing according to service manual specification. **NOTE** When a Teflon or nylon U-cap seal is used, treat it in hot water to make it pliable, then work quickly to install it.

Lubricate the piston rod and piston rod packing well before sliding the cylinder head onto the piston rod. Install the O ring and backup washers. Make certain the O ring and washer are not twisted and are properly located in the groove. Install to the piston the piston packings, as well as the wear rings, and make certain that they are correctly located and correctly positioned according to the service manual.

Install the O ring to the piston rod and then install the piston and torque the self-locking bolt or nut to the specified torque. Again lubricate the cylinder and the piston assembly well before sliding the cylinder barrel over the piston (see Fig. 10-22) or sliding the piston into the barrel. Be very careful that the piston packing is not damaged because of a cocked piston or because the barrel end is threaded or has a lock ring groove. When recommended, install a piston ring compressor to the piston to ensure a trouble-free installation. Most modern barrel designs do not require a ring compressor for safe assembly of the piston. If appropriate, align the cylinder head with the supply tube before pushing it into its position and secure the head with a snap ring, or align the cylinder head by supporting the piston rod to ensure that the cylinder head starts properly in the barrel without risk of cross-threading.

Lubricate the O ring just before it enters the barrel so that it will remain in its place and be forced to rotate with the cylinder head.

CYLINDER INSTALLATION Avoid lifting, carrying, or installing, by yourself, any cylinder that is heavier than 60 lb [27.24 kg]. Use a hoist or ask for a helper.

Using a sling around the cylinder barrel, lift

the rebuilt cylinder into position so that you can align and mount the piston end of the cylinder to the machine. Do not connect the hoses at this time.

CAUTION Under no circumstances start the engine or operate the directional control valve to extend or retract the piston rod. To do so may cause an accident and/or damage the rebuilt cylinders.

To align and connect the rod end eye with the mounting bore, remove the protection caps from the cylinder ports and push or pull the piston rod to make the proper alignment. On larger cylinder assemblies this method of alignment is not possible, for you require a hoist or a crane to lift or lower the equipment to make the alignment. The next step is to connect the hoses according to the identification tag on the cylinder ports.

Check and when necessary refill the reservoir. Start the engine and operate the directional control valve to remove the air from the cylinder and to check for leaks at the hose connection and rod packing.

Recheck the oil level and, if required, refill to the proper level before turning the machine over to the operator.

Hydraulic Motors (Rotary Actuators) The hydraulic motor is gaining wider acceptance in today's hydraulic systems because manufacturers have increased the efficiency of the hydraulic pumps, as well as the motors. Although this motor is well known to industry as a power source, it is far from reaching its full potential.

The design of hydraulic motors and pumps is basically the same. In fact, most hydraulic pumps could be used as hydraulic motors with very few modifications, even though the hydraulic pump needs a power source to produce an oil flow, whereas the hydraulic motor converts the fluid flow and pressure into rotary motion and torque.

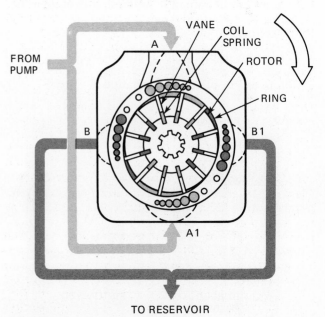

Fig. 10-23 Operations of high-performance vane motor. (*Sperry Vickers Division of Sperry Inc.*)

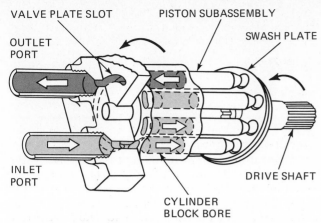

Fig. 10-24 Schematic view of a swash plate hydraulic motor. (*WABCO, An American-Standard Company*)

Hydraulic pumps are rated by their ability to pump fluid at a given speed against a fixed resistance. Hydraulic motors are rated in terms of displacement, pressure, and torque. Displacement refers to the quantity of oil in cubic inches (in³) or liters (l) necessary to rotate the motor one revolution, or gallons or liters per minute. Torque is expressed in pound-feet, pound-inches, and newton-meters (lb·ft, lb·in [N·m]) at a fixed pressure. That means the hydraulic motor can develop a torque of an X number of lb·ft [N·m] at a given pressure.

The preventative maintenance and servicing procedure for a hydraulic motor, and the procedure to determine the cause of motor failure, are the same as that for a hydraulic pump and therefore are not repeated here.

OPERATION Oil from the pump is directed through a directional control valve to either port of the motor and returns to the directional valve, or the pump oil outlet and inlet ports are connected to the motor ports. When the oil flow from and to the hydraulic pump is direct to the motor, it is called a "closed system." The oil enters the inlet port of the motor and fills the spaces formed between the gear teeth, housing, and end plate or the space formed between the vane, rotor, cam ring, and pressure plates. The resistance of the drive shaft causes a pressure rise within the pockets and creates a force onto the gear teeth, or onto the vanes, forcing the gears or rotor to rotate. At the same time the gear teeth mesh at the outlet port, or the vanes retract, forcing the oil out of the outlet port back to the directional control valve or to the inlet side of the pump (see Fig. 10-23).

When a nine-axial piston motor is used, four pistons are over the inlet slot, four pistons are over the outlet slot, and one piston is between the inlet and the outlet slots. This condition exists at all times (see Fig. 10-24), whether or not the motor is operating. When oil enters the inlet port, the resistance to drive shaft rotation causes a pressure rise within the hydraulic lines and the inlet line port valve slot and against the four piston areas positioned over the inlet valve slot. The four pistons are then forced outward against the swash plate, and because of the swash plate angle, the piston slides on the swash plate to the left. At this point the force of the four pistons is higher than the resistance of the drive shaft and causes the cylinder barrel and drive shaft to rotate also to the left. As the cylinder barrel starts to rotate, the other four pistons slide down the swash plate, causing them to discharge the oil into the outlet slot. At the same time the ninth piston cylinder bore opening (which was in neutral) moves over the motor inlet slot. The adjacent cylinder opening, which has just completed its discharge, moves into the neutral position. The piston that has completed its power stroke moves its cylinder bore opening over the discharge slot. Oil from the discharge slot goes to the outlet port, to the directional control valve, or to the inlet side of the hydraulic pump.

Review Questions

1. What is the purpose of an actuator?

2. The two main types of actuators are (a) the hydraulic cylinder and (b) the hydraulic motor. What is the major difference between them?

3. Although the single-acting cylinder and the hydraulic ram can perform the same operation, they have several different features. Describe these features.

4. Calculate the force reduction on the piston rod and on the piston when the pressure is 2000 psi, the piston area 8 in², and the rod area 3 in².

5. Explain the action of a limiting travel valve when the piston nears the end of its stroke.

6. Explain why the first piston of a telescoping piston must move to the end of its stroke before the second piston is forced out.

7. If the piston packing assembly shows excessive wear of about 1 in over the total length, to what would you attribute this condition?

8. If the piston packing assembly shows excessive wear on the lower or upper half, to what would you attribute this condition?

9. What are the advantages of using V or chevron packing?

10. Explain how you would verify that the piston rod packing is not tight, or is too loose, when the packing adjustment is made through the rod packing nut or shims.

11. Why are the inlet and outlet ports of a hydraulic motor equal in diameter?

12. What are the five main advantages of using a hydraulic motor instead of a mechanical drive?

Unit 11
Hydraulic Circuits

When traveling by automobile from one destination to another, it is best that you use the most recent road map available. In addition to the routes, maps include symbols to tell you the type of road construction you will encounter and the size of villages, towns, cities, and so forth.

When tracing the problems of a hydraulic system, you should also have an up-to-date and relevant "map," and this is provided by the service manual. The appropriate service manual includes exploded or perspective views or diagrams of the entire system, comparable in usefulness to any road map. It also includes various diagrams and cutaway views of major components and schematically outlines the oil flow within the system, among other things. Individual components, whether depicted by photographs or simplified drawings, are also identified by name.

As with the traveler's road map, your service manual is the best way to familiarize yourself sufficiently with the system's components and oil flow that you can service the system. Studying it carefully and following the outlined instructions is the quickest and most accurate way to learn the operation and interrelation of each particular system. Possessed of this knowledge, you can easily diagnose and evaluate system failure.

When developing a service manual, manufacturers address them to the user who has a basic knowledge of their product or products of similar construction. To help you gain this fundamental understanding and working knowledge of hydraulic systems, several are now illustrated and discussed, commencing with one used on a 120-ton rear dump truck.

Truck Hoist and Steering System   The purpose of this hydraulic system is to raise, hold, lower, and float the dump box safely and also, with the assistance of two steering cylinders, to steer the truck. An emergency steering supply system is an inherent part of the system to facilitate steering in event the main supply system fails.

A view of a truck hoist and steering system is shown in Fig. 11-1. Note that in this system the flow control valve is part of the hoist directional control valve, and the four-position directional control valve is actuated manually. When the system is equipped with accumulator steering, an air cylinder, controlled by a hoist control valve, is used. The hoist directional control valve is a three-way, four-position (down, hold, dump, and float positions), spring-centered valve. The reservoir holds 120 gal [454.0 l] and is pressurized from the truck's air system. This pressure is controlled by an air pressure regu-

lator that maintains a pressure of about 20 psi [137.8 kPa] within the reservoir. The pressure relief valve is set to about 25 psi [172.2 kPa] to protect the reservoir against damage if the air pressure at any time exceeds the set pressure.

The three-way air valve mounted to the reservoir is used to allow air to pass into the reservoir and to bleed air from the reservoir. The outlet oil filter has a 100-μm rating, and the return oil filter, a 30-μm rating. The two cartridge-type balance vane pumps supply a flow rate of 160 gal/min [605.6 l/min] at 2500 psi [17,225 kPa]. The working pressure is 1500 psi [10,335 kPa] at rated load. The two hoist cylinders are of the three-stage, double-acting cylinder

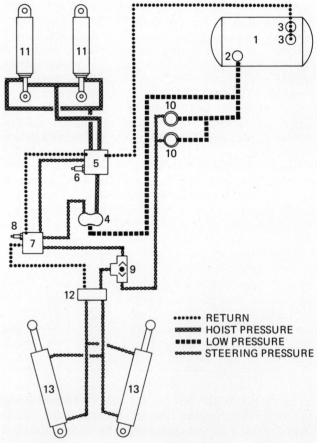

```
······ RETURN
▭▭▭▭ HOIST PRESSURE
■■■■ LOW PRESSURE
◌◌◌◌ STEERING PRESSURE
```

1. Reservoir	7. Flow divider (control valve)
2. Screen	8. Steering relief valve
3. Filters	9. Shuttle valve
4. Hydraulic pump	10. Emergency steering pump
5. Hoist control valve	11. Hoist cylinder
6. Hoist relief valve	12. Steering gear
	13. Steering cylinder

Fig. 11-1   Truck hoist and steering system schematically illustrated. (*WABCO, An American-Standard Company*)

design. There are two electric motor-driven emergency pumps which can supply oil to the steering system at 25 gal/min [94.62 l/min] at rated rpm if the main pump fails to supply oil.

OPERATION AND OIL FLOW When the engine is operating, oil at a pressure of 20 psi [137.8 kPa] is forced from the reservoir through a single line, into both vane pumps. The oil displaced by the small pump is directed to the flow divider valve, and when the steering valve is in neutral, the divider valve redirects the oil to the hoist control valve to join with that of the large pump. The oil displaced by the large pump is directed to and through the hoist control and back to the reservoir. When the hoist control lever is moved in the dump position, the hoist valve spool moves into the raised position, and oil is directed through the flow control valve into the hoist cylinders. Any time the operator releases the hoist control lever, the spring force of the hoist control valve spool forces the spool to the hold position and stops the dump action. When the hoist control valve lever is moved to the power lowering position, the oil flow is reversed. The dump box is then lowered by the hydraulic pressure because the flow control valve restricts the return oil flow. See the discussion of telescoping cylinders in Unit 10 for the hoist cylinder action and oil flow.

Dozer Hydraulic System The purpose of the dozer's hydraulic system is to hold, raise, lower, and float the blade; to tilt it inward or outward; or to hold it in a fixed position.

Figure 11-2 shows the location of the dozer's hydraulic system components, as well as of the cylinder connections. Note that only the ripper and tilt circuits use secondary relief valves and the anticavitation valve is effective only for the dozer circuit.

The reservoir has a capacity of 28 gal [94.62 l]. It is pressurized through the expansion of the oil and is protected by a pressure relief valve against over-pressurizing.

The multistage outlet screen has a 100- and a 40-mesh screen and the return filter is of a 25-μm rating. The directional control valve is bolted to the reservoir, and the return oil can pass directly into the reservoir. The dual-stage external gear pump supplies 79 gal/min [299 l/min] at rated pressure. The two main relief valves are set at a pressure of 2000 psi [13,780 kPa], and all secondary relief valves open at 2300 psi [15,847 kPa]. All cylinders are of the double-acting design. The dozer lift cylinders have quick-drop valves and limited travel valves (see the discussion of actuators in Unit 10).

OIL FLOW When the engine is operating and the three-valve spools are in hold position, the oil output of the large pump (front section) enters the control valve at the bottom, passes by the main relief valve, and then passes through the dozer's valve spool. Part of the oil flows into the right oil return passage and returns directly to the reservoir. The remaining part of the oil flows past the (floating) anticavitation valve and merges with oil flowing from the smaller (rear section) pump.

The output of the smaller pump enters the control valve at the top center. Oil passes by the second main relief valve and then merges with oil from the large pump to return through the left oil return passage to the reservoir.

When the dozer's valve spool is moved to the raised position, oil from both pumps is directed to the dozer's valve spool and flows past the load check valve into the rod end of the cylinder. Oil displaced by the piston returns to the valve spool and flows through and into the right return oil passage, while part of the oil passes the anticavitation valve and moves on through the left return oil passages (however, all the oil eventually reenters the reservoir).

The oil flow to the valve spool follows the same route whether in power-down position or in raised position. However, in the latter position the oil pressure closes the anticavitation valve. This closes the return passage, and oil then flows to the piston end of the cylinder, lowering the blade. **NOTE** No load check valve is used in this circuit. Oil displaced by the piston reenters the valve spool, opens the load check valve, and returns through the left and right passages to the reservoir. When applied pressure exceeds the main relief valve setting, one or both main relief valves open, allowing oil to flow into the return passage, reducing the pressure. When the pistons come to the end of their stroke, the limiting travel valves are open, reducing the applied pressure within the cylinder. However, if the blade drops quickly (the oil pressure from the pump being lower than the return pressure), the anticavitation valve moves downward because of the higher return pressure and allows return oil to merge with pump oil. In addition the quick-drop valves function simultaneously, preventing hesitation and cavitation (see the discussion of actuators in Unit 10).

When the dozer's valve spool is moved to float position, the detent holds it in this position. Owing to the spool position (and porting), the oil output from both pumps enters and passes through the dozer's valve spool, although some of it returns to the right return passage back to the reservoir. The remaining oil passes by the anticavitation valve into the left return passage back to the reservoir. The (low) oil pressure at the rod end and piston end of the cylinder is the same as that in the reservoir and maintains the cylinders full of oil but allows the blade to move up and down to follow the contour of the ground.

When the operator moves the tilt valve spool to tilt the blade forward (left) or backward (right), output oil from the large pump flows unrestricted through the dozer's valve spool into the right return passage and then back to the reservoir (see Fig. 11-3). Part of the oil flow passes the anticavitation valve, flows into the left return passage, and then returns to the reservoir. The small pump supplies oil only to the tilt cylinder valve spool (reducing the tilt speed), and when the applied pressure is higher than the load, the load check valve opens, allowing oil to flow into the cylinder. Return oil from the cylinder

126

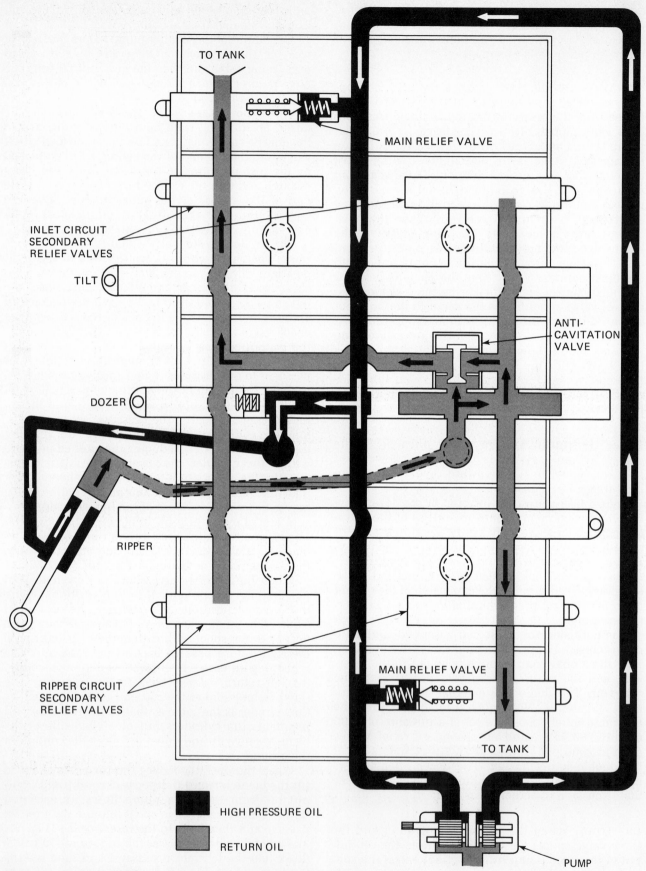

TO TANK

MAIN RELIEF VALVE

INLET CIRCUIT
SECONDARY
RELIEF VALVES

TILT

ANTI-
CAVITATION
VALVE

DOZER

RIPPER

RIPPER CIRCUIT
SECONDARY
RELIEF VALVES

MAIN RELIEF VALVE

TO TANK

HIGH PRESSURE OIL

RETURN OIL

PUMP

Fig. 11-2 Dozer hydraulic system; oil flow in raised position. (*Fiat-Allis*)

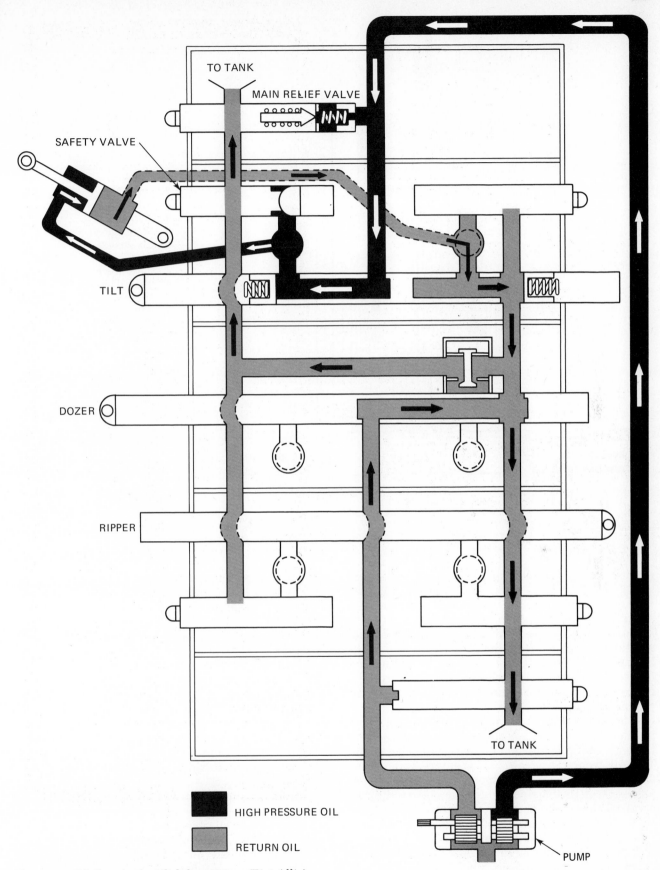

TO TANK

MAIN RELIEF VALVE

SAFETY VALVE

TILT

DOZER

RIPPER

TO TANK

HIGH PRESSURE OIL

RETURN OIL

PUMP

Fig. 11-3 Oil flow in the tilt left position. (*Fiat-Allis*)

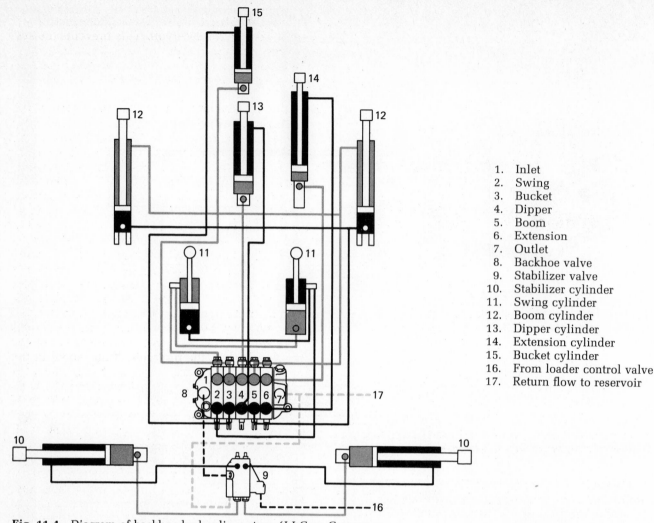

1. Inlet
2. Swing
3. Bucket
4. Dipper
5. Boom
6. Extension
7. Outlet
8. Backhoe valve
9. Stabilizer valve
10. Stabilizer cylinder
11. Swing cylinder
12. Boom cylinder
13. Dipper cylinder
14. Extension cylinder
15. Bucket cylinder
16. From loader control valve
17. Return flow to reservoir

Fig. 11-4 Diagram of backhoe hydraulic system. (*J I Case Company Agricultural Equipment Division*)

reenters the valve spool, opens the other load check valve, and then flows through the left and right return passages back to the reservoir. The purpose of directing the return oil through the load check valve is to prevent a reverse oil flow when the valve spool position is changed from the tilt-forward to the tilt-back position. When the top main relief valve setting is reached by the system's pressure, it opens and the oil returns to the reservoir, reducing the applied pressure.

When the operator moves the ripper valve spool to the lower or raised position, only the flow from the large pump is directed to the ripper valve spool. The oil from the small pump enters and passes through the dozer's valve spool, and part of the oil passes through the right return passage to the reservoir. The remainder of the oil passes by the anticavitation valve, to and through the left return passage, and back to the reservoir.

The oil from the large pump enters the ripper valve spool, opens the load check valve, and passes on to the ripper cylinder. Return oil from the cylinder reenters the valve spool, opens the load check valve, and returns to the reservoir, through the left and right return passages. When the ripper or tilt valve spool is in neutral and the pressure in the tilt or ripper circuits exceeds the secondary relief valve

setting, the valve opens. When the valve opens, pressure in the tilt or ripper circuits is reduced, and this in turn protects the cylinders and also prevents excessive strain on the equipment.

Backhoe Hydraulic Circuit The purpose of a backhoe hydraulic system or excavator hydraulic system is to raise, lower, and hold the boom; to extend and retract the dipper; to roll the bucket in and out; to swing the boom to the left or to the right; and to raise, lower, and hold each individual stabilizer in a fixed position. With the combined effort of all individual circuits the operator can excavate the soil and move it to one side or the other or load it into a truck.

The hydraulic circuits are protected by high- or low-pressure secondary relief valve(s). Regeneration (anticavitation) valves are used to prevent hesitation and cavitation. Many backhoes are designed with extending booms to increase their digging depth, in which case an additional control valve section and cylinder is added. This type of backhoe can then extend, retract, and hold the boom extension in a fixed position. **NOTE** Most modern backhoes and excavators also have a boom lock valve which increases their load-handling capacity. A diagram of a backhoe hydraulic system is shown in Fig. 11-4.

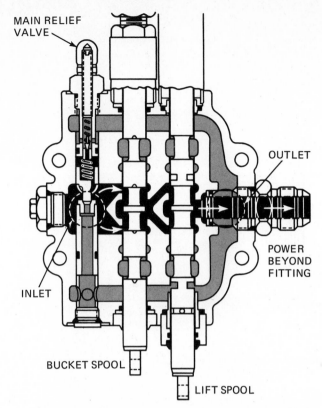

MAIN RELIEF VALVE

OUTLET

POWER BEYOND FITTING

INLET

BUCKET SPOOL

LIFT SPOOL

Fig. 11-5 Schematic illustration of oil flow with the loader control valve in neutral. (*J I Case Company Agricultural Equipment Division*)

Its reservoir has a capacity of 17 gal [64 l] and it is atmospherically vented. The return filter has a 40-μm rating, and the outlet filter is a 100 wire mesh screen. The single-stage external gear pump supplies a flow of 24 gal/min [91.1 l/min] at 2000 rpm. The main relief valve is set at 2000 psi [13,780 kPa] and the high-pressure secondary relief valve of the dipper and bucket and the raise circuit of the boom cylinders are set at 2400 psi [16,536 kPa]. The secondary relief valve of the boom cylinder's down pressure circuit is set at 700 psi [4823 kPa] and the swing circuit's secondary relief valves are set at 1800 psi [12,402 kPa]. The sectional control valve assembly is of the open center spool design and includes a regeneration valve and check valve. The swing control valve section has, in addition, two anticavitation valves. The specially designed stabilizer directional control valve is of a fail-safe design.

NOTE All hydraulic cylinders are of the double-acting design.

OIL FLOW WHEN VALVE IS IN NEUTRAL Oil from the hydraulic pump is directed to and through the loader directional control valve, then flows through the stabilizer control valve, to and through the sectional control valve assembly of the backhoe, and then back to the reservoir.

To protect the entire hydraulic system from series pressure buildup between the two directional control valves, only the first directional control (loader) valve has a main relief valve and a power-beyond fitting. The fitting is installed to provide a series oil flow to the backhoe control valve and separate return oil flow from the loader and backhoe directional control valve to the reservoir. This prevents the system pressure from rising to the relief valve setting of the combined pressure of the loader and backhoe main relief valves (see Fig. 11-5).

OIL FLOW IN THE POWER-BEYOND CIRCUIT When both directional control valves are in neutral, oil from the pump enters the loader valve and passes through the center passage, then through the power-beyond fitting, and on to the backhoe directional control valve. It then flows through the center of the backhoe directional control valve and back to the reservoir. When one valve spool in the backhoe directional control valve is activated, the oil flow is stopped in the center passage. The pressure rises in the parallel passage, opening the load check valve and allowing oil to flow out of one port to the actuator, while return oil (from the actuator) enters the other port and flows through the return passage, back to the reservoir. If the pressure rises above the main relief valve setting, the main relief valve opens and directs oil into and through the return passage, out of the valve, and back to the reservoir. If one spool in the loader directional control valve is fully actuated, the flow is stopped at the center passage and there is no oil flow to the backhoe directional valve. The pressure rises in the first directional valve parallel passage, opens the load check valve, and allows the oil to flow to the actuator.

If the spool in the loader directional control valve is only partly moved to activate the cylinder, the oil flow in the center passage is only partly restricted, reducing the supply to the actuator, reducing the actuating speed, but allowing the remaining pump oil to pass on to the backhoe directional control valve and to be used to actuate a cylinder.

The action and the oil flow of the individual valve section, as well as the action and oil flow of the high- and low-pressure secondary relief valve, is the same in all valve sections. However, oil flow and action within the swing section directional control valve is slightly different because it has two additional anticavitation valves (see Fig. 11-6). (See discussion of sectional control valves in Unit 9.) These valves prevent voids or air pockets from occurring when the swing valve spool is placed in neutral position, but the boom continues to move of its own inertia. The additional movement, owing to the unequal movement of the piston within the swing cylinders, results in a pressure rise in the return line (15), unseats the low-pressure relief valve (19), and allows the oil to flow into the return passage. This unseats the anticavitation valve (21) and redirects the oil to the other side of the swing pistons.

NOTE One of the anticavitation valves opens when the valve spool is actuated and the pressure in the parallel circuit is below the set pressure of the regeneration valve.

The hydraulic swing circuit of an excavator is much the same as that of a backhoe except, of course, that the swing cylinders are replaced with a single- or dual-stage hydraulic motor that drives the swing transmission.

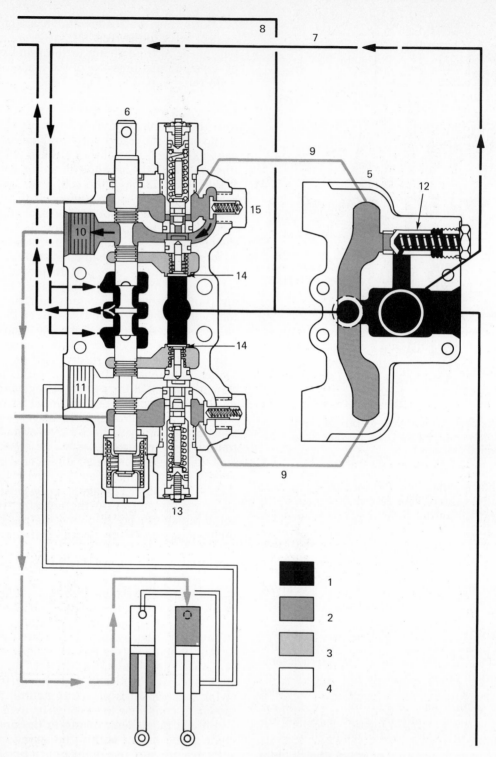

1. Pump flow
2. Return oil
3. Static oil
4. Oil displaced from swing cylinders
5. Inlet
6. Swing
7. Open center passage (internal)
8. Parallel passage (internal)

9. Return passage
10. A port
11. B port
12. Regeneration check valve
13. Secondary relief valve open
14. Load check valve
15. From pump via loader control valve and stabilizer control valve

Fig. 11-6 Oil flow with boom swinging to the right and stopping.
(*J I Case Company Agricultural Equipment Division*)

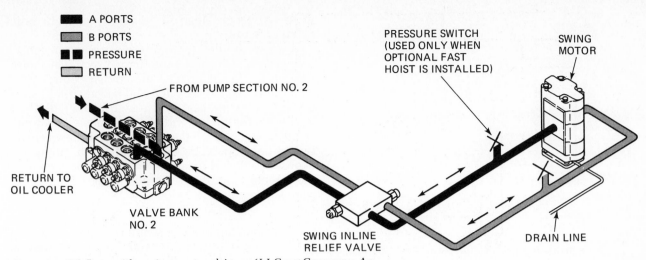

■ A PORTS
▨ B PORTS
■▬ PRESSURE
▬ RETURN

FROM PUMP SECTION NO. 2

PRESSURE SWITCH
(USED ONLY WHEN
OPTIONAL FAST
HOIST IS INSTALLED)

SWING
MOTOR

RETURN TO
OIL COOLER

VALVE BANK
NO. 2

SWING INLINE
RELIEF VALVE

DRAIN LINE

Fig. 11-7 Oil flow with swing motor driven. (*J I Case Company Agricultural Equipment Division*)

Commonly, the anticavitation valves and the lower pressure relief valves are removed from the swing section of the directional control valve and are combined with and placed into a separate valve body which is then inserted in the line of the swing motor circuit (see Fig. 11-7). Instead of the two secondary relief valves and anticavitation valves, two high-pressure secondary relief valves are installed in the directional control valve.

OPERATION When the operator moves the swing valve spool to make a right-turn swing, oil is directed unrestricted through the swing relief valve into the hydraulic motor(s) and flows back from the hydraulic motor(s) to the swing relief valve, directional control valve, and then back to the reservoir. If at the start of the oil flow the pressure rises above the set pressure of the swing relief valve (which is about 70 percent of that of the main relief valve), or the oil flow to the swing motors is suddenly stopped, or the oil flow is reversed, one relief valve opens and directs oil into the low-pressure line. As a result the swing action is cushioned and cavitation is avoided by redirecting the oil to the low-pressure side.

When the swing valve spool is in neutral and an external side force is exerted onto the upper structure, the oil pressure in one hydraulic line increases and the swing relief valve responds to the high pressure and redirects the oil into the low-pressure line. However, if the external force is higher and the swing relief valve cannot handle the high volume of oil that has to be released to reduce the pressure, the pressure rises, causing one of the high-pressure secondary relief valves to be forced open and allowing additional oil to be directed into the return passage of the directional control valve.

The combined action of both relief valves protects the superstructure from being damaged and at the same time prevents cavitation.

Boom Lockout As mentioned previously, most modern excavators or backhoes have a boom lockout system to increase the load-handling capacity of the boom (see Fig. 11-8). These valves are simple direc-

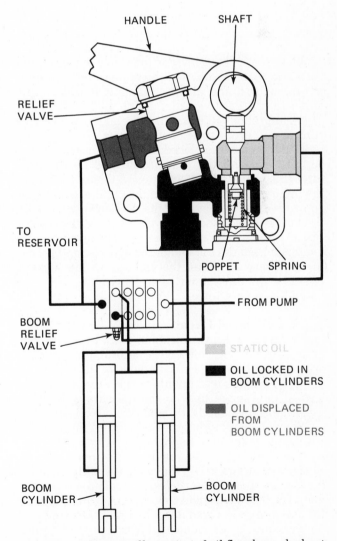

HANDLE   SHAFT

RELIEF
VALVE

TO
RESERVOIR

BOOM
RELIEF
VALVE

POPPET   SPRING

FROM PUMP

STATIC OIL

OIL LOCKED IN
BOOM CYLINDERS

OIL DISPLACED
FROM
BOOM CYLINDERS

BOOM
CYLINDER

BOOM
CYLINDER

Fig. 11-8 Schematic illustration of oil flow boom lockout circuit, in lockout position. (*J I Case Company Agricultural Equipment Division*)

132

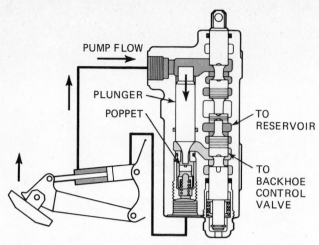

Fig. 11-9 Schematic view of oil flow to raise the stabilizer. (*J I Case Company Agricultural Equipment Division*)

tional control valves having a poppet valve (instead of a valve spool) and a built-in relief valve. The poppet valve is opened and closed through an eccentric shaft.

OPERATION AND OIL FLOW The lockout valve is placed in series with the rod end circuit of the boom cylinder.

When the lockout lever is placed to the right, the eccentric shaft rotates, and the plunger lifts the poppet off its seat and allows an unrestricted oil flow either to or from the rod end side of the cylinders. The main relief valve and the secondary relief valve control and protect the boom circuits.

When the lever is placed to the left, as shown, the spring force and the pressure created by the load force the poppet to seat, closing off the oil flow from the rod ends of the boom cylinders to the directional control valve. However, if the pressure (created by the load) exceeds the relief valve setting of 2750 psi [18,947.5 kPa], the valve opens and allows some oil to escape from the rod end of the cylinder and return to the reservoir. When the valve is in the lockout position, the directional control valve can raise the boom but cannot lower it hydraulically.

Stabilizer Control Circuit In the interest of safety of the operator and the machine, most hydraulic circuits which would otherwise be prone to accident are equipped with a fail-safe device. These devices may be a single-, or a double-check valve or a valve specially designed to hold the pressure within the circuit until the load is lowered through oil pressure.

When an even higher safety factor is required, the valve is installed directly to the actuator. In this case, since no hydraulic lines are used to connect the cylinder ports to the valve, the valve instantly closes if a hydraulic line breaks. Because oil cannot leave the cylinder, the load is held stationary. Furthermore the load cannot be lowered until the line is repaired and oil pressure is activated to lower the load under power. **NOTE** When the load creates a higher pressure than the setting of the main relief valve, it is very difficult to lower the load, in which case you

must reduce the load or increase the main relief valve pressure.

A valve similar to the single- or double-check valve is used within the stabilizer directional control valve (see Fig. 11-9). The directional control valve is of the open center design and has a spring-loaded poppet valve and seat positioned in the outlet port leading to the piston end of the actuator. A plunger is positioned above the poppet valve between the two outlet ports. The upper end of the plunger is exposed to the oil pressure leading to the rod end of the actuator, and the lower end of the plunger rests against the poppet valve.

OIL FLOW When the operator moves the valve spool to lower the stabilizer, oil from the pump forces the poppet valve off its seat and allows the oil to pass to the piston end of the actuator, lowering the stabilizer. The oil displaced by the piston returns to the directional control valve and then returns directly to the reservoir.

As soon as the valve spool returns to the hold position, the pressure created by the load closes the poppet, blocks the return flow, and the stabilizer piston is then held in a fixed position.

When the operator moves the valve spool to raise the stabilizer, the oil passes by the upper spool land and into the rod end of the cylinder. The pressure rises and the force on the plunger increases, but nothing happens until the force on the plunger is higher than the opposing force created by the load on the poppet valve. When this occurs, the plunger forces the poppet valve from its seat, allowing the oil from the piston end to return to the reservoir.

Loader Hydraulic System The purpose of a loader hydraulic system is to hold, raise, lower, and float the bucket and to hold and tilt the bucket forward and backward.

An illustration of an articulated loader hydraulic system is shown in Fig. 11-10. The reservoir has a capacity of 105 gal [397.4 l] and serves a dual function, because it is at the same time the power steering reservoir. The return filter has a micron rating of 80, the pump inlet screen has a 100 wire mesh rating, and both are located within the reservoir. The reservoir is pressurized from the engine air box, and a check valve is placed in the line to prevent a reverse air flow. A combination pressure relief and vacuum valve is located on top of the reservoir to protect it against high and low pressure (not shown). A single-stage external gear pump having a rating of 68 gal/min [257.3 l/min] at a pressure of 2100 psi [14,469 kPa] is used. The directional control valve is of the open center design with the main relief valve built in. A separate tilt cylinder relief valve is inserted in the actuating line of the tilt cylinder piston ends. The return line from the tilt cylinder relief valve is connected to the common system return line. A one-way check valve is used to prevent lift cylinder cavitation. It is inserted between the common return line and the actuating line of the lift cylinders' rod ends (not shown).

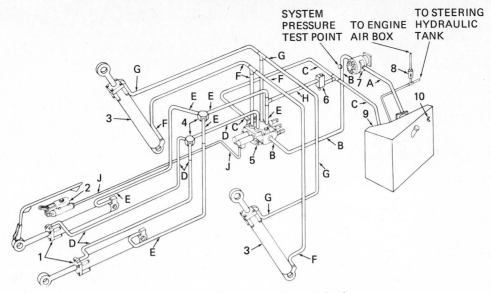

1.	Tilt cylinders
2.	Bucket leveler master cylinder
3.	Lift cylinders
4.	Manifolds
5.	Control valve
6.	Tilt relief valve
7.	Pump
8.	Check valve
9.	Hydraulic tank
10.	Pressure release cock

A Pump inlet line
B Pump outlet line
C Return line
D Line connecting the bucket cylinder (rod end) with the directional control valve
E Lines connecting the bucket cylinder (piston end) with the directional control valve
F Lines connecting the lift cylinder (piston end) with the directional control valve
G Lines connecting the lift cylinder (rod ends) with the directional control valve

Fig. 11-10 Schematic view of a loader hydraulic system. (*Terex Division of General Motors Corporation*)

OPERATION As soon as the engine is operating, air from the air box pressurizes the reservoir to about 5 psi [34.45 kPa]. When all valve spools are in neutral, the oil from the hydraulic pump is directed into and through the directional control valve and back to the reservoir. When the lift cylinder valve spool is moved to raise the bucket, oil is directed onto the load check valve, and when the oil pressure is higher than the pressure created by the load, the check valve is forced open and oil flows to the piston end of the lift cylinders. The piston rod then extends and the bucket is raised. Oil returning from the rod end of the lift cylinders is directed back to the directional control valve and from there back to the reservoir. If, for one reason or another, an additional load is placed on the bucket which would cause the applied pressure to increase beyond the main relief valve setting, this valve opens but maintains the maximum pressure. When the lift cylinder valve spool is placed into the lowering position, the oil flow reverses. Pump oil is directed to the rod end of the lift cylinders and the oil displaced by the piston returns to the valve spool and from there back to the reservoir. If, under this circumstance, the return oil pressure increases to more than the applied pressure (pump pressure) because the engine is at low idle and/or the bucket has dropped quickly, the higher return pressure opens the check valve and directs return oil into the rod ends of the lift cylinders. Cavitation is then prevented and the likelihood of air's passing by the piston rod packing is minimized.

When the lift valve spool is placed in the float position, the spool position allows the pump oil (which is under very low pressure) to flow back to the reservoir and also directs oil to the rod end and piston end of the lift cylinder. This oil flow maintains full cylinders at all times and allows the bucket to follow the contour of the ground.

The oil flow to and from the bucket tilt cylinders, when in the tilt-back or dump position, is the same as that in the lift cylinder circuit.

To protect the tilt cylinders, the bucket, the loader arms, and the machine from being damaged, the bucket dump circuit is protected through a secondary relief valve. When the tilt valve spool is in neutral position and an additional load is added to the bucket (owing to shock loads, binding, or loading conditions), the pressure increases in the piston end of the cylinders, as well as in the lines leading to the directional control valve and tilt relief valve. The relief valve is forced open, relieving the high pressure.

Automatic Lift Control Many modern hydraulic lift circuits, as well as fork lifts and lift trucks, use mechanical, hydraulic, electrical, or air-actuated lift controls which automatically limit the lift height of the bucket or of the forks. This control device shortens the lifting and lowering cycles and at the same time allows the operator free use of one hand to handle the machine more safely.

An electrical control system consists of a solenoid

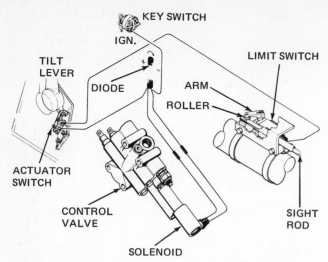

Fig. 11-11 Schematic view of an electrical control system. (*J I Case Company Agricultural Equipment Division*)

attached to the lift cylinder spool valve and of an actuating switch attached to the loader frame. An actuating lever is bolted to the loader lift arm, and either the lever or the actuator switch is adjustable to adjust the lift height (see Fig. 11-11).

OPERATION When the engine is operating, current is present at one switch terminal. When the lift valve spool is placed in the raised position, the loader arms and tilt lever pivot, and as the lever comes into contact with the actuator switch, the control closes and the electric circuit is completed over the limited switch to ground, energizing the solenoid. This action pulls or pushes the spool valve to neutral, stopping the hydraulic action. To increase or lower the lift height, the switch or the lever is moved to close the switch earlier or later.

Air-Actuated Lift Control System An air-actuated lift control system consists of an air kickout valve and an air kickout cylinder. The kickout valve is bolted to one side of the loader frame so that the kickout valve lever rests against the lift arm kickout cam, which is adjustably attached to the lift arm (see Fig. 11-12). The kickout cylinder is screwed to the directional control valve lift spool, and they are connected by an air line. The inlet port A of the kickout valve is connected through an air line with the air brake reservoir.

OPERATION When the lift valve spool is placed in the raised position, the detent holds the spool, causing the loader arms to rise and rotate the kickout arm. As soon as the cam moves the lift arm kickout lever, the exhaust valve closes and the inlet valve is forced open. Air is directed to the kickout cylinder, forcing its piston assembly to the right and pushing the lift spool into the neutral position. When the lift valve spool is placed into the lowering position, the kickout cam rotates as the loader arms are lowered, allowing the lever to move to the right. The air inlet valve closes and the exhaust valve opens, releasing the air pressure from the kickout cylinder.

Automatic Tilt-back Stop (Bucket Leveler) As the name indicates, these devices are used on loader bucket tilt-back circuits to speed the loading and unloading cycle and to allow the operator free use of one hand. These devices could also be mechanical, hydraulic, electrical, or air controlled.

A hydraulic bucket leveler consists of an actuating lever and a conventional master cylinder. The master cylinder is bolted to the loader arm and connected with a hydraulic line to the tilt plunger cover. The actuator lever is bolted at one end to one tilt cylinder piston rod, and the other end rests on a lever that is pivot-fastened to the master cylinder and master cylinder push rod (see Fig. 11-10).

OPERATION When the tilt valve spool is placed in the tilt-back position, the valve spool is held by its detent, causing the bucket to tilt backward until the firm cam on the actuator rod pivots the lever and moves the pushrod. This action displaces fluid from the master cylinder onto the tilt plunger piston, moves the valve spool out of its detent, and the valve spool spring positions the spool valve in neutral position. If the valve spool is moved again to the tilt-back position, the first cam allows the master cylinder to come to the neutral position, releasing the applied pressure. As the second cam on the actuator rod pivots the lever again, the master cylinder is actuated, and the bucket rollback is again stopped just before the pistons are fully retracted.

TROUBLESHOOTING, TESTING, AND PREVENTIVE MAINTENANCE

When a hydraulic system does not perform adequately, the defect may be within (1) the oil supply circuit, (2) the hydraulic pump, (3) the control valves, (4) the cylinders, or (5) the hoses and fittings.

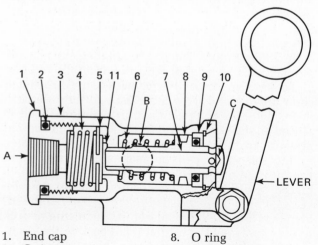

1. End cap
2. O ring
3. Valve body
4. Spring
5. Inlet valve
6. Spring
7. Plunger
8. O ring
9. Seal assembly
10. Snap ring
11. Exhaust valve
A. Inlet port
B. Port to kickout cylinder
C. Exhaust port

Fig. 11-12 Schematic view of an air-actuated lift kickout valve. (*Terex Division of General Motors Corporation*)

Preliminary Checking Before commencing any checks or tests, review the vehicle's service records, if available, to determine what work has already been done. Also interrogate the operator to ascertain (1) what the general problem is, (2) when the trouble was first noticed, (3) whether or not any unusual noise preceded the trouble, (4) when the filter was last changed and the screen cleaned, (5) when the last maintenance checks were performed, (6) how the engine reacts when lifting a heavy load or when forcing the dozer blades into the ground, (7) whether the entire hydraulic system has lost its operating speed or only one circuit is faulty, (8) whether the entire hydraulic system has lost its power or only one circuit is causing problems, (9) whether or not the actuators are spongy.

Evaluation of the information gathered will disclose to you the component or components causing the problem. If it is not possible to interrogate the operator, you should first check the areas most likely to cause problems, such as the oil level and the condition of the oil. Check the general condition of the engine, as well as the mechanical and hydraulic condition of the machine.

Worn pins and bushings or a bent or twisted loader arm, dump box, boom, or dipper stick will cause additional friction. Check for damaged hydraulic tubes, fittings, or hoses which cause increased restriction and reduced speed and pressure.

NOTE When fittings are pulled from the hose ends or a hose is broken, check the hose installation. The hose may be too short or too long or may be twisted, the fitting may be overtorqued, or the secondary relief valve may not have been operating or may have been set above the recommended opening pressure.

Then check the operating condition of the engine. If necessary, adjust high idle. Retract one actuator fully, so that the engine has to operate against the maximum relief valve pressure. Note the engine response and the rpm. If necessary, consider stall testing the engine by using the power shift transmission.

When all checks have been made and evaluated and the cause of the problem narrowed down to, say, the oil supply, the pump, the control valves, or the cylinders, confirm your diagnosis and the percentage of wear or malfunction within the component or system by making several circuit tests with a flowmeter or by using the cycle and drift test.

Flowmeters With the use of a flowmeter you can simulate the load condition of the hydraulic system encountered by the machine during operation. This instrument measures the flow rate, the temperature, and the pressure against which the oil is flowing. By evaluating these measurements, when testing under a prescribed procedure, you can not only locate the problem but also determine the efficiency of the components.

CONSTRUCTION A flowmeter Fig. 11-13 consists of a mechanical or electric measuring device that has the capacity to measure the flow rate (lpm or gpm)

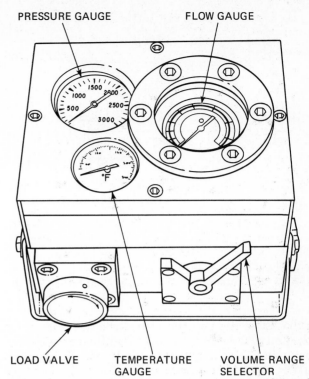

Fig. 11-13 Flowmeter. (*J I Case Company Agricultural Equipment Division*)

and to transmit its measurement to a scale so that an instant readout can be made. A temperature gauge indicates the temperature of the oil flowing through the tester. A valve or switch is able to select a low and high scale, for example, 10 and 100 gal/min [37.85 and 378.5 l/min]. The pressure with which the oil is forced through the flowmeter is recorded by the pressure gauge. A metering valve within the flowmeter, in the form of a load control valve, is able to increase or decrease the flow and thereby control the pressure simulating the load.

HOOKUP The flowmeter can be connected to the system in any one of three ways: (1) direct hookup, (2) T hookup, or (3) combination hookup (see Fig. 11-14).

When the flowmeter is connected directly to the system, you are able to test only the oil supply system and the efficiency of the pump, leaving the balance of the system unknown. When the flowmeter is connected to the system, in a T hookup, you are able to test the hydraulic circuit, including the main relief valve and low-pressure secondary relief valve. You cannot, however, properly test the oil supply system or the efficiency of the pump. The T hookup, then, can be used only when the efficiency of the oil supply system and pump is known, for example, if you have previously tested the oil supply system and the pump.

A complete system test can be made with a combination hookup in which the flowmeter is connected in T hookup and a shutoff valve is installed after the T. This setup is disadvantageous in that it is not always possible to obtain, for all hydraulic systems, the fittings needed to connect the shutoff

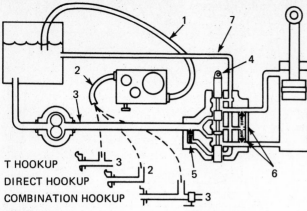

T HOOKUP

DIRECT HOOKUP

COMBINATION HOOKUP

1. Flowmeter return
2. Flowmeter in
3. To system
4. Directional control valve
5. Main relief valve
6. Secondary relief valves
7. System return

Fig. 11-14 Three ways of flowmeter connection.

valve to the system. However, the advantage is that the entire system can be tested with one hookup.

INSTALLATION   Before loosening any lines, lower or rest all hydraulic equipment on the ground and check the oil level and the engine high-idle rpm. Remove the pressure from the reservoir and the cylinders by moving the directional valve spools back and forth.

Install the flowmeter inlet hose and the shutoff valve at a convenient place between the pump and the directional control valve so that the shutoff valve is between the flowmeter and the control valve. Position and fasten the flowmeter return line so that the end of the hose is below the reservoir oil level. Finally, fully open the load control valve and the shutoff valve.

When the combination hookup is made, record the test specifications from the service manual and transfer them to the checksheet. If you are not familiar with the hydraulic circuit or with its valve design, operation, or location, refer to your service manual and study it carefully.

Assume that, for an angle, tilt dozer, and ripper hydraulic circuit (with no quick-drop valve or limiting travel valve), you have the following test specifications: hydraulic system refilling capacity, 41 gal [155.2 l]; engine rpm high idle, 2000 rpm; converter stall, 1780 ± 30 rpm; pump volume (no load, 2000 rpm), 79 gal/min [299.0 l/min]; main relief valve, 2000 psi [13,780 kPa]; secondary relief valve down pressure, 1500 psi [10,335 kPa]; all safety valves (secondary relief valves), 2300 psi [15,847 kPa]; normal oil temperature, 190°F [88°C].

Start the engine and operate it at 1000 rpm and close the load control valve to obtain a pressure of about 500 psi [3445 kPa]. When the engine is at the operating temperature, increase the engine speed to high idle and adjust the load control valve to obtain a pressure of about 1500 psi [10,335 kPa]. Now operate the control valves to bring the oil temperature to at least 100°F [38°C] above the ambient temperature. When the oil is at the recommended temper-

ature, you are ready to make the first three essential tests: (1) the oil supply system, (2) the efficiency of the pump, and (3) the main relief valve. Next, test the efficiency of the individual circuits.

Testing the Oil Supply System   The purpose of testing the oil supply system is to determine the efficiency of the circuit between the pump and the reservoir (the oil supply circuit). To perform this test, open the load control valve fully and close the shutoff valve. This causes all the oil from the pump output to flow through the flowmeter and back to the reservoir with no load (pressure) imposed on the pump. Next, operate the engine at high idle. The pressure on the pressure gauge should read zero, and the flowmeter should indicate 79 gal/min [299.01 l/min]. If the reading is less than 79 gal/min [299.01 l/min] during this test, there are three possibilities to be considered: (1) the oil supply to the pump may be restricted, (2) there may be air in the system, or (3) the pump may be worn.

Pump supply restriction could arise from (1) plugged filters or screen, (2) a collapsed pump inlet line, (3) a crimped inlet line, (4) an internally damaged hose, or (5) foreign particles in the inlet line or reservoir outlet line.

Air in the inlet line displaces an equal volume of oil, and therefore, the air reduces the flow to the pump. Air could enter the inlet side of the pump through a damaged pump seal, loose connections, or a damaged hose.

To determine whether the reading is below specification, say, 60 gal/min [227.1 l/min], owing to an inlet restriction or to the presence of air in the system, close the load control valve until the pressure gauge reads about 1200 psi [8268 kPa].   **NOTE** Be very careful when closing the load control valve to obtain system pressure, because the main relief valve is not in the circuit while the shutoff valve is closed.

If the flow rate is low, say, 60 gal/min [227.1 l/min], owing to an inlet restriction, the pressure gauge would be relatively steady at 1200 psi [8268 kPa]. If there is air in the system, the flowmeter would also indicate the same flow rate, but the pressure gauge would fluctuate rapidly. If, however, the pump is worn, the flow rate would drop off because of the increased pressure.

Testing the Efficiency of the Pump   In this test you are seeking to determine the pump's rate of efficiency or its percentage of wear, and yet this test is often overlooked, and as a result, components are often exchanged unnecessarily or the pump is serviced without cause. Close the load control valve to obtain a pressure of 2000 psi [13,780 kPa]. Check the engine rpm and take the flowmeter reading. If a pump delivers 79 gal/min [299.0 l/min] at no load and 74 gal/min [280.0 l/min] at a rated load of 2000 psi [13,780 kPa], it is said to be operating at 100 percent efficiency, because pump manufacturers generally allow 10 percent flow reduction at the rated load. In effect this means that a pump rated at 79 gal/min [299 l/min] would be accepted as 100 percent efficient even when it delivers 71.1 gal/min [269.11 l/min] at 2000 psi [13,780 kPa].

When the pump's effectiveness is seriously reduced or it is noisy, it may be because (1) the oil is contaminated; (2) the oil level is too low; (3) the oil supply is inadequate; (4) the oil viscosity is inapplicable; (5) there is air in the oil; (6) the pump and the drive are misaligned; (7) the housing is damaged or cracked; (8) the bearings, gears, vanes, piston, or wear plates are worn; (9) (if applicable) a reservoir inlet filter is causing a restriction; (10) (if applicable) the reservoir relief valve is not operating properly; or (11) a worn drive coupling is causing slippage.

When a pump has external oil leaks, it may be because of (1) worn bearings, (2) worn or damaged pump shaft or seal, (3) plugged drain passage to the inlet of the pump, or (4) a damaged wear plate seal.

Testing the Main Relief Valve   It is essential to test the main relief valve, because its setting controls the working power available to the system. It is also important to check the cracking point of the pilot valves. When the cracking point (pressure) is higher than 10 percent of that of the relief valve setting, the pressure variation within the system is too high. Power is lost through either of these problems.

To check the cracking point and the fully open point of the main relief valve, open the shutoff valve and the load control valve. Operate the engine at high idle and lift the ripper off the ground so that the piston rod is fully retracted. Hold the control valve in this position. All the oil from the pump will then flow through the tester, and the flowmeter should be recording 79 gal/min [299 l/min]. Gradually close the load control valve and note when the needle of the flowmeter begins to move down scale. This is the point where the pressure has lifted the pilot valve off its seat and is called the *cracking pressure* of the main relief valve.

Next, fully close the load control valve to stop the flow through the tester. The oil from the pump is now forced to flow through the open main relief valve. The pressure gauge reading is the main relief valve setting.

If the flowrate has fallen off during the test, say, to 69 gal/min [261.1 l/min], the cause could be (1) internal leakage between the valve spool and bore, (2) incorrect positioning of the valve spool owing to adjustment or to worn or damaged detents, (3) failure of the secondary relief valve to seat, (4) damaged or worn main relief valve or seals, or (5) damaged or worn hydraulic cylinder piston seal packing.

If the cracking pressure is higher than 10 percent, the cause could be an internal leak in the main relief valve or a damaged pilot valve.

If the main relief valve setting is lower than specified, the cause could be (1) too low an adjustment, (2) a broken main relief valve spring, (3) a sticking or dirty valve or piston, or (4) a setting of the secondary relief valve lower than that of the main relief valve.

If the main relief valve opens above specification, the cause could be (1) a dirty main relief valve, (2)

a sticking relief valve, (3) too high an adjustment, or (4) a restricted return line.

Individual Circuit Testing   To test the efficiency of each individual circuit—in other words, to check the directional control valves and the cylinders for leakage—first open the shutoff valve and the load control valve and operate the engine at 1500 rpm. Next, actuate the valve spool (to lift the dozer blade) and then gradually close the load control valve to develop a pressure which will retract the piston. When the piston is fully retracted, adjust the load control valve so that the pressure gauge indicates 1000 psi [6890 kPa] or is as specified in the service manual. When the circuit is under this condition, the cylinder cannot accept any more oil. All oil from the pump must flow through the flowmeter. If there are no internal leaks in the control valve or cylinder(s), the flowmeter reading should be the same as it was when the efficiency of the pump was being tested, that is, 74 gal/min [280 l/min]. If this is the case, you can conclude that there is no oil leakage in the circuit being tested.

Now actuate the valve spool in the opposite direction to extend the piston rod fully. The flowmeter again should record the same. If there is less flow, say, 60 gal/min [227.1 l/min] recorded by the tester when the control valve is actuated in either or in only one direction, the oil (14 gal/min [52.9 l/min]) not accounted for has been lost through internal circuit leakage. The internal leakage could originate from damage within the control valve or be due to a damaged secondary relief valve, piston seal, or cylinder barrel.

To determine where the leak is, disconnect the supply line leading to the cylinders and cap the ports and the lines. Then repeat the test. If the flowmeter reading remains 60 gal/min [227.1 l/min], the leak is in the control valve. If the reading improved, say, to 70 gal/min [265 l/min], there is an oil leak of 4 gal/min [15 l/min] in one or both cylinders, and 10 gal/min [37.8 l/min] is lost within the control valve.

To determine which cylinder is leaking, reconnect the supply line to one cylinder and disconnect the cylinder crossover line. Cap the lines but do not cap the cylinder port. Repeat the test. If the reading improves, say, to 62.6 gal/min [237 l/min], then you can assume that the cylinder being tested is allowing 2.6 gal/min [10 l/min] to pass from one side of the piston to the other. You will also notice that the oil is leaving the cylinder port being tested.

Possible causes of control valve leakage are (1) excessive clearance between the valve spool and bore, (2) a damaged valve spool or valve body lands, (3) an improperly positioned valve spool, or (4) a damaged secondary relief valve or its being held open by dirt.

If the valve spool has excessive resistance when activated in either direction or does not return to neutral, the cause could be (1) a bent valve spool, (2) nicks or burrs on the valve spool or spool bores, (3) a distorted valve body due to overtorquing the mounting bolts or misaligning the valve body and mounting flange, or (4) a broken centering spring.

If the load drops when activating the valve spool, the cause could be a damaged or worn load check valve or improper positioning of the valve spool land in relation to the valve body.

If the load drops (drifts) with the control valve in neutral, the cause could be (1) damaged piston seals or cylinder barrel, (2) improper seating of the load check valve, (3) failure of the valve to seat properly when a quick-drop valve is used, or (4) the valve's being damaged or having dirt underneath the seat when poppet or limited-travel valves are used.

If the problem is within the cylinder, it could be due to (1) worn or damaged piston seal or packing, (2) loose piston on piston rod or seal damage, (3) damaged quick-drop valve (if used) or its being held open by dirt, (4) damaged poppet or limited travel-valve (if used).

If the piston rod is bent, check for (1) misalignment of the piston rod to the mounting bore, (2) a worn pin or bushings, (3) inadequate lubrication of the pivot points, or (4) too high an adjustment of the secondary or main relief valve.

Testing Low-Pressure Secondary Relief Valves   To test the low-pressure secondary relief valve of the dozer's lift cylinder (down pressure), operate the engine at about 1000 rpm, close the shutoff valve, and, using the load control valve, create a pressure of about 1500 psi [10,335 kPa]. Then increase or decrease the engine rpm to create a flow of 40 gal/min [151.4 l/min] (about half of the main flow) and maintain a pressure of 1500 psi by varying the position of the load control valve.

The reason why a reduction of flow volume is recommended is that in most cases a secondary relief valve is not able to pass the full pump output through its opening.

Having established these conditions, open the shutoff valve, actuate the valve spool to pressurize the low-pressure secondary circuit, and close the load control valve. This causes all pump-delivered oil to be dumped through the fully open secondary relief valve. The pressure indicated on the pressure gauge is the fully open secondary relief valve pressure.   **NOTE**   Any circuit using a low-pressure secondary relief valve can be tested in the same manner.

Testing Poppet Valves   When the dozer's lift cylinders are equipped with poppet, or limited-travel, valves, install the recommended adapter or make a device that prevents the piston from completing its full stroke. Then test the cylinder as previously outlined.

NOTE   If there is a volume loss, it is not possible to determine if the piston seal or poppet valve is causing the reduction in the lpm reading.

When the cylinders have been tested, remove the adapter and repeat the test. When you are testing, the pressure should drop to the service manual specification, for example, to 800 psi [5512 kPa] as the pistons come to the end of their stroke. If such is the case, the poppet valves are operating satisfactorily.

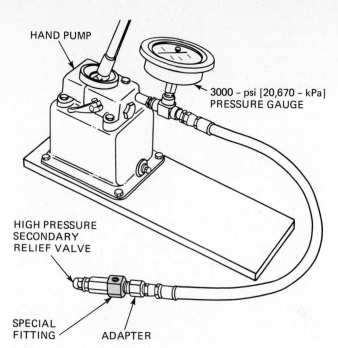

Fig. 11-15   Testing a secondary relief valve by using a special fitting. (*J I Case Company Agricultural Equipment Division*)

Testing High-Pressure Secondary Relief Valves   To test the high-pressure secondary relief valves (cracking pressure) of the tilt and ripper circuits or any other type of high-pressure secondary relief valve, a hand pump with a pressure gauge is required. The secondary relief valve can be tested when installed in the directional control valve, or it can be removed and installed to an adapter and then tested and adjusted. See Fig. 11-15.

To test the cracking pressure of the ripper secondary relief valve, remove the pressure from the circuit by operating the valve spool back and forth. Disconnect the hose at any convenient place between the directional control valve and the cylinder port. Install the hose of the hand pump by using a T fitting. Start the engine and move the control valve back and forth to fill the lines with oil and to remove any air that may have entered. Make certain that the oil temperature is 100°F [38°C] above ambient temperature and then stop the engine. Operate the hand pump to increase the pressure to open the relief valve. The gauge reading is the cracking pressure of the secondary relief valve, though not the fully open pressure of the relief valve.

To adjust the cracking pressure, refer to the appropriate service manual for the method applicable to the machine being tested.

Repeat the same test procedure for the remaining secondary relief valves.

Failure of the secondary relief valves to operate properly could be due to (1) a damaged or worn valve or valve seat, (2) a broken spring, (3) a sticking valve, or (4) damaged seal rings.

Testing Circuit Efficiency by Using Cycle Time   When a flowmeter is not available, the efficiency of the individual hydraulic circuits can be checked and evaluated by measuring the cycle time of each circuit. For this purpose most service manuals provide cycle time specifications.

When using the cycle-time method to test the individual circuits, bring the oil to operating temperature and check (and, if necessary, adjust) the main relief valve. To test the swing circuit cycling time, for example (operating the engine at the specified rpm), raise the boom and operate the control valve so as to swing the boom to its full left and right positions. For checking the lifting and lowering of the loader bucket, boom, or dipper stick or for checking the bucket dump from the full rollback to the full dump position, it is usually recommended that the bucket be filled to the normal load capacity so that the system pressure will be near maximum and the test results will, therefore, be valid. As you move the valve spool to start the swing action, the loader lift or the bucket dump action activates the stop watch. When the piston comes to the end of its stroke, you then stop the watch. Compare the time taken with that specified in the service manual. From this comparison you can establish the swing cycle, the lifting and lowering cycle, and the dump and rollback cycle. If it has taken more time to complete the cycle than specified in the service manual, you then know that there is a volume loss, although this test does not indicate where the loss occurred or what volume was lost—in the hydraulic pump, the control valve, or the cylinder(s).

Drift Testing By using the drift test you can evaluate, to some extent, the condition of the valve spool, the directional valve, and the hydraulic cylinder and thereby compare the drift test results with the cycling time to calculate the hydraulic pump loss volume.

To perform the drift test on a loader, dozer, boom, or dipper stick lift cylinder, the hydraulic oil must be brought to 100°F [38°C] (minimum) above ambient temperature. Raise the bucket, the blade, or the boom about 4 ft [1.22 m] off the ground and allow the valve spool to spring to neutral (hold position). With a felt pencil or equivalent device, mark on the piston rod a distance of, say, 2 in [50.8 mm] from the cylinder head. After a time lapse of 1 min, measure the distance from the mark on the piston rod to the cylinder head. The retraction of the piston rod(s) is called "drift," and it should not exceed the specification given in the service manual. If the drift is higher than specified, you know that the leakage is excessive, but you have no indication of the origin of the leak. The defect may be a damaged load check valve, or the secondary relief valve may be leaking, or the cylinder or the piston packing may be worn or damaged. It is therefore best, whenever possible, to use a flowmeter to test the hydraulic system. (The two test methods just outlined should be used only in an emergency.)

Preventive Maintenance If a hydraulic system is not properly maintained, its service life will be less than anticipated and the cost of operation and downtime will be excessive. Following are some maintenance procedures, but they should be used as a guide only. Service manual instructions should be followed implicitly. Remember also that the major cause of component wear and system failure is contaminated oil. Other causes of system failure are improper adjustments and overworking of the machine. Manufacturer imperfections actually cause very little downtime.

When servicing a hydraulic system or repairing hydraulic components, make certain that you do the following:

1. Keep your hands, the tools, the components, and the working area as clean as possible.
2. Cap all openings when removing hydraulic components for service.
3. Lubricate all parts adequately before you reassemble them (this prevents damage to the spools, pistons, and bores).
4. Check the oil level daily and in accordance with service manual instructions; do not miscalculate because of the equipment position.
5. Stop any oil leaks promptly by immediately replacing the seals, gaskets, fittings, or hoses. Even a small leak could, midway through the working shift, reduce the oil level to a point where the oil cooler no longer controls the temperature, and the excessive temperature would increase pump slippage and result in additional wear and loss of power.
6. Keep the pivot points well greased to reduce friction and wear. Wipe off excessive grease to prevent dirt and dust from collecting and contaminating surfaces between the pins and bushings.
7. Change the oil filters and clean the screens at regular intervals. When necessary, cut open the filter and analyze the trapped contaminants to determine the serviceability of the components.
8. When you are changing the filters, do not replace original filters with others of a higher or lower micron rating. A filter replaced by one with too high a micron rating would allow foreign particles to pass into the system whereas too small a micron rating would restrict the flow.
9. Change the oil (by draining and refilling the reservoir), as specified in the service manual, after 1000, 1500, or 2000 hours of operation. If there is evidence of oil contamination, you should flush the entire system. This may appear to be time consuming, but it is time saving over the long run.

NOTE Refill the system only with the oil type recommended by the manufacturer.

10. Remove dirt and water, etc., daily if necessary, from the exposed ends of the directional control valves. This prevents the valve spool ends from becoming oxidized or corroded, the valve from being damaged, and dirt or air from entering the system.
11. Replace worn or damaged bucket teeth or cutting edges. Since dull edges require more power, the pump has to operate against a higher pressure, and this, in turn, increases component wear.
12. Immediately service any components that have lost their efficiency. This is extremely important, for it prevents further contamination of the system, pre-

vents damage to the remaining components, and reduces repair costs and machine downtime.

Flushing Procedure Position and block the hydraulic equipment so that you can remove the reservoir, the pump, and the cylinders without too much interference from the other components. Operate the control valve to remove the pressure from the lines and the air pressure from the reservoir. To drain the entire system, first drain the reservoir and then remove the connecting line from the pump and cylinders. Use a drain pan to collect the oil, then cap the openings. (When possible, remove the reservoir.) Remove the filter, the screens, and the control valve from the reservoir (if applicable) and steam-clean them thoroughly. Reinstall the components to the reservoir and mount the reservoir to the machine.

Remove, disassemble, inspect, and reassemble all cylinders, pumps, and/or motors. Service all serviceable parts and replace worn parts, as well as seals and packings. To flush the tubings and hoses, connect the lines of each circuit so that they form a complete loop "from" the control valve and "to" the control valve. The method used to flush the system will vary according to your shop equipment. If, for instance, you have no special flushing equipment, you would be forced to use the hydraulic pump and the machine's reservoir. To do this, install the hydraulic pump and connect the lines to the reservoir and to the directional control valve. Install new filters and fill the reservoir with a solution having a 50:50 ratio of diesel fuel to engine oil. Start the engine and operate it at half throttle. Move one directional control valve spool in one direction to full open position and hold it there for 2 min. Then move the spool valve in the opposite direction, again to full open position, and again hold it for 2 min. Repeat this procedure with the remaining control valve spools.

When the system is thoroughly flushed, disconnect all lines so that the reservoir, pump, and lines can drain properly. Some manufacturers recommend that, after flushing the system, you should, in addition, service the control valves. When this is the case, remove, disassemble, inspect, and service all control valves as previously outlined. When servicing is completed, install them to the machine. Reconnect all lines and again replace all filters. Refill the reservoir (see the discussion of reservoirs in Unit 7 for startup procedure) and bring the hydraulic oil to operating temperature. Recheck for leaks and, if

they are present, stop them. Recheck the oil level. Readjust the main relief valve and the low-pressure secondary relief valves.

Review Questions

1. Basically all hydraulic systems are similar, since they all perform the same work—pushing the piston inward or outward. What, then, are the differences among hydraulic systems?

2. Select, from your shop, service manuals which cover the hydraulic systems of (i) a dump truck, (ii) a wheel- or track-type dozer and loader, (iii) a backhoe, (iv) a scraper. (a) Compare and record the hydraulic systems in regard to type of pump(s), control valves, cylinders, hydraulic hoses, and fittings; (b) trace the oil flow of each machine in the neutral, raised, and lowering positions.

3. What action would take place if an additional weight were dumped on the bucket when (a) the bucket is in the tilt-back position, and (b) when the operator tries to lift the machine with the bucket off the ground?

4. Describe the hydraulic action which would take place within the control valve if the operator placed the load lift spool into the lowering position, and, owing to the weight and load in the bucket, it fell quickly to the ground.

5. What is the purpose of a power-beyond fitting?

6. What is the purpose of a boom lockout?

7. Why do some loaders use an automatic tilt-back and lift control?

8. Why is it recommended to periodically check (a) the general condition of the engine, (b) the mechanical and hydraulic condition of the machine?

9. It is nearly impossible to find the cause of trouble in a modern hydraulic system and to determine the remaining lifespan of the components without a flowmeter. What makes the flowmeter such a valuable test instrument?

10. Select a shop machine and to it connect a flowmeter in such a way that you can make the recommended test with one connection. List the steps you took to connect the flowmeter as outlined earlier.

Unit 12
Tires, Wheels, and Rims

TIRES

The tires used on on- and off-highway equipment are specially designed pneumatic tires, mounted onto a rim or disk wheel. When a conventional tire is mounted and inflated, the air pressure is contained within the tire tube, whereas, with a tubeless tire, the air pressure is contained in the space between the tire and the rim. Some small forklifts and other small commercial vehicles use solid rubber tires or tires filled with rubber particles and then treated in an oven, which causes the rubber to foam. After a precise curing time it forms into a tough cellular core and becomes equivalent in pressure and load-carrying capacity to a conventional tire. The purpose of either type tire is to support the vehicle and the load and to transmit the torque from the drive axle to the road surface with the most effective traction and with the least rolling friction. In addition the pneumatic tire, owing to its inherent flexibility, absorbs road shocks and provides flotation with resultant comfort to the driver or operator.

The pneumatic tires used on on- and off-highway equipment have reached a high degree of perfection, but nevertheless they need careful and regular maintenance to ensure maximum service life and to reduce wear and tear on the vehicle. Pneumatic tires are specially composed and designed for specific operating conditions. For example, off-highway tires are rugged enough in design and have a sufficient load-carrying capacity to operate under conditions that would damage on-highway tires or farm tractor tires within the first few hundred meters of service. On the other hand, because of their increased sidewall flexing, these tires generate more heat than tires intended for on-highway use. In fact, if the tires were operated at a speed greater than the maximum rated speed, their temperature would reach or exceed the vulcanizing temperature, and they would, therefore, disintegrate. In conclusion, pneumatic tires are composed and designed to give maximum performance under specified operating conditions when properly maintained.

Facts About Tires   Before contemplating tire design, tire size, and related terminology, here are some basic facts about tires worthy of review.

- When pneumatic tires are mounted to a disk wheel or rim, are correctly inflated, and do not contact the road surface, they are perfectly round and have a specified diameter called the overall diameter.
- Tires which rest on the road surface assume a different shape by deflecting at the road contact area. As a result of this deflection the distance from the center of the axle to the road surface is somewhat less than half of the overall tire diameter. This reduced radius is called static load radius.
- The static load radius varies according to the load placed on the tire, the tire inflation pressure, and the road crown angle.
- Any of these factors alter the static load radius and therefore alter the tire revolutions per mile.
- When the vehicle is in operation, the tires act like a roller chain and therefore stand still at the point of contact with the road surface.
- The tire speed at the spindle height conforms to the vehicle speed, and the tire speed opposite from the road contact surface reaches twice the speed of the vehicle.
- The centrifugal force acting on the tire varies constantly, and this deforms the tire.
- The vehicle steering, the transmitting of torque, and braking torque, occur through the tire footprint, also called the contact patch.
- The contact patch varies with the static load radius, the tire design, the overall tire diameter, and the tire width.
- All the foregoing affect the traction.
- Under all normal operating conditions the traction force of a tire is equal in all directions (with the exception of some agricultural drive wheel tires).

Tire Design and Terminology   Although hundreds of types of tires are available, all are similar in design and construction. There are four major tire classes: car and small truck; on-highway truck, trailer, and bus; off-highway (earth-moving equipment, graders, loaders, and dozers); and agricultural (front tires, drive wheel tires and implement tires) (see Figs. 12-1 to 12-4). Each major class may be additionally divided into three subclasses: (a) bias ply, (b) bias-belted, and (c) radial ply. These may be again subdivided into tubeless and tube-type tires.

A tire requiring an inner tube is almost identical in design to a tubeless tire. The tube-type tire requires, of course, an inner tube which, when inflated with air, supports the load. It also has a tube flap that protects the inner tube and prevents it from coming out of shape. Tubeless tires usually have a toe strip or rim chamfer to improve sealing and also have an inner liner which substitutes for the missing inner tube. The air is confined by the tire and rim assembly.

A tire is composed of the body ply cords, which are made up of rubber-coated textile (rayon, nylon, polyester), and/or steel wire strands (the plies), and

Fig. 12-1 Car tire. (Firestone Tire and Rubber Company of Canada, Limited)

Fig. 12-3 Off-highway dump truck tire. (Firestone Tire and Rubber Company of Canada, Limited)

Fig. 12-2 Truck tire. (Firestone Tire and Rubber Company of Canada, Limited)

Fig. 12-4 Farm tractor tire. (Firestone Tire and Rubber Company of Canada, Limited)

the inner lines (see Figs. 12-5 to 12-7). The ends of the plies and the inner liner are wrapped around the bead. The bead, or beads, are one or more wire bundles made of high tensile steel wires. With the cord they form in shape to fit the rim through the bead flange area, through the heel and the toe, and through the bead face. When the tire is properly inflated, it seats and remains firm (against the rim base, bead seat band, and inner and outer flange) under load stress, on uneven terrain, and during acceleration, deceleration, and braking.

PLIES Two methods are used to apply the plies to the bead to form the cord body (carcass)—the bias and the radial method (see Fig. 12-8).

A bias ply cord is one in which the ply cords run from bead to bead at an alternate angle substantially less than 90° across the center line of the cord body. A radial ply cord is one in which the plies run from bead to bead at an angle of 90° across the center line of the cord. It appears as though the plies start from the center of the carcass. The carcass is the tire structure without the rubber of the tread and sidewalls. Belts, also called brakers, are placed around the outer circumference of the carcass. They may be constructed of the same material as the plies. The belts increase stabilization, improve the footprint and the tire strength, and protect the cord (by distributing the road shocks throughout the tire).

A tire of the bias-belted or radial belted design rolls on the road with less resistance. However, a radial belted tire is much more superior and has a longer tread life. The trucking companies claim to get up to 150,000 miles [241,340 km] from a radial front axle tire and 110,000 miles [176,990 km] from a drive axle tire. The reason is that the tread design does not vary as it makes its footprint on the road, whereas the tread design on bias ply or bias-belted tires does (see Fig. 12-9). In addition, a radial tire runs cooler than a bias ply tire; it requires less repair and is safer; and it needs only a rim or disk wheel, or, sometimes, a tube. Moreover, a bias ply tire re-

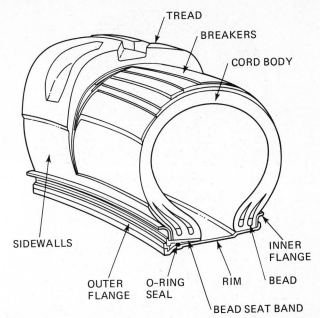

Fig. 12-6 Sectional view of a tubeless tire and rim assembly (off highway). (*Terex Division of General Motors Corporation*)

quires at least four more parts: the tube; the tube flap, the disk wheel, or rim; a loose flange; and a lock ring. The weight of the assembly is therefore increased.

TREAD AND SIDEWALL The tire tread and sidewall rubber are vulcanized to the carcass. The tire tread and sidewalls are made of an elastomer compound of natural and synthetic rubber, with chemicals and filler added to meet the stresses placed on it and to improve its durability and wearability.

That portion which contacts the road surface is called the tread face. Numerous tread designs are used to fulfill the tire's operating objectives. They vary in tread depth, from regular to super depth, and also vary in tread compound. The base tread or the

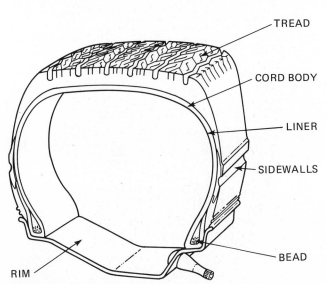

Fig. 12-5 Sectional view of a car tire and rim. (*Firestone Tire and Rubber Company of Canada, Limited*)

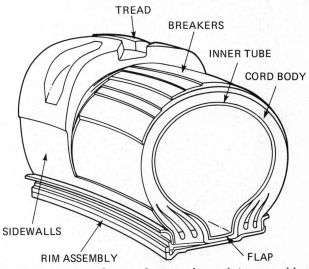

Fig. 12-7 Sectional view of a tire, tube, and rim assembly. (*Terex Division of General Motors Corporation*)

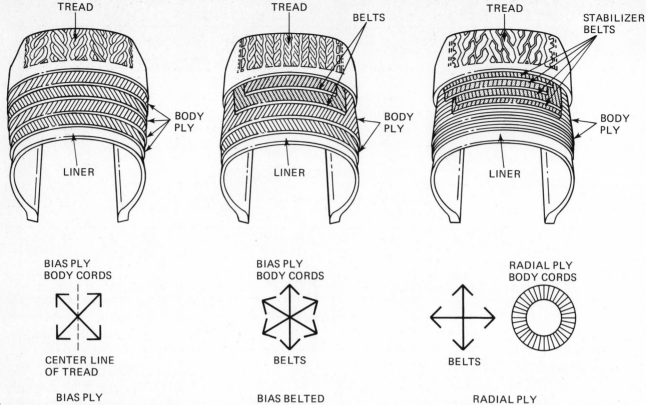

Fig. 12-8 Cord body construction.

under tread is the portion of the tread that protects the plies or breakers. The major tread groove or void is the space between the adjacent tread. The sidewall rubber protects the cord and is that portion from the tread surface to the bead or rim flange. It may be divided into the upper, middle, and lower sidewalls.

NOTE The middle section is the point of the maximum tire width.

Load Range To identify the load range of a given sized tire in relation to the minimum and maximum designed inflation pressure, a lettering system from A to L is used for on-highway vehicles, and the ply rating is used for off-highway equipment. The ply rating (not the plies) is in direct proportion to the load range (see Table 12-1).

Samples of load-carrying capacity versus the inflation pressure for passenger cars, trucks, farm tractors, and earthmoving vehicle tires are shown in Table 12-2.

Tire Size The tire size to be used on a given vehicle is based on the load it has to carry, the traction (footprint), and the anticipated operating revolutions per mile. On all tires, the size, the load range, and the maximum pressure are molded into the sidewalls. For example, on a tire marked 10.00-20 G100, the first set of numbers imprinted on the sidewall indicates the approximate height of the tire

Table 12-1 LOAD RANGE—PLY RATING CONVERSION TABLE

Load range	Replaces	Ply rating
A		2
B		4
C		6
D		8
E		10
F		12
G		14
H		16
I		18
J		20
K		22
L		24

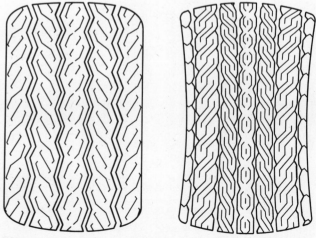

Fig. 12-9 Footprints of radial ply tire (left) and bias ply tire (right).

Table 12-2 LOAD AND INFLATION TABLE FOR TIRES; LOAD LIMITS GIVEN IN POUNDS PER TIRE

For Tires Used on Passenger Cars and Station Wagons

Load range B (4-ply rating) ——————————→
Load range C (6-ply rating) ——————————————→
Load range D (8-ply rating) ————————————————————→

Tire size (interchangeability is not implied)									Cold inflation pressures, psi											
Bias		Bias and belted bias				Radial														
1965 -on	Pre-1965	'78 Series'	'70 Series'	'60 Series'	Metric	'78 Series'	'70 Series'	'60 Series'	20	22	24	26	28	30	32	34	36	38	40
6.95-14					175R14				950	1000	1050	1100	1140	1190	1230	1270	1310	1350	1390
		C78-14	C70-14			CR78-14	CR70-14		950	1000	1050	1100	1140	1190	1230	1270	1320	1360	1400
	6.50-14								930	990	1030	1080	1130	1170	1210	1250	1300	1330	1370
9.15-15					235R15				1510	1600	1680	1750	1830	1900	1970	2030	2100	2160	2230
		L78-15	L70-15	L60-15		LR78-15	LR70-15		1520	1600	1680	1750	1830	1900	1970	2040	2100	2170	2230

For Bias Ply Tires Used on Type I, II, and III Rims

Tire size	Us-age	Tire load limits at various cold inflation pressures														
		45	50	55	60	65	70	75	80	85	90	95	100	105	110	115
9.00-20	D	3120	3310	3510	3690	3870	4040(E)	4200	4360	4520(F)	4670	4820	4970(G)			
	S			3560	3770	4000	4210	4410	4610(E)	4790	4970	5150(F)	5320	5490	5670(G)	
11.00-22	D		4350	4600	4840	5080	5300	5520(F)	5730	5940	6140(G)	6330	6530	6720(H)		
	S			4960	5240	5520	5790	6040	6290(F)	6530	6770	7000(G)	7220	7440	7660(H)	

For Radial Ply Tires Used on Type I, II, or III Rims

Tire size designation		Us-age	Tire load limits at various cold inflation pressures															
Tube type	Tubeless		35	50	55	60	65	70	75	80	85	90	95	100	105	110	115	120
8.25R15TR		D	2030	2170	2310	2440	2570	2700	2810	2930	3040	3150	3260(F)	3360	3470	3570(G)		
		S			2310	2470	2630	2780	2930	3080	3200	3340	3470	3590	3720(F)	3830	3960	4070(G)
11.00R22	12R24.5	D			4350	4600	4840	5080	5300	5520(F)	5730	5940	6140(G)	6330	6530	6720(H)		
		S				4960	5240	5520	5790	6040	6290(F)	6530	6770	7000(G)	7220	7440	7660(H)	

For Wide-Base, Bias Ply Tires Used on 15° Tapered Rims

Tire size	Us-age	Tire load limits at various cold inflation pressures														
		30	35	40	45	50	55	60	65	70	75	80	85	90	95	100
15-22.5	D				5000(E)	5320	5620	5910(F)	6200	6480	6740(G)	7000	7250	7500(H)		
	S						5680(E)	6040	6390	6720(F)	7040	7360	7660(G)	7950	8240	8520(H)
18-22.5	D				6430	6850	7230	7610	7980	8330	8680(H)	9010	9340	9650(J)		
	S						7310	7780	8220	8650	9070	9470	9860(H)	10240	10610	10970(J)

Rear Tractor Tires Used as Singles

Tire size	Tire loads at various inflation pressures							
	12	14	16	18	20	22	24	Pressures as indicated
14.9-24	2470*	2700[4]	2920	3130	3330[6]	3520	3700	3880 @ 26[8]
18.4-34	....	....	4970[6]	5320	5660[8]	5980	6290	6600 @ 26[10]
18.4-38	....	....	5250[6]	5630	5990[8]	6330	6660	6980 @ 26[10]
								7880 @ 32[12]

Earthmover Tires on Drive-away Vehicles

Tire size	Tire load limits at various cold inflation pressures															
	25	30	35	40	45	50	55	60	65	70	75	80	85	90	95	100
16.00-24		13 660	14 050	14 770	15 820	16 830[12]										
27.00-33	18 880	21 030	22 990	24 860	26 640[24]	28 330	29 970[30]	31 520	33 040[36]							
36.00-51	40 380	44 990	49 170	53 160	56 970	60 600	64 100	67 420[42]	70 680	73 810[50]	76 820	79 770	82 660[58]			
40.00-57	51 470	57 280	65 220	67 780	72 610	77 220	81 650	85 900[52]	90 030	94 020[60]						

Notes:
1. Letters in parentheses denote load ranges for which loads and inflations are maximum. (See Load Range-Ply Rating Conversion Table.)
2. For tire loads at various maximum speeds other than 60 mph and special operating conditions.
3. Vehicles to be stopped for a period of 30 min for each 50-mile distance, or every 2 hr.
4. Use 40-psi minimum for end dump trucks. All other vehicles use 25-psi minimum.
5. Small index numbers denote ply ratings for which loads and inflations are maximum.

(from the bead to the tread face (10 in, 254 mm); the second number indicates the diameter from bead to bead base (rim size) (20 in, 508 mm); the letter G indicates the load range at the maximum pressure 6040 lb [2745.4 kg], and the last number indicates the maximum inflation pressure 100 psi [689.0 kPa].

Although the tire section and the sidewall flex area of a tube tire 10.00-20 and that of a tubeless tire 11.0-22.5 (shown in Fig. 12-10) are practically the same, they differ in size. The reason for the 2.5-in [63.5-mm] increase in the designation of the bead diameter size is that a tubeless truck tire is supported on a 15° tapered bead seat. This raises the bead heel by 1.250 in [31.7 mm] from the lowest point of the rim. On a 5° tapered rim the bead heel diameter is the same as the actual rim diameter size.

Small truck and car tires of the bias ply design use the same tire size identification as on- and off-highway tires. For example, they may be identified as 6.50-16 B36. Small truck and car tires of the bias-belted or radial design, however, are classified differently. An example of their size identification may be HR 78-15 D40. The first letter used may range from A to N. It identifies the overall tire width. H, for example, indicates 8.65 in [219.7 mm]. The second letter identifies the tire as a radial ply. The next set of numbers (60, 70, 78, or 83) represents the tire series. These numbers express the percentage of the tire height to the tire width and are called the aspect ratio. In other words, a tire of the series 60 is only 60 percent in height to the tire width, and a series 70 is only 70 percent, a 78 is 78 percent, and an 83 is 83 percent in height to the tire width. In the example used, therefore, the tire height is 78 percent of 8.65, which equals 6.05 in [153.7 mm].

The width of tires for on- and off-highway trucks, trailers, or agricultural equipment usually equals the height. However, some new radial truck tires and also some off-highway tires are now greater in width than in height. The reason for using this low-profile tire is to improve the load-carrying capacity, the traction, and the road-handling performance. A tire data sheet showing several tire designs (and sizes) is shown in Table 12-3. **NOTE** The tire size and design establish the type of rim to be used, as well as the rim width. Table 12-3 also shows the load-carrying capacity, the static load radius, the revolutions per mile, and the footprint area.

Off-highway and Agricultural Equipment Tires
Tires used for off-highway and agricultural equipment are identifiable by their size, and a lettering and numbering system identifies the purpose for which the tire is designed.

Agricultural steering tires use the code letter F with the numbers 1, 2, or 3 to identify the tread design. F-1 is a single-rib tire, F-2 a dual- or triple-rib tire, and F-3 a multirib tire or an industrial design tread (similar to a traction truck tire).

Agricultural drive wheel tires use the code letter I and a numbering system of 1, 2, 3, and 6. I-1 is a rib tread tire, I-2 a moderate-traction tire, I-3 a traction implement tire, and I-6 a smooth implement tire.

Off-highway tires are also coded by a letter and numbering system to identify the purpose for which they were designed.

Code Letter C identifies a compactor tire. Code C-1 is a compactor tire having a smooth tread, and C-2 is one having a grooved tread.

Code Letter E is used to identify earthmover service tires followed by a number to identify the designed purpose. E-1 is a rib tread tire, E-2 a traction tread tire, and tires identified E-3 to E-6 are of a rock tread design, varying from moderate to maximum in heat resistance. E-7 is a tire having a flotation tread

Table 12-3 NEW TIRE DIMENSIONS

Size identification	Load range	Design rim width, in	Design tire width, in	Overall diameter, in	Static loaded radius, in	Overall tire width in use, in	Revs per mile	Footprint area, in²
				Car tire				
LR 78-15	C	6.50	9.03	29.31	12.93	6.63		
CR 78-14	B	5.00	6.95	25.54	11.60	5.20		
				Truck tires				
9.00 × 20	E	7.00	10.36	40.1	18.9	11.3	523	
11.00R × 22	F	8.00	11.71	44.7	21.2	12.8	466	
				Wide oval truck tire, tubeless				
18-22.5	H	14.00	18.00	45.3	20.9	20.1	458	
				Duplex tires				
15-22.5	H	11.25	15.2	42.3	20.0	16.9	486	
				Off-highway tires				
16.00 × 24E7	24	11.25	17.19	58.4	27.2	18.8		192
27.00 × 33E3	36	22.00	29.04	87.9	40.1	33.0		626
37.5 × 33L4	30	32.00	38.25	94.1	40.5	43.7		1024
40.00 × 57E4	60	29.00	43.20	141.48	65.1	48.8		1492
				Rear traction tire				
14.9-24(R4)	4	413	14.9	49.3	21.8			
18.4-38(R2)	6	D416	18.4	69.0	31.1			

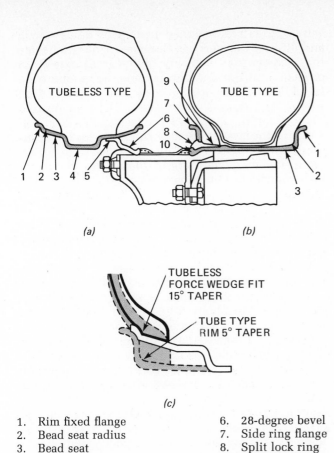

(a)   *(b)*

TUBELESS
FORCE WEDGE FIT
15° TAPER

TUBE TYPE
RIM 5° TAPER

(c)

1. Rim fixed flange
2. Bead seat radius
3. Bead seat
4. Rim gutter
5. Inflation ledge
6. 28-degree bevel
7. Side ring flange
8. Split lock ring
9. Lock ring toe
10. Gutter tip

Fig. 12-10 (*a*) 15° full drop center; (*b*) three-piece flat base rim; (*c*) bead seats of tubeless and tube tire rims.

design so that it can operate in sand or as a free rolling wheel where flotation is of maximum importance.

Tires designed for grader service have the code letter G followed by a number. G-1 identifies a rib tread design, G-2 a traction tread design, and G-3 a rock tread design.

Tires designed for loaders and for dozer service are coded with the letter L followed by a number for their design or special purpose. L-2 is a traction tread design, whereas L-3, L-4, and L-5 are rock tread designs varying in tread depth.

Tires designed for logging service (log skidders) are coded LS. They may be of the same tread design as the drive wheel tractor tires (R), but the tread is deeper. Furthermore, the tread and sidewalls are of different rubber compounds and have two or more steel cord plies. Some have shredded steel under the body of the tread and sidewall to resist cuts and snags.

Car, Truck, Trailer, and Bus Tires   Car, truck, trailer, and bus tires are identifiable by their size and design. They are specifically named by the tire manufacturer to indicate the tread design and/or the core and belt material composition. As an example, Tiger Paw, Radial 721 and Silver Town are some names used for car tires. The names Transteel Milesaver and Hi-miler refer to tires used for truck service.

CAR TIRES   Four car tires of varying designs are shown in Fig. 12-11. No. 1 is an NR 78-15 C40 steel-belted tubeless radial tire having rib blade tread de-

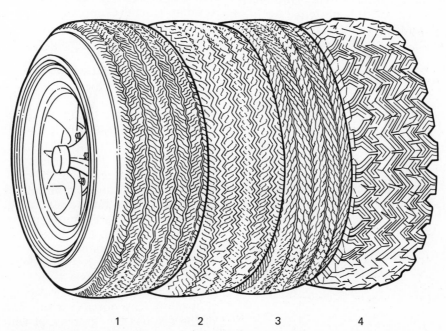

            1   2   3   4

Fig. 12-11   Various car tire designs. (*Firestone Tire and Rubber Company of Canada, Limited*)

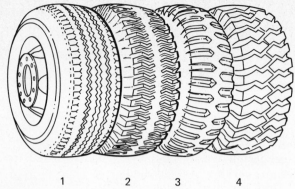

Fig. 12-12 Various truck tire designs. (*Firestone Tire and Rubber Company of Canada, Limited*)

sign and two radial polyester body plies. It has two steel cord stabilizer belts, and the inner liner is laminated. *No. 2* is an L 78-15 B36 bias ply tubeless tire having a rib blade tread design and two polyester plies. It has two fiberglass belts, and the inner liner is laminated. *No. 3* is a 6.95-14 B36 bias ply tubeless tire having a rib blade tread design. The body plies are either polyester or rayon, and the inner liner is laminated. *No. 4* is a D 78-15 B36 bias-belted tubeless tire having a mud and snow tread design and is provided with stud holes. It has two polyester body plies and two fiberglass stabilizer belts. The inner liner is laminated.

TRUCK TIRES Four truck tires of various design are shown in Fig. 12-12. *No. 1* shows a radial steel-belted truck tire usable for all positions and for all types of highway service. The common truck tire sizes are from 8.25-15 to 1100-22 (tube type). The tubeless tire design range from 10R-22.5 to 12.75R-22.5, with a load range up to G. **NOTE** See sample load range chart. *No. 2* shows a traction tire having wide, heavy, and deep tread bars for good traction and high speed durability. It has a nylon cord body. *No. 3* is a nondirectional tire. It is designed for rugged terrain, and owing to its tread design, it can be rotated in either direction without sacrificing traction. *No. 4* shows a duplex all-traction 15-22.5 tire.

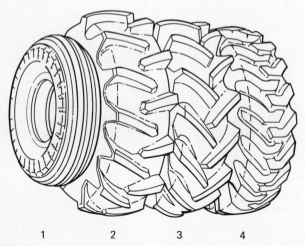

Fig. 12-13 Agriculture tires. (*Firestone Tire and Rubber Company of Canada, Limited*)

Duplex tires are designed to replace duals for on- and off-highway service. Because of the tire design, the load-carrying capacity of the front axle is increased, and the flotation or mobility is improved. In addition it provides a more comfortable ride, it weighs less than a set of duals, and as a result it reduces the possibility of fire hazard. No rocks can lodge in the duplex as they can between the duals, there are no dual matching problems, and furthermore, the manufacturers of these tires claim that they contribute to fuel saving.

Duplex tires are manufactured in sizes from 10-16.5 to 18-22.5. They vary in load range from C to J. The tread design also varies from an all-position traction tire to a super rock grip tire having two additional steel tread plies over the nylon core body.

AGRICULTURAL TIRES Four agricultural tires are shown in Fig. 12-13. *No. 1* is an 1100-16 8-ply having a nylon cord body. The tread is designed to accommodate the steering axle and/or the free rolling wheels. *No. 2* is an R-1 20.6-38 8-ply, deep-tread tire, having a bar angle of 23°. It has wide, flat treads for more shoulder-to-shoulder contact to increase traction. *No. 3* is an R-2 23.1-34 8-ply tire with very deep traction bars. It is built for wet soil farming. *No. 4* is an R-4 16.9-26 10-ply designed for tough on- and off-highway road operation. The traction bars are wide to give moderate traction, good flotation, and long wear.

OFF-HIGHWAY TIRES Five off-highway tires are shown in Figs. 12-14 and 12-15. *No. 1* is an L-5 37.25 36-ply. This tire has extra deep-rock tread with a shredded wire undertread. *No. 3* is an L-2 23.5-25 16-ply traction tire. *No. 2* is an E-7 16-20 20-ply flotation tire of large, thick, boldface tread design. *No. 4* is an E-2 33.5-33 38-ply traction tread tire designed to operate on soft, sandy, or rugged surfaces. Figure 12-15 is a beadless tire especially designed by Caterpillar Tractor Company for use on loaders where a conventional tire would not stand up to the operating conditions and would therefore deteriorate rapidly.

At present, only two tire sizes are manufactured by Caterpillar Tractor Company—one with a rim diameter of 48.9 in [124.2 cm] and the other with a rim diameter of 39.8 in [110.1 cm]. The total weight of the large tire assembly is 7440 lb [3380 kg].

BEADLESS TIRES The beadless tire (see Fig. 12-15) has many advantages over the conventional tire and rim assembly: a nearly unlimited load-carrying capacity and speed but no ply rating, it has a low operating temperature, more provision for traction, longer service life, and lower initial cost and less subsequent maintenance.

The beadless tire is a one-piece oval air chamber (the carcass), which is a 1-ply, helically wound design, reinforced with steel cables for strength and protection. The outer circumference (tread surface) of the tire has five grooves in which the mounting belt protrusion lugs rest. Hoops, rather than tire beads, are formed on each lower sidewall. The hoops

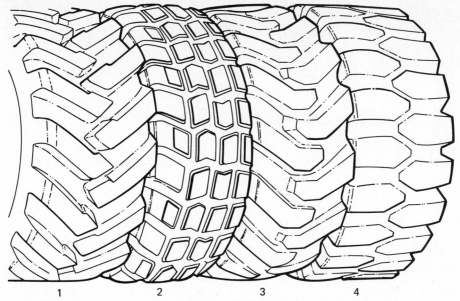

Fig. 12-14 Off-highway tires. (*Firestone Tire and Rubber Company of Canada, Limited*)

are contoured to the bead seat radius, the fixed rim flange, and the rim base, preventing the tire from rolling off the rim. The high inflation pressure forces the inner carcass and hoops against the rim base and rim flange and thereby holds the tire firmly to the rim. The rubber mounting belt is circumferentially wound with layers of steel cables and anchor plates molded to the outside of the belts (to which the steel shoes are bolted). The steel shoes, which provide traction, overhang the belt and thereby protect the carcass. The two-piece rim of the beadless tire is similar in design to that used on a semipneumatic or a solid rubber tire. However, the rim flange, the bead radius, and the bead seat design differs, since the rim need not anchor the beads or contain air pressure. Furthermore, the bolts which fasten the two rim halves to a unit also bolt the rim to the wheel hub. The high inflation pressure of 120 psi (826.8 kPa) gives a firm ride but also provides good flotation.

DISK WHEELS AND RIMS

The purpose of a demountable rim is to support the tire safely and to facilitate mounting the tire to the wheel hub. A rim is a fabricated circular steel or an aluminum frame formed to the shapes shown in Fig. 12-10a. Special rim clamps are used to center and fasten the rim to the wheel hub.

A disk wheel is a rim to which a steel or aluminum permanent center member (called a disk or a spider) is fastened. It provides the mount for the disk wheel to the hub. Special wheel bolts, wheel nuts, or wheel studs with nuts of various designs are used to center and fasten the disk wheel to the wheel hub.

To identify the intended application of the disk wheel or rim, manufacturers must label them and label the additional parts (the bead, bead band, the outer flange, and the lock ring). On each part is

stamped the manufacturer's name and the date manufactured; rim width and diameter; and rim type (whether for tube or tubeless tires, bias or radial, dual type disk or rim type, drop-center dual disk or rim type; or single semidrop-center disk wheel or rim type), as well as maximum load rating and inflation pressure.

Design Manufacturers of tires and wheels select and test the tires and disk wheels or rims that best

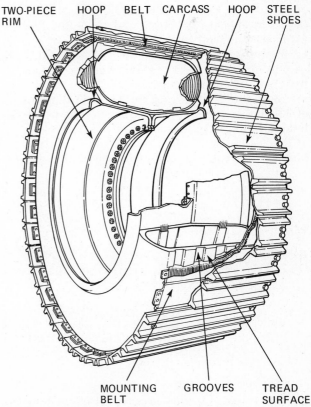

Fig. 12-15 Beadless tire design. (*Caterpillar Tractor Co.*)

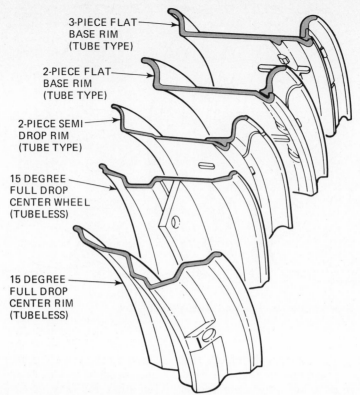

3-PIECE FLAT
BASE RIM
(TUBE TYPE)

2-PIECE FLAT
BASE RIM
(TUBE TYPE)

2-PIECE SEMI
DROP RIM
(TUBE TYPE)

15 DEGREE
FULL DROP
CENTER WHEEL
(TUBELESS)

15 DEGREE
FULL DROP
CENTER RIM
(TUBELESS)

Fig. 12-16 Tube and tubeless rim designs. (*Motor Wheel Corporation—Goodyear*)

suit the particular vehicle and the conditions under which it will operate. Whether a disk wheel or rim must be used depends upon the wheel hub design. The tire size and design govern the type of rim that must be used.

There are various rims and disk wheels designed for use on cars, trucks, buses, and agricultural equipment, etc., as well as those especially designed for off-highway equipment. Rim or disk wheel designs vary in dimension and contour to accommodate the tire size and their location on the wheel hub. Furthermore the designs vary in regard to the number of bolt holes, the bolt circle diameter, and the centerbore (hub pilot diameter). See Fig. 12-18.

Trucks, trailers, and buses, whether their tires are tube or tubeless, use one of the eight rim designs shown in Figs. 12-10 and 12-16. Each of these designs is also available as a disk wheel.

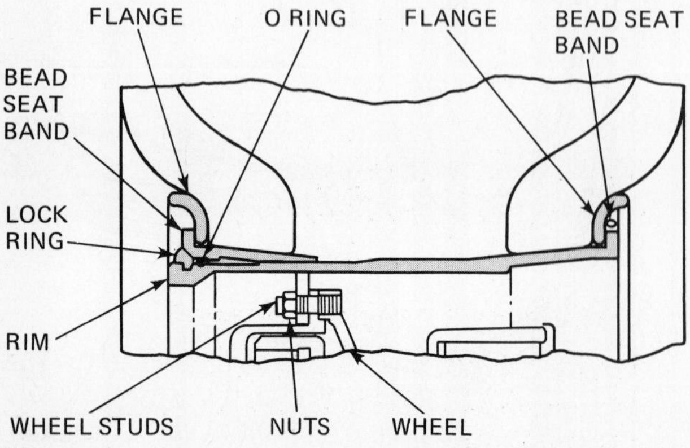

For off-highway equipment, usually a five-piece rim design is used (see Fig. 12-17). Industrial or agricultural disk wheels or rims (tube or tubeless type) are of the drop-center design (one-piece), varying in size from 12-3.00 to 22 × 16.00 (see Fig. 12-18).

NOTE Most two- and three-piece rim designs use a 5° tapered bead seat to increase the seating capacity of the tapered bead tire.

Small equipment using semipneumatic tires or solid rubber tires use split disk wheels for easier mounting. The split disk wheel is manufactured in two equal parts and then bolted as a unit.

Wheel Studs and Nuts When a disk wheel is to be fastened to the wheel hub, five, nine, or more specially designed wheel studs are threaded (or pressed) into the hub flange in a circular fashion and precisely spaced (see Fig. 12-19). Three basic wheel studs are used: the headed type, which is either serrated or has a flat edge on the head to prevent it from turning in the wheel hub bore; the wheel bolt type, which is commonly used on farm equipment and small vehicles, it has a hexagon head with a tapered (ball) seat, and, when screwed into the hub, supports and positions the wheel on the hub; and the threaded shoulder type, which is threaded on both ends, one end fitting snugly in the wheel hub and brake drum bore. The flat which is machined on the shoulder fits in the stud groove and prevents it from turning.

FLANGE   O RING   FLANGE   BEAD SEAT
BAND

BEAD
SEAT
BAND

LOCK
RING

RIM

WHEEL STUDS   NUTS   WHEEL

Fig. 12-17 Cutaway view of a typical off-highway rim assembly. (*Terex Division of General Motors Corporation*)

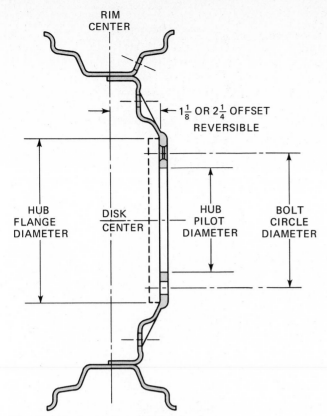

Fig. 12-18 Agricultural disk wheel.

The brake drum is fitted over the studs and is held in position with special self-locking nuts. The single rear disk wheel, or front disk wheel, is mounted over the outer stud and is supported and positioned by special single-wheel cap nuts. When dual disk wheels are mounted to the wheel hub, special inner cap nuts having inner and outer threads support and position the inner disk wheel. The outer disk wheel is mounted over the inner cap nuts and the outer cap nuts support and position the outer disk wheel. The tapered (ball seats) wheel stud holes in the disk and the ball faces on the inner and outer wheel cap nuts are precision-machined, to ensure wheel-to-axle centricity and correct alignment. **NOTE** Usually left- and right-hand-threaded studs are used to increase the safety of the wheel. The left-hand-threaded studs are used on the left side (driver's side) and, of course, the right-hand-threaded studs on the right side. With increased load-carrying capacity the stud diameter increases from $\frac{1}{2}$ to $1\frac{15}{16}$ in [12.7 to 49.1 mm] and even higher on specially designed equipment.

Failure and Servicing Disk wheels and rims originate from the manufacturer without a flaw, to run true and hold the tire firmly to its base, and to withstand difficult operating conditions. Therefore many mechanics, drivers, and operators pay little attention to the disk wheels, rims, and tires (see Fig. 12-20). They assume these parts will operate trouble-free indefinitely but subsequently discover that inadequate maintenance has caused very expensive failure. A good maintenance program to prevent wheel failure

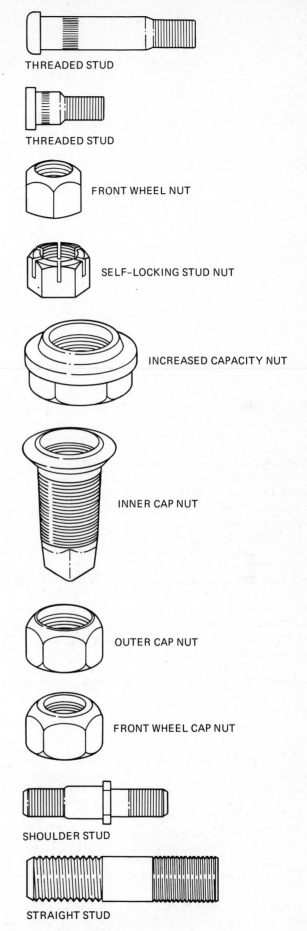

Fig. 12-19 Wheel attaching parts.

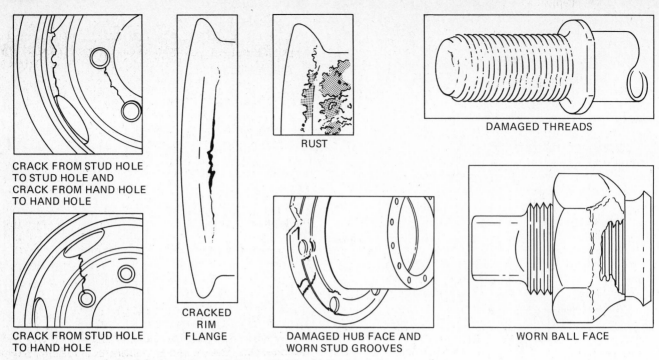

CRACK FROM STUD HOLE
TO STUD HOLE AND
CRACK FROM HAND HOLE
TO HAND HOLE

CRACK FROM STUD HOLE
TO HAND HOLE

CRACKED
RIM
FLANGE

RUST

DAMAGED THREADS

DAMAGED HUB FACE AND
WORN STUD GROOVES

WORN BALL FACE

Fig. 12-20 Rim, wheel, hub, and stud failure. (*The Budd Company*)

cannot, therefore, be overemphasized if costly downtime is to be prevented.

Preventive maintenance could begin with a daily check of the inflation pressure and the general condition of the tires. **NOTE** Make certain that you replace the valve cap.

While checking the tire, also visually check for a disk crack running from stud hole to stud hole, or worn stud holes—which would indicate a loose mounting condition; disk cracks from hand hole to hand hole, or from hand hole to stud hole—which would indicate that the wheel was operated in an overload condition; cracked rim or rim flange—which may be caused from the overload condition or from improper tire size or improper seating of side ring or lock ring; rust—which, if present around the cap nuts and ball seats or around the rim clamps, is indicative of a loosely mounted rim, as is a polished appearance around each side of the rim locks; and damaged or improperly seated lock ring.

NOTE See the discussion of tire mounting and demounting and disk wheel and rim installation in this unit.

Whenever the wheels are removed for tire changes, servicing the brakes, etc., check the mounting surfaces for dirt, paint, grease, and nicks and burrs and check that the brake drum retainer screws are properly seated; otherwise excessive wheel runout or loose mountings could result. Clean the stud bolts and cap nuts and check them for damage and wear. Screw the nuts onto the studs to determine if the threads are worn or damaged. If a stud bolt thread is damaged (perhaps from an overtorqued cap nut or because the disk wheel was placed over the stud bolts), refer to the applicable service manual, since many companies recommend that all studs be

replaced. Others suggest replacing only the stud bolt opposite the broken one. In any case, make certain that the correct stud bolt is reinstalled.

As you well know, all precision parts seat after a period of time under operating conditions. This is also true for disk wheels and rims. It is therefore recommended that, upon conclusion of the first day of operation, or after the first trip, the cap nuts or the rim clamp nut of the disk wheel or rim be retorqued in the sequence designated by the manufacturer. Furthermore, many manufacturers suggest removing the disk wheel or the rim, to check the cap nuts, ball seat, rim holes, and stud threads for paint, dirt, or damage before new equipment is placed into service.

Removal and Installation Of prime importance in a preventive maintenance program is the correct installation of the disk wheel or rim. The cap nuts or rim clamp nuts must be correctly torqued and tightened in the sequence recommended by the manufacturer. In the interest of safety, meticulous care in this procedure cannot be overstressed.

Before raising the vehicle, break the cap nut loose with a gear wrench having a 3:1 torque multiplication or use a socket and extension handle. In either case, support the end of the tool so that the socket does not slip off the cap nut. When using an air wrench, make certain you use the air sockets.

CAUTION The threads of the wheel stud bolts on the right-hand side have right-hand threads and those on the left side have left-hand threads.

Once the cap nuts are loose, block the vehicle and raise it (only) to the height necessary to remove the disk wheel or rim from the wheel hub. Block the

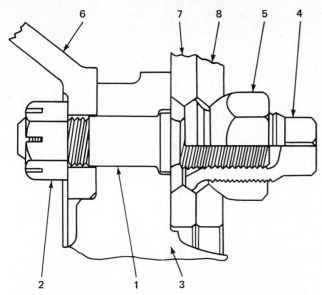

1. Shoulder-type stud
2. Jam nut
3. Wheel hub
4. Inner cap nut
5. Outer cap nut
6. Brake drum
7. Inner disk wheel
8. Outer disk wheel

Fig. 12-21 Dual disk wheel mounting. (*The Budd Company*)

vehicle so that it rests safely on stands or blocks. There should be adequate working space. Equipment should be available to facilitate lifting the tire from the wheel hub without damaging the tire, the disk wheel, or the rim.

Place a wheel dolly under the tire. Raise the dolly so that it rests firmly under the tire and then secure the tire to the dolly frame with the chain. (If you do not have a wheel dolly, use a piece of plywood on which some hand soap has been applied at the tread contact surface. Lower the vehicle so that the tire just contacts the plywood and then remove the cap nuts.) If necessary, before removing the disk wheel from the stud bolts, raise or lower the wheel dolly (or the vehicle) so that the disk holes are free from the stud bolts. You can then slide out The dolly or tire.

The only difference in procedure when removing a single or dual rim from the wheel hub is to position the rim lugs face upward. This will protect the tire valve during removal of the rim. After you have removed the stud nuts, you can then remove the rim clamps. If a dual rim is mounted to the wheel hub, first remove the rim spacer and then the inner dual.

When removing the inner disk wheel cap nuts of a dual installation, place a triangular-shaped wooden block in front of the tire if you are working on the right-hand side of the vehicle. If you are working on the left-hand side (driver's side) of the vehicle, place it behind the tire. In this way the tire will be safely locked (wedged) when the cap nuts are broken loose.

Installing a Dual Disk Wheel After making the recommended service checks, slide the inner dual tire over the wheel hub stud bolts. Take care not to

damage the stud threads. Hold the disk against the wheel hub and then run the inner cap nuts' ball face against the ball seat of the wheel stud holes (see Fig. 12-21). **NOTE** When installing the aluminum disk wheel, lubricate the stud threads with the recommended grease and make certain the end of the socket wrench is smooth. Otherwise it will damage the disk around the cap nuts' surfaces.

Use a torque wrench and, in the recommended sequence, tighten the cap nuts to about one-third of the specified torque (see Fig. 12-22). Next, tighten the cap nuts (again in the same sequence) to the recommended torque.

This is the opportune time to check the radial and lateral runout of the rim and tire to ensure that the tire will run true and therefore give maximum tread life. To check the radial runout, first clean the rim and tire and then position the spindle of the dial indicator as shown in Fig. 12-23, position A. Zero the dial. While slowly rotating the tire, mark on it the maximum and minimum radial runout. If the total runout is more than 0.090 in (22.86 mm), reposition the dial indicator to Position B. Again, rotate the tire slowly and again indicate on the tire the minimum and maximum runout. Check your runout against the maximum allowable radial and lateral runout recommended in your service manual. If the runout is more than 0.045 in [11.25 mm], replacement of the disk wheel is suggested. If the radial runout is less than 0.045 in, remount the tire in a way that the maximum runout of the tire aligns with the low mark of the rim runout. Recheck the radial runout. However, before remounting the tire, check the lateral runout of tire and rim by positioning the

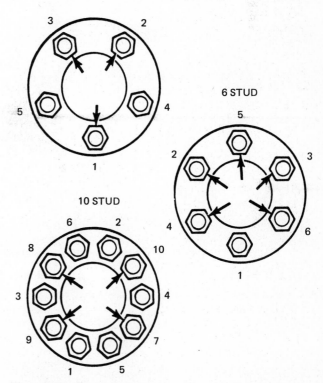

Fig. 12-22 Torque sequence.

154

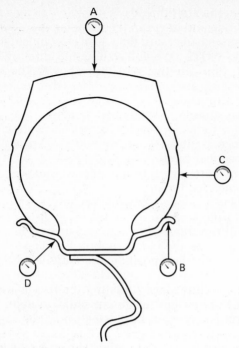

Fig. 12-23 Checking radial and lateral wheel and tire runout using a dial indicator.

dual indicator as indicated in Fig. 12-23, position C. If the lateral runout is more than 0.090 in, check the runout of the rim by repositioning the dial indicator as shown in Fig. 12-23, position D. If the runout is more than 0.045 in, the tire should be replaced. Once the inner dual wheel is mounted, slide the outer disk wheel over the inner cap nuts. Take care not to damage the threads. **NOTE** The tire valves should be 180° apart. To install the inner disk wheel, follow the procedure outlined to install the outer disk wheel.

Installing Dual Demountable Rims Make the rim checks recommended in your service manual. Clean

away any dirt or rust from the rim spacer and wheel hub and then, if necessary, repaint them with a fast-drying paint. Position the inner rim, the rim spacer, and the outer rim to the wheel hub in such a way that the tire valves are 180° apart. Place the rim clamps on the stud bolts and tighten the nuts finger-tight (see Fig. 12-24). (If necessary, raise or lower the wheel dolly to achieve a close rim-to-spoke alignment.) Next, use a torque wrench to tighten the nuts (in the correct sequence) to half of the recommended torque and then, in the correct sequence, tighten them to the specified torque. It is important at this time to check the radial and lateral runout of the demountable rim. If the lateral runout is greater than specified and the same runout is recorded on the tire, loosen the rim clamp stud nuts 180° opposite from the high runout and then tighten the nuts at the high runout. Next, retorque all nuts and recheck the lateral runout. If the lateral runout is not within specification, the rim may be bent or twisted, or the tire may be defective. At this point you may have to consider whether or not it is worthwhile to remount the tire.

CAUTION When using a gear wrench or torque multiplier, make certain that you take into account the ratio of the wrench. For example, assume the cap nuts are to be torqued to 500 lb·ft [677.5 N·m] and that you are using a torque multiplier having a ratio of 3:1. The reading on the torque wrench equal to the recommended torque would be only 166.66 lb·ft [225.83 N·m] 677.5 ÷ 3 − 225.83 N·m. An air impact wrench is a timesaver, but its advantage is offset by the fact that it may overtorque or undertorque the cap nuts. In either case, wheel failure would eventually result.

Removing Demountable Rim from Off-highway Equipment When removing a rim from an off-highway vehicle, observe the same safety rules and take the same precautions as if it were a truck. Gen-

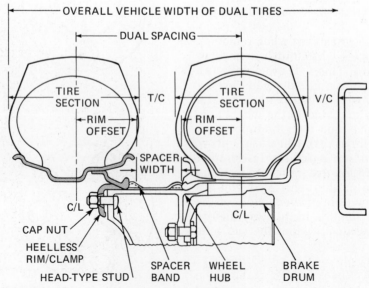

Fig. 12-24 Installation of demountable rim. (*Firestone Tire and Rubber Company of Canada, Limited*)

Fig. 12-25 Removing front wheel assembly.

erally speaking, the removal procedure is similar, but because of the weight of the off-highway tires and rims, even greater caution should be exercised.

To remove the rim from a rear dump truck having dual rims, first position the vehicle so that you can use a lifting device or a forklift to remove the rim from the wheel hub. Next, block the front tires and then bleed the air pressure from the system. Raise the rear section of the truck until the tire just clears the ground and then block it securely. Chain the inner dual wheel to the truck frame so that it cannot tilt on the wheel hub when the rim clamp nuts are loosened. In most cases the next step is to disconnect the inner and outer valve stem extension from the holding bracket. Now attach a sling, as shown in Fig. 12-25, to the outer tire. Position the lifting device so that it takes up the slack and causes most of the tire and rim weight to hang on the sling. Remove the wheel nuts and rim clamps and then carefully raise or lower the tire so that it can slide off the wheel hub without damage to the wire, the rim, the valve stem extension, or the inflation line. If the inner dual is to be removed, attach a sling to the rim spacer and then lift it from the wheel hub. Next, remove the inner tire in the same manner in which you removed the outer tire. The installation procedure for dual tires is precisely reverse to removal.

CAUTION Take care not to damage the inflation line of the inner dual wheel and make sure that it is positioned correctly in the channel on the wheel hub.

When positioning the rim spacer, make certain that it rests firmly against the inner rim, and when positioning the outer rim, make sure the tire valve bracket is aligned with the inner dual inflation line.

Install the rim clamps and the wheel nuts and tighten them in the specified sequence to the recommended torque. After the truck has made one haul or has operated for about a half hour, the wheel nuts should be retorqued. **NOTE** If you use a forklift to remove the tire assembly, chain the tire to the forklift mast. Remember, too, when using a forklift for removal or installation of tire assemblies, that, as the forklift backs away (or backs into position), the height of the ground surface may vary and thereby lower or raise the tire (see Fig. 12-26).

TIRE MAINTENANCE

Tires are usually the third highest cost factor in operating a vehicle. The driver's or operator's wages rate first; the fuel and oil rate second. Nevertheless, if tire maintenance is neglected, their continuous replacement cost could exceed that of fuel. On the other hand, you, the mechanic, can lower the deterioration rate of tires and also reduce the wear on the equipment by following the manufacturer's recommended procedures and precautions when storing, installing, or removing tires.

Storage To prevent deterioration, begin with the storage area for the tires and tubes. Store them on a tire rack and in a room where the temperature ranges between 40°F [4.44°C] and 60°F [15.6°C]. Make sure that no moisture, oil, dirt, or fuel can come in contact

Fig. 12-26 Installing wheel, using a fork lift.

with them while they are in storage. Do not expose them to excessive daylight or air current over a prolonged period of time. Never store tires in an area where electrical equipment generates ozone. This is a powerful oxidizing agent, and it accelerates the oxidation of rubber.

If the vehicle is not to be used over a long time, raise and block it so that the tires are off the ground and deflate them to about 5 psi [34.47 kPa]. If the vehicle cannot be raised and blocked, raise the tire pressure by about 10 psi [68.9 kPa] and check the pressure at regular intervals. In addition, entirely cover the tires with a dark, weatherproof material so that neither moisture nor daylight will contact them. If the tires and wheels are removed as a unit from the vehicle, clean the tires thoroughly and then deflate them to 5 psi [34.47 kPa]. If the tires and tubes are removed from the rims, clean them thoroughly and inspect them for damage. If any repairs are necessary, attend to them before storing the tires. Cover exposed cord areas with a rubber compound to prevent moisture from being absorbed by the fabric, for this could lead to bead and cord separation.

The tubes must be fully deflated and folded so as to avoid kinks. They should be placed in dark, weatherproof material. Since tubes deteriorate for the same reasons that tires do, retain new tubes in their original packings. Do not stack them too high, for the weight on the lower packings may cause them to crumble, and this could cause creases along the folds of the tubes.

Selection   Another step in preventive maintenance is to correctly select the tire in regard to the vehicle's load-carrying capacity and anticipated operating speeds. Decide whether a tube type or tubeless tire would be more appropriate and in some cases even choose between tread designs.

Inflation   The most common cause of premature tire wear is improper inflation (see Fig. 12-27). From this graph you can see its effect on the tires, as well as the effects of overloading and excessive speed.

NOTE   The correct tire pressure is shown on the inflation table in regard to tire size and load.

If possible, check the tire pressure daily, but if this cannot be done, then check it at least weekly. The checks and adjustments should be done with an accurate tire gauge when the tires are cold. When a new tire is inflated to the recommended pressure, it loses some pressure because it stretches and the inflated air cools. You must therefore recheck the tire pressure after 24 hours.

When a vehicle travels on an underinflated tire it creates excessive heat because of the higher tire deflection. In addition, the tire wears excessively on the outsides of the tread face. This may also cause separation of the plies or tread from the tire body. When one tire is flat or underinflated on a dual installation, the resultant internal and external friction could create heat buildup so intense that the tire could disintegrate or burst into flames. The other dual tire would then become overloaded and may also fail.

An overinflated tire is hard and rigid and therefore more vulnerable to road hazards such as cuts, snags, punctures, etc. It will show excessive wear on the center of the tread face (see Fig. 12-28). It may also lead to ply, body, or cord breakage and to rim damage.

Interchanging   To reduce tire deterioration rate of an on-highway vehicle, interchange the steering axle tires (which wear irregularly) with each other or move them to the drive axle or trailer axle and install new tires on the front axle. Do not install recapped tires. Replace any tire when only $\frac{2}{32}$ in (1.58 mm) of the tread remains or if the tire is damaged. A worn tire loses traction (increases in slippage), wears abnormally, and is more vulnerable to damage. A damaged tire is unsafe.

If a set of duals are worn unevenly or if one dual is worn more than the other, interchange the dual tires or move them to the other side of the axle.

Matching and Spacing   Another means of lowering tire mortality rate and reducing differential wear and interaxle differential wear is to match and space the dual tires properly. If, for example, one dual tire had an overall diameter of 28.3 in [718.8 mm] and a static load radius of 13.4 in [340.4 mm], it would make 737 revolutions per mile. If the other tire had an overall diameter of 29.5 in [749.3 mm] and a static load radius of 13.9 in [353 mm], it would make 711 revolutions per mile. To cover the same distance, the small tire would have to slow down, or the larger tire would have to speed up, but this is not, of course, not possible, because they are mounted to the same wheel hub. In fact, the smaller tire must slip over the road about 94.56 ft [28.75 m] per mile to make up the difference in tire circumferences. Static load radius $\pi \times 26 = 13.9 \times 3.14 \times 26 = 94.56$ ft [28.74 m] per mile.

The increased slippage results in increased tread wear and in an irregular pattern. It also causes an

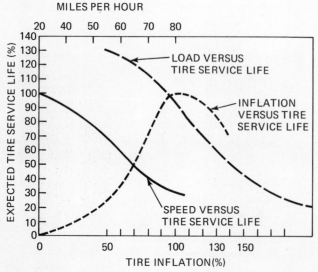

MILES PER HOUR

Fig. 12-27   Tire life versus speed, inflation, pressure, and load.

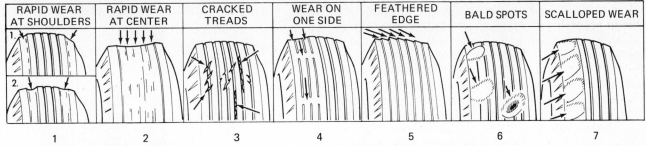

RAPID WEAR AT SHOULDERS	RAPID WEAR AT CENTER	CRACKED TREADS	WEAR ON ONE SIDE	FEATHERED EDGE	BALD SPOTS	SCALLOPED WEAR
1	2	3	4	5	6	7

1. Under-inflation or lack of rotation
2. Over-inflation or lack of rotation
3. Under-inflation or excessive speed
4. Excessive camber
5. Incorrect toe
6. Unbalanced wheel
7. Lack of rotation of tires, or worn, or out-of-alignment suspension

Fig. 12-28 Tire wear patterns. (*Chrysler Corporation*)

increase in temperature of the smaller tire and may cause ply or tread separation, or the tire may totally disintegrate. In addition, the larger tire must carry more weight, which leads to overheating and possible failure. If the left and right dual sets are not of the same diameter, the differential must work continuously to compensate for the difference in revolutions per mile, which, of course, increases differential wear. If the tires of a front or a rear tandem axle do not have the same diameter, the smaller diameter tires will wear faster and irregularly because the larger tires drive the vehicle while the smaller tires increase in slippage. However, if an interaxle differential is used, the drive axle having the smaller tires is allowed to make 737 revolutions per mile and the larger tires on the other drive axle are allowed to make 711 revolutions per mile because of the interaxle differential.

Before a set of tires is measured and selected for a single or a tandem drive axle, they must have been inflated for at least 24 hours. You must also know the recommended maximum allowable tire circumference or diameter difference and then check the tires against these specifications. A difference of $\frac{1}{4}$ in [6.35 mm] in diameter or $\frac{3}{4}$ in [19.05 mm] in circumference is usually the maximum allowable difference recommended by the tire and truck manufacturers.

There are many ways in which to measure or match a set of tires, but a positive way is to measure the circumference with a tape measure. A tire caliper or matching caliper will also give you an accurate measurement. If the tires are already installed to the vehicle, you may use a straight edge or hold a string across the tires to determine the variation, but this will not give you an accurate measurement of the difference between the circumferences of the tires (see Fig. 12-29).

When mounting dual tires, make certain you have the specified spacing between the tires. If the spacing is too small, the tire sidewalls may come in contact with each other as the tire makes it footprint on the road. Such contact will develop excessive heat and lead to ply separation or to thread separation from the cord body.

Abnormal Tire Wear Abnormal tire wear can also result from improper tire-to-rim installation, a bent rim or disk wheel, a twisted or egg-shaped rim or disk, or excessive runout due to improper tightening sequence or unevenly torqued wheel nuts. See discussion of disk wheels and rims, removal and installation in this unit.

Another contributor to reduction of tire life is suspension trouble or wear caused by broken or weak springs which allow the load to shift to the side of the vehicle where the spring is weak. This increases the load on the tires on the side where the spring is weak. Worn spring shackles, broken center bolts, worn tire rod ends, king pin bushings, or wheel and a bent axle housing each results in axle misalignment (tracking), and this, in turn, causes the tires to wear abnormally. Faulty brakes, that is, oversensitive, misadjusted, or improperly installed brakes, also cause abnormal tire wear. Other causes are misalignment of the front axle, toe-in, camber, or caster; a loose or misadjusted steering gear; or worn tie rod ends, king pin bushings, or wheel bearings. A bent axle affects the front-end steering geometry and may thereby change the toe-in, camber, and caster. Too much toe-in feathers the inside edge of the tread ribs like hacksaw teeth, and too

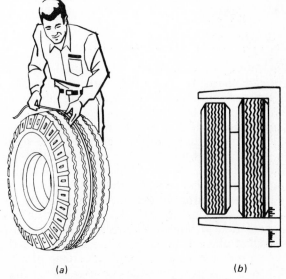

(a)   (b)

Fig. 12-29 Measuring tire circumference: (*a*) using a tape measure; (*b*) using a matching caliber. (*Mack Canada Inc.*)

158

much toe-out shows feathering on the outside edges of the tread ribs. Too much positive camber due to misadjustment or due to a bent spindle or axle wears the outside tread edge. Conversely, too much negative camber due to misadjustment, loose wheel bearings, worn king pin bushings, or bent axles wears the inside tread surface. Uneven or excessive tire wear due to insufficient, excessive, or uneven caster may be caused by a twisted axle or misadjusted caster. Furthermore, a front axle with uneven caster causes the vehicle to pull to one side, whereas excessive caster may cause shimmy tire wear, and insufficient caster may cause wandering and result in spotty tire wear.

Tire failure or excessive wear over which you have little or no control is that of overloading, or the load's being wrongly placed on the vehicle, or abusive driving practices. Overloading is very common on off-highway trucks, tractors, and trailers, even though it is costly and unsafe. Tires which are required to carry a load greater than that recommended flex more than usual. The core in the interior lower sidewalls or near the tread surface then breaks, and as a result there may be air pressure loss, which can gradually lead to total destruction of the tire. Overloading, misplaced load, or abusive driving may also cause wheel or rim failure or wheel hub failure.

Another tire-destroying factor over which the mechanic has no control is the condition of the haul road. Often the costs for tires and vehicle repair would have been saved many times over if more time, money, and effort had been spent to maintain the off-highway haul road.

When off-highway tires show minor cuts, snags, or punctures, they should be repaired as soon as they are discovered to prevent further tire deterioration or total tire failure. To repair a minor tire defect, take a sharp-pointed knife and skive the damaged tread. The angle of the knife, while cutting, should be about 45°, which is sufficient to prevent foreign material from lodging in the cut. The knife should reach the bottom of the hole or cut, but it should not go deeper than the first breaker. If the defect extends beyond the first breaker, the tire must be removed for service.

Tire Tubes   When a tire tube is inflated with air, it is forced against the inner tire walls, the tire flap, or the rim and thus supports the load. The tubes for car tires or for light truck tires are usually made from a butyl compound, and for heavy-duty applications they are made from chloro-butyl compound to give the tube a higher heat resistance. Tubes made from natural rubber are used mainly where the ambient temperature is near or below the freezing level. This is because a synthetic tube loses much of its flexibility at these temperatures. Most tubes have external vent ribs to release the air that is trapped between the tube and inner tire walls during inflation.

The production method and the shape of a tube used for a bias ply tire (small or large) are different from those used for a radial tire. It is therefore essential that you use a radial tube with a radial tire.

Fig. 12-30   Sectional view of tire valves.

Tube sizes are identifiable by a code number so that they may be matched to the correct tire. The manufacturer's name is also shown. Radial tubes are further identified with an R. An example of a tube identification code may be as follows: code number XXXX, or the tire size 1800-25 and the manufacturer's name DOE COMPANY. Car and light truck tubes may be used for more than one tire size, for example, a tube having a code number XXXX could be used with a 6.70-15, 7.10-15, 7.75-15, or 8.15-15 tire.

Tube Valves   Tube valves are used to confine the air pressure within the tube and to make a link from the tube to the outside of the rim (or as a link from the rim to the outside) so that the air chuck can be connected to inflate the tube or tubeless tire. The tube valve consists of the tube spud (valve base), valve stem, valve core, and the valve cap (see Fig. 12-30). The tube spud is vulcanized onto the inside or the outside of the tube. Valve stems of different lengths are screwed to the spud and sealed with an O ring.

NOTE   The large valve stem, when new, is straight and it must therefore be bent with a special bending tool to fit the intended application. The valve spud and valve stem on small tubes are usually a single unit.

Another type of valve (used on large tubes) is one in which the tube spud is vulcanized from the inside or outside to the tube. A steel collar is placed over the outside of the spud, and a nut secures the collar to the spud. The valve stem or valve stem extension is screwed to the spud and sealed with an O ring (see Fig. 12-31).

There are as many different valves which are sealed to the rim for tubeless tires as there are tube valves. In all cases the rim has one hole varying in size in which the base of the snap-in valve or tubeless spud is positioned. The base design of the snap-on valve holds it firmly and airtight in the rim hole,

Fig. 12-31 Spud assembly for tube valves.

whereas the spout is sealed to the rim with one or two rubber grommets, and a ring washer and nut holds the assembly to the rim. The valve extensions or valve stems, also varying in length, are screwed to the spud. An O ring is used to seal between the spud and the stem.

Whether a tube valve or a tubeless valve (see Fig. 12-32) is used, the valve core is screwed with a special tool into the end of the valve stem or extension. The valve core is a simple one-way check valve consisting of the seat, stem, and valve spring. It allows air to enter the tube or tire but allows it to escape only when the valve stem is manually lifted off its seat. The valve cap acts as a secondary air valve and

Fig. 12-32 Tubeless tire valves.

also protects the valve core from contamination since the rubber seal rests against the end of the valve stem (when installed).

Agricultural or other equipment where liquid ballasts may be used has a specially designed valve stem to accommodate the special hydro valve. When dry ballasts are used, a special valve and valve core are also installed.

Truck Tire Flaps All tube-type tires require a tire flap to protect the tube and to prevent tube distortion. The tire flap is contoured to the particular rim design on which it will be used. The flap size marking 20-8, for example, indicates the nominal rim diameter (20 in [508 mm]) and the actual flap width (8 in [203.2 mm]). When the valve hole is off-center, it is marked with a star. **NOTE** Radial tires require special flaps.

Tire-Handling Safety Tips Conforming to safety rules should rate first in the procedures to remove wheels or to mount and demount tires of any kind. Following the suggestions listed here will minimize injury to yourself or to others. **NOTE** An inflated tire has the potential force of dynamite.

- Make certain the vehicle is safely blocked on both sides (not only the side on which you are working) to prevent the vehicle's slipping on the blocks or stands.
- When raising a vehicle which is not positioned on a cement floor, place hardwood blocks under the jacks and stands.
- Allow yourself adequate room to remove the disk wheel or rim and to demount or mount the tire.
- Keep the floor clean and dry.
- Hang a sign on the steering wheel "DO NOT START ENGINE." (The vibration of the engine could rock the vehicle from the blocks on which it stands.)
- Do not take short cuts by eliminating safety procedures.
- Whenever possible, use a (safe) lifting device.
- If no lifting device is available, roll the tire to the work area; do not try to carry it.
- If you must lift a tire, or disk wheel, or rim, lift it from a squat position. (Lifting from a waist-bend position can cause back injury.)
- Do not drop an inflated tire. It will bounce with great force and may cause injury to yourself or to others.
- Deflate the tire before you remove it from the wheel hub.
- Do not inflate a flat or seriously underinflated tire when the disk wheel or rim is mounted to the vehicle. Remove it for service.
- When deflating a tire, first depress the valve core stem to reduce most of the pressure, after which you can remove the valve core. If you remove the valve core when the tire is inflated, even to 70 psi [482.3 kPa], it would have a force of about 376 lb [1670.9 N], which is equivalent to the force of a bullet fired from a rifle.
- Demount or mount drop-center rim tires by using

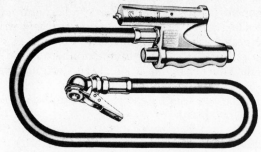

Fig. 12-33 Button control chuck gauge with clip-on air chuck. (*Schrader Automotive Products Division Scovill*)

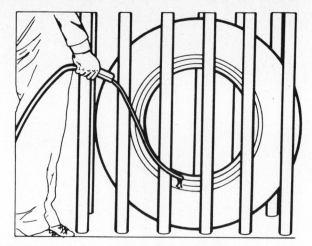

Fig. 12-34 Safety device to be used while inflating tire.

a tire-changing machine and *follow* the instructions provided in the machine's operating manual.

- When using the special tire iron, keep your hands free of oil and grease. Grip firmly so that it will not slip from your hands.
- Use only those tools which were especially designed for the job you are undertaking. Makeshift tools such as a standard prybar screwdriver, etc., may not only injure you but may also damage the rim and/or tire bead.
- When demounting or mounting a tire of a two-, three-, or five-piece split-rim design, follow the recommended steps outlined in the tire or rim manufacturer's manual. Make certain the rim sets are matched. Do not use components from another manufacturer or of a different size.
- Do not attempt to repair disk wheels or rim parts by welding, heating, or brazing. Do not reuse a deformed, badly rusted, or cracked lock ring, side ring, or rim or disk wheel. Such a rim or disk wheel could fly apart during inflation or after being placed in service.
- Do not use a cut or scarred tire before having it repaired.
- When using a wire buffer to remove contaminants and rust, wear a face shield to protect yourself from the subsequent flying scales.
- Use a rubber-covered steelhead hammer to reduce the force of flying pieces of steel that may break off from the hammer or rim.
- Before inflating a tire, attach a remote-control clip on air valve chuck (see Fig. 12-33) to the valve stem so that you can stand on one side of the tire (not in front of or over the tire) during inflation. Make certain all component parts are properly seated before inflating the tire.
- When the rim assembly seats as the tire is inflated, attach a portable safety device or use a tire cage to prevent the possibility of injury from a flying lock ring or rim flange. (A portable safety device is the safer; see Fig. 12-34).

DEMOUNTING AND MOUNTING TIRES

There are various methods to mount and demount tires, dependent on the types of rims and tires, and therefore, only the general procedures will be cov-

ered. In all cases, however, the proper tools are essential if you are to guarantee your work and not endanger yourself or damage the rim or tire (see Fig. 12-35).

In addition to the tools, you will need a wire hand brush or power brush, emery cloth, steel wool, a pair of vise grips, fast-drying paint, the recommended rubber lubricant, wooden blocks, a portable safety device or a tire cage, and a mounting and deflating tool. **CAUTION** When mounting a tire to an aluminum rim, do not use any rubber lubricant. Use only soapy water (and use regular soap, NOT detergent).

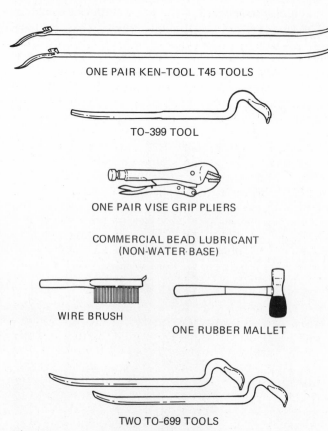

ONE PAIR KEN-TOOL T45 TOOLS

TO-399 TOOL

ONE PAIR VISE GRIP PLIERS

COMMERCIAL BEAD LUBRICANT (NON-WATER-BASE)

WIRE BRUSH

ONE RUBBER MALLET

TWO TO-699 TOOLS

Fig. 12-35 Tools required to demount and mount on-highway tires. (*Motor Wheel Corporation—Goodyear*)

CENTER MAST

DEMOUNTING TOOL

HOLD-DOWN SCREW

Fig. 12-36 Tire mounted to power tire changer (removing upper tire bead).

Demounting Small Tubeless Tires When demounting a tubeless tire from a car or a small truck, use a power tire changer (see Fig. 12-36). Place the fully deflated tire over the center mast, and one wheel stud hole over the side pin, and then screw the cone adapter against the centerbore of the disk to secure it to the machine. Activate the air valve to bring the upper and lower half-moon-shaped bead breaker arms against the tire, near the rim flange. This forces the beads loose from the rim flange and bead seat. Now push the flat end of the demounting tool over the rim flange and under the tire bead with the slot of the demounting tool over the flat end of the center mast. Push the other side of the tire bead into the drop center of the rim and then operate the air valve to rotate the center mast. At the same time place one hand onto the other end of the demounting tool to prevent the tool from sliding from the mast. This rotation will cause the upper tire bead to be lifted over the rim flange. Now lift up one side of the tire and place the demounting tool between the upper rim flange and the lower tire bead and again lift the slot over the flat end of the center mast. With one hand raise up the opposite side of the tire, place the other hand onto the demounting tool, and then activate the valve to rotate the mast. The lower bead will then slide over the top rim flange. Remove the tire valve from the rim with a hammer or with a knife and cut off the base of the tire valve. Remove the rim from the tire changer machine and with a wire hand brush or a power brush clean the entire rim surface. You can also use a sand blaster if you have one; it is faster and more efficient.

After cleaning the disk wheel, examine it thoroughly, as previously outlined. If necessary, remove nicks and burrs with a file and straighten out any small dents with a rubber-covered hammer. Clean the rim flange and bead seat with steel wool. However, if they are excessively rusted or pitted, the whole assembly must be replaced because the bead would not be seated airtight and would therefore cause tire failure. If necessary, clean, dry, and paint the bare metal surface of the rim. (Use a flat-drying metal primer and paint.)

Mounting the Small Tubeless Tires Fasten the disk wheel to the center mast. Using a new valve, screw the mounting tool onto the valve stem. Lubricate the valve base and push the valve tool handle through the rim hole, from the inside to the outside. With a sharp pull on the handle, seat the valve into its bore. Lubricate the tire beads, the rim bead seat, and the rim flange. Place one side of the tire over the rim so that its lower tire bead rests in the drop center. Force the other side of the lower tire bead over the rim flange. Press one side of the upper tire bead into the drop center and place the other side of the demounting tool between the bead and rim flange. The slot must come over the center mast.

Activate the control valve to rotate the center mast. The rotating tool will cause the tire bead to slide over the rim flange. Remove the tool. Lift and rotate the tire to position it onto the bead seat. Attach a remote control inflation chuck to the valve stem and inflate air into the tire. The air leaving the circle ring blows against the air leaving the tire at the lower bead. As a result, the pressure rises within the tire and forces the lower and upper bead to seat. If the tire changer does not have the lower ring, place a tire-mounting band around the center of the tire tread and engage it. This compresses the center of the tire tread, spreading the beads against the rim bead seat. Give the tire a few quick shots of air to seat the bead properly. Remove the inflation tool, install the valve core, and inflate the tire to the recommended pressure. Replace the valve cap onto the valve stem.

Demounting a Tubeless Truck Tire Because tubeless truck tires are less flexible and much heavier than car tires, a larger power tire changer must be used. When this is not stocked, you must demount them with a tire iron (see Fig. 12-37), which is a more complex procedure. In this case, start by laying the fully deflated tire flat on the floor. Try to loosen the beads from the rim flange and bead seat by walking on the tire with the heels close to the rim flange. If this does not loosen the beads, place the flat of the curved end of tool B between the rim flange and bead so that the handle end is in a vertical position. With a rubber mallet, hammer onto the curved neck of the tire tool until it is driven between the rim flange and the bead, causing them to separate. Repeat this procedure a few inches further along the rim flange. After you have broken both beads loose, place the tire so that the wide side of the top rim faces downward and then thoroughly lubricate the top bead. Place the spoon ends of the tire irons about $\frac{1}{2}$ in [12.7 cm] from each side of the valve stem (between the rim and the top bead) so that the stop shoulder rests against the rim flange. Next, stand on the opposite side of the tire to bring the top bead to the height of the drop center. Pull one tire iron tool toward the center of the rim and place one foot on the tire. Pull the other tool toward the center of the rim and move your foot from the first tire iron onto the second one.

Remove the first tire iron, insert it between the rim flange and the bead (about $\frac{1}{2}$ in in front of the

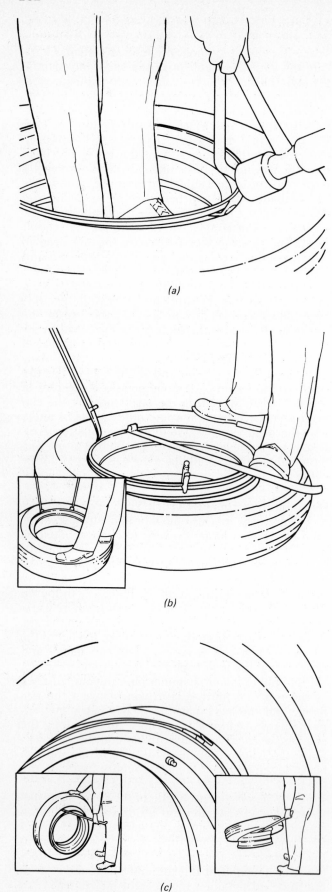

(a)

(b)

(c)

Fig. 12-37 Removing a tubeless truck tire. (a) Breaking the first bead loose. (b) Removing the first bead from the rim. (c) Removing the rim from the tire. (*Motor Wheel Corporation—Goodyear*)

second iron), and then pull it toward the center of the rim. Repeat these steps until the top bead lifts over the rim flange. You can now stand the tire upright and lubricate the second bead and rim flange.

Lean the tire so that the rim falls toward you and the lower tire bead is in the drop center. Insert the straight end of the tire iron at the top between the rim and bead. Lubricate the bead and rim area where the tire and rim meet. Next, hold the tire firmly and let the assembly fall toward you. Rock the tire to pry out the disk wheel or insert the other tire iron close to the first one to pry it out.

Mounting a Tubeless Truck Tire Once the tire is removed, take out the valve and clean and inspect the disk wheel as previously outlined. Before replacing the valve, place the disk wheel with the wide side downward, on the floor. (Make certain the floor is clean.) Lubricate the first bead and upper rim flange and bead seat. Place the tire over the rim so that one side of the first bead lies in the drop center. Insert the straight end of the tool with the stop against the rim flange close to the point where the bead contacts the rim flange. Place your foot onto the tire at the point where the bead contacts the rim flange. Now push the tire iron outward. This will move the bead over the flange and pull the other side into the drop center. Again insert the tire iron where the bead contacts the rim flange, move your foot close to the tire iron, and then push it outward.

Repeat the procedure until the first bead comes over the rim flange. Lubricate the rim flange and outer tire bead. Stand full weight on one side of the tire to force the outer bead into the drop center. You may, at this time, have to relubricate the bead and rim flange. Next, insert the curved end of the tool between the bead and rim flange at a point close to where the bead and rim flange meet and then force the stop against the rim flange. While pushing the tool outward, follow along with the weight of your foot, to aid the installation and to hold the bead in position. If the other side of the tire bead slips out of position, place a vise grip onto the rim flange but take care not to damage the inner rim flange surface. Repeat the procedure (using one tool) until about 17.9 in [45 cm] of bead remains near the rim flange. Lubricate the bead and rim flange and then insert two tire irons to force the remaining bead over the rim flange (see Fig. 12-38).

Roll the tire into a tire cage or install a safety removal device. Connect the remote-control clip-on air valve chuck to the valve stem. Apply air to the tire to seat the beads. It may be necessary to rotate the disk wheel or rim or to install a tire-mounting band to help seat the beads. Once the beads are seated, install the valve core and then inflate the tire to the recommended pressure. Check the valve for air leakage before placing the valve cap onto the valve stem.

Demounting a Tubeless Off-highway Tire Tubeless (or tube-type) tires of off-highway vehicles having a drop-center disk wheel or rim or a five-piece rim design can be demounted and mounted safely

163

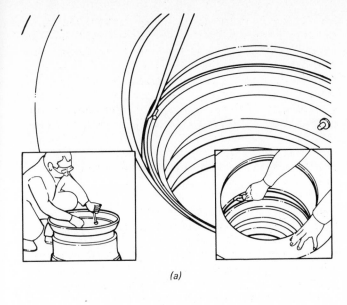

(a)

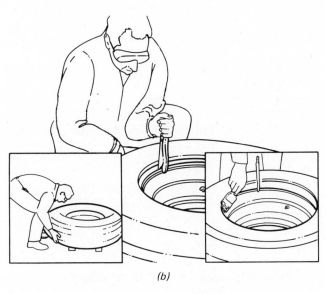

(b)

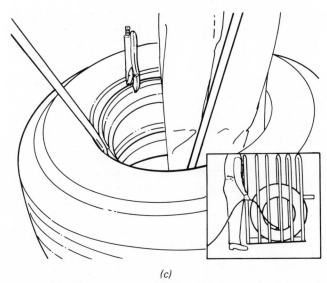

(c)

Fig. 12-38 Installing a tubeless truck tire. (a) Preparing the rim and tire for mounting. (c) Installing the first bead. (c) Preparing to install second bead. (c) Installing second bead and inflation. (*Motor Wheel Corporation—Goodyear*)

with the rim or disk wheel fastened to the wheel hub. However, you will require special hydraulic actuating tools and adapters to minimize the time required to break the beads loose and demount the tire (see Fig. 12-39).

To demount a tubeless tire having a five-piece rim design (see Fig. 12-40), first deflate the tire completely (applying all safety rules). Next, place a sling around the tire, attach a lifting device to the sling, and take up the slack. Install the clamp tool and securely tighten any adjusting screws at the bottom of the jaws. Set the hand screws against the lock ring and adjust them until the jaw assembly is at a right-angle position to the plane of the flange. Retract the hydraulic ram and insert it between the open sides of the frame. Place the spade tip between the tire bead and rim flange. Raise the ram assembly until the trunnion engages the frame shoulder support and then screw the stop screw into the support ram. Apply pressure to the ram (by means of the hydraulic pump) until the spade has moved the tire bead on the bead seat band far enough to place a bead wedge between the beads and the rim flange on each side of the spade.

Release the pump pressure. Relocate the (spade) assembly about 60° from the first installation (either to the left or to the right).

Repeat the entire procedure several times until the tire bead comes loose from the bead seat band. Now move the bead seat band away from the lock ring so that you can remove the lock ring. To do this, place the hook end of the special prybar in the groove of the rim and between the two ends of the lock ring. Next, place a pipe over the bar to increase leverage and then pry upward. Near the first prybar, place the hook end of a second prybar between the lock ring and the bead seat band, and then move the first bar in front of a second bar. Pry upward as in Fig. 12-39*b*.

Repeat this entire procedure all the way around the lock ring so that the lock ring can be removed.

To remove the lock ring, place the flat end of the prybar in the groove of the rim and pry the tool downward (to lift the end of the lock ring over the rim). Next, use two prybars and work around the rim to remove the lock ring from the rim. Remove the O ring from the rim and discard it.

Place the two hook ends of the prybar between the outer rim flange and bead seat band. Lift the tool upward to pry the bead seat band away from the rim flange. Remove the band and outer rim flange from the rim. Now, using the same procedure, break the inside bead loose from the rim. Remove the tire from the rim and then remove the inner rim flange.

After the tire is removed, use a sand blaster or a wire brush to remove any rust, dirt, or rubber particles. Replace any parts that are damaged, twisted, or cracked. If the surfaces of the rim flanges, the rim, the O ring groove, or the bead seat band are eroded sufficiently to cause an air leak or to secure the lock ring inadequately, these parts must be replaced.

If it appears necessary, paint the rim assembly parts with a fast-drying metal primer and then install a new valve spud. However, before installing it,

164

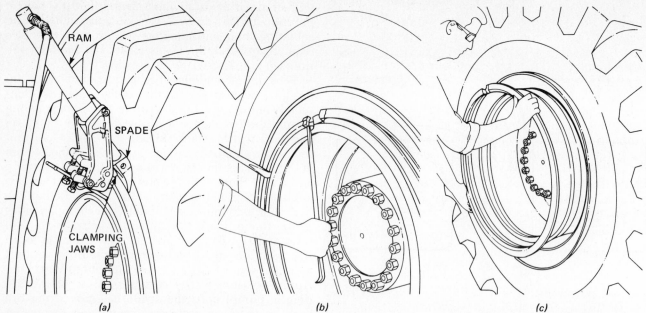

Fig. 12-39 Demounting a tubeless off-highway tire. (a) Breaking the bead loose; (b) removing locking ring; (c) removing bead seat band. (*Terex Division of General Motors Corporation*)

check the rim bore, lubricate it and the spud rubber grommet, and push the spud from the outside through the rim hole.

CAUTION Take care not to damage the grommet or the valve spud threads. Screw the spud nut securely to the spud. Lubricate the O ring on the valve extension insert. Align and then fasten it to the spud.

Mounting a Tubeless Off-highway Tire First, place the inner flange over the rim base so that the drive lug rests on the slot of the rim base. Lift the tire and place it over the rim base firmly against the inner rim flange. Place the outer rim flange onto the rim and align the drive lug with the slot in the rim base. Then push the tapered bead seat band over the rim base and underneath the tire bead and outer

rim flange. At the same time align and engage the slot with the drive lug. Now, using tire irons or the forks of a forklift, push the tapered bead seat band past the O ring groove in the rim. **NOTE** Place wooden blocks between the tire and ends of the forks to prevent sidewall damage.

Align the lock ring drive lug with the slots in the bead seat band and the rim base and then, using the tire tool, install the lock ring. Make certain it is seated properly in its groove (and that the lug seats properly in the rim base slot).

Lubricate the O ring and O ring grooves with the recommended lubricant and then place the O ring in the lower rim groove. Spread it over the lock ring and into the O ring groove. Make certain that the O ring is not rolled or twisted. If it is rolled or twisted, use a pencil or similar object and place it underneath

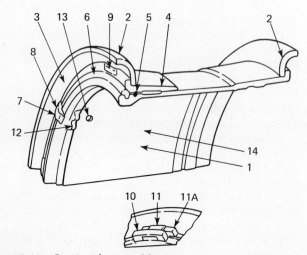

1. Rim base
2. Flanges (side ring)
3. 5° bead seat band, tapered ring
4. Bead seat band toe
5. O-ring gasket
6. Lock ring
7. Lock ring driver
8. Gutter notch for lock ring driver
9. Pry bar slot
10. Outboard driver pocket (rim base)
11. Locking driver key
11A. Outboard driver pocket (bead seat band)
12. Locator—demountable rim only
13. Tubeless valve hole
14. Stub valve slot (not shown)

Fig. 12-40 Sectional view of five-piece rim assembly. (*Terex Division of General Motors Corporation*)

the O ring. With the pencil under the O ring and resting on the rim, move it in a complete circle to take out the twist or roll; with the other hand, guide the O ring back into its groove. After the O ring is installed, again lubricate it and its surrounding area. Pull the tapered bead seat band and the outer rim flange outward and over the O ring, against the lock ring. Check that all parts are correctly positioned and that the lugs are engaged in their slots before inflating the tire to the pressure recommended to seat the beads. Once the beads are fully seated, deflate the tire and install the valve core and then reinflate the tire to the recommended cold pressure. Finally, check for possible air losses by using the soapy water and brush method.

NOTE Take all safety precautions outlined earlier in this unit under the heading "Tire-Handling Safety Tips."

Demounting and Mounting a Tube-type Off-highway Tire The primary difference between demounting an off-highway tube-type tire and an off-highway tubeless tire is in the removal and installation of the tire flap and, of course, the tube.

To remove the tube flap and tube, use a tire spreader or a hydraulic jack to spread the beads apart. Pry and roll first the flap and then the tube from the tire casing. After cleaning and then inspecting the tube, the tire flap, the valve stem, and the inner casing for breaks and bruises, lubricate the casing, the tube, and flap with an approved dry lubricant such as soapstone.

When preparing to mount the tire, first hang the tube over your shoulder so that the valve stem is at the bottom and faces in the intended direction, that is, to the outside or the inside, as it will be installed. Next, place the tube in the bottom of the tire casing and gradually work it (to the left and to the right) into the casing. Apply some air to the tube as you progress, to hold it in place and to prevent tube wrinkles.

After the tube is installed, rotate it so that the valve stem is in the correct position. Place the valve stem through the flap hole and work the flap ends between the tube and the tire beads, but make certain the tube is centered and free of wrinkles. When placing the tire over the rim base, make certain the valve stem aligns properly with the slot in the rim and that it has not been damaged during installation.

CAUTION Do not apply the inflation pressure until you have pulled the tapered bead seat band and outer rim flange out over the lock ring.

NOTE Double inflation is necessary to ensure that the tire tube and flap are located properly within the tire casing. This will prevent wrinkles which could lead to premature tire failure.

Demounting a Tube-type Tire from a Two-piece Rim Lay the fully deflated tire assembly with the side ring flange facing upward on the clean floor. To break the outside tire bead loose from the rim seat and side ring, hammer the curved end of the tire tool

between the tire bead and side ring flange. This will loosen the bead from the side ring and rim seat. Continue inserting and prying one or both tools progressively around the tire until the bead is completely free from the bead seat (see Fig. 12-41).

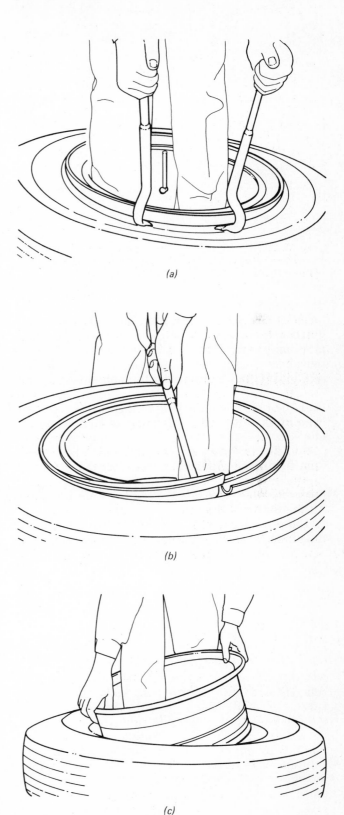

(a)

(b)

(c)

Fig. 12-41 Demounting the tire from a two piece rim. (a) Loosening the bead. (b) Removing the side ring. (c) Removing the rim. (*Motor Wheel Corporation—Goodyear*)

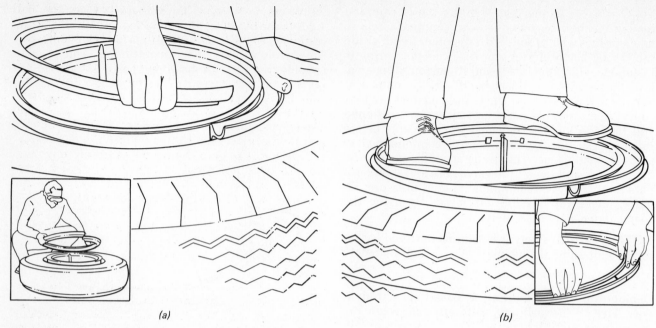

Fig. 12-42 (a) Mounting the tire; (b) placing side ring in place, and installing. (*Motor Wheel Corporation—Goodyear*)

To disengage the side ring flange from the rim gutter, insert one rim tool in the tool slot of the side ring and pry the ring upward and outward. The removal can be accelerated by inserting the hook end of a second tool between the tire and side ring and then prying downward on the tire to free the ring from the tire bead. Continue in this manner around the rim until the side ring flange is completely removed.

Turn the tire over and unseat the tire bead in the same manner in which you broke loose the first bead. Lift the rim (the side opposite from the valve stem), push the valve stem through the rim hole, and then lift the rim from the tire.

The procedure to remove the tire flap and tube is the same as that outlined for off-highway tires.

NOTE You are advised against using an old tube with a new tire, because the old tube will have stretched and will therefore wrinkle when installed.

Mounting a Tube-type Tire on a Two-piece Rim After a new tube and tire flap have been placed within the tire casing, lay the rim on the clean floor, with the valve slot facing upward. Align the valve with the rim valve slot and place the tire onto the rim. Tilt it slightly to insert the valve through the valve slot. Now place the side ring flange onto the rim base so that the side ring split is opposite the valve stem. Force the leading end of the ring into the rim gutter by placing one foot at or near the split and the other foot (close to the first one) onto the side ring. Progressively work the side ring into place (see Fig. 12-42). Check the seating of the side ring; if it is satisfactory, place the tire into a safety cage and inflate the tire to 10 psi [68.9 kPa] or install a portable safety device before inflating.

Again check to ensure proper engagement of the side ring. If the assembly is not properly engaged, deflate the tire and reinstall correctly. Never hammer on an inflated or partially inflated tire and rim assembly to correct the engagement, for an accident may result.

After the assembly is properly inflated (to the recommended pressure) to seat the beads, recheck the beads to see that they are properly seated. If so, completely deflate the tire to prevent wrinkling of the tube, install the valve core, and then inflate the tire to the recommended cold pressure. Install the valve cap.

Demounting a Tire from a Three-place Rim Assembly Place the fully deflated tire assembly on the clean floor, with the lock ring facing upward. Starting opposite the valve stem, hammer the hook end of the first tire tool and then the hook end of the second tire tool between the side ring flange and the tire bead (see Fig. 12-43).

Next, remove one tool and place it about 3.9 in [10 cm] from the other, into the space between the side ring flange and the tire bead. Press the tool down onto the sidewall of the tire to free the bead. Work around the tire until the entire bead is loosened from the bead seat and side ring flange. Once the bead is broken loose, straddle the tire by standing on the side ring flange and tire sidewalls. This will force the side ring flange down and expose the lock ring. While in this position, disengage the lock ring from the rim gutter by inserting the rim tool in the removing notch near the split in the lock ring. Push downward to pry the ring up. If necessary, a second tool may be used to aid the removal.

Move progressively around the rim until the lock ring is free and then lift off the lock ring and the side ring flange. Turn the tire assembly over. Unseat

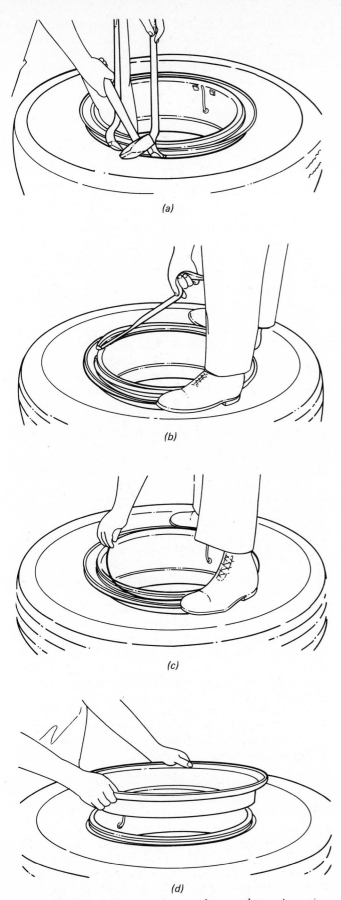

Fig. 12-43 Demounting the tire from a three-piece rim. (a) Starting to break bead loose from side ring flange. (b) Removing locking ring. (c) Removing O ring. (d) Removing side ring flange. (*Mack Canada Inc.*)

the tire bead in much the same manner as you did when breaking the first bead loose. Stand the tire in a vertical position and rock the rim from the tire.

Mounting a Tire on a Three-piece Rim Assembly
Remove the old valve and then clean and inspect the rim or disk wheel. After installing a new valve, place the rim on the clean floor with the fixed rim flange downward. Lubricate the base of both tire beads, place the tire over the rim, and place the removable side ring flange onto the bead of the tire and over the rim base. Make certain that the side ring does not bind on the rim base (see Fig. 12-44).

Stand on the side ring flange and sidewall to position the ring about 1.9 in (4 cm) below the rim gutter. Maintaining this position, insert the tapered toe of the lock ring between the bead and rim base and then place one end of the lock ring into the rim gutter.

Put one foot on the lock ring and hammer the end of the ring into position with a rim mallet. Using both feet to hold the lock ring, continue progressively around the rim, hammering the lock ring into the rim gutter. After checking the seating of the rings, inflate the tire to 10 psi [68.9 kPa].

The final inspection steps are identical to those previously outlined.

Ballast On agricultural equipment, where the weight of the tractor alone is insufficient for use of the maximum power of the engine—a condition that thereby prevents the equipment from reaching the maximum draw bar pull—additional ballast is added to the tractor, to reduce tire slippage. The additional weight can be added by specially designed cast iron weights mounted to the rear wheel hub, to the disk wheel, or to the frame. However, because of the cost factor, cast iron is not always used, but rather, a liquid or a dry ballast is placed inside the tire. Although the use of cast iron places the weight where it is most effective and reduces tire wear, more power is not needed to move this additional weight. Nevertheless dry or liquid ballast is more commonly used, and when further weight is needed to achieve the maximum draw bar pull and to maintain the tire slippage within 9 percent, cast iron weights are added.

The liquid ballast is water with a certain percentage of calcium chloride to prevent freezing. It is pumped into the tire tube through a special tube valve with the aid of a special hydrofloating adapter (see Fig. 12-45). The tire should not be filled more than 75 percent if it is to retain the inherent characteristics of a pneumatic tire and also withstand damage.

Dry ballast in the form of lead powder, although more expensive than liquid ballast, is less expensive than cast iron. In addition, it is claimed to have several advantages over liquid ballasts. It is said that dry ballast has about 10 percent less traction than its same weight in cast iron but has about 20 percent more traction than liquid ballast of the same weight.

A tractor having dry ballast requires less power than one having liquid ballast because the tire rolls

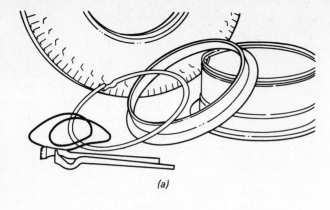

(a)

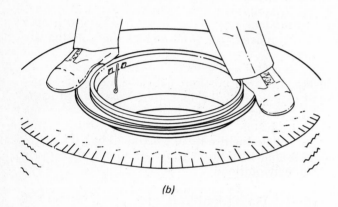

(b)

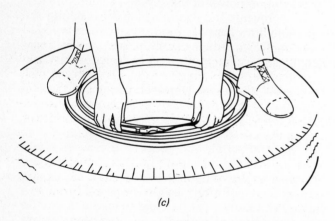

(c)

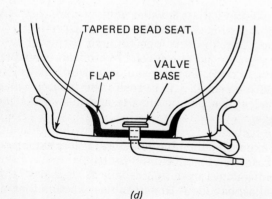

TAPERED BEAD SEAT

FLAP

VALVE BASE

(d)

Fig. 12-44 Mounting the tire on a three-piece rim. (a) Preparing for mounting. (b) Positioning side ring flange. (c) Installing O ring. (d) Proper position of tube flap. (*Mack Canada Inc.*)

easier, since it does not have to move the water uphill while the tire is rotating. In addition, the tractor gives a smoother ride, which accounts for the gain in traction and the better draw bar pull, and there is less tire wear. Its disadvantage is that most shops are not equipped to remove or refill the dry ballast in the event the tire is to be replaced.

Removing and Filling a Tire with Liquid Ballast
Assume you have to remove a 20.8-38 tire, the liquid ballast of which is 114 U.S. gal [431.49 l] of water and 258 lb [570 kg] of calcium chloride. Assume also that you have the equipment to make this tire and liquid ballast change. Your first task would be to remove the liquid from the tube. To remove the liquid, first raise the tire off the ground and then safely block both sides. Rotate the wheel so that the valve stem is at the top. Remove the valve cap and then loosen the valve core about two turns. Next, fasten the hydro-floating adapter A to the valve stem and then fasten part B to part A.

Reverse the direction control valve on the water pump and pull the bleed tube out before moving part C inward to engage it with the nut of the valve core. Turn the knob to unscrew the valve core nut. Once the nut is removed from the valve stem, pull part C outward to remove the valve core from the valve stem. Next, push the vent tube inward. Turn the tire so that the valve stem is at the bottom and then start the motor to operate the pump.

During the removal of the liquid, the vent tube equalizes the pressure within the tire tube and thus prevents a low-pressure buildup within the tube. With proper care and attention, 99 percent of the liquid can be withdrawn.

The tire-filling procedure repeats many of the steps taken to remove the liquid. Begin by rotating the wheel so that the valve stem is positioned at the top. Attach the valve core nut firmly to part C and pull part C outward. Next, connect part A to the valve stem and connect part B to part A. Position the vent tube in the 75 percent level of the tire as shown in Fig. 12-45.

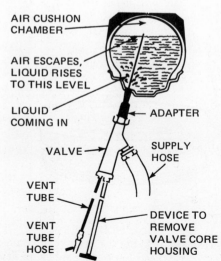

AIR CUSHION CHAMBER

AIR ESCAPES, LIQUID RISES TO THIS LEVEL

LIQUID COMING IN

ADAPTER

VALVE

SUPPLY HOSE

VENT TUBE

VENT TUBE HOSE

DEVICE TO REMOVE VALVE CORE HOUSING

Fig. 12-45 Hydro-flation procedure (*Firestone Tire and Rubber of Canada, Limited*)

To achieve the recommended mixture at the 75 percent level and maintain a freezing protection against −53°F [−47°C], you should mix 258.55 lb [570 kg] of calcium chloride with 114 gal [31.49 l] of water. After these ingredients are thoroughly mixed and cooled, start the motor to operate the pump.

During the pumping operation the vent lines will cause reduction of the pressure within the tire, and when the solution reaches the vent line level, it will leave the tire through the vent line. As soon as some solution leaves the tire, immediately stop the pumping action and move part C gently inward so that the valve core reaches into the valve stem bore. Promptly turn part C in a clockwise direction to engage the valve core nut with the valve stem. When this has been done, remove part B from part A and remove part A from the valve stem. Finger-tighten the valve core nut (do not use a pair of pliers) and inflate the tire to the recommended pressure.

NOTE Use a tire pressure gauge which is designed for this purpose. After use, wash it thoroughly in warm water to remove the salt solution; otherwise the gauge could deteriorate to uselessness.

Wheel Balancing Wheel balancing is the precision placement of the wheel weight onto the rim flange so as to offset any uneven distribution of the tire and wheel assembly weight and to counteract misalignment of rotating parts and moving load mass. An unbalanced wheel assembly having the heavy spot at or near the center line of the tire results in static imbalance (see Fig. 12-46a) causes hopping (wheel tramp) because the heavy spot, when approaching the top, has the effect of trying to lift the tire before driving it into the ground. Furthermore, as the heavy spot approaches the bottom (road surface), it causes the tire tread to flatten and thereby increases its footprint.

A wheel assembly (having the heavy spot at any point other than the area near the center line) is dynamically unbalanced (see Fig. 12-46b) and can be dangerous because it can cause the tire to wriggle or the wheel to shimmy. With rotation, the heavy spot influences the tire to turn to the left or to the right as the weight approaches the spindle height. Then, as the spot approaches the top of the tire, the tire moves back to the center line position. As it continues to rotate, the tire is again influenced to the right or to the left as the spot once more approaches the spindle height. It then moves back again to the center line position as the heavy spot returns to the bottom. How much the tire would tramp and/or shimmy depends largely on how much the assembly is out of static and/or dynamic balance. To give an example—if a truck tire size 1100-20 had a heavy spot of, say, only 3 oz [84 g] about 2 in (5.08 cm) from the center line of the tire, at a speed of about 60 mph [96.6 km/h], the tire would be lifted and lowered with a force of about 50 lb [222 N]. At the same time it would be caused to move (to the left or to the right) with a force of about 20 lb [88.8 N]. When such forces constantly act on the tire, the entire motor vehicle shakes and vibrates.

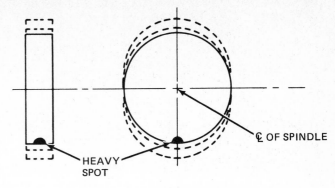

(a) WHEEL TRAMP

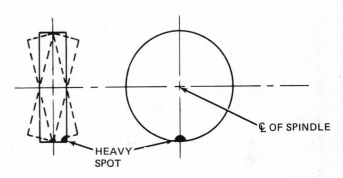

(b) WHEEL SHIMMY

Fig. 12-46 (a) Statically unbalanced wheel assembly; (b) dynamically unbalanced wheel assembly.

A wheel that is in balance rolls with low resistance over the road surface, whereas an unbalanced wheel assembly hops and wriggles. The driver feels how poorly the vehicle steers or handles, and he may also find that it is noisy or that it vibrates and shakes. Furthermore, the unbalanced condition causes excessive tire and suspension wear.

NOISE, VIBRATION, AND SHAKE Before attempting to diagnose the cause of noise, vibration, or shake, you should first consider what these terms mean to a mechanic.

Noise may be identified as any disturbing sound, particularly if it is accompanied by shake or vibration, although the latter sounds are secondary. Noise can emanate from the tire as it makes its footprint on the road, or it can be caused by a flat or soft spot on the tire. It can also originate from the drive line, front axle, or brakes. However, tire noise or whine is easily distinguishable from other noises, which vary in pitch as the speed of the vehicle varies. Tire noise remains relatively the same over a greater speed range.

Shake is a rapid, irregular, to-and-fro movement which mechanically should not exist.

Vibration, on the other hand, though similar to shake, happens with a constant frequency to generate a characteristic sound which will vary as the speed changes. It could originate from an unbalanced wheel assembly, a soft spot on the tire, a tire's having too large a radial or lateral runout, or under-

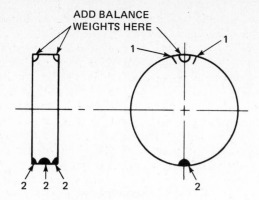

ADD BALANCE
WEIGHTS HERE

1) CHALK LINE 1 AND 2
2) THE LOCATION OF THE HEAVY POINT
   ON THE WHEEL ASSEMBLY

Fig. 12-47 Static balancer.

inflation or overinflation of the tires. It could also come from the drive line, frame, brakes, suspension, loose or damaged wheel bearings, or the engine or accessories.

When a driver complains of poor steering, difficult handling, noise, shake, or vibration, you should first visually inspect for damaged, broken, worn, or misadjusted springs, shackles, drive line, and center bearing and for a bent frame. Also check the inflation pressure of the tires and the tires' condition. Check for oil leaks at the clutch transmission, drive pinion shaft(s), axle seals, and shock absorbers. If no defect is found in these areas, raise the vehicle off the ground and block it safely. Next, check the wheel bearing adjustment, the tie rod ends, steering arm, drag link steering gear, and king pins, or ball joints for wear. If these components check out satisfactorily, check the wheel assembly to see if it is in balance.

NOTE A wheel assembly should be automatically checked for balance after about 20,000 miles [32,000 km], when the tires are rotated, and after a tire is remounted.

There are two general methods to balance a wheel assembly: on the vehicle or off the vehicle. The former method is more precise because it permits balancing, not only the wheel assembly, but also the rotating components, that is, the brake drum or rotor and the wheel hub. Using the former method, you can, in most cases, balance only the wheel assembly.

Static Balancing If your shop has no dynamic wheel balancer, then you can balance the wheel assembly only by the static method. Static wheel balancing (see Fig. 12-47) is the equal distribution of weight around the axis of the rotation (spindle) so that the wheel assembly will not rotate by itself, regardless of the position in which it is placed.

Before a wheel assembly is static balanced, several checks have to be made and the following steps taken:

- Clean all dirt from the assembly.
- Check the radial and lateral runout, and if it ex-

ceeds specification, replace the tire and/or rim or disk wheel or remount the tire.
- Remove imbedded stones from the tread grooves.
- Check the inflation pressure.
- Check the wheel bearing adjustment.
- If necessary, back off the brake adjustment.
- On wheels having hydraulically actuated disk brakes, remove the cover from the master cylinder and remove some brake fluid from the primary master cylinder reservoir before prying the brake pads away from the rotor. (This is necessary to avoid overflow.)

NOTE Do not forget, after the wheel balancing, to apply the brakes before adding fluid to the "full" level.

When the aforementioned procedures have been followed, chalk a horizontal line static mark precisely on the top sidewall of the tire (as a reference mark) because the tire now rests with the heavy spot at the bottom. Rotate the tire 90° and allow it free play until it comes to rest. Note the speed with which it returns and pendulates. When at rest, chalk another reference line on precisely the top of the tire. Now, rotate it 90° in the opposite direction and again let it come to rest. When it comes to rest, make a third line on the tire.

You now have three lines on the tire. Erase the center line, measure the distance between the remaining two lines, and find the center. Chalk mark this point and erase the two outside lines. You now have located the light spot of the tire and have noted the speed with which the tire came to rest. Unfortunately, you do not know the location of the heavy spot. It may be in the middle, to the left, or to the right side of the tire or on the wheel assembly. Furthermore, you do not know the weight of the heavy spot.

Selecting the correct weight is a matter of trial and error. If the assembly quickly comes to rest, select a 2-oz (56.70 gm) weight, and if it comes to rest slowly, select a weight 3 oz (85.05 gm) or more.

In any event, at precisely the marked line, tap the selected weight onto the rim flange. Turn the tire 90° in either direction. If the tire remains in this position, you have positioned and selected the correct static weight.

If the tire rotates upward, your selected weight is too light. If the tire rotates downward, the selected weight is too heavy.

If the total selected weight, when a small tire is balanced, is more than 2 oz (6 oz [170.10 g] or more, on a truck tire), place about two-thirds of the total weight onto the inside rim flange and one-third to the outside rim flange. If the weight is placed on only the inside or the outside, it may drastically upset the dynamic balance.

Bubble-type Tire Balancing The bubble-type balancer is a simple (off-vehicle) static balancer. It has a cone-shaped wheel support that rests on a needlepoint which is part of the stand. In the center of the wheel support is a bubble under a convex glass on which a crosshair is marked. A lever, when at

Fig. 12-48 Bubble-type wheel balancer.

rest, holds away the weight of the cone-shaped wheel support from the needlepoint. When released, it rests on the point (see Fig. 12-48).

To balance the tire, first rid the tire of all dirt, stones, and weights. Place the disk wheel center bore onto the cone-shaped wheel support as you would place it onto the wheel hub. Press the lever down. The tire will float in the plane and find its balance. If the tire is in balance, the bubble will center below the crosshair. If the bubble moves off-center, the tire is heavily spotted. The heavy spot will be on the side opposite that from which the bubble has moved.

Select a weight which you think would level the tire. Lay it onto the rim flange and watch the reaction of the bubble. Add or remove weight, or move the weight to the left or to the right, to bring the bubble under the crosshair. **NOTE** Also split the weight as outlined in this unit under the heading "Static Balancing."

Dynamic Balancers There are many dynamic wheel balancers on the market. Some are more expensive than others and some are more effective than others. Nevertheless it is not the machine alone that balances the wheel assembly. Balancing is achieved through the combined effort of the technician and the machine.

All dynamic balancers have a spindle to which the disk wheel or the wheel assembly can be fastened. The methods used to fasten the disk wheel or wheel hub (see Fig. 12-49) or to drive the spindle are much the same. The main differences are in the manner in which they sense the imbalanced condition of the tire assembly and in how this information is transmitted to the indicator.

One of many dynamic wheel balancers is shown in Fig. 12-50. The spindle of this balancer is supported on ball bearings which rest in their floating supports. Sensing pickups, which are adjusted

through an indicator dial knob, rest against the support. The balancer drive shaft is driven by a V belt and can be engaged or disengaged with the spindle. The drive shaft wheel has numbers from 0 to 9 which correspond with the spark dial. When the handle is in the vertical position and the motor is operating, the drive shaft is driven at low speed. When moved to a horizontal position, the drive shaft is driven at a high speed. When the lever is moved to the right, a brake is applied to stop the wheel and at the same time reduce the tension on the drive belt.

Before attempting to balance the wheel assembly, remove the inner and outer wheel bearing cones and seal. Clean away any excessive grease from the inside of the hub. Check the tire pressure and make certain the assembly is clean.

Select the small spindle for car and small truck tire assemblies and the large spindle for larger wheel or tire assemblies.

From the side (opposite the drive) of the spindle, remove the ball bearing by screwing the spindle nut against the ball bearing. Select the required cones and/or adapters. Securely fasten the wheel hub assembly to the spindle so that the wheel is at or near the center of the spindle and so that the brake drum faces toward the drive shaft. Install the ball bearing, pull out the drive shaft, and open the safety covers (located over the floating bearing supports).

Turn the knurled knobs of the adjusting dial about three turns, counterclockwise, to move the spring-loaded contact away from the floating bearing support. With a hoist, lift the assembly and then place the bearings into the pockets of the floating supports.

Mount a dial indicator in such a fashion that you can measure the radial runout and then the lateral runout. If the runout in either case exceeds the service manual specifications, remount the tire or replace the disk wheel and/or the tire. Now static balance the assembly as outlined previously.

Dynamic Balancing When the wheel assembly is in static balance, engage the drive shaft with the spindle. Start the electric motor to spin the assembly at low speed (lever in vertical position). Compare the oscillatory movement of each side of the bearing support. If the left side oscillates more, slowly turn the left adjusting dial until a spark flashes on the spark dial. Take note of the flashed number on the spark dial. Stop the electric motor. Pull the lever to the right to engage the brake and stop the wheel assembly.

NOTE Do not disengage the drive shaft. Turn the tires so that the number on the drive shaft wheel correlates with the number flashed on the spark dial, and aligns with the pointer in the window, and then locate the static mark (see Fig. 12-51). It can be anywhere—on the upper or lower half of the tire, or on the side facing you, or on the opposite side.

Say, for instance, that the static mark is at the spindle height and is on the side of the tire facing you. This indicates that the assembly is not in static balance and more weight is needed at the static point. If the static mark is at spindle height but is on

172

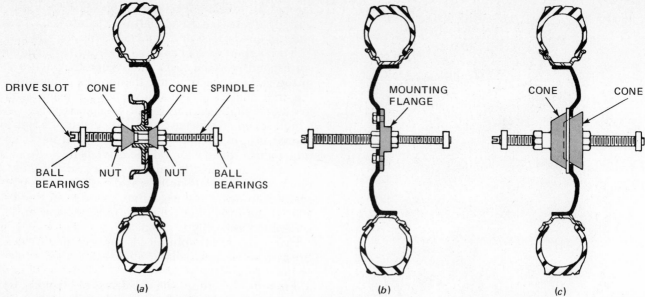

Fig. 12-49 Methods used to fasten tire or wheel hub to spindle: (a) using cones and nuts to hold and center wheel hub, (b) bolting disk wheel to mounting, (c) using cone and nuts to hold and position disk wheel.

the side of the tire facing away from you, again, the tire is not in static balance. There is too much weight at the static point.

NOTE Make certain when changing the weight that it is placed precisely at the static point, which in this case is at the spindle center line. If all the static weight is on one side and additional weight is required, the added weight must be counterbalanced by placing an equal amount of weight on the other side of the rim at exactly 180° opposite the

static point to maintain static balance. If any weight is added, you must recheck the static balance.

CAUTION Before disengaging the drive shaft, take note of the number aligned with the pointer window. When reengaging the drive shaft, make certain it is in the original (pointer) position. If the static mark is in any other position, rotate the tire so that the spark flash number on the number disk aligns with the pointer in the window. Position one dynamic weight to the left rim flange (at spindle

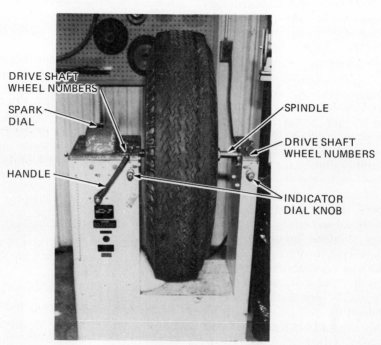

Fig. 12-50 Tire mounted to Bear dynamic wheel balancer.

STATIC WEIGHT

SPINDLE CENTER LINE

Fig. 12-51 Wheel assembly positioned to the spark number. (*Bear Applied Power Inc.*)

height) and an equal amount of weight to the right-side rim flange (at spindle height), precisely 180° from the left-side weight.

NOTE The correct dynamic weight is selected by the trial-and-error method, but your skill in selecting improves rapidly with balancing experience.

To recheck the dynamic balance, back off the left adjusting dial. Spin the wheel at a higher speed by placing the lever in a horizontal position. To determine if the assembly is in dynamic balance, open both bearing safety covers and check the movement of the floating bearing supports. If there is no movement, the assembly is in dynamic balance. If there is any movement, either at the left or the right, proceed as follows.

Turn left or right adjusting dial until the spark flashes on the spark dial. Note the number.

Stop the motor and assembly and rotate the wheel assembly so that the number on the drive shaft wheel, which aligns with the pointer in the window, correlates with the number flashed on the spark dial.

If the left dynamic weight is at spindle height and is pointing toward you, both dynamic weights are too light. In this case, increase both weights by equal amounts. If the right dynamic weight is pointing toward you, both dynamic weights are too heavy. Reduce both weights by equal amounts. If the left-side weight is within 45° of the center line of the spindle, move the left weight down about 1 in [25.4 mm]

and move the right-side weight upward by the same amount.

Recheck the dynamic balance. If the left-side weight is 45° or less below the center line of the spindle, move the weight about 1 in upward. Move the right-side weight by the same distance downward and recheck the dynamic balance. However, when the left dynamic weight is within the 45° above the spindle, the weights have to be removed and the entire balancing procedure must be repeated.

Two-weight Method of Wheel Balancing The two-weight method of balancing a tire or a wheel assembly is quick and often requires less weight than the other method. To apply the two-weight method, first balance the assembly dynamically and then statically. Assume that the assembly is clean, the stones are removed, and the assembly is mounted, and the radial and lateral runout is within specification.

Spin the assembly at low speed and open both bearing safety covers. Determine which side has the most oscillatory movement. Say it is the left side. Slowly turn the left adjusting dial until a spark flashes on the spark dial. Note down the number. (If more than one number is flashing, select the middle number.)

Say, for instance, the flashing numbers are four and five. Position the wheel assembly so that the pointer in the window is pointing at 4½. When this is positioned, scribe a line precisely at the spindle height onto the tire side wall. Install at this point to the rim flange the weight you think necessary to offset the dynamic imbalanced condition. Back off the left adjusting dial and again spin the assembly at low speed to recheck the oscillatory movement of the dynamic side (left side). If the bearing support does not oscillate, the assembly is in dynamic balance. However, if there is still movement, turn the adjusting dial until a spark occurs in the spark dial and note the number. Stop the assembly and turn it so that the spark number aligns with the pointer in the window. If the dynamic weight is pointing away from you, although not more than 45° above or below the center of the spindle height, you have selected a dynamic weight that is too heavy. Install a lighter weight at the same point and repeat the procedure to determine where the spark occurred. If the dynamic weight is facing you but is within 45° above or below the spindle height, more weight must be added (at precisely the same point). However, if the dynamic weight is on the top or the bottom but within 45° from either side of the vertical center line of the tire, move the weight on the rim flange about 1 in [25.4 mm] toward the spindle. Again repeat the balancing procedure and weight adjustment until all the left bearing support oscillatory movement ceases (see Fig. 12-52).

When you dynamically balance a car or light truck wheel assembly, move the speed handle slowly to the horizontal position to check the dynamic condition of the assembly at high speed.

NOTE Do not spin a truck wheel assembly at high speed.

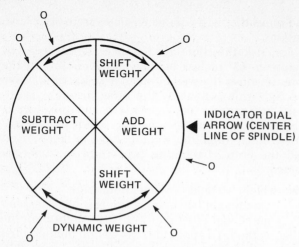

Fig. 12-52 Weight change to be made when using the two-weight method of balancing. Zero indicates weight position. (*Bear Applied Power Inc.*)

When the assembly is in dynamic balance, you must now static balance the wheel assembly by adding weights to the right side. To do this, follow the same steps as outlined in this unit under the heading "Static Balancing"; however, note all weights must be added to the right-hand side rim flange.

After the assembly is in static balance, engage the drive shaft and spin the assembly at high speed. If there is any oscillatory movement at either bearing support, dial the side which has the most movement and balance the wheel assembly, following the procedure to correct the wheel assembly for a dynamically imbalanced condition.

Wheel Balancing on the Vehicle   There are as many on-vehicle wheel balancers as there are off-vehicle balancers. They, too, vary in design, ranging from a very simple unit to a drive-on electronic unit. However, whether simple or sophisticated, they all operate on the same principle; that is, they pick up the vibration force caused by the unbalanced wheel assembly and transmit it to a measuring and locating device.

One of the simplest balancers is the remote-mounted electronic wheel balancer shown in Fig. 12-53. It consists of a static and dynamic pickup, an electronic unit, and a wheel spinner. The ends of the dynamic pickup have permanent magnets, and in addition, one end has a transducer assembly. When it is properly positioned to a wheel assembly which is out of dynamic balance and the wheel assembly is rotating, the dynamic vibration force causes the transducer end to move in and out. This opens and closes a set of points, sending a signal to the electronic unit which produces a powerful flash of light.

The static pickup has the appearance of a hydraulic jack, but instead of having a set of points, it uses a crystal as its sensing unit.

The electronic unit is designed and operated like a timing device. It has two speed scales—one for small car tires and one for truck tires; it has a weight scale calibrated in ounces; and it has one selector knob for choosing the dynamic or static pickup. The

wheel spinner is a low-profile cart having an electric motor and a drive drum. When engaged with the tire tread surface, the friction between the drum and the tread surface drives the wheel assembly.

To operate this unit, first prepare the front wheel assembly for balancing by checking the lateral and radial runout. Position the static pickup under the axle as close as possible to the king pin or below the lower control arm. Screw out the nut from the static pickup so that, when the vehicle is lowered, part of its weight rests on the pickup. Turn the steering wheel until the spindle comes to rest against the wheel stop. Position the transducer end at spindle height (as forward as possible) to the backing plate or to any other part of the assembly. At the same time loosen the adjusting nut and extend the length of the pickup. Place the other end as level as possible against the frame or against something firm, to wedge the spindle against the wheel stop, and then lock the extended rod with the nut. Position the wheel spinner and check that the tire does not contact part of the frame or pickup. Make the electrical connection. Turn the right-hand knob to the tire size; turn the left-hand knob to the tachometer position and then with a piece of chalk, scribe a line on the tire sidewall. Now spin the wheel at about 60 mph [100 km/h].   **CAUTION**   If a severely imbalanced condition exists; that is, if the vibration is excessive, spin the assembly only at moderate speed. When the desired speed is reached, release the spinner and wait a few seconds to allow the assembly to find its own vibration. During the waiting period, switch from tachometer to static position. Locate the chalk mark with the flash. Note the position of the chalk mark on the tire and at the same time check the weight scale to determine the weight needed to statically balance the assembly.

Stop the wheel assembly with the wheel spinner. Never try to stop it manually or with any other tool— a serious injury could result. Next, place the tire so that the chalk mark is in the same position as it was when the wheel assembly was spinning. Assume it was at 10 o'clock—you know that at 6 o'clock the tire is heavier than at 12 o'clock, by the weight indicated on the weight scale; therefore, the weight must be placed precisely at 12 o'clock. If the indicated weight is more than 1 oz [28.35 g] (for a car or light truck tire) or 6 oz [170.10 g] (for a truck tire), place about one-third of the weight onto the outside rim flange and the remaining weight onto the inside rim flange. Again, spin the wheel assembly and check the static weight. Note the position of the weight spot and the needle position on the scale. If the meter needle is within the green area and the weight wanders slowly around the tire, or if there is no flash, the wheel assembly is within its static balance limit and you can proceed with the dynamic balancing of the assembly.

However, if the static weight is on top between 10:30 and 1:30 o'clock, more static weight is required at the static point. If the static weight is between 4:30 and 7:30 o'clock, it is too heavy and must be reduced. If the static weight is anywhere between 1:30 and 3:30 o'clock or between 7:30 and 10:30

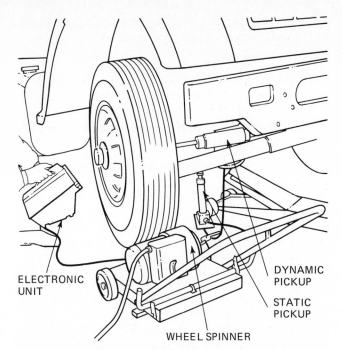

Fig. 12-53 Electronic wheel balancer. *(FMC Corporation)*

meter needle is within the green area, the wheel assembly is in dynamic balance. If the meter needle is not within the green area, stop the wheel assembly and place the tire so that the chalk mark is in the same position as it was when the wheel assembly was spinning. Now install, at spindle height, about 1 oz [28.55 g] of weight (for car and small truck tires) or about 4 oz [109.40 g] of weight (when balancing a truck tire) onto the inside rim flange, and equal amounts of weight onto the outside rim flange directly in line with the inside weight. **NOTE** The placement of the dynamic inside weight is determined by the position of the dynamic pickup because the flash occurs as the dynamic force of the wheel assembly moves the pickup inward. Therefore the inside weight is placed where the dynamic pickup is located. When the dynamic pickup is located in front of the axle, the weight is placed forward. When the pickup is located behind the axle, the weight is placed rearward.

Let us assume the dynamic pickup was located in front of the axle. Again, spin the wheel assembly and observe the chalk mark position and the meter needle. If the meter needle is in the green area, the assembly is in dynamic balance. However, if it is not in the green area, stop the wheel assembly, reposition the chalk mark, and note the location of the outside dynamic weight. If the outside weight is between 1:30 and 4:30 o'clock, both the inside and outside weight must be decreased by equal amounts. If the weight is between 7:30 and 10:30 o'clock, both inside and outside weights must be increased by the same amount. If the outside weight is between 10:30 and 1:30 or between 4:30 and 7:30 o'clock, move both weights an equal amount (about 1 in [25.4 mm]) toward 3 or 9 o'clock (see Fig. 12-55).

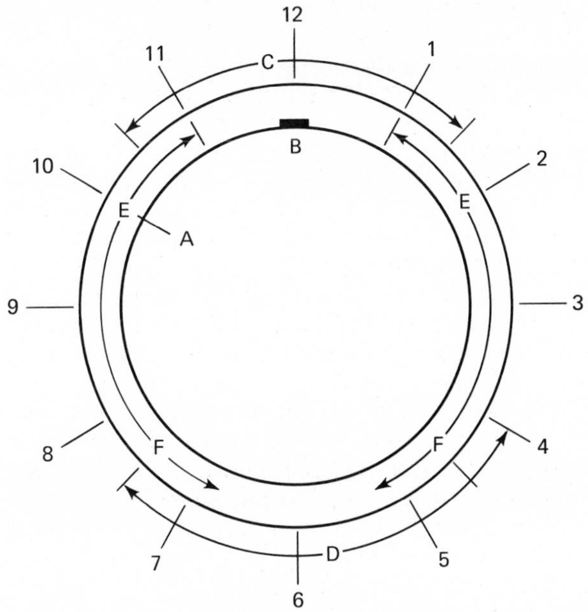

o'clock, move the weight toward the top. **NOTE** Move a small weight about 2 in [50.8 mm] and a heavy weight about 1 in [25.4 mm] (see Fig. 12-54). Before respinning the wheel assembly to check the dynamic balance condition, check the position of the dynamic pickup and turn the knob to the tachometer. Spin the wheel. When it reaches the desired speed, turn the knob to dynamic position. Pick up the chalk mark on the tire with the flash. Note its position and note the weight scale needle. If the

A — 10 o'clock flash
B — static weight
C — add weight
D — remove weight
F — move weight in direction of arrow

Fig. 12-54 Correction of static weight location.

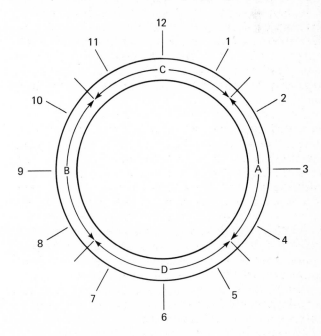

A — remove weight
B — add weight
C and D — move weight away(toward 3 or 9 o'clock)

Fig. 12-55 Correction of dynamic weight position.

Rear Wheel Balancing The procedure to balance the rear wheels of a small or large truck is the same as that when balancing the front wheel assembly. However, because you must spin the wheel assembly with the power of the engine, the following precautions must be taken to prevent accidents.

Lock the front wheels of the vehicle. Raise all rear tires off the ground and place jack stands under the axles as close as possible to the wheel assembly. You can then prepare the wheel assembly for balancing. When this is done, raise one wheel assembly from the jack stand and position the static and dynamic pickup. Start the engine and shift the transmission into direct drive. From this point on the procedure is the same as that to balance a front wheel assembly.

Review Questions

1. List the four functions of a tire other than to support the vehicle and/or load.

2. List four conditions under which the static load radius of a tire could vary.

3. (a) What terminology is used to describe the contact area a tire makes on the road surface? (b) List four factors which could vary this area.

4. List three advantages of a radial-type tire over a bias-type tire.

5. How is the tire load range identified on: (a) highway equipment, (b) off-highway equipment?

6. Interpret the following car tire code: CR 78-14.

7. Why is the tire designed by Caterpillar (see text) superior to a conventional loader or dozer tire?

8. Outline the maintenance checks you would perform to prevent: (a) tire failure, (b) wheel assembly failure.

9. Explain why you should: (a) use a torque wrench to tighten the wheel nuts and (b) tighten the nuts in a specific sequence.

10. List four causes of high radial runout and four causes of high lateral runout.

11. How would you determine if the abnormal tire wear were caused by incorrect: (a) toe-in, (b) toe-out, (c) camber, (d) overinflation, (e) misalignment?

12. Why is it essential to place wooden blocks or a plank under the jack or jackstand when the motor vehicle or equipment is not on solid ground?

13. Outline the steps to demount an inflated small truck tubeless tire, using only tire tools.

14. List three reasons why weight is more effective when fastened directly to the drive axle or wheel than when in the form of a wet ballast in the tube.

15. List three advantages in balancing the wheel on equipment that operates at more than 25 mph [40.2 km/h].

16. At what position within the tire is the excess weight when the tire assembly is: (a) in static unbalance, (b) in dynamic unbalance.

17. What is the (tire movement) result of a wheel assembly when it is: (a) statically unbalanced, (b) dynamically unbalanced?

18. Using a dynamic wheel balancer, dynamically balance a mounted wheel assembly and then list the steps you followed to achieve this.

Unit 13 Wheel Hubs, Dead and Live Axles

A wheel assembly consists of the spindle, the wheel hub with wheel bearings and wheel bearing seal, the brake drum or rotor, the wheel or rim, and the tire. Numerous wheel assemblies are used on on- and off-highway equipment to accommodate the differences in various vehicles' load-carrying capacity, the methods used to drive the wheels, wheels mounted to a live axle or a dead axle, and the differences in foundation brake designs. However, all wheel assemblies have the same purposes—to support the vehicle's weight, to reduce rolling friction, and to transmit brake torque to the tire. In addition, wheels that are mounted to a live axle transmit the drive torque from the drive axle shaft to the wheels and also retard torque from the tire to the drive axle.

Dead Axles   A dead axle is a nondrive axle (a front axle or a trailer axle), and the wheel hub is mounted with antifriction bearings to the spindle or axle housing and can rotate freely in either direction.

A trailer axle may have a straight or curved axle beam (see Fig. 13-1) and could be made of tubular steel, cast iron, or prefabricated steel. The machined induction-hardened spindle is fastened to the axle. The spring and/or suspension mounting brackets are welded to the axle beam as are the necessary mounting brackets.

A nondrive steering axle is commonly of the I-beam design; that is, the axle beam is of a forged steel construction; however, some are of a tubular or prefabricated design. To attach the steering knuckle or spindle to the axle beam, three different axle ends have been designed. When the axle ends form two yokes and the steering knuckle is positioned between them, this axle is known as the Elliot type (see Fig. 13-2). If the steering knucle ends form two yokes and the knuckle is positioned over the axle end bore, it is known as a reverse-Elliot axle (see Fig. 13-3). When the spindle forms an L shape and is positioned into the bore of the axle beam end, it is known as a Lemoin-type axle (see Fig. 13-4).

Live Axles   When the wheel hub is mounted to a live axle of the full-floating design, the wheel hub is mounted with antifriction bearings to a fixed axle housing or spindle, and the assembly carries the ve-

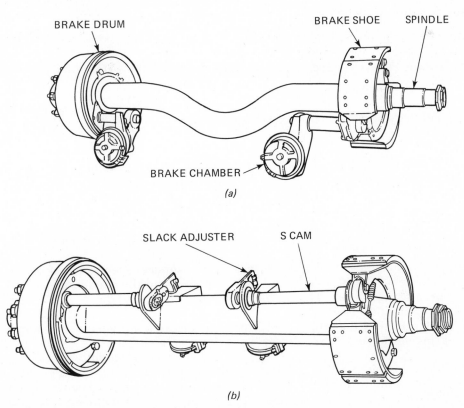

(a)

(b)

Fig. 13-1   Trailer axles: (a) tubular design; (b) square axle beam design. (*Rockwell International, Automotive Operations*)

177

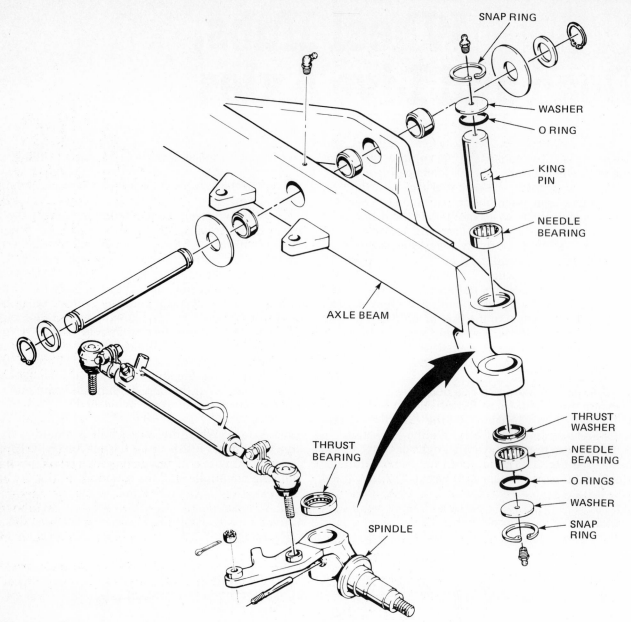

SNAP RING

WASHER

O RING

KING PIN

NEEDLE BEARING

AXLE BEAM

THRUST WASHER

NEEDLE BEARING

O RINGS

WASHER

SNAP RING

THRUST BEARING

SPINDLE

Fig. 13-2 Elliot steering axle. (*J I Case Company Agricultural Equipment Division*)

hicle weight. The axle shaft flange is fastened to (and drives) the wheel hub. On a planetary drive axle the sungear is splined to the axle shaft, and it drives the planetary carrier which is bolted to the wheel hub. In either case the drive axle only drives the wheel but carries no vehicle weight (see Figs. 13-30 and 13-35).

When the wheel hub is mounted to a semifloating axle, the hub is fastened to the axle shaft, and the wheel and brake drum are bolted to it. The axle shaft is supported by an antifriction bearing in the axle housing; therefore 50 percent of the vehicle's weight is carried by the axle housing and 50 percent by the axle shaft.

When the wheel hub is mounted to a $\frac{3}{4}$ floating axle, the axle shaft is so supported that three-fourths of the vehicle weight is carried by the axle housing and one-fourth of the weight is carried by the drive axle shaft.

Wheel Hubs Whether or not the wheel hub is used on a live or dead axle, it is supported by antifriction bearings on the spindle, axle housing, or axle shaft. It is the mounting base for the brake drum or rotor, and the wheel or rim. The wheel hub is machined to accommodate the inner and outer wheel bearing cups and the wheel bearing seal. In addition the outer surfaces are machined so that the brake drum or rotor and the single- or dual-disk wheels can be mounted in alignment with the center of the wheel hub and spindle. The fastening method varies according to the intended load-carrying capacity, and whether a single- or dual-disk wheels are to be fastened to the wheel hub.

The brake drum is either inboard mounted behind the hub flange or outboard mounted (see Fig. 13-5). When outboard mounted, the drum is placed over the face of the wheel hub and attached with countersunk screws to the hub but positioned and sup-

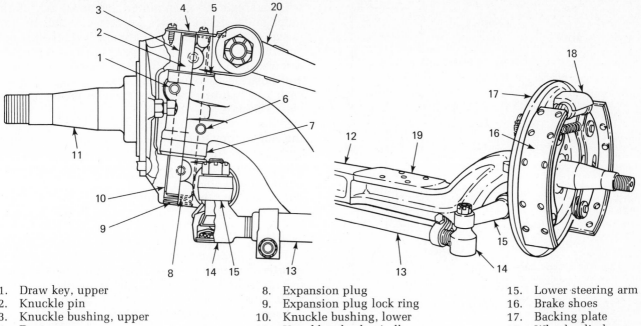

1. Draw key, upper
2. Knuckle pin
3. Knuckle bushing, upper
4. Dust cover
5. Spacing washer and shim
6. Draw key, lower
7. Thrust bearing

8. Expansion plug
9. Expansion plug lock ring
10. Knuckle bushing, lower
11. Knuckle wheel spindle
12. I beam axle beam
13. Cross tube (tie rod)
14. Tie rod end

15. Lower steering arm
16. Brake shoes
17. Backing plate
18. Wheel cylinder
19. Spring seat (saddle)
20. Upper steering arm

Fig. 13-3 Reverse-Elliot axle, having a straight kingpin. (*International Harvester Company*)

ported through the wheel studs. The advantage of this arrangement over the inboard mounted drum is that the brakes can be serviced without removing the wheel hub. When the wheel hub is used on a full-floating axle, special drive-axle-to-hub retainer studs are threaded into the wheel hub, or the drive axle is splined into the hub splines and a hub cap is used to seal the wheel hub.

SPOKE WHEELS   When the tire is mounted to a de-

mountable rim, the wheel hub design differs slightly. On trucks, tractors, and trailers, spoke-wheel hubs are used. A spoke-wheel hub is a one-piece casting having three, five, or six extended-rim mounting surfaces. The brake drum is inboard mounted to the wheel hub, but apart from this a spoke-wheel hub is no different in design than any other wheel hub (see Fig. 13-6).

When dual rims are mounted to the spoke wheel, the inner ends of each spoke are beveled 28°, and

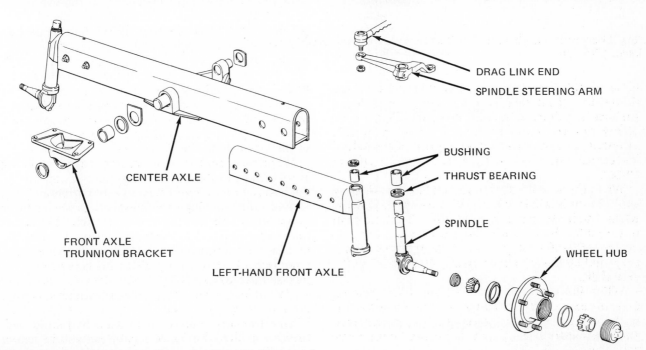

Fig. 13-4   Lemoin-type steering axle. (*Deere & Company*)

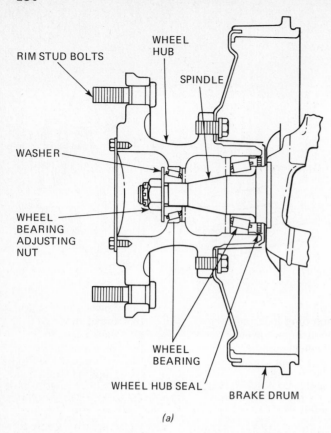

WHEEL HUB

SPINDLE

RIM STUD BOLTS

WASHER

WHEEL BEARING ADJUSTING NUT

WHEEL BEARING

WHEEL HUB SEAL

BRAKE DRUM

(a)

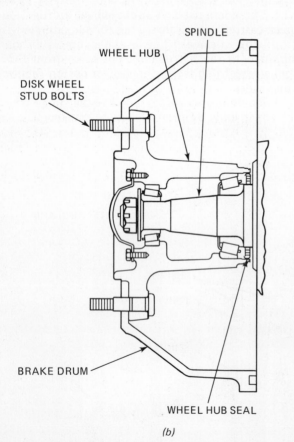

SPINDLE

WHEEL HUB

DISK WHEEL STUD BOLTS

BRAKE DRUM

WHEEL HUB SEAL

(b)

Fig. 13-5 Brake drum positions: (a) inboard; (b) outboard. (*General Motors Corporation*)

when a single rim is mounted to a spoke wheel, the outer ends of the spokes are beveled 28°. In both designs there is a threaded bore in the outside outer end, and special wheel bolts, or wheel studs, are screwed into this bore. Special rim clamps support and position the rim to the spoke wheel. However each rim manufacturer has its own individual rim clamp design.

When a single rim is mounted to the spoke wheel, the rim clamps force the rim at the outer circumference against the tapered end of the spokes. This positions and supports the rim. When dual rims are mounted to a spoke wheel, the rim clamps force the outer rim against the rim spacer, which in turn forces the inner rim with its taper against the tapered end of the spokes. (See the section on disk wheels and rims, removal and installation.)

Farm equipment having a semifloating or a three-quarter-floating drive axle uses rims, but they are usually bolted to a steel disk, and the disk is bolted with wheel bolts to the drive axle flange.

Nearly all large-wheel equipment (including rear dump trucks) uses rims, mainly because a disk wheel would not stand up to the high load weight, and also because it is very difficult to mount a disk wheel to a large live or dead axle.

Front or Trailer Axle Wheel Hub and Bearing
When the wheel hub or spoke wheel is mounted to a front axle or trailer axle, the inner and outer wheel bearing fits snugly on the machine spindle, and the wheel bearing seal rests on the seal shoulder of the spindle. The wheel bearing adjusting nut maintains the recommended bearing adjustment. A dust cap may be pressed into the hub, or the cap may be fastened with screws to the wheel hub. The wheel bearings are lubricated with grease or oil.

DISASSEMBLY When servicing a front or trailer axle wheel hub, you should first position the vehicle so that you have adequate room in which to work. Next, lift the axle to raise the tires off the floor and place floor stands under the axle(s) to support the vehicle safely. Disconnect the battery ground cable. **NOTE** On vehicles equipped with air brakes, drain the air tanks and, when applicable, manually release the spring brakes to prevent the brakes from self-applying. Before removing the disk wheel or rim, slack off the brake adjustment slightly to allow easier removal of the wheel hub.

When servo brakes are used, remove the adjusting screw hole plug located at the inner lower side of the backing plate. Insert a small screwdriver into the slotted hole and push the automatic adjuster lever away from the adjusting screw star wheel. Insert a brake adjusting tool (or large screwdriver) so that the tool contacts the star wheel. Manipulate the tool upward to back off (turn) the adjusting screw and thus release the brakes. **NOTE** Do not try to release the brake unless the adjusting lever is disengaged from the star wheel.

To release the brakes which use a hydraulic non-servo brake, first turn the front adjusting screw

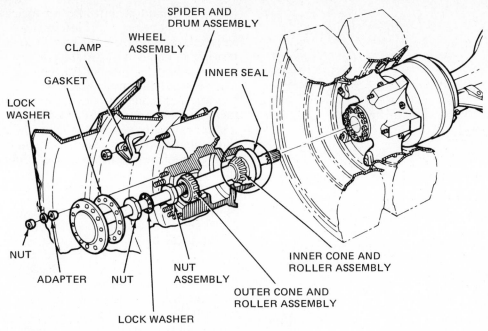

Fig. 13-6 Schematic view of a rear wheel hub and drum assembly. (*Ford Motor Company*)

clockwise and then the rear adjusting screw counterclockwise.

To release brakes having an air or hydraulic wedge-type foundation brake, first remove from the wheel cylinder the hollow cap screw, spring, and guide pawl. Next, rotate the actuator counterclockwise to back off the brake shoe from the drum.

To release the brakes of a cam foundation brake system (hydraulic or air), turn the slack adjuster adjusting screw counterclockwise. This turns the slack adjuster and the cam, releasing the brakes. When the brakes are released, remove the disk wheel or rim (see the discussion of wheels and rims). To remove the wheel hub, remove the cotter pin, the adjusting nut, and retainer, in that order. Rock the wheel hub to force the outer wheel bearing cone loose from the spindle. To remove the wheel hub from larger front axles or trailer axles having oil-lubricated wheel

bearings (see Fig. 13-7), drain the oil and remove in sequence the lock nut, the washer, or the locking ring, or the adjusting nut. Always wrap the bearing in wax paper or in a lint-free cloth for protection immediately after removal. Where smaller equipment is concerned, use your hands to lift the wheel hub with brake drum or rotor from the spindle. On larger assemblies, use a sling and a lifting device to lift the assembly from the spindle. In either case take care not to damage the spindle, bearings, or brake shoes or to drag the inner bearing over the spindle thread. After the assembly is removed, tape the spindle threads with masking tape for protection.

Use a prybar or hammer puller to remove the wheel bearing seal. When removed, lift from the hub the inner bearing cone and also wrap it in wax paper or in a lint-free cloth.

Using a steam cleaner, remove all old grease or

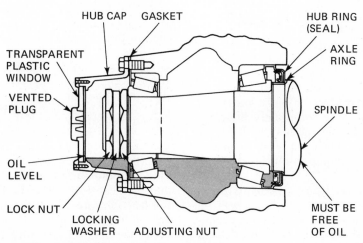

Fig. 13-7 Oil-lubricated front wheel assembly. (*Mack Canada Inc.*)

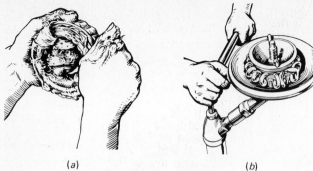

Fig. 13-8 (a) Hand packing bearings, (b) power packing.

oil from the hub and when necessary dry it with compressed air. Use a vacuum cleaner and wire brush to clean the backing plate and use solvent to remove old oil and grease from the spindle. Then cover the assembly to prevent any damage or to prevent dirt from falling onto the assembly.

INSPECTING   Inspect the bearing cups for pitting, galling, discoloration, unusual wear, and evidence of seal bore and stud thread damage. At the same time inspect the foundation brakes (see the discussion of brake drum service). If the brake drum must be replaced, check the appropriate service manual before replacing because of the various methods used to fasten the brake drum to the wheel hub. Also check the wear of the king pin, king pin bearings, and tie rod ends for excessive wear. If one bearing cup is damaged, both cups should be replaced, since the other bearing will have operated under misaligned conditions.   **NOTE**   See the discussion of bearings with regard to replacing bearing cups or cleaning and inspection.

Packing Wheel Bearings   When packing wheel bearings, it is important to use only the best lubricant available and to work it thoroughly into the spaces between the inner and outer races, for this will, in the long run, save downtime and money. Of even greater importance to the life of wheel bearings is adherence to the recommended procedure when installing and adjusting the wheel bearings. Also, before hand packing or power packing (see Fig. 13-8) a bearing, make certain that it is clean and that it has been dried with compressed air.

To hand pack a tapered roller bearing, hold it so that the open end of the large end of the bearing faces upward. Scoop up a handful of grease and knead it forcefully from the palm of your hand into the spaces between the rollers or balls and races. Make certain that all space is completely filled, for an inadequately packed bearing may fail prematurely. Following this, if the bearing is not to be used immediately, wrap it in wax paper to protect it from contaminants.

It is advantageous to use a bearing packing device since it completely fills all spaces inside the bearing. When using a bearing packing device, make certain the cup, the cone, and the top of the packer are clean. Place the bearing onto the cup and screw the cone finger-tight against the bearing. Next, pump grease

(using the hand pump) into the space between the inner and outer races or between the inner race and rollers. When the grease being expelled from the bearing is about 0.46 in (12 mm) in length, cease pumping and then smear it evenly (with light pressure) around the outer surface of the (taper roller) bearing and cage, or between the inner and outer races (ball bearing).   **NOTE**   Check the service manual in regard to greasing the wheel hub inner cavity. Most manufacturers recommend applying only a light coat of grease to the inner surface to prevent rusting.

Studs and Seals   To replace a damaged, serrated, or flat shoulder wheel stud, first place the wheel hub on the press bed so that both sides are evenly supported. Next, press the damaged stud out and press a new one into place.   CAUTION   Make certain that the new stud starts straight in its bore, that it fits tight in its bore, and that it comes to rest against the hub flange shoulder. Do not "drive" the stud in or out, for this will damage the bore and result in a loose stud fit.

After the inner bearing cone is placed in position, install the wheel bearing seal. If the OD of the seal is not coated already, place a thin coat of nonhardening sealing compound around the seal bore. Use a seal driver to position the seal according to the appropriate service manual. In any event, make certain it is installed parallel to the hub bore surface. Coat the lips with a multiple-purpose grease and cover the wheel hub to prevent dirt or grit from accumulating on the greased surfaces and brake drum.

Check the spindle for damaged threads or worn or damaged bearings or seal surfaces. If the threads are damaged, use a thread file to restore them and use fine emery cloth to restore the seal and bearing surfaces. If the bearing surface is worn to the extent that the bearing or bearings are loose on the spindle, the spindle must be replaced.

To decrease the rolling friction, to increase the service life, and to reduce maintenance costs, wheel bearings are now commonly oil lubricated, in which case a special wheel bearing seal and wheel hub cap are used. (See components installed in Fig. 13-7.) When installing this type of seal into the hub, use the special seal driver to prevent damaging it and to ensure that the seal slides straight into its bore and bottoms evenly. Also pack grease into the spring cavity to prevent the spring from dislodging during installation. Before driving the axle ring (or in this case the deflector ring) with the special driver onto the spindle, make certain there are no nicks or burrs on the seal surface.

Installing Wheel Hub   Apply a light coat of oil or grease to the entire spindle surface (to prevent rust) and then carefully lift the hub over the spindle. Keep the hub centered on the spindle during installation and hold it in this position until the outer bearing cone has been placed on the spindle. This precaution is necessary to prevent any damage to the hub seal, bearing, and spindle threads.

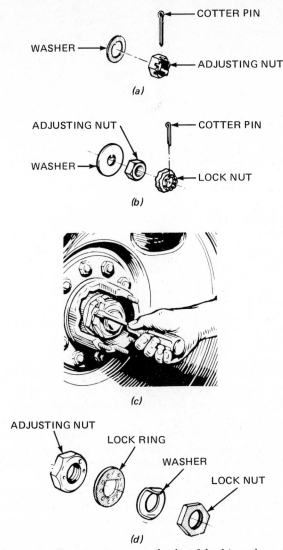

Fig. 13-9 Four common methods of locking the wheel bearing adjustment. (a) Internal tang retainer washer and adjusting nut. (b) Similar to (a) but with stamped castle nut. (c) Metal lock with bending tabs. (d) Pin-type adjusting nut and matching lock ring. (*Ford Motor Company*)

Wheel Bearing Adjustment As a general rule of thumb the procedure for adjusting the wheel bearings is the same, and all wheel bearings have either zero or only a small amount of end play. However, the method used to hold the wheel bearing adjusting nut to the spindle in the adjusted position varies. Four common methods (see Fig. 13-9) used are as follows: (1) A retainer washer having an internal tang is placed in the keyway of the spindle against the outer wheel bearing cone, and the slotted adjusting nut is screwed against it. After the wheel bearings are properly adjusted, a cotter pin is used to pin the adjusting nut to the spindle. (2) The second method is similar to the first one; however, a stamp castle nut is placed over the adjusting nut, and the cotter pin fastens the castle nut to the spindle. The following methods are used on large front axles and on nearly all full-floating axles, as well as on trailer axles. (3) The third method is to use a metal lock having tangs or a round metal lock. It is

placed against the adjusting nut, and the lock nut is torqued against the lock. One part of the metal lock is then bent against one flat of the lock nut, and one part is bent against the flat of the adjusting nut. (4) In the fourth method the adjusting nut has one pin. The lock ring has the same size holes drilled into the outer diameter and has an internal tang. After the wheel bearings are adjusted, the lock ring tang is placed in the keyway of the spindle and onto the adjusting nut pin. The hole of the lock ring must slide over the pin. If it does not, turn the lock ring over and try once more to slide the lock ring over the pin. If it still will not slide over, turn the wheel bearing adjusting nut and increase the torque (to make the alignment). Install and torque the lock nut to specification. Following are some examples of wheel bearing adjustments.

When you are adjusting the wheel bearings of a 5000-lb [2270-kg] axle, it is recommended that you tighten the adjusting nut with a socket and torque wrench to 15 lb·ft [20.4 N·m] (to seat the bearings) while rotating the wheel in both directions. At this point you should feel a slight drag. Back off the nut one flat and insert the cotter pin. If the adjusting nut and spindle hole do not align, back off the nut to make the alignment. The cotter pin should be so installed that the long tang can be bent over the end of the spindle end. Next, cut the other tang, leaving just enough length to bend it against the side of the adjusting nut. Adjusting the bearings as outlined will provide for 0.000 to 0.006 in [0.000 to 0.15 mm] bearing end play.

Assume now that the wheel bearings of a 18,000-lb [3632-kg] axle are to be adjusted. Using a socket and torque wrench, tighten the adjusting nut to 125 lb·ft [170 N·m] while rotating the wheel in both directions to seat the bearings. Next, loosen the adjusting nut one complete turn (360°), then retighten the nut to 50 lb·ft [68 N·m] while rotating the wheel in both directions. Align the cotter pin hole or mark the nut position. Next, back off the adjusting nut one flat, or so that it aligns with the next cotter pin hole. When the bearings are thus adjusted, the wheel will rotate freely within the limit of 0.001 to 0.010 in [0.025 to 0.25 mm] end play. **NOTE** When the wheel bearing adjustment is held by the lock nut method, make certain to check the rotation of the wheel, after the lock nut is torqued to specification. The bearings can preload when the adjusting nut or the spindle threads are worn.

Because of the possibility of bearing preload many manufacturers recommend that you check the wheel bearing end play with a dial indicator. To do this, fasten the magnetic base to the wheel hub so that the spindle of the dial indicator can be placed onto the spindle. Zero the dial, then try to rock the wheel back and forth on the spindle. The dial needle travel will indicate the bearing end play (see Fig. 13-10).

After the wheel bearings are adjusted and locked, install the dust cap. When the wheel is oil lubricated, install the special hub cap, remove the filler plug, and fill the wheel hub with the recommended oil to the level indicated on the hub cap.

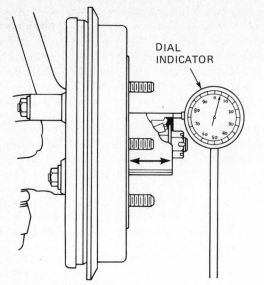

Fig. 13-10 Checking wheel hub bearing end play by using a dial indicator.

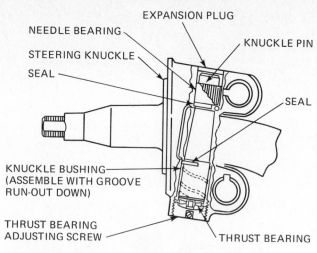

Fig. 13-12 Sectional view of a steering knuckle and axle having a tapered kingpin. (*Mack Canada Inc.*)

Kingpins The kingpins are the pivot points of the steering knuckles on a nondrive steering axle. If the clearance due to wear on the kingpins and bushings or bearings increases, the front wheels come out of alignment (toward negative camber) and thereby reduce steering efficiency and increase tire wear.

The two most common types of kingpins are the straight and tapered types (see Figs. 13-11 and 13-12). Either may be supported by bushings made from nylon or bronze or by needle bearings. On a reverse-Elliot axle the bushings or bearings are pressed into the bores of the steering knuckle yoke bores, and on an Elliot or Lemoin-type axle they are pressed into the bores of the axle ends.

A straight kingpin fits tightly into the axle end bore and is held in place through a tapered pin (kingpin lockpin). To prevent dust and dirt from entering the bushings or bearings, expansion plugs or

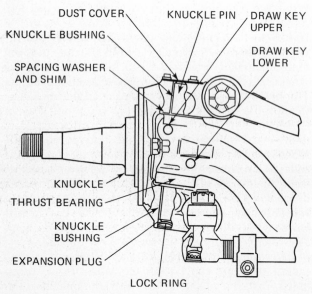

Fig. 13-11 Sectional view of steering knuckle and axle having a straight kingpin. (*Mack Canada Inc.*)

cover plates are used. The cover plates are fastened to the steering knuckle ends by screws or cap screws, and the plugs are either held in place by a snap ring or are flattened against the bore surface.

To ease steering (reduce rotation friction between the axle and steering knuckle), a thrust bearing is placed between the lower steering knuckle yoke and axle end. The bearing carries the vehicle load placed on the front axle. The thrust bearing could be of a ball, roller, or tapered needle bearing design.

When a tapered kingpin is used, the axle ends have a slightly tapered bore (enlarged at the bottom), and the tapered kingpin is pulled into the axle taper either by the kingpin nut or by the adjusting screw.

SERVICING To check the kingpin and bushings or bearings for wear, try to force the spindle end up and down, and if you can feel excessive play, the assembly must be serviced.

On the assumption that the wheel hub is removed, the next step is to remove the drag link and tie rod ends, the brake backing plate or the brake assembly, and then wire it to the frame. Next, remove the kingpin locking device, the cover plates, and if expansion plugs are used, drill a 0.250-in (6-mm) diameter hole in the plugs and then with a punch pry them out. Next, drive out the kingpin. **CAUTION** Do not hammer directly on the pin—use a drift.

NOTE Tapered kingpins are driven downward. If the kingpin is frozen, use a press to remove it. Do not use heat to expand the axle bore in order to remove the pin, for this could damage the bore. When the pin is removed, lift the steering knuckle, thrust bearing, and shims from the axle end; thoroughly clean the steering knuckle and discard the thrust bearing. Examine the steering knuckle carefully for any imperfection or damage—if possible Magnaflux the assembly to locate hidden cracks. In some states and provinces it is a regulatory requirement to Magnaflux or x-ray the steering knuckle. If the steering knuckle is reusable, press out the bushings or bear-

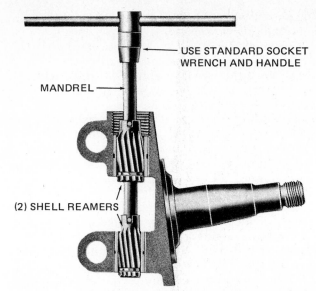

Fig. 13-13 Reaming steering knuckle bushings by using two shell reamers. (*Mack Canada Inc.*)

ings by using an arbor press, and before pressing new ones in place, thoroughly clean the bores. When bushings are used, make certain the bushing holes align with the lubricating hole in the steering knuckle before pressing the bushings in place. Next, clamp the steering knuckle in a vise and, with the specified reamer, line-ream the bushings (see Fig. 13-13). This is particularly essential when the upper and lower bushings are different in size. If, however, the bushings are of equal size, a power stroke honing machine could be used (see Fig. 13-14). After the bushings are reamed or honed, thoroughly clean the assembly and dry it with compressed air. When needle bearings are used, press on the identification side of the bearings; otherwise you could damage them while pressing them into position. Using the new kingpin, check the axle end bore. If the bore is tapered or elongated, the axle must be replaced. Do not use heat to shrink the bore.

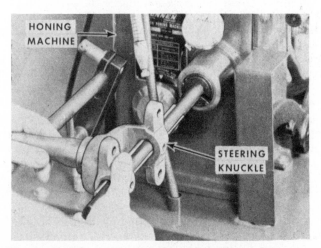

Fig. 13-14 Honing steering knuckle bushings by using a power stroke honing machine. (*International Harvester Company*)

INSTALLATION Position the steering knuckle over the axle end and then place the thrust bearing with the retainer lip down, between the lower axle end face and the lower knuckle yoke face. Place a jack under the lower yoke to raise the steering knuckle and at the same time align the bores until the clearance is taken up between the lower yoke, thrust bearing, and the lower bore face of the axle end. With a feeler gauge measure between the top face of the upper axle end and the lower face of the lower yoke. Insert shims to reduce the clearance to the specification given in the service manual. Again align the bore and the kingpin, push the pin through the top yoke bore onto the axle end bore, and drive it into position. Install the lock pin, the cover plates or plugs. **NOTE** When reinstalling a tapered kingpin, check the service manual with regard to axle center-to-steering knuckle clearance (see Fig. 13-12).

Full-floating Axle Wheel Hubs In general terms the removal, service, and installation of a wheel hub to a full-floating front or to a rear axle is similar to that of removing, servicing, and installing a wheel hub to a front or a trailer axle. There are some differences, however, because of the additional parts needed to drive the wheel hub.

SERVICING A FULL-FLOATING REAR AXLE WHEEL HUB The additional parts just mentioned could be the axle shaft, the tapered dowels, and the axle hub retainer studs and nuts. On other designs the axle shaft is splined to the internal splines of the wheel hub, and the hub cap is bolted to the wheel hub (to seal and cover the axle shaft), or the axle shaft flange is bolted with special axle shaft bolts to the wheel hub (see Fig. 13-15).

To service the wheel hub, the same preliminary steps and precautions must be taken as those outlined when servicing a nondrive axle wheel hub. After the disk wheel or rim is removed and the brake

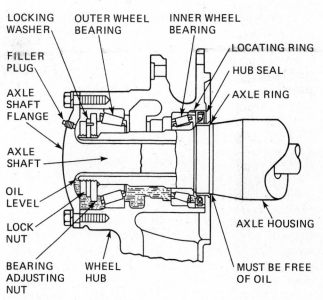

Fig. 13-15 Sectional view of wheel hub mounted to a full-floating axle. (*Mack Canada Inc.*)

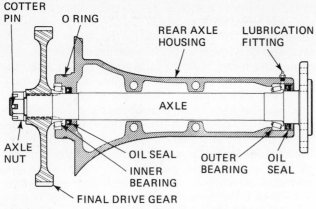

COTTER PIN

O RING

REAR AXLE HOUSING

LUBRICATION FITTING

AXLE

AXLE NUT

OIL SEAL

INNER BEARING

OUTER BEARING

OIL SEAL

FINAL DRIVE GEAR

Fig. 13-16 Schematic view of a rear axle housing. (*J I Case Company Agricultural Equipment Division*)

adjustment is backed off, position a suitable container under the hub to catch any oil that may spill from the hub. Next, remove the axle shaft hub nuts or cap screws. If tapered dowels are placed over the studs into the axle flange, use a sledge hammer and strike the flange with a sharp blow. This will loosen the dowels, as well as the axle shaft. Remove the dowels and slide the axle shaft from the axle housing and store it in a secure place. If no "tapered" dowels are used, fasten a hammer puller to the threaded holes in the axle shaft flange to pull the axle shaft from the housing. Under no circumstances should you drive a chisel or screwdriver between the flange and wheel hub to loosen the flange from the hub, for this will damage the hub surface. If the axle shaft is splined to the hub, fasten a hammer puller to the splined axle shaft flange to pull the shaft from the hub spline.

Before installing the axle shaft, make certain that the surfaces of the hub and axle shaft flange are free from any nicks and burrs, the axle studs are tight in the wheel hub, the stud threads are undamaged, and the old gasket material is completely removed from the hub and axle surfaces.

Place a new gasket over the axle studs onto the hub surface and then slide the axle shaft into the axle housing. Start the splined end into the differential side gear and the axle flange over the wheel hub studs. Install the dowels and axle nuts and tighten the nuts to the specified torque. When the wheel bearings are oil lubricated, fill the hub with the recommended gear oil and then secure the filler plug.

Wheel Hubs and Bearings (Semifloating Axle)
Small trucks and farm tractors are often equipped with a semifloating axle (see Fig. 13-16). In this design the axle shaft flange is the wheel hub. On farm tractors, small loaders, and other small equipment, the axle shaft is usually supported in the rear axle housing by the inner and outer tapered roller bearing and only the disk wheel is bolted to the axle flange. A lip-type seal is pressed into the outside bore of the rear axle housing to seal the axle shaft. Occasionally an inner seal is also used, in which case the rear axle housing becomes the oil reservoir for the axle bear-

ing, because the seal separates the rear axle housing from the carrier housing.

On small trucks the brake drum is located over the wheel studs and is usually attached to the flange with two or three retainers. The disk wheel is mounted on the same studs, and both the drum and wheel are supported and positioned to the axle flange by the wheel nuts or wheel bolts. The axle shaft is supported at one end (on the outside) by a roller, a ball, or a tapered roller bearing which is pressed onto the axle shaft close to the inside of the axle flange. The bearing is held in position by the retainer clinch ring. The other end of the axle shaft is splined into the differential side gear (see Fig. 13-17). The axle shaft is either retained to the rear axle housing by a retainer plate bolted to the axle housing flange, or it is held with a C lock to the differential side gear. When tapered-roller or roller-type axle shaft bearings are used, a lip-type seal is pressed into the outer bore of the axle housing to seal the axle shaft (but without preventing lubricant from reaching the bearing). When a single- or double-row sealed-type ball bearing is used, the lip-type seal is positioned (inboard) in the axle housing to seal the axle shaft, and in this case, lubricant cannot reach the wheel bearing.

SERVICING If the wheel bearing is noisy, the axle seal is damaged and oil leaks onto the brake shoes and drums. If the axle flange or the wheel studs are damaged, the axle shaft must be removed for service. Such servicing includes the same preliminary steps required to service a front or a full-floating axle, such as lifting the rear of the truck to the desired working height, placing floor stands securely under the axle housing or frame, and backing off the brake adjustment and removing the wheel cover and the disk wheels.

You must then unscrew the two or three drum retainers from the wheel studs and lift off the brake drum. When the axle shaft is held by the wheel bearing retainer or cover to the axle housing, turn the axle shaft so that the large bore in the axle shaft flange aligns with the nuts that secure the wheel bearing retainer to the axle housing flange and then work through the bore to remove the nuts. When the nuts are removed, slide the axle shaft out of the axle housing, but make certain the backing plate remains in position. When the axle shaft is removed, secure the backing plate (with one nut) to the axle housing.

When removing an axle shaft held with a C clamp to the differential side gear, the differential pinion shaft must first be removed (in order to remove the C clamp). Obviously, before this is done, the carrier area should have been steam-cleaned to prevent dirt and foreign matter from entering the carrier.

To drain the oil from the carrier housing, place a drip pan under the carrier, loosen the cover bolts, and then tap the cover loose.

After removing the cover, remove the differential pinion shaft lock (or screw) and the pinion shaft. Push the axle shaft toward the carrier. This may automatically drop the C clamp from the axle shaft. If it does not, push the differential side gear against

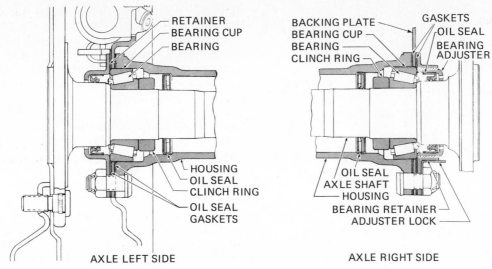

Fig. 13-17 Sectional view of a semifloating rear axle with bearing ring end play adjustment. (*International Harvester Company*)

the differential case to expel the C lock from the counterbore in the side gear. Remove it and slide the axle shaft from the axle housing. If you reuse the bearing and seal, take care not to damage them, since both remain in the axle housing.

Use a slide-hammer puller to remove the seal and the roller bearing. Place the jaws of the puller past the roller bearing cage and then extend them so that they lock behind the roller cage. Now slide the hammer with force outward to remove the seal and bearing out of the axle housing bore. To prevent damage to the housing bore, do not use any other method to remove the seal and roller bearing.

Clean and then check the bearing and seal bores for nicks and burrs and elongations. If the bores are enlarged or elongated to the extent that the seal or bearing is loose in the bore, the axle housing must be replaced.

Lubricate the bearing and bearing bore before driving the new roller bearing into the bore firmly against the bore shoulder. Pack the cavity between the seal lips and seal housing with wheel bearing grease before driving it into its bore against the bearing cage. Use a seal driver of the correct diameter to install the bearing and seal; otherwise you may damage them during installation.

Examine the axle shaft splines and the bearing and seal surfaces for excessive wear and surface damage. If the bearing surface is rough or pitted, the axle shaft must be replaced.

Check the axle shaft flange surface for damage and for straightness. If the wheel studs are loose or the threads are damaged, replace them also.

REASSEMBLY Thoroughly clean the axle shaft, coat the seal and bearing surfaces with grease, and then screw one wheel nut onto one wheel stud. Place a long-extended socket wrench onto the nut. Take care, when placing the axle shaft onto the axle housing, not to damage the seal lips or rollers. Using the socket wrench extension as a lever, lift the end of the axle shaft to engage its spline with the splines

in the differential side gear. Push the axle shaft fully inward and push the side gear against the differential housing; then install the C clamp into the axle shaft groove. Pull the axle shaft outward to lock the C clamp in the side gear counterbore.

Reinstall the pinion shaft and lock. Clean away any old gasket material from the carrier and cover surface and, if necessary, clean the interior of the carrier housing and gears with a flushing gun.

Install a new gasket and put back the cover. Torque the bolts in a crosswise pattern to the specified torque, so that the gasket will not leak. Fill the rear carrier with the recommended gear oil to the specified level, and torque the filler plug to the specified torque. Reinstall the brake drum and disk wheel and if necessary readjust the brakes. When the axle shaft is supported by a sealed ball bearing, always replace the inner axle shaft seal whenever the axle shaft is removed. With a slide-hammer puller, remove the inner axle shaft seal according to the procedure given previously. For installation, see recommendations previously outlined.

To remove either a sealed ball bearing or a tapered roller bearing from the axle shaft, you must first remove the bearing retainer (clinch ring). To do this, drill a ¼-in [6-mm] hole only to a depth of three-fourths of the retainer thickness so that the drill does not reach the axle shaft. Place the retainer on a solid surface (anvil) and then place a cold chisel across the hole and strike it sharply. This will split the retainer. Some manufacturers merely recommend making several deep nicks with a cold chisel on the retainer to expand it sufficiently to slide off the shaft (see Fig. 13-18).

To press the wheel bearing (ball or tapered roller bearing) from the axle shaft, assemble the two half collets so that the inner circle flange rests behind the bearing race. Secure this position by tightening the through bolts. Now place the collet and axle shaft on the press bed and, for protection in the event the bearing explodes, wrap a shop towel around the bearing before pressing the shaft from the collet. In-

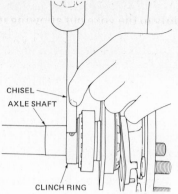

Fig. 13-18 Removing clinch ring. (*International Harvester Company*)

spect the machined surfaces of the axle shaft and axle housing for surface damage or other irregularities which could affect bearing and seal action. Check the axle in the manner outlined previously.

Bearing Installation Lubricate the axle shaft bearing surface and the bearing bore and, if applicable, fill the cavity between the seal lips and seal housing with grease. Place the bearing retainer plate and the bearing in the correct direction on the axle shaft. If a tapered roller bearing is used, place the new axle shaft seal and then the bearing cone onto the axle shaft. **NOTE** The small outer diameter of the bearing must face toward the splined end of the axle shaft.

Press the bearing onto the axle shaft by using an adapter that adequately supports the bearing and then apply sufficient force to seat the bearing against the axle shaft shoulder. Lubricate the bore of the bearing retainer and press it firmly against the bearings (see Fig. 13-19). **NOTE** Do not press the bear-

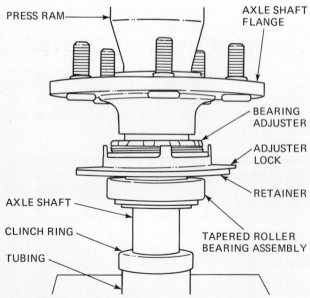

Fig. 13-19 Installing clinch ring onto axle shaft. (*International Harvester Company*)

ing and bearing retainer onto the axle shaft simultaneously. This could damage the bearing and create a loosely fitted retainer. Some off-highway equipment manufacturers recommend heating the bearing retainer to 300°F [149°C] and then placing it in position. The retainer shrinks as it cools, securing it to the axle shaft.

Axle Shaft Installation (Ball Bearing) Before installing the axle shaft, make certain that the old (axle housing flange) gasket material is removed from the flange, that the backing plate and both surfaces are free of nicks and burrs, and that the backing plate and mounting surface are not twisted or bent. Next, place the new gaskets between the housing flange and backing plate. Follow the installation procedure previously outlined to install the axle shaft. When the bearing bottoms against the housing bore shoulder, position the bearing retainer, then install and tighten the nuts to specified torque. **NOTE** Some manufacturers also use a gasket between the bearing retainer and backing plate.

Axle Shaft Installation (Tapered Roller Bearing) Before installing the axle shaft, thoroughly clean the surfaces of the axle housing bore, flange, and backing plate. Pack the wheel bearing with grease and then place the bearing cup onto the bearing cone.

NOTE Some manufacturers recommend lubricating the bearing cone with the same axle lubricant used in the carrier.

Grease the seal lips, the outer surface of the bearing cup, and the bearing bore. Make certain that no inner axle shaft seal is installed in the axle housing, for this would prevent lubricant from reaching the wheel bearing. To facilitate engaging the splines with the side gear splines, use the procedure previously outlined in this unit for installing the axle shaft.

Before bottoming the bearing cup against the housing bore shoulder, pull the seal away from the corner of the bearing cup into the retainer. This action slightly reduces the outer seal diameter so that it starts straight into the axle housing bore with ease. Now bottom the bearing cup against the bore shoulder and position the bearing retainer plate. Install the nuts and tighten them to the specified torque (see Fig. 13-20). Install the brake drum, the drum retainers, and the disk wheel.

FRONT AXLE DRIVE WHEEL HUB

The purpose of a front axle drive is to provide additional tractive effort. With four or six wheels capable of driving, all the weight of the vehicle and payload is used to give maximum tire traction. Although front axle drives are full-floating, they are not all consistent in design. Modifications are made to accommodate the vehicle's load-carrying capacity, its foundation brake design, and a planetary drive or locking wheel hub if these are included in the design.

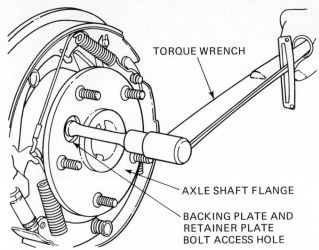

Fig. 13-20 Tightening backing plate and retainer plate. (*International Harvester Company*)

Design The ball yoke is bolted or welded to the axle housing, and the bearing cups are located in the outer end of the ball yoke, or a tapered hole is machined in the lower end of the ball yoke and a tapered adjusting sleeve is threaded into its upper outer end, to which the ball joints are fastened (see Fig. 13-21).

A bushing is pressed into the ball yoke to support the outer end of the inner axle shaft. A one-piece steering knuckle is positioned to the ball yoke with tapered roller bearings and kingpins; otherwise, ball joints are used to fasten the steering knuckle to the ball yoke. In either design the steering knuckle is fastened rigidly to the yoke but allowing it to swivel. Shims are used to adjust the kingpin bearing end play, or the adjusting sleeve is used to adjust the ball joint end play. **NOTE** Not all upper steering knuckle supports are identical. Some designs use a tapered kingpin and a tapered nylon bushing, while others use a straight kingpin and a brass bushing. On the front axle shown (see Fig. 13-22) the universal joint area is not lubricated with oil. A seal located between the spindle and steering knuckle seals the wheel hub toward the universal joint area; therefore the ball joints or kingpins are lubricated with grease. On some large equipment the steering knuckle is manufactured as two halves and then bolted to a unit over the yoke. See the discussion of front axle planetary drive wheel hub later in this unit.

The steering arm is either bolted or pinned to the steering knuckle. A seal, fastened to the inside of the steering knuckle, seals the wheel hub. The backing plate and spindle are bolted to the steering knuckle. A flange-type bushing is pressed into the spindle to support the inner end of the outer axle shaft and absorb the axle shaft side thrust; or a needle bearing supports the inside of the outer axle shaft, and the spacer acts as the thrust washer. The splash plate and spindle are bolted to the steering knuckle.

The wheel hub is supported on the spindle by tapered roller bearings. The wheel bearings are adjusted by one of the methods outlined earlier in this unit or by shims. The wheel bearing seal seals the area between the wheel hub and spindle. The brake drum or rotor is fastened to the wheel hub, and the

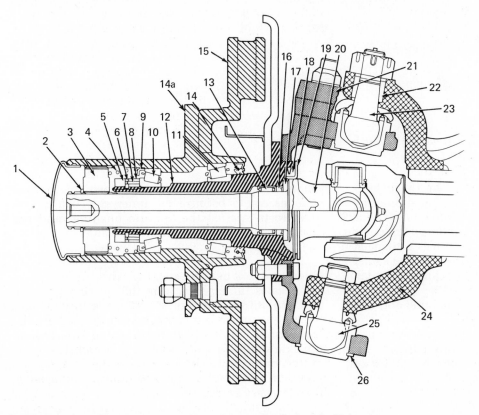

1. Hub cap
2. Snap ring
3. Hub drive gear
4. Spring
5. Lock nut
6. Lock-adj. nut
7. Pin-adj. nut
8. Adjusting nut
9. Pressure plate
10. Outer-wheel bearing
11. Inner-wheel bearing
12. Spindle
13. Spindle bearing
14. Seal
14a. Wheel hub
15. Wheel hub disk (rotor)
16. Oil seal
17. Spacer
18. Dust seal
19. Deflector
20. Axle outer shaft
21. Knuckle
22. Adjusting sleeve
23. Upper ball joint
24. Yoke
25. Lower ball joint
26. Retaining ring

Fig. 13-21 Sectional view of a front drive axle (locked hub) having ball joints. (*International Harvester Company*)

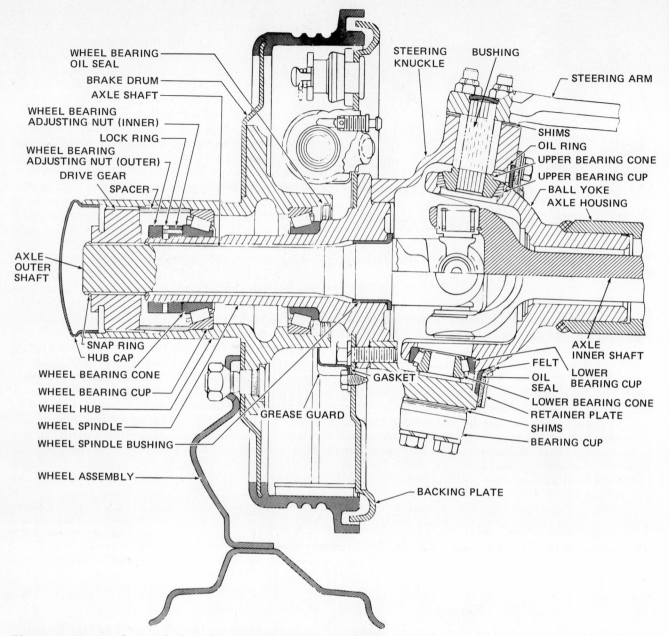

Fig. 13-22 Sectional view of a front drive axle having kingpins (non-locking hub). (*International Harvester Company*)

outer axle shaft is splined into the drive flange bolted to the wheel hub, or it may be splined to a drive gear splined into the wheel hub or it is splined to the axle shaft hub of the manual or automatic locking hub. When the front axle uses a planetary gear set, the axle shaft is splined to the sungear (see the discussion of planetary drive wheel hubs later in this unit).

Axle shaft assemblies (that is, the inner and outer axle shaft and the universal joint) may be slightly different to some degree, dependent on the type of universal joint used. There are three types of universal joints—the Cardan type (see Figs. 13-20 and 13-21), which is of the nonconstant velocity design, and the Rzeppa and the Weiss types, which are of the constant velocity design. (See the discussion of planetary drive and drive lines later in this unit.)

Each outer axle shaft has a snapring groove and

when the snapring is installed, it positions the axle shaft assembly because the inner side of the axle yoke rests against the spindle bushing, and the snapring rests against the drive flange, the drive gear, or the sungear.

Operation   When the steering wheel is turned, it semirotates the steering arm, the steering knuckle, and the spindle on the kingpin bearings or ball joints. The power is transmitted as follows: from the front carrier pinion to the differential side gear to the axle shafts. From the outer axle shaft it is transmitted onto the wheel hub (or to the locking hub and then to the wheel hub) or from the sungear to the planetary carrier.

Servicing the Front Axle Drive   Before removing the wheel hub, the axle shaft assembly, or the steer-

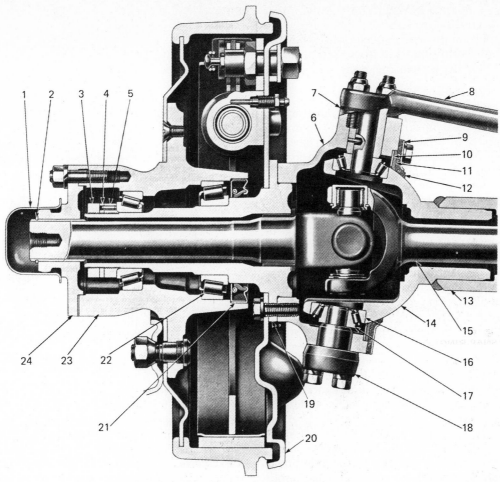

1. Hub cap
2. Snap ring
3. Lock nut
4. Lock ring
5. Adjusting nut
6. Steering knuckle

7. Shims
8. Steering arm
9. Seal retainer
10. Felt seal ring
11. Rubber seal
12. Felt seal

13. Axle housing
14. Ball yoke
15. Axle shaft
16. Bearing cap
17. Bearing cone
18. Bearing cap

19. Spindle
20. Brake backing plate
21. Wheel bearing seal
22. Wheel bearing, inner
23. Wheel hub
24. Drive flange

Fig. 13-23 Sectional view of steering knuckle and wheel hub. (*General Motors Corporation*)

ing knuckle, check the components as you would a nondriving wheel hub (previously outlined) to determine if the assembly needs to be serviced or merely adjusted. Additionally, check the wheel assembly for oil leaks, and check for loose or worn kingpin bearings or ball joints.

If the drive must be serviced, first steam-clean the area on which you intend to work. Obey all safety rules as you prepare the vehicle, following the steps outlined in the discussion of front or trailer axle wheel hub and bearing in this unit. The procedure should be modified, of course, according to the part of the wheel assembly being serviced and the weights involved, when you are removing the components.

To service a complete assembly of the type shown in Fig. 13-23, start by removing the wheel nuts and wheel and the three countersunk screws that position the brake drum to the wheel hub and then lift the brake drum from the wheel hub. Remove the hub cap, the snapring from the outer axle shaft, and the stud nuts and washers, in that order. Lift off the

drive flange and gasket, the wheel bearing lock nut, lock ring and adjusting nut, and the outer wheel bearing cone. **NOTE** While removing the outer wheel bearing cone, hold the wheel hub so that the spindle threads, the inner wheel bearing, and the wheel bearing seal cannot be damaged and then lift the wheel hub from the spindle. Remove the bolts and lock washers that hold the backing plate and spindle to the steering knuckle. Take care, when removing the backing plate, not to twist the brake hose or suspend the backing plate. It is suggested that you wire the backing plate to the frame to protect the brake components. Next, pull the spindle from the steering knuckle and slide it over the outer axle shaft and pull the axle shaft assembly from the axle housing. Remove the bolts that hold the seal assembly (seal retainer, felt seal, and rubber seal) and lay the seal assembly onto the axle housing. Remove the drag link from the steering arm and the tie rod from the steering knuckle. Remove the lower bolts and lock washers that secure the lower kingpin bearing cap. Remove the cap and shims and wire them to-

192

gether. Remove the nuts from the studs of the upper bearing cap or steering arm and lift the bearing cap or steering arm from the studs and steering knuckle. Then slide the steering knuckle from the ball joint. DO NOT let the lower bearing cone fall on the ground.

Cleaning and Inspection   Wearing protective glasses, clean all parts in solvent and dry them with compressed air. Scrutinize all machined surfaces for indication of wear, stress, pitting, and score marks. Check the axle shaft splines (drive hub) for wear, pitting, or broken splines. Check the bushing and seal surfaces for wear, pitting, or rough spots. Replace the axle housing and spindle bushings and discard all seals and gaskets. See the discussion of bearings in regard to cleaning, inspecting, removing, and installing.

Use a press or a puller arrangement and the appropriate adapters when removing or installing press-fitted parts. Replace any damaged nuts, bolts, and studs, including the wheel studs. If the universal joint is sticking or feels rough when the shafts are misaligned then it must be serviced.

Reassembly   First, make certain that all parts are clean. Remove nicks, burrs, and rough spots by using an oil stone or fine emery cloth. Service the foundation brakes.

Start the reassembly by placing shims of equal thickness onto the lower and upper bearing retainer (cap) and place the retainers close to the axle housing on a clean shop towel. Place the seal assembly over the axle housing, and the bearing cups in the bores of the ball yoke. Lubricate the bearing cones with the recommended axle oil and then place one into the upper cup. While holding the lower bearing cone in the lower cup, slide the steering knuckle over the ball yoke. Align the upper bores and install the upper bearing cap or steering arm into the bearing cone and steering knuckle bore. Secure the cap with bolts and lock washers and torque the bolts to specification.

Next, install the lower bearing cap. Secure it (loosely) with bolts and lock washers—do not torque the bolts at this time.

To check the bearing preload, place a socket onto one upper bearing cap bolt head and then, with a torque wrench, measure the torque required to start or maintain the motion needed to pivot the steering knuckle. Check your service manual for detailed procedure. If the steering knuckle can be turned with ease, tighten the bolts evenly in a cross pattern and at the same time move the steering knuckle. If the effort increases beyond the torque specification, remove the lower bearing cap, add a shim, and then repeat the procedure.

If the starting torque is too low after both caps are torqued to specification, remove a shim from the lower bearing cap. **NOTE** If shim thickness of more than 0.010 in [0.25 mm] is required to achieve the starting torque, place an equal amount of shim thickness below the upper and lower bearing cap to maintain the spindle in center with the axle shaft.

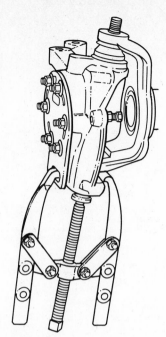

Fig. 13-24   Removing knuckle from yoke. (*International Harvester Company*)

This will reduce wear on shaft and bushing. When the preload is checked and adjusted, lightly lubricate the outer surface of the ball yoke and then install the rubber seal and the felt seal and retainer and secure it with bolts to the steering knuckles. Make certain you use a torque wrench to tighten the bolt to specified torque; otherwise the seal will leak.

To complete the assembly, take precisely the reverse steps you took when disassembling. Do not forget to fill the wheel hub with the recommended axle oil to the level specified and to check the front carrier oil level.

Driving Front Axle Wheel Hub with Ball Joint and Disk Brakes   The primary differences in servicing a ball joint and disk brake front driving axle wheel hub, as opposed to one having kingpins and a brake drum, lie in the procedure to remove the disk brake caliper, the testing procedure, and the servicing of the ball joints. On this type of driving axle, the rotor is inboard mounted, and furthermore, a splash shield rather than a backing plate is bolted to the spindle and steering knuckle. Apart from this, the removal, servicing, and installation procedures are the same (see Fig. 13-21).

SERVICING   To service the aforementioned front axle, first remove the axle shaft assembly and then remove the spindle from the ball joints. To remove the spindle, first remove the cotter pin and then the nut from the upper ball joint stud. Remove the self-locking nut from the lower ball joint socket, as well as the snapring. Now attach the puller adapter plate to the steering knuckle splash plate surface and puller jaws onto the shoulder of the lower steering knuckle (see Fig. 13-24). Position the puller screw with its adapter against the flat surface of the lower ball joint socket. Turn the puller screw to force the

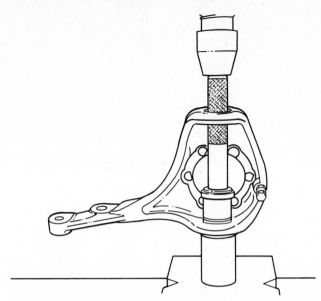

Fig. 13-25 Removing top ball socket from knuckle. (*International Harvester Company*)

two ball joint sockets out of their steering knuckle bores. **NOTE** If the upper ball joint socket should remain in the steering knuckle, press it out or use a puller attachment to remove the ball joint studs from the yoke. Do not drive them out; use a puller attachment (see Fig. 13-25); otherwise you will damage the ball yoke. Next, remove the ball stud's threaded sleeve with a pin wrench, discard it, and then thread in a new one, leaving about two threads visible.

REASSEMBLY Clean the steering knuckle and yoke with solvent and dry them with compressed air. If the bores are damaged or elongated, or if the eyes are bent or twisted, the steering knuckle and/or housing must be replaced.

Start the reassembly by pressing a new ball joint socket into the lower steering knuckle bore and another one into the upper bore (see Fig. 13-26). Make certain that both ball joint sockets seat firmly against the shoulder of the steering knuckle. Install a new snapring into the lower socket groove and then slide the ball joint studs into the tapered bores of the yoke. Screw a new nut onto the lower ball joint stud and torque the nut to specification. Next, torque the threaded sleeve to the specified torque, install the nut, and then torque the nut to the specified torque. Align the cotter pin holes but do not loosen the nut for hole alignment.

To check that the ball joints are correctly pre-loaded and that the steering knuckle has the specified turning resistance, attach a spring scale to the specified point on the steering knuckle and turn it in a straight ahead position. Next, pull on the spring scale and read from the scale the kilogram or pounds pull required to keep the steering knuckle turning after the initial movement. When the turning effort is too great, loosen the threaded sleeve slightly, and when the knuckle moves too easily, increase the torque to achieve the recommended turning effort. When it is correctly adjusted, reinstall and retorque

the upper ball joint stud nut and install the cotter pin.

LOCKING WHEEL HUBS

The purpose of a locking wheel hub is to reduce wear on the tires, the axle shaft assembly, the front carrier, and the drive line. It provides a means of controlling the engaging and disengaging of the front wheel hubs with/from the axle shafts. When the locking hub is in the engage position (manual or automatic), the axle shaft drives the wheel hub. when it is in the disengage position, the axle shaft is free from the wheel hub. The wheel can therefore rotate (at a speed governed by the tire-to-ground contact).

There are two types of locking wheel hubs on front-drive axles, the manual locking wheel hub or an automatic locking wheel hub (Lock-o-matic). Although each type has several different designs, their basic operating principles remain the same.

When the front axle has a manual locking wheel hub, the following precautions should be observed. Do not drive the vehicle unless both wheel hubs are correctly positioned in either "lock" or "free" position or the wheel lock is in lock position when the transfer case is in low gear (otherwise there would be too much torque in the rear drive line). Never force the control in either position with a tool—use only your fingers.

Manual Locking Wheel Hub One design of a locking wheel hub is shown in Fig. 13-27; it is a spring-loaded type. This design obviates the need to move the wheel in the event the engagement is not being completed, but it permits the control dial to be positioned in lock or free position, and when the vehicle moves slightly, the engagement or disengagement occurs.

DESIGN When the manual locking hub is assembled to the wheel hub, the body locking hub and

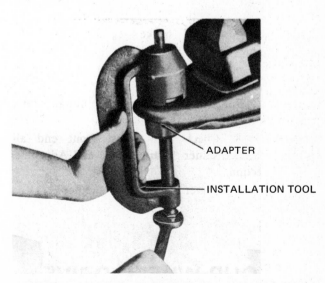

Fig. 13-26 Installing lower ball joint. (*General Motors Corporation*)

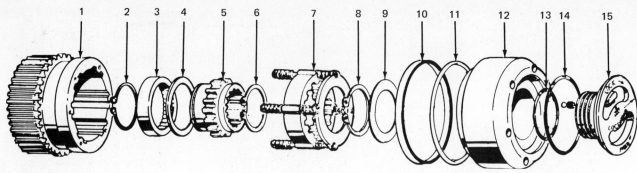

1. Body locking hub
2. Snap ring
3. Needle bearing
4. Wear shim
5. Axle shaft hub

6. Axle shaft snap ring
7. Clutch assembly w/springs ring
8. Snap ring
9. Disk shim
10. Retainer ring

11. O-clutch cap ring
12. Clutch body cap
13. Outer O ring
14. Oil seal
15. Control with spring and ball

Fig. 13-27 Exploded view of spring-loaded manual type locking hub with socket head mounting screws. (*International Harvester Company*)

clutch body are bolted to the wheel hub, and the axle shaft hub is splined to the axle shaft. The axle shaft hub is supported inside the body locking hub by a roller bearing and is held in place by the snapring. A thrust washer (wear shim) is placed between the roller bearing and the axle shaft hub to absorb the side thrust during engagement. A snapring maintains the assembly on the axle shaft. The clutch ring assembly has five pins. Each pin has a coil spring on each side. The left sides of the pins rest against the body locking hub, and the right sides of the pins are fastened to the ring. Large splines on the outside of the clutch ring assembly fit into the splines of the body locking hub. When the control dial is set to the free position, the coil springs have positioned the clutch ring so that there is a space between them and the axle hub. The control dial is positioned inside the clutch body cap and sealed with two O rings. It is held to the body cap by the screw that is fastened with a countersunk screw to the control dial. A thrust washer (disk shim) lies between the screw face and the bottom of the body cap. The screw is threaded into the clutch ring.

OPERATION When the control dial is in the free position, the clutch ring is in the position as outlined earlier (see Fig. 13-28). When the control dial is rotated clockwise (about 45°), the large screw forces the ring to the left, compressing the right coil springs. This moves the clutch ring in the large splines of the body locking hub to the left. If the internal splines of the clutch hub and the external splines of the axle hub do not mesh, because of misalignment, the coil spring tension increases until the control is in the lock position.

As soon as the wheel moves slightly, the clutch hub slides over the splines of the axle hub, locking the wheel hub to the axle shaft. The power can now be transmitted from the axle shaft to the axle shaft hub, to the clutch ring, to the body locking hub, and to the wheel hub.

When the control dial is turned to free position,

the screw moves the ring to the right, increasing the force on the left coil springs, and if there is no torque on the axle hub and clutch ring, the spring force disengages the clutch hub from the splines of the axle shaft cup. Otherwise the engagement occurs with the first movement of the axle shaft.

Lock-o-matic The principal advantage of a Lock-o-matic over a manual locking hub is that it automatically locks the axle shaft with the wheel hub the moment torque is applied to the axle shaft and disengages as soon as the torque is removed. When the front axle wheels are to be used to transmit engine retardation to the wheels or to control steep downhill steering, the control must be set manually to lock position.

DESIGN The Lock-o-matic hub components (18 to 30), shown in Fig. 13-29, are similar in design to the manual locking hub, and the location of the components within the clutch body is also relatively the same. However, the clutch body shown here has internal grooves, and the clutch ring has external grooves in which the drive pins are located. The purpose of all these components is to manually lock the internal splines of the clutch ring to the short external splines of the axle shaft hub.

Components 1 to 15 (a one-way clutch) are required to automatically engage and disengage the axle shaft hub with the hub body. The axle shaft hub has 10 tapered external ramps, and the hub body has an internal steel ring; 10 rollers are positioned in the 10 right-angular slots in the roller cage and are held to the roller cage by the centering spring. The friction shoes are positioned in the circular right-angular slots and held in the roller cage slots by the friction shoe spring. The shoe drag ring is positioned inside the friction shoe and is threaded onto the spindle. The axle shaft hub is held to the roller cage by two Spirolox lock rings. The thrust washer rests against the counter bore shoulder in the hub body, and a Spirolox lock ring holds it to the hub.

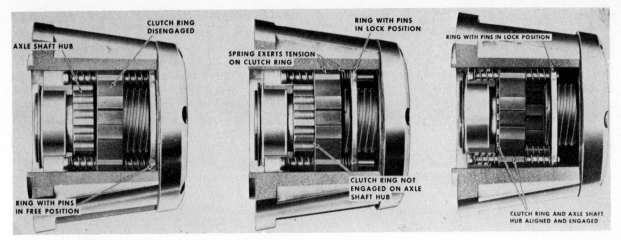

Fig. 13-28 Three-stage operation of spring-loaded manual locking hub. (*International Harvester Company*)

OPERATION When the control is turned to the lock position, the screw has moved the clutch ring, and when the splines of the clutch ring and axle shaft hub align, an engagement is achieved. If the splines do not align, an engagement will not be made, and you will sense this lack of engagement. Furthermore, the arrow on the control dial will not be in line with the dot on the clutch body.

To complete engagement, first raise the tire off the ground and then turn the wheel slightly as you move the control dial to the full lock position. You will sense engagement as it takes place. The power can now be transmitted from the axle shaft hub, to the clutch ring gear, to the drive pins, to the clutch body, and finally to the wheel hub.

When the control dial is placed in the free posi-

tion, the clutch ring is disengaged from the axle shaft hub. Whenever the axle shaft is turned in a forward direction, the friction between the shoe drag ring and friction shoes causes a positioning of the roller cage on the axle shaft hub, bringing the rollers to the lowest position on the axle shaft hub ramps. Moreover, when the wheel rotates faster than the axle shaft, the friction from the internal steel surface to the roller surfaces maintains the rollers in the low position. However, as soon as the rotating speed of the wheel, and likewise the hub body, is less than that of the axle shaft hub, it causes the roller cage to move, moving the roller on the hub ramps and forcing them outward against the inner (steel) surface of the hub body. The rollers are then wedged between the inner body hub surface and axle shaft hub ramps.

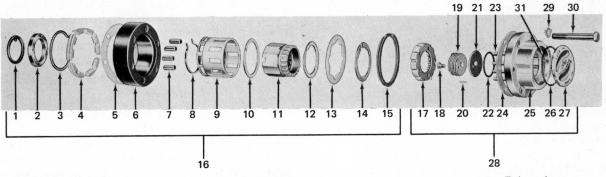

1. Spindle lock washer	12. Lock ring	23. Drive pin
2. Drag shoe	13. Thrust washer	24. Clutch gasket
3. Friction shoe spring	14. Lock ring	25. Clutch body
4. Friction shoe	15. Lock ring	26. U ring, oil seal
5. Gasket	16. Hub assembly body	27. Assembly control
6. Hub body	17. Clutch ring	28. Clutch assembly body
7. Roller	18. Flat head screw	29. Lock washer
8. Centering spring	19. Clutch screw	30. Bolt
9. Roller cage	20. Dowel pin	31. Stop pin
10. Lock ring	21. Disk	
11. Axle shaft hub	22. U ring, oil seal	

Fig. 13-29 Exploded view of locking wheel hub (Lock-o-matic). (*International Harvester Company*)

The power from the axle shaft is now transmitted from the axle shaft hub to the rollers, to the hub body, and to the wheel hub.

Troubleshooting   The main reasons why a manual or an automatic locking hub will not manually engage or why it will not engage or disengage properly are insufficient lubrication, loose wheel bearing adjustment, and seized or damaged control dial. It may also be due to wear or damage of the clutch, axle shaft hub splines, and/or the clutch ring. Then, too, if the axle hub roller bearing were damaged or worn, it would allow the axle shaft hub to misalign with the clutch ring.

The main reasons why a Lock-o-matic may fail to operate properly are insufficient lubrication, loose wheel or worn wheel bearings, worn friction shoes and/or worn shoe drag ring, or grooved, pitted, or corroded rollers or ramp surfaces.

Servicing a Lock-o-matic   To service a Lock-o-matic, it is not necessary to raise the vehicle off the ground or to remove the wheels. The assembly can be removed as a unit by removing the six bolts that secure the locking hub to the wheel hub.

After the bolts are removed, separate the clutch body assembly from the hub body assembly by removing parts 17 to 27 (see Fig. 13-29). Then remove the axle snapring and slide the hub body assembly from the axle shaft.

To disassemble the clutch body assembly, remove the countersunk screw that secures the screw to the control dial. Lift it and the clutch ring from the dowel pin and unscrew the clutch ring. Remove the drive pins, gasket, and dowel pin from the clutch hub. Remove the disk from the bottom center. Using your finger, press the control dial from the clutch body and remove the inner and outer O rings.

NOTE   If the steel ball and spring that lock the control dial in free or lock position are damaged, the control dial must be replaced.

Wash all parts in solvent and dry them with compressed air. Discard all seals and gaskets. Check all parts for wear or damage. Particularly check the screw and clutch ring for damaged or worn threads and the splines and drive pin grooves for wear. Before or during the assembly coat all parts lightly with the specified grease and then start the reassembly.

REASSEMBLY   Commence reassembly (see Fig. 13-29) in an order precisely the reverse of disassembly. When correctly assembled, the screw edge will be flush with the back edge of the clutch ring, and the control dial will turn freely from lock or free or vice versa and will snap smartly into position. This allows the clutch ring to move freely on the screw and drive pin. When the clutch ring is in free position, it barely bottoms against the clutch body. The countersunk screw and dowel pin should then be staked (locked) so that they cannot come out.

To disassemble the Lock-o-matic unit (see Fig. 13-29), first mark the axle shaft hub gear position on the hub body. Next, in precisely this order, proceed

as follows: remove the lock rings that hold the axle shaft hub into the hub body and pull the axle shaft hub and roller cage from the hub body. Take out the centering spring and remove the rollers from the cage and the Spirolox lock ring from the second groove in the axle shaft hub. Now slide the roller cage from the hub. (You may have to twist it slightly to align the hub corners with the friction shoe grooves.) Remove the friction shoe spring and the friction shoes from the roller cage and remove the Spirolox lock ring and thrust washer from the hub body.

Clean all parts in solvent and dry them with compressed air. Inspect all machined surfaces for pitting, grooving, and score marks. If the clutch hub or axle shaft ramps are damaged to any extent, they must be replaced; otherwise the one-way clutch will not disengage. If the splines of the hub are worn or chipped, they must be replaced. Always replace the friction shoes.

REASSEMBLY   Reassemble the Lock-o-matic parts to the clutch hub in precisely the reverse order of disassembly (see Fig. 13-29). However, first lubricate the parts lightly with the recommended grease. **CAUTION**   The center ring spring must be placed into the longest roller slot in the roller cage. Moreover, before installing the Lock-o-matic to the wheel hub, check the wheel hub flange surface for nicks and burrs, the threaded bores for damaged threads, and the shoe drag ring for wear. Always make certain that the drag shoe is properly secured.

If you wish to replace the shoe drag ring, first loosen the hexhead set screw and unscrew the drag shoe from the spindle and then check the condition of the snapring. Screw a new shoe drag ring onto the spindle until it seats against the snapring and then tighten the set screw. Use grease to affix the gasket to the left side of the clutch and hub body.

Place the axle shaft hub onto the splines of the axle shaft and secure it to the shaft with a snapring. Align the hub body bores with the wheel hub threaded bores, and then place the clutch hub onto the hub body; secure both to the wheel hub.

TESTING   After tightening the bolts to the specified torque, check the manual operation and the Lock-o-matic operation. To make these checks, first raise the front axle sufficiently to lift the tires off the ground. Secure the front axle by using floor stands. To check the manual lock operation, place the control dials in lock position, turn one front wheel in either forward or reverse direction, and observe the rotation of the other front wheel. It should turn in the direction opposite that of the turning wheel.

To check the operation of the Lock-o-matic, turn the control dials to free position and then turn each front wheel in a forward direction—they should rotate freely. When you are rotating the front wheel in a backward direction, the wheel should lock up, and the locked wheel should drive the other front wheel in forward direction. This opposite-direction rotation is caused by the differential in the front carrier.

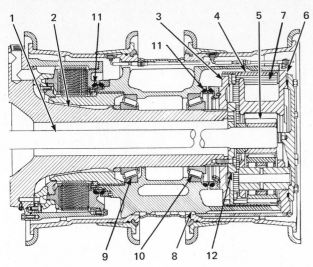

1. Axle shaft
2. Spindle
3. Final drive hub
4. Ring gear
5. Sun gear
6. Planetary carrier
7. Planetary carrier gear(s)
8. Wheel hub
9. Inner wheel bearing
10. Outer wheel bearing
11. Duo-cone floating seal
12. Retainer

Fig. 13-30 Sectional view of a final drive planetary wheel hub. (*Caterpillar Tractor Co.*)

PLANETARY DRIVE WHEEL HUBS

Planetary drives, also called planetary final drives, are usually used only on off-highway tractors, trucks, and loaders, although a few large on-highway tractors also use them. A unique feature of a planetary drive axle is its ability to perform the final torque multiplication at the point at which the torque is applied to the drive wheel. It is compact, and yet, because of its design, it can transfer a greater torque than a single set of gears.

To grasp the concept of the planetary drive wheel hub, you must recognize that it is necessary to multiply the engine torque several times before it reaches the drive wheel to efficiently use a compact engine. The torque is multiplied in the transmission and by the rear carrier(s) through reduction gearing. When a torque converter is used, through hydrodynamics the torque is again multiplied before the power enters the transmission.

However, all this torque multiplication is insufficient for most off-highway equipment. An additional reduction is required to achieve the desired multiplication of about 140:1. The use of a planetary gear set in a drive axle wheel hub is the most efficient way in which to achieve this objective. If the torque multiplier (a gear set) were located at any other place within the power train, the components located after the additional gear set, such as the axle shaft, axle housing, carrier, and/or drive line, would be required to transmit a greater torque. This increased torque would necessitate stronger components which would, in turn, increase the equipment costs and weight. More significantly, a smaller portion of the engine power would be available to move the load.

Rear Axle Planetary Drive Design   The planetary gear set is located in the outer portion of the wheel hub and is usually splash lubricated (refer to Fig. 13-30). The oil is supplied from the planetary drive compartment and in some cases is supplied from the carrier housing. The planetary drive axle is also of the full-floating design. The sungear is splined to the outer end of the drive axle shaft, and the inner end of the drive axle is splined to the side gear of the differential. The planetary ring gear is splined to the final drive hub, which is splined to the spindle and, therefore, does not rotate. The planetary carrier gears (located in the planetary carrier housing) are supported on the gear shaft by roller bearings. The carrier housing is bolted to the wheel hub, and the wheel hub is supported by tapered roller bearings on the spindle.

The spindle is bolted to the carrier housing. One duo-cone floating seal ring seals between the final drive hub and the wheel hub. The other duo-cone seal seals between the wheel hub and the brake hub, keeping the lubricant within the final drive and brake cavity. The wheel bearings are shim adjusted. The cover is bolted to the planetary carrier housing, and in conjunction with the O ring it seals the planetary gear set. The cover has three internal lugs, and when it is bolted to the carrier, the lugs rest in the carrier gear shaft cutouts and thereby prevent them from turning within the carrier housing.

OPERATION   When the rear carrier pinion is rotated, it rotates the ring gear, the differential housing, and with it, the side gears, the axle shafts, and the sungear. When the tires have equal traction and the truck is moving straight ahead, then the ring gear of the carrier and sungear rotate at the same speed. The sungear drives the planetary carrier gears in a direction opposite to the rotation of the sungear. The planetary gears are forced to travel within the stationary planetary ring gear and thereby rotate the planetary carrier and the wheel hub in the same direction as the sungear (but at a lesser speed).

TROUBLESHOOTING   When malfunction occurs within the planetary final drive, it may be noticeable by (1) excessive noise due to insufficient or contaminated lubricant; (2) excessive noise due to worn gear teeth or to worn or chipped shafts or bearings; (3) loose wheel bearing adjustment, causing the wheel to tilt and the planetary carrier gear to misalign; (4) overheated planetary gear set, due to reduced lubrication, foaming, or contaminants in the lubricant; (5) seal and O ring failure.

An oil leak could emanate from seal failure or from loose bolts and nuts, inadequate wheel bearing preload, or a wheel bearing damaged owing to careless installation. In each of these cases the planetary final drive has to be serviced.

SERVICING   To service the planetary final drive, first steam-clean the area on which you intend to work. Next, position the truck to accommodate your lifting device in the event you have to remove the wheel and the wheel hub. When the truck or loader, etc.,

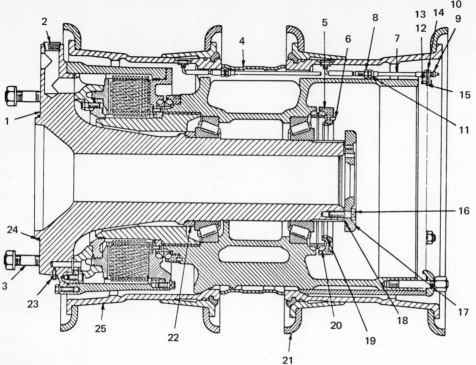

1. Spindle assembly
2. Plug
3. Stud
4. Band
5. Retainer assembly
6. Pin
7. Extension assembly
8. Nut
9. Cap
10. Core
11. Nut
12. Bolt
13. Lockwasher
14. Washer
15. Bracket
16. Bolt
17. Retainer
18. Shim
19. Seal
20. Seal assembly
21. Flange
22. Spacer
23. Screw
24. Seal
25. Base

Fig. 13-31 Sectional view of rear wheel and brake assembly. (*Caterpillar Tractor Co.*)

is positioned, lift the axle housing so that the tires just clear the ground and then safely block it in this position.

Do not forget to drain the air tanks. Turn the wheel hub until the final drive drain plug is at the bottom and then drain the final drive lubricant. Remove the cover nuts and washers and then screw three ⅜-in NC bolts into the provided holes to force the cover from the planetary carrier. Check the O ring in the cover. As a unit, slide the sun gear, the axle shaft, and the washer from the axle housing. Screw two ½-in NC eyebolts into the carrier, attach a hoist to it, and then take up the slack. Place a rubber-covered pipe (about 5 ft [1.52 m] long) between the carrier gears to improve the carrier's balance during the removal. Pull the carrier gears out of the ring gear. **CAUTION** Do not let the carrier gear pin fall out of the carrier housing while removing the carrier or when placing the carrier on the workbench for servicing.

To remove the wheel hub (shown in Fig. 13-31), attach a sling and hoist to it, take up the slack, and then remove the retainer bolt, the retainer with O ring, and shims from the final drive hub and spindle. Slide the final drive hub, as well as the planetary gear and seal retainer, from the spindle. Before sliding the wheel hub from the spindle, remove from it the seal, the seal retainer, the metal floating ring seals, the toric seals, and the outer wheel bearing cone. To protect the floating-ring seal rings and to ensure that the two halves are not interchanged, tape them together. Carefully slide the wheel hub from the spindle, and when it is removed, lift the floating ring seals and the toric seals from it and the brake

assembly hub. From the wheel hub remove the seal retainer, and from the spindle remove the inner bearing cone.

Before cleaning the components, disassemble the planetary carrier. To do this, place the planetary carrier on two blocks with the cover studs upward. The carrier gear pins are slide-fitted into the planetary carrier bore. To remove the carrier gear pins, push them upward or downward and then slide out the planetary carrier gears. With them should come two steel spacers, and two nonmetallic washers.

CAUTION Take care not to let the roller bearings or spacer fall to the floor.

INSPECTING, CLEANING, AND REASSEMBLING Clean all planetary carrier parts in solvent and dry them with compressed air or use a hot tank. In the latter case, follow all the recommended safety rules.

You should start your inspection by examining all machine surfaces for scoring and pitting and the splines and gear teeth for wear, burrs, and broken or chipped teeth. At this time replace any parts that cannot be reused for service. If the ring gear or final drive hub needs to be replaced, remove the mounting bolts and then lift the final drive hub from the splines of the ring gear. The spacer and washer must be flat and not scored; otherwise they will have to be replaced. See the discussion of bearings in regard to cleaning, inspection, and installing.

Clean the steel floating ring seals with an oil-free chemical such as alcohol or naphtha and then examine (without touching) the seal surface. There should be no evidence of nicks or burrs, and the

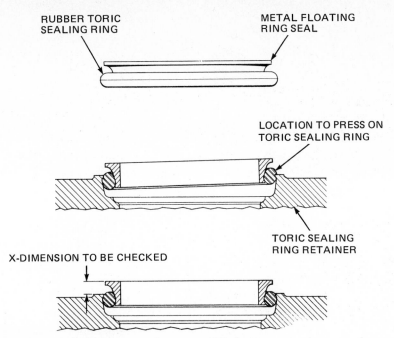

Fig. 13-32 Installing floating-ring seal and toric sealing ring. X is the dimension to be checked. (*Caterpillar Tractor Co.*)

wear pattern should not pass the halfway mark of the seal surface; otherwise the two halves will have to be replaced because they are lap fitted. If the toric seal rings are deformed, deteriorated, or cracked, they must be replaced.

The reassembly procedure is precisely the reverse of disassembly. Make certain all components are clean (and kept clean) and that they are well lubricated during assembly. Use a sling and hoist to lift the heavy components into position. (Do not attempt to lift them manually.)

Cool the bearing cups to ensure trouble-free installation. Follow the manufacturer's instructions precisely when installing the floating ring seals; otherwise your wheel may leak.

If no service manual is available and there is no seal installing tool, install the toric seal rings (by using your fingers only) against the lower seal seat (see Fig. 13-32). Next, place the floating ring seal into the inner diameter of the toric seal ring. Make certain it is placed parallel with the mounting surface and do not touch the floating seal ring surface. If you accidentally touch the ring surface, clean it again with alcohol. Do not interchange the two halves, and before matching up the set, lightly coat the seal surface with engine oil.

As you may be aware, a misadjusted wheel bearing on your car will cause trouble. A misadjusted wheel bearing on a truck that may carry 60,000 lb [27,273 kg] on one wheel would be even more serious. It must be adjusted precisely in accordance with the procedure recommended by the manufacturer.

For example, using the wheel assembly described earlier, with the wheel hub still supported on the spindle by the sling and hoist or jack, install the outer wheel bearing cone and the retainer (without the shims) and torque the bolts in a cross pattern to

50 lb·ft [67.8 N·m] while rotating the wheel assembly (see Fig. 13-33). This will have forced the retainer and the outer wheel bearing cone and the wheel hub toward the inner wheel bearing cone (preloading them as recommended by the manufacturer). Recheck the torque, slack off the sling, and rotate the wheel to ensure that the wheel bearings have seated properly. Now screw two long set screws with lock nuts into the threaded holes provided in the retainer. Finger-tighten them against the spindle and lock the position of the set screw with the lock nuts. Raise the hoist to take the load from the spindle and then remove the retainer. Take care not to disturb the position of the set screws. Next, measure the protrusion of the set screw with a depth micrometer or lay a straight edge across the set screws and, with a feeler gauge, measure the distance between the edge of the straight edge and the face of the retainer (see Fig. 13-34). Suppose your measurement was 0.080 in [2.0 mm] and say that the service manual indicated to add 0.010 in [0.25 mm] to the measurement—in other words, this would be 0.090 in [2.25 mm]. Therefore you must install 0.090-in shims to achieve the recommended wheel bearing preload. Place the shims on the retainer, bolt the retainer into position, and torque the bolts to 150 ± 20 lb·ft [204 ± 27.12 N·m] and then lockwire the bolts.

To install the axle shaft, first remove the sun gear from the shaft. Place a pipe over the shaft to gain sufficient leverage to engage the inner shaft splines with the differential side gear.

Carefully install the cover. Make certain the lugs fit in the cutout of the carrier gear shaft so that the cover will not break when you are torquing the bolts to specification.

Finally, fill the planetary drive housing with the recommended oil. To do this, turn the wheel hub so

200

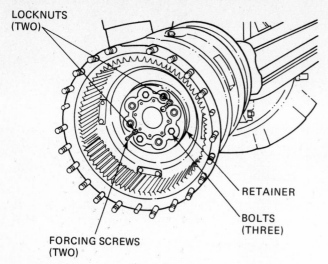

Fig. 13-33 Preloading wheel bearings. (Caterpillar Tractor Co.)

that the level plug is parallel to the floor. Then continue filling the planetary drive housing with the recommended oil until the oil runs out of the filler plug. Do not forget to check the oil level in the rear carrier.

Front Axle Planetary Drive Wheel Hub Although the components of a front axle planetary drive are very similar to those of a rear axle planetary drive, some differences and additional components exist because it is a steering axle (see Fig. 13-35).

DESIGN AND OPERATION The trunnion (ball yoke) is bolted to the axle housing. Two large-diameter pins (sockets) are fastened to the ball-shaped outer end of the trunnion, and a bushing and seal are pressed inside its center bore. The bushing supports the inner axle shaft, and the seal seals the planetary drive from the axle housing. This prevents lubricant from leaving or entering the other compartments.

The inner and outer flange halves are placed over the trunnion and are bolted together to form a unit. The inner flange half accommodates a seal, a seal

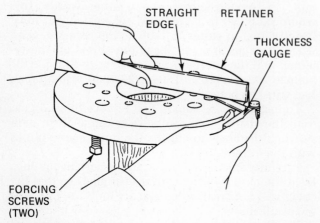

Fig. 13-34 Determining shim requirements. (Caterpillar Tractor Co.)

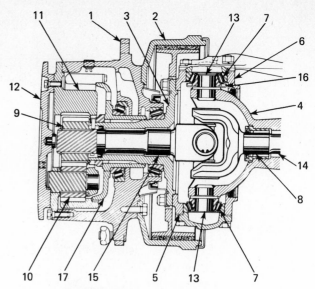

1. Wheel hub
2. Brake drum
3. Spindle
4. Trunnion flange (bolted to the axle beam)
5. Trunnion flange half (outer)
6. Trunnion flange half (inner)
7. Trunnion flange bearings
8. Shaft assembly bushing and seal
9. Sun gear
10. Carrier gear
11. Carrier
12. Cover
13. Pins
14. Inner axle shaft
15. Outer axle shaft
16. Grease retainer
17. Planetary ring gear hub

Fig. 13-35 Planetary drive steering axle. (J I Case Company Agricultural Equipment Division)

retainer, and a snap ring. The snap ring holds the components in the flange's outer bore, and the seal seals the planetary drive externally. The spindle is bolted to the outer flange itself.

To fasten the spindle quite rigidly while allowing it nevertheless to be moved horizontally (left or right), a grease retainer and a tapered roller bearing are placed on each trunnion socket, and the bearing cups are placed into the bores of the (now single-unit) trunnion flange. Shims are used to adjust the bearing preload. The spindle has external splines and an internal bushing.

The planetary ring gear is splined to the planetary hub, which in turn is splined to the spindle (see Fig. 13-36). The planetary ring gear's internal splines fit loosely on the splines of the ring gear hub, allowing the planetary gear to float into the orbit of the ring gear and thereby ensure uniform loading on the planetary gears. Lock plates and screws secure the position of the planetary ring gear to the gear hub.

A seal retainer, with seal, is bolted to the spindle, with the seal lips resting against the sealing surface of the wheel hub, sealing the planetary drive toward the brake drum. The outer axle shaft is supported by the bushing in the spindle, and the wheel hub is

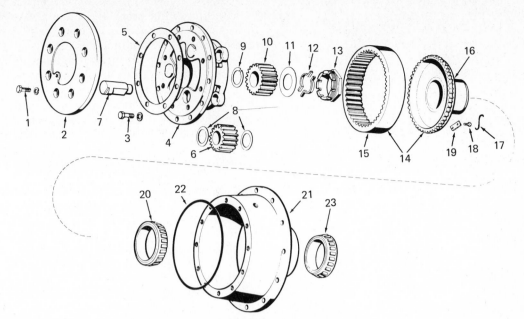

1. Cap screws
2. Cover
3. Cap screws
4. Planetary carrier housing
5. Gasket
6. Planetary carrier gears
7. Carrier gear shaft
8. Thrust washers
9. Snap ring
10. Sun gear
11. Thrust washer
12. Wheel nut locks
13. Wheel nut
14. Planetary ring gear assembly
15. Ring gear
16. Planetary ring gear hub
17. Lock wire
18. Screw
19. Lock plate
20. Outer wheel bearing
21. Wheel hub
22. O ring
23. Inner wheel bearing

Fig. 13-36 Exploded view of the planetary gear set and wheel hub.
(*J I Case Company Agricultural Equipment Division*)

supported by tapered roller bearings. The inner bearing cone is placed on the spindle, and the outer bearing cone is placed on the planetary gear hub. The wheel bearing adjustment is made through a castle nut and secured by two locks to the spindle.

The brake drum is bolted to the right side of the wheel hub and the planetary carrier to the left side. The three planetary gears are supported by the pinion shafts which are positioned in the bores of the carrier housing. Special truss washers (one on each side of the carrier gears) prevent the gears from coming in contact with the planetary carrier housing. The gasket and cover seals the planetary gear set and the internal cover locks and prevents the pinion shafts from turning in their bores.

The inner axle shaft is supported on the universal yoke side by a bushing pressed into the trunnion. The other side of the shaft is splined to the differential side gear, which also supports it.

The universal yoke side of the outer axle shaft is supported by a bushing pressed into the spindle, and the left side is supported by the sun gear splined to it. The universal cross and bearings join the two axle shafts to form an assembly. **NOTE** This type of universal joint is called a Cardan universal joint.

The operation, that is, the drive from the front carrier to the wheel hub, is the same as that of a rear planetary drive wheel hub, as long as the tractor is moving in a straight line. However when the steering wheel is turned to the left or to the right (see the discussion of hydrostatic steering), the wheels turn to the left or to the right. Under this condition the inner and outer axle shafts are no longer in the same plane. They operate at an angle, and as a result the rotating speed between the inner and outer axle shaft varies because only a Cardan universal joint is used in this installation. See the discussion of universal joint and drive line.

CONSTANT-VELOCITY UNIVERSAL JOINTS To increase the turning radius and to maintain equal rotating speed, a constant-velocity universal joint is used (see Fig. 13-37). This type is called a Rzeppa universal joint (bell type). In this application the outer axle shaft has an outer race bell at its inner end, and the inner axle shaft is splined to the inner race and is held there by a snapring. Both axle shafts are drivably connected through steel balls located in the six meridional grooves in the races and positioned in the constant-velocity plane by the cage. Consequently, when the inner section shaft angle changes, the balls continue to change their position within their grooves but maintain equal speed.

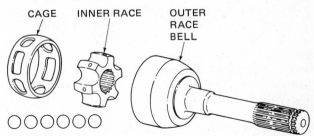

CAGE   INNER RACE   OUTER RACE BELL

Fig. 13-37 Exploded view of a Rzeppa universal joint.
(*J I Case Company Agricultural Equipment Division*)

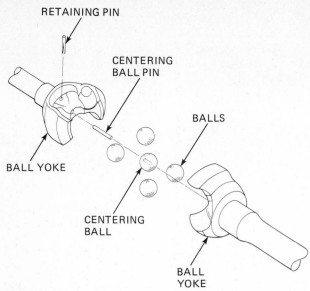

RETAINING PIN

CENTERING
BALL PIN

BALLS

BALL YOKE

CENTERING
BALL

BALL
YOKE

Fig. 13-38 Schematic view of a curved, grooved Weiss universal joint. (*J I Case Company Agricultural Equipment Division*)

Another type of constant-velocity universal joint used on front drive axles, either with or without a planetary drive, is the Weiss universal joint (see Fig. 13-38). The inner and outer axle shaft each has a yoke drivably connected through steels balls located in the constant-velocity plane. However, as you can see from the illustration, the steel balls lie in non-concentric, intersecting grooves symmetrically positioned in radial planes that are machined in the two yokes. To maintain the alignment, absorb the end thrust, and retain the assembly, a piloted centering ball is located on a pin between the two ball sockets in the yokes. To maintain the ball in contact with the yoke sockets, thrust washers located behind the yokes are used.

However, all three universal joints are limited in regard to their operating angle. To prevent damaging the universal joints during operation, the operating angle is limited through an adjusting device.

SERVICING The service procedure of a front axle planetary drive (see Fig. 13-35) is very similar to that of a rear axle planetary gear and the latter was previously outlined (see Fig. 13-30).

After the planetary carrier is removed, remove the snapring to slide the sun gear and washer from the axle shaft. Wrap a sling around the wheel hub and with a hoist take the weight from the spindle. Now lift out the two wheel bearing adjusting nut locks and remove the nut. Insert puller screws into the planetary ring gear hub to pull the hub from the spindle splines. Slip the outer wheel bearing cone from the hub and then slide the wheel hub with brake drum from the spindle. Remove the inner wheel bearing from the wheel hub. Remove the bolts that hold the seal retainer to the spindles. Remove the nuts from the stud bolts on the outer flange half and then remove the spindle. You can now pull the axle shaft assembly from the trunnion and axle housing.

To remove the inner and outer flange halves, remove the snapring, seal retainer, and seal from the inner flange half counter bore (see Fig. 13-39). Remove the bearing cap bolts, the bearing cap, shims, and bearing cups from the flange bores. Remove the nuts from the bolts that secure the two flange halves. Remove the nuts from the axle housing studs, so that you can remove the trunnion and from it the O ring, inner flange half, seal, seal retainer, and snapring.

CLEANING AND INSPECTION Clean all parts in solvent and dry them with compressed air. Discard all seals and O rings. Scrutinize all parts for indications of wear, stress, pitting, and score marks. Inspect the axle shaft splines for wear, pitting, and broken splines and the bushing and seal surfaces for wear. Replace all nuts that have rounded edges or damaged threads and all bolts or studs that have damaged threads. Remove all nicks and burrs from the machined surfaces and check the threaded bores for worn or damaged threads. Using the appropriate adapter, replace the inner axle shaft bushing and seal, as well as the outer axle shaft bushing. Use a press and the appropriate adapter when assembling the components (See the discussion of bearings in regard to cleaning, inspection, and installing.)

SERVICING THE RZEPPA UNIVERSAL JOINT When there is evidence that the universal joint is sticking when the shafts are misaligned or that the balls or grooves show pitting, the universal joint must be serviced.

NOTE If the universal joint is damaged, check the steering angle adjustment, for this is usually the cause of universal joint damage.

The inner race must be driven from the inner axle shaft, since the snapring that holds the shaft cannot be removed. To do this, clamp the inner axle shaft in a vise which has protected jaws so that the outer shaft faces straight downward. With a brass punch, drive the inner race from the axle shaft (see Fig. 13-40).

To remove the inner race and cage from the outer race bell, tilt the inner race so that one steel ball can be lifted out and then tilt the inner race until another ball can be lifted out. Repeat this procedure until all balls are removed.

To remove the inner race and cage, position them so that the two elongated holes in the cage align with two opposite teeth in the bell. To separate the cage from the inner race, turn it at right angles to the cage so that one tooth passes into one elongated hole in the cage. Now roll the opposite side of the inner race out of the cage (see Fig. 13-41).

INSPECTING AND REASSEMBLING Inspect the inner raceways of the outer race bell and the outer raceways of the inner race for surface cracks, scores, and pit marks. Inspect the bearings, seal surfaces, and splines for excessive wear and damage. The steel balls must be replaced if they are damaged, scored, or pitted, and the shafts must be replaced if the splines are worn or broken. If the cage is deformed or cracked, it must be replaced.

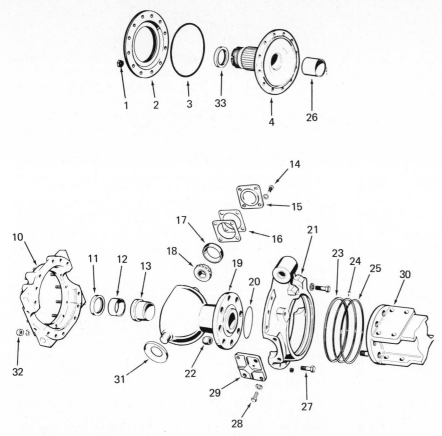

1.	Self-locking nut
2.	Oil seal and retainer
3.	O ring
4.	Spindle
10.	Outer flange
11.	Oil seal
12.	Bushing
13.	Axle support bushing
14.	Cap screws
15.	Bearing caps
16.	Shims
17.	Bearing cups
18.	Trunnion socket bearings
19.	Trunnion flange (ball yoke)
20.	O ring
21.	Inner trunnion flange half
22.	Self-locking nuts
23.	Trunnion flange seal
24.	Seal retainer
25.	Snap ring
26.	Spindle bushing
27.	Trunnion socket flange bolts
28.	Trunnion flange
29.	Bearing cap
30.	Axle housing
31.	Grease retainer
32.	Lockwashers and nuts

Fig. 13-39 Exploded view of the wheel hub assembly. (*J I Case Company Agricultural Equipment Division*)

The reassembly procedure is precisely the reverse of disassembly. Note, however, that, before driving the inner axle shaft into the inner race, you must install a new snapring to the axle shaft; otherwise the shaft will come out of the inner race during operation.

REASSEMBLING THE PLANETARY DRIVE AXLE Assume that all damaged or worn parts have been replaced, that the reusable parts have been cleaned, and that the planetary gear set, the brake drum, and the foundation brakes were checked or serviced. Commence reassembly by placing the snapring, retainer, seal, and inner flange half over the axle housing. Place one grease retainer on one trunnion socket, press the bearing cone firmly against it, and then install the other bearing. Place a new O ring into the groove of the trunnion, bolt it to the axle housing, and then torque the nuts to the specified torque. **NOTE** Do not, at this time, install the seal into the counter bore of the inner flange half.

Position the inner and outer flange halves onto the trunnion bell, align both flange halves, and then

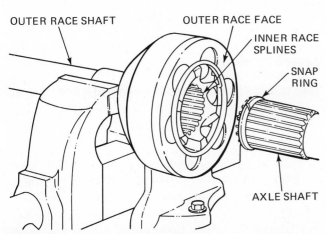

Fig. 13-40 Removing inner race from inner axle shaft. (*J I Case Company Agricultural Equipment Division*)

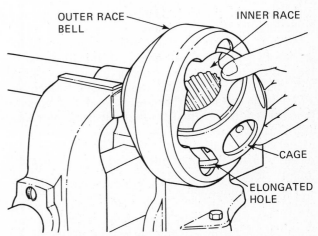

Fig. 13-41 Removing inner race. (*J I Case Company Agricultural Equipment Division*)

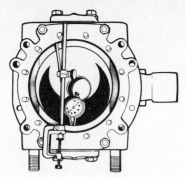

Fig. 13-42 Method used to determine trunnion bearing end play. (*J I Case Company Agricultural Equipment Division*)

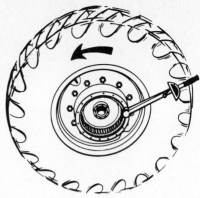

Fig. 13-43 Method used to determine wheel bearing preload.

bolt them together. Place the bearing cups into the bores of the flanges to aid in alignment. At this time lubricate the socket bearing with axle lubricant and then place the bearing cup onto it. Place an equal thickness of shims between the bearing cap and the trunnion socket flange. Bolt the bearing caps loosely in place to ensure that the socket bearings are not excessively preloaded. The shim thickness should be at least 0.010 in [0.25 mm] more than that used when the bearings are new, to arrive at the specified end play more quickly. Say, for example, that you have installed 0.100-in [2.54-mm] shims under the top and bottom bearing cap. You should then torque the lower bearing cap bolts to the specified torque. Next, install a dial indicator (magnetic base or as shown in Fig. 13-42) to the bearing cap and adjust the dial gauge so that the dial spindle rests on the inner surface of the trunnion bell, opposite from the magnetic base. Zero the dial and check the end play of the bearings. If there is end play, gradually tighten the other bearing cap bolts to the specified torque while continuing to check the end play. Let us assume that the end play (after the cap bolts are torqued) is 0.050 in [1.25 mm] but that the specified end play should not exceed 0.005 in [0.012 mm]. You would then have to remove from each bearing cap 0.02 n [0.57 mm] of shims. **NOTE** Do not remove the total amount of shims required from only one bearing cap to achieve the specified end play, for this would bring the axle shaft out of alignment. As a result the life of the bushing, the axle shaft, and the universal may be shortened.

After the socket bearing preload is adjusted, lubricate the trunnion bell and seal. Install the seal, the seal retainer, and the snapring to the inner flange half counterbore. Reinstall the axle shaft assembly and bolt the spindle to the outer flange half. Reinstall the seal retainer to the spindle by using a new seal and O ring. Also use a new wheel hub and a new planetary ring gear hub O ring. Next, tighten the wheel bearing adjusting nut to 100 lb·ft [136 N·m] to seat the wheel bearings.

The recommended procedure for checking the wheel bearing adjustments varies among manufacturers. The procedure as given by one manufacturer, for instance, for measuring the rolling torque of the wheel is as follows. First, you must install the wheel to the wheel hub and then screw a bolt into the planetary carrier housing so that you can place a socket (with torque wrench) onto the bolt head. Next, slightly loosen the wheel bearing adjusting nut and then, using your hands, start the motion of the wheel. At the same time try to maintain the rotation by using the torque wrench. Read from the torque wrench scale the torque required to keep the wheel in motion. If the rolling torque is too great, loosen the adjusting nut. If it is too little, tighten it to achieve the specified rolling torque. **NOTE** Do not use this method to adjust the wheel bearing when there is ballast in the tires. The wheel bearing adjustment will be too loose (see Fig. 13-43).

After the wheel bearing is adjusted, install the locks into the adjusting nut and spindle, and the washer, the sun gear, and the snapring onto the outer axle shaft. Install the planetary carrier and place a new gasket onto the planetary cover. Position the cover and gasket and then tighten the cover bolts to the specified torque.

Turn the wheel until the filler plug is on the top and the level plug is on the bottom. Now fill the planetary (which includes the wheel hub) with the recommended axle oil, until the oil appears at the level plug. Reinstall and tighten both plugs to the specified torque. Use a grease gun loaded with the specified grease and apply about three strokes to each socket bearing to ensure efficient lubrication. Recheck the carrier oil level.

Review Questions

1. List the five major components of a front wheel assembly.

2. What is the main difference between a full-floating axle and a semifloating axle?

3. On a planetary drive axle, which is the drive component and which is the driven component?

4. Outline the essential steps you must follow and/or the precautions you must take prior to removing a front axle or trailer wheel hub which has a nonservo foundation brake.

5. Why should you (a) wrap the removed wheel bearings in wax paper or lint-free cloth and (b) cover the spindle and brake assembly with a cloth?

6. What is the advantage of using a bearing packing device rather than hand packing?

7. When checking the spindle for its serviceability, what damage, wear, or flaws may be revealed?

8. Before installing the wheel assembly, why should you (a) pack grease into the wheel bearing seal cavity (b) coat the spindle with either oil or grease?

9. Check and record the wheel bearing adjustment procedure and specifications in the following service manuals: (a) car, (b) motor truck, (c) off-highway machine.

10. How can you visually determine that the kingpin and/or bushing are worn and need to be replaced

11. What is the difference between a "reverse-Elliot" axle and an "Elliot" axle?

12. When placing the thrust bearing into position, (a) in which direction is the thrust face placed and (b) why in this direction?

13. Name the three types of universal joints used on the front axle shaft.

14. What is the purpose of a locking wheel hub?

15. Which part or components act as the clutch (a) in the manual locking wheel hub, (b) in the Lock-o-matic?

16. Why should you tape the two halves of a floating ring seal together?

17. List two reasons why the larger front axle drives use constant-velocity universal joints.

18. Explain why the constant-velocity joints illustrated in the textbook can maintain equal wheel speed when the axle shaft is out of alignment.

Unit 14 Fundamentals of Braking and Hydraulic Brakes

A brake is any mechanism capable of checking motion. Many different devices are used on on- and off-highway equipment to reduce the rotating speed of a wheel, winch, drum, track, or transmission or to reduce the engine speed. However, most brake devices use friction linings, pads, or plates which are forced against a rotating or fixed-reaction surface. The force derived from the brake fluid or from atmospheric air, oil pressure, or mechanical linkage is controlled by the driver or the operator, through a control device. The braking effort or retardation is increased by increasing the applied force or is decreased by reducing the force.

Power Requirement for Braking   To drive a truck, dozer, or winch, etc., heat from combustion or electric or hydraulic energy are converted into energy of motion (*kinetic energy*), which is measured in foot pounds (ft·lb) [newton meters (N·m) or joules (J)]. In order to reduce motion, the kinetic energy is converted back into heat by the vehicle's brakes and is released into the atmosphere.

The power required to stop a particular vehicle from a known speed can be calculated in two steps. First the vehicle's kinetic energy is calculated. The kinetic energy is combined with the time allowed to stop the vehicle to determine the required power.

EXAMPLE   Say a 60,000-lb [27,240-kg] highway truck has a diesel engine that develops about 300 hp [223,800 W], and is able to accelerate to 60 mph [97 km/h] in about 45 s. Assume also that the truck's braking system can slow the truck at a rate of 15 feet per second per second (15 ft/s^2) [4.6 meters per second per second (4.6 m/s^2)]. This will bring the truck to a full stop from 60 mph in 5.86 s (60 mph = 88 ft/s; 88 ft/s ÷ 15 ft/s^2 = 5.86 s). If we ignore the effects of mechanical engine friction, gear ratios, rolling friction, and wind resistance, we can calculate the power needed to stop the vehicle.

Begin by finding the truck's kinetic energy, with the formula:

$$KE = \tfrac{1}{2}\,(w/g)v^2$$

where KE = kinetic energy (foot pounds), w = the truck's weight (pounds), g = the acceleration of the earth's gravity (a constant equal to 32.2 ft/s^2), and v = the truck's velocity (feet per second.) The truck's speed is 60 mph; this is

$$\frac{60 \text{ mph} \times 5280 \text{ feet per mile}}{3600 \text{ seconds per hour}} = 88 \text{ ft/s}$$

So,

$$KE = \tfrac{1}{2} \times \frac{60,000}{32.2} \times (88)^2 = 7,214,906 \text{ ft·lb}$$

Use the following formula to find the power needed to convert energy of motion to heat in the approximately 6 s it takes to stop the truck:

$$\text{Power (horsepower)} = \frac{KE \text{ (ft·lb)}}{550 \times t}$$

(where t = deceleration time)

$$= \frac{7,214,906}{550 \times 6} = 2186.3 \text{ hp}$$

or about 7.2 times the power needed to accelerate the vehicle. If the truck is a 6 × 4 tractor, each set of wheels must generate 2186.3 ÷ 8, or approximately 273 hp.

NOTE   These formulas only apply when using the units of measure shown. To calculate the power in watts, use the formulas

$$KE \text{ (N·m or J)} = \tfrac{1}{2}mv^2$$

where m = mass of vehicle (kilograms) and v = velocity (meters per second), and

$$\text{Power (watts)} = KE/t$$

Notice that if either the time allowed to stop the vehicle decreases or the kinetic energy increases then the power required for braking must increase. Since kinetic energy increases as the square of the velocity (that is, if the velocity doubles kinetic energy increases by four), an increase in speed has a much greater effect on the required braking power than an increase in the weight of the vehicle.

Stopping Distance   Stopping distance is based on the deceleration of the truck. Deceleration depends on the design and effectiveness of the braking system, the speed and weight of the truck, the tire diameter and width, and the road surface.

The kinetic friction between tire and road surface is the only friction that actually retards the speed and eventually stops the truck. When one or more wheels lock up, the kinetic friction becomes static (sliding) friction (between the road surface and the tire) and as a result the retarding or stopping effect is reduced. The friction reduction creates uncon-

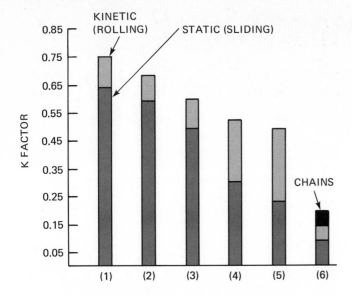

Fig. 14-1 Maximum tire-to-road surface coefficient of friction (K factor).

(1) SMOOTH CONCRETE — DRY

(2) ASPHALT — DRY

(3) SMOOTH CONCRETE — WET

(4) ASPHALT — WET

(5) SMOOTH CONCRETE — WET, OILY

(6) ICE — DRY

trolled braking, lengthens the stopping distance, and increases the tire wear. The decelerating rate (stopping distance) therefore is greatly influenced by the type of road surface and the condition, size, and width of the tire. This means that a tire and a given road surface can maintain only a certain percentage of retarding force (the K factor). On an average a retardation force of 0.60 to 0.65 K is about the limit on dry concrete highways and about 0.55 K on dry asphalt. In other words, for every 100 lb [45.36 kg] of weight there is only 60 lb [27.21 kg] of retarding force (see Fig. 14-1).

An object falling freely (acted on only by the force of gravity [its weight]) accelerates at a rate of 32.2 ft/s² or 9.8 m/s². Therefore, to decelerate an object at this same rate, you would require a coefficient of friction of 1.0. However, even under ideal conditions, you may have a coefficient of only 19.32 ft/s² [5.88 m/s²] 0.6 K. The maximum deceleration rate, therefore, cannot exceed 32.2 × 0.6 = 19.32 ft/s² (9.8 × 0.6 = 5.88 m/s²); otherwise the tire would skid over the road surface. Only in an emergency would you attempt to decelerate at this rate because the wheels of the truck would lock up. A deceleration of 15 ft/s² [4.6 m/s²] would be a severe deceleration rate and would also, in some applications, lock the wheels. The average deceleration rate is about 10 ft/s² [3.04 m/s²].

To calculate for a moving object the distance required either to gain or reduce speed at a given acceleration or deceleration rate, the following formula is used:

$$d = \frac{v_2{}^2 - v_1{}^2}{2a}$$

where d = distance
v_1 = initial velocity
v_2 = final velocity
a = rate of acceleration (positive for an object that is speeding up, negative for one that is slowing down)

The stopping distance for the 60,000-lb truck discussed previously is, therefore,

$$d = \frac{(0 \text{ ft/s})^2 - (88 \text{ ft/s})^2}{2\,(-15 \text{ ft/s}^2)}$$

$$= 258.13 \text{ ft } [78.88 \text{ m}]$$

The time needed to stop the truck is calculated with another formula:

$$t = v_1/a$$
$$= 5.85 \text{ s}$$

Coefficient of Friction Friction is the resistance to movement between any two surfaces which are in contact with each other. The two basic forms of friction are friction of rest, also known as coefficient of static friction, and friction of motion, also known as coefficient of kinetic friction. The coefficient of static friction or kinetic friction is the ratio of force to weight, expressed in percentage, giving the amount of force required to move an object (or to maintain it in motion) while it remains in contact with another. For example, if 50 lb [222.4 N] of force is required to move an object weighing 100 lb [45.36 kg], the coefficient of static friction would be 50/100 = 0.5. However, to keep the object in motion (kinetic friction), only 40 lb [177.9 N] may be required. Therefore the coefficient of kinetic friction would be 40/100 = 0.4 **NOTE** Static friction is always higher than kinetic friction (see Fig. 14-2).

Brake Lining Friction The coefficient of kinetic friction of a brake lining must be sufficient to safely stop the vehicle. In addition, the brake lining must also have the capability to withstand the heat (created by the friction) until it dissipates and the ability to maintain its friction regardless of speed. The lining coefficient of friction is important, but so are the drum or disk design and the metal alloy used. When the lining material is poor, the coefficient of friction varies considerably with the contact surface's condition, with its temperature, with the relative motion of the drum, and with a change in pressure placed on the material under friction.

If the coefficient between the lining and drum, or disk, is too high, the wear rate increases and the brake may "grab." If the coefficient of friction is too low, a higher pressure is required to bring the vehicle in motion to a stop. Furthermore, a higher tem-

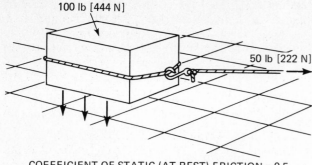

COEFFICIENT OF STATIC (AT REST) FRICTION = 0.5

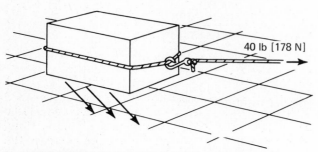

COEFFICIENT OF KINETIC (IN MOTION) FRICTION = 0.4

Fig. 14-2 Coefficient of friction. Static (at rest) coefficient = 0.5. Kinetic (motion) coefficient = 0.4.

perature develops when the brake is applied, and this may cause it to "fade."

Brake fade occurs when the brake temperature increases to the point where a reduction in the coefficient of friction takes place. Antifade is a reverse condition—with increased temperature, the coefficient of friction increases. If the increase of friction is high, the lining or block effectiveness may become unpredictable (see Fig. 14-3).

Another type of fade, though infrequent, is water fade. Water fade occurs when the brake lining is exposed to an unusual amount of water.

The vehicle and brake lining manufacturers test the applicable equipment and accordingly select the most suitable lining material, drum design, and metal alloy having the best braking action within a low wear rate. However, in some cases where the operating condition (logging or dump truck) demands special lining material, the wear rate of the drum, disk, and lining increases, but this has to be sacrificed to achieve a more effective braking.

NOTE Although the lining and drum coefficient of friction is an important factor, others must be considered, such as (1) lining-to-drum contact, (2) lining and drum area, (3) heat dissipation, (4) drum or disk design, (5) vehicle weight and speed, (6) engine and gear ratio, (7) tire size (diameter and width), (8) coefficient of friction between the tire and road surface, (9) type of brake system, (10) leverage factor of force to shoe or band, and (11) brake adjustment.

Heat Dissipation The heat developed from braking a logging truck could be as high as 600°F [316°C] under normal conditions, and this must be dissipated as fast as possible into the atmosphere.

Generally speaking, there are two routes in which this heat can travel to reach the atmosphere. One is from the lining or brake blocks to the brake shoes,

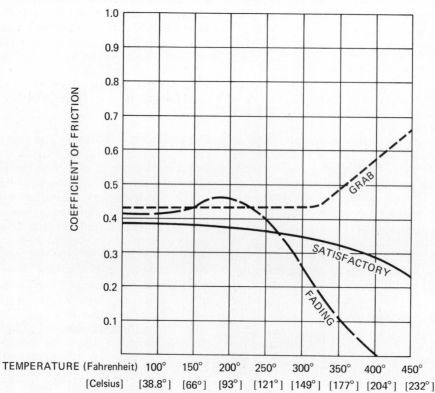

Fig. 14-3 Temperature effect on three types of linings.

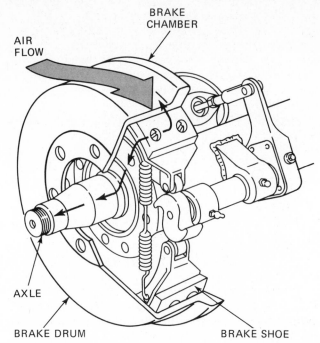

AIR FLOW

BRAKE CHAMBER

AXLE

BRAKE DRUM

BRAKE SHOE

Fig. 14-4 Arrows show heat dissipation through a drum brake.

and then to the backing plate or spider, and finally to the axle. The other route which dissipates most of the heat is from the drum or disk to the atmosphere and the wheel hub (see Fig. 14-4). Also see the discussion of brake drums and brake shoes in Unit 16 for further information on special metal alloy and drum design to improve heat dissipation.

Since all the heat that develops from braking is placed on the lining and the brake drum, the producers must take into consideration in its manufacture an adequate lining-to-drum contact so that they can absorb and dissipate the heat quickly. However, it is up to you, the mechanic, when servicing the brakes, to make sure that the lining has full contact with the brake-drum surface. If there is incomplete contact, the brake effectiveness is reduced, a greater heat develops, and consequently the brakes may fade, char, grab, squeal, or pull, or because of the increased temperature the brake drum may crack, be forced out-of-round, or become barrel- or bell-mouthed. Additionally, incomplete lining-to-drum contact may result in lining or block glazing, lining or block charring, or the lining's coming loose from the shoe table (see Fig. 14-5).

Brake Torque (Stopping Power)   The torque that drives the wheels originates from the engine and is transmitted to the transmission, the rear carrier, the drive axles, on to the wheel hubs, and then to the wheels. The stopping torque originates from the brake and drum shoes (or disk pads and disks) and is transmitted to, and absorbed by, the front wheels, the kingpin, axle suspension, and frame. The stopping torque is transmitted and absorbed at the rear wheels by the axle, housing, suspension, and frame.

The stopping torque capacity that a given type of brake system can develop depends on the following

factors: the amount of actuating force that can be placed on the shoes or disk pads, the friction area, the drum diameter, the coefficient of friction between the drum or lining, the shoe lever action, and the amount of the shoe's self-energization (type of brakes). The stopping torque capacity needed is determined by the weight and speed of the vehicle and the tire size (the coefficient of friction between the tires and road surface).

Take, for example, a truck having 11-20 tires, a static load radius of 20 in [508 mm], a brake drum diameter of 18.0 in (radius-9 in), a total lining area of 220 in² (559 cm²) (a lining coefficient of 0.34), and a distance from the applied force to the anchor of 16 in [406.4 mm]. When the brakes are applied under these conditions and the force on each brake shoe is 3000 lb [13,344 N], then the brake torque would be $3000 \times 220 \times 0.34/8.00 = 28,050$ lb · in [3167.3 N · m] and the braking force to the tire would be $28,050.0/20 = 1402.5$ lb [6238.32 N].

If the static load radius of the tire were less than 20 in but the drum diameter remained the same (18.0 in), the braking force-to-tire would increase. However, excessive brake torque does not increase the overall braking effect, but it could make the brake more sensitive under light load conditions, under normal deceleration, or on a slippery road surface (see Fig. 14-6).

Retarding Action of Engine   While traveling you may have noticed, as you approached long downhill grades, safety signs which instruct truckers to "check brakes and use low gear." The "check brakes" warning is to indicate that, in the interest of safety, the driver should stop the vehicle and check the entire brake system. He should not start the downhill approach until he is ensured that the brake drums are cool, the air system has full pressure, and the brakes are properly adjusted. On such steep and/

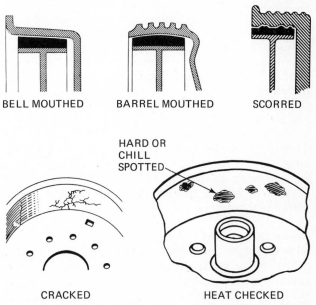

BELL MOUTHED

BARREL MOUTHED

SCORRED

HARD OR CHILL SPOTTED

CRACKED

HEAT CHECKED

Fig. 14-5 Defects in brake drums which reduce brake efficiency and cause lining wear. (*International Harvester Company*)

210

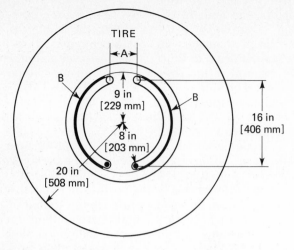

FORCE APPLIED TO BRAKE SHOES (A) = 3000 lb [13,344 N]
BRAKE LINING AREA (B) = 100 in² [0.064 m²]

Fig. 14-6 Brake torque and tire braking force.

or lengthy declines, deteriorating brake systems could cause the driver to lose control of his truck, and could result in a runaway vehicle. The instructions are also to "use low gear." Using the lowest gear ratio accelerates retardation.

A diesel engine has unrestricted air supply, and its speed is altered by varying the quantity of fuel injected per cycle. Therefore, when the fuel injection system is in the idle fuel position, the only retarding force transmitted to the transmission is the mechanical friction of the engine. As no doubt you know, when the engine speed (at idle fuel consumption) increases, the mechanical friction increases. For example: A 350 hp [260.96 kW] diesel engine at rated speed has a mechanical friction of about 80 hp [59 kW] and only 35 hp [26 kW] at 1000 rpm. Therefore, at rated speed, the retarded input torque of 80 hp [59 kW] to the transmission equals 44,000 ft · lb/s (80 × 550 = 44,000 ft · lb/s). If the total gear ratio of the transmission and the rear carrier were, say, 20:1, then the total retarding force would be 880,000 ft · lb/s (44,000 × 20 = 880,000 ft · lb/s). This obviously reduces the work the brakes would otherwise have to perform. However, when the engine speed is reduced, the mechanical friction is lessened or, when the transmission is placed in a higher gear, the ratio is varied, and more brake effort (work) is needed to retard the vehicle's speed.

Tire-to-Road Contact To effectively brake the speed of any vehicle, the tire must maintain static friction with the road surface. If one or more tires convert to kinetic friction (skidding), the stopping distance increases.

Brake Design Objectives Braking systems are designed so that the control and braking effectiveness of the tractor, trailer, truck, bus, etc., is not lost during normal deceleration. These objectives are achieved in the following ways: (1) by varying the tire size, (2) by increasing or decreasing the drum diameter and/or the drum width (friction surface), (3) by increasing or decreasing the lining material coefficient, (4) by increasing or decreasing the lining

friction area (in²), (5) by increasing the lining area at the rear wheels (the reverse on cars), (6) by increasing or decreasing the mechanical leverage (foundation brake design), (7) by increasing or decreasing the applied force to the front wheel brakes, (8) by increasing or decreasing the maximum applied force (oil, fluid, or air pressure or piston area), (9) by using an antiskid device, and (10) by varying the type of foundation brakes.

However, when the weight on the front or rear tires exceeds specification, or the payload weight shifts (to the front or rear, or from the left to the right side), the tires lose weight force and may, therefore, have less road contact and thereby reduce the effectiveness of the brake and control of the vehicle.

HYDRAULIC BRAKES

There are so many varieties and types of hydraulic brakes used on on- and off-highway equipment that it would be impractical to attempt to cover them all in this text. Reference is therefore restricted to the more common types.

On all hydraulic brake systems, the activating force by the operator or driver is transmitted over a lever to a piston called the *master cylinder*. The force moves the piston and displaces brake fluid into the hydraulic lines, which are connected to four-, six-, and eight-wheel cylinders. Depending on the area of the master cylinder piston, the applied force increases or decreases the line pressure. See Unit 6, "Introduction to Hydraulics." The displaced fluid (under low pressure) enters the wheel cylinders. As the resistance increases, the pressure increases. This forces the brake shoes against the brake drum and thereby provides the braking action. When the pedal force is increased, it increases the system pressure, which, in turn, forces the brake shoe more rigorously onto the brake drums. When the applied pedal force is removed, the force on the master cylinder piston is released, reducing the pressure within the brake system. The brake shoe retraction (or return) springs retract the brake shoes from the drums, forcing the wheel cylinder pistons to move inward. Each wheel cylinder then displaces its fluid back to the master cylinder (see Fig. 14-7).

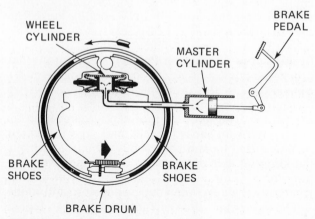

Fig. 14-7 Schematic view of a conventional hydraulic brake system. (*Wagner Electric Sales Corporation*)

Master Cylinders The master cylinder is multi-purpose. It stores fluid, it displaces the fluid necessary to actuate the wheel cylinders to develop the required pressure, it recharges the system after each brake release, it returns excessive fluid to the reservoir when the pedal is pumped, and it maintains a fixed line (residual) pressure.

There are two types of master cylinders—the single and the tandem designs. Both types perform the same functions and operate on the same principle. The single master cylinder is now used only on off-highway equipment, whereas the tandem master cylinder must be used on all on-highway equipment.

TANDEM MASTER CYLINDER Tandem master cylinders are sometimes misnamed "dual master cylinders." In actual fact, dual master cylinders are two single master cylinders, side by side, in a single or separate housing, whereas the two master cylinders of the tandem type are aligned one behind the other. Each individual master cylinder of the dual or tandem master cylinder supplies fluid to an individual hydraulic circuit. For example, one of the dual master cylinders can be used to actuate the clutch slave piston, and the other, the brakes, or one of the dual master cylinders supplies fluid to the left side brakes, and the other supplies fluid to the right side brakes. In a tandem master cylinder, the primary section supplies fluid to the front wheel brakes, and the secondary section supplies fluid to the rear wheel brakes.

On some large truck applications where each wheel has two wheel cylinders, the front wheel cylinders may be connected with one of the rear wheel cylinders. On vehicles having tandem rear axles, one master cylinder supplies fluid to the front axle wheel cylinders, and the other supplies fluid to the rear axle of the tandem rear axle wheel cylinders.

The maximum pressure requirement, in conjunction with the quantity of fluid required to stop a given vehicle, determines the ratio of the actuating lever, the area of the master cylinder piston, and the area of the wheel cylinders. The maximum hydraulic pressure (normal pedal force) for a system without power assist is about 800 psi [5512 kPa], whereas 1500 to 2000 psi [10,335 to 13,780 kPa] is common for larger brake systems or when disk brakes or non-self-energizing brakes are used.

SINGLE MASTER CYLINDER Most master cylinder bodies are made from cast iron, although some recent models are made from steel. The body is divided into two parts—the reservoir and the cylinder. The reservoir is closed off by a vented filler cap. Two ports connect the reservoir with the cylinder—a small one (the compensating or bypass port), and a large one (the inlet port). The secondary cup seal, piston, piston return spring, primary cup seal, and the residual check valve are located inside the cylinder bore. A washer and snapring are used to limit the rearward motion of the piston. The piston return spring serves two functions: it returns the primary cup and piston to their rest position whenever the brake force is released, and it holds the residual

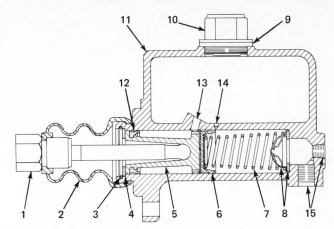

1. Plunger
2. Plunger boot
3. Snap ring
4. Retaining washer
5. Piston
6. Piston (pressure) cup
7. Piston spring
8. Valve and seat
9. Gasket
10. Filler cap
11. Housing reservoir
12. Outer cup
13. Inlet port
14. Compensating port
15. Brake line fitting connecton

Fig. 14-8 Sectional view of a single master cylinder. (*Fiat-Allis*)

check valve on its seat to achieve residual line pressure (see Fig. 14-8).

The right side of the cylinder bore is threaded to connect the brake line fitting with the master cylinder. The left side is made dustproof by a rubber boot. The push rod passes through the boot opening and rests in the recess of the master cylinder piston.

Tandem Master Cylinder Design The tandem master cylinder has two independent reservoirs, each having an intake port and compensating port, and two pistons with primary and secondary cup seals. The first master cylinder assembly (toward the push rod) is called the primary section and the other is called the secondary section. A rubber diaphragm and cover seal the reservoirs from the atmosphere.

The primary and secondary pistons are equipped with return springs. **NOTE** Some manufacturing companies make the primary return spring slightly stronger than the secondary piston spring.

The circles (see Fig. 14-9) at the left side of each piston indicate the location of the residual check valves and outlet threaded openings. A locating (stop) screw positions the secondary piston and prevents it from moving toward the primary piston. A snapring holds the washer and therefore limits the rearward movement of the primary piston.

Master Cylinder at Rest (Release Position) Assume that the master cylinder is at rest, the brake lines are free of air, and the reservoir is filled to the specified level. Under this circumstance, both residual check valves are held closed by their springs and thereby hold a pressure in the application lines. The pressure is from 6 to 18 psi [41.34 to 124.02 kPa], depending on the predetermined vehicle requirements. This residual pressure ensures that the wheel cylinder cup seals with additional force on the lips and thus further minimizes the possibility of air's

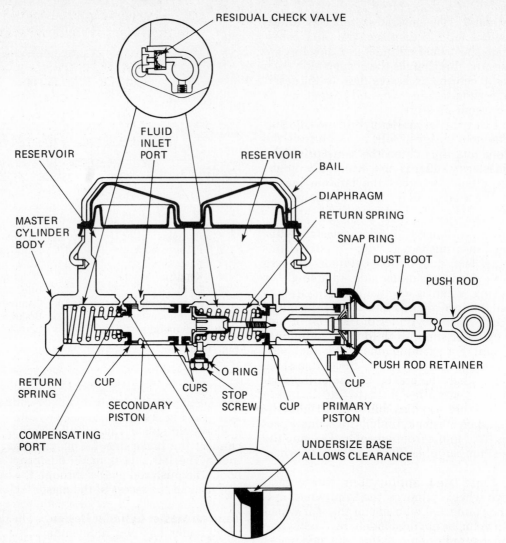

Fig. 14-9 Sectional view of a tandem master cylinder. (*International Harvester Company*)

entering the system. The pressure also ensures a quick brake response when the brakes are being applied, and with the additional pressure the vapor point of the brake fluid is increased. The piston return springs hold the pistons against their maximum rearward stop position.

Atmospheric pressure can enter between the cover and diaphragm. This pressure acts on the surface of the diaphragm to maintain the atmospheric pressure within the reservoir and the cylinder bore. The cup seals are purposely designed to force the seal lips against the cylinder bore to prevent fluid from leaking from the secondary to the primary section and from the cylinder at the push rod end.

Normal Master Cylinder Operation   When the operator moves the brake pedal (about 1 in [25.4 mm]), the pedal movement causes the push rod to move against, and subsequently to move, the primary piston and cup seal. Any additional pedal travel moves the primary cup seal past the compensating port and closes it. During the forward movement of the primary cup seal, fluid is allowed to escape through the compensating port (see Fig. 14-10). This loss of fluid

reduces the pressure in front of the cup seal and thereby prevents the seal lips from being forced into the hole of the compensating port. Permanent damage to the seal lips is therefore retarded and a dangerous braking condition averted.

When the compensating port is closed, an immediate pressure buildup begins. As the primary

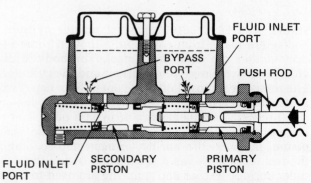

Fig. 14-10 Schematic view of a dual master cylinder during the start of brake application. (*Wagner Electric Sales Corporation*)

piston continues to move forward, the primary piston spring and pressure simultaneously move the secondary piston. The fluid trapped between the primary and secondary piston seals, and that trapped between the secondary piston seal and the forward end of the cylinder, builds up in pressure until it forces the residual check valves open and then enters into the individual hydraulic systems. During the forward movement of both pistons, fluid can enter or leave the intake port, to maintain atmospheric pressure between the primary and secondary piston seals.

HOLD POSITION When the operator maintains the same pedal position, no further pressure buildup occurs, and the fluid is under static pressure. Both residual check valves are now closed, and the brake shoe force neither increases nor decreases.

RELEASE ACTION Any slight retraction of the brake pedal reduces the applied pedal force and allows the pistons to follow the retracted pushrod. In consequence the pressure in the front of the piston area is reduced in proportion to the increased volume of the cylinders. The wheel cylinders then have a higher pressure, and the fluid is forced back to the master cylinder, equalizing the pressure. The residual check valves open and allow a reduction in pressure, but the applied pressure in the primary and secondary systems remains higher by the amount of force exerted by the residual check valve spring (see Fig. 14-11).

When the brake pedal is fully released, the force the piston springs causes them to return to their rest position against their stops. However, the fluid from the wheel cylinders does not return as quickly as the piston retracts. As a result, the pressure in front of the primary cups is lower than atmospheric pressure. The higher atmospheric pressure now forces fluid through the charging ports (passages in each piston) and then around the lips of the primary cups into the lower pressure area (see Fig. 14-12). **NOTE** Fluid also flows through these holes during bleeding of the system. It also flows through when the brake pedal is pumped (when the brakes are not

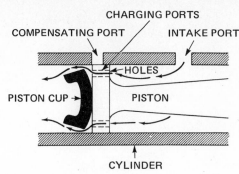

Fig. 14-12 Primary cup action during brake release. (*Wagner Electric Sales Corporation*)

properly adjusted), allowing sufficient fluid displacement to provide adequate braking effect.

As soon as the pressure in the master cylinder is lower than that of the line pressure, the residual check valves are forced off their seats. This allows the fluid to return into the primary and secondary cylinder bores, flow through the compensating ports, and return into the reservoirs.

When the applied pressure drops to that of the residual pressure, the check valve spring force closes the valves, holding the desired pressure in the application lines (see Fig. 14-13).

System Failure If the primary system fails to build up sufficient pressure after the brakes have been applied, the secondary system nevertheless operates properly. However, the pedal travel and subsequent manual exertion must be increased. The reason for this is that the primary piston must travel about 0.250 in [6.35 mm] before the projected primary piston pin contacts the secondary piston and moves the secondary piston mechanically rather than by hydraulic force. The increased force and pedal travel should warn the operator that a failure has occurred; also the warning light should indicate that one system has lost its pressure. See the discussion of warning light switch and combination valve in Unit 15. For this reason alone, it is imperative that the brakes always be correctly adjusted to maintain adequate brake pedal height. Otherwise, in case of a failure, the brake pedal could descend to the floor board before sufficient pressure builds up within the braking system.

When the secondary system fails after the brakes are applied, the secondary piston moves (or has already moved) to the right by the fluid pressure from the primary piston and comes to stop against the end of the cylinder. This increases the distance (and therefore the volume) between the primary piston cup and the secondary piston. The primary piston must then travel a greater distance to build up sufficient pressure for braking. See Fig. 14-14. Also see the discussion of troubleshooting for master cylinder failure in Unit 17.

Master Cylinder Service Whenever the brakes are to be relined (see Fig. 14-15), the master cylinder and wheel cylinder should be serviced and the sys-

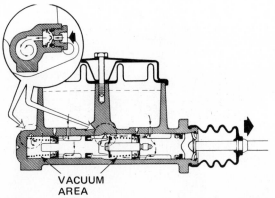

Fig. 14-11 Schematic view of a dual master cylinder during the brake release action. (*Wagner Electric Sales Corporation*)

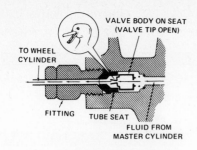

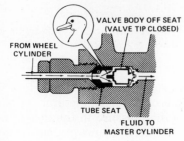

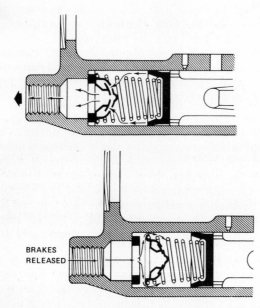

Fig. 14-13 Sectional view of two types of residual check valves during the brake applied and released action. (*Wagner Electric Sales Corporation*)

tem thoroughly flushed to remove the old fluid and any contamination from the system.

Before removing a master cylinder from a vehicle, first steam-clean the area on which you intend to work. Park the vehicle safely by blocking the wheels and positioning the hydraulic equipment so that it does not interfere with the master cylinder removal. Disconnect the brake tubings and cover the openings. Remove the connecting pins from the pedal arm and push rod and remove the mounting bolts. Lift the master cylinder from its position. If you inadvertently spill brake fluid on the painted exterior, always clean it up immediately to prevent the paint from peeling.

If necessary, reclean the master cylinder before removing the cover and diaphragm. Dump the fluid from the reservoir and, by using the push rod, pump the master cylinder empty of fluid. Mount the cylinder in a vise which has protective jaws and take care that the force of the vise does not distort the cylinder.

Next, remove the secondary piston stop screw (which may be located externally or internally) by moving the piston at least 0.5 in [12.7 mm] forward, to give adequate screw clearance, and then remove the boot to get access to the piston stop. The piston stop could be in the form of a retainer ring, snapring, or retainer cover held by a countersunk screw. Remove the retainer after first moving the piston forward. When it is removed, allow the piston return springs to expand slowly, to force the primary piston from its bore. If the secondary piston fails to slide out, tap the cylinder lightly on a piece of wood, or, with exceptional care, you can use compressed air. When using the latter method to remove the secondary piston, hold the cylinder bore about 0.5 in [12.7 mm] over a piece of wood and then apply the air pressure to the secondary outlet port. The piston discharges from its bore.

Remove the outlet ports' check valve retainer nuts and the check valves. If the check valves are press-fitted into the outlet ports, use a simple seat puller or tap a thread into the bore of the seat. Then place a large washer with a small hole over the outlet port and screw a ¼-in screw into the thread to retract the residual check valve seat. (You can also use a self-

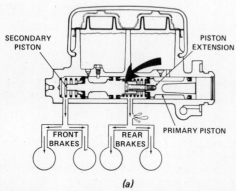

(a)

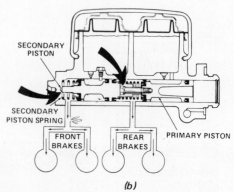

(b)

Fig. 14-14 Master cylinder actions when the primary (a) and secondary (b) brake systems have lost pressure (fluid). (*Wagner Electric Sales Corporation*)

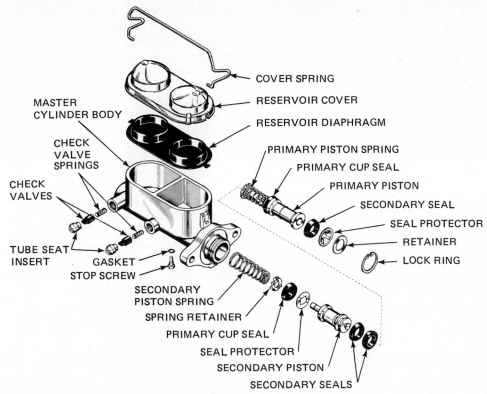

Fig. 14-15 Exploded view of tandem master cylinder components. (*International Harvester Company*)

threading screw and screw it into the seat-bore opening.) Use two screwdrivers and pry evenly under the flat washer to remove the valve (see Fig. 14-16).

When the push rod is fastened to the primary piston by either a rubber grommet or a nylon clip, place the push rod in a vise and then place two large screwdrivers between the piston and vise jaws to pry the piston loose from the push rod.

CLEANING AND INSPECTION Although all rubber parts should be replaced, they should be examined before being discarded so that you can assess the condition of the system generally. If the cup edges are worn or the cup sides have longitudinal scratches, this indicates that the fluid contains fine-particle contaminants. When the cups are swollen or cracked, it indicates that a fluid was used that was below specification or that the fluid was diluted.

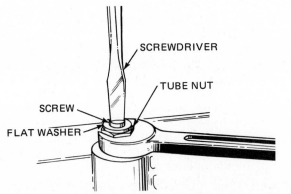

Fig. 14-16 One method of removing the residual check valves. (*Wagner Electric Sales Corporation*)

After examining the dismantled components, clean the internal surface of the master cylinder body in alcohol or in brake fluid and dry it with compressed air. Do not dry with cloth. Cloth can leave lint or fiber sticking to the walls which will clog the compensating port. This could cause cup leakage or master cylinder failure.

After cleaning and drying the master cylinder, hold the cylinder bore against a strong light so that you can examine the bore for wear spots, corrosion, pitting, or scratches. If there is damage which you think can be rectified through honing so that the bore is then under the maximum wear specifications, there is no need to replace it. Remember to check the internal surface of the reservoir for oxidation. If oxidation is present, the master cylinder must be replaced.

To hone the master cylinder (see Fig. 14-17), mount it so that the cylinder bore and center line of the drill can be placed in a straight line. Chuck a $\frac{3}{8}$-in electric drill with a three-stone deglazing hone. Insert the hone into the bore and adjust the stone tension. Start the drill and readjust the stone tension as necessary so that the stones do not vibrate when rotated. Use brake fluid as cutting oil while moving the drill slowly forward and backward. (Take care to prevent the stones from bottoming against the end of the master cylinder or from coming out of the master cylinder bore.) To remove the hone, stop the drill, press the hone arms together, and then check the effectiveness of your honing.

When the bore is satisfactorily honed and the body and cylinder bore are cleaned, check the piston clearance. The clearance for a cylinder bore of less

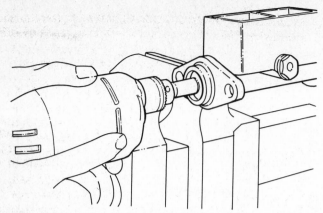

Fig. 14-17 Honing the master cylinder bore. (*Wagner Electric Sales Corporation*)

than $1\frac{1}{4}$ in [31.75 mm] I.D. should not be increased more than 0.006 in [0.15 mm]. For a $1\frac{1}{4}$-in bore it should not be more than 0.007 in [0.17 mm], and for a $1\frac{1}{2}$-in [38.10-mm] (or more) bore, not more than 0.008 in [0.20 mm].

To check the clearance between the pistons and the bore, place a small strip of feeler stock, the thickness of the maximum specified clearance, into the bore. Try pushing the piston into the bore. If the piston can be inserted, the bore is oversize and the master cylinder must be replaced. **NOTE** Whenever a master cylinder is honed, the compensating port must be deburred because honing makes the port edges knifelike. To deburr the port, insert the burring tool tip from the cylinder bore side into the compensating port and oscillate the top while holding it firmly in the port.

REASSEMBLY Again, clean all parts and dry them with compressed air. Generously lubricate the bore and parts with brake fluid before placing them into the master cylinder bore. **NOTE** The lighter spring is the secondary piston return spring. All cup lips must face forward with the exception of the secondary rear cup, which must face toward the primary piston (rearward) (see Fig. 14-18). Take care not to cut the cups on the intake ports; you may use a small hardwood stick to guide them past the ports. Also make certain that you install the secondary piston stop screw before placing the primary piston retainer in position, and a residual check valve in the primary piston port when the front axle has disk brakes.

Bleeding the Master Cylinder It is good practice to bleed the master cylinder before reinstalling it to the vehicle. The bleeding operation at this time is more convenient, and you can check that the pistons stroke freely and return with ease against their stops.

To bleed the master cylinder, connect short nylon

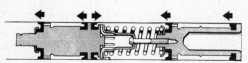

Fig. 14-18 Sectional view of correct installation of the piston seal. (*Wagner Electric Sales Corporation*)

or copper tubings, to the outlet ports and place the ends in the reservoir (see Fig. 14-19). Fill the master cylinder with the recommended brake fluid and then, by hand or with a screwdriver, push the primary piston forward. This also moves the secondary piston forward and displaces the air and fluid from the cylinder bores.

Allow the opposing spring force to return both pistons. Repeat this action until no more air comes from the tubings and then refill the reservoir to the specified fluid level, install the diaphragm, and secure the reservoir cover.

Installing the Master Cylinder Before installing the master cylinder, check the mounting surfaces and bolts for damage. Check the brake pedal bushings for wear and make certain that the brake pedal return spring brings the pedal back against the stop without binding. Check the operation of the stoplight switch.

If all checks are satisfactory, place the master cylinder in position and finger-tighten the mounting bolts or nuts. Remove the bleed lines, one at a time. Finger-tighten the brake line fittings, tighten the mounting bolts to specified torque, and then, using a flare nut wrench, finish tightening the brake line fittings.

To check or adjust the brake pedal free play (brake pedal travel), hold the push rod bore(s) in line with the bore(s) of the brake pedal. The connecting pin should slide into the bores without binding. If it does not, then adjust the yoke until it does. Now have someone depress the pedal while you observe the action within the reservoir. When the free play is properly adjusted, you will notice a fluid swirl within the reservoir while the brake pedal is depressed. The fluid motion should stop when the brake pedal has traveled about 1 in [25.4 mm]. When the free play is more than 1 in, it reduces the stroke available for braking, and this is particularly risky when a tandem master cylinder is used. When the free play is less than 1 in, the compensating port may become partially blocked. The brakes would then be slow to release, or they may drag or lock up completely (see the discussion of bleeding brakes in Unit 17).

BRAKE DRUMS AND BRAKE SHOES

Although many types of brake drums and shoe arrangements (foundation brakes) are used on on- and off-highway equipment to attain the relevant force needed to stop the equipment, they are, nevertheless, very similar in design. The differences which occur appear in the brake shoe design and arrangement, the design and size of the brake drum, the capacity to transmit the actuating force to the brake drum, and the method of actuation. A common characteristic of all designs is the requirement of some type of anchor to hold the shoe in position when the brake shoe(s) come in contact with the rotating drum.

Most significant in any type of drum brake system

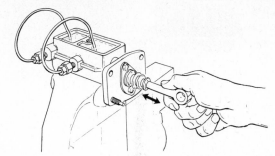

Fig. 14-19 Bleeding the master cylinder. (*Wagner Electric Sales Corporation*)

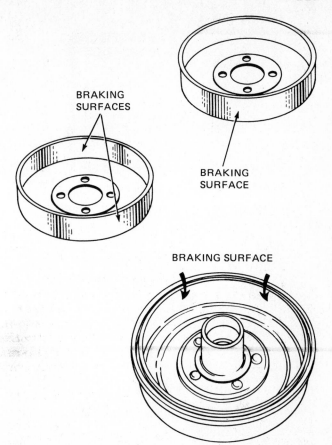

BRAKING
SURFACES

BRAKING
SURFACE

BRAKING SURFACE

Fig. 14-20 View of brake drum. (*FMC Corporation*)

are the brake shoes, the lining, and the drums. Much expertise on the part of engineers and metallurgists goes into the design of brake drums, brake shoes, and lining for a given vehicle so that it will withstand the applied pressure and the heat and maintain effective braking.

It is relatively simple to make the brake drums and brake shoes strong enough to withstand the applied pressure and to make the brake drums a good heat conductor. To maintain effective braking, however, is much more complex. As you know, brake drums heat owing to the braking action, sometimes enough to cause drum expansion (increasing its diameter). However, the brake shoes do not absorb heat through the brake lining as quickly as the drums do. The heat occurs on the outer surface of the shoe, and consequently the brake shoe's radius decreases. With the drum diameter increased and the shoe radius decreased, the total affected lining area is reduced, retarding the brake force. On the other hand, between braking applications, the drum cools faster than the brake shoes, contracting the drum to (or near) its original diameter. At the same time the brake shoes have absorbed heat from the brake drum and expand, enlarging their radius. Under this circumstance it is possible for the shoe's radius to become greater than the drum's radius, and therefore, when the brakes are applied, a reduced brake force could again result. Because of the many obvious factors to be considered in the design of brake drums and shoes they are manufactured in great variety.

Brake Drums   The two most basic types of brake drums are the internal type, in which the brake shoe's friction surface is the internal circumference of the brake drum, and the external type, in which the shoe or brake band is placed over the outer brake drum's friction surface.

Another class of brake drum used on some off-highway equipment is the internal-external type. This drum type has an inner and outer machined friction surface (see Fig. 14-20).

The brake drum diameter, the friction surface width, and the design, in regard to construction, type of material, bolt size, and bolt pattern, are all correlated to the brake requirement and intended application. Brake drums used for the braking system on on- and off-highway equipment are bolted or riveted to the wheel hub. On many other brake applications the brake drum is splined to the input or

output shaft of the transmission, or is bolted to a flange of the transmission, or is splined or bolted to a winch drum or differential shaft.

The most common brake drum designs are pressed steel, cast iron alloy, cast iron alloy friction ring with steel disk, cast iron alloy friction ring with steel drum, and cast iron alloy friction ring with aluminum alloy drum (see Fig. 14-21).

The pressed steel brake drum is formed from a sheet of steel. The manufacturing cost is low, but it also has a low coefficient of friction, has a low heat dissipation rate, and distorts or deforms during excessive brake application. This design is therefore limited to certain applications only. For example, it is used for parking brakes, small winch drums, and farm tractors (see Fig. 14-21(1)).

The cast iron alloy drum is used mostly on larger vehicles because of its inherent qualities. By varying the casting method and the alloy used, it is possible to improve the drum's friction quality, increase its heat dissipation capacity, increase its strength, and lessen wear and scoring. In addition, cooling ribs or air fins can be cast or machined to the drum's outer surface to further increase heat dissipation capacity and improve the drum's strength. Although this type is not easily distorted, extreme heat and quick cooling cause it to crack or permanently deform (see Fig. 14-21(2)).

The combination brake drum used on small trucks and on farm tractors may have a steel disk fastened

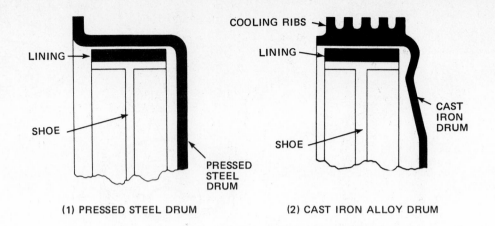

(1) PRESSED STEEL DRUM

(2) CAST IRON ALLOY DRUM

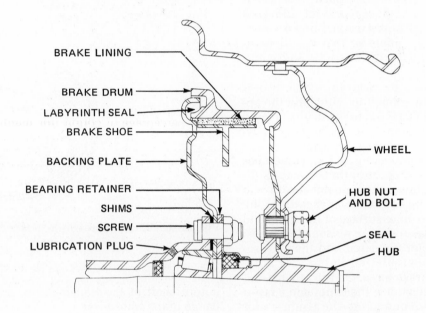

(3) CAST IRON ALLOY FRICTION RING WITH STEEL DISK

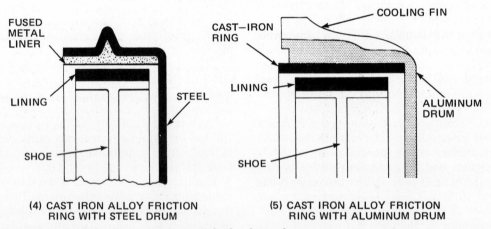

(4) CAST IRON ALLOY FRICTION
RING WITH STEEL DRUM

(5) CAST IRON ALLOY FRICTION
RING WITH ALUMINUM DRUM

Fig. 14-21 Sectional view of the five most common brake drum designs. (*FMC Corporation*)

to a cast iron ring which has cooling ribs, or it may be a die-formed steel drum to which the cast iron braking surface is centrifugally cast or fused (see Fig. 14-21(3)).

A drum which, because of the higher cooling efficiency, is becoming more popular on large braking systems is one designed basically the same as the steel drum having the cast iron friction surface. However, the production method and drum metal have changed (see Fig. 14-21(4)). The aluminum alloy drum is formed and fused to the cast iron ring. This design has, therefore, the quality of a cast iron

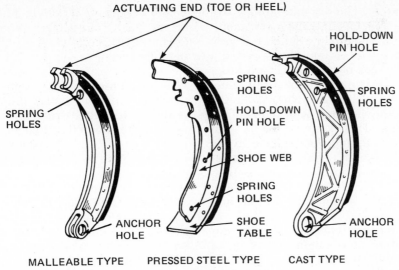

ACTUATING END (TOE OR HEEL)

HOLD-DOWN PIN HOLE

SPRING HOLES

HOLD-DOWN PIN HOLE

SPRING HOLES

SPRING HOLES

SHOE WEB

SPRING HOLES

ANCHOR HOLE

SHOE TABLE

ANCHOR HOLE

MALLEABLE TYPE   PRESSED STEEL TYPE   CAST TYPE

Fig. 14-22 Schematic view of the three most common brake shoe designs. (*FMC Corporation*)

brake drum and, because of the aluminum alloy covering, has a higher heat dissipation capacity (see Fig. 14-21(5)).

NOTE All vehicles equipped with backing plates have a labyrinth seal between the outer circumference of the backing plate and the drum (see Fig. 14-21(5)). The seal shape may vary; however its purpose remains the same—to keep water and damaging particles out of the inner drum assembly in order to prevent excessive lining and drum wear.

Brake Shoes The most popular shoe design for smaller braking systems is the prefabricated brake shoe made from steel. On larger brake systems, cast iron alloy, aluminum alloy, or malleable iron alloy brake shoes are used. Apart from this, the brake shoes for large or small systems are otherwise very similar (see Fig. 14-22).

A brake shoe consists of a table and shoe web. The lining or brake blocks are fastened to the table through bonding, riveting, or bolting. The shoe web supports the table and the shoe return spring. Some accommodate the automatic adjuster guide and lever. The hold-down pin passes through one web hole. One end of the shoe web (the heel) is the anchor bore or the anchor rest path. The other end (the toe) is the actuating end. Depending on the brake shoe arrangement, the shoe may be called the primary, secondary, forward, or reverse brake shoe (see the discussion of foundation brake design in this unit).

Brake Lining Material The basic types of lining used are woven linings, rigid molded linings, and dry mix-molded linings.

Each of these three types uses asbestos as its main substance because of its high friction quality, high heat resistance, and strength.

WOVEN LININGS Woven linings are usually used on winch drums, for wet and dry clutches, and on cars and small trucks as primary shoe linings. The woven linings are made chiefly from asbestos fibers with a small percentage of cotton (for manufacturing purposes). In addition a small percentage of bronze, lead, zinc, copper, and graphite may be added to modify the lining to the desired friction coefficient and to the desired heat and fade resistance. The compound is then impregnated with a bonding agent (resin), woven to the desired width and thickness, and then compressed into a rigid or semipliable product. It is ground to the desired width and thickness and to the desired drum arc. It is then drilled and countersunk for the bolts or rivet holes and checked for correct fit (see Fig. 14-23).

RIGID MOLDED LINING The rigid molded lining is the most common lining type used for light- and medium-duty applications because it can be produced to nearly any friction coefficient and also has a high resistance and effective fade resistance. In addition its close manufacturer tolerances make it easier to perform a reline brake job because the lining may not have to be arced to the drum diameter.

This lining is made chiefly of short asbestos fibers and asbestos powder. Moreover, to improve fade and heat resistance and the coefficient of friction, powdered sulfur, powdered nut shells, and a small quantity (of one or more) of brass, copper, lead, rubber, and zinc are added.

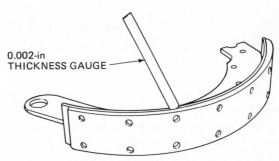

0.002-in THICKNESS GAUGE

Fig. 14-23 Checking tightness of molded lining. (*International Harvester Company*)

DRY MIX-MOLDED LININGS The dry mix-molded lining is used on off- and on-highway equipment, where a high fade resistance and a quick recovery are mandatory. Good-quality linings of this type are made chiefly from asbestos fiber with friction properties added such as aluminum, silicas, lead, zinc, graphite and a small amount of rubber. After the asbestos fiber and additives have been blended together, resin is added. This combination is then pressed into slabs, treated, and then shaped to the desired arc and dimension at a controlled temperature and pressure. The semifinished block is then cut to the specified width and again treated. Finally it is ground to a specific dimension, drilled, and countersunk.

Because of the numerous types and sizes of on- and off-highway equipment, a single type of brake lining would not be effective for all applications. Brake manufacturers therefore produce some six or seven types of lining, including an all-around good-performance-quality lining for normal service use. There is a special lining for heavy-duty operation, one for wedge brake design, and one specially designed for extra-heavy-duty operation. The latter is recommended for any multistop application (transit buses). Other types of brake linings are those manufactured for logging truck operations, in which the drums are water-cooled, and those designed for vehicles equipped with an antiskid system (121), and yet another for farm tractors, dozers, shovels, and graders, etc.

METALLIC FRICTION BRAKE BLOCKS The metallic friction brake blocks are specially designed for logging trucks or other applications operating under conditions in which braking power is of paramount importance. However, these metallic brake blocks should not be confused with the sintered bronze clutch plates used in power shift transmissions or with clutch plates used in the steering and brake systems of a track machine.

The metallic lining is made chiefly of steel supplemented with friction fiber properties and various metal alloys. The coefficient of friction is extremely high, as is the fade resistance. They have exceptionally good wet friction characteristics and withstand temperatures beyond 650°F [343°C]. Unfortunately, the wear rate of the drums' friction surface is higher than when conventional brake linings are used.

Identification of Coefficient of Friction To identify the coefficient of a brake lining, a lettering system is used. The first letter indicates the normal friction coefficient, and the second letter, the hot friction coefficient.

C = 0.15
D = over 0.15 to 0.25
E = over 0.25 to 0.35
F = over 0.35 to 0.45
G = over 0.45 to 0.55
H & Z = over 0.55

As an example, a brake lining, or a block having the lettering code FG could have a minimum coef-

ficient of friction of 0.35 to a hot friction coefficient of, say, 0.50, indicating that the lining or block coefficient of friction increases to this extent as the temperature increases.

Wheel Cylinders The purpose of the wheel cylinder is to convert hydraulic pressure into force which is then transmitted from the pistons to the piston link and to the brake shoe (see the introduction to hydraulics in Unit 6). In most cases the wheel cylinder is bolted to the backing plate of the brake assembly.

Basically, two types of wheel cylinders are used—straight-bore double-end (two opposed pistons) and the single-end single-piston wheel cylinder (see Fig. 14-24). The double-end step-bore wheel cylinder is no longer used on modern brake systems.

The double-end wheel cylinder has a cast iron body having a straight cylindrical bore, into which two pistons are loosely fitted. Two piston cup seals are used to seal the cylinder wall. Where a reduction of fluid volume is necessary, U-ring piston cup seals are used instead of the conventional piston cup seals. However, this type of seal must seal the piston, as well as the cylinder wall. Piston cup expanders are now seldom required because of the improved cup design and the synthetic material used.

A coil spring placed between the pistons is used to maintain the cup, the piston, and the piston link in constant contact with the brake shoe web. A dust boot seals each end of the cylinder bore, although the piston link or shoe web passes through the boot to maintain contact with the piston.

Two passages lead from the outside into the center area of the cylinder. One passage connects the bleed screw with the cylinder area to enable air to be removed from the system. The second passage leads from the center area to the threaded inlet bore.

Wheel Cylinder Cup Action When the brakes are released, the resilience of the synthetic rubber and the residual line pressure of 6 to 18 psi [41.34 to 124.02 kPa] hold the cup lips against the cylinder wall. When the brakes are applied, the pressure in the brake lines and wheel cylinder rises. The piston, piston cups, piston links, and shoes are then pushed outward against the force of the shoe return springs. Because of the low pressure at the beginning of the brake application, the cup lips are allowed to slide along the cylinder wall with very low friction. When the cylinder bore is even slightly damaged, the cup will wear at the damage points and perhaps cause a leak at a future date. Cylinder bore damage can also cause the cup or piston to stick, delaying the brake application to the wheel.

As the brake shoes come in contact with the brake drum, the pressure increases, forcing the lips of the cup against the cylinder wall and holding the cup in a fixed position. However, the increased pressure forces the piston and the brake shoes a few thousandths of an inch [hundredths of a millimeter] further outward. Under this condition the cup stretches at the cup-tapered base because its diameter is slightly smaller than the lip diameter (see the dis-

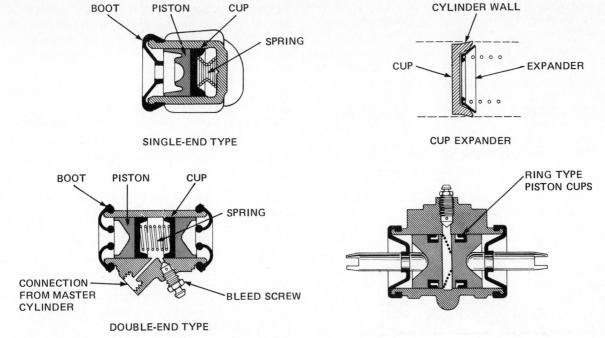

BOOT PISTON CUP

SPRING

SINGLE-END TYPE

CYLINDER WALL

CUP — EXPANDER

CUP EXPANDER

BOOT PISTON CUP

SPRING

CONNECTION FROM MASTER CYLINDER

BLEED SCREW

DOUBLE-END TYPE

RING TYPE PISTON CUPS

Fig. 14-24 Sectional view of three types of wheel cylinders. (*Wagner Electric Sales Corporation*)

cussion of dual master cylinder in this unit). Only under extreme pressure applications and drum deflection does the sealing portion of the cup stretch. It is therefore very important not to oversize the wheel cylinder bore beyond specification. When the bore exceeds the specification, the wheel cylinder cup expands, may rupture, and damage the cup lips, or fluid may leak past the lips.

When the brake pedal is released, the pressure in the system reduces, and the shoe return springs pull the brake shoes away from the brake drum surface, pushing the piston link, the piston, and the piston cup inward. Fluid is then displaced back into the master cylinder reservoir.

During the cup retraction the pressure on the cup lips is low, but the knife edge of the lips wipes the fluid from the cylinder wall with very little friction. However, if the cylinder bore is oversize, if the wall is damaged, or the fluid contaminated, the seal lips may deteriorate generally and become cut or needlessly worn, so that fluid seeps by and the walls are no longer wiped clean.

A single-wheel cylinder is actually one-half of a double-end wheel cylinder, the difference being that the cylinder bore is closed off on one end. The action within the single-wheel cylinder is the same as that within a double-end wheel cylinder, except that the force is exerted in only one direction.

Servo Brakes The most common brake shoe arrangement used on cars and small trucks is the servo foundation brake. A servo brake is a self-energizing brake assembly in which the primary brake shoe friction helps to force the secondary shoe into tighter contact with the drum, and when the vehicle is operating in reverse and the brakes are applied, the secondary shoe becomes the energizing shoe. The additional force due to the self-energizing action im-

proves performance of the brake assembly. **NOTE** When the rotation of the drum tends to force the brake shoe toward the anchor, the inward movement of the shoe not only reduces the friction but also resists the actuating force. This action is described as deenergizing force.

In a servo foundation brake the shoes are assembled to form a ring or unit, linked through an adjusting device (see Fig. 14-25). The base of the assembly is the backing plate which is bolted to the axle housing or front spindle. The backing plate has four or six shoe tables (guide paths or raised flat surfaces) on which the brake shoes rest or slide when the brakes are actuated or released. The brake shoes are held to the backing plate by one or more spring-loaded hold-down devices. The double-end wheel cylinder and the anchor are fixed and bolted to the backing plate.

The forward shoe of the servo brake is called the primary shoe and the rearward shoe is called the secondary shoe. There are two shoe return springs—one end of each spring is hooked to the upper part of the primary and secondary brake shoe web, and the other two ends are hooked to the anchor. The adjuster screw (star wheel) is placed between the heel of the primary and the toe of the secondary brake shoe. The automatic adjuster lever (pawl) is hooked to the secondary shoe web, and the adjuster lever return spring holds the lever arm snug to the starwheel of the adjuster screw. The adjuster cable spring is hooked to the adjuster lever on one end, and the other end of the cable is placed over the anchor. The cable guide hooked to the upper part of the secondary shoe web guides the cable.

Servo Action When the hydraulic pressure rises within the system, the wheel cylinder pistons are forced outward, and as a result, the toe of the pri-

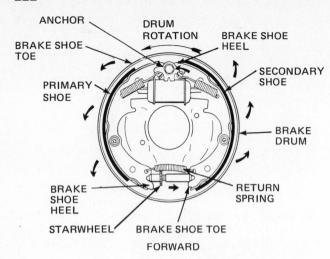

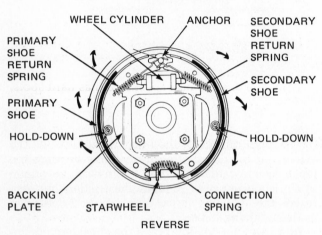

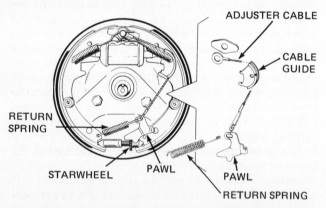

Fig. 14-25 Sectional view of a servo foundation brake in forward and reverse drum rotation. (*Wagner Electric Sales Corporation*)

mary shoe is forced to the left and the heel of the secondary shoe is forced to the right, away from the anchor and against the drum. The primary shoe is then forced to move in the direction of the rotating drum, causing the adjuster screw to transmit the motion to the secondary shoe. Consequently, the heel of the secondary shoe pushes the wheel cylinder piston inward and comes to rest against the anchor. The primary shoe now places an additional force onto the secondary shoe and thereby compounds the brake's effectiveness.

NOTE The arrows (Fig. 14-25) indicate the direction of force when the brakes are applied while the truck is traveling in reverse. The secondary shoe acts as the primary shoe, and the brakes are nearly as effective as in the forward direction.

When the brake pressure is released, the brake shoe return springs retract the brake shoe from the drum surface and bring the toe of the primary shoe against the anchor.

AUTOMATIC ADJUSTING ACTION Automatic adjustment occurs only when the vehicle is moving in reverse, the brakes are applied, and the lining-to-drum clearance is disproportionately large. Under these circumstances, the secondary shoe moves further away from the anchor. The distance from the anchor to the adjuster lever increases, lifting the adjusting lever to the point where it will engage into the next tooth on the adjusting screw starwheel. As the brake is released, the adjusting spring pulls the adjusting lever back to its original position. The adjusting screw starwheel then turns, increasing (by a few hundredths of a millimeter) the distance between the heel of the primary shoe and the toe of the secondary shoe.

If the brakes are applied (when correctly adjusted), the secondary shoe moves only a short distance away from the anchor. This expanse is inadequate to sufficiently move the adjuster lever so that it hooks into the next tooth of the starwheel. When the brakes are released, the shoe return spring pulls the secondary shoe against the anchor, and the adjuster spring pulls the adjuster lever back into the same tooth of the starwheel.

Preliminary Checks and Inspection When brake trouble exists, there may be a defect or malfunction in the hydraulic system components or in the foundation brakes. Brake ineffectiveness can also originate from the tires, wheel bearings, suspension, shock absorbers, and the steering mechanism. Service, therefore, should not be restricted to the brake system alone. The source of the trouble must be determined and the defective part serviced so that brake failure will not recur (see the discussion of troubleshooting in Unit 17).

Before attempting any service work to the drum or brake assembly, you should first position the vehicle so that you have adequate work area. Next, lift the vehicle's front axle and place floor stands under the axle to support the vehicle's weight. Repeat this procedure with the rear axle. Slack off the foundation brake's adjustment, release the parking brakes, and then check the wheel bearings by rotating the tire backward and forward to sense the rolling action of the bearings. Also rock the tire left and right and move it inward and outward to determine if there is adequate adjustment or whether the steering system is loose or worn.

Commence service by removing the wheels and the brake drum (see the discussion of tires, wheels and rims in Unit 12). Vacuum away any contaminants and dust from the brake drum and brake as-

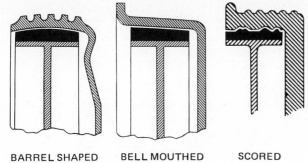

BARREL SHAPED   BELL MOUTHED   SCORED

Fig. 14-26 View of a barrel-shaped brake drum, a bell-mouthed brake drum, and a scored brake drum. (*Wagner Electric Sales Corporation*)

sembly and then check the wear pattern of the lining and drum to assess their general condition. For instance, determine if the brake drum is scored, barrel shaped, bell mouthed or grooved (see Fig. 14-26). When the drum is barrel shaped, the center of the lining is less worn than the two sides. When it is bell mouthed, the lining is worn more on the outside than on the inside. In either case, the problem may be a distorted shoe, bent or loose backing plate, or grooved backing plate tables, or the shoe hold-down device may be missing.

When the lining and drum are scored, the drum to backing plate seal has allowed contaminants to enter the assembly. You should therefore check the backing plate for alignment and the drum for heat checks and cracks. If only heat checks exist, the drum can be serviced (see Fig. 14-27); however, if it is cracked or split, the drum must be replaced. If the lining and/or drum is saturated with fluid, grease, or oil, check the wheel cylinder, drive axle seal, and wheel hub seal for damage and check the oil level and/or grease. The level may be too high, or an inferior grade of grease may have been used.

When the lining is worn to $\frac{1}{32}$ in above the rivet head on small trucks (about $\frac{1}{16}$ in on larger on- or off-highway equipment) or when it is loose on the shoe table, it must be replaced. **NOTE** Do not try to rerivet or rebolt a loose lining, because the lining holes are elongated and will not remain in place. Also, never replace one shoe lining only and never replace one wheel assembly only. To do so will offset the braking balance of the vehicle.

If the lining shows more wear on the heel than on the toe, check for a loose or bent anchor (see Fig. 14-

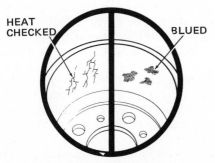

Fig. 14-27 Schematic view of a blued and heat-checked brake drum. (*Wagner Electric Sales Corporation*)

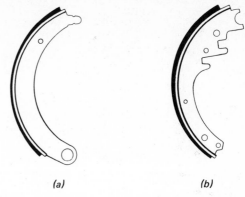

Fig. 14-28 Schematic view of (a) normally worn brake lining and (b) lining worn more at the heel owing to loose, bent, or misadjusted anchor. (*Wagner Electric Sales Corporation*)

28). (If there are small surface cracks on the lining, do not concern yourself with them—they do not reduce the lining's effectiveness.)

When the drum is heat checked or has hard spots, the lining is usually scored. **NOTE** A heat-checked or hard-spotted drum surface requires grinding because the cutting tool will jump over the spot; it will not cut the hardened material. The heat-check discoloration, blued, or hard spots on the drum are the result of excessive heat due to severe brake usage, as a result of overloading, of poor or inadequate lining contact to drum, of inadequate heat dissipation due to an oversize drum, or of a corroded or dirty outer surface of the drum.

Before removing the brake shoes from the backing plate, check the adjuster lever's alignment with the starwheel. Check the cable guide. Check that the shoe return springs are correctly located and aligned—if the springs are spread or the shanks twisted, they should be replaced. Also at this time check the shoe hold-down device and take note of the component locations (see Fig. 14-29). Start the removal of the brake shoes by pulling the adjuster link down and toward the rear of the vehicle to unhook it from the adjusting lever. Remove the link from the anchor and then use a removal tool to remove shoe hold-down clips.

Remove the shoe guide plate by spreading the shoes away from the anchor and then lift the assembly from the backing plate.

To separate the primary from the secondary shoe, move the shoes toward each other to unhook the spring.

Regardless of the condition of the wheel cylinder, it must be removed for service whenever the brakes are to be relined. The reason is that the new linings cause a repositioning of the wheel cylinder cups within the wheel cylinder bore, and this area may have become pitted or gummed. Such a defect would prevent the cup from sealing.

To remove the cylinder, first remove the clip that holds the hose to the frame (see Fig. 14-30), and then, using two flare nut wrenches, loosen the hose-to-tube fitting. With a six-point socket wrench remove the two cap screws.

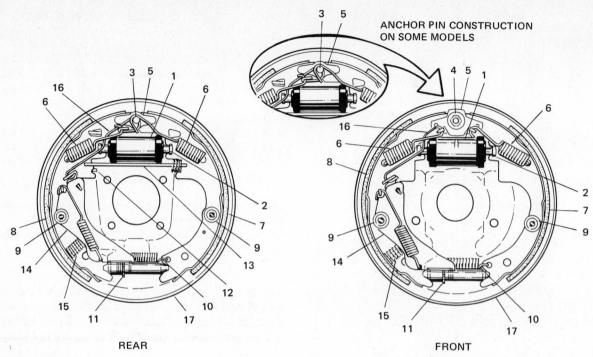

ANCHOR PIN CONSTRUCTION
ON SOME MODELS

REAR

FRONT

1. Wheel cylinder (see exploded view)	7. Primary shoe	13. Parking brake strut
2. Cylinder link	8. Secondary shoe	14. Adjusting lever and pivot assembly
3. Anchor pin	9. Hold-down cup and spring	15. Lever return spring
4. Anchor bolt	10. Shoe connecting spring	16. Adjusting link
5. Anchor plate	11. Adjusting screw assembly	17. Backing plate
6. Return spring	12. Parking brake lever	

Fig. 14-29 Schematic view of the front and rear self-adjusting brake assemblies (right-hand side). (*Wagner Electric Sales Corporation*)

To remove the brake tube fitting from the rear wheel cylinder, first apply penetrating oil to the fitting before attempting to loosen it. This prevents the tube from turning with the fitting while it is being loosened.

Inspecting and Servicing Servo Brakes When the drum is not cracked or split and the wear pattern is not very deep, measure the diameter of both front

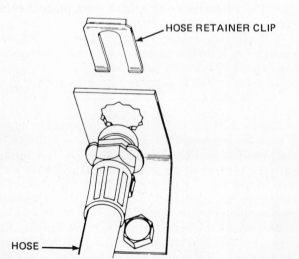

HOSE RETAINER CLIP

HOSE

Fig. 14-30 Schematic illustration of hose and hose retainer.

and rear drums to determine if they can be resurfaced. Record on the drums the drum measurements and their position on the vehicle. The reason for this precaution is that each set of drums must be machined to the same diameter and returned to the same spindle or axle to ensure balanced braking.

Before attempting to measure the drum diameter, first check the micrometer to make sure it is properly adjusted and then adjust it to the drum diameter. (Make certain the adjustment is locked in.) Place the micrometer flat onto the edge of the drum and then move the end (on which the dial gauge is located) to the left and right, to gain the highest needle movement. The gauge reading at its highest level equals the maximum diameter. Again measure the drum 90° from the first measurement to determine diameter variation (out-of-roundness; see Fig. 14-31).

If the diameter size falls within 0.010 of an inch of the maximum oversize specification (see the relative service manual because of the variations in allowable oversize) but has deep grooves, or if it is out-of-round beyond specification, then the drum may not be resurfaced; it must be replaced. However, if the drum is only 0.003 in [0.076 mm] out-of-round and its surface nearly perfect, an 80-grit emery cloth can be used to roughen the surface and thereby allow the new lining to seat faster.

If the drum surface is rough or grooved but the drum is nevertheless resurfaceable, commence restoration by removing the inner wheel bearing and

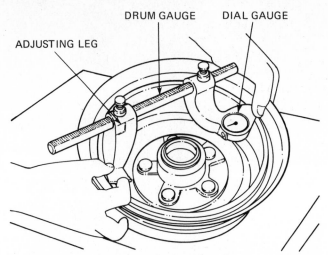

Fig. 14-31 Measuring the brake drum diameter. (*Wagner Electric Sales Corporation*)

seal. If your brake drum lathe is small, you may have to remove the disk wheel, in which event you should retorque the wheel nuts to prevent drum distortion while it is being machined.

If the brake drum is heavily oxidized (rusted), remove the wheel and sandblast the drum to acceptable cleanliness. You can also use a scraper and wire brush to clean the drum and the labyrinth seal groove to ensure good heat dissipation and backing plate-to-drum sealing.

Resurfacing the Drum The following general procedure may have to be modified according to the drum lathe used or to conform to the manufacturer's instructions (see Fig. 14-32). First make certain that the cutting tool is sharp and that it is correctly aligned to cut close to the back of the drum brake surface. Or if a grinding stone is used, it must be dressed and must have the correct angle.

Mount to the lathe the front or rear drum having the largest diameter. Use the supplied adapter but take care not to overtorque the nut, for this could damage the bearing race or distort the drum. Install

the rubber vibration damper around the drum's outer surface and set the lathe at fast-feed cut position. Set the cutting tool (or grinding wheel) close to the smallest drum diameter and then start the motor that turns the drum (and the grinder). Manually feed the cutting tool (or grinder) in and/or out to find the smallest drum diameter. It is usually at the bottom end and at the rim end of the drum. Move the cutting tool close to the back of the drum brake surface, manually feed the cutting tool or grinder outward about 0.005 in [0.12 mm], and then position the lathe on automatic. Mark the micrometer setting on the lathe. When the cut is completed, reset the lathe to take a fine cut. After the last cut has been made, hold the emery cloth against the drum surface (while continuing to turn the drum), until the cutting marks are no longer visible.

When turning the other drum, front or rear, make certain that the final cut has the same lathe micrometer setting so that the diameter of both drums is the same. After turning or grinding the drum, steam-clean it or wash it in hot soapy water and then dry it with compressed air. If the drums are not installed immediately, wipe the drum surface with wood alcohol to prevent it from oxidizing.

Servicing Brake Shoe Assembly Shoe return springs having coil separation, or coils or shanks that are twisted, oxidized, or corroded must be replaced. Brake shoes with any of the following defects must be replaced: worn or out-of-round anchor radius, broken weld (table loose on the web), excessive rusting or pitting of the table or web, or worn shoe table due to drum contact. Brake shoes must also be replaced if there is any other damage which has weakened the shoe structure.

To remove the old lining rivets, use a tool similar to the one shown in Fig. 14-33. The use of a punch and hamer could damage the shoe table and/or elongate the holes.

Select a die having the same or a slightly smaller diameter than the rivet and place it into the upper holder. Select an anvil having a bore slightly larger than the rivet head, place it into the lower holder, and then adjust the anvil height. Next, place the shoe

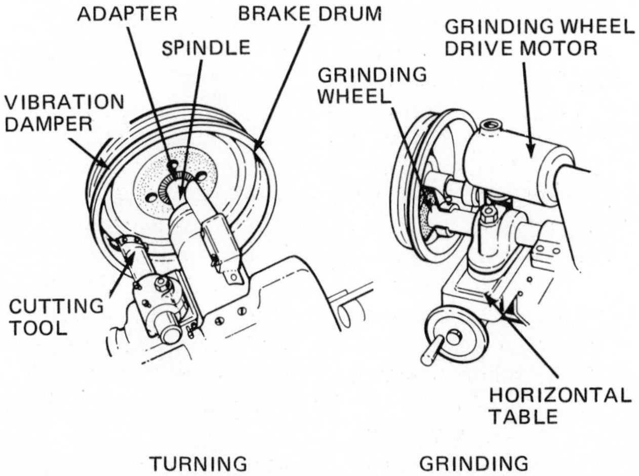

Fig. 14-32 Schematic view of two methods of resurfacing a brake drum. (*Wagner Electric Sales Corporation*)

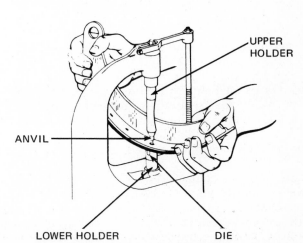

Fig. 14-33 Method of removing brake lining rivets.

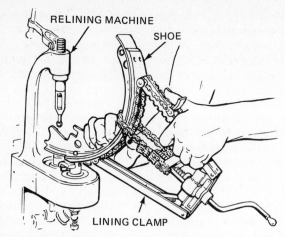

Fig. 14-34 Riveting lining to brake shoe. (*International Harvester Company*)

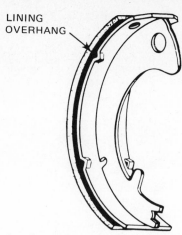

Fig. 14-35 Clean-up lining overhand, shoe table, and web edges.

so that the rivet head rests on the anvil and the die rests on the rivet and then eject the rivet by actuating the lever.

After removing the old lining, degrease and clean the shoes by using a wire buffer or a sand or glass blaster, etc. If necessary, use a file to smoothen the table surface. Repaint the shoes by using the recommended paint. Check the lining-to-shoe fit—the rivet holes must align with the table holes, and the lining must not overhang the shoe table.

Select and install the correct anvil and crown rivet head into the lining tool, and with a C clamp or a lining clamp, clamp the lining to the shoe table (see Fig. 14-34). Place a rivet into a center hole and the rivet head onto the anvil. Adjust the tool so that the lining rests firmly against the shoe table when the rivet is set (clinched). If the rivet is set too tightly, the lining may crack or bulge away from the shoe table, and if set too loosely, they could break away from the table. Continue riveting the lining to the shoe table, alternately, toward the toe and heel.

Check that the rivets are evenly and firmly set and that the heads are not cocked to one side. With a feeler gauge check the lining-to-shoe table fit (see service manual specification). Before grinding (sizing) the shoes to the drum diameter, check the lining overhang. If necessary, use sandpaper or a file to remove any overhang (see Fig. 14-35) and at the same time remove the paint from the shoe tables.

Grinding the Shoe Lining All new linings must be ground to remove the slight but inevitable contour distortions and to ensure a minimum drum surface contact of 80 percent. Furthermore, servo brakes must have a toe and heel clearance of at least 0.005 in [0.12 mm] to ensure a smooth brake application. When the lining is high spotted, it distorts the shoe, reduces braking efficiency, and creates a higher temperature, any of which may lead to lining fade. If there is lining contact at only the toe and heel, it pinches the lining ends and causes the brakes to squeal, pull, or grab. Again, this reduces the braking efficiency and also raises the brake temperature.

Special shoe grinders have been developed to grind the shoe to the desired diameter. One that is

able to grind the shoe diameter to a slightly smaller size than the drum diameter is referred to as a cam or contour grinder (see Fig. 14-36). In using this type of grinder, the basic steps to grind the shoe to the required diameter are as follows.

Measure the drum diameter by using a drum micrometer. Say it measured 12.040 in [305.8 mm]. Set the grinder to the drum diameter 12 in [304.8 mm] and then turn the micrometer adjuster to 0.040 in [1 mm]. Since this setting would grind the shoe concentrically and servo brakes require a toe-and-heel clearance, the shoe diameter must be reduced. To do this, reduce the micrometer setting about 0.20 in [5.08 mm].

After the grinder is adjusted, set the movable anchor in the correct position and then clamp the shoe in place. Make certain the shoe rests against the anchor and the table rests against the clamp stops (not shown). Using a chalk, scribe several longitudinal marks on the lining so that the ground area is more apparent.

Start the motor and turn the handle to bring the shoe lining in contact with the abrasive disk. Swing the shoe back and forth across the disk. When the chalk marks are just barely removed, the ground shoe should fit perfectly against the drum contour and square to the drum surface.

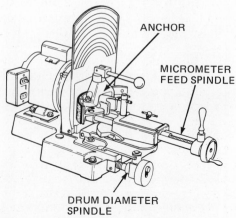

Fig. 14-36 Schematic view of a cam brake shoe grinder. (*Wagner Electric Sales Corporation*)

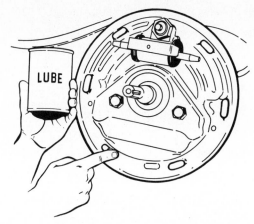

Fig. 14-37 Applying lubricant to the shoe tables

To check the fit (that is, the toe and heel clearance), place the shoe into the resurfaced drum and with a feeler gauge measure the clearance at the toe and heel. **NOTE** Store the drum and shoe so that no oil or grease can contact the lining or drum surface.

Backing Plate When checking the backing plate, check the anchor for looseness, galling, and wear and the backing plate tables for grooves and distortion. Place a straight edge across the tables to measure the backing plate for distortion. If the tables are slightly worn, use a file to restore the surface. If the surface cannot be restored, the backing plate must be replaced; otherwise the brake shoes may hang up during application or may not release fully.

Use solvent, or when rusted, use a wire (power or hand) brush to thoroughly clean the backing plate and then, if necessary, paint it. Remove the paint from the backing plate tables and apply a small amount of specified grease to the tables and anchor (see Fig. 14-37).

Clean the adjuster screw, nut, and cup. Check the starwheel teeth and threads for damage. **NOTE** The letters L and R stamped on the adjuster indicate left- and right-hand threads. Take care not to interchange the adjuster and thereby cause a left-hand-threaded starwheel to be installed to the left side brakes because this would allow the automatic adjuster to release the adjustment. Finally, apply a small amount of grease to the adjuster screw and then turn it all the way into the nut.

Wheel Cylinder The service procedure, that is, cleaning, honing, and measuring the maximum wear limit of a wheel cylinder, is much the same as that for a master cylinder.

The maximum wheel cylinder wear limit for a $\frac{3}{4}$- to $1\frac{3}{16}$-in cylinder bore is 0.005 in [0.12 mm]. For a bore diameter of $1\frac{1}{4}$ to $1\frac{7}{16}$ in it is 0.006 in [0.15 mm], and for a bore diameter about $1\frac{1}{2}$ in it is 0.007 in [0.17 mm]. Some additional steps are to remove and clean the bleeder screw and to check the threads and flare seat. When servicing a single-end wheel cylinder, place a washer inside the cylinder to protect the stone from damage while honing.

When the pistons are eroded or gummy and no replacement is available, wash and clean them in hot, soapy water but do not use emery cloth or a wire brush, for they would remove the protective coating.

REASSEMBLY To reassemble the wheel cylinder, first make certain all parts are clean. Next, wet the bore and dip the cups and piston in brake fluid. Install one cup, with the lip facing inward into the cylinder bore, and then place the piston with its flat side against the cup and install the dust boot over the end. Turn the cylinder over, place the spring against the first cup, and then insert the second cup and piston into the cylinder bore. While holding the piston in the bore, place the dust boot over the cylinder bore end. Install the bleeder screw finger-tight and cap the inlet port opening.

INSTALLATION Hold the cylinder to the backing plate and remove the protective caps. Start the brake line fitting into the threaded bore and then finger-tighten the fitting to prevent cross-threading the fitting. Now bolt the wheel cylinder to the backing plate and, with a flare nut wrench, tighten the fitting.

When installing the front wheel cylinder, use a new copper gasket on the male end of the hose before screwing it into the wheel cylinder inlet. Then fasten the tube fitting to the other hose end after making certain the hose is not twisted. Also make sure the hose does not interfere during spring deflection or rebound or during maximum degree of front wheel turns.

Reassembly of Brakes Make certain that all brake components, including the wheel hubs, are serviced, that the components of one wheel are not interchanged with another wheel, and that no parts are missing. Next, lay out the foundation brake components so that the primary shoe is facing forward and place the socket end of the adjuster screw between the shoe web ends. Check that the star wheel aligns with the adjusting hole in the backing plate. When necessary, install a light spring so that the shoes remain as a unit. Position the assembly to the backing plate so that the toe and heel rest against the anchor and then attach the two shoes to the backing plate by means of the shoe hold-down pin, spring, and cups (see Fig. 14-38).

Place the shoe anchor plate onto the anchor and then place the cable end onto the anchor pin (according to the service manual recommendation).

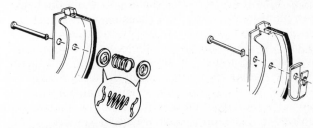

Fig. 14-38 Schematic view of two common brake shoe hold-down components.

Insert the cable guide into the hole of the secondary shoe web. Lubricate the guide with grease and lift the cable over and into the guide groove. After verifying that it is in the groove, install the primary and secondary shoe return springs. Use the proper tool to guide the springs onto the anchor pins. Again, refer to the service manual in regard to location of the shoe return springs because some brake assemblies use color-coded springs and others are different in length and shape.

Hook the cable to the adjuster lever and hook the spring to the primary shoe web. Pull the adjuster lever downward and backward to hook it into the web of the secondary shoe. To check the action of the automatic adjuster, use a prybar and move the secondary shoe away from the anchor to lift the adjuster lever to the next star wheel tooth. It should snap into the tooth. When the shoe returns to the anchor, the spring force should move the lever, turning the star wheel one tooth.

Before reassembling the rear wheel brake assembly, check the parking brake cables, and links for freeness and then lubricate them. Fasten the parking plate lever to the secondary shoe before positioning the shoe to the backing plate. When the shoes are attached to the backing plate through a hold-down device, push the large end of the antirattle spring onto the strut against its shoulder. Place the strut spring end into the web of the primary shoe and the other end of the strut into the parking brake lever (see Fig. 14-39).

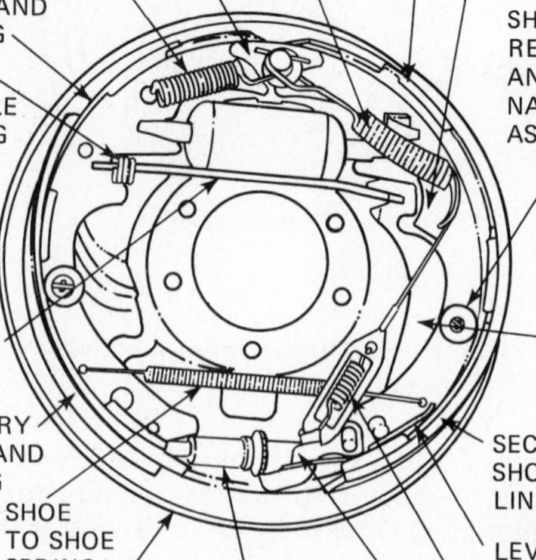

Anchor Adjustment If the old linings are worn unevenly (say, more so on the heels than on the toe) and the anchor is of the adjustable design, the alignment should be checked and, if necessary, adjusted. To make this adjustment, install a dummy drum (cutaway drum) over the assembly and place a 0.015 in [0.38 mm] feeler gauge about 1½ in [37.5 mm] from the adjuster, between the secondary lining and drum. Adjust the star wheel until the feeler gauge cannot be removed and then turn the star wheel in the opposite direction only enough to withdraw the feeler gauge. Now insert the feeler gauge about 1½ in from the anchor between the secondary shoe and drum. The 0.015 in [0.38-mm] feeler gauge should have a slightly heavier drag. When the looseness of the feeler gauge exceeds 0.003 in [0.07 mm], loosen the anchor nut and tap or turn the anchor to achieve the desired clearance. See service manual for specification applications. **NOTE** Always recheck toe and heel clearance after the anchor nut is tightened.

If a dummy drum is not available, loosen the anchor nut and tap it to free the anchor from the backing plate. Install the drum assembly and adjust the shoes so that the drum can barely be turned. Tap the anchor to center the brake shoes to the drum. You may have to adjust the shoes once more and again tap the anchor before tightening the anchor nut.

If the brake adjustment is mechanical, back off the starwheel adjuster 12 notches. If the adjustment is automatic, back off the starwheel 20 notches.

The fastest way to preadjust the shoe is to use a shoe gauge, since modern servo brakes need only

Fig. 14-39 Sectional view of the left rear brake assembly. (*General Motors Corporation*)

the initial adjustment. Thereafter the automatic adjuster will maintain the correct lining to drum clearance (see Fig. 14-40).

To make the adjustment, loosen the knurled screw of the gauge and place the legs, with the cutout, against the drum surface. Next, adjust the gauge to the drum diameter and lock the measurement securely, and then, using the other pair of legs, place the gauge over the brake lining. Expand the shoes by turning the star wheel until the gauge legs rest against the shoes. **NOTE** When adjusting the rear brake shoes, make certain the parking brake is fully released.

Installing Wheel, Hub, and Drum Before sliding the wheel hub onto the spindle or the brake drum onto the drive axle, recheck the foundation brake and make certain it is assembled according to the service manual instructions and that all parts are secured, lubricated, adjusted, and operating properly. When the wheel hub is in place, slide the outer wheel bearing and washer onto the spindle and secure it with the nut.

The general procedure to adjust the wheel bearing is outlined in Unit 13.

Nonservo Brakes A nonservo brake is one which is so assembled that its brake action is not compounded. A nonservo brake used on a four-wheel drive loader is shown in Fig. 14-41 and 14-45. The primary differences between the illustrated brake and the servo brake is that each brake shoe on the nonservo brake has its own adjustable (eccentric)

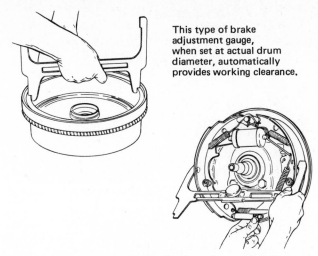

This type of brake adjustment gauge, when set at actual drum diameter, automatically provides working clearance.

Fig. 14-40 How to use the brake adjustment gauge to preadjust the brake shoes. (*Wagner Electric Sales Corporation*)

anchor and eccentric cam adjuster. Only one shoe return spring and one double-end wheel cylinder are used. In this brake shoe arrangement, the brake shoes are referred to as the forward shoe and the reverse shoe.

NOTE When the anchor center punch marks reach the point where they face each other, the eccentric anchors have then moved the shoes the farthest distance away from the drum surface. Note also that no shoe hold-down clamps or shoe tables are used, because of the strong anchors and because the bore in the shoe web is wide enough to ensure alignment.

Brake Application (No Servo Action) As the pressure rises in the wheel cylinders, both brake shoes are forced against the brake drum surface and pivot on both anchors. Because the anchors are farther

away from the drum than they are from the brake lining, a lever is formed, and the anchors become the fulcrum and assist in the braking effort. Note that the arrows (Fig. 14-41) indicate the direction of force, and that the forward shoe is self-energizing, and the reverse shoe is deenergizing.

There are two other nonservo brake arrangements to be found on some smaller trucks and on off-highway equipment: where two single-end wheel cylinders are used and where two double-end wheel cylinders are used.

When two single-end wheel cylinders are used (see Fig. 14-42), two shoe return springs are required. Both shoes are called forward shoes because each has self-energizing action when the vehicle is moving in the forward direction. When the vehicle moves in the reverse direction, there is deenergizing action on the shoe facing rearward; therefore, there is a great difference in the braking effort when the vehicle moves in the forward or reverse directions.

The anchors of the self-centering brake shoes are the opposite-wheel cylinders, and the heels of the brake shoe can slide within the groove of the wheel cylinders. In some applications an automatic adjusting mechanism that is fastened to both brake shoe webs is used to maintain the proper running clearance.

Brake Action When the brakes are released, the return springs have moved the brake lining away from the brake drum surface and have forced the shoe web against the adjusting wedge or eccentric cam adjuster. When the hydraulic pressure rises, the toe of each brake shoe is forced outward and comes in contact with the drum. This causes the shoe heel to be forced outward and against its anchor. Because of the shape of the anchor, the shoe is forced against

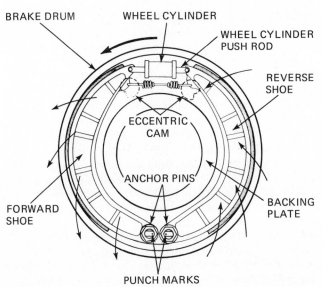

Fig. 14-41 Schematic view of a nonservo foundation brake. (*J I Case Company Agricultural Equipment Division*)

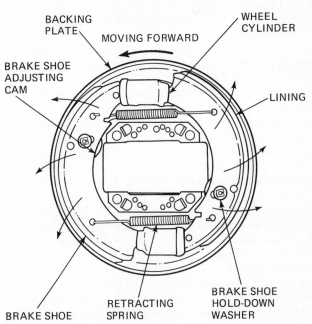

Fig. 14-42 Schematic view of a nonservo foundation brake using two single-end wheel cylinders. The brake cylinders are of the self-centering design. (*Wagner Electric Sales Corporation*)

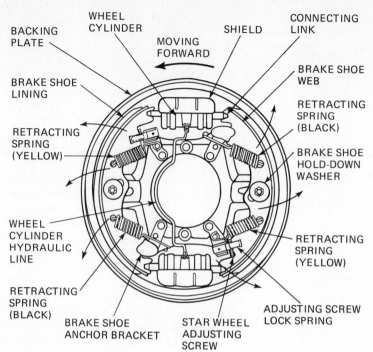

Fig. 14-43 Schematic view of a nonservo final drive brake using two double-end wheel cylinders. (*Wagner Electric Sales Corporation*)

the drum surface. Again a lever is formed where the anchor becomes the fulcrum, increasing the applied force. **NOTE** The arrows indicate the direction of force arrows (Fig. 14-42).

When the brakes are released, both shoe return springs pull the brake shoes away from the drum. The wheel cylinder piston retracts, and the heels of the shoes slide inward on the anchors.

The nonservo brake shoe arrangement shown in Figure 14-43 is used on medium-sized on-highway trucks, as well as on off-highway equipment. This type of brake uses two double-end wheel cylinders, and therefore the applied force is equal at the heels and toes of the shoes. Since both shoes are self-energizing, the brake effort is equal in the forward or in the reverse direction (Fig. 14-43). The arrows indicate the direction of force.

Although the brake shoe heel anchors are fixed to the backing plate, they are slotted to allow the shoe web to slide in or out when the brakes are applied or released. The brake shoe toe anchors are the screws of the adjuster and become the fixed anchors when the vehicle moves in reverse direction. When the brakes are equipped with an automatic adjuster, the crank is fastened to each heel anchor pin (see Fig. 14-44). At one end a short link is hooked to the crank. The other end of the short link is hooked to the eccentric adjustment hex on the shoe web. A long link is hooked from the other end of the crank into the slot of the star wheel's adjusting lever. The lever can pivot on the pin fastened to the backing plate support. The other end of the star wheel's adjusting lever rests in one tooth of the star wheel. The combination of links and lever ratio senses lining clearance with respect to the movement of the brake shoe heel when the vehicle is in the reverse direction and the brake is applied.

When the linings are somewhat worn, the crank

lever pivots farther than when the brakes are correctly adjusted. This additional lever movement allows the lever to engage with the next tooth on the star wheel. Although an adjustment may not occur immediately (because the shoe force has increased the friction on the threads of the adjusting screw), as soon as the brakes are released, the adjustment takes place.

Servicing a Nonservo Brake Any time the nonservo brakes on an axle of the four-wheel-drive loader type are to be serviced, the planetary drive must first be removed. (See the discussion of planetary drive in this unit.) Removing the planetary drive (which includes the brake drum) exposes the brake assembly (see Fig. 14-45). At this point, examine the splines, threads, seals, and inner wheel bearing for damage and wear. It is recommended at this time to remove the bearing from the spindle, the wheel hub, and the hub seal (planetary housing seal). To protect the drive axle, spindle splines, and spindle threads, bind them with masking tape. Cover the seal opening also, using masking tape to prevent contaminants from entering the axle housing.

Turn both eccentric cam adjusters clockwise until the wheel cylinder push rods are loose enough to be removed and then install a wheel cylinder clamp. Next, turn the eccentric cam counterclockwise to retract the brake shoes and remove the brake shoe return spring. Remove the cotter pin, nut, and shoe links and lift the brake shoes from the anchor.

The inspection and service procedure of the nonservo brake drum is the same as that for a servo brake drum. However, on this type of brake when the brake drum has to be rebored (turned), you must oversize the drum so that either a 0.064-in [1.6-mm] or a 0.0128-in [0.32-mm] oversize lining can be used since shimming is not recommended.

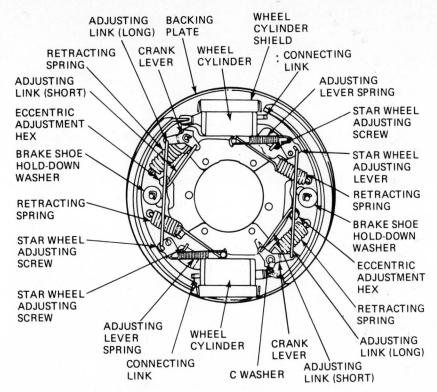

ADJUSTING
LINK (LONG)

BACKING
PLATE

WHEEL
CYLINDER
SHIELD

RETRACTING
SPRING

CRANK
LEVER

WHEEL
CYLINDER

CONNECTING
LINK

ADJUSTING
LINK (SHORT)

ADJUSTING
LEVER SPRING

ECCENTRIC
ADJUSTMENT
HEX

STAR WHEEL
ADJUSTING
SCREW

BRAKE SHOE
HOLD-DOWN
WASHER

STAR WHEEL
ADJUSTING
LEVER

RETRACTING
SPRING

RETRACTING
SPRING

BRAKE SHOE
HOLD-DOWN
WASHER

STAR WHEEL
ADJUSTING
SCREW

ECCENTRIC
ADJUSTMENT
HEX

STAR WHEEL
ADJUSTING
SCREW

RETRACTING
SPRING

ADJUSTING
LEVER
SPRING

WHEEL
CYLINDER

CRANK
LEVER

ADJUSTING
LINK (LONG)

CONNECTING
LINK

C WASHER

ADJUSTING
LINK (SHORT)

Fig. 14-44   View of a self-adjusting double-end wheel cylinder foundation brake. (*International Harvester Company*)

Before removing the brake linings, check the wear of the anchor pin bores and anchor pins. If the anchor pins are loose or worn, the pins must be replaced. If the bores are worn, the shoes must be replaced. It is permissible to enlarge the bushing bore and press a new oversize bushing into the bore, but if this is done, make certain when placing the shoe on the anchor that it is perfectly aligned. Do not neglect to check, for wear, the surface on which the eccentric cam acts. After the linings are removed, hold the shoe with a punch or bar and then tap it

with a hammer to reveal hidden flaws and cracks (see Fig. 14-46). The shoe will have a bell sound if it is not cracked. If the shoe has no flaws or cracks, degrease and sandblast it and, if necessary, file the shoe table smooth.

To rivet the lining to the shoe, you will need a $\frac{3}{8}$-in hand riveting tool set because of the rivet size. While riveting, use several C clamps to hold the lining to the table to ensure good lining contact.

When the lining is aligned and clamped to the shoe table, use a $\frac{7}{16}$-in flat head drift and drive two

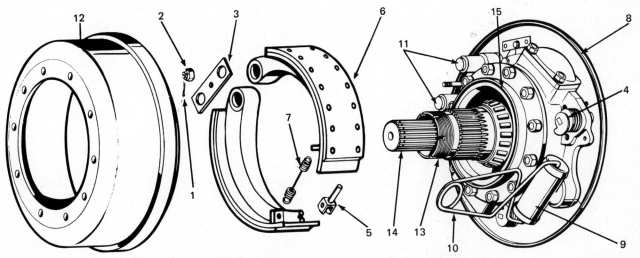

1. Cotter pin	5. Wheel cylinder push rod	9. Wheel cylinder	13. Wheel hub
2. Nut	6. Forward brake shoe	10. Wheel cylinder clamp	14. Drive axle
3. Brake shoe link	7. Brake shoe return spring	11. Adjustable anchor pins	15. Seal
4. Eccentric cam	8. Backing plate	12. Brake drum	

Fig. 14-45   Schematic view of a nonservo brake assembly. (*J I Case Company Agricultural Equipment Division*)

Fig. 14-46 Method used to check the brake shoe for hidden flaws. (*FMC Corporation*)

rivets into the first two holes close to the anchor bore. Turn the shoe so that the rivet heads rest flat on the $\frac{7}{16}$ anvil while you form the rivet head with a $\frac{13}{64}$-in tubular rivet set. Continue riveting toward the toe of the shoe (see Fig. 14-47).

When checking the lining-to-shoe table fit (clearance), follow the procedure outlined for checking servo brakes. The wheel cylinder can be serviced and also honed without removing it from the brake assembly.

It is imperative that you check the alignment of the backing plate and the flange and the outer circumference of the backing plate. If the backing plate is bent, or if the flange is damaged, contaminants such as dust, sand, gravel, etc., can enter the brake assembly and cause excessive wear and a reduction in brake efficiency.

Check the eccentric cam for wear and also for

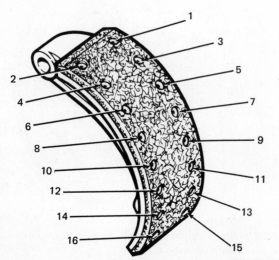

Fig. 14-47 Sequence of riveting the lining to the brake shoe. (*J I Case Company Agricultural Equipment Division*)

turnability. At this point loosen the two anchor nuts and turn the anchor pin so that the center punch marks face each other and then retighten the nuts.

REASSEMBLING, ADJUSTING, AND GRINDING Before starting the assembly, first check the trunnion bearing play (kingpin). Otherwise, if an adjustment or bearing replacement were necessary after the brakes were reassembled, you would once more have to remove the brake shoes. Always reassemble components in an order precisely the reverse of that of disassembly.

To ensure at least an 80 percent contact between the lining and drum, the linings must be ground by use of a concentric grinder before they are installed to the vehicle or by use of a spindle-mounted grinder to ensure a concentric shoe-to-drum fit (see Fig. 14-48). To grind the lining, fasten the grinder attachment to the spindle so that the grinder can be rotated freely on the spindle while remaining square to the shoes and firm to the spindle. Then adjust the electric motor so that the abrasive disk covers the lining. Now measure the drum diameter. Say, for example, it is 17.280 in [438.9 mm]. Loosen the hand nuts on the grinder adjusting arm, turn the adjusting handle so that the micrometer reads 0.280 in [0.71 mm] and the pointer is slightly past 17, and then lock the setting. Now rotate the grinder so that the abrasive disk is near the heel of the rearward shoe. Turn the eccentric cam to bring the lining toward the disk. Reposition the disk near the toe of the rear brake shoe and turn the anchor to bring the lining near the disk. Recheck the lining-to-disk contact at the heel, readjust, and then recheck and readjust the toe. When the forward and rear shoes are adjusted so that the linings at the toe and heel contact the abrasive disk, you can then start the dusty job of grinding the brakes. Although the grinding machine has its own vacuum cleaner, a second vacuum cleaner should also be used. It is mandatory that you use a spray paint mask and goggles to protect your eyes and your lungs from the asbestos dust.

After donning mask and goggles, start the electric motor and rotate the grinder on the spindle to remove the high spots from the linings. After each grind-rotation, reduce the diameter of your grinder by turning the micrometer feed. Continue turning the micrometer after each revolution until it reads 17.265. The shoe diameter is then reduced by 0.070 in [1.778 mm], which is the recommended running clearance between the lining and drum. A closer running clearance may cause brake drag and would reduce power. After the grinding is completed, remove all dust from the brake assembly with a vacuum cleaner—do not use compressed air.

When the lining cannot be ground because no grinder is available, the brakes can be adjusted only after the drum and planetary drive are reassembled and the bearing preload is adjusted.

At this point in the reassembly, rotate the hub and simultaneously turn one eccentric cam in clockwise rotation until the lining comes in contact with the drum and slightly drags. Now loosen the anchor nut and turn the anchor (in either direction) to take away

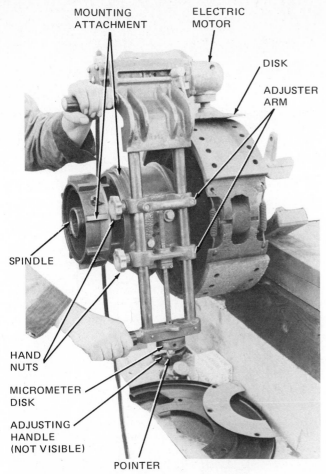

MOUNTING ATTACHMENT

ELECTRIC MOTOR

DISK

ADJUSTER ARM

SPINDLE

HAND NUTS

MICROMETER DISK

ADJUSTING HANDLE (NOT VISIBLE)

POINTER

Fig. 14-48 View of spindle-mounted shoe grinder installed.

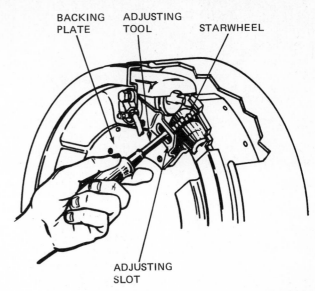

BACKING PLATE

ADJUSTING TOOL

STARWHEEL

ADJUSTING SLOT

Fig. 14-49 Adjusting the brakes. (*International Harvester Company*)

the drag. Once again turn the eccentric cam until a drag is felt and again rotate the anchor until the drag is removed.

Repeat this adjustment procedure until the rotation of the anchor will no longer release the drag. When this occurs, tighten the anchor locknut while holding the anchor and then turn the eccentric cam counterclockwise to remove the drag. Repeat this entire procedure with the other brake shoe of the same wheel.

Brake Adjustment: Two Double-end Wheel Cylinders After the brake shoes are concentrically ground to fit the drum diameter and reinstalled to the backing plate, the wheel hub mounted and adjusted, and the brakes bled (see the procedure for bleeding brakes in Unit 17), you can then adjust the brakes.

To adjust the brakes (see Fig. 14-49), insert the adjusting tool or a screwdriver into one adjusting slot (in the backing plate) to engage with the star wheel. Now move the tool upward to rotate the star wheel and repeat this procedure until the brake drags, and then repeat this procedure with the other shoe. Next, apply the brakes several times to center both shoes and once again make the adjustment until both brake shoes drag. Now remove the drag by turning the star wheel five notches in the opposite direction.

Review Questions

1. Define the term *brake* as it relates to on- and off-highway equipment.

2. Which six factors, to some extent, adversely affect the deceleration (stopping distance) of a motor vehicle or equipment?

3. Briefly outline six methods to increase the brake torque of any type of foundation brake.

4. List the major components of a hydraulic brake system.

5. What are the functions of the (*a*) compensating port, (*b*) residual check valve in the master cylinder?

6. (*a*) Explain why, when the primary system has lost all its brake fluid, the secondary system operates and applies the brakes. (*b*) Which brakes are applied—the front or the rear?

7. Outline the preparation and bleeding procedure of a dual-master cylinder.

8. List some of the differences among the various

9. (*a*) List the basic parts of a brake shoe. (*b*) What method is used to identify the coefficient of the brake lining or brake block? (*c*) Outline the methods used to attach the shoe linings or blocks to the brake shoes.

10. What is the function of (*a*) the wheel cylinder, (*b*) the wheel-cylinder piston, (*c*) the piston cup?

11. Define (*a*) servo-foundation brake, (*b*) nonservo foundation brake.

    hydraulic-actuated drum-type foundation brakes.

12. List the parts or components which could contribute to reduced brake efficiency, other than hydraulic or foundation brake failure.

Unit 15
Disk Brakes

A disk brake assembly (floating or fixed caliper design) consists of a wheel hub and disk assembly, caliper with wheel cylinder (floating or fixed to the adaptor or anchor plate), one set of lining pads, and a splash plate.

Disk Brakes Versus Drum Brakes   Although drum foundation brakes provide the necessary braking torque to stop a vehicle safely, all disk brakes have inherent characteristics which provide for greater safety and effectiveness. One reason a drum brake is inferior to the disk brake is that it dissipates heat less readily. Again, where disk brakes are concerned, brake fade due to overheating is nearly impossible. On designs where it is possible, the brake is oil cooled. With disk brakes, water fade is also very minimal because the air current and disk rotation dry the moisture from the disk surface, and the lining contact against the rotor surface wipes the lining clean.

In summary, because of their design, disk brakes versus drum foundation brakes have superior stopping performance and higher braking torque, are easier to maintain, and are lighter in weight.

Further advantages of disk brakes over drum brakes are that (1) higher application pressure is possible because the brake assembly cannot be distorted and (2) disk brake contact between the rotating and stationary friction surface is always parallel. The applied force acts, therefore, directly 180° on the friction surface, allowing greater friction efficiency and less brake torque variation. On drum brakes, both friction surfaces are curved, and the applied force from the brake shoe to the drum is always on an angle, reducing the friction efficiency.

The operating principle is the same for all disk brakes, regardless of design, size, or method of actuation. The mechanical force, hydraulic force, or air pressure forces the stationary or rotating friction lining pads or plates against the stationary or rotating reaction surfaces.

Floating and Fixed Caliper Disk Brakes   Many of you will be familiar with floating and fixed caliper disk brakes since they are small enough to be used on cars. Both straddle the rotor. However, the floating caliper differs from the fixed caliper in that the former generally has one or two wheel cylinders positioned in the inboard side of the caliper housing and it is supported by two guide pins which are fastened to the adapter or by guides machined to it. The adapter is bolted to the steering knuckle or the axle housing. Because the caliper slides on the guide pins or adapters, an even force is placed on the disk when the brakes are applied (see Fig. 15-1).

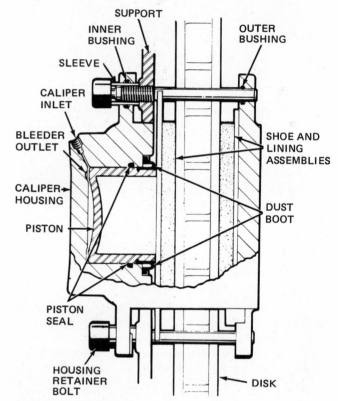

Fig. 15-1 Sectional view of a floating caliper and disk. (*Chrysler Canada Ltd.*)

A fixed caliper is bolted to the steering knuckle or to the axle housing. It consists of two units—the inboard caliper housing and the outboard caliper housing, both having a one- or two-wheel cylinder. When the brakes are applied, the inside and outside piston move out, forcing the lining pads against the disk (see Fig. 15-2).

When the truck is equipped with disk brakes on the front axle and conventional drum brakes on the rear axle, the braking system requires an additional valve—the combination valve, which improves balance and braking control. Furthermore, in the event that one system loses its pressure, this valve is instrumental in causing a warning light to signal the operator of the impending pressure loss.

Combination Valve   The combination valve (see Fig. 15-3) is composed of more than one valve and serves multiple functions. Some braking systems use a combination valve having only two valves. On earlier cars and trucks the valves located within the combination valve were separate single units.

NOTE   When testing a combination valve, always conform to the specifications in the applicable ser-

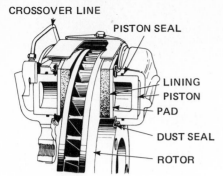

Fig. 15-2   Cutaway view of a fixed caliper and disk.

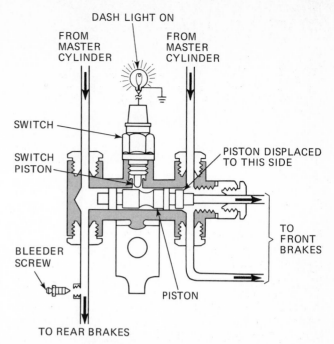

Fig. 15-4   Sectional view of a warning light switch. (*Wagner Electric Sales Corporation*)

vice manual because the recommended test pressures sometimes vary among manufacturers.

As mentioned previously, the purpose of a dual braking system is to prevent total loss of braking power in the event the primary or secondary system loses its braking pressure. One of the valves located within the combination valve is the warning valve (sometimes called the pressure differential valve or system effectiveness indicator). It senses the pressure loss and closes the electric circuit. This causes the warning light switch to effect illumination of the instrument panel.

Warning Light Switch   The warning light switch (see Fig. 15-4) consists, in part, of the sliding piston with tapered ramps on both ends and a mechanically actuated electric switch. Some designs have a bypass valve incorporated which leads to the rear brakes. When the brakes are released, residual line pressure acts on the left side of the sliding piston, but the switch spring holds the spool in position. Under normal braking conditions, because of the equal pressure in the primary and secondary systems, the spool remains in this position.

If the secondary line pressure is lost, the spool is forced to the lower pressure side (the left). The switch pin, then being forced out of its groove, closes the switch and the electric circuit.

When the pressure is lost in the primary system, the spool shifts to the right, opens the small port,

and allows full application pressure to flow through the bypass port to the rear wheel cylinder. When the cause of failure is eliminated and the brakes are bled, the sliding spool, on the first brake application, automatically returns to its rest position.

NOTE   Some warning light switches operate slightly differently in that the valve, when moved by unequal pressure, remains in that position until it is moved mechanically. (See service manual for specific operation.)

Proportional Valve   Another valve within the combination valve is the proportional valve (also called a pressure ratio or pressure control valve). The purpose of the proportional valve is to improve balance of front-to-rear braking by reducing the application pressure to the rear wheel cylinder when the brakes are severely applied. This limits the tendency of the rear wheels to skid earlier than the front wheels.

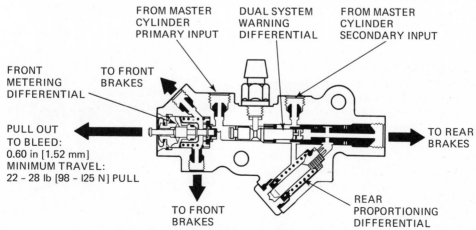

Fig. 15-3   Sectional view of a combination valve. (*Wagner Electric Sales Corporation*)

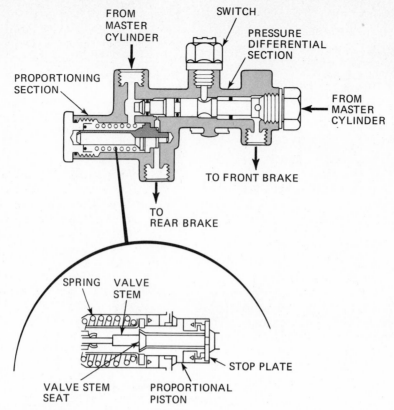

Fig. 15-5 Sectional view of a warning light and proportional valve. (*Wagner Electric Sales Corporation*)

The proportional valve consists of the components shown in Fig. 15-5. When at rest, or during normal brake application, the spring maintains the proportional piston to the right, and the valve stem rests against the stop plate. During normal brake application, fluid up to approximately 300 to 500 psi [2067 to 3445 kPa] flows from the master cylinder into the spring portion of the valve, through the space between the valve stem and proportional piston, around the stop plate, and out to the rear wheel cylinder.

NOTE The pressure applied from the primary and secondary master cylinder is equal.

When the system pressure increases, say, to 400 psi [2756 kPa], the force on the large area of the proportional piston is then greater than the spring force on the piston. The piston moves to the left, seats (or partially seats) the valve stem reducing the fluid flow and the pressure to the rear wheels, to a ratio slightly below 2:1. To cite an example: If the valve is to restrict the flow at 500 psi [3445 kPa], then the secondary pressure would be 800 psi [5512 kPa], when the primary pressure is 1000 psi [6890 kPa].

Metering Valve The third valve in the combination valve is the metering valve, also called the disk balance valve or holdoff valve. The function of this valve is to delay the brake application to the primary circuit until the system pressure approaches about 120 psi [826.8 kPa]. The secondary pressure then

overcomes the shoe return spring force and lightly applies the rear brakes, before the disk brakes are applied. This ensures controlled braking and good steering control at the beginning of braking.

The metering valve consists of the components shown in Fig. 15-6. When the brakes are not applied, the check valve is held open by the stem through the diaphragm, allowing fluid to flow to and from the primary master cylinder reservoir and pass

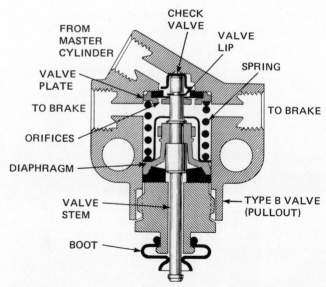

Fig. 15-6 Sectional view of a metering valve in the brake-release position. (*Wagner Electric Sales Corporation*)

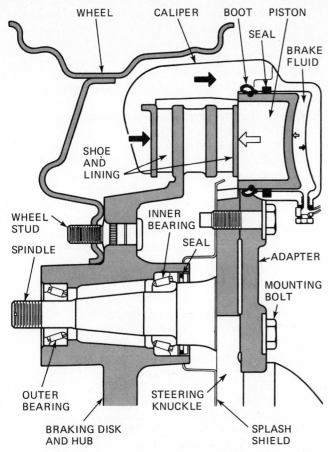

WHEEL CALIPER BOOT PISTON
SEAL
BRAKE
FLUID
SHOE
AND
LINING
WHEEL
STUD
SPINDLE
INNER
BEARING
SEAL
ADAPTER
MOUNTING
BOLT
OUTER
BEARING
STEERING
KNUCKLE
BRAKING DISK
AND HUB
SPLASH
SHIELD

Fig. 15-7 Sectional view of a floating caliper disk brake assembly. (*International Harvester Company*)

rise in the primary circuit to equal the secondary pressure. After both pressures rise and approach 500 psi [3445 kPa], the secondary pressure should then read less than the primary circuit pressure. **NOTE** See the applicable service manual for the specific pressure.

The pressure on various brake applications must conform with the pressures specified in the service manual if the combination valve is to be qualified as operational.

Floating Caliper Disk Brake Design The disks, or rotors, of floating caliper disk brakes may be of cast iron or of steel. They may be bolted to the wheel hub or may form part of the wheel hub (see Fig. 15-7). The rotor may be solid or have cooling fins (between the machined friction surfaces) which cause an air flow to cool the disks when the wheel rotates. The rotation and subsequent centrifugal force remove contaminants from the rotor friction surface.

The disk is protected on one side by the tire and disk wheel and on the other side by a splash plate (shield) bolted to the steering knuckle or axle housing. The caliper slides in grooves machined on the caliper and adapter or floats on two guide pins or bolts supported in the adapter or anchor plate. Machined guide pads on the anchor and caliper align the caliper with the adapter. **NOTE** The guide pins do not anchor the brake shoes. The lugs on the brake shoes rest against the caliper and act as anchors.

When the brakes are applied, the braking torque is transmitted from the outboard shoe lug to the caliper, and from the inboard shoe lug directly to the adapter. The caliper housing is usually a one-piece casting with one- or two-wheel cylinder bores. The wheel cylinder bore diameter varies between $1\frac{1}{2}$ to $3\frac{1}{2}$ in [28.1 to 88.9 mm], depending on the application force. The pistons are usually of a cup design, minimizing the heat transfer from the piston to the brake fluid. They are made basically of steel and then chrome- or nickel-plated to prevent corrosion.

A square cross-sectional O ring located in the square-cut groove of the piston seals the piston to the cylinder wall. Otherwise the piston seal is installed in a square-cut groove in the cylinder bore. A dust boot fits into or over the end of the cylinder bore. The inner lip of the dust boot rests either on the reduced-diameter surface of the piston or in a groove within the piston, preventing contaminants from entering the piston and cylinder bore.

The brake linings or brake pads are riveted or bonded to the shoes. Not all brake shoes of the floating caliper design are identical—the lugs differ in location and shape, and on some disk brakes the outboard shoe is longer than the inboard shoe.

OPERATION When the brakes are applied, the pressure within the system rises, moving the piston outward. This moves the inboard shoe against the disk. As the force against the disk increases, the caliper, guided by the guide pins or groove (see Fig. 15-8), is forced inward and thus forces the outboard and inboard shoes against the disk. Both shoes now clamp the disk.

through the orifice in the valve plate. As soon as the pressure approaches about 10 psi [68.9 kPa], it forces the check valve downward against the force of the diaphragm and against the valve plate, closing the orifice and cutting off the fluid flow to the front brakes. As the system pressure approaches 120 psi [826.8 kPa], it acts on the check valve and valve plate surfaces, forcing the stem along with the valve plate downward and creating a clearance between the valve plate and seat. A metered amount of fluid then flows to the disk brakes. As the system pressure increases, the clearance increases, permitting greater fluid flow.

When the pressure reaches 500 psi [3445 kPa], the valve is fully open. Now, with no flow restriction, the primary and secondary pressures are equal.

Testing the Metering and Proportional Valves When the driver complains that the brakes are oversensitive, the combination valve may be defective. If it is, it must be replaced, for it is a nonserviceable unit. It is therefore important that you prove to yourself that this valve is, in fact, defective. To make this assessment, install one pressure gauge into the primary and one into the secondary brake circuit and then apply the brakes very slowly and observe both gauges. They should indicate no pressure in the primary circuit until the secondary circuit reaches the specified pressure, say, about 120 psi [826.8 kPa]. Not until then should the pressure

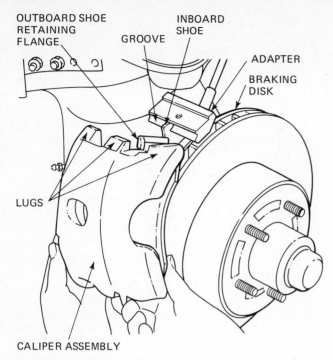

Fig. 15-8 View of caliper partly removed showing the groove in the adapter and mating guide lugs on the caliper. (*Chrysler Corporation*)

On both types of disk brakes the outboard shoe transmits its torque to the caliper and from the flat machined surface or the grooves onto the adapter. The inboard shoe transmits its braking torque directly to the adapter. As the wheel cylinder starts to move outward, the hydraulic pressure locks the square seal ring to the piston groove and the cylinder wall, deflecting the seal ring (see Fig. 15-9). As the pressure is released within the cylinder, the distorted seal pulls the piston into its bore. The displaced fluid then returns to the reservoir. **NOTE** Automatic adjustments occur whenever the piston relocates outwardly owing to lining wear.

Fixed Caliper Disk Brakes   The main difference between the fixed and floating caliper brakes is that

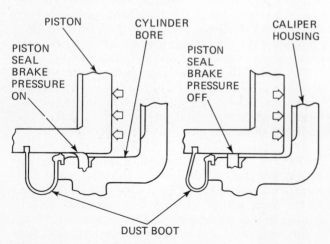

Fig. 15-9 View of seal action during the applied and release positions. (*Chrysler Corporation*)

the fixed caliper is solidly fastened and therefore cannot move. Furthermore, the fixed caliper consists of an inboard and an outboard housing bolted to a single unit. Each caliper half has either one- or two-wheel cylinder bores with pistons and dust boots similar to the floating caliper. Some models use square piston seals, whereas others use U cup or L-shaped cups as piston seals. When any type of piston seal other than the square O ring is used, each piston has a light coil spring to maintain a low friction contact between the lining and disk surfaces. Internal passages or an external tube connects the inboard with the outboard wheel cylinder. Small O rings are used as fluid seals to seal the passages between the two caliper halves. The brake shoes are usually identical in shape and size and are retained by various pins or clip arrangements (see Fig. 15-10).

Disk Brake Service   The most common complaints associated with disk brake failure are noise, chatter, and pedal pulsation. Often major brake service is not required, and a replacement of the brake lining or readjustment of the wheel bearings or freeing of the caliper on its guides, guide pins, or bolts is all that is required.

Nevertheless, a truck which has front disk brakes and rear drum brakes can encounter problems parallel to those of a truck with servo brakes. (See instructions for inspecting and servicing servo brakes in Unit 14). In addition, however, there could be malfunction of the combination valve.

To service disk brakes, first raise the truck and support it safely. Mark the position of the front wheels and then remove them. The disk brake assembly will then clearly be visible (see Fig. 15-11).

Before starting to disassemble the brakes, make the checks recommended in the instructions for inspecting and servicing servo brakes in Unit 14. In addition, check the wear of the outboard and inboard lining and the surface condition of the disk and measure the disk thickness, the taper, and the runout before starting to disassemble the brakes. If the inboard shoe is worn much more than the outboard shoe, this indicates that the caliper movement is restricted.

NOTE   The inboard shoe normally shows somewhat more wear than the outboard shoe because it first comes in contact with the disk, and it moves the caliper to engage the outboard shoe with the disk. If the linings are worn to a taper, this indicates that the caliper is misaligned or the guide, guide bushing bolts, or pins are worn, bent, or loose. If the vehicle has been out of service for a time, the disks may be rusted. When the vehicle is placed in service, the rust can score the disk and become imbedded in the linings. A pulsating brake pedal or one with a long stroke indicates a distorted disk or high runout. Again, the combination valve may be defective or the wheel bearing loose. When any of these symptoms is evident, or when the brake lining is worn past the maximum specified wear limit, the caliper must be removed.

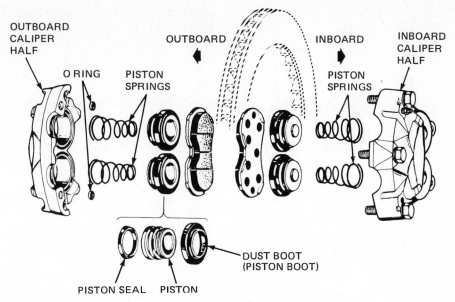

Fig. 15-10 Exploded view of a fixed caliper disk brake. (*Wagner Electric Sales Corporation*)

Removing a Floating Caliper A general procedure for removing a floating caliper is applicable to all types and makes. Start by cleaning the entire brake assembly, including hose and tube fittings. Remove about two-thirds of the fluid from the primary master cylinder reservoir, to avoid an overflow as you force the piston inward to gain clearance between the linings and disk. Next, loosen and remove the mounting bolts that hold the caliper to the adapter (see Fig. 15-12) and lift the caliper from the disk. Remove the inboard shoe and dislodge the outboard shoe. Use a rope or wire to hang the caliper to the suspension or frame but make certain not to twist or bend the hydraulic hose. Next, check the caliper piston for fluid leakage and for damage on the machined mating surfaces of the caliper and adapter. If the caliper checks out satisfactorily, clean it and then install new shoes, implicitly following the manufacturer's service manual recommendations relevant to replacement of guide bushings, sleeve, seats positioners and pins, and shoe position. If there is evidence of a fluid leak or if the machined mating surfaces are worn, the caliper must be replaced and sometimes also the adapter. To replace the adapter, first remove the special mounting bolts that hold it to the spindle support and bolt a new one in place. **NOTE** Since the mounting bolts used are especially designed for the adapter, they should never be replaced with any other type. They must also be torqued precisely to specification.

Before reinstalling the caliper to the adapter, you should always check the disk for surface damage (rust or scoring) and measure the disks for parallelism, runout, and wear. To do this, remove the dust cap and the cotter key and then tighten the spindle nut to remove the existing wheel bearing end play. Install a dial indicator as shown in Fig. 15-13. The indicator spindle should be about 1 in [25.4 mm] from the disk edge. Zero the dial indicator and then rotate the disk to check the runout. If the runout exceeds that specified in the service manual (which is about 0.004 in [0.10 mm], the disks must be resurfaced or replaced. **NOTE** If disks are to be resurfaced, mark the maximum runout point. If one

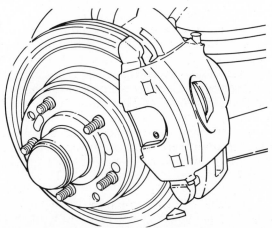

Fig. 15-11 View of disk brake assembly with tire removed. (*Wagner Electric Sales Corporation*)

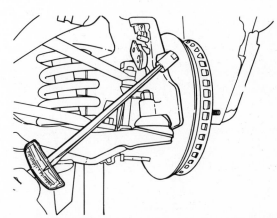

Fig. 15-12 Removing mounting bolts from caliper. (*Wagner Electric Sales Corporation*)

240

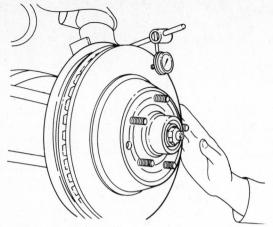

Fig. 15-13 Checking disk for lateral runout. (*Wagner Electric Sales Corporation*)

Fig. 15-15 Disk installed on machine for resurfacing. (*Wagner Electric Sales Corporation*)

disk needs to be resurfaced, you must also resurface the other one to ensure balanced braking.

If both disks pass these checks, measure thickness variation 1 in [25.4 mm] from the edge at four or more places around the disk and compare the measurements with the service manual specification (see Fig. 15-14). If either disk is not within specification, both disks must be resurfaced. If either disk is worn beyond the maximum wear limit, both disks must be replaced because the worn condition will reduce heat dissipation.

Finally, measure the disk taper at four or more places along the outer friction surface and the inner friction surface. If the measurements vary more than 0.003 in [0.076 mm], the taper is excessive and both disks must be resurfaced.

Resurfacing the Disk   If you have a good disk lathe to resurface the disk, you may do the resurfacing; otherwise, you should replace the disks. **NOTE** Resurfacing is a precision job not to be taken lightly.

Commence by removing the dust cap, cotter key, and spindle nut. Tap on the outer disk circumference to loosen the outer wheel bearing from the hub and spindle. Next, remove the wheel hub, and from it remove the seal and the inner wheel bearing. Clean

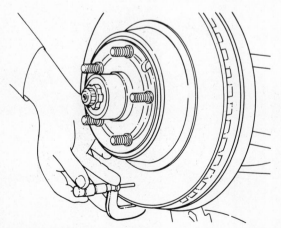

Fig. 15-14 Measuring rotor thickness and/or taper. (*Wagner Electric Sales Corporation*)

away any grease or rust from the assembly and then dry it with compressed air.

The general procedure to resurface a disk is as follows (after making sure your two cutting tools are sharp [see Fig. 15-15]):

1.   Using the correct adapter, mount the wheel hub to the spindle so that the disk is centered between the two tool holders. You may have to reposition the tool holders and the holder bracket to achieve the desired position.
2.   Install a dial indicator so that the dial spindle is 1 in [25.4 mm] from the edge of the outer disk and then slowly turn the disk. The dial indicator must show the same runout reading, at the same point as when it was mounted to the spindle. If the disk runout is not the same and not at the same point, you must reposition the wheel hub on the spindle until it comes within the runout.
3.   Set both micrometer adjusting screws to a full number or line and then mount the cutting tools so that each tip rests against the disk surface. Turn each micrometer knob counterclockwise one even number to retract the cutting tools from the disk.
4.   Manually turn the spindle handle so as to move the cutting tool table to the innermost friction surface.
5.   Start the electric motor and adjust the cutting tools to the zero setting or one line above. Now manually turn the handle to move the cutting tool table outward (to take the high spots from both sides of the disk).
6.   When you have accomplished this, bring the cutting tool table inward again and reset both cutting tools evenly one graduation or more. Start the motor and position the lever to automatic feedout.
7.   When the final cut is made, hold emery cloth (100 grit) to both surfaces to remove the cutting tool marks.

NOTE   Avoid removing more surface from one side of the disk than from the other, for this could affect braking, and never use one which is below or machined below minimum thickness.

After resurfacing the disk, clean it and the wheel

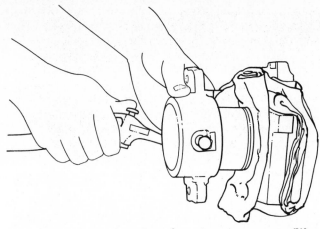

Fig. 15-16 Removing piston by using air pressure. (*Wagner Electric Sales Corporation*)

hub thoroughly. Clean, check, and repack the wheel bearings. Insert the inner wheel bearing and install a new hub seal. Before placing the wheel hub onto the spindle, check it and the splash shield for damage and twist. Next, slide the assembly onto the spindle. Install the outer wheel bearing, washer, and nut and tighten the nut to the torque specified in the service manual. **NOTE** if this is your first attempt to resurface, you should take the precaution to recheck the disk runout.

Caliper Servicing   If it is apparent that the caliper needs to be serviced, prepare to disassemble it first by cleaning your workbench and tools. Dismount the brake hose from the caliper and proceed as follows. If you have not previously done so, remove the shoe support spring from the piston, the bleeder screw from the inboard ear, the sleeve, the rubber bushing from the groove in each of the four caliper ears, and the inlet protection cap. Fully drain the wheel cylinder and discard the fluid and then remove the dust boot from the cylinder groove. Carefully mount the caliper in a soft-jaw vise without distorting the piston bore. Use a piston retracter to remove the piston. If this tool is not available, use a piece of ¾-in [19.05-mm] plywood (5 in by 6 in [127 by 152.4 mm]) wrapped in a shop towel and place the plywood between the piston and outboard legs. Use just enough shop air pressure to ease the piston from its bore (see Fig. 15-16). Proceed with caution so as to avoid cuts or abrasions to your hands. With a small plastic or wooden pointed stick, remove the piston seal from the cylinder bore.   **CAUTION**   Do not use a metal tool, for it could burr the edges of the groove or scratch the surfaces.

CLEANING AND INSPECTING   Remove dust and dirt from the caliper exterior and then wash the components in hot, soapy water. Dry them with compressed air.

Inspect the piston and the cylinder bore for scoring, pitting, and for corrosion marks. If the marks are deep, the caliper must be replaced. Light scores, pits, and stains can, however, be removed with crocus cloth. When polishing the piston or cylinder bore, use rotary motion only. Do not forcefully slide the cloth in or out.   **NOTE** Although some manufacturers recommend nothing more than crocus cloth, others recommend a special hone to polish the cylinder bore.

When the pistons and bores are polished, clean the seal and dust boot grooves with a bronze wire brush and brake fluid and then clean with compressed air. Wash all parts with brake fluid (or a cleaning fluid recommended by the manufacturer) and dry them with compressed air. Also, blow dry the passageways and grooves. If black stains are still present on the piston or cylinder walls, do not replace the parts. Black stain is caused merely by the piston seals and is harmless.

If the cylinder bore has been honed, check the piston clearance with a feeler gauge. If it is worn beyond service manual specifications (0.006 in [0.15 mm] is about the limit), the caliper must be replaced.

REASSEMBLY   First, make certain all components are clean. Next, dip the piston seal in brake fluid and install it into the cylinder groove. This is done by placing part of the seal into the groove and then gently working around with your finger until the remainder of the seal slides into the groove. The seal must not be twisted or rolled. Lubricate the dust boot with brake fluid and then start working it (with your fingers) into the groove. The boot may at first appear to be too large, but with a little patience it installs snugly into the groove.

To install the piston, first install the bleeder screw and plug the inlet opening. Next, generously coat the piston, the seal, and the dust boot with brake fluid. Place the piston above the dust boot so that part of the piston is inside the dust boot. Simultaneously push the inserted piston downward to the side and rotate it while you finger-press on the outer circumference of the dust boot. The trapped air below the piston forces the remaining part of the dust boot lip outward and around the piston. As the piston is forced further inward, the boot lips snap into the piston groove. You can then remove the bleeder screw and force the piston inward until it bottoms. Reinstall the bleeder screw or use the method shown in Fig. 15-17 to install the piston boot. Next, install

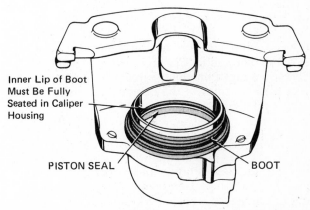

Inner Lip of Boot Must Be Fully Seated in Caliper Housing

PISTON SEAL   BOOT

Fig. 15-17 Installing caliper piston boot. (*General Motors Corporation*)

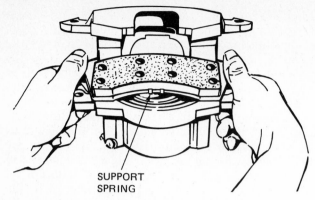

Fig. 15-18 Installing inward shoe. (*GMC Truck and Coach Division of General Motors Corporation*)

the inner and outer rubber bushings and the sleeves according to the service manual instructions. **NOTE** Dip the bushings in water to allow for easier insertion and positioning. Install the brake shoe support spring. Position the inward shoe into the adapter (see Fig. 15-18) and the outward shoe into the caliper after making certain the shoes are fully recessed in the caliper and adapter. While holding the outward shoe in position, guide the caliper downward, over the disk and onto the adapter. Slide new bolts through the sleeve and through the mounting bracket (adapter) so that the bolts pass under the retaining ears of the inboard shoes. Then push them through the holes in the outboard shoes to engage the bolt thread with the threaded bores in the outboard caliper ears and then tighten the bolts to specification. **NOTE** Some manufacturers suggest (to ensure good alignment) bleeding the caliper and then applying the brakes before torquing the mounting bolts or guide pins to specification.

Always use new brake hoses when performing a major brake service to preclude surfacing of hidden hose flaws at a later date. When installing the hose, make sure you place the specified number of gaskets in the correct position and that you do not overtorque the fitting.

Servicing a Fixed Caliper Disk Brake Although the procedure to service a fixed caliper disk brake (see Fig. 15-19) is much the same as that for a single- or dual-piston sliding caliper, there are a few minor differences. For instance, with the former you can usually remove the brake pads without removing the caliper simply by forcing the piston back into the cylinder bores and then removing the antirattling clip. You can then remove the two disk pads. The procedure to remove the caliper, the disk, the dust boot, and the piston is the same, as is that for the piston and cylinder bore service (see Figs. 15-11 to 15-17).

NOTE When assembling a caliper where the piston has the seal groove, make certain the seal lip points in the correct direction. Also take care not to cut or damage the seals while inserting the piston. Do not forget to install the O rings into the grooves of the crossover passages if the unit is so designed.

Mechanical Disk Brakes The mechanical disk brake shown in Fig. 15-20 is used on some farm tractors, on smaller track machinery, and as a parking brake. Although it is the earliest of the disk brakes, it has undergone considerable modification during the last 30 years, but on the whole, its operating principle remains the same. Two disks, each having the friction material riveted or bonded to them, are splined to the drive shaft, drive axle, or differential shaft. An actuating unit consisting of two actuating disks is located between the two brake lining disks. The inside of the brake cover and housing are the brake reaction surfaces. On the inside of the two actuating disks four equally spaced, tapered oval inserts are positioned in which the steel actuating balls lie. The two actuating disks are held together by four coil springs. A link fastened to each half is centrally joined and is connected with a pin to the actuating rod. When the mechanical disk brake is installed, the housing cover and the brake pin (not shown) become the brake torque stop lugs.

BRAKE RELEASE When the brake pedal is released, the pressure in the wheel cylinder is reduced to the residual pressure. This allows the coil spring to pull the brake lever downward and the four coil springs to hold the two actuating disks together and thereby forces the four steel balls to their lowest point in the oval recess. Under these circumstances (when prop-

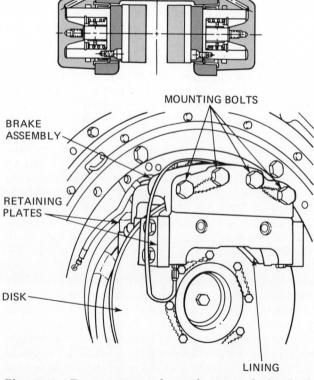

Fig. 15-19 Front section and outside views of a fixed caliper disk brake used on a large dump truck. (*WABCO, An American-Standard Company*)

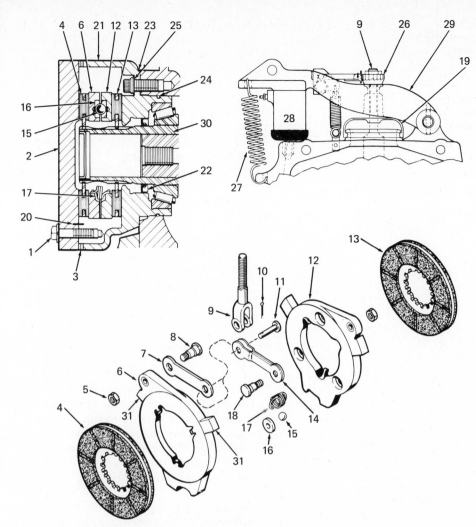

1. Cap screw with lock washer
2. Brake cover
3. Shims
4. Outer brake lining disk
5. Nut
6. Actuating disk (outer)
7. Link
8. Bolt
9. Brake rod
10. Cotter pin
11. Yoke pin
12. Actuating disk (inner)
13. Inner lining disk
14. Link
15. Balls
16. Inserts
17. Springs
18. Spring stud
19. Dust cap
20. Roll pin
21. Brake housing
22. Seal
23. Gasket
24. O-ring seal
25. Cap screw
26. Automatic adjuster
27. Return spring
28. Wheel cylinder
29. Brake lever
30. Differential shaft
31. Torque lugs

Fig. 15-20 Sectional and exploded views of a mechanical disk brake. (*J I Case Company Agricultural Equipment Division*)

erly adjusted) the friction disks have the necessary clearance between the four friction surfaces. When the brakes are applied, the wheel cylinder moves downward, pivoting the brake lever and pulling the brake rod upward. The latter then pulls on the two links, causing the two actuating halves to rotate toward the pull rods. This action causes the four steel balls to roll up on their ramps. Consequently, both actuating units are forced apart and the two lining disks are forced against the four friction surfaces. When this occurs, the actuating unit rotates slightly. The torque lugs come to rest against the lugs in the housing and against the brake pin and thereby transmit the brake torque to the housing.

When the brake is being released, the wheel cylinder retracts, the brake lever and the pushrod are pulled downward by the coil springs, and the four disk springs pull the two actuating disks toward each other. The four steel balls then retract on their ramps to the lowest point in the oval recesses.

A modified version of this type of disk brake which has greatly improved the brake torque is shown in Fig. 15-21. The modification consists of (1) an actuating disk splined to the drive axle or differential shaft; (2) an actuating drum which has an external friction surface fastened with coil

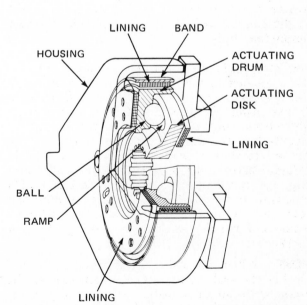

Fig. 15-21 Schematic view of the modified mechanical disk brake. (*J I Case Company Agricultural Equipment Division*)

springs; (3) lining material riveted to the outside surface of the actuating disk and actuating drum; (4) four equally spaced elliptical recesses inside the actuating disk and actuating drum (tapered downward toward the center) in which the actuating steel balls rest; (5) a brake band (see Fig. 15-22) surrounding the actuating drum, whose ends are connected to the links; (6) an adjusting nut screwed to the actuating rod, and the self-adjusting device (see Fig. 15-23) fastened to the brake lever. When correctly installed, adjusted, and in the release position, the retraction springs hold the brake band away from the actuating drum at a specified clearance. The brake cylinder fastened to the brake lever retracts, as does the pushrod, allowing the brake lever to pivot and the actuating rod to move downward.

BRAKE APPLICATION   When the tractor moves forward or in reverse, the actuating drum and disk rotate as a unit. When the brake is applied, the brake cylinder piston moves outward. This outward movement lifts the brake lever, which pulls on the pullrod and the inner and outer link. The brake band is then pulled against the actuating drum. The friction between the brake band lining and the drum friction surface causes a slight misalignment between the disk and actuating drum. The tapered recesses then come out of alignment, and the steel balls roll up on the tapered ramps, forcing the actuating disk and the actuating drum to separate and forcing the friction surfaces against the reaction surfaces. Because the actuating disk is splined to the drive axle or the differential shaft, retardation takes place. With increased brake force, a greater brake band friction is accomplished, and greater misalignment between the actuating disk and actuating drum is achieved. As a result the separating force increases, causing higher friction between the friction lining and the reaction surface. **NOTE**   When the tractor is moving, whether or not the brakes are applied, the actuating drum and disk rotate as a unit. The brake band is used, not only to cause the misalignment between the disk and the drum, but also to add to the retardation.

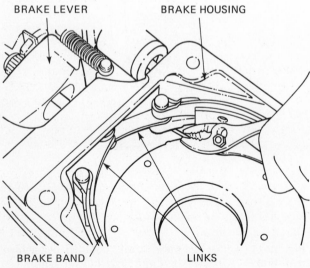

Fig. 15-22   View of brake band (installed).

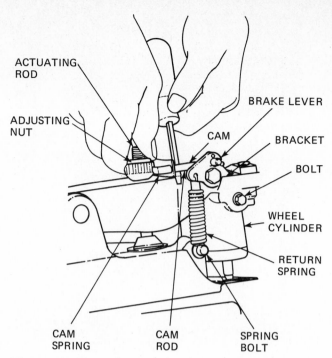

Fig. 15-23   View of automatic adjuster.

AUTOMATIC ADJUSTMENT   When the brake is applied, the brake cam pivots (owing to the lifting action of the brake lever) and causes the cam rod to move horizontally. When the brake is released, the nose of the camrod is held (through a small spring) in one notch of the ratchet nut (adjusting nut). As the brake band, actuating disk, and the actuating drum lining surface wear, the actuating rod travel increases. The brake cam then pivots even more so, causing the cam rod to move a greater distance. If the cam rod nose moves into the next notch of the ratchet nut, an adjustment takes place as the brake is released because the brake lever retracts (through its return spring) to its rest position, causing the brake cam to pivot. As the cam rod moves, the ratchet adjusting nut turns.

Multidisk Brakes   Multidisk brakes are used on large vehicles and track equipment to increase the braking torque. They are oil-applied, or they are air-over-oil-applied, and therefore oil-cooled. Let us take, for example, the brakes used on a 60-ton dump truck (see Fig. 15-24). The drive axle is of the planetary design (see the discussion of planetary drive wheel hub in Unit 13). The multidisk brake consists of two main assemblies, the brake assembly and the brake cylinder assembly. The brake assembly includes the outer gear (also called the drum), which is splined and bolted to the spindle. The hub is bolted to the outer side of the outer gear, and an O ring forms a seal between the hub and the end of the outer gear. The inner splines of the outer gear mesh with the outer splines of the steel reaction plates. The inner gear has two sets of outer splines and one set of inner splines. The right outer splines mesh with the wheel assembly, and those of the left set mesh with the internal friction disk splines (see Fig. 15-25).

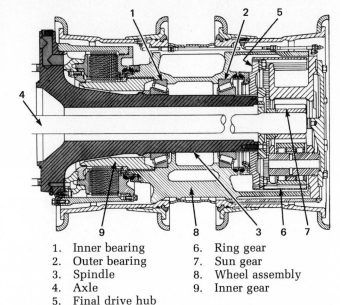

1. Inner bearing
2. Outer bearing
3. Spindle
4. Axle
5. Final drive hub
6. Ring gear
7. Sun gear
8. Wheel assembly
9. Inner gear

Fig. 15-24 Sectional view of final drive and brake assembly on a 60-ton truck. (*Caterpillar Tractor Co.*)

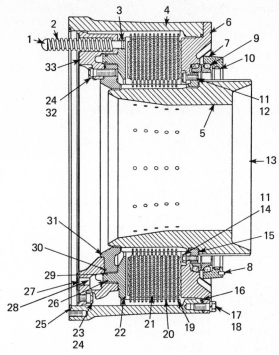

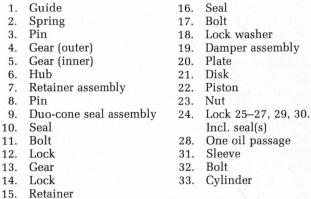

1. Guide		16. Seal
2. Spring		17. Bolt
3. Pin		18. Lock washer
4. Gear (outer)		19. Damper assembly
5. Gear (inner)		20. Plate
6. Hub		21. Disk
7. Retainer assembly		22. Piston
8. Pin		23. Nut
9. Duo-cone seal assembly		24. Lock 25–27, 29, 30.
10. Seal		Incl. seal(s)
11. Bolt		28. One oil passage
12. Lock		31. Sleeve
13. Gear		32. Bolt
14. Lock		33. Cylinder
15. Retainer		

Fig. 15-25 Sectional view of a multidisk brake assembly. (*Caterpillar Tractor Co.*)

The brake assembly, including the cylinder, is splined to the spindle, and the guides rest on the spindle. Three oil passages, sealed by an O ring, connect the brake assembly with the housing. One passage connects the master cylinder to the piston cavity. The piston flange fits into the sleeve and is sealed with two seal rings. Six cylinder guides are used to direct the piston as it moves out under oil pressure and retracts by the spring force when the oil pressure is reduced. **NOTE** When the brake is not applied, there is no air pressure in the rotary air chamber and no oil pressure in the master cylinder or brake piston cavities.

The oil that cools and lubricates the disk brakes and aids in the operation of the disk and plates is supplied by a vane pump. Whether or not the brakes are applied or released, the cooling oil passes through the second passage and is directed between the disk and the plate because of the spiral and radial grooves in the friction material. The third passage allows the oil from the final drive to return to the reservoir.

APPLIED POSITION As the air supply actuates the power piston, oil displaced by it enters the brake cylinder (see Fig. 15-25). The brake piston is then pushed out, forcing the disks and plates against the hub. Since the plates are splined to the stationary outer gear (drum), and the disks are splined to the rotating inner gear (hub), the friction created between the disks and plates retards wheel rotation. If the applied air pressure is increased, the oil pressure increases the force against the brake piston and thereby increases the friction between the plate and disk.

BRAKE RELEASE When the air pressure of the air control valve (application valve) is reduced or fully released, the air pressure in the rotary chamber and the hydraulic pressure in the master cylinder and in

the brake cylinder cavity are reduced or released. Subsequently, the lubricating pressure and spring force separate the plates and the disk, partly or fully releasing the brakes.

Servicing Multidisk Brakes A complete brake service is essential when the truck will not stop within the recommended distance or hold the vehicle on a specified grade or when routine test results do not measure up to the service manual specifications. Before starting the disassembly, place a drip pan under the assembly to catch the oil runout as the wheel assembly is separated from the mounting face of the spindle.

To service the brake assembly, remove the tire and rim, planetary drive, and wheel hub, as outlined in connection with servicing the planetary drive in Unit 13. Once the outlined components are removed, the brake assembly is exposed. Attach a sling and a hoist to the brake assembly and take up the slack. Screw two $\frac{1}{2}$-in [12.7-mm] NC 6-in [212.4-mm] guide pins into the end of the outer gear. The use of

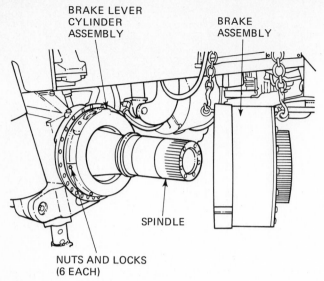

BRAKE LEVER CYLINDER ASSEMBLY

BRAKE ASSEMBLY

SPINDLE

NUTS AND LOCKS (6 EACH)

Fig. 15-26 Removing the brake assembly. (*Caterpillar Tractor Co.*)

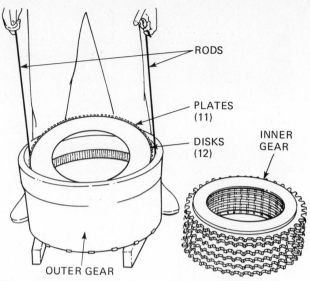

RODS

PLATES (11)

DISKS (12)

INNER GEAR

OUTER GEAR

Fig. 15-28 Removing plates and disks. (*Caterpillar Tractor Co.*)

guide pins ensures alignment and prevents damage to the splines, the bearing surface, the outer gear, and the brake cylinder. Next, remove the bolts that fasten the brake assembly to the spindle and pull the brake assembly (the inner splined gear) from the spindle (see Fig. 15-26). Attach a sling and hoist to the brake cylinder assembly to take up the slack, remove the nuts and locks, and then lift the assembly from the mounting surface of the spindle.

BRAKE CYLINDER ASSEMBLY To remove the piston from the cylinder, you must first remove the piston release springs. To release the spring force, place the brake cylinder assembly (springs facing downward) on a flat surface. Force the piston downward just enough to compress the springs so that the pins can be removed. Release the force and then screw three $\frac{3}{8}$-in [9.51-mm] NC screws into the piston to push it out of the cylinder. Remove the inner and outer piston seals and the bolts and locks that secure the sleeve to the cylinder. Lift out the sleeve and O ring. Finally, remove the piston guide and release springs (see Fig. 15-27).

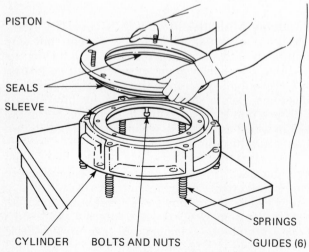

PISTON

SEALS

SLEEVE

CYLINDER

BOLTS AND NUTS

SPRINGS

GUIDES (6)

Fig. 15-27 Removing piston. (*Caterpillar Tractor Co.*)

Clean all parts in solvent and dry them with compressed air or clean them by the hot tank method. If the latter method is used, take precaution to follow all safety rules. Examine all parts for serviceability. If the piston surface is warped, bent, or cracked or if the seal grooves are damaged, the piston must be replaced. If the sleeve or guide is worn or damaged, it must be replaced. If the springs are bent or the height does not come within service manual specifications, they also must be replaced. The reassembly order is precisely the reverse of disassembly.

CAUTION When installing the piston seals, make certain the flat-face surface faces downward and that it is well lubricated before the piston is placed into the cylinder. Before lifting the cylinder onto the spindle, check that both mounting flanges are clean and install three new O ring seals into the grooves of the oil supply passages.

BRAKE ASSEMBLY When disassembling, place the brake assembly on two blocks so that the inner gear does not touch the floor surface. Lift out the inner gear and then using two $\frac{1}{8}$-in [3.17-mm] welding rods bent to form hooks, lift the plates and disks from the outer gear splines (see Fig. 15-28). Stack them on a clean bench in the order in which they were removed. **NOTE** The first plate you remove (that is facing toward the piston brake cylinder) has a friction surface bonded to the plate. The last plate also has a friction surface bonded to one side, and it faces toward the hub.

If it becomes necessary to remove the outer gear from the hub, first remove the mounting bolts and then use a sling and hoist to lift it from the hub. Discard the hub seal. If it becomes necessary to separate the inner gear from the hub, remove the six mounting screws threaded into the half-circle retainer to allow the hub to be lifted from the inner gear. Remove the toric seal rings (O rings) from the hub groove. Clean all parts in solvent and dry them with compressed air.

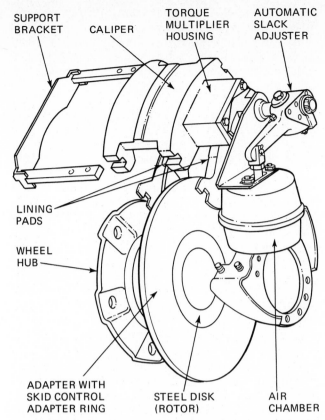

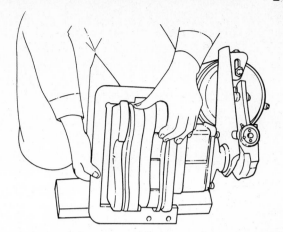

Fig. 15-30 A caliper assembly removed. (*B. F. Goodrich Engineered Systems Co.*)

REASSEMBLY Reassembly is precisely the reverse of disassembly. Before reassembling, make certain the components are spotlessly clean, that the plates and disks are well lubricated, and that all mounting bolts and nuts are torqued to specification. **NOTE** See the discussion of planetary drive in Unit 13 for installing duo-cone floating seals, wheel assembly, and bearing adjustment.

Air-Actuated Disk Brakes Because of the advantages of air-actuated disk brakes over drum brakes, the resultant marketability has brought manufacturers to produce several air-actuated disk brakes. Their brake torque ranges up to 85,000 lb · in [9597.91 N · m].

DESIGN All air-actuated disk brakes (see Fig. 15-29) are basically similar in design to a floating caliper disk brake having a single hydraulic piston. The greatest difference lies in the transmission of the actuating force from the air chamber to the input shaft (the torque-multiplying actuating device). Air-actuated disk brakes consist of a welded steel or cast iron disk which is fastened to an adapter. The adapter is fastened to the wheel hub. **NOTE** The adapter has the antiskid control exciter ring fastened to it.

The torque plate or bracket is bolted to the axle housing. The support brackets are bolted to the torque plate. The caliper is supported in rectangular slots in the support brackets, allowing the caliper, the lining pads, torque, multiplier, slack adjuster, and air chambers to slide freely along the support bracket rails. The outboard lining pad rests against the inside of the caliper, and the inboard lining pad rests against the actuating piston. The extended lining pad lugs rest on the support bracket rails. The torque-multiplying housing and air brake chamber bracket are bolted to the caliper. The automatic slack adjuster (or simply a lever) is splined to the power screw or input shaft (see Fig. 15-30).

The actuator or torque-multiplying device is a sealed unit located within the torque multiplier housing. Some designs also have an automatic adjusting device to maintain correct lining-to-rotor clearance, whereas others use an automatic slack ad-

Fig. 15-29 View of an air-actuated mechanical disk brake. (*B. F. Goodrich Engineered Systems Co.*)

INSPECTING AND MEASURING Inspect the inner and outer gears for external damage and the splines for 1(wear) grooves. If the splines are sufficiently grooved to cause the disk or plates to hang up, the gears must be replaced. This also holds true when the outer splines of the inner gear are worn to this extent.

NOTE Use a new plate when checking the wear of the inner splines of the outer gear and use a new disk when checking the wear of the outer spline on the inner gear. Also check the threaded bore of the outer gear for worn or damaged threads.

When inspecting the hub, check the toric seal ring bore for nicks and burrs. If any are present, remove them with an oil stone. Examine the friction surfaces of the plates for heat spots and cracks and the teeth for damage and wear. With a straight edge and feeler gauge determine if the surface is warped (coned).

Inspect the disk friction surfaces for deterioration, heat spots, warpage, and worn or damaged teeth. If the disk friction material starts to break loose from the plates, the disks should be replaced.

Measure the total height of the friction assembly, that is, the 2 one-sided bonded plates, 11 plates, and 12 disks. If the total height is below minimum specification, examine and measure the thickness of each disk and plate to determine which plates can be reused.

NOTE If the disk and plates are within their maximum wear limit but the total height is below minimum height, you may, in some instances, install one additional disk or plate.

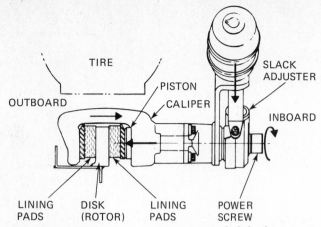

Fig. 15-31 View of a power screw air disk brake operating mechanism. (*B. F. Goodrich Engineered Systems Co.*)

juster for this purpose. The force-multiplying mechanism may be of a power screw, a wedge or helical-ramp design. In each case it converts the semirotation of the input shaft or the power screw shaft into a clamping force within the caliper. Simultaneously it multiplies the applied air chamber force needed to develop the required braking torque.

OPERATION; POWER SCREW When the air pressure is released from the air chamber (refer to Fig. 15-31), the slack adjuster semirotates the power screw in a counterclockwise rotation which, in turn, causes the power screw and piston to retract and the caliper to move to the left. This increases the distance between the piston and the left inside surface of the caliper. The clamping force then releases, to allow for a predesigned clearance between the rotor and the lining pads.

When the operator actuates the application valve, air under pressure enters the air chamber. Instantly the pushrod is moved outward and semirotates the slack adjuster. This rotation turns the power screw within the caliper assembly in a clockwise direction, forcing the piston outward and the inside lining pads against the rotor. The opposite force of the power screw slides the caliper on the support bracket to the right. An equal force is then exerted on both lining pads, and the frictional force moves the lining pads against the support bracket. The braking torque is then transferred to the torque plate or bracket. Any increase of air pressure increases the clamping force and brake torque because a greater torque is placed on the power screw shaft.

The primary difference between the torque-multiplying mechanism of the power screw design and the helical-ramp design is that the input torque from the air chamber is multiplied 16 to 1 by the helical ramp on the actuator and stator. Further, the stator and thrust spindle are responsible for converting the rotational motion to linear motion and for transmitting it onto the lining pads. Moreover, the friction within the stator and thrust spindle serves as the automatic adjusting device.

OPERATION; HELICAL RAMP In the release position (refer to Fig. 15-32) the air pressure is released from

the air chamber. The input shaft and the actuator have turned counterclockwise, placing the helical ramps, the stator, and the actuator in their lower position. This causes the stator to move to the right, removing the clamping force. If the driver actuates the application valve, the air pressure activates the pushrod, which rotates the lever arm, the input shaft, and actuator in a clockwise direction. The rotation of the actuator causes the actuator ramp to slide on the stator ramp and thereby move the stator and thrust spindle in a linear direction to the left. This forces the inboard lining pad against the disk (rotor). The caliper moves simultaneously in the opposite direction, pushing both lining pads with equal force against the disk surfaces. Each time the stator moves to the left, the motion is transmitted to the friction clutch. If the load on the thrust spindle is less than the predetermined holding power of the friction clutch, the nut turns on the thrust spindle and an adjustment occurs. However, if the thrust spindle load is higher, the clutch slips and no adjustment is made.

SERVICING Relining an air-actuated disk brake is a simple process, and no special tools are required. Furthermore, only the wheel assembly needs to be removed.

To replace or to resurface the rotor, it is necessary to remove the wheel hub. When replacing any of the following parts: the lining pads, parts of the caliper, the torque-multiplying unit, the torque plate, or the support bracket or the disk, prepare the vehicle as you would when servicing drum brakes. Next, drain the air tank and then remove the outer and inner dual wheels or remove the front wheels. If you are working on the rear axle, you must manually release the spring brakes to remove the spring force from the pushrod (see the discussion of parking brakes in Unit 18).

Remove the service line and the spring brake air line from the air chambers. Remove the four nuts and bolts from the support bracket and then slide the caliper assembly (including the air-actuating component of the rotor) from the rotor. **CAUTION** The unit is heavy.

To remove the lining pads, slide the support

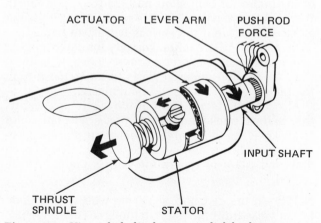

Fig. 15-32 View of a helical ramp air disk brake operating mechanism.

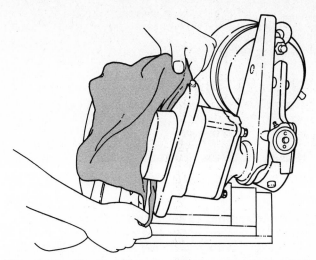

Fig. 15-33 Cleaning the power piston. (*B. F. Goodrich Engineered Systems Co.*)

bracket from the caliper and lift the pads from the support bracket. If it is necessary to service the service air chamber and spring, brake air chamber, or the slack adjuster, remove them from the assembly by pulling out the pushrod cotter pin, the pushrod pin, and the lock ring from the screw shaft and remove the nuts from the chamber stud bolts (see the discussion of slack adjuster and air chamber service in Unit 18).

Clean the remaining assembly, particularly the piston assembly, before turning the screw shaft to fully retract the piston (see Fig. 15-33). If the automatic slack adjuster is not already removed, turn its adjusting nut until you are able to retract the piston and then place the new lining pads into the caliper. Slide the support bracket into the caliper groove and between the lugs of the lining pads. **NOTE** It may be expedient at this point to repack and readjust the wheel bearings.

Reposition the caliper and torque the nuts to the specified torque. When reconnecting the air lines, make certain the delivery line is connected to the service air brake chamber and that the air lines are not twisted or in a position to rub against the frame or axle.

Before reinstalling the disk wheel or rim, turn the slack adjuster screw until the lining pads rest firmly against the rotor and then back off the adjusting nut until the wheel hub can be turned freely. Manually release the spring brakes and adjust the wheel senser.

Review Questions

1. List six reasons why a disk foundation brake is superior to a drum foundation brake.

2. List the major types of disk brakes.

3. Name the three valves positioned within the combination valve.

4. What is the purpose of each valve positioned within the combination valve?

5. Explain the hydraulic and mechanical action of a floating caliper disk brake when the master cylinder displaces fluid into the system.

6. List the three most common operator complaints associated with disk brake failure.

7. Why must you measure and make the disk run-out before removing it for resurfacing?

8. Why do manufacturers recommend, when resurfacing the disk, that you resurface both sides at the same time and, when possible, remove an equal amount of material?

9. On what operating principle does the brake application of a mechanical disk brake rely?

10. Explain why nearly all types of foundation brakes have some kind of automatic adjustment.

11. What advantage has a multidisk brake over any other type of disk or drum foundation brake?

12. Outline the differences and the advantages of an air-actuated disk brake over a hydraulically actuated disk brake.

Unit 16 Cam, Wedge, and Internal-Expanding Tube-Type Drum Brakes

CAM BRAKES

A cam foundation brake assembly has, generally, the same components as a single- or double-anchor hydraulic brake having a double-end wheel cylinder. However, in place of the hydraulic wheel cylinder, the cam foundation brake uses an S or flat cam to force (spread) the brake shoes against the friction surface of the brake drum (see Fig. 16-1). In addition it requires a device (slack adjuster) that changes the linear applied air or hydraulic force into rotary motion (torque). In so doing, it acts as a torque multiplier, increasing the applied force. As the name indicates, the slack adjuster serves an additional purpose, that is, to adjust the brakes.

Although most cam foundation brakes are air activated, there are some which are hydraulically activated. The hydraulically activated cam brakes can be used on trucks and tractors up to 62,000 lb [28,123.3 kg] GVW and may eventually be used on off-highway equipment.

Because of their activation and brake shoe arrangement, cam foundation brakes are nonservo brakes. Each brake shoe may have its own anchor, or both shoes may be placed onto one anchor. Depending on the desired brake torque, the drum diameter of an air- or hydraulically activated cam brake ranges from 12 to 22 in [274.8 to 558.8 mm], and the lining thickness and lining width alter proportionately with the diameter change. The lining width ranges from $2\frac{1}{2}$ to 22 in [63.50 to 558.8 mm], and the lining thickness ranges from $\frac{5}{16}$ to $\frac{3}{4}$ in [7.90 to 19.05 mm]. In comparison the servo or nonservo hydraulic foundation brake has a drum diameter range of $7\frac{1}{4}$ to 16 in [184.15 to 406.4 mm] and a lining thickness range of $\frac{1}{4}$ to $\frac{3}{8}$ in [6.35 to 9.51 mm]. However, the diameter of a wedge brake drum ranges from $12\frac{1}{2}$ to 42 in [317.5 to 1066.8 mm]. The brake lining width ranges from $2\frac{1}{4}$ to 20 in [57.15 to 508 mm] and the lining thickness ranges from $\frac{3}{8}$ to 1 in [9.51 to 25.4 mm].

Design The brake backing plate (bolted to the spindle or axle housing) is the foundation of a small cam brake assembly, whereas on the larger brake assemblies the foundation is the cast malleable brake spider which is riveted or bolted to the spindle or axle housing. A typical on-highways cam brake assembly, which may be air or hydraulically activated, is shown in Fig. 16-2. When used on on-highway equipment, two dust shield segments, bolted to the spider, are added to prevent contaminants from entering the brake assembly. When the cam brake assembly is used on off-highway equipment, one or

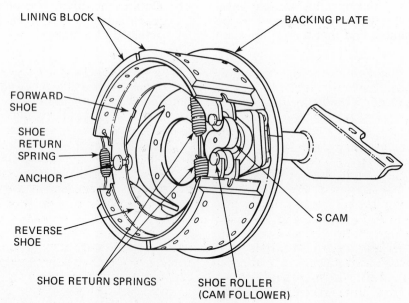

Fig. 16-1 View of a single anchor S cam foundation brake. (*Eaton Corporation*)

250

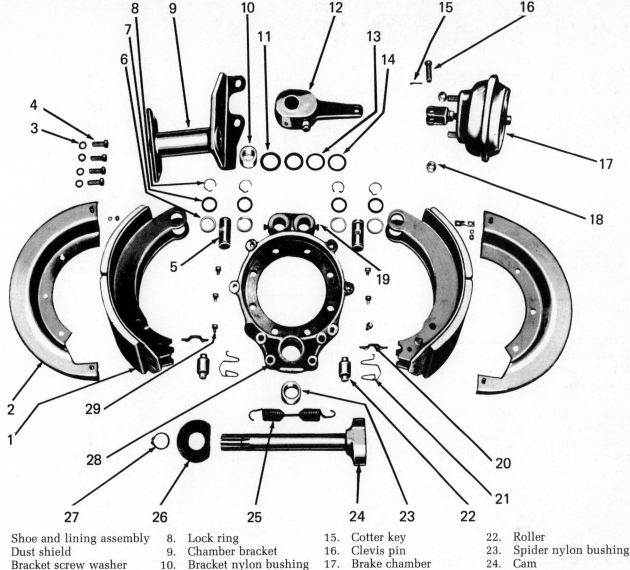

Fig. 16-2 Exploded view of S cam brake assembly. (*GMC Truck and Coach Division of General Motors Corporation*)

1. Shoe and lining assembly	8. Lock ring	15. Cotter key	22. Roller
2. Dust shield	9. Chamber bracket	16. Clevis pin	23. Spider nylon bushing
3. Bracket screw washer	10. Bracket nylon bushing	17. Brake chamber	24. Cam
4. Bracket cap screw	11. Felt spacing washer	18. Stud nut	25. Return spring
5. Anchor pin	12. Slack adjuster	19. Anchor pin lock screw	26. Cam washer
6. Felt retainer	13. Thin spacing washer	20. Return spring pin	27. Lock ring
7. Felt	14. Thick spacing washer	21. Roller spring clip	28. Spider
			29. Dust shield cap screw

both dust shield segments are usually removed so that road gravel, etc., will not become trapped inside the assembly. On the larger brake assemblies, the cam support (chamber) bracket is bolted to the spider. It not only supports the cam but also acts as the mounting surface for the hydraulic wheel cylinder or air chamber. Two nylon or bronze bushings or needle bearings are pressed into the housing in which the cam shaft is supported. Two cam seals, one on each end, retain lubricant and prevent contaminants from lodging between the cam shaft and the bushings. A washer or wear indicator or adjusting stop is placed between the slack adjuster and end of the cam support bracket. The slack adjuster is splined to the cam shaft, which is retained by a cotter pin or a lock ring. Shim washers, placed between the retainer and the slack adjuster, are used to adjust the end play.

The slack adjuster is a lever that is used to convert linear force (from the pushrod) to rotary motion (torque), to multiply the application force, and also to adjust the brakes. The lever length is usually around 5 to 6 in [12.7 to 15.24 cm]. The cam used is of a single, double S, or flat design. The brake shoes have split table webs, and each shoe anchor end rests against its anchor pin. To accommodate the brake shoe arrangement, the anchor bores on the spider are offset. A cam roller rests in each half moon cutout in the brake shoe web. Its purpose is to reduce friction. A shoe return spring is hooked onto each shoe web pin to maintain the shoe webs against the S cam. **NOTE** The shoe return or retaining springs are identified by a color code to signify which spring is to be used with which type of brake shoe.

A heavy duty S cam brake is shown in Fig. 16-3. The primary differences between it and the single-

252

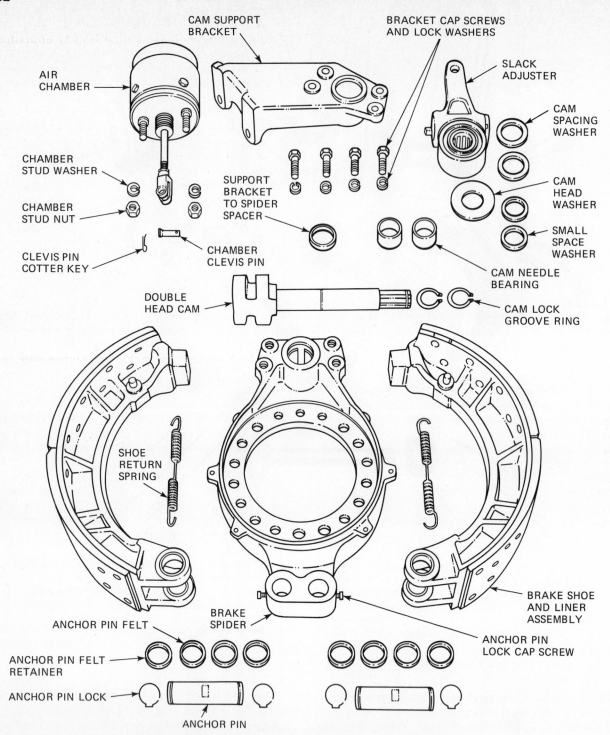

CAM SUPPORT BRACKET

BRACKET CAP SCREWS AND LOCK WASHERS

AIR CHAMBER

SLACK ADJUSTER

CAM SPACING WASHER

CHAMBER STUD WASHER

SUPPORT BRACKET TO SPIDER SPACER

CHAMBER STUD NUT

CAM HEAD WASHER

SMALL SPACE WASHER

CLEVIS PIN COTTER KEY

CHAMBER CLEVIS PIN

CAM NEEDLE BEARING

DOUBLE HEAD CAM

CAM LOCK GROOVE RING

SHOE RETURN SPRING

BRAKE SHOE AND LINER ASSEMBLY

ANCHOR PIN FELT

BRAKE SPIDER

ANCHOR PIN FELT RETAINER

ANCHOR PIN LOCK CAP SCREW

ANCHOR PIN LOCK

ANCHOR PIN

Fig. 16-3 Exploded view of a heavy duty S cam foundation brake. (*Rockwell International Automotive Operations*)

anchor brake assembly are that (1) it has malleable cast iron brake shoes with each brake shoe placed onto its own anchor, (2) the shoe anchor bores have replaceable bushings, (3) the anchor pins are positioned and held in place through a lock cap screw, (4) a felt ring and a retainer are positioned on each side of the anchor pin (they rest against webs, preventing contaminants from entering the anchor pin, and are held with pin locks to the anchor), (5) hardened cam pressure pads are used on the brake shoes instead of cam rollers, (6) the shoe return springs are hooked to pins on the shoe webs, and (7) the cam is

of a double S design and is supported by needle bearings in the housing.

Operation When the brakes are released, the shoe return spring(s) pull the brake shoes away from the drum surface, and the cam rollers or cam pressure pads (flats) rest firmly against the S cam. When either the pushrod of the air chamber or the hydraulic wheel cylinder influences the slack adjuster to rotate, it partly rotates the cam shaft and the S cam (see Fig. 16-4). **NOTE** The rotation (clock-

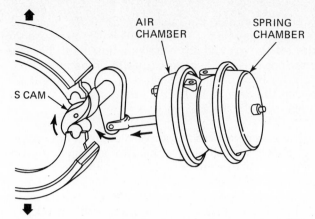

Fig. 16-4 Schematic view of cam brake actuation. (*Wagner Electric Sales Corporation*)

wise) of the cam in relation to the rotation of the wheel and the cam shaft is about 17° when the brakes are properly adjusted. This semirotation causes the cam rollers to roll on the S cam. Because of the S design, the cam rollers (or flats) are forced outward. The distance from the cam center to the cam roller contact surface increases with increased cam rotation. The shoes spread, forcing the brake lining in contact with the brake drum surface. The forward shoe is partly self-energized and transmits its brake torque to the anchor, whereas the reverse shoe is deenergized and transmits its brake torque to the cam. With an increase in the air or hydraulic force, the torque increases and the brake shoes exert greater force against the brake drum friction surface. When the applied force is reduced or fully removed, the cam is allowed to rotate in a counterclockwise direction. This decreases the distance between the cam rollers and the center of the cam, reducing the spreading force. When the application force is fully removed, the shoe return springs hold the cam roller in contact with the cam, away from the drum.

Troubleshooting The most common brake complaints are uneven brake torque, brakes' applying or releasing too slowly, or brakes' fading, grabbing, or squealing. Generally each of these malfunctions can be traced to brake misadjustment or insufficient lubrication of the cam shaft.

Another common cause of brake shortcomings emanates from damaged or worn components, such as the spider (distorted), the brake backing plate, brake shoe, drums and brake shoe anchors, cam shaft or cam, cam rollers and/or roller pin, slack adjuster, and wheel bearing (loose or damaged). Brake deterioration also occurs if leaking oil contaminates the brake drums and lining. Although oil seal or grease seal deficiency is not common, when it does occur, it causes uneven brake torque or brake grabbing and thereby reduces brake friction.

When a vehicle is brought in for brake service, you should promptly examine the slack adjuster adjustment and the lining wear (see Fig. 16-5). Check the wear indicator (or the slack adjuster stop, when so equipped). Remove the dust shield and examine the lining to determine lining wear. **NOTE** All linings which are uniform in thickness when new, will, when worn, be thicker at the toe end of the forward shoe and at the heel end of the reverse shoe. All linings that are tapered when new are uniform in their thickness when overly worn. You should therefore measure the lining thickness at the center and compare the measurement with that specified in the service manual.

An alternate method of determining whether or not the brakes should be relined is to remove the brake drum and visually examine the lining at the bolt or rivet head. When the lining is worn to nearly the surface of the bolt or rivet head, relining is mandatory.

While checking the lining for wear, pry the brake shoes apart at a suitable place, if possible, to check

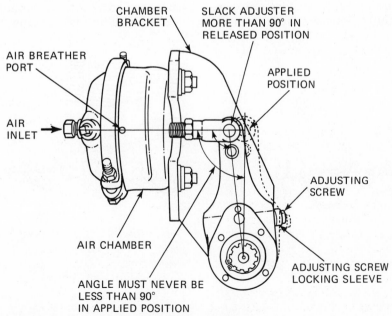

Fig. 16-5 View of brake chamber and slack adjuster. (*International Harvester Company*)

Table 16-1 CHAMBER STROKE AT WHICH BRAKE SHOULD BE READJUSTED

Chamber size effective area, in	Diaphragm, in	Brake chamber, in	Roto-chamber, in
9	$1\frac{3}{8}$	$1\frac{1}{2}$	$1\frac{1}{2}$
12	$1\frac{3}{8}$	$1\frac{1}{2}$	$1\frac{1}{2}$
16	$1\frac{3}{4}$	$1\frac{3}{4}$	$1\frac{7}{8}$
20	—	$1\frac{3}{4}$	$1\frac{7}{8}$
24	$1\frac{3}{4}$	$1\frac{3}{4}$	$1\frac{7}{8}$
30	2	2	$2\frac{1}{4}$
36	$2\frac{1}{4}$	$2\frac{1}{2}$	$2\frac{5}{8}$
50	—	—	3

the condition of the anchor, the anchor bore, the cam and cam bushing, and the cam rollers.

If, upon checking the lining condition, you find no evidence of grease or oil on the lining, apply the brakes and hold the application pressure. Now, measure the pushrod stroke length (see the discussion of slack adjusters in this unit). Each stroke should be of an even length 1 in [2.54 cm], and the angle between the pushrod and the center line of the slack adjuster should be 90°, or very close to it (see Table 16-1).

Pushrod Adjustment   If the pushrod strokes are not even in length and the center line of the slack adjuster is not 90°, adjust each brake so that the pushrod stroke is 1 in [2.54 cm] and the applied angle is 90°. This adjustment is made by first pushing the locking sleeve inward and then turning the slack adjuster screw until it is tight. Next, back off the screw about two or three flats (clicks) and let the sleeve lock the screw and then tap the drum with a steel tool. If the lining is not in contact with the drum (no brake drag), the drum will give a clear ringing sound. If the sound is dull, loosen the adjusting screw one more flat.

CAUTION   If the brake return springs are damaged or the anchor pins or bores are worn, or if the cam shaft and/or the bushings are worn, your adjustment may be too loose.   **NOTE** Do not raise the tire off the ground for a brake adjustment, because any looseness of bearings (due to adjustment or to spindle bore wear) will cause a misalignment between the drum and lining surfaces and may cause brake misadjustment.

If for some reason the applied angle is not 90° but the brakes nevertheless appear to be adjusted properly, loosen the pushrod lock nut and remove the pushrod pin. Now, while holding the pushrod with a pair of vise grips, turn the yoke counterclockwise sufficiently to decrease the angle or turn it clockwise to increase the angle. Reinstall the pushrod pin and, while holding the pushrod, tighten the lock nut and then readjust the brakes.

Brake Service   If the foundation brakes require service, remove the disk wheel or rim and the brake drum (see the discussion of wheels, tires, and wheel hubs in Unit 13). Upon removing the brake drum, you may remove the cam rollers and the shoe return spring(s) from the web pins and then remove the lock rings, the retainers, and the anchor pin felts (see Fig. 16-6). Cut the lock wire from the anchor pin lock screws. Remove the screws, anchor pin, and shoe assemblies. Now, if so equipped, unhook the cam rollers' retainer spring from the brake shoes and lift off the cam rollers.

If the cam, cam shaft, or bushings (bearings) are worn more than the maximum wear limit of 0.020 in [0.50 mm], remove (see Fig. 16-7), in order, the following: the camshaft retainer, snap ring, slack adjuster, and the cam spacer washer. Slide the cam shaft out of the bracket assembly. Slide the cam shaft head washer from the cam shaft.

If the cam shaft bushings (bearings) are worn, remove the hydraulic cylinder or the air chamber from the bracket assembly and remove the cap screws that secure the bracket to the spindle.

The procedure to examine, measure, and service

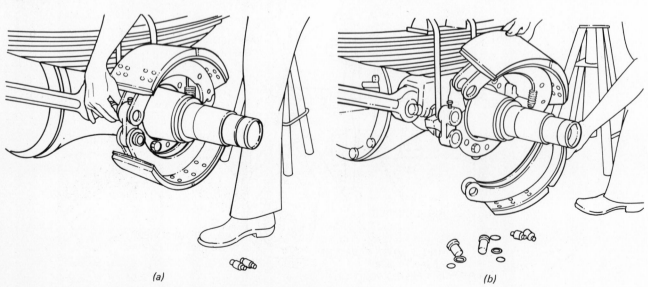

(a)   (b)

Fig. 16-6 (a) Removing web pin, (b) removing brake shoes. (*Eaton Corporation*)

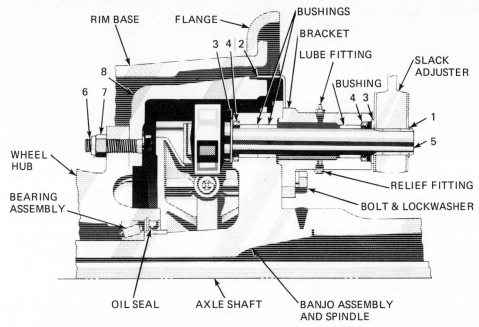

Fig. 16-7 Sectional view of camshaft installation. (*Terex Division of General Motors Corporation*)

1. Lock ring
2. Backing plate
3. Washer
4. Seal
5. Camshaft
6. Wheel stud
7. Wheel nut
8. Brake drum

the brake drum and brake shoes of a cam foundation brake is the same as that for nonservo hydraulic brakes. However, since a cam and cam roller is used to spread the shoes, it is important that you check the shoe span. Use the gauge supplied by the manufacturer to determine whether or not the span has enlarged (see Fig. 16-8). If you do not have a gauge, check the shoe span by placing the anchor and the cam roller into position and then measuring the distance from the center of the anchor to the center of the roller. Compare the measurement taken with that shown in the service manual. Once a shoe is spread, it must be replaced because a shoe cannot be bent back into shape.

If the brake lining is to be bolted to the brake shoe table, use new lock washers and a torque wrench to tighten the nuts to the specified torque (see Fig. 16-9).

NOTE Three-eighths-inch brass bolts require a torque of 18 to 23 lb · ft [24.39 to 31.16 N · m]; $\frac{1}{4}$-in brass bolts require a torque of 7 to 8 lb · ft [9.48 to 10.84 N · m]. Also check the manufacturer's in-

formation data. Some manufacturers recommend using a different lining coefficient on the reverse shoes.

If the drums require reservicing, increase the drum diameter by 0.060 in [2.12 mm] or by 0.120 [3.04 mm], since lining manufacturers furnish oversize linings in $\frac{1}{16}$-in increments. Obviously, when the drum diameter is increased, the corresponding oversize lining must be used.

NOTE Refer to service manual specifications to determine the maximum permissible oversize.

If the dust shields are twisted, bent, or badly rusted, replace them. When the anchor pins are worn

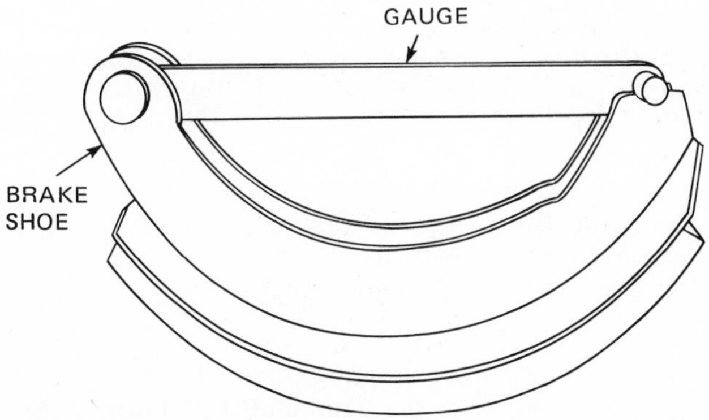

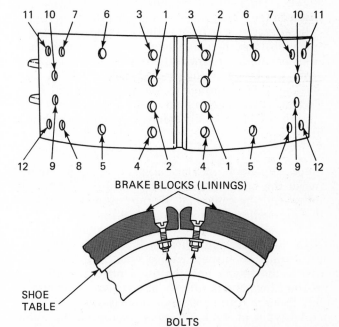

Fig. 16-9 Sequence of bolting the brake blocks to shoe table.

Fig. 16-8 Checking brake shoe for spread.

or loose, or the brake backing plate or the spider is distorted, cracked, or badly rusted, they should also be replaced.

To remove a riveted spider from the spindle or axle housing, carefully center-punch each rivet head and then drill a centering hole. Use a drill about 0.030 in [0.76 mm] smaller than the rivet shank to drill through the head. Use a portable press to press the rivet out. (A punch and hammer will not remove the rivet.) Because of numerous difficulties in cold riveting the spider to the spindle, special replacement bolts, nuts, and washers are furnished to facilitate installation.

Following are some recommendations which will help prevent cam overroll:

- Use standard cam rollers with standard linings and drum.
- Use $\frac{1}{16}$-in oversize cam rollers when servicing standard linings which are reusable despite the drum diameter's enlargement to about 0.060 in [2.12 mm] due to wear.
- Use $\frac{1}{8}$-in oversize cam rollers when standard linings are to be used with an oversize resurfaced drum.
- When $\frac{1}{16}$-in oversize linings and drum are used and the linings are worn more than 50%, $\frac{1}{4}$-in oversize cam rollers should be installed.
- When $\frac{1}{8}$-in oversize linings and drum are used and the linings are worn to about 50 percent, $\frac{1}{2}$-in [12.7-mm] oversize cam rollers should be installed.

After the brakes are reassembled, circle grind the linings to provide for a minimum of 80 percent lining-to-drum contact. To circle grind linings, follow the procedure outlined in Unit 14, but, further, grind the brake shoe diameter 0.070 in [1.78 mm] smaller than the drum diameter.

NOTE The cam rollers must be in the lowest position on the S cam while you are grinding the shoes.

If, after circle grinding the linings, the contact area is still less than 80 percent, then adjust the slack adjuster one flat to force the brake shoes apart. Regrind the brake lining. **CAUTION** Wear a face mask as protection against asbestos dust and have a second man vacuum up dust during grinding. Vacuum the brake assembly before reinstalling the brake drum.

Slack Adjusters A slack adjuster is the nexus between the brake chamber, or hydraulic wheel cylinder, and the cam shaft. Its purpose is to multiply the application force and to adjust the brakes.

Generally speaking, there are two main types of slack adjusters: one whereon the adjusting mechanism must be turned with a wrench to make the brake adjustment, and the other on which the adjusting mechanism adjusts automatically wherever the lining-to-drum clearance increases.

All types of slack adjusters, including the automatic, use a worm and gear as the adjusting device. The biggest difference among slack adjusters lies in

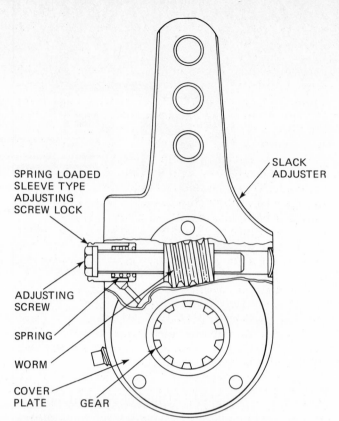

Fig. 16-10 Sectional view of a slack adjuster. (*International Harvester Company*)

the torque limit specification, which ranges from a limit of 15,000 lb · in [1693.75 N · m] torque to 50,000 lb · in [5645.83 N · m] torque. All slack adjusters have 10 internal splines, but the inside diameters are $1\frac{1}{8}$, $1\frac{1}{4}$, or $1\frac{1}{2}$-in so as to fit the various diameters of the cam shafts. They also differ in their lever length. Furthermore, the lever arm may be different in shape or may be offset or made to a special configuration to accommodate various installation requirements.

Manual Slack Adjuster The manual slack adjuster body includes a lever with a gear bushing. Inside the body is a gear which has external (curved) teeth and internal splines. The worm shaft is positioned in the cross-drilled bore within the body. The worm gear is pressed to the worm shaft on which the spring and lock key are positioned. The cover with the gear bushing, which encloses and seals the assembly, are riveted to the body (see Fig. 16-10).

To turn the adjusting screw, place a $\frac{3}{4}$-in box end wrench over the adjusting screw. Depress the adjusting lock sleeve to release the adjusting screw lock so that you can rotate the worm shaft in either direction. After the adjustment is made, release the force from the adjusting lock sleeve to allow it to engage with the hexhead of the worm shaft head. You may have to turn it slightly to achieve a positive engagement.

NOTE When the adjusting screw is turned in a clockwise direction, the cam shaft is rotated clockwise, spreading the brake shoes. When the adjustment is made in a counterclockwise rotation, the brake shoes are released.

Automatic Slack Adjuster   A cam foundation brake will lose brake torque with each brake application. Also, with each application, slightly more air is required to apply the brake. The time in which they become effective (brake applied) is extended. Also, with each application a slightly higher air pressure is needed to achieve the previous brake torque, and therefore more time is needed to apply the brake. This is because, as the drum and the brake linings wear, the pushrod stroke increases, causing the angle between the slack adjuster and the pushrod to change. Since any lever is at its greatest advantage at an angle of 90°, the pushrod and the center line of the slack adjuster, to be most effective, must form a 90° angle when the brakes are applied.

For example, assume the air chamber is 30 in² [0.193 m²], the slack adjuster is 6 in [0.1524 m], and the applied air pressure is 60 psi [413.4 kPa]. In this case the pushrod force would be 30 × 60 = 1800 lb [7992.0 N], and the torque onto the cam shaft would be 1800 × 6 = 10,800 lb · in [1219.5 N · m]. However, when the pushrod stroke is increased (due to lining or drum wear or to misadjustment), the lever arm will no longer be 6 in (see Fig. 16-11). It may be shortened by 0.25 in [6.35 mm]. Therefore the torque would be: 1800 × 5.750 = 10,350 lb · in [1168.68 N · m], a loss of 450 lb · in [50.81 N · m] torque.

In addition, the increased pushrod stroke requires more air, which increases the time to apply the brakes and therefore increases the stopping distance. Furthermore, the compressor has a shorter rest period, which accelerates its rate of deterioration. Hotter air enters the reservoir, and sludge buildup

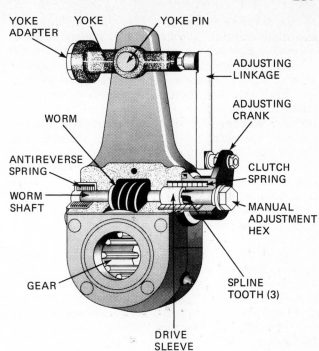

Fig. 16-12   Cutaway view of an automatic slack adjuster. (*International Harvester Company*)

within the air system increases, resulting in early component failure. More important, however, is the fact that a greater pushrod force is needed to achieve the same braking torque, and this amount of force may cause brake drum distortion or cause the brake backing plate or the brake spider to deflect or become permanently distorted.

To ensure that the lining-to-drum clearance is as recommended at all times, that it is equal on all wheels, and that the pushrod-to-slack adjuster maintains an angle of 90°, automatic slack adjusters are used. One type of automatic slack adjuster is shown in Fig. 16-12. The main difference between a standard and an automatic slack adjuster is that the former requires the automatic adjusting parts.

DESIGN   The adjusting crank is connected to the slack adjuster yoke through a ball socket adjusting link. The clutch spring located in the body is left wound and fitted snugly onto the drive sleeve, whereas the other end of the clutch spring is press-fitted into the pocket of the adjusting crank. An antireverse spring is pressed into the worm shaft cap and fitted snugly onto the end of the worm shaft. The manual adjusting screw has three external splines which fit into the three internal drive sleeve splines.

OPERATION   When the brake is released, the worm shaft is held in a fixed position by the antireverse spring. The center line of the adjusting crank and the center line of the slack adjuster form an angle of about 45°. As the air chamber pushrod causes the slack adjuster to rotate, the cam shaft rotates in a clockwise direction. At the same time, the rotation of the slack adjuster moves the adjusting linkage, which in turn causes the adjusting crank and clutch

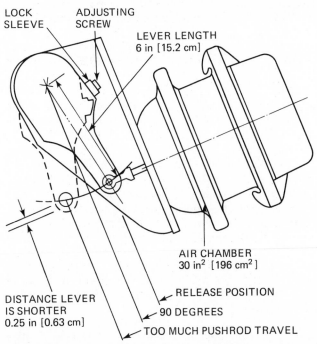

Fig. 16-11   Torque effect due to misadjusted slack adjuster.

spring to rotate in a clockwise direction. The clock-wise rotation winds the spring tight against the outer surface of the drive sleeve. As the spring turns, it takes up the free play between the three external manual-adjusting screw splines and the three internal drive sleeve splines. When the lining-to-drum clearance is corrected, no further action takes place, because the free play between the internal and external splines is directly correlated to the exact lining-to-drum clearance. Nevertheless, the clutch spring still exerts torque onto the drive sleeve and the worm shaft. However, the brake linings have made contact with the drum surface, and the torque on the gear is too high to allow the worm to turn the gear. This is because the gear torque now exceeds the force of the friction between the drive sleeve and the clutch spring, causing the clutch spring to slip on the drive sleeve. If, at this time, the brake linings have not contacted the brake drum's inner surface, the worm shaft will be rotated (and the antireverse spring unwound). The worm will rotate and, in turn, rotate the gear and the cam shaft and thereby adjust the brakes.

As the brakes are released, the slack adjuster and the cam shaft turn in a counterclockwise rotation and unwind the clutch spring, allowing it to slip on the drive sleeve, because the antireverse spring has now wound itself onto the worm shaft and holds it stationary. If the antireverse spring did not hold the worm shaft, the brake adjustment would back off.

The automatic slack adjuster can be manually adjusted by turning the adjusting screw. The adjusting screw rotates the worm shaft and the worm and thereby rotates the gear. The clutch spring then allows the drive sleeve to slip.

TROUBLESHOOTING A slack adjuster may fail to hold its adjustment or may be difficult to adjust when it is insufficiently lubricated, since lack of lubricant causes the bushings to wear and the gear to come out of mesh with the worm. Spline wear and lever arm bushing wear or damage are usually the result of severe operating conditions. An automatic slack adjuster which fails to maintain proper lining-to-drum clearance may bring about a bent linkage and/or a bent crank, worn ball sockets, or dirt within the drive clutch assembly or may eventually brake the antireverse spring.

Replacing a Slack Adjuster To extend the service life of the slack adjusters, you should lubricate them every 25,000 mi [40,225 km] with a multipurpose grease, grades 1 or 2. If it requires service, remove it with caution. Hydraulic or air brake systems use spring brakes, and, when working, the brakes may apply automatically as the air pressure leaks down or as the emergency line is disconnected (see the discussion of servicing spring brakes in Unit 18).

Before servicing the slack adjuster, always block the wheels and then manually release the spring brakes. Drain the air reservoirs and then remove the cotter pin and the pushrod pin, the retainer, and the washer from the end of the cam shaft. Note the position of the slack adjuster relative to the cam shaft

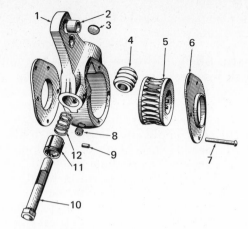

1.	Body slack adjuster	7.	Rivets
2.	Bushing	8.	Plug or fitting
3.	Welch plug	9.	Guide pin
4.	Worm	10.	Worm shaft
5.	Gear	11.	Lock sleeve
6.	Cover plate	12.	Spring

Fig. 16-13 Exploded view of a slack adjuster. (*International Harvester Company*)

and then slide the slack adjuster from the cam shaft splines. If a wear indicator and/or adjusting stop is used, mark its position relative to the cam shaft.

If a new or a serviced slack adjuster is to be installed, make certain that it is one of the same configuration, that it has the same lever length and the same torque rating, and that the spline diameter is correct. When all these qualifications have been met, slide the slack adjuster (with the adjusting screw facing away from the pushrod) onto the splines of the cam shaft. The center line of the pushrod and slack adjuster should form an angle of about 100°.

Install the washer and the retainer and, with a feeler gauge, check the end play of the cam shaft. It should be within specification. If the end play exceeds specification, install an additional washer. Now install the pushrod pin and cotter pin. Adjust the brakes and release the spring brake.

Servicing a Slack Adjuster To service a slack adjuster (refer to Fig. 16-13), first clean the assembly in solvent and dry it with compressed air. With a chisel, cut off the rivet head and drive out the rivets. Remove the cover(s). With a punch, remove the welsh plug. Use a press to push out the worm shaft from the welsh plug side of the worm and body.

NOTE The worm will remain in the body, but the sleeve lock and spring come out with the shaft.

After removing the worm shaft, lift out the worm and gear. Clean and inspect all parts. If, upon examining components of the slack adjuster, you find evidence of excessive wear, cracks, or chipped parts, the defective parts must be replaced. If the worm shaft bearing surface is worn or the corners of the head is rounded off, the worm shaft must be replaced. If the lever arm bushings are loose in the bores or out-of-round or damaged in any other way, press them out and replace them with new ones.

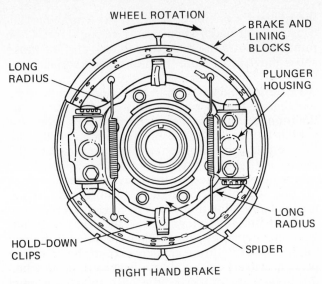

WHEEL ROTATION

BRAKE AND LINING BLOCKS

LONG RADIUS

PLUNGER HOUSING

LONG RADIUS

HOLD-DOWN CLIPS

SPIDER

RIGHT HAND BRAKE

Fig. 16-14 View of a 17-in wedge brake. (*International Harvester Company*)

NOTE The replacement bushing must be reamed to the size specified in the service manual.

If there is any damage to the lock sleeve, replace it. Always replace the lock sleeve spring.

The reassembly procedure is precisely the reverse of the order of disassembly. When pressing the worm shaft into the worm, make certain the lock sleeve groove aligns with the pin and body and that the worm shaft end is the specified distance from the body surface. While lubricating the slack adjuster, turn the adjusting screw (worm shaft) at least 50 revolutions to ensure satisfactory lubrication of all gear pockets.

WEDGE BRAKES

The wedge hydraulic brake actuating mechanism and brake shoe arrangement are used on off- and on-highway trucks up to 300 tons. It is a nonservo brake arrangement and usually has a shoe action equiva-

lent to foundation brakes having two double-end wheel cylinders. Both brake shoes also perform as forward shoes because of the self-energizing action in the forward and reverse directions.

The size of the components and lining areas of a 300-ton dump truck staggers the imagination. For instance, the front drums have a diameter of 36 in [91.74 cm] and a width of 12 in [30.48 cm] and the rear drums have a 42-in [106.6 cm] diameter and are 18 in [45.72 cm] wide. The total lining surface is 7690 in² [49,613 cm²]. The truck, when loaded, weighs about 727,540 lb [330,010 kg]. Its maximum speed is about 24 mph [38.64 km/h].

Design The spider, which is bolted to the axle housing or splined to the spindle, is the foundation of the wedge brake assembly (see Fig. 16-14). Whether bolted or splined, it has two wheel cylinders and is of the automatic adjustment design. The toe end of the shoes rests in the slotted adjusting bolt, and the heel ends rest in the slotted solid plunger. Shoe retainers (two for each shoe) are used to guide and position the shoes while in rest position and while the brakes are being applied or released. Two return springs are hooked (near the toe and heel) to the shoe web and to the spider. The larger radius end of the shoe web must be placed into the adjusting bolt. Also note that the shoe lining blocks are tapered toward each end (toe and heel). The sectional view of a plunger housing that is part of the spider is shown in Fig. 16-15. Each plunger housing has one adjusting plunger and one solid plunger. The solid plunger acts as the anchor in the forward direction. It is retained and guided in the bore by the screw (plunger guide), whereas the adjustable plunger is retained and guided by the guide pawl. Rollers, although positioned in the roller cage, can move within the plunger slots. A wedge rests between the two rollers, and the wedge rod rests against the wheel cylinder piston (see Fig. 16-16). The plunger and the wedge angles may vary 10 to 16° from application to application, depending on the brake model. When the wedge brake is air actuated, the air chamber is screwed into the plunger

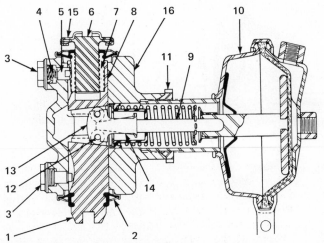

1. Solid plunger
2. Plunger seal and retainer
3. Screw
4. Spring
5. Adjusting pawl and plunger guide
6. Adjusting bolt assembly
7. Adjusting sleeve (actuator)
8. Adjusting plunger
9. Wedge assembly
10. Air brake chamber
11. Collet nut (lock nut)
12. Rollers
13. Roller cage
14. Wedge
15. Adjusting bolt assembly
16. Plunger housing

Fig. 16-15 Sectional view of a plunger housing and air chamber. (*International Harvester Company*)

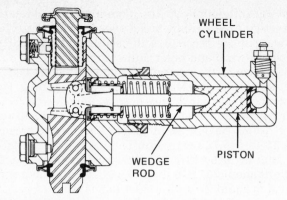

Fig. 16-16 Sectional view of a hydraulically actuated wedge brake. (*International Harvester Company*)

housing (spider), and the wedge rod rests in the air chamber pushrod.

The adjusting sleeve (actuator) is loosely fitted inside the adjusting plunger, and the adjusting bolt is threaded into the adjusting sleeve. The guide pawl has sawlike teeth which rest on the helical teeth of the actuator.

Brake Action   When the hydraulic pressure rises in the wheel cylinders, the piston forces the wedge (downward) deeper between the rollers, and this moves the plungers evenly apart and thereby forces the shoe linings into contact with the drum surface. The brake linings' contact causes the drum to drag the shoes around slightly, and as a result the heel of each shoe is forced inward. This moves the solid plunger, the wedge, and the adjusting plunger and forces the toe of each shoe outward to a distance equivalent to that to which the heels are moved inward (see Fig. 16-16). The solid plunger now becomes the anchor and transmits the brake torque to the spider. When the hydraulic pressure is released, the wedge spring forces the wedge, the rollers, and

the hydraulic piston upward. At the same time, because of the brake shoe return spring's force, the plunger follows the retracting rollers, and the brake shoes move away from the brake drum surface.

Automatic Adjuster   With each brake application, whether in the forward or in the reverse direction, the plungers move outward. Furthermore, when the vehicle is geared in the reverse direction, the adjusting plunger instantly retracts once the brake lining comes in contact with the drum. However, when the vehicle is geared in the forward direction with the brakes applied, the adjusting plunger, the actuator, and the adjusting bolt are forced even farther outward after the linings contact the drum. This outward movement lifts the guide pawl out of its helical tooth contact with the actuator. When the adjusting plunger travels only a short distance (that is, when the brakes are properly adjusted), the guide pawl cannot reseat into the next tooth. Therefore, when the brakes are released, the guide pawl slides back into the same tooth and no adjustment is made.

When the outward movement of the adjusting plunger increases owing to lining wear, the guide pawl reseats into the next tooth. In this case, when the brake is released, the plunger moves inward, causing the actuator to rotate. The adjusting bolt then moves minutely outward, reducing the lining-to-drum clearance.

A different type of automatic wedge brake adjuster is shown in Figs. 16-17 and 16-18.

DESIGN   The adjuster piston and anchor piston have a ramp machined on one end in which the wedge rollers are guided. The pistons, positioned by index pins, fit loosely in the actuator bore. The adjuster cap nut has hacksawlike teeth and fits loosely over the outside of the adjuster nut. The automatic overloading spring fits in the slots of the adjuster cap nut and adjuster nut.

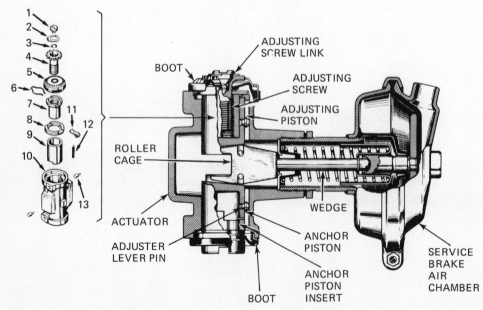

1. Adjusting screw link
2. Detent spring
3. Link retainer
4. Adjusting screw
5. Boot
6. Automatic adjuster overload spring
7. Adjusting nut
8. Adjusting nut cap
9. Piston
10. Actuator
11. Automatic adjuster lever
12. Adjuster lever spring
13. Adjuster lever pin

Fig. 16-17   Sectional view of actuator and air chamber. (*Bendix Heavy Vehicle Systems Group*)

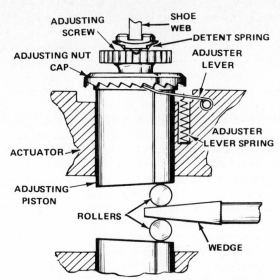

Fig. 16-18 Schematic view of automatic adjuster components.

The purpose of the overload spring is to transmit the motion from the adjuster cap nut to the adjuster nut and to prevent adjuster lever damage. When the vehicle then comes to a stop, a slight rockback occurs, and if (before the rockback) the adjuster lever has advanced in the next tooth, the adjusting nut cannot rotate, because of the additional force placed on the adjuster screw. Under this condition, only the adjuster cap nut rotates by collapsing the overload spring. The adjuster screw link is held to the adjusting screw by the link retainer, the detent spring being situated between them. One end of the detent spring rests in a notch in the adjusting screw, and the elongated opening fits into the cutout of the adjuster screw link. This arrangement not only holds the adjusting screw but also prevents it from turning when an automatic adjustment is made. If the spring is broken, no adjustment can be made, because the adjusting screw would turn with the adjuster nut.

NOTE The lower end of the shoe web slot must face toward the axle.

OPERATION The application principle of this type of wedge brake design is the same as that of the brake previously covered. When the brakes are applied and the lining clearance is correct, no adjustment is made. However, when the lining clearance is excessive, the adjuster piston moves out an additional distance, and the adjuster lever can lock into the next tooth on the adjuster cap nut (see Fig. 16-19). As the brakes are released, the wedge spring forces the wedge to the right, and the shoe return springs force the adjuster and anchor piston inward. The inward movement of the adjuster piston pivots the adjuster lever on its pin, and the pivot action turns the adjusting cap nut. The semirotation of the adjusting cap nut is transmitted to the overload spring and then onto the adjuster nut. Since the adjusting screw is held by the detent spring, the screw is moved outward about 0.001 in [0.025 mm], decreasing the lining clearance. **NOTE** If the threads on the screw or nut are dirty, damaged, or worn, or the overload spring is broken or damaged, no adjustment can be made, because the thread friction is too high and the overload spring cannot transmit the torque.

Brake Servicing Most wedge brakes, hydraulic or air, can be serviced by one person. However, it is impossible for one person alone to service the stop master brakes on a 300-ton rear dump truck, since any part that must be disassembled is extremely huge and heavy. The front wheel brakes are simpler to service than the rear wheel brakes since they are not dual wheels and do not have a planetary drive; hence we commence service procedure for the front brakes.

To begin with, you need a good jack and good cross-blocking material since the weight on the front axle is 110,479 lb [50,113 kg]. Commence service by raising the front axle to a height sufficient to remove the weight from the tires and then block it firmly. Next, bleed the air from the air reservoir since the brake system is air over hydraulic. Remove the cap screws and then the wheel cover and wheel

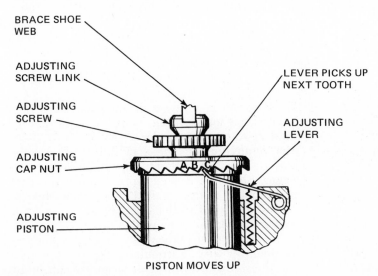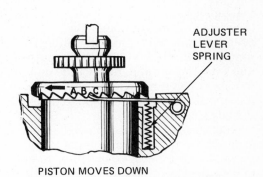

Fig. 16-19 Automatic adjuster operation. (*Bendix Heavy Vehicle Systems Group*)

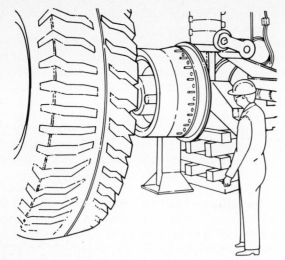

Fig. 16-20 View of wheel hub after wheel and tire are removed. (*WABCO, An American-Standard Company*)

cover bracket. To the tire attach a sling and hoist (see the discussion of tires, wheels, and rims in Unit 12) and take up the slack. Remove the wheel stud nuts and lugs that secure the rim to the wheel hub and then slide the rim from the wheel hub (see Fig. 16-20). Attach a sling and hoist to the wheel hub and take up the slack. **NOTE** If only the brakes are to be relined, you do not have to remove the wheel and tire. In this case secure the top portion of the tire to the truck frame using a chain and come-along.

To release the brakes, first remove the guide pawls (automatic adjuster) from each wheel cylinder. To do this, remove the hollow cap screw spring and with a magnet lift out the guide pawl. You can now rotate the actuator counterclockwise to back off the shoes from the brake drum.

Disconnect the brake lines from the wheel cylinders and cover all openings to prevent contaminants from entering. Remove the cap from the drain pipe and drain the oil from the wheel hub. Always use a deflector shield to prevent oil from running onto the lower brake shoes. Bend the lock plate away from the bolt heads and then remove the four cap screws and lock washers that secure the retainer plate to the spindle. Remove the lock plate retainer plate and slings. Install puller bolts to pull the brake support plate and brake assembly from the splined spindle end. Remove the wear sleeves from the brake support plate and the O ring from the spindle. Remove the cap screws and lock washers and then the retainer and oil seal from the wheel hub and lay them over the axle; then carefully slide the wheel hub from the spindle. **NOTE** While pulling the wheel hub from the spindle, remove the outer wheel bearing cone. The inner wheel bearing cone remains on the spindle. Use masking tape to protect the spindle threads (see Fig. 16-21).

After the assembly is removed, examine the brake drum. If the drum is to be replaced, loosen and remove all cap screws, except three to hold the drum to the wheel hub. Slip a sling around the brake drum and take the weight from the hub. To loosen the drum from the wheel hub, remove the remaining

three cap screws and turn the puller screws into appropriate threaded holes.

Before installing the new drum, refer to the applicable service manual to confirm location of the specially hardened washer and the torque specification.

Brake Assembly Inspection and Servicing When examining the brake support plate, give special attention to the condition of the internal splines. Check the bolt holes for elongation and the washers for excessive wear and cracks. If there is any external damage or if cracks are visible, replace the assembly. If there is any external damage to the spider assembly, it must be replaced.

When removing the lining from the brake shoes, use an impact wrench and a socket to spin the nuts from the brake shoe bolts. If the screw turns, use a flex handle and a screw driver socket to hold it. Clean the brake shoes and check them for serviceability.

After cleaning and planing or sanding the table surface, align one lining block with the table holes. The tapered side of the lining block faces toward the toe or heel of the shoe. Install all screws and new lock washers and nuts and then tighten the nuts to 50 lb · ft [67.75 N · m] torque, in the sequence outlined in the service manual. Install the second lining block. It is essential that you use a torque wrench to tighten the brake shoe nuts. If the nuts are too loose, the brake blocks could rock loose, elongate the holes, and break away from the shoes. If they are overtorqued, the blocks could crack.

New linings require no contour grinding when new brake drums are installed, since they are precision ground by the manufacturer. Furthermore, the shoes are self-aligning. However, when oversize linings are installed, they must be contour ground.

Wheel Cylinder and Automatic Adjuster Servicing Before removing any part of the assembly, mark the adjuster-plunger side of the spider (see Fig. 16-22). Remove the set screw that holds the wheel cylinder in position and then turn the wheel cylinder counterclockwise out of the spider bore. Remove the bleeder screw. Remove the piston, piston cup, spacer, and spring from the cylinder housing bore. Remove the O ring from the piston. You may have to use compressed air or hydraulic pressure to remove the piston.

The inspection and servicing procedure of a wedge brake wheel cylinder is the same as that for any hydraulic wheel cylinder.

After removing the wheel cylinder, lift out the wedge assembly. Compress the spring to remove the E washer. Slide the washer, spring, and spring retainer from the wedge shaft. Use a screwdriver to pry the wedge head (roller retainer) apart and thus remove the rollers and the wedge.

After cleaning all parts with a glass blaster, examine them for wear. Particularly examine the rollers and the wedge for pitting or for marks caused by the wedge action. Replace all defective parts and reassemble, unit by unit, in precisely the reverse or-

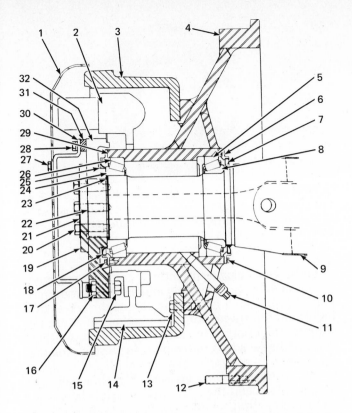

1. Wheel cover
2. Brake assembly
3. Brake drum
4. Wheel hub
5. Inner bearing cup
6. Seal retainer
7. Seal
8. Inner bearing cone
9. Spindle
10. Cap screw and lock washer
11. Breather
12. Wheel mounting stud
13. Cap screw
14. Brake shoe
15. Cap screw
16. Nut and washer
17. Cap screw and lock washer
18. Seal
19. Retainer plate
20. Cap screw
21. Lock plate
22. Shims
23. O ring
24. Outer bearing cone
25. Sleeve
26. Outer bearing cup
27. Cap screw and lock washer
28. Cap screw and lock washer
29. Gasket
30. Hub bracket
31. Spacer
32. Brake support plate

Fig. 16-21 Sectional view of front wheel and brake assembly. (*WABCO, An American-Standard Company*)

der of disassembly. **NOTE** Coat well all parts of the wheel cylinder and adjuster with the recommended grease before reassembly and again while they are being reassembled.

To remove the anchor plunger, first remove the plunger guide bolt. To remove the adjusting plunger, remove the hollow cap screw spring and then use a magnet to remove the guide pawl if it has not been removed previously. Pry the plunger seals loose and then remove the seals and the plungers.

From the adjusting plunger remove the actuator and then unscrew the adjusting bolt.

After thoroughly cleaning all these parts with a glass blaster, examine them for damage and wear. Always replace all seals and gaskets. When the angle surface of the plungers, the plunger threads, the adjusting bolts, the pawl, the retainers, or the washers are worn or damaged owing to pitting or corrosion, they must also be replaced. Check the plunger bores for pits, grooving, nicks, and corrosion. Remove

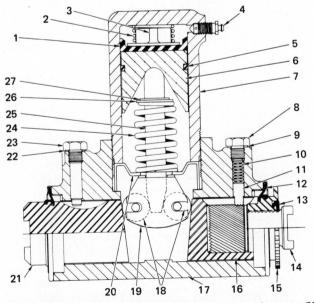

1. Piston cup
2. Spring
3. Spacer
4. Bleeder
5. O ring
6. Piston
7. Cylinder housing
8. Cap screw
9. Lock
10. Spring
11. Guide pawl
12. Diaphragm seal
13. Adjusting bolt seal
14. Adjusting bolt
15. Actuator
16. Adjusting plunger
17. Spider
18. Rollers
19. Roller cage
20. Spring retainer
21. Anchor plunger
22. Lock
23. Plunger guide
24. Wedge spring
25. Wedge
26. Washer
27. E washer

Fig. 16-22 Wheel cylinder and automatic adjuster. (*WABCO, An American-Standard Company*)

264

small defacements on the bore surface with emery cloth.

Reassembly First, tape the shoe web slot to protect the seal lips before placing the seal onto the anchor plunger. Make certain the double lips of the seal rest in their respective grooves or shoulders. Before placing the plunger into the bore, pack additional grease in the seal cavity and then slide the plunger (with the guide slot toward the opening of the plunger guide) into its bore. **CAUTION** Make certain that the L-marked anchor plunger is used on the left-hand brake assembly, and the R-marked anchor plunger on the right-hand brake assembly. The heel of the brake shoe then rests against the plunger and the adjusting plunger is in the correct side of the bore. Screw the plunger guide into the threaded bore so that the end engages in the anchor plunger slot and tighten the guide screw to the specified torque. When installed, check the plunger. It must be able to move unrestricted within its bore.

Slide the actuator into the adjusting plunger and then, with a magnet, place the pawl into the bore so that the 45° bevel faces toward the wedge. This ensures that the pawl and the actuator helical teeth are aligned and that the flat of the pawl fits into the plunger slot.

Next, install a new spring and gasket. Install and finger-tighten the hollow cap screw. To check if the automatic adjuster is working properly (the pawl and actuator should mesh smoothly), turn the activator in a clockwise rotation. If properly installed, a clicking sound can be heard and the mating can be felt.

Check the freeness of the plunger. Torque the cap screw to specification and then place the plunger seal over the shoulder of the actuator. Use the recommended seal driver to seat the seal in the plunger housing bore. Thread the adjusting bolt into the actuator but take care not to damage the seal or to bottom the bolt against the seal. Place the wedge assembly into the spider bore and then push down the wedge to make certain that the rollers and the

Fig. 16-24 Sectional view of wheel cylinder and automatic adjuster. (WABCO, An American-Standard Company)

plunger seats engage correctly. If correctly engaged, the plunger moves smoothly and easily outward (see Fig. 16-23). If such is the case, thread the wheel cylinder into the spider bore until bottomed. Align the cylinder inlet port in the direction of the brake lines and use the set screw to secure the cylinder. Remove the protection caps and then connect the brake lines to the cylinders. Apply grease to the shoe web, the plunger slots, and the adjusting bolt slots before installing the brake shoes and brake shoe return springs. Place the shoe web with the longest radius (toe end) into the slot of the adjusting bolt (see Fig. 16-24). Fasten the spider to the brake support plate and then torque the nut to specification. Remove the masking tape from the spindle and then grease the spindle and the brake support plate splines.

Install a new O ring and gasket. Lift the assembly into position and slide the brake support plate onto the splined spindle. If new wheel bearings are installed, adjust the wheel bearings as outlined in Unit 13, "Wheel Hubs, Dead and Live Axles." However, if the bearings are not being replaced install the same number of shims as removed, and place the retainer into the spindle end. Install and torque the cap screw to about 100 lb · ft [135.5 N · m].

Remove the chain that holds the tire against the truck frame and, while rotating the wheel, torque the cap screw in three sequences to the specified torque.

Adjusting the Wedge Brake The fastest way to make the brake adjustment is to center the brake shoe (use a pry-bar) and then place two strips 0.070 in [1.778 mm] of feeler gauge stock at the toe and heel between the lining and drum surface. Turn the actuator star wheel clockwise while keeping the shoe centered, until both feeler gauge stocks drag evenly when you are moving them in and out. Repeat this adjusting procedure with the other brake shoe.

Another method, though slower, is to center the brake shoe and turn the star wheel until the linings are tight against the drum. Remove the hollow cap screw spring and pawl and back off each actuator eight notches. Reinstall the guide pawl spring and hollow cap screws. This method could, however, dislodge the pawl and thereby prevent the automatic adjuster from operating.

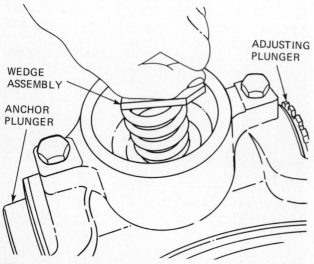

Fig. 16-23. Checking plunger movement. (WABCO, An American-Standard Company)

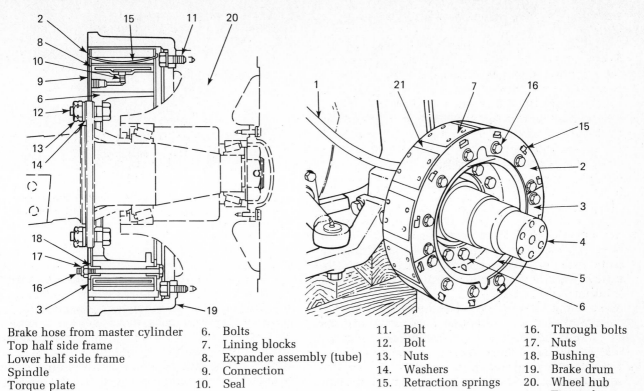

1. Brake hose from master cylinder
2. Top half side frame
3. Lower half side frame
4. Spindle
5. Torque plate
6. Bolts
7. Lining blocks
8. Expander assembly (tube)
9. Connection
10. Seal
11. Bolt
12. Bolt
13. Nuts
14. Washers
15. Retraction springs
16. Through bolts
17. Nuts
18. Bushing
19. Brake drum
20. Wheel hub
21. Torque bars

Fig. 16-25 Sectional and side views of an internal expander tube brake assembly. (*Caterpillar Tractor Co.*)

Reinstall the drain cap or the drain pipe and then turn the wheel to position it to fill the wheel hub with the recommended oil. Remove the filler cap and the level cap and fill the housing with the recommended oil until the oil runs out of the level port. Cap the ports. After securing both caps, install the wheel cover bracket and the cover. **NOTE** See the instructions for bleeding brakes in the discussion of air-over-hydraulic brakes in Unit 17.

INTERNAL EXPANDING TUBE-TYPE BRAKES

Internal expanding tube-type brakes (Fig. 16-25) are used on large off-highway equipment, on winches, and as a clutch. This type of brake can be actuated by air, by oil, or by air over oil. All types of internal expanding tube brakes consist of basically the same components and parts and operate on the same principle.

Design The brakes to be covered are those used on the front axle of a rear dump truck. The torque plate is bolted to the spindle and transmits the brake torque from the torque plate onto the spindle. Thru-bolts and bushings are used to bolt the two half-circle side frames to the torque plate. The side frames have equally spaced torque bars. The lining blocks are riveted to the shoe table and placed from torque bar to torque bar, between the side frames. Thin steel shields are fastened to the shoe tables or torque bars to gap the space between the torque bars, as well as to prevent expander tube extrusion. A leaf retraction spring lies in the cutout formed by the lining and

shoe table, and the ends of the spring are placed into the cutout in the side frame. This arrangement retracts the lining from the brake drum whenever the pressure in the expander tube is reduced.

The brake drum is bolted to the wheel hub. Tapered roller bearings support the wheel hub on the spindle, and bearing preload is adjusted by shims. A metal floating seal ring prevents oil from leaking out of the wheel hub assembly or contaminants from entering it.

Operation Whenever the air control valve is activated, a metered amount of air, under pressure, enters the rotary chamber, moving the power piston in the master cylinder. The oil displaced by the master cylinder is forced into the expander tube, and consequently, the tube expands, forcing the lining blocks against the drum friction surfaces. As the lining and drum make contact, the lining moves against the torque bar, transmitting the brake torque to the torque plate. With increased air pressure, a greater power cylinder displacement is achieved, which causes the oil pressure to rise within the application line and expander tube and increases the lining force against the drum. Any reduction in the applied air pressure retracts the power piston in the power cylinder and thereby decreases the oil pressure. The lining force against the drum decreases accordingly. See the discussion of air-over-oil power assist in Unit 17.

Troubleshooting The internal expanding tube-type brake is very little trouble per se. However, if the wheel bearings are too loose or damaged, or the

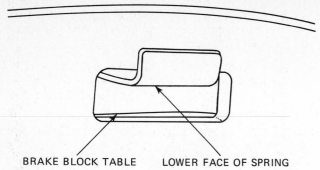

Fig. 16-26 View onto retraction spring cutout. (*Caterpillar Tractor Co.*)

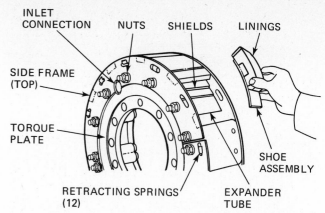

Fig. 16-27 View of brake shoe assembly (removed). (*Caterpillar Tractor Co.*)

floating seal ring is worn or damaged, the resultant oil leakage contaminates the brake blocks. The brake torque may be reduced because the wheel may tilt, and this would bring about a misalignment between the drum and linings.

The lining wear can be evaluated by applying the brakes and then examining the spring cutout at the inside side frame. When the linings are new, the brake shoe tables are below or in line with the lower leaf spring openings (see Fig. 16-26). When they are severely worn, the brake shoe tables are almost in contact with the leaf springs' lower surface. **NOTE** Linings should never be allowed to deteriorate to this dangerous level.

To service the expander tube or brake assembly or merely to replace the lining, the tire and wheel hub must be removed. Refer to the discussion of planetary drive wheel hubs in Unit 13 for procedure to remove the wheel hub and rim and adjust the bearing.

After removing the rim and wheel hub, scribe a line across the side plate and the torque plate and from the torque plate to the spindle to expedite component reassembly. Do not disconnect the oil inlet line fitting from the top inside torque plate if you intend only to replace the linings.

Drain the oil (using the drain screw to reduce the pressure). With a screwdriver, force the end of the leaf spring toward the center of the spindle, to bring the bent end over the opening in the side plate. Drive the spring toward the other side plate and then remove it. Lift one side of the brake shoe assembly and then slide it toward the raised side so that the extended shoe table can slide from below the torque bar. Repeat this procedure with the remaining 11 brake shoe assemblies (see Fig. 16-27).

If the torque plate has to be replaced, remove the self-locking nuts from the thru-bolts. Remove the bushing and then lift off the side frames. **NOTE** The thin steel shields may come off with the side frame, or they may stick on the expander tube. To remove the expander tube, first remove the two O rings and the inlet connector from the torque plate. To remove the torque plate, remove the torque plate mounting bolts and then lift it from the spindle.

Inspection and Reassembly It is good practice to replace the expander tube, the shields, the retraction springs, and the expander tube O ring seals, when-

ever the brake linings are to be replaced. Clean all other parts in solvent and dry them with compressed air or clean them in a hot tank. Examine the machined surface for cracks, nicks, and burrs. Examine the threaded and nonthreaded bores for damaged threads and elongation. If the torque bars are broken away from the side frame or are excessively worn, the side frame should be replaced. See the procedure for replacing brake linings in Unit 14. If it is necessary to reuse the expander tube, first clean it with alcohol and then examine it for loose fabric, leakage, and other signs of deterioration.

The reassembly procedure is precisely the reverse order of disassembly. However, when placing the individual shields underneath the torque bar, fasten them with N°2 Permatax and make sure that both shield ends are equal in distance from the sides of the torque bars.

To install the leaf retraction spring, use a $\frac{1}{8}$-in flat iron bar (one which is nearly the same width as the leaf spring). Position it through one leaf spring slot so that the inserted end points outward. Slide the leaf spring through the opposite slot so that the bent end rests against the flat bar. Now drive the leaf spring through the other slot. Remove the flat bar to allow the bent end to spring outward and lock to the side frame.

NOTE Follow the same bleeding procedure that you would for any hydraulic brakes but note that more oil is used when bleeding expanding tube-type brakes.

Review Questions

1. List the differences between a cam (air or hydraulically actuated) brake and a hydraulically actuated double-anchor foundation brake.

2. What is the purpose of (a) the cam (S or flat), (b) the slack adjuster?

3. Explain the mechanical action of a cam foundation brake, once the slack adjuster is forced to rotate.

4. What factors, other than the most obvious "misadjustment," would contribute to reduced brake torque?

5. Explain why (a) the travel of the air chamber push rods must be equal on all chambers, and (b) the angle of the slack adjuster must be 90° when the brakes are applied.

6. List the most apparent differences which can be found among slack adjusters.

7. List the main differences between a cam foundation brake and a wedge foundation brake.

8. Outline the mechanical action of a wedge brake from the point when the wedge is forced to move in order to apply the brakes.

9. What are the major differences between the two types of automatic wedge adjusters referred to in your textbook?

10. Refer to the service manual for an automatic wedge foundation brake. Write out the procedure to adjust (a) the air chamber, (b) the brake's shoe-to-drum clearance.

11. List the major components of an internal expanding tube-type drum brake.

12. Through which means can the extent of wear on the internal expanding tube lining be determined?

Unit 17 **Power-Assist Brakes, Brake Fluid, and Troubleshooting**

VACUUM-SUSPENDED POWER ASSIST BRAKE BOOSTER

Vacuum-suspended power assist brake boosters are used on small trucks and on light- to medium-size on- and off-highway equipment. They are designed to minimize the driver's effort as he applies the brakes to increase the brake pressure. However, it is possible to apply the brakes mechanically (without the assisting power source) in the event the power assist unit should fail, notwithstanding the shape, design, internal construction, or method of activation of the power assist unit.

The operating principle of all vacuum-suspended power assist units is the same, in that the power (force) is assisted by the atmospheric pressure on one side and the lower pressure (vacuum) on the other side, the latter being controlled by a valve mechanism. The vacuum on a gas engine emanates from the intake manifold and on a diesel engine from a vacuum pump.

NOTE A gas engine in good condition readily pulls 16 to 24 in [54.17 to 81.26 kPa] of mercury, whereas a vacuum pump in good condition readily pulls 28 in [94.80 kPa] of mercury.

Basic Design A vacuum-suspended power assist unit (direct mounted) consists of a large cylindrical housing internally divided by a piston or diaphragm. A rod is fastened to the piston or diaphragm and rests against the primary master cylinder piston or power cylinder piston. The rod is sealed to prevent atmospheric air from entering the vacuum half of the cylindrical housing. A coil spring in the vacuum side of the cylinder forces the piston or diaphragm toward the atmospheric side. A combination of hydraulic tubing and hoses connects the intake manifold or vacuum pump with the vacuum side of the cylinder and with the actuating valve mechanism. The actuating valve mechanism is a self-contained unit consisting of a vacuum valve and an atmospheric valve, each having a balance spring. The valves are actuated by the pushrod connected to the brake pedal (see Fig. 17-1).

Operation When the engine is operating and the brakes are released the vacuum valve is open and the atmospheric valve is closed. Equal (low) pressure then exists in both halves of the cylinder. The coil spring has forced the piston or diaphragm into the release position (to the left) and has allowed the

master cylinder pistons to move into the release position, opening compensating ports.

Assume that the diaphragm area is 60 in² [387 cm²] and that the vacuum pump has created a low pressure of 26 in [100.36 kPa] of mercury in both chambers. The remaining pressure in both halves would then be roughly 2 psi [13.78 kPa]. The pressure differential between the inside (vacuum) and the (outside) atmospheric pressure would be about 13 psi [89.57 kPa].

On an average day the barometric pressure is about 29.9 in [101.24 kPa] of mercury, which is equal to 14.7 psi rounded off to 15 psi [103.35 kPa]. Assume the truck is operating under this condition. If the vacuum valve were now closed and the atmospheric valve were open, atmospheric pressure of about 15 psi [103.35 kPa] would be acting on the 60 in² [387.0 cm²] diaphragm area. On the other hand, a pressure of 2 psi [13.78 kPa] would be acting on the opposite side of the diaphragm area. The effective pressure would, therefore, be only 13 psi [89.57 kPa], creating a pushing force of 780 lb [3463.2 N] on the pushrod and onto the master cylinder piston.

If the atmospheric valve were open for only a short time, so that only a low pressure of 20 in [67.72 kPa] of mercury (10 psi) could build up in the left side of the cylinder, then the force acting on the diaphragm and pushrod would be only 180 lb [799.2 N] because the pressure differential would be only 8 psi [55.12 kPa].

These calculations have demonstrated that, by controlling the atmospheric pressure, you control the applied force. To increase the applied force, the affected piston or diaphragm area is increased, or dual diaphragm power assist units are used.

Hold and Release Positions When the drive holds the brake pedal in a fixed position, the atmospheric valve closes (balanced position), and the existing application pressure is maintained. When the driver releases the brake pedal just a little, the vacuum valve opens to reduce the pressure within the atmospheric side of the cylinder. As a result the diaphragm moves to the left, as does the master cylinder piston, reducing the application pressure. When the brake pedal is fully released, the vacuum valve opens, reducing and equalizing the pressure to 2 psi [13.78 kPa] in both cylinder halves.

To maximize the safety of a vacuum-suspended power assist unit in the event that the vacuum line breaks, the gas engine operates at a wide-open throt-

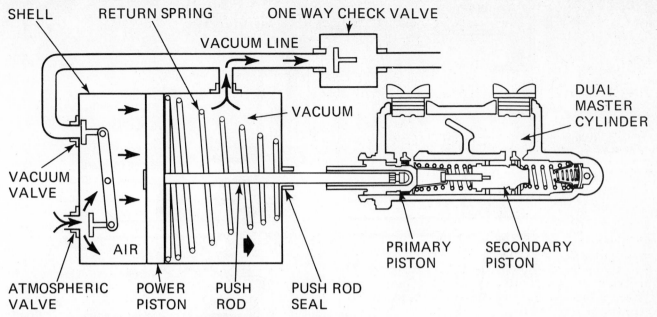

Fig. 17-1 Schematic view of a simplified vacuum-suspended brake booster.

tle. To compensate in the event of a damaged vacuum pump, a one-way check valve is installed to the inlet side of the vacuum connection. On larger brake systems an additional vacuum tank is used. **NOTE** On some on- and off-highway equipment the primary and secondary circuit each has a power assist unit.

Single and Tandem Power Cylinders The most common power cylinders used on small trucks are the single and the tandem vacuum-suspended power cylinders. A single-diaphragm power assist unit is shown in Fig. 17-2. With these cylinders one end of the valve rod is fastened, through a pin, to the brake lever mechanism, and the other end rests in the valve body socket. The power cylinder is usually mounted inside the engine compartment to the firewall, and a dual master cylinder is bolted to the

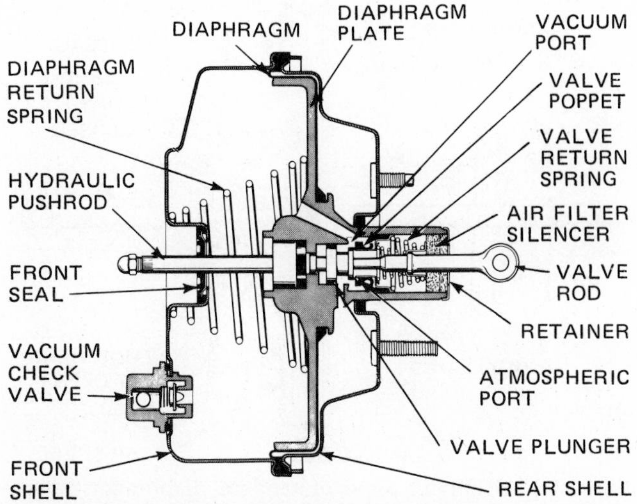

Fig. 17-2 Sectional view of single-diaphragm power cylinder. (*International Harvester Company*)

power unit. The pushrod, which is the link between the power unit and master cylinder, comprises part of the power unit.

The main difference between a single and a tandem power cylinder is that the tandem unit has two diaphragms and therefore has twice the force of a single unit with the same diaphragm area.

A tandem diaphragm vacuum-suspended power unit consists of the components shown in Fig. 17-3. The check valve fastened to the front shell serves as the inlet connection. The pushrod seal is press-fitted into the rear shell. The front diaphragm, which serves as the seal between both shells, is fastened to the front diaphragm plate. The hydraulic pushrod and the reaction disk rest in the bore of the front plate. The end of the front diaphragm plate is threaded into the rear diaphragm plate and is sealed with an O ring. The seal of the center plate and the rear diaphragm plate slide on the outer cylinder surface. The rear diaphragm is fastened to the center plate and to the rear diaphragm plate. The cylindrical extension of the rear diaphragm plate passes through the rear shell. A rear seal prevents atmospheric air or dirt from entering the shell. This arrangement creates four sealed chambers.

The diaphragm return spring holds the diaphragm to the right (in release position). The control valve assembly extends inside the cylindrical rear diaphragm plate. As shown, the left end of the valve plunger passes through the bore in the front diaphragm plate and the right side of the rod plunger forms the seat of the atmospheric port. The valve return spring and the poppet return spring force the valve plunger against the seat of the poppet valve and thereby close the atmospheric port and open the vacuum port. **NOTE** The vacuum port seat is formed in the hub of the rear diaphragm plate. The poppet valve is made of a flexible rubber. The valve rod rests in the socket of the valve plunger and ex-

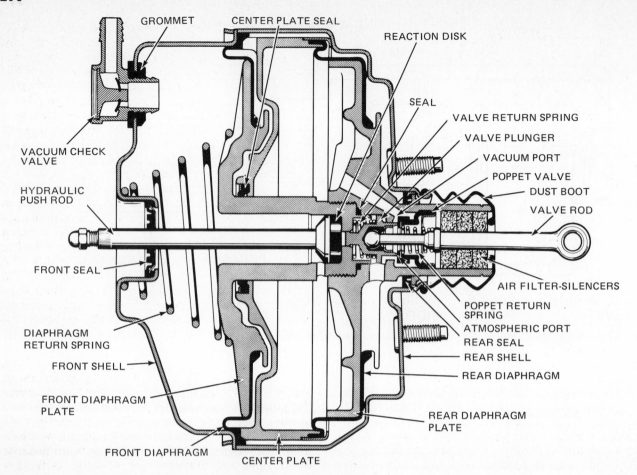

Fig. 17-3 Sectional view of tandem diaphragm power cylinder in the release position. (*International Harvester Company*)

tends to the right. The air filter (silencer) is held inside the rear diaphragm bore by the dust boot.

OPERATION—BRAKES RELEASED AND ENGINE RUNNING
When the engine is operating and the brakes are released, the valve return spring has moved the valve plunger, as well as the valve poppet, opening the vacuum port. The low pressure (vacuum) in the intake manifold reduces the pressure within the four chambers via the vacuum check valve in chamber 1 passage 1; in chamber 3 passage 2; in chamber 4, around the rear diaphragm and center plate. Passage 4 releases pressure out of chamber 2, and through passage 3 out of chamber 3. The diaphragm return spring holds the front diaphragm center plate and the rear diaphragm plate to the right.

APPLICATION When the driver depresses the brake pedal, the valve rod and valve plunger move to the left. The tip of the valve plunger comes to rest against the reaction disk. At the same time, the poppet valve spring forces the poppet to the left, closing the vacuum port. Chambers 2 and 4 are then closed off from chambers 1 and 3 (see Fig. 17-4).

Any additional brake pedal application moves the valve plunger away from the poppet valve (presently resting against the vacuum port seat) and opens the atmospheric port. The valve plunger tip, which is resting against the reaction disk, then moves the hy-

draulic pushrod. This increases the force on the primary master cylinder piston and moves the floating secondary piston to the left. Furthermore, with the atmospheric valve open, atmospheric air enters through the air filter, flows around the atmospheric port, and moves through passage 3 into chamber 4.

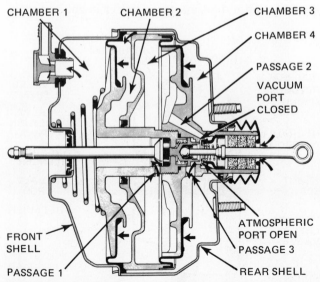

Fig. 17-4 Sectional view of tandem diaphragm power pistons in the applied position. (*International Harvester Company*)

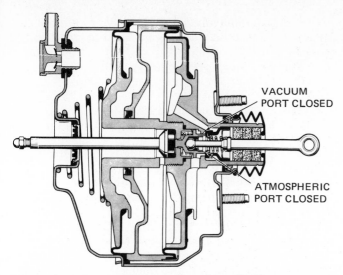

Fig. 17-5 Sectional view of tandem diaphragm power pistons in the hold position. (*International Harvester Company*)

It continues to flow around the outer circumference of the rear diaphragm and center plate, passage 4, to move into chamber 2.

With the atmospheric pressure in chambers 2 and 4, and with low pressure (vacuum) in chambers 1 and 3, the front and rear diaphragm plates move to the left, as does the hydraulic pushrod. As hydraulic pressure develops within the hydraulic system, the counterforce acting on the pushrod and reaction disks increases. This force is transmitted to the valve rod, to the brake lever linkage, and to the brake pedal.

Because of the valve mechanism design, the applied brake force is in direct proportion to the hydraulic system pressure developed within the brake system. The driver can, therefore, sense the amount of brake force applied.

HOLD POSITION While the brake is being applied, the hydraulic force against the hydraulic pushrod, the reaction disk, and the valve plunger reacts in

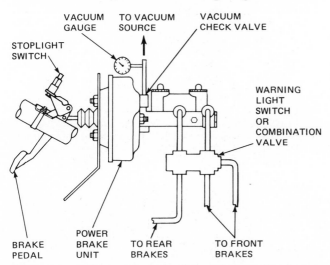

Fig. 17-6 Schematic view of brake assembly being checked for vacuum leak. (*International Harvester Company*)

opposition to the driver force on the brake pedal— in effect, attempting to close the atmospheric port. As soon as the brake pedal movement ceases, the diaphragm plate and poppet valve move an additional (about $\frac{1}{32}$ in, 0.79 mm) distance to the left. This is just far enough to close the atmospheric port. With both ports closed the diaphragm plates remain in a fixed position. **NOTE** When the maximum pedal force is applied, the atmospheric port does not close. Maximum atmospheric pressure is admitted to chambers 2 and 4 (see Fig. 17-5).

When the brake pedal is released, the valve rod moves to the right, allowing the hydraulic force to move the valve plunger. The plunger moves the poppet valve and opens the vacuum valve. This again connects chambers 2 and 4 with chambers 1 and 3, reducing the pressure within chambers 2 and 4. The diaphragm plates, the hydraulic pushrod, and the primary and secondary master cylinder pistons then move to the right, reducing the hydraulic pressure within the brake system. If the brake pedal movement stops before it is fully released, the power unit comes to the hold position.

LOSS OF VACUUM In the event of engine failure or a break in the vacuum line, the existing vacuum within the chambers of the power unit provides two or three brake applications. When the vacuum no longer exists, the driver is not entirely without brakes; however, he has less braking force because he now has only the pedal force acting on the hydraulic pushrod.

TESTING A vacuum-suspended power unit or any other type of power assist unit is seldom the cause of brake trouble; however, if there is indication it is cause for concern, the following checks should be made before removing the units: (1) inspect the brake pedal linkage to determine if it is binding, (2) check the valve rod to determine if it is bent or binding, (3) look for dirt in the air filter, (4) check the vacuum line to see if it is loose or broken or has deteriorated, (5) inspect the inlet grommet for damage and the seal for deterioration.

If these areas have checked out satisfactorily, install a vacuum gauge and operate the engine to check the vacuum (see Fig. 17-6). Stop the engine to check for vacuum leaks. While the engine is stopped, apply the brakes several times to remove the vacuum. With the brakes applied, start the engine. If the power assist unit is operating satisfactorily, the pedal should fall away slightly. In essence the valve mechanism of the power assist unit is operating and comes to the hold position.

If, when following up a complaint of dragging brakes, you find the foundation brakes to be operating satisfactorily, it will then be necessary to remove the power unit. By removing the power unit you can determine if the diaphragm return spring is broken, the valve assembly is dirty, the power unit needs to be lubricated, or the hydraulic pushrod has come out of adjustment.

If the complaint is reduced brake force or a hard pedal, again the power unit must be removed and

272

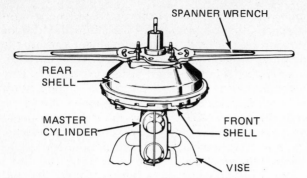

Fig. 17-7 Separating the front from the rear shell. (*International Harvester Company*)

serviced. Each of these problems can evolve from dirt in the valve mechanism, insufficient lubrication, or damage to one or both diaphragms.

SERVICING Before removing any type of power assist unit, always block the wheels to ensure safety and then clean the unit and the surrounding work area. **NOTE** Whenever the power unit is to be serviced, also service the master cylinder.

Remove the vacuum line and the hydraulic line from the master cylinder and the power unit. Cover all openings to prevent entry of foreign matter. Disconnect the pedal linkage and remove the mounting nuts and washers from the studs and then lift the power assist unit from the firewall. Next, remove the fluid from the reservoirs and bores; remove the dust boot, and then clean the unit thoroughly. From this point on the disassembly procedure varies slightly, depending on manufacturer model.

On many models the front and rear shells are locked together. To separate them, apply brake fluid to the outer circumference. Scribe a line across both shells, another line from the master cylinder to the front shell, and a third line on the front shell. Marking of the shells designates alignment of the check valve and mounting studs and therefore expedites reassembly.

Clamp the master cylinder in a vise (which has protective jaws) so that the rear shell points upward. Place the special spanner wrench holes over the rear shell studs and fasten the wrench to the studs. Force the wrench downward while turning it counterclockwise until the cutouts in the rear shell align with the locking lands in the front shell. Slowly release the downward force to allow the diaphragm return spring to separate the shells (see Fig. 17-7).

Remove master cylinder mounting nuts and washers from the studs of the front shell. Remove the master cylinder, drive out the seals with a seal driver, and take care not to damage the check valve. If the check valve is damaged or the grommet (seal) deteriorated, pull the valve (straight) out of its grommet. If you were working with a tandem diaphragm power assist unit, you would first remove the rear shell diaphragm, then the hydraulic pushrod, and then the return spring.

Next, remove the boot from the rear shell. When removing the valve rod end from the grommet, dampen the rubber grommet with brake fluid or al-

cohol to ease removal; clamp the valve rod in a vise (placing a prybar between the vise and the stud bolt) and force the rear shell, in parallel position, away from the vise. Take care not to pry on the plastic rear diaphragm plate, for it may crack or chip.
CAUTION Do not allow the rear shell to fall to the floor.

Once the valve rod is removed, lift out the retainer, the air filter, the poppet return spring, the spring retainer, and the poppet valve from the rear diaphragm hub. Carefully remove the spring retainer and lift the rear diaphragm from the rear plate.

To separate the front diaphragm plate from the rear plate, clamp a $1\frac{1}{16}$-in [26.98-mm] hex bar in a vise and place the hex opening in the front diaphragm plate, over the hex bar. Now, holding the outer edge of the rear diaphragm plate, twist it counterclockwise to loosen it and then carefully unscrew it from the front plate.

Remove the square O ring seal, the valve return spring, and the valve plunger from the rear diaphragm plate. Slide the center plate out from the front diaphragm plate and remove the front diaphragm.

CAUTION Do not damage the center plate seal. It is not individually replaceable.

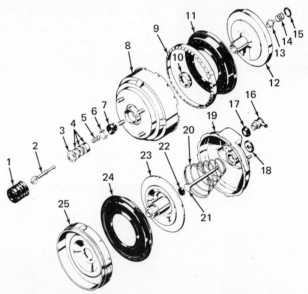

1. Boot
2. Valve rod
3. Filter-silencer retainer
4. Air filter-silencer
5. Poppet return spring
6. Poppet spring retainer
7. Valve poppet
8. Rear shell
9. Rear diaphragm retainer
10. Rear vacuum bearing seal
11. Rear diaphragm
12. Rear diaphragm plate
13. Valve plunger
14. Valve return spring
15. Seal
16. Vacuum check valve
17. Check valve grommet
18. Front vacuum seal
19. Front shell
20. Diaphragm return spring
21. Hydraulic push rod
22. Reaction disk
23. Front diaphragm plate
24. Front diaphragm
25. Center plate

Fig. 17-8 Exploded view of tandem diaphragm power unit. (*International Harvester Company*)

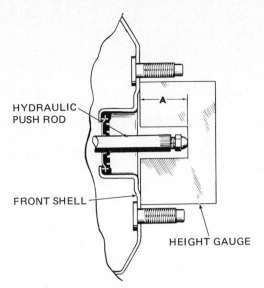

Fig. 17-9 Measuring pushrod protrusion. Distance A must be within limits outlined in service manual specifications. (*International Harvester Company*)

To remove the rear seal, place the shell studs on a flat surface and then use a seal driver to push the seal out of its bore (see Fig. 17-8).

CLEANING AND INSPECTION After the power assist unit is disassembled, clean all metal parts with solvent. Use compressed air to dry them and to remove any remaining dirt or fluid from the passages and surfaces. Rubber or plastic parts should be cleaned with alcohol.

CAUTION Plastic parts crack or chip easily.

Automatically discard all used parts that are duplicated in the repair kit. Check the serviceability of the remaining parts. If the diaphragms have kinks or cracks, they must be replaced.

REASSEMBLY Reassemble components in precisely the reverse order of disassembly. Use a seal driver to install the front and rear seal, and make certain

the seals seat properly against the shoulder. Furthermore, the front seal lip must face toward the master cylinder and the rear seal lip toward the mounting bracket.

Apply a light coat of the recommended lubricant to the following components: the diaphragm hubs, the front and rear seal, the seal of the center plate, and the valve plunger. Do not lubricate the plunger grommet. Do not forget to tighten the rear diaphragm plate to the specified torque.

Dust the rear shell with talcum powder and apply a light coat of lubricant to the outside of the rear diaphragm plate and to the cutouts around the edge of the front shell. Make certain, when placing the diaphragm assembly into the rear shell, that the lugs align with the lines on the rear shell. When locking the rear shell to the front shell, make sure that the scribe marks align.

Next, measure the protrusion of the hydraulic pushrod (see Fig. 17-9). If it is not within service manual specifications, adjust the self-locking screw until it comes within the recommended limits. Before installing the dust boot, swab the openings with alcohol to ease installation.

To service and bleed the master cylinder, follow the procedure previously outlined for the master cylinder.

Before installing the power unit, make the following checks: the brake pedal mechanism for extent of wear, the bushing for looseness and/or wear, the vacuum line for damage, and the brake light switch for effectiveness.

Frame-Mounted Power Brake Assist Unit Another type of vacuum-suspended power brake assist unit is the frame-mounted type known as the Hydrovac. This type is a power multiplier and is hydraulically activated. It is used on light- and medium-size on- and off-highway equipment. When used on a truck having a dual master cylinder, either a single or dual diaphragm power assist unit or two or four single units could be used (see Fig. 17-10).

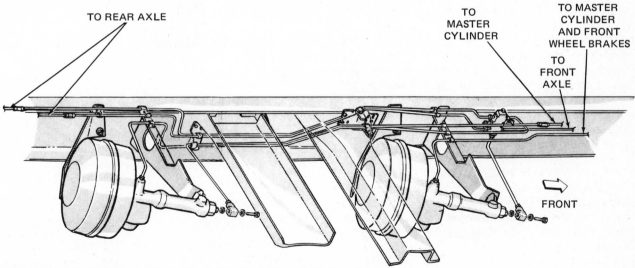

Fig. 17-10 View of frame-mounted single-diaphragm brake booster installed. On larger units the same installation is on the right frame rail. (*Chrysler Corporation*)

274

When the truck has a diesel engine, a vacuum pump is necessary to create low pressure (vacuum). The power assist unit may have a diaphragm or may be of the piston design. In either case the design and operation of the control valve mechanism and of the hydraulic power cylinder are very similar.

DESIGN OF A SINGLE-DIAPHRAGM UNIT   The power chamber is fastened to the hydraulic cylinder and is sealed by a flange gasket. The power chamber consists of a left shell and a right shell, and the diaphragm which divides it into two sealed chambers. A plate and pushrod are fastened to the diaphragm. The pushrod extends into the hydraulic cylinder bore, where it is pinned to the hydraulic piston. The diaphragm return spring holds the diaphragm to the left (when the brakes are released). The left chamber shell is connected with the valve body. Inside the cylinder bore is a bearing and seal. The bearing is used to support the pushrod, the seal prevents hydraulic fluid from leaking into the right chamber, and the lip seal seals the pushrod.

The hydraulic piston stop limits the pushrod travel, the hydraulic line connects the master cylinder to the fluid inlet port, and the hyraulic piston seal is used to trap the fluid in the hydraulic cylinder when the brakes are power applied. The residual check valve and spring are used to maintain a residual pressure within the hydraulic system.

The control valve consists of the control valve piston (which is fastened to the control valve diaphragm) and two seals. It is used to control vacuum and atmospheric pressure. The lower half of the control valve piston has a center passage and a cross-drilled opening leading to the vacuum port and right side of the diaphragm chamber. The control valve diaphragm separates the lower valve body into halves, and the diaphragm extension becomes the vacuum poppet seat.

The control valve diaphragm return spring always applies upward force to the diaphragm. The first-stage atmospheric poppet is fastened to the vacuum poppet extension. The vacuum poppet return spring holds the first-stage and the second-stage atmospheric poppet on its seat, limiting the upward travel (but opening the vacuum port). The atmospheric tube is connected to the engine air cleaner or to a separate air cleaner.

OPERATION—BRAKES RELEASED AND ENGINE RUNNING   With brakes released and engine running, the master cylinder line pressure is about the same as atmospheric pressure; therefore the diaphragm return spring has moved the diaphragm and control valve piston upward against the piston stop. The vacuum poppet return spring has moved the vacuum poppet upward and has closed the first- and second-stage atmospheric ports. The atmospheric pressure in the left and right power chambers is reduced by the engine or by the vacuum pump. The atmospheric air is drawn from the left chamber via the control tube, via the center passage and port in the control valve piston (see Fig. 17-11), and then through the vacuum port in the control valve body. The atmospheric air

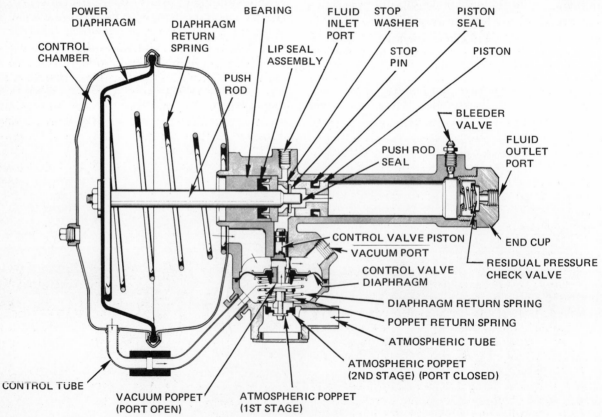

Fig. 17-11 Sectional view of a single-diaphragm hydrovac power booster. (*International Harvester Company*)

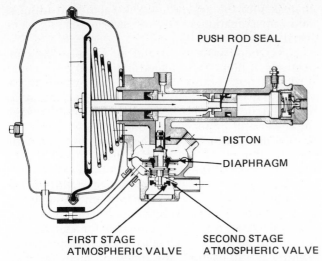

Fig. 17-12 Schematic view of power cylinder in the application position. (*International Harvester Company*)

is drawn from the right chamber via port A, through and around the control valve piston, and then mixes with the air from the left chamber. The diaphragm return spring holds the diaphragm and pushrod to the left within the limits set by the pin and piston stop. As a result the seal on the end of the pushrod does not rest against the hydraulic piston. Expanding and contracting brake fluid is therefore allowed to flow through the open passage to and from the hydraulic cylinder.

APPLICATION As the brake pedal is depressed, the fluid displaced by the master cylinder increases the (fluid) pressure on the control valve piston and within the hydraulic cylinder, forcing the piston and diaphragm downward. The piston bottoms against the vacuum poppet, closing the vacuum port and closing off the vacuum source to the left power chamber. **NOTE** The right power chamber cannot be isolated.

Any additional downward movement of the piston and diaphragm moves the vacuum poppet downward. The first-stage atmospheric poppet is then forced off its seat and allows atmospheric pressure to pass by the open port into the control tube and into the left chamber. Atmospheric pressure now acts on the lower area of the diaphragm, forcing the diaphragm and piston upward. The increased pressure in the left chamber moves the power diaphragm and pushrod to the right. The end of the pushrod seal butts against the hydraulic piston, closing off its fluid passage and trapping the fluid within the hydraulic cylinder. At the same time the second-stage atmospheric poppet is forced open, allowing the atmospheric air to rush into the left chamber. Because of the two-stage atmospheric poppet arrangement, the brake application is very smooth (see Fig. 17-12).

With the hydraulic piston passage closed, and with additional diaphragm movement, the pressure within the cylinder increases. The residual check valve opens and the pressure within the brake system increases. However, the push rod force is not

the only force that acts on the hydraulic piston—the master cylinder also exerts pressure on its left side.

To cite an example: say the pressure differential between the left and the right side of the power chamber is 10 psi [68.9 kPa], the area of the diaphragm is 50 in² [322.5 cm²], and the area of the hydraulic piston is 1 in² [6.45 cm²]. There would then be a pressure of 500 psi [3445 kPa] within the hydraulic system; (10 × 50)/1 = 500 psi.

Assume that the pressure created by the master cylinder is 300 psi [2067 kPa]. The total pressure acting on the hydraulic piston would be 500 + 300 = 800 psi [5512 kPa].

HOLD AND RELEASE POSITIONS When the brakes are applied, the hydraulic pressure acts on the control valve piston area and creates a downward force. The atmospheric pressure and the diaphragm return spring acting on the area below the diaphragm create an upward force. As soon as both forces are equal, the vacuum poppet return spring upsets the balance, moves the control valve upward, and closes the atmospheric ports. The force from below the control valve (atmospheric pressure) is transferred first to the control valve piston, then to the master cylinder, and finally to the brake pedal, so that the driver senses the applied brake force.

Any additional master cylinder pressure, due to increased force on the brake pedal, forces the atmospheric valves to reopen, increasing the atmospheric pressure within the left chamber. As soon as the forces equalize again, the valve closes. Any reduction in the master cylinder pressure moves the diaphragm and control valve piston upward, opening the vacuum port, until a new point of balance is reached (see Fig. 17-13).

If the brake pedal is fully released, the master cylinder pressure falls to atmospheric pressure, removing the force from the control valve piston. Atmospheric pressure acting on the diaphragm return spring moves the diaphragm upward and opens the vacuum port. The left chamber is then connected with the vacuum source, reducing the pressure within the chamber.

As the pressure is reduced within the left cham-

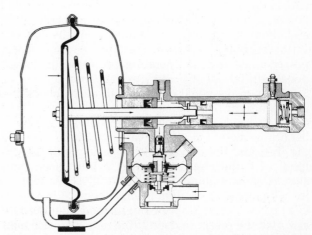

Fig. 17-13 Schematic view of power cylinder in the hold position. (*International Harvester Company*)

ber, the applied hydraulic pressure forces the hydraulic piston, the pushrod, and the diaphragm to the left, reducing the applied hydraulic pressure within the cylinder bore. The system pressure opens the residual check valve and thereby reduces the system pressure. As the hydraulic piston comes to rest against its stop, the pushrod and the diaphragm continue to move to the left because of the force of the power diaphragm return spring. The return spring's force ceases when the pin in the pushrod contacts the left side of the pin bore in the hydraulic piston.

The final pushrod movement is approximately $\frac{1}{16}$ in (2.13 mm) before the pushrod end opens the fluid passage in the piston, allowing the fluid to pass back to the master cylinder reservoir. The residual check valve then closes and maintains the residual system pressure.

If the vacuum source becomes depleted, there is sufficient vacuum within the chamber to allow one or two power assist brake applications. When using a vacuum tank, the system has a reserve of five to seven power assist brake applications. When the vacuum is depleted within the chamber or reservoir, or when the atmospheric supply is completely restricted owing to a clogged air cleaner, the master cylinder acts as the safety system, supplying the necessary fluid displacement to create the pressure required to activate the brakes. However, this pressure is greatly reduced, regardless of the physical effort exercised by the driver. In this latter situation the fluid displaced by the master cylinder flows through the fluid passage in the hydraulic piston, into the cylinder area (opening the residual check valve), and then into the hydraulic lines and wheel cylinder.

TROUBLESHOOTING AND TESTING   Before removing the power assist unit for service, verify that it is the cause of the brake trouble by conducting several checks and tests. Start by test driving the equipment to evaluate the condition of the brakes.

If the operator complained of "poor brakes" but inspection and checks reveal satisfactory foundation brakes, proceed as follows:

1.   Check the condition of the vacuum lines and connections.
2.   With the engine shut off, pump the brakes several times to remove all vacuum from the system. With the brakes applied, start the engine. If the power assist unit is operating properly, the brake pedal will fall away about $\frac{1}{2}$ in [12.7 mm].
3.   If the brake pedal does not fall away, check the air cleaner for restriction.
4.   Install a vacuum gauge into the left power chamber or reservoir to check the vacuum source, the supply line, and the power unit for leaks. Start the engine; with the engine running at idle speed, you should register about 20 in [67.72 kPa] of mercury (or when using a vacuum pump, about 28 in [94.80 kPa] of mercury). Stop the engine and note the rate at which the pressure rises. If the rate is greater than 2 in [6.77 kPa] of mercury per min, the leak is excessive, and the unit must be serviced. If there is no air leak into the system but the vacuum reading is below specification, check and service the engine or service the vacuum pump.
5.   Use soapy water to detect air leaks at the connections. If none are revealed here, then the air leak is in the power unit, or one or both atmospheric valves may be damaged, or the flange gasket may be damaged, or there may be a leak at the joint between the lower and upper valve body.
6.   If the vacuum source, the power unit, and the vacuum line check out satisfactorily, install a 2000 psi [13,780 kPa] pressure gauge (at any convenient place) into the hydraulic system. Start the engine and apply the brakes with maximum pedal force. Your pressure gauge reading should equal the specified psi [kPa], which on an average for a single unit is about 1600 psi [11,024 kPa]. If the pressure gauge reading is satisfactory, the brake problem must lie in the foundation brake. If the pressure is below specification, the problem could stem from any of the following conditions: power diaphragm damaged, pushrod seal not sealing the hydraulic fluid passage, hydraulic piston seal damaged, control valve piston seal damaged, pushrod seal damaged, brake fluid draining into the engine, bent pushrod, or the primary seal in the master cylinder leaking.

If the operator complained that the brakes would not release, the trouble may be a damaged residual check valve, or the control valve piston may be binding, or the hydraulic piston or pushrod may be binding on the return stroke.

REMOVING THE POWER ASSIST UNIT   The preliminary removal procedures to be followed and the precautions to be taken are the same as those outlined for servicing the direct-mounted power assist unit.

After the unit has been cleaned and the brake fluid removed from the cylinder bore, scribe a line across the front and rear shells and scribe another line across the front shell and hydraulic cylinder housing. Clamp the hydraulic cylinder in a vise with the left shell facing upward. Loosen and then remove the control tube and the clamp band while pressing the left shell downward. Slowly ease off the force and then lift off the shell (see Fig. 17-14).

Manually compress the diaphragm return spring and, with snap-ring pliers, remove the lock ring that holds the bearing guides in place. You can now lift off the diaphragm with plate and pushrod, and the diaphragm return spring. Next, remove the pushrod seal, the lock ring, stop washer, bearing guide with seal, hydraulic piston stop, retaining ring, the hydraulic piston from the right shell, and the hydraulic cylinder. Carefully slide the diaphragm return spring over the hydraulic piston (see Fig. 17-15). Remove the three screws that hold the right shell to the hydraulic cylinder body and lift the shell from the cylinder. Remove the hydraulic cylinder, the end fitting, the seal, residual check valve, spring, washer, and the snap ring. It is expedient at this time to remove the bleed screw also.

Remove the four screws that hold the valve body to the hydraulic cylinder and then remove the valve body. Remove from the valve body the valve body

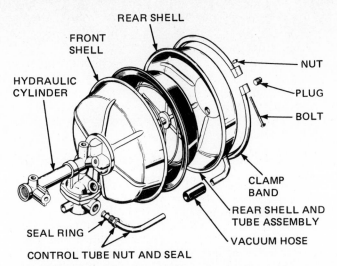

Fig. 17-14 Removal of control tube, clamp band, and rear shell. (*International Harvester Company*)

cover, the first- and second-stage atmospheric poppet, the valve return spring, the spring retainer, diaphragm, control valve, washer, and the control valve piston.

Remove the cup seals from the piston. Remove the vacuum poppet and poppet return spring from the body (see Fig. 17-16).

The procedure for cleaning and inspecting is the same as that outlined for the single and tandem power cylinders.

REASSEMBLING AND INSTALLING Reassemble each part in an order precisely the reverse of that in which you disassembled them. **NOTE** Your work area and parts must be kept immaculately clean during reassembly.

Before reassembling, lubricate all hydraulic seals and cups thoroughly with brake fluid. Lubricate the power diaphragm (with the recommended lubricant) where it contacts any metal surfaces. Do not forget to align the scribe marks before fastening the parts together and take care to turn the nuts or screws to the specified torque.

Before installing the left shell, coat both sides of

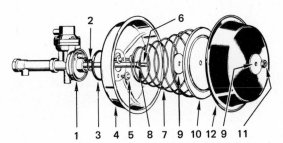

1. Hydraulic cylinder	7. Diaphragm return spring
2. Lock ring	8. Nut
3. Seal	9. Washer
4. Front shell	10. Diaphragm plate
5. Bolt	11. Nut
6. Hydraulic pushrod	12. Diaphragm

Fig. 17-15 Removing diaphragm, spring, front shell, and gasket. (*International Harvester Company*)

the power diaphragm with the recommended lubricant or talcum powder to ease installation. Cap all openings.

After installing the power unit make certain that the mounting bolts are torqued to specification, the vacuum lines are not damaged or twisted, the connections are correctly fastened, and the hydraulic lines are not bent or the fittings cross-threaded. Finally, check the air cleaner and the air cleaner connections.

BLEEDING PROCEDURE

NOTE The power assist unit cannot be bled until after the master cylinder is bled.

To bleed the power assist unit, attach two bleed hoses to the bleed screws—one close to the right shell and the other at the cylinder. Immerse the free end of the drain tube into a container partly filled with brake fluid. Open the first bleed screw (close to the right shell) one complete turn and then depress the brake pedal several times until the fluid is free of air bubbles. Next, tighten the first bleed screw and then proceed with the second bleed screw as you did the first. You must then bleed the wheel cylinder.

Vacuum Pump Equipment using a diesel engine requires a vacuum pump to maintain a constant supply of vacuum to operate the vacuum power assist devices. The vacuum pump used is of the unbalanced vane pump design. It is usually driven by the engine through a belt and pulley and therefore operates any time the engine is running. Some differences (see Fig. 17-17) between a hydraulic pump and a vacuum pump are the following:

The rotor of the vacuum pump has only three vanes and the vanes are of a carbon compound, the vacuum pump requires lubrication, the inlet port is connected to a vacuum reservoir, the inner housing at the inlet and outlet ports is slotted and combines into a chamber leading to the inlet and outlet ports, the outlet port is connected to the engine oil pan or oil return, and the engine oil pressure provides the required lubrication and sealing.

Lubrication oil enters the rear end plate and passes through the hole in the bronze bushing to lubricate the shaft.

There are three radial holes at the bushing end of the rotor shaft and six radial holes in the center area of the shaft, two of which lead into the rotor vane slots. There are three holes in the baffle plate which allow oil to pass onto the ball bearing for lubrication.

The inner housing has five oil discharge slots which open to the oil and air (discharge) outlet port. For correct alignment the front and rear end plates are doweled to the housing and fastened with through bolts and nuts to the center housing. The front end plate accommodates the baffle plate, the ball bearing, and two lip seals back to back. A passage within the end plate allows return of the oil (used for lubricating the bearing) to the outer circumference in the housing near the inlet port. The arrangement is used to aid in the lubrication of the

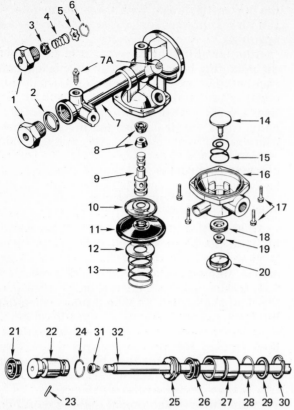

1. End fitting	17. Valve body screw
2. Seal	18. Atmospheric poppet (2nd stage)
3. Residual pressure check valve	19. Atmospheric poppet (1st stage)
4. (R.P.C.V.) spring	20. Valve body cover
5. Washer	21. Hydraulic piston cup
6. Snap ring	22. Hydraulic piston
7. Hydraulic cylinder	23. Piston-to-pushrod pin
7A. Bleed screw	24. Retaining ring
8. Control valve piston cup	25. Hydraulic piston stop
9. Control valve piston	26. Stationary seal
10. Washer	27. Guide bearing and seal
11. Control valve diaphragm	28. O-ring seal
12. Spring retainer	29. Stop washer
13. Valve return spring	30. Lock ring
14. Vacuum poppet	31. Pushrod seal
15. Poppet return spring	32. Pushrod and seal assembly
16. Valve body	

Fig. 17-16 Exploded view of control valve and hydraulic piston components. (*International Harvester Company*)

inner housing because the vacuum on the outer side of the bearing increases the oil flow.

OPERATION When the engine is running, lubrication oil under pressure enters the rear end plate and passes through the hole in the bronze bushing. When one of the three holes in the rotor shaft aligns with the hole in the bushing, metered oil enters the center passage of the rotor shaft. It then flows through the two holes into the rotor vane slots to lubricate the vanes and through one of the three

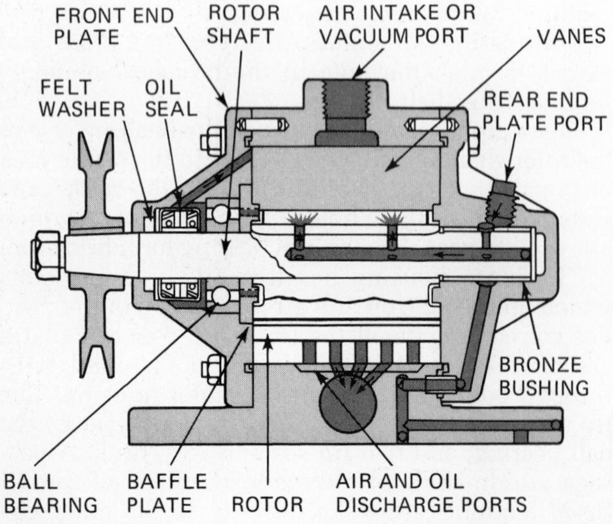

holes in the baffle plate to lubricate the bearing. The oil pressure and centrifugal force hold the vanes against the inner circumference of the pump housing.

The rotor vane A (see Fig. 17-18) is in the center of the inlet port slots, allowing air from the reservoir to enter between the vanes C and A and C and B. At the same time, rotor vane B is in the center of the outlet discharge port. As the rotor turns counterclockwise, vane C passes point A, and vane B passes point C.

The sealed pocket formed between vane C and vane B, along with the housing and the end plates, creates a low pressure (vacuum) as the vanes rotate and draw air from the reservoir. At the same time the pocket created between vane A and vane B and the housing and end plate opens to the outlet discharge port. Vane C is then between the outlet port and the inlet port, and vane A has started to discharge oil and air into the discharge slots and port. **NOTE** The discharge of the compressed air begins as the vane passes point C, which is close to the beginning of the discharge slots.

TROUBLESHOOTING AND TESTING Preliminary checks and tests should first be made to determine whether or not the vacuum pump is the cause of the low vacuum. Commence by visually inspecting the vacuum pump. Check for oil leaks at the end plates and housing—the square seal ring may be damaged or the through bolts may be loose. Check for oil leaks at the rotor shaft and front end plate—the front seal

Fig. 17-17 Sectional view of a vacuum pump. (*J I Case Company Agricultural Equipment Division*)

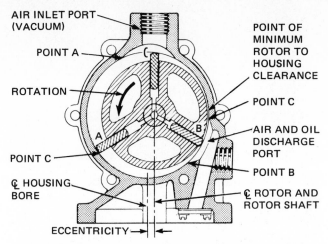

Fig. 17-18 Vacuum pump operation. (*International Harvester Company*)

may be damaged. Check the fan belt—a loose fan belt can cause low rotor speed. Check the connecting lines and fittings leading from the pump to the reservoir and to the power unit.

When no oil leaks are visible and no other malfunctions are noticeable, connect the vacuum gauge to the reservoir and check the vacuum and the system for air leaks. **NOTE** Inadequate lubrication, too much lubricant, or a restricted return line also reduces the efficiency of the pump. You must therefore check the volume of oil supply and oil return. If the oil return is severely restricted, drive belt slippage occurs. If the oil return is extremely high, reduce the flow; otherwise it may cause the rotor shaft to break.

If the vacuum pump does not draw the specified vacuum and yet no oil leaks are evident, then check for the following: worn or damaged vanes, surface damage to the inner housing or the end plate, or excessively worn bushings, bearing, or shaft. (The latter would increase the clearance between the rotor and housing.) If any of these defects is suspected, the pump must be removed for service.

REMOVAL Whenever possible, steam-clean the area in which you intend to work. Remove the pump by loosening and removing the inlet air line and the inlet oil and return line. Cap all openings. Loosen the pump adjusting nut and pump mounting bracket to release the drive belt tension and then remove the drive belt from the pump pulley. Remove the pump mounting bolts and lift the vacuum pump from the mounting plate (see Fig. 17-19).

SERVICING Again, clean the pump before removing the cotter key and the castellated nut from the rotor shaft. Use a puller to remove the pulley since it is keyed and has a tapered seat. Scribe a line across the front end plate and housing and the rear end plate and housing before loosening and removing the nuts and bolts. With the aid of a soft-face hammer, loosen the end plates from the housing but do not remove the dowels. Slide the rotor from the housing and remove the ring from the rotor. Use a hammer puller

to remove the baffle plate, ball bearing, seal rings, and seals. If a hammer puller is not available, lay the end plate on a wooden block and drive out these parts with a $\frac{3}{8}$-in punch, taking care not to damage the rotor face or seal surface. Before inspecting the components for their serviceability, clean them thoroughly and dry them with compressed air. Discard all seals and O rings (see Fig. 17-20).

INSPECTION Check the front and rear end plate surfaces for excessive wear. The amount of wear can be ascertained with the aid of a straight edge and a feeler gauge. The maximum wear limit is specified in the applicable service manual.

If the surfaces are not too badly scored, they can be restored by lapping. However, if the bearing, or the seal bore, or the bushing in the rear end plate is loose or the bushing is worn, the entire rear end plate must be replaced (because the bushing cannot be separately purchased).

If the baffle plate is worn or fits loosely in the front end plate, the baffle plate and/or front end plate must be replaced because the two components are press-fitted together.

When inspecting the housing, check for damaged inlet and outlet port threads and check the inner housing surface for excessive score marks or burrs. Small marks may be removed with fine grit emery cloth or with a cylinder deglazing hone.

Measure the length of the housing at four different places and compare the measurement with the service manual specification. Inspect the rotor shaft at the seal, bearing, and bushing surfaces. If any of the surfaces are rough, clamp the shaft in a lathe, rotate it and, using fine emery cloth (at least 600 grit), pol-

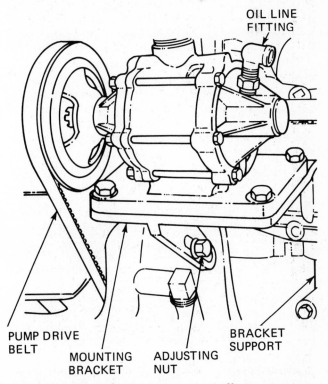

Fig. 17-19 Typical vacuum pump installation. (*International Harvester Company*)

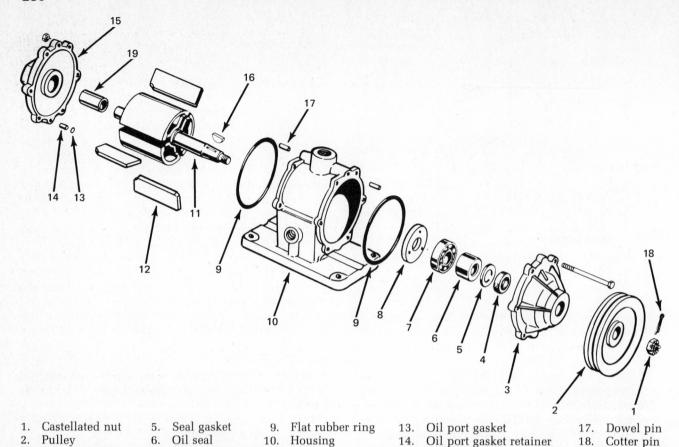

1.	Castellated nut	5.	Seal gasket	9.	Flat rubber ring	13.	Oil port gasket
2.	Pulley	6.	Oil seal	10.	Housing	14.	Oil port gasket retainer
3.	Front end plate	7.	Ball bearing	11.	Rotor	15.	Rear end plate
4.	Felt washer	8.	Baffle plate	12.	Vane	16.	Key

17.	Dowel pin
18.	Cotter pin
19.	Bushing

Fig. 17-20 Exploded view of vacuum pump components. (*J I Case Company Agricultural Equipment Division*)

ish the surface in a shoeshine motion. Take care not to undersize the shaft below specification. The ends of the aluminum rotor should show no uneven wear, and the length should not measure less than that specified in the service manual (see Fig. 17-21).

If the vane slots are worn or damaged or if the clearance between the slots and vane exceeds specification, the rotor assembly must be replaced. Inspect the curved edges of the vane that come in contact with the housing. There should be no excessive groove or wear marks. Check the side surface for wear, scoring, or embedded metal particles. **NOTE** The length of the vane must not exceed the length of the rotor.

REASSEMBLING Before commencing reassembly, re-clean all parts and dry them with compressed air.

Reassemble the vacuum pump parts in an order precisely the reverse of that in which they were disassembled. During the assembly dip all parts that require lubrication in high-grade engine oil.

Insert the vanes into the rotor slots with care. To prevent damaging the vanes, first install the front end plate to the housing. Position the rotor with one vane slot upward. Slide the vane (with the notch edge toward the rotor shaft) into the vane slot. The notch of the vane will then slip over the vane guide and the baffle plate.

Next, turn the rotor until the other vane slot is top

side and then install the second vane. Repeat this procedure with the third vane. The vane must not come rearward while you are turning the rotor, and when the rear end plate is positioned, the rotor must turn freely before the nuts are tightened to the specified torque.

CHECKING ROTOR CLEARANCE To ensure efficient pump action, the rotor-to-housing clearance must be between 0.003 and 0.006 in [0.076 and 0.152 mm] and must be equal at both front and rear.

To measure the clearance, insert a long 0.006 in [0.15 mm] feeler gauge through the inlet port. Manipulate it (toward the front end plate) to the nearest

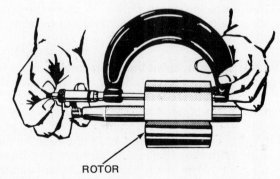

ROTOR

Fig. 17-21 Measuring rotor to determine its serviceability. (*J I Case Company Agricultural Equipment Division*)

point between the rotor and housing. If the feeler gauge will not go through this point, use a smaller gauge.

To check the complete outer rotor circumference, turn the rotor carefully so that the feeler gauge is not forced out. Repeat this procedure but this time place the feeler gauge toward the rear end plate.

To equalize or increase the clearance, you must move the end plate or plates. If, for example, the clearance toward the rear end plate is too great, move both end plates (using a soft-face hammer) horizontally toward the maximum clearance space. You may have to loosen the nut to make this move.

If the clearance is too great toward the front end plate, drive only the front plate (horizontally) to the minimum clearance. Do not forget to retighten the nuts after the adjustment has been made.

CHECKING ROTOR-TO-END-PLATE CLEARANCE To check the end play, install a dial indicator so that its stem contacts the end of the rotor shaft. After you have moved the rotor shaft back and forth, the dial should indicate a clearance less than maximum specification (see Fig. 17-22).

Repeat the dial installation in at least four places, 90° apart. When the vacuum pump is correctly installed and adjusted, the rotor should rotate with little effort. If the rotor binds at one point or another, loosen the nuts and then retighten them in three steps in a cross pattern to the specified torque. Before capping the openings, pour about three tablespoons of engine oil into the inlet port and rotate the rotor several times in both directions to ensure initial lubrication.

INSTALLATION Place the pump on the mounting bracket and tighten the mounting bolts finger-tight. Align (with the aid of a straight edge or string) the pump pulley with the drive pulley and then tighten the nuts to the specified torque.

Check the drive belt and the engine pulley for damage and wear. If they check out satisfactorily,

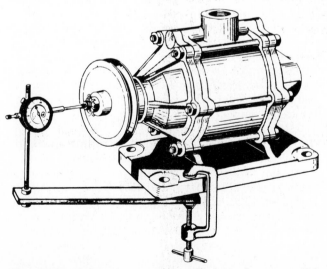

Fig. 17-22 Measuring rotor-to-end-plate clearance. (*J I Case Company Agricultural Equipment Division*)

lay the belt over the engine pulley and pump pulley and then tighten it to specification.

Connect the inlet air line, lubrication line, and return line to the pump and then retest the vacuum pump to evaluate its effectiveness.

HYDRO BOOSTERS (OIL OVER HYDRAULIC)

Several types of hydro boosters are manufacturered, each intended to increase the brake system's safety and the brake pressure. They are used on heavy cars, trucks, and buses, up to 42,000 lb [19,050 kg] GVW. All units are basically the same in design, performance, and operating principle. They use the power steering fluid as their power source and thereby provide about 30 percent more brake pressure than that of a current single-vacuum power assist unit, that is, about 2000 psi [13,780 kPa]. Furthermore, they provide one or more reserve power source(s) in event the engine stalls. Some units have an accumulator, or an electrically driven hydraulic pump, or a vacuum assist power unit.

One complete hydro brake system is shown in Fig. 17-23. It consists of the power steering pump, power steering unit, Hy-power booster (that is bolted to the master cylinder), hand control valve, relief valve, a diverter valve, check valve, relay valve, electrohydraulic pump, axle Hy-park actuator, and the front wheels with the cam actuator.

The purpose of the hand control valve is to send pilot oil pressure to the relay valve or to remove the pilot pressure from the relay valve.

The relief valve prevents the oil pressure from exceeding 120 psi [826.8 kPa]. If the power rises above this pressure, the valve opens and oil is directed back to the power steering reservoir. A pilot line is connected to the pressure control valve, which is part of the diverter valve. System pressure through this line is exerted onto the pressure control valve to maintain a pressure of about 80 psi [551.2 kPa] within the system. If the pressure drops below 80 psi, the diverter valve reduces the return oil flow, and more oil flows toward the hand control valve to maintain the desired pressure.

The check valve retains line pressure to the hand valve and relay valve whenever the engine is stopped and the park brake is released.

The relay valve directs oil back to the reservoir when the hand valve has directed pilot oil onto it. The relay valve also directs oil to the Hy-park actuators when the pilot pressure from the hand valve is removed.

The Hy-park actuator provides the vehicle with service brakes and parking brakes.

Design The hydro booster consists of the components shown in Fig. 17-24. The power piston inside the body is sealed to the cylinder bore. The control valve seat fits into the (reaction) piston counterbore and is held to the piston with a retainer ring. The piston fits in the bore of the control valve and power piston and is sealed with O rings to the bores. Its spring, positioned between it and the power piston,

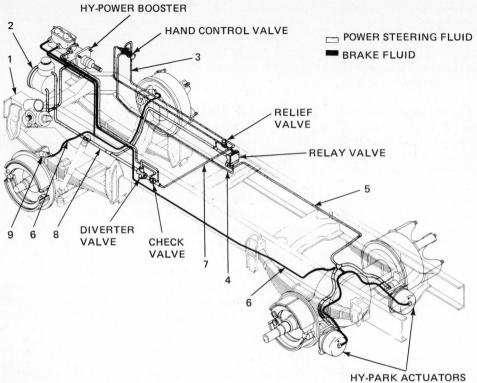

HY-POWER BOOSTER

HAND CONTROL VALVE

POWER STEERING FLUID
BRAKE FLUID

RELIEF VALVE

RELAY VALVE

DIVERTER VALVE

CHECK VALVE

HY-PARK ACTUATORS

1. Power steering
2. Power steering pump
3. Pressure line
4. Pilot pressure line
5. Hy-park actuating lines
6. Brake lines
7. Pilot lines
8. Return line
9. Cam brake wheel cylinder

Fig. 17-23 Schematic view of a Hy-park brake-actuating system. (*GMC Truck and Coach Division of General Motors Corporation*)

holds the reaction piston against the (control) valve, the latter being supported and sealed in the right body end. The seals are retained by a retainer (not visible in illustration). The taper on the valve protrudes through the bore in the control valve seat, and the smaller (round end) rests against the reaction piston.

The control valve spring holds the valve away from the seat. A dust boot protects the control valve and the extension link. The output end cap (left side) and the seal assembly are screwed to the main housing. The seal assembly seals the cylinder bore, as well as the pushrod. Supported within the cap, the piston rod rests—one end in the primary master cylinder piston and the other end in the power piston. To the right, against the body shoulder, the power piston is held by the power piston return spring.

Hy-Park Actuator The cam brake actuator shown in Fig. 17-25 is used on the rear axles of trucks and buses up to 62,000 lb [28,148 kg] GVW. It has two independent actuating systems built as one unit— the service brake system and the parking (or emergency brake) system.

DESIGN The two halves of the actuator body are bolted to make one unit, and the diaphragm is clamped between the two mating surfaces. The inner circle of the diaphragm is fastened to the park apply sleeve, which is supported within the left body half, and supported on the outer circumference by the hydraulic cylinder. It is sealed to the left housing with two seals located within the housing, and an O ring is used to seal between the park apply sleeve

and the hydraulic cylinder. The two stud bolts, screwed into the left body half, fasten the actuator to its mounting bracket. The dust boot fits into the groove of the pushrod collar and over the body housing, preventing contaminants from entering the actuator, as well as protecting the sleeve externally. The park apply piston rests against the diaphragm and in the recess area of the park apply sleeve. The piston has two threaded bores in which the manual release bolts are screwed, to release the park brake. One side of the park apply spring rests in the piston, and the other side rests against the right body housing, which has two manual-release access slots. The hydraulic cylinder, which is fastened to the right body half, has one threaded bore to accommodate the inlet fitting. The hydraulic piston within the hydraulic cylinder is sealed to the cylinder bore with two cup seals. One end of the pushrod rests in the pushrod guide in front of the hydraulic piston. The clevis is screwed to the other end of the pushrod. **NOTE** The front wheel actuators have no parking brake components.

OPERATION When the engine is running and the brake pedal is released, oil from the power steering pump enters the power steering valve, passes around the control valve spool, and leaves the outlet port. It is then directed into the power booster inlet port, flows into chamber A, between the control valve and the control valve seat, into the reaction piston spring area. Oil also passes into chamber B through openings in the power piston. From there it flows through the outlet port and flow switch, where it is diverted into two lines. One line directs oil to the diverter

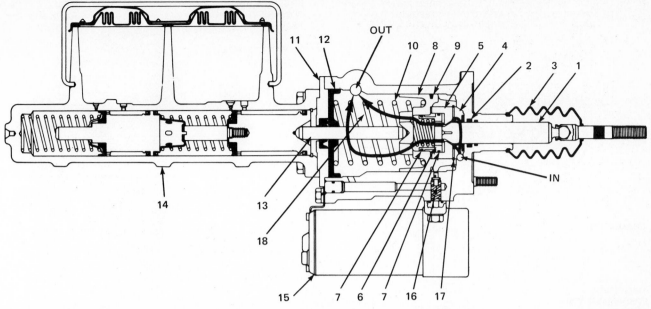

1. Valve	4. Retainer	7. Piston seal	10. Spring	13. Piston rod	16. Check valve
2. Seal	5. Seat	8. Power piston	11. Cap	14. Dual master cylinder	17. Chamber A
3. Boot	6. Piston	9. Power piston seal	12. Seal assembly	15. Electric pump	18. Chamber B

Fig. 17-24 Sectional view of a Hy-park power brake booster. (*GMC Truck and Coach Division of General Motors Corporation*)

valve, and the other line directs oil to (and through) the check valve, onto the hand control valve, where the oil flow ceases (see Fig. 17-26).

System pressure is exerted through the pilot line onto the pressure control valve, and when the pressure is about 80 psi [551.2 kPa], the pressure control valve reacts, the diverter valve opens, and oil is then directed back to the power steering reservoir to maintain the pressure of 80 psi.

A T connection directs the oil to the relay valve and from there to the Hy-park actuators, releasing the parking brakes. A second T connection directs oil to the relief valve and from there back to the power steering reservoir. The oil return line from the relay valve connects with the return line from the pressure relief valve. A pilot line from the hand control valve is connected to the relay valve.

When the hand control valve is placed in the open position (park brake applied), pilot oil pressure is exerted onto the relay valve. As the relay valve responds by opening a passage which allows the oil from the power booster park chambers to return back to the power steering reservoir, it also closes the oil flow to the park actuators (see Fig. 17-27). Oil from the left chamber side of the Hy-park actuators can now flow through the relay valve and into the return line, completely eliminating the pressure within the chambers. As the pressure is dropping within the chambers, the energy of the spring forces the piston, the diaphragm, and the park applied sleeve to the left. This causes the sleeve to push against the pushrod collar and forces the pushrod to move laterally, rotating the slack adjuster with a force of about 1500 lb [6660 N].

If the hand control valve is closed, the relay valve responds, the return oil flow to the reservoir is

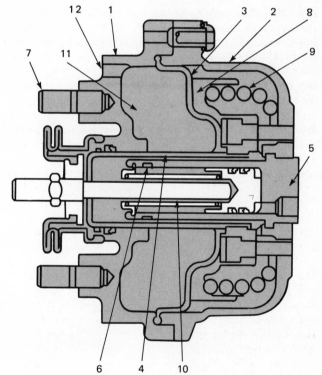

1. Front (body half)	7. Studs	
2. Rear (body half)	8. Park applied piston	
3. Diaphragm	9. Park applied spring	
4. Park applied sleeve	10. Pushrod guide	
5. Hydraulic cylinder	11. Parking brake oil chamber	
6. O ring	12. Parking brake inlet port	

Fig. 17-25 Schematic view of the cam brake actuator. (*GMC Truck and Coach Division of General Motors Corporation*)

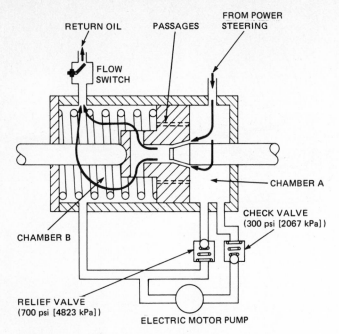

Fig. 17-26 Schematic view of the power booster when the brake is released and the engine is operating.

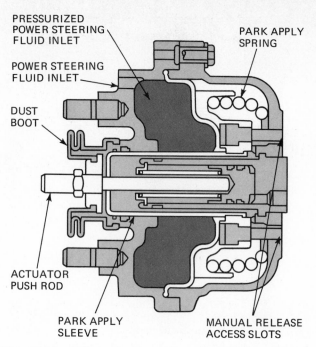

Fig. 17-28 Schematic view of parking brake released. (*GMC Truck and Coach Division of General Motors Corporation*)

blocked, and the oil is directed to the actuators. As the pressure rises, the force moves the diaphragm, the piston, and the park applied sleeve to the left, compressing the spring. This action removes the force from the pushrod and the brake shoe return spring(s) pull the shoes away from the drum, rotating the camshaft and slack adjuster and pushing the pushrod to the right (see Fig. 17-28).

BRAKE APPLICATION—ENGINE NOT RUNNING When the engine is not running and the electro hydraulic pump is not operating, the primary and the secondary master cylinder pistons supply brake fluid to their respective systems through the direct action of

the brake pedal. Then as the brake pedal is forced downward, the extension and the control valve are forced to the left until the control valve comes to rest against the control valve seat. This forces the power piston and the piston rod to the left and causes the primary and secondary master cylinder pistons to move to the left. The displaced fluid from the master cylinders is forced into the primary and secondary system. As the pressure increases, the hydraulic piston (in the actuators) moves outward, forcing the pushrod outward. The slack adjuster and camshaft rotate, causing the brakes to apply (see Fig. 17-29). When the brake pedal force is reduced (or fully re-

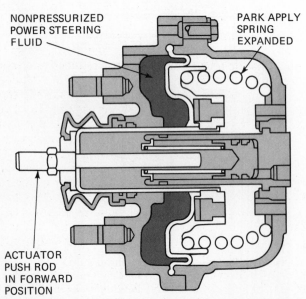

Fig. 17-27 Schematic view of parking brake applied. (*GMC Truck and Coach Division of General Motors Corporation*)

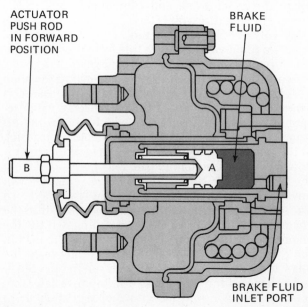

Fig. 17-29 Schematic view of a service brake application. (*GMC Truck and Coach Division of General Motors Corporation*)

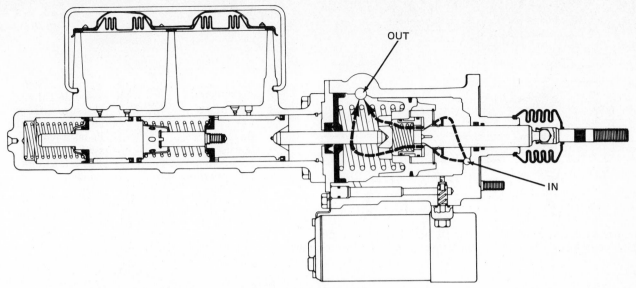

Fig. 17-30 Sectional view of the power booster in the application position when engine is operating. (*GMC Truck and Coach Division of General Motors Corporation*)

moved), the power piston return spring forces the power piston, the control valve seat, the control valve, and the extension to the right, and the brake pedal return spring moves the control valve away from the control valve seat. As the piston rod moves to the right, the hydraulic force causes the master cylinder piston to follow the piston rod. This allows the brake shoe return springs to retract the shoes from the brake drum surface, and as a result the camshaft rotates and the slack adjuster forces the pushrod and the actuator pistons to retract in their bores.

BRAKE APPLICATION—PRIMARY SYSTEM UNDER OIL FLOW When the primary system is under oil flow and the brake pedal is forced down, with a force of, say, 75 lb [333 N], the control valve closes the space between it and the control valve seat and moves the reaction piston to the left. Pressure instantly builds up within chamber A because of the resultant flow restriction. As the pressure increases and overpowers the power piston return spring, the power piston and the pushrod are forced to the left, moving the primary and the secondary master cylinder pistons to the left, causing the brakes to apply (see Fig. 17-30).

As the power piston and the control valve seat move to the left, a space is created between the valve and seat through which pump oil flows. A constant flow of oil also passes through the piston passages to maintain the desired application pressure in chamber A. The movement of the power piston indirectly applies the brakes, placing a counterforce on the piston rod and the power piston, which brings the power piston to a stop before it moves slightly to the right, to increase the flow restriction.

When the driver holds the brake pedal in a fixed position, the power piston and control valve seat are also in a fixed position. This creates a limited amount of space between the control valve and the seat, and a fixed pressure in chamber A. **NOTE** This

pressure is about 2.8 times lower than the hydraulically applied pressure.

If the driver increases the pedal force, the space between the control valve and the seat is reduced, increasing the pressure in chamber A. The control valve seat and the power piston then move to the left, increasing the force on the master cylinder pistons. When both forces (oil pressure in chamber A and piston force on the power piston) are equal, the power piston movement comes to a stop and a fixed restriction is achieved, resulting in a fixed oil pressure and a fixed hydraulic brake line pressure.

If the pedal force is partly removed, the control valve increases the space between the valve and the seat and as a result the pressure within chamber A is reduced. The higher force from the master cylinder pistons is then exerted onto the piston rod, forcing the power piston and control valve seat to the right. This reduces the space between the valve and the seat and maintains a lower pressure.

As the master cylinder pistons move to the right, the hydraulic brake line pressure is reduced and less force is exerted on the brake shoes. **NOTE** Under all circumstances (with the engine operating) the full power steering pump flow occurs between the control valve and the valve seat. However, as the restriction increases, the oil velocity increases.

When maximum pedal force, about 150 lb [666 N], is applied, the control valve remains seated against the control valve seat, and when the pressure in chamber A reaches about 700 psi [4823 kPa], the relief valve is forced open. About 4 gal/min U.S. [15.14 l] of oil passes by the valve at high idle and about 2.5 gal/min [9.46 l] at low idle and is directed into chamber B, where it returns to the power steering reservoir via the outlet port and flow switch. **NOTE** When the chamber pressure is 700 psi, the pressure in the brake line is about 2000 psi [13,780 kPa] because the power piston area is approximately 2.8 times larger than the master cylinder piston area.

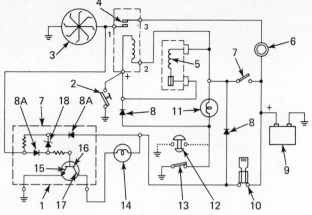

1.	Sensor	10.	Ignition switch
2.	Flow switch	11.	Tell-tale 1 (bulb)
3.	E.H. pump	12.	Pressure differential
4.	Relay		switch (S-models)
5.	Buzzer	13.	Pedal travel (safety)
6.	Starter solenoid		switch
	connection	14.	Tell-tale 2 (bulb)
7.	E.H. pump switch	15.	Emitter
	(brake pedal)	16.	Base
8, 8.A	Diodes	17.	Collector
9.	12-V battery	18.	Zener diode

Fig. 17-31 Schematic view of the Hy-park brake's electrical system. (*GMC Truck and Coach Division of General Motors Corporation*)

Reserve Power System   If, for any reason, the power steering pump oil flow seizes, the electrohydraulic pump automatically energizes. As soon as the motor starts to rotate, the vane pump draws oil from chamber B and pumps it over the check valve into chamber A. The reserve power system supplies a maximum oil pressure of only about 380 psi [2618.2 kPa] because some of the oil flows through the inlet port and back to the power steering and then to the inlet side of the power steering pump. However, this pressure allows adequate brake application with a maximum hydraulic line pressure of about 1000 psi [6890 kPa].

To energize the DC motor as soon as the oil flow from the primary system stops and to warn the driver that he must immediately stop the motor vehicle, three warning devices (two warning lamps and a buzzer, mounted on the dashboard) are used. When the primary system (power steering) has failed or is not operating, lamp 1 glows and the buzzer sounds. When the reserve system has also failed, the other lamp glows.

ELECTRIC COMPONENTS AND CIRCUITS   The reserve power system consists of the components shown in Fig. 17-31. Note that the battery voltage is always present at the relay's terminal 3. The relay, the buzzer, and light 1 are connected in parallel, as are the ignition switch and the electrohydraulic pump switch.

The electrohydraulic pump switch is open when the brake pedal is released. The flow switch is closed when there is no flow. Since diodes, a zener diode, and a transistor are involved, the electron theory applies to the operation of the system.

If the brake pedal is released when the ignition switch is in the off position, the electrohydraulic pump switch is also in the off position and therefore no light glows, and the buzzer does not sound. However, when the ignition switch is on, or when the brake pedal is forced down approximately 1.5 in [38 cm], the electrohydraulic switch closes, the buzzer sounds, and lights 1 and 2 glow. In either circumstance the circuits are closed, and the electrons flow

from the flow switch ground to relay terminal 4, through the relay coil, out of terminal 2, to buzzer terminal 5, through the coil, out of terminal 6, to junction A, through diode 8, over the light 1, to junction B, over either the ignition switch or the electrohydraulic switch, to the positive side of the battery. The relay coil's magnetic force pulls the armature down, closing the contacts, and allowing the electrons to flow from the ground of the DC motor through the field windings and the armature windings, over the points, to the starter solenoid, to the positive side of the battery. The motor rotates, supplying oil to the power booster; however, the flow switch remains closed because the oil flow within the Hy-power brake unit is reversed. At the same time the base circuit is completed from the ground of the motor, to terminal 9, over the resister, the zener diode, another resister, to terminal 7, over light 2, to junction C, over the ignition switch, to the positive battery terminal. This allows the electrons to flow from the ground of the sensor to the emitter, to the collector, over light 2, to junction C, over the ignition switch, to the positive battery terminal.

When the engine is operating, the flow switch is forced open and causes the light, the buzzer, and the relay circuit to open. With the relay circuit open the motor circuit is also open, and the high voltage from the zener diode is removed. This causes the base circuit to open and the transistor to switch off, and light 2 goes out. If the primary system is operating, but electrical problems arise within the electric pump motor, light 2 glows because a higher voltage is asserted on the zener diode, and this causes the electrons to flow from the motor ground, through the field and armature windings, through the resister, the zener diode, another resister, over the base, to the collector, over light 2, to junction C, over the ignition switch, to the positive battery terminal. This switches the transister on and commences the electron flow from ground, to the emitter, to the collector, at a higher voltage, causing the light to glow.

Troubleshooting   Trouble in the brake system could arise from any one of the four independent systems, that is, the hydraulic brake system, the primary and secondary booster systems, and the electric system. (The troubleshooting procedure for the hydraulic system need not be repeated.)

If the operator reports reduced braking or excessive pedal travel, visually check for the following: a loose pump drive belt, low oil reservoir fluid level, evidence of oil leaks, and pinched or twisted hydraulic lines. If an oil leak is apparent between the master cylinder and the booster, the high-pressure seal is damaged. If there is oil seepage at the control valve, the control valve seal or valve surface is damaged. If oil is noticeable at the electromotor pump flange and booster, the cap screws are loose or the O rings are damaged. If there is an oil leak at the end plate of the electric motor, the motor must be serviced.

When the operator complains of excessive pedal travel or of slow brake release or brake drag, check the adjustment of the brake pedal and make certain the pedal is fully returning against the stop. Incorrect adjustment can reduce the space between the control valve and seat and cause a pressure buildup within chamber A.

If, after the visual checks are made, the trouble has not been found, install a flowmeter and test the power steering pump flow against that specified. Check for flow restriction and for air in the system. If air is in the system, check for loose connections. Next, apply maximum brake pedal force and check the pressure. If the oil flow is below specification, check the filter first before servicing the power steering pump. If the pressure is below specification, service the power steering pump pressure relief valve and/or service the power brake booster pressure relay valve, for either relief valve may be faulty. If both flow and pressure are within specification, the cause of reduced brake action is within the power brake booster. The power piston seal may be damaged, the piston scored, or the cylinder bore scored or pitted.

To check the operation of the reserve power system, first turn on the ignition switch. If the pump is noisy or chatters, there is air within the secondary circuit. To remove it, lightly depress the brake pedal several times to actuate the booster and brakes. If the noise remains after several pedal actuations, and the hydraulic lines are not restricted or leaking, or if the fittings are not loose, the electrohydraulic motor must be serviced. If the motor rotates at a slow speed, proceed as follows: check the battery terminals and, if necessary, clean them; measure and test the battery and note the battery voltage; measure the voltage at the starter solenoid; and measure the voltage at terminal 1 and 3 of the relay and motor terminals. The voltage at each point should be not less than 0.3 volt of the open-battery voltage.

To check the relay contacts, measure the voltage drop by connecting a voltmeter to terminals 1 and 3. If there is a voltage drop, the points are pitted and the relay must be replaced. If the voltage at the motor terminal is correct, measure the ground side of the motor circuit. If the voltage checks out satisfactorily, the problem may be due to worn motor brushes and/

or commutator, or the bearings may be damaged or worn. A damaged vane pump can also cause the motor to rotate slowly.

Electric Failures   If electric failure occurs, first check the condition of the light bulbs and then check the battery voltage, the voltage at the ignition switch, and the electric hydraulic pump switch. If these check out satisfactorily, turn on the ignition switch and measure the voltage at terminals 2, 4, 5, 6, 7, 8, and 9, and at junctions A, B, and C. The voltage reading at each point should equal battery voltage reading.

To check the resistance of the electric hydraulic motor switch, connect a voltmeter across the switch and apply the brakes. The voltmeter should read zero voltage. If voltage is present, there is resistance within the switch and it should be replaced.

To check the operation of the flow switch and for high resistance, connect a voltmeter across the switch, turn on the ignition switch, or apply the brakes. If the switch is in good working condition, the voltmeter will read zero voltage.

If light 1 does not glow, or the buzzer does not sound when the ignition switch is turned on, diode 8 or 8A is open, or the relay coil is open. Replace the diodes or the relay. If light 2 fails to glow when the engine is not running, the cause must be within the sensor, on the assumption that there is battery voltage at the terminal 7.

Hydro-Booster Power Brakes   Another type of power booster system is shown in Fig. 17-32. Some variations between this power booster and the Hypark system previously described are that (1) the oil from the power steering pump is directed first to the power booster and then to the power steering; (2) a spring-loaded accumulator is used at the reserve power source instead of the electrohydraulic motor; (3) a return line from the accumulator leads back to the power steering reservoir, allowing the oil that could pass by the O ring and teflon ring to drain; (4) an accumulator valve and a check valve are used

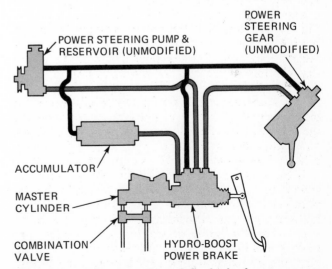

Fig. 17-32 Schematic view of the hydro-booster power brake system. (*Ford Motor Company*)

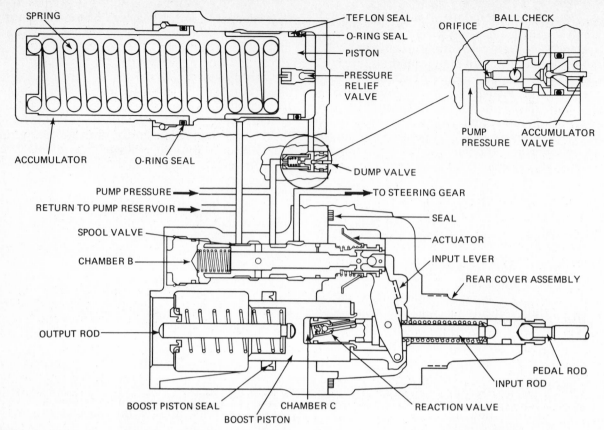

Fig. 17-33 Sectional view of the hydro-booster. (*Ford Motor Company*)

to charge the accumulator. (The check valve (having an orifice) is used to prevent accumulator oil from flowing in the reverse direction when the pump pressure decreases to less than the accumulator pressure. The function of the orifice is to allow only a small amount of oil to enter the accumulator and thereby minimize the flow effect to the power steering); (5) the oil flow to the booster piston (and to the power steering) is controlled through the open-center spool valve, which is center-drilled, cross-drilled, and spring-centered; (6) the spool valve is indirectly actuated through the input lever that is linked, through the piston bracket, to the input rod; (7) the pedal rod is linked to the input rod through a grommet which is sealed to the cover. A spring (with the assistance of the spring force of the piston's return spring and spool spring) holds the pedal rod to the right to allow the booster piston, piston bracket, and input lever to come to the rest position (neutral) (see Fig. 17-33).

MANUAL BRAKE APPLICATION   In the event of engine failure or power steering pump malfunction, the driver can stop the truck manually, although it takes greater effort and achieves less braking force. Under either of these circumstances, when the driver forces the brake pedal down, the motion is transmitted first to the brake pedal rod, and then to the input rod, the piston bracket, the booster piston, the output rod, and onto the primary master cylinder piston. Although the spool valve has moved to the left, it has

no effect on the manual brake application. The driver senses the brake effort in direct proportion to the applied pedal force and the counterforce of the master piston.

OPERATION WITH ENGINE RUNNING   When the engine is running (at high idle, low idle, or any other speed), a fixed flow of oil enters the power booster, flows around the spool valve, and out of the port leading to the power steering. No oil can flow into the boost pressure chamber, because the spool valve lands have closed off the flow. It then flows into the power steering control valve, out of the return port, and back to the power steering reservoir.   **NOTE** The oil flow at this time is under low pressure; therefore only a very small amount of oil would pass through the orifice by the check valve and into the accumulator.

The oil can flow in and out of pressure chamber A, through the cross end, and into the center-drilled passage in the spool valve and reenters through the inlet port.

When the power steering is actuated or the brake pedal is forced down, the oil flow is restricted either by the power steering or (booster) spool and sleeve assembly, and the pressure rises to maintain the same flow rate. The oil then passes through the orifice, opening the check valve and entering the accumulator. The system pressure forces the accumulator piston to the left, compressing the spring. If the system pressure at this point has not reached the pressure of the relief valve setting, the accumulator would be only partly charged. As soon as the system pressure is equal to that of the accumulator, the check valve closes through its spring force. **NOTE** To fully charge the accumulator, apply maximum brake force or turn the steering wheel to the left or to the right stop position.

In the event that the accumulator pressure exceeds maximum system pressure, the accumulator relief valve is forced off its seat and oil can return to the power steering reservoir.

BRAKE APPLICATION WITH ENGINE RUNNING   As soon as the pedal free play is taken up, the pedal motion is transmitted as outlined in the description of manual brake application in Unit 14. Now, however, the movement of the spool valve to the left closes the return oil flow from the pressure chamber, and for a fraction of a second most of the pump oil flows through the spool valve into pressure chamber A. This causes a quick pressure buildup in the line from the power steering pump to the pressure chamber, and as the pressure increases within chamber A, the booster piston is forced to the left, moving the output rod and master cylinder pistons to apply the brakes. During this time the pressure in chamber B is moving the spool to the right against its spring force, allowing more oil to flow to the power steering and some oil to flow from the pressure chamber A back to the reservoir to maintain the desired oil pressure in pressure chamber A. Within this same time (or a split second later) the booster piston, owing to the counterforce of the applied braking force, is moved slightly to the right. This pivots the input lever (on the top) to the right, removing some force from the spool spring. At the same time as the input rod was moved, the ring moved the reaction valve off its seat and allowed oil to enter reaction chamber C. The reaction of the pressure chamber gives the operator the feel of the applied brake force. When the force of the oil pressure on the booster piston is equal to the counterforce from the master cylinder piston, all movement stops within the power booster and a fixed pressure is maintained in chamber A.

NOTE   A passage from the pressure chamber leads onto the accumulator valve, and if the oil pressure in chamber A is higher than that within the accumulator, the accumulator valve is forced off its seat, and more oil enters the accumulator, increasing the pressure within. If, during a brake application, a higher pressure is required for steering, the spool valve shifts as the pressure from the pump to the steering control valve rises. This allows more oil to flow to the steering control valve and from the pressure chamber to maintain a lower brake pressure (see Fig. 17-34).

BRAKE RELEASE   If the brake pedal is partly released, the mechanical force from the output lever is removed and several actions take place simultaneously. The input rod spring forces the pedal rod to the right, the spool valve spring pivots the input lever, and the spool valve moves to the right, in-

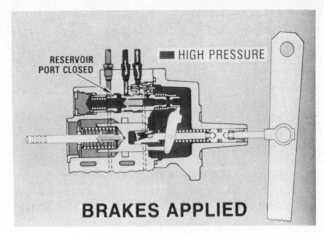

Fig. 17-34 Sectional view of brakes applied (engine operating). (*Ford Motor Company*)

creasing the return oil passage and allowing more oil to flow to the power steering. As a result of these mechanical reactions the line pressure and the pressure in chamber A are reduced, the master cylinders force the booster piston to the right, and the movement of the master cylinders reduces the brake pressure. As the two forces come into balance, the valve spool again positions itself to maintain a flow into and from pressure chamber A, to hold a fixed pressure on the booster piston.

RESERVE POWER   If, for one reason or another, the engine or the power steering pump fails to operate, two or three reserve power applications are available through the stored oil (under pressure) within the accumulator. When the brake pedal is then forced down, the spool valve closes the pump inlet passage and restricts the return flow passage. At the same time the actuator contacts the plunger of the accumulator valve, opens the valve, and allows additional oil to flow into the pressure chamber. This additional oil increases the pressure within the chamber, aiding effectiveness of brake application.

TROUBLESHOOTING AND TESTING   The same preliminary checks and tests must be made that were outlined for the other power booster. If, after the power steering pump and the hydraulic brake system have been checked and tested, the driver nevertheless reports a slow or incomplete pedal return, recheck the pedal and linkage for binding and for kinked or twisted return lines. With the engine stopped, apply the brakes several times to remove the accumulator pressure and then hold a moderate force on the brake pedal while starting the engine. If the power booster is operating correctly, the pedal should fall away slightly and then come back, and you should feel the applied force. If no force is noticeable, the power booster must be serviced to determine if any of the following components is worn or damaged: the spool valve, the bore, the seals, or the power piston or bore.

If the pedal is pulsating, or the brake application is very sensitive, the power booster must be serviced, for the spool valve or spring is worn or damaged and thereby causes the faulty spool action.

To determine if the accumulator, the check valve, or the accumulator valve is leaking or otherwise performing unsatisfactorily, stop the engine and apply the brakes several times to reduce the accumulator pressure. Next, start the engine, turn the steering wheel to the stop position, and hold it there for several seconds to fully charge the accumulator. (You may hear a hissing sound as the oil passes through the orifice.) Stop the engine and apply the brakes several times. There should be at least two power assist brake applications before the brake effort increases. If you have no power assist, there may be a leak in the check valve, the accumulator valve, or the accumulator piston seal, or the accumulator spring may be broken. To be sure that none of these components is faulty, recharge the accumulator, stop the engine, let it stand for about an hour or so, and again apply the brakes. If you have at least two power assist brake applications, then the assembly is satisfactory. If not, one of the just-mentioned components is faulty, and the accumulator must be serviced.

POWER BRAKES (OIL)

Oil-applied brakes are presently used only on off-highway equipment, that is, on crawler tractors and carriers and on large-wheel tractors. There are several reasons for using oil under pressure, namely: to increase the brake force, to increase safety, to speed up brake effectiveness, and to reduce the effort required of the operator.

More than one method and brake valve are used to apply the brakes, by using the oil flow from an existing source. In fact, the oil flow could come from the power shift transmission, the hydraulic system, the power steering, or the steering system of the crawler tractor.

Generally, the oil pressure from the main supply system is reduced to the designed brake pressure. Whether one system or another is used to supply the oil flow, the brake valve spool is actuated through a lever or a pedal to control the brake pressure. Furthermore, the foundation brake may be a servo, a nonservo, a single-disk or a multidisk brake design.

One of the simplest brake valves is shown in Fig. 17-35. It is used on a wheel tractor having servo foundation brakes, the oil being supplied from the power steering system. The brake system operates at a reduced pressure of about 950 psi [6545.6 kPa]; however the operation of the power steering has no effect on the operation of the brake or, alternately, the operation of the brake has no effect on the power steering. This is because the actuation of the brake valve requires only a very small amount of oil and the application pressure is less than that of the power steering.

Brake Design The master cylinder is bolted to the right side of the valve body. The residual check valve, the piston return spring, and the piston cup seal are located inside the cylinder. The large diameter of the master piston is supported within and sealed to, the body bore, and its small diameter is positioned in the master cylinder bore. The inlet port is connected with the master cylinder through a passage within the body and through the compensating port. Fitted in the bore of the body, the manual brake actuating sleeve is sealed with an O ring seal to the left side of the body bore. It is slotted at the top and bottom, and the bottom slot holds and guides it through the sleeve guide. A cross-drilled passage leads from the inlet port to the outlet port. In addition it has two internal valve lands.

A pressure-regulating spool, which is center-drilled and has two valve lands, is located in the bore of the manual actuating sleeve. The reaction

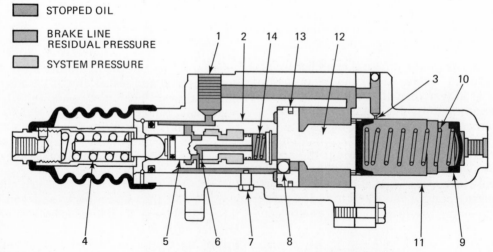

1. Return port to tank	5. Pressure regulating spool	9. Residual valve	13. Piston seal
2. Manual brake actuating sleeve	6. Orifice	10. Piston return spring	14. Reaction spring
3. Compensating port	7. Sleeve guide	11. Master cylinder	
4. Pressure regulating spring	8. Check valve	12. Master cylinder piston	

Fig. 17-35 Sectional view of a brake valve in neutral with engine operating. (*Caterpillar Tractor Co.*)

spring is positioned between a plug fastened to the manual actuating sleeve and the pressure-regulating spool. The pressure-regulating spring within the pressure-regulating sleeve rests against the pushrod shoulder and the connecting link threaded into the regulating sleeve. The pushrod socket rests against the pressure-regulating spool.

Manual Brake Application   When the engine is stopped, and the power steering pump or any other hydraulic component has failed and thereby prevented oil from flowing to the brake valve, it is possible for the driver to apply the brakes manually; however, a greater effort is needed and a greater pedal travel is noticeable.

In this case, when the operator forces the brake pedal down, the motion is transmitted to the pressure-regulating sleeve, to the manual brake actuating sleeve, and onto the master cylinder piston. The piston is then forced to the right, causing the piston cup seal to pass by the compensating port and pressurize the master cylinder. As the pressure overcomes the residual check valve spring, oil is forced into the hydraulic lines and wheel cylinders, applying the brakes.

If the operator releases the brake pedal force, the pressure-regulating sleeve is pulled to the left, allowing the master cylinder piston to be forced to the left. This action reduces the pressure within the application lines and the wheel cylinders. Furthermore, as the master cylinder piston moves to the left, oil passes by the cup seal lips into the space vacated by the master piston. As the piston cup seal passes by the compensating port, oil is forced from the master cylinder and returns to the power steering reservoir. When the pressure in the application line has reached about 18 psi (124 kPa), the residual check valve spring closes the valve and holds the line under this pressure.

NOTE   The check valve opens to allow the oil to flow from the chamber when the master cylinder is moved manually.

Power Brake Application   When the engine is running, oil from the power steering pump enters the inlet port and flows into the top slot of the manual brake actuating sleeve. It then passes through the cross-drilled passages to the power steering port and also flows around the regulating spool, into the lower slot, and acts on the master cylinder piston. Oil also passes into the upper passage and then down through the compensating port into the master cylinder.

When the brake pedal is forced down, the motion is transmitted to the pressure-regulating sleeve and the manual actuating sleeve, causing the pushrod to move the pressure-regulating spool. This places the spool such that it restricts the flow to the steering control valve, groove C, and at the same time opens groove B and closes groove A. This causes the pump pressure to rise and the oil to flow through the orifice and center-drilled passage, into the pressure-regulating spool, and then into the reaction chamber. During this time the oil passes into the lower slot of the manual activating sleeve and into the large area of the master cylinder piston. The oil pressure causes the check valve to close, and the oil pressure acting on the master cylinder piston moves it to the right, applying the brakes. The same pressure that applies the brake also exists in the reaction chamber, forcing the pressure-regulating spool slightly to the left, against the energy of the pressure-regulating spring. When spring force and oil pressure are equal, the pressure-regulating spool takes a fixed position insofar as restricting the flow (but not the volume) to the power steering control valve. A fixed oil pressure on the master cylinder piston is then achieved. If the pedal force does not change, from this point on, the oil flow past groove B and through the orifice controls the pressure in the reaction chamber and in turn the pressure on the master cylinder piston. Although the pressure on the reaction area and that on the large area of the master piston are equal, the brake line pressure is double because of the smaller size of the master cylinder bore (see Fig. 17-36).

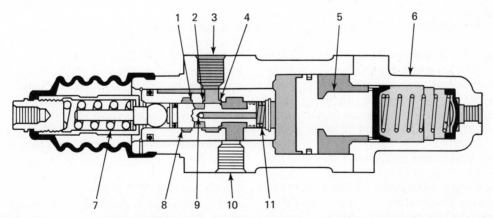

1. Groove edge A
2. Groove edge B
3. Inlet port from pump
4. Groove edge C
5. Master cylinder piston
6. Master cylinder
7. Pressure regulating spring
8. Pressure regulating spool
9. Orifice
10. Port to power steering
11. Reaction chamber

Fig. 17-36 Sectional view of brake valve activated with power steering in neutral. (*Caterpillar Tractor Co.*)

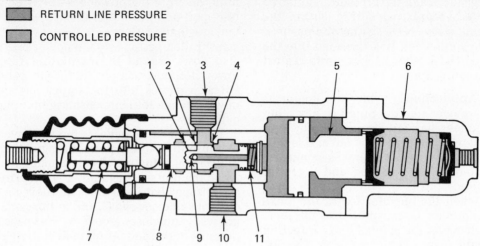

1. Edge groove A
2. Edge groove B
3. Inlet port from pump
4. Edge groove C
5. Master cylinder piston
6. Master cylinder
7. Pressure regulating spring
8. Pressure regulating spool
9. Orifice
10. Outlet port to power steering valve
11. Reaction chamber

Fig. 17-37 Sectional view of brake valve when the steering system pressure is equal to brake line pressure. (*Caterpillar Tractor Co.*)

When the brake is applied and the power steering is actuated, but the power steering warrants a higher pressure, the pressure increases within the reaction chamber, which in turn moves the pressure-regulating spool to the left, reducing groove edge B and opening groove edge A, to allow the oil to flow through the groove edge A, and through the orifice, into the reaction chamber. However, as groove edge C increases in clearance, the pressure to the power steering increases.

When the brake pedal is released, the spring force is removed from the pressure-regulating spool, and the oil pressure and spring force move the spool to the left. This action increases the opening of groove edge C, closes groove edge B, and opens groove edge A. With groove edge A enlarged, oil can flow out of the reaction chamber and from the left side of the master cylinder piston, reducing the pressure within both chambers. The master cylinder return spring plus the applied pressure move the master cylinder to the left against the body shoulder (see Fig. 17-37).

Testing and Troubleshooting When faulty brakes are reported, first check the foundation brakes for external leaks at all line connections, especially the wheel cylinders, the power steering pump, the power steering control valve, and the brake valve. Perform all preliminary checks and tests as previously noted.

If foundation brake tests and power steering are satisfactory, check the power brake operation. Apply moderate force on the brake pedal and then start the engine. If the valve is operating correctly, the pedal should fall away slightly and then return.

If the pedal falls gradually away, the problem may be a worn or damaged master cylinder piston, seal, or bore, or it may be that the check valve is leaking. In any circumstance the operator should also have complained of ineffective brakes. Inferior brakes can also be caused by a damaged or scored pressure-regulating spool, a damaged or scored bore, a broken return spring, a plugged orifice, or a broken pressure-regulating spring.

If the pedal travel is too great, and yet the brakes are adjusted correctly, the residual check valve may be leaking. If the brake release is too sluggish, the master cylinder piston may be sticking, the master cylinder return spring may be broken, the pressure-regulating spool may be sticking, the spool return spring may be broken, or there may be dirt in the power steering oil. If the brake application is too sensitive, the pressure-regulating spool spring may be broken. However, under this circumstance the operator should also have complained of ineffective brakes.

BRAKE FLUID

It is well known that fluid can transmit force undiminished, and it is to this end that fluid is used in hydraulic brake systems. The fluid used in brakes, however, must not only perform as an agent to transmit force but must also, in the interests of safety, have properties which will enable it to protect the brake components over a long time.

Two types of fluids are used for on- and off-highway braking systems—petroleum base fluid and synthetic fluid. Synthetic fluid is by far the more commonly used.

The Society of Automotive Engineers (SAE) has made recommendations about the minimum properties that should be accepted in synthetic brake fluid if it is to meet the requirements of today's demanding braking systems. If the quality of a brake fluid is inferior to the set standards, the brakes deteriorate more rapidly because the parts composed of steel, aluminum, and cast iron corrode, and the piston seal, cups, or hoses swell, soften, or disintegrate.

This is not to say that high-quality brake fluid does not eventually become contaminated after lengthy service, just as engine oil becomes contaminated from water, dust, and particles within the system (or owing to inadequate servicing).

Other sources contributing to deterioration of brake fluid are poor maintenance, which allows petroleum base fluid to enter the system and cause cup swelling and softening, or improper storage, which can adversely affect even high-quality brake fluid.

In addition to the brake properties, you should also be concerned (and perhaps even more so) with the fluid's minimum boiling point. If the fluid boils and vaporizes owing to heat from braking, the vapor pressure displaces some fluid back to the reservoir. If the brakes are then applied, the pedal stroke may only compress the vapor, and very little force would therefore be applied to the wheel cylinder and brake shoes. If an extreme amount of fluid turns to vapor, you may run out of pedal travel. **NOTE** Fluid stability (boiling point) changes after the brake fluid becomes heated during braking.

When handling high-quality brake fluid, make sure the container in which it is stored is kept covered at all times. This is essential because brake fluid having a high boiling point quickly absorbs moisture (as a sponge) from the atmosphere. When the moisture is absorbed by the fluid, the boiling point is lowered. For example, when a high-quality brake fluid is exposed for 24 hours to the atmosphere, it could absorb enough moisture to lower its boiling point from 550°F to 350°F [288°C to 177°C]. Since moisture so adversely affects brake fluid, the system should be flushed at least once a year or with every brake relining job. When checking the brake fluid level, make certain, therefore, that you clean the surrounding area thoroughly to prevent contaminants from entering the fluid. Never leave the cover off for an extended period of time. Also make certain that the diaphragm is correctly positioned.

Bleeding Hydraulic Brakes Bleeding a hydraulic brake system is the process of forcing brake fluid into the system and thereby removing the air, to ensure 100 percent transfer of force from the master cylinders to the wheel cylinders.

There are two methods of bleeding the system, namely, manual bleeding and pressure bleeding. The manual bleeding method requires two persons (to expedite bleeding)—one to operate the brake pedal and the other to open and close the bleed screw. The pressure bleeding method is therefore quicker—only one person is required to perform the task, and the master cylinder reservoir does not have to be checked or refilled during this procedure. In either case, some manufacturers recommend removing the brake light warning switch prior to bleeding the system, because an unequal pressure exists during bleeding which could conceivably shift the piston sufficiently to break the pin.

Most manufacturers recommend bleeding the brakes in the following order: first the right rear

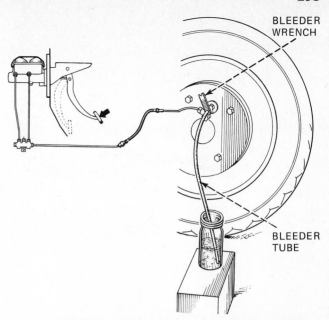

Fig. 17-38 Manually bleeding the brake system. (*International Harvester Company*)

brake and then the left rear brake; next, the right front brake and then the left front brake.

MANUAL BLEEDING Your first step when manually bleeding the brakes system is to place one end of a short hose onto the bleed screw and submerge the other end in a glass jar partly filled with brake fluid. This prevents brake fluid from leaking over the brake assembly and suspension or from contacting you during the bleeding. It also prevents air from entering the system.

Assume now that the master cylinder is serviced and bled, that the pedal linkage is checked and adjusted, that all hydraulic lines are connected, and that a bleed hose is connected to the bleed screw. To avoid a restriction which may not allow the air to escape from the wheel cylinder, open the bleed screw at least one full turn. Now ask your assistant to depress the brake pedal slowly. (A quick pedal action could mix air and fluid within the line, and this would prolong the bleeding procedure.) After the stroke is completed, request a slow release of the pedal. Repeat the procedure until the fluid that leaves the bleed line and enters the glass jar is free of air (see Fig. 17-38). **NOTE** If the pedal is released too quickly, fluid may be drawn into the system from the jar. If this happens, close the bleed screw after each applied stroke and then open it again on the down stroke. Repeat the procedure with the other rear wheel. If the brake assembly has two wheel cylinders, bleed the wheel cylinder that is last in line or that is located at the highest point of the brake assembly. During the bleeding procedure frequently check the fluid level within the secondary reservoir.

When the vehicle is not equipped with a metering valve or a combination valve, the bleeding procedure for the front wheel cylinders having drum or disk brakes is the same as that for the rear wheel brake cylinders. However, when a metering valve or

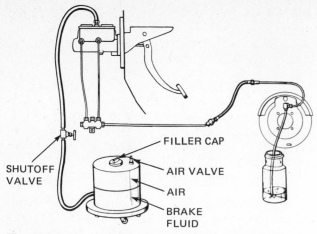

Fig. 17-39 Pressure bleeding the brake system. (*International Harvester Company*)

combination valve is used, you must depress the metering valve bleeder button to allow the fluid to bypass the metering piston. Use the special clamp to hold the button in, but do not use a C clamp. This could damage the valve, since the force required to push the button inward (depending on the manufacturer of the valve) is between 10 lb to 17 lb [44.4 N to 75.48 N].

If applicable, reinstall the brake warning light switch or reset the brake warning light switch. The brake warning light switch on a vehicle having a combination valve can be reset by applying a pedal force of about 500 psi [3447 kPa].

PRESSURE BLEEDING A pressure bleeder is a tank separated by a diaphragm. The lower half of the pressure tank stores the brake fluid, and a hose with a shutoff valve connects the tank with the adapter to the master cylinder. The upper half (which has an air gauge and an air coupling) is the air chamber.

Before connecting the pressure bleeder, check that the bleeder tank contains sufficient fluid to complete the bleeding. Pressurize the tank to about 30 psi [207 kPa] and then remove the master cylinder cover. Install the correct adapter and connect the hose to the adapter. Now open the shutoff valve to allow brake fluid from the tank to enter the two reservoirs (see Fig. 17-39). From this point on the bleeding procedure is the same as that outlined for manual bleeding. Before bleeding the front brakes, check the air pressure, and if it is less than 10 psi [69 kPa], recharge the tank. At this time do not disconnect the pressure bleeder. Apply the brakes several times to ensure that the disk brake pads rest firmly against the disk, that there is a "hard" pedal, and that you have adequate pedal height. Then check the brake pads to see if they align properly with the rotor.

After the vehicle is bled, close the shutoff valve on the pressure bleeder. Cover the fast breakaway coupling with a shop towel before disconnecting the hose. Remove the adapter from the master cylinder and check the reservoir level. If necessary, add or remove fluid to achieve the specified fluid level. Place the diaphragm and the cover onto the master cylinder and secure the cover to the master cylinder.

Road Testing On the assumption that all recommended checks have been made, including a tire pressure check, lower the vehicle to the ground and warm up the engine. Start the vehicle moving and make several low-speed stops to determine the braking effectiveness. If, after you have applied the brakes, the pedal is low, make several stops while moving in reverse to adjust the drum brakes. Now make several hard stops to seat the disk pad to the disk. You are now ready to proceed with road testing the vehicle.

During the road test check for pull, grab, lockup, squeal or other abnormal noises, pedal vibration or pulsation, and brake drag. For information on any of these problems, refer to the following discussion.

TROUBLESHOOTING HYDRAULIC BRAKES

The ability to analyze and therefore accurately assess the cause (or combination of causes) leading to brake failure requires an intimate knowledge of the hydraulic components, the brake assembly (foundation brakes), and other components that counteract the torque produced by the brakes. Moreover, since each type of foundation brake has characteristic inherent engineering qualities, broad mechanical experience is needed to pinpoint a problem.

Your first approach in diagnosing the cause of brake failure should be to systematically eliminate improbables until you are left with only those systems, components, or parts which could be contributing to the problem. Ask questions of the operator relating to his complaint: When did the trouble start? What were the operating conditions when the problem first occurred? When was the last maintenance check? Were the tires, wheels, steering, suspension, or brakes ever checked or serviced? Are the brakes (or any of the wheels) noisy, and do they "chatter"? Are the brakes now poor or their effectiveness reduced, or does this condition occur only after a long downhill grade? Is the brake pedal low? Hard? Spongy? Do the brakes pulsate? Do the brakes pull to one side when applied? If so, does the pull occur at low speed? Or high speed? Are the brakes too sensitive? Do the brakes drag or release too slowly? Were the brakes wet when they failed?

Another source of information is the shop service record, which outlines what was done and when.

Other preliminary steps are a visual inspection of the general condition of the tires, equality of tire size, and a tire pressure check.

Next, check for fluid, grease, or dirt on the brake drums. Check for bent or twisted hydraulic lines and for worn parking brake linkage, cables, or levers. If possible, accompany the operator on a test drive or operate the vehicle yourself to confirm or further evaluate the condition of the brakes.

Apply the brakes with light force and hold this position for a few seconds. If the pedal falls away, there is a fluid leak somewhere in the system. If you are checking a power assist unit, deplete all vacuum, apply the brakes lightly, and then start the engine. If the pedal falls about $\frac{1}{2}$ in [12.7 mm], the power unit is operating properly. **NOTE** See the material on vacuum-suspended and air-over-hydraulic power assist for troubleshooting checks and tests.

Visual Checks If the cause of failure has not yet been determined, lift the vehicle, machine, etc., off the ground and secure it safely with floor stands. Check for worn, broken, bent, or damaged springs. Check the condition of the bolts, shackles, control arms, kingpins (or ball joints), tie rod ends, steering gear, and shock absorbers. Check the wheel bearing adjustment. Check the exterior of the brake drums for excessive rust or dirt. (This could reduce brake effectiveness because the drums would not dissipate the heat fast enough.)

Checking Drum for Out-of-roundness Check the brake drums for out-of-roundness by having a helper lightly apply the brakes as you rotate each wheel to feel out any high spots on the drums. The helper should increase or decrease the brake application pressure to achieve a light lining-to-drum contact. Set one wheel to the low spot. If you are then unable to turn the wheel 360° it is badly out-of-round. Repeat this procedure with each wheel. **NOTE** No matter what quality brake lining you use, brake problems will persist if the drum is more than 0.010 in [0.25 mm] out-of-round.

Brake Noise If brake application produces noise or squeal, there may be improper lining-to-drum contact, the drum may be eccentric, contaminants may be embedded in the lining, or the lining may be loose. This noise could also come from a loose backing plate, anchor, wheel cylinder, or brake drum.

The following also produces noise or squeal: the brake shoe scraping on the shoe tables because of weak or broken hold-down spring, bent or twisted brake backing plate or shoes, wrong anchor position, or a damper spring missing from the drum.

When the brakes chatter, there may be too much lining clearance, the automatic adjuster may be partly seized, the shoe return spring may be weak or broken, or the drum deformed. Possibly the brake shoes are twisted or bent, or the lining or drum may be contaminated. Chatter can also occur from a loose brake backing plate, a loose anchor, wheel cylinder, or loose or damaged wheel bearings. Excessive disk (rotor) runout or varied disk (rotor) thickness also brings on this condition.

When the brakes grind or scrape, the rivets or the bolt heads may be contacting the drum. There may be foreign matter embedded in the lining or between the lining and drums. The edges of the disk (rotor) and/or caliper may be contaminated, the caliper may be misaligned, or the brake pads may be worn.

If there is an audible clicking or rattling noise, it may be that the brake shoe moves away from the shoe table and snaps back (because of a threaded drum surface). This sound would also occur if the hold-down spring were weak or missing, or if the shoe table were grooved. Clicking and rattling can also come from a loose backing plate or a loose an-

chor or wheel cylinder. It also occurs if the lining clearance is excessive, the axle support is weak owing to a broken spring, the U bolt is loose, or the shock absorbers are weak.

Brake Pull When brake application causes the vehicle to pull to one side, the casters, cambers, tire diameters, or tire pressures may be unequal. Unbalanced wheels or mismatched dual tires also cause side pull. Other causes of pull are a weak or broken spring, broken center bolt, loose U bolt, worn shackles, loose steering gear or tie rods, or weak shock absorbers.

Check the lining and drum surface for contamination; check for mismatched linings, that is, the primary lining installed in a secondary position; and check for loose lining. Brake pull occurs also when the diameter of one drum is larger than the other, when the drum surface has an uneven finish, or when one drum is cracked or deformed or has a high spot on its surface. Further causes are a weak or missing shoe return spring, grooved shoe tables, bent or twisted brake shoes, uneven lining-to-drum contact due to improper lining arc, misadjusted or loose anchor or wheel cylinder, or a bent brake backing plate.

Brake Drag When the operator's complaint is brake drag, check for one or more of the following: a loose or damaged wheel bearing, a weak or broken brake shoe return spring, a seized wheel cylinder, overadjusted brakes due to adjuster failure, distorted brake shoe, distorted drum, grooved shoe tables, misadjusted parking brake, clogged compensating port, pedal linkage binding, weak pedal return spring, inadequate free play, seized caliper piston, distorted pad, improper caliper pad alignment, loose caliper or guide pin, damaged rotor surface, or uneven thickness of rotor.

Reduced Brake Effectiveness When the brake effectiveness is badly deteriorated, the power assist may not be working, or the lining or pads may be worn or glazed. Check also for a heat-checked rotor or drum or for brake drag causing over-heating of the drum. Moreover, the rotor may be machined too thin; there may be excessive lining clearance; the primary shoe may be installed in the secondary position; or the vehicle may be overloaded.

Brakes Too Sensitive If the brakes are too sensitive (when metering valve and proportional valve are used), install a pressure gauge into the primary and secondary system and check the action of the valve. If brake application allows the pedal to reach too close to the floorboard, there may be too much free play or excessive lining clearance. In either case the brakes need to be adjusted. On the other hand, the residual check valve may not be holding the desired pressure, or in the case of disk brakes, the wheel bearings may be loose, the rotor may have excessive runout, or the rotor thickness may not be even.

If the pedal drops, look for external fluid leaks or excessive drum expansion due to overheating conditions.

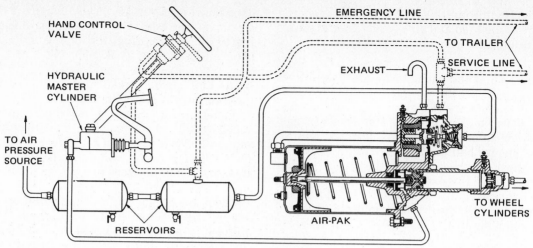

Fig. 17-40 Bendix air pack installation. (*Bendix Heavy Vehicle Systems Group*)

Brake Pedal Pulsation or Spongy Brakes If the complaint is pedal pulsation, the drums may be excessively out-of-round, the wheel bearings damaged or loose, the rotor distorted or of uneven thickness, or the runout excessive.

A spongy pedal is often the result of air in the system due to a damaged seal. It can also be caused by vapor pockets in the wheel cylinder or in the lines because of low-quality brake fluid or by too much water being absorbed by the brake fluid. Another reason for a spongy brake pedal is an excessively thin brake drum or a too thinly machined rotor causing excessive heat). Also, if the linings are not arced properly, the shoe spreads when brake force is applied.

A less common but nevertheless a possible cause of a spongy brake pedal is a brake hose which expands under application pressure.

AIR-OVER-HYDRAULIC POWER ASSIST UNIT

As the name indicates, the air-over-hydraulic power assist unit depends on compressed air rather than atmospheric pressure as its source of power to actuate the hydraulic piston and thereby the brakes. The air pack (see Fig. 17-40) is one of the oldest type of power assist units in existence. Its design and operation are much the same as for the frame-mounted vacuum-suspended power assist unit covered earlier in this unit. However, because it uses compressed air, a greater force is placed on the components and parts; therefore the parts are manufactured from different material to make them more durable. This air pack unit also uses hydraulic pressure from a single master cylinder or from a dual master cylinder to actuate the control valve.

As you can see from the illustration, the component part names have changed to relate more closely to their functions. This unit is just as versatile in its application as the frame-mounted vacuum power assist unit. Some brake designs use one air pack unit per wheel, which means the equipment or truck could have six power units. **NOTE** The air com-

pressor, governor, reservoir, and lines are covered in Unit 18.

Operation When the Reservoir is Charged and the Brakes are Released, the hydraulic pressure in the lines between the master cylinder and the control valve and in the master cylinder is near atmospheric pressure because the primary cup in the master cylinder has opened the compensating port. The residual check valve in the air pack holds the residual pressure in the application lines. With no force on the control valve piston, the exhaust valve is held open, allowing atmospheric air into the left and the right side air chambers. With equal pressure in both chambers the air piston return spring has forced the air piston to the left. As a result the pushrod has moved away from the hydraulic piston and allowed it to come against its stop. Brake fluid, due to expansion and retraction, can then enter or leave the master cylinder, the hydraulic cylinder, and the control valve area (see Fig. 17-41).

Brake Application and Hold Position As the brake pedal is depressed, the fluid displaced by the master cylinder enters the hydraulic cylinder via the check valve and also passes through passage A behind the control valve piston. As the hydraulic pressure builds up, the control valve piston is forced to the right, closing the exhaust valve and subsequently closing off the left air chamber from the atmosphere. As the hydraulic pressure rises, it moves the control valve piston, opening the inlet valve and allowing compressed air to pass by the valve into the air control tube and into the left air chamber. The air piston and pushrod are then forced to the right. The pushrod contacts the hydraulic piston and moves it to the right, closing the check valve. The hydraulic piston then displaces fluid past the residual check valve into the brake system to apply the brakes.

NOTE The air force acting on the air piston and the hydraulic force from the master cylinder (on the back side of the hydraulic piston) comprise the total force on the hydraulic piston.

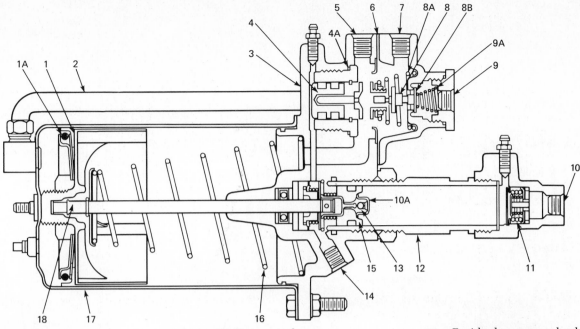

1. Air power piston
1A. Piston seal
2. Control tube
3. End plate
4. Valve hydraulic piston
4A. Piston seals
5. Air exhaust port
6. Diaphragm

7. Trailer control port
8. Atmosphere poppet
8A. Balance spring
8B. Air poppet
9. Air supply port
9A. Spring
10. Hydraulic fluid outlet port
10A. Yoke

11. Residual pressure check valve
12. Hydraulic cylinder
13. Ball check valve
14. Hydraulic fluid inlet port
15. Hydraulic piston
16. Piston return spring
17. Air power cylinder
18. Pushrod

Fig. 17-41 Sectional view of air pack. (*Bendix Heavy Vehicle Systems Group*)

For example, if the air piston area is 20 in² (129 cm²) and the applied air pressure is 60 psi [413.4 kPa], the hydraulic piston area is 1 in² [6.4 cm²] and the hydraulic pressure from the master cylinder is 300 psi [2067.0 kPa]. The force on the hydraulic piston due to the air pressure is then 20 × 60 = 1200 lb [5328 N].

The total force on the hydraulic piston is therefore 1200 + 300 = 1500 lb [6660 N].

NOTE The check valve in the hydraulic piston is seated and remains seated.

When the hydraulic pressure that acts on the control valve piston and the air pressure and spring force that act on the diaphragm are equal in force, the air valve spring closes the air intake valve. The atmospheric air displaced from the right chamber by the movement of the air piston leaves via port B around the diaphragm adapter and moves out into the atmosphere through the exhaust port. Any additional brake pedal force offsets the balance of the valve and opens the air valve to increase the application force until a balance in force is again achieved.

Release Position When the brake pedal force is reduced, it also reduces the hydraulic line pressure and likewise the force on the control valve. Under this circumstance, the applied air force acting on the diaphragm is greater than the hydraulic force on the control valve piston, causing the exhaust valve to open. This allows the compressed air from the left chamber to escape into the atmosphere. When the forces between the applied air pressure acting on the control valve piston are equal, the exhaust valve spring closes the exhaust valve.

Since the frame-mounted vacuum-suspended power assist unit and the air pack unit are so alike, there is no need to discuss service and testing procedure for the air pack unit.

AIR-OVER-HYDRAULIC POWER CLUSTER

The air-over-hydraulic power cluster converts air pressure into the mechanical force which moves the hydraulic piston in the master cylinder, displaces the brake fluid, and finally activates the brakes. The most significant difference between the power cluster and the air pack is that the power cluster requires an air control valve to meter the applied air pressure to achieve the desired actuating force. On the air pack unit, the control valve that meters the applied air pressure is hydraulically activated; therefore the air pack unit can apply the brakes hydraulically in the event of air pressure loss. The power cluster unit cannot, however, activate the brakes when there is no air pressure.

Two major types of power clusters are used—one that has a conventional single master cylinder bolted to the air chamber (see Fig. 17-42) and the other that has the hydraulic cylinder of the power pack unit

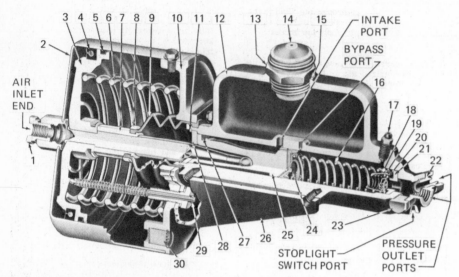

1. Reducer bushing
2. Air cylinder shell
3. Air piston and rod
4. Piston cup
5. Piston wiper
6. Piston return spring
7. Grommet
8. Boot strap
9. Boot
10. Cylinder head
11. Retainer
12. Hydraulic cylinder
13. Adapter
14. Filler cap
15. Gasket
16. Return spring
17. Bleeder valve
18. Spring retainer
19. Valve spring
20. Check valve
21. Valve seat
22. Connector
23. Plug
24. Primary cup
25. Hydraulic piston
26. Mounting support
27. Secondary cup
28. Stop plate
29. Stroke indicator
30. Air filter

Fig. 17-42 Sectional view of a power cluster using a conventional master cylinder. (*Terex Division of General Motors Corporation*)

screwed into the end cover of the air chamber (see Fig. 17-43). **NOTE** The latter unit also has no hydraulic control valve, the brake fluid reservoir is remote mounted, and the hydraulic supply line from the reservoir is connected to the end cover. On both power clusters the air line coming from the air control valve is connected to the end of the air power cylinder.

The number of power clusters used per vehicle is not always the same. On some equipment one power cluster may serve the front and another may serve the rear wheels. Yet on other equipment there may be one unit for each wheel cylinder: this means that eight power clusters (one for each wheel) may be used.

Operation Applying, holding, or releasing the air pressure from the air cylinder is the same on all power clusters because it is controlled by the air control valve.

The mechanical and hydraulic action within the power cluster having the conventional master cylinder is the same as that of a vacuum-suspended power booster having a single master cylinder. The mechanical and hydraulic action within the power cluster having the hydraulic cylinder is identical in operation to the power pack unit.

Troubleshooting and Testing Although with either type of power cluster very little brake failure or diminished brake force occurs, many service manuals nevertheless stress that it is good maintenance practice to install a complete repair kit whenever the brakes are relined.

If the checks and tests indicate that the cause of brake failure lies in the power cluster, install an air

gauge to the air chamber or application line and a 3000 psi [20,670 kPa] pressure gauge into the hydraulic application line.

To check the air and hydraulic line pressure (and at the same time to check for air and hydraulic leaks), bring the air pressure up to the governor cutout pressure and then apply the brakes. The psi [kPa] reading on the air gauge should be consistent with the reading on the pressure gauge in the driver compartent. There should be no air exhausting from the air chamber shell or end cover. If there is air emission, the seal is damaged. If air exhausts through the bronze air filter in the end cover, the piston cup seal is damaged.

When the air pressure in the chamber shows less (pressure) than the reservoir pressure, there is some malfunction in the air control. When the hydraulic pressure is below service manual specifications but the applied air pressure is nevertheless correct, this indicates that there may be a fluid leak between the hydraulic cylinder and the wheel cylinder or that the primary cup is damaged, allowing fluid to bypass (the seal).

To check the effectiveness of the residual check valve, release the brakes and note the hydraulic pressure. The gauge reading should correlate with that given in the service manual.

Removal and Service First, steam-clean the area wherein you intend to work and then drive the equipment to your work location. When it is safely blocked, lower or raise the hydraulic equipment to permit easy removal of the hydraulic components. Also block the wheel to prevent the equipment from moving. Bleed all air from the service reservoir but not from the air starting system reservoir, if used.

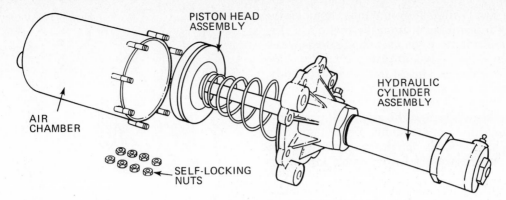

Fig. 17-43 Partially disassembled power cluster using hydraulic cylinder assembly. (*WABCO, An American-Standard Company*)

Disconnect the air line from the power cluster, the brake fluid supply line, and the hydraulic application line(s). Drain the fluid into an adequate container to prevent it from leaking onto other components or parts. Cap all openings to prevent contaminants from entering the cluster or hydraulic lines.

From this point on, the service procedure between the two units changes. To remove the power cluster (see Figs. 17-43 and 17-44), remove the mounting nuts or bolts and lift the assembly from the mounting bracket. Again, clean the power cluster thoroughly and blow it dry with compressed air before mounting it in a vise which has protected jaws. Take care not to damage the hydraulic cylinder. Clamp the cluster by its mounting flange lugs. Scribe a line across the shell and end cover before removing the eight self-locking nuts from the air chamber shell's stud bolts.

To remove the piston head assembly, place a large-blade screwdriver in the end of the slotted shaft. Hold it firmly while loosening and removing the shaft nut.

CAUTION The piston return spring is under a light pressure. If not handled carefully, it could injure you, as well as damage the piston.

Separate the piston assembly by lifting the piston follower, expander ring, piston cup, piston felt, and ring from the pressure plate. Before loosening the two lock nuts on the hydraulic cylinder, scribe a line across the cylinder, lock nut, and end cap and scribe a line across the cylinder lock nut and end cover to expedite reassembly.

After the lock nuts are loosened, screw the end cap from the hydraulic cylinder and unscrew the hydraulic cylinder from the end cover. Hold on to the (air piston) shaft and remove the cylinder tube.

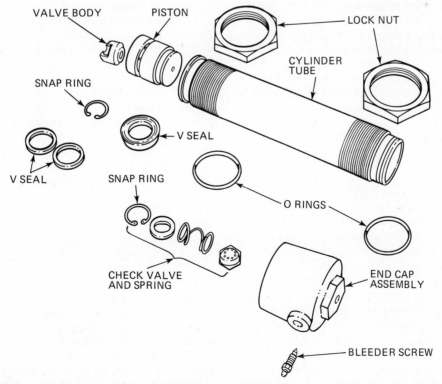

Fig. 17-44 Exploded view of a power cluster. (*WABCO, An American-Standard Company*)

Remove the two O rings from the tube. Remove the piston and the piston shaft from the end cover. Remove the snap ring from the valve body, to separate the air piston valve body and piston from the valve body. Remove the valve insert from the valve body. Remove the V ring seals. Remove the bronze air breather from the end cover.

Discard all seals, O rings, the air breather, and the end cap, since these components are contained in the repair kit. Clean all remaining parts, and dry them with compressed air. Inspect each part for its serviceability. Remove small nicks and burrs with an oil stone. If the cylinder tube or the air chamber shell's inner surfaces are rough or slightly scored, use a cylinder deglazer hone to refinish them. Do not neglect to check all thread bores and external threads for damage and also check the end cover flange and mounting locks.

Reassembly and Installation   The order of reassembly for the power cluster is precisely the reverse of disassembly.

Always use a new air breather, a new end cap, and new residual check valve components. During the reassembly, coat the expander, the cup lips, the piston grooves, and the felt with the recommended grease. Coat the inner surface of the shell with engine oil. Coat the hydraulic seals (including the surface of the hydraulic tube) with brake fluid. Make certain the lock nuts are tight against the end cap and end cover. After the power cluster is reinstalled, the air and fluid lines are connected, and the fittings tightened, fill the reservoir with brake fluid.

To bleed the brakes, loosen the bleed screw, connect a bleeder hose to it, and then immerse the hose end into a container partly filled with brake fluid. Close the air tank drain valves and build up the reservoir pressure. Apply a pressure of about 20 psi [137.8 kPa] and hold this pressure. Repeat the procedure until no air bubbles are visible as the fluid leaves the bleed hose. When the cluster is bled, close the bleed screw and remove the hose. **NOTE**   Do not forget to bleed the wheel cylinder as outlined in the procedure for bleeding hydraulic brakes.

AIR-OVER-OIL POWER ASSIST UNIT

An air-over-oil power assist unit differs from an air-over-hydraulic power cluster unit in that the former requires a rotary air chamber because a greater stroke is needed. Moreover, the master cylinder has a greater diameter and is longer than a master cylinder of the power cluster unit. The air-over-oil power assist, of course, uses oil, whereas the hydraulic power cluster uses brake fluid. Although the master cylinders and brake chambers vary among equipment manufacturers, their operation is nevertheless similar (see Fig. 17-45).

Operation—Release   When the air control valve is in the release position, the air from the rotary chamber has already exhausted into the atmosphere. The diaphragm return spring has moved the diaphragm,

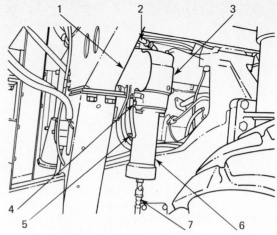

1. Hydraulic fluid reservoir
2. Air inlet line
3. Brake chamber
4. Bolts (2)
5. Hydraulic fluid inlet line
6. Master cylinder
7. Hydraulic line to front wheel brakes

Fig. 17-45   View showing air-over-oil power assist unit installed. Operation sequence: 2, 5, 7, 4. (*Caterpillar Tractor Co.*)

the inner clamp, the guide, the pushrod, and the power piston to the left. The power piston has opened the passage from the check valve and the makeup valve. The oil can enter or leave the hydraulic oil cavity at any time (owing to the expansion and retraction of the oil) via the makeup valve and the ball check valve passage (see Fig. 17-46).

When the air control valve is activated, a metered amount of compressed air enters the rotary chamber, forcing the diaphragm and power piston downward. The power piston closes the passage to the reservoir. As the hydraulic pressure builds up, the check valve and makeup valve are forced shut, trapping the oil in the cylinder cavity.   **NOTE**   The piston is sealed through the seal assembly and not by the wear ring. Therefore oil under pressure is in the groove between the seal and the wear ring.

With any additional movement of the power piston, more oil is displaced by the power piston into the multidisk brake assembly or into the expanding tube. The increased volume of oil in the disk brake piston or in the expanding tube moves the brake piston, forcing the disks together, or the expanding tube forces the lining into contact with the brake drum. With more air pressure applied to the rotary chamber, more oil is displaced, and this thereby increases the hydraulic pressure.

For example, when the diaphragm area is 30 in² [193 cm²], the applied pressure is 60 psi [413.4 kPa], the power piston area is 2 in² [12.9 cm²], and the disk brake piston has an area of 90 in² [580 cm²].

The force that compresses the multidisk brakes is equal to 8100 lb [35964 N].

When 60 psi [413.4 kPa] acts on an area of 30 in² [193 cm²] the pushrod has a force of 1800 lb [7992 N] onto the piston (60 × 30 = 1800 lb). Since the area of the power piston is 2 in² [12.9 cm²], a pressure of 900 psi [6201 kPa] is developed:

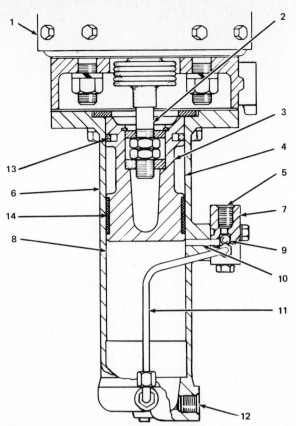

Fig. 17-46 Sectional view of a master cylinder. (*Caterpillar Tractor Co.*)

1. Air chamber
2. Pushrod
3. Power piston
4. Cavity
5. Inlet port connected to hydraulic oil supply tank
6. Cylinder
7. Check and makeup valve
8. Hydraulic oil cavity
9. Ball check
10. Passage
11. Makeup oil line
12. Outlet port to rear wheel brakes
13. Seal
14. Wear ring

$$P = F/A = 1800/2 = 900 \text{ psi } [6201 \text{ kPa}]$$

With a line pressure of 900 psi [6201 kPa] acting on the 90 in² [580 cm²] disk piston area, the force is

$$F = P \times A = 900 \times 90 = 8100 \text{ lb } [35,964 \text{ N}]$$

When the air control valve balances; that is, when the valve actuation has stopped, no air enters or leaves the air control valve, and therefore no air enters or leaves the rotary chamber. **NOTE** The driver senses the brake application through the air control valve. When the air control valve reduces the application pressure by any amount, the hydraulic force moves the power piston upward. This increases the volume of the hydraulic oil cavity and thereby reduces the applied pressure.

If the pressure is fully released, the hydraulic pressure and the diaphragm return spring move the diaphragm pushrod and the power piston to the release position.

Servicing To check the air chambers for leaks and to check the hydraulic pressure, perform the steps outlined for testing the air-over-hydraulic power assist unit.

The preliminary steps and the safety rules referred to in connection with the air-over-hydraulic power-assist unit also apply when you are servicing the air-over-oil power assist unit.

After the assembly is cleaned and dried with compressed air, clamp the master cylinder in a horizontal position in a vise having protected jaws. Remove the bolts that secure the master cylinder to the brackets. Connect an air supply line having a pressure regulator to the air chamber and then gradually apply the air pressure until it separates the master cylinder from the bracket (see Fig. 17-47). For safety reasons, place a 3.9-in [10-cm] wooden block in the space created. Remove from the master cylinder the retainer that stops the power piston's rearward movement, remove the wooden blocks, and slide the master cylinder away from the bracket.

With a pair of snap-ring pliers, remove the retainer from its groove and then slide the piston, retainer, and washer from the pushrod. Slowly release the air pressure to retract the pushrod and then remove the makeup line and the makeup and check the valve housing.

If the rotary brake chamber shows any kind of leakage, the pushrod may be bent or the mounting

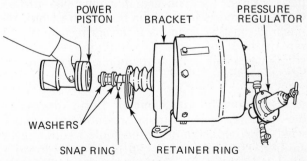

Fig. 17-47 Removing power piston from air brake chamber pushrod. (*Caterpillar Tractor Co.*)

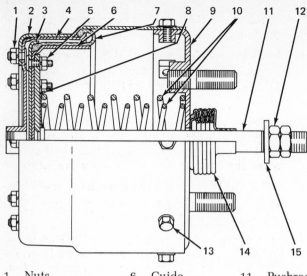

Fig. 17-48 Sectional view of the rotary air chamber. (*Caterpillar Tractor Co.*)

1.	Nuts	6.	Guide	11.	Pushrod
2.	Body	7.	Diaphragm	12.	Nuts (2)
3.	Inner clamp	8.	Guide	13.	Bolts (8)
4.	Outer clamp	9.	Cover	14.	Boot
5.	Nuts (8)	10.	Springs	15.	Washer

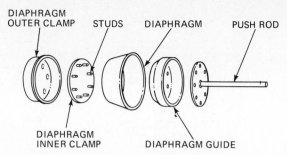

Fig. 17-49 Exploded view of rotary air chamber components. (*Caterpillar Tractor Co.*)

studs in the cover may be loose. The air chamber must be serviced. Start the air chamber service by removing the eight nuts that secure the outer clamps to the chamber body (see Fig. 17-48). Remove the first washer, the two nuts, and the second washer from the pushrod and then remove the dust boot from the cover. Next, place the chamber (with the mounting studs facing upward) on the press bed and lay two wooden blocks across the cover. Bring the hydraulic piston in bare contact with the wood. This safety procedure is necessary to prevent the spring from forcibly ejecting the cover from the body, once the bolts are removed. Now remove the eight bolts that secure the cover to the chamber body. Gently tap the body with a soft-face hammer to loosen the cover. Slowly release the hydraulic force while holding the chamber body. Lift from the body, as a unit, the pushrod, the diaphragm guide, and the diaphragm inner clamp and outer clamp. If any of these components is worn or damaged, remove the nuts from the diaphragm, remove the inner clamp studs, and move to one side the parts to be replaced. Clean all nonrubber parts in solvent, clean the rubber parts in alcohol, and dry all parts with compressed air.

If the diaphragm is kinked, deteriorated, or damaged in any way, it must be replaced. If the metal parts are rusted or damaged, they must be replaced. If the pushrod is bent or the threads are worn, the pushrod must be replaced. If the springs are rusted, replace them, too, but make certain the replacement spring carries the same parts number, to ensure balanced braking.

Reassembling the Air Chamber During the assembly apply air brake cylinder grease to any location where the diaphragm comes in contact with a metal surface. Place the small end opening of the diaphragm in the diaphragm's inner clamp. Place the

diaphragm guide onto the diaphragm and over the inner stud bolts. Place the pushrod onto the stud bolts and then install and tighten the nuts to specified torque. Now place the diaphragm's outer clamp ring over and onto the outer stud bolts of the diaphragm's inner clamp. Roll the end of the diaphragm back and over the rolled shoulder of the outer diaphragm clamp (see Fig. 17-49).

Slide the subassembly into the body and guide the outer diaphragm clamp studs through the holes in the body. Install and tighten the nuts to specified torque. Install the diaphragm guide into the body and place the two springs over the pushrod. Position the cover over the pushrod and then align the holes with the threaded bore in the body. Compress the spring to install the bolts. Tighten the bolts to the specified torque.

Install the dust boot onto the cover, place a new washer onto the pushrod, and screw the two nuts onto it. Install the bracket and tighten the nuts to specification.

To ensure that the power piston does not cover the passage opening from the check valve, the first washer must be positioned at a specified distance from the bracket. To achieve the precise position, adjust the first nut until the distance is as specified and then use the second nut to lock in the adjustment (see Fig. 17-50).

Master Cylinder Service Clean all parts in solvent and dry them with compressed air. Inspect all parts for their serviceability. Discard wear ring and seals. If the cylinder bore is scored or rough, use a cylinder hone to restore the inner surface. If the power piston is chipped or excessively worn, it should be replaced.

Check that the threaded bores, the check valve, makeup valve, and makeup line are not damaged. Before placing the wear ring or the seals onto the piston, fasten the power piston to the pushrod. To do this, extend the pushrod (using compressed air) and over it place the piston, washer, and retainer ring and then install the retainer ring.

Lubricate the piston and master cylinder bore with engine oil and install the wear ring and seals. Now guide the master cylinder over the power piston but take care not to damage the seal assembly.

Position the washer in the counter bore of the master cylinder before pushing the master cylinder onto the bracket. **NOTE** You may have to remove some air pressure from the air chamber to retract the

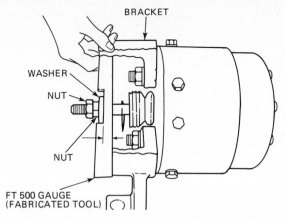

BRACKET

WASHER

NUT

NUT

FT 500 GAUGE
(FABRICATED TOOL)

Fig. 17-50 Cutaway view: Measuring pushrod adjustment. (*Caterpillar Tractor Co.*)

pushrod before the master cylinder bottoms against the bracket. Install and tighten the bolts to specified torque and install the check valve body and makeup line.

Bleeding the Brakes   After the master cylinder assembly is installed, the supply line to the reservoir connected, and the reservoir filled with the appropriate oil (not brake fluid), open the bleed screw on the power assist unit. Connect a drain hose over the screw and place the other end of the hose into a large container partly filled with oil. Now apply the brakes. When oil and air stop flowing from the bleed hose, release the brakes. Wait several minutes to allow oil from the reservoir to flow into the master cylinder and then repeat the procedure.

NOTE   When oil is drawn from the container into the master cylinder as the brakes are released, close the bleed screw before releasing the brakes. On an average, about 1 gal [3.785 l] of oil bleeds off before the system is clear of air.

Review Questions

1. List three reasons why a power assist brake booster is used.

2. On a vacuum-suspended power assist unit: (*a*) Which is the power assist source? (*b*) Which valve controls the assist power? (*c*) Which two sources could create the low pressure? (*d*) What is the maximum power assist (in psi) that could be achieved?

3. Explain the operation of the power assist unit shown in your text as Fig. 17-1 when: (*a*) the brakes are applied, (*b*) when in the hold position.

4. If the vacuum-suspended power assist unit fails or loses some of its assist power, five

checks should be made before removing it for service. List these checks.

5. List the two most obvious differences between a regular vacuum-suspended power assist and a "Hydrovac" vacuum-suspended power assist unit.

6. Explain the operation of a Hydrovac-brake booster: (*a*) when the master cylinder displaces fluid into the system to apply the brakes, (*b*) when the Hydrovac is in the hold position.

7. What checks and/or tests must be made to determine whether or not a Hydrovac power assist booster needs to be serviced?

8. (*a*) Why are there three holes in the rear bushing of the vacuum pump? (*b*) Why are the inlet and outlet slots in the body or housing elongated?

9. Explain why the hydro-booster is now being used more often than vacuum-suspended power assist brake boosters.

10. What two methods are used to provide emergency power supply (oil flow) for the hydro-booster?

11. (*a*) Define the term *power brake*. (*b*) What are the two main power sources of a power brake?

12. List four advantages of an oil power brake system over any other power assist system.

13. On an oil power booster, which valve, sleeve, or piston controls the oil pressure to actuate the master cylinder?

14. List the primary differences between an oil-over-hydraulic cluster and an air-over-hydraulic power cluster.

15. Explain why synthetic brake fluid is used in preference to petroleum base fluid.

16. Why are the master cylinder reservoirs closed off from the atmosphere?

17. Outline the procedure to: (*a*) bleed the brakes manually, (*b*) use a power or pressure bleed device.

18. (*a*) Outline, in order of most common occurrence, the causes of brake failure. (*b*) Outline, in order of most common occurrence, the components which could cause brake failure.

19. Name the parts or components that could cause: (*a*) undue noise to occur when the brakes are applied, (*b*) the motor vehicle to pull to one side when the brakes are applied, (*c*) the operator to complain of "brake drag," (*d*) the operator to complain of reduced brake efficiency, (*e*) the operator to complain of a spongy or pulsating brake pedal.

Unit 18
Air Brakes

Air brakes have long been used on heavy vehicles. Their popularity with on- and off-highway equipment can be accredited to the following: moderate effort by the driver or operator can be multiplied to near unlimited brake force; they can be applied to any motor vehicle, equipment, or machine; their unlimited safety factor is unequaled; they have unlimited energy supply; and they can tolerate some leakage and minute component failure without noticeable reduction in the brake efficiency.

Air brake systems of on-highway motor trucks, truck tractors, and trailers have advanced technologically over the years, particularly since 1975 with the advent of the FMVSS (Federal Motor Vehicle Safety Standard 121).

To fulfill the requirements of FMVSS 121, which for instance, require a tractor trailer combination to stop within a 12-ft [3.66-m] lane at 60 mph [96.6 km/h] within a stopping distance of 295 ft [89.97 m], the manufacturers had to convert to a dual air brake system. This system has seen many changes in valves and air line connections, including increases in the number and the capacity of the reservoirs and changes to the wheels, drums, lining, and axles (particularly the front axle). Furthermore, spring-applied parking brakes must be used to meet the parking brake requirements.

The brake systems of off-highway motor trucks, tractors, or other vehicles have also advanced technologically, but not to the same extent as on-highway vehicles. They, too, are now more complex to meet today's safety requirements.

THE BASIC AIR BRAKE SYSTEM

The components which make up a basic air brake system are the compressor, governor, reservoir, application valve (brake valve), relay valve, actuator, the foundation brakes, and the hydraulic lines (air lines) (see Fig. 18-1).

The air brake system's originating energy source is the motor vehicle's engine, which drives, directly or indirectly, an air pump, called the compressor. The compressor is connected to a tank known as the reservoir. When the engine is operating, the compressor discharges air into the reservoir, increasing the reservoir's pressure. A pressure-sensing device, called the governor, monitors the reservoir pressure. When the air pressure within the reservoir reaches the desired cutout pressure, which could be from 105 to 130 psi [723.45 to 895.7 kPa], the governor sends a signal to the compressor and the pumping action stops. As the reservoir pressure drops, owing to brake application, and the cut-in pressure is reached, which is about 20 psi [137.8 kPa] below the maximum reservoir pressure, the governor responds by sending a signal to the compressor, and the pumping action starts again.

The stored air under pressure becomes the potential energy of the air brake system. However, the volume of stored air (reservoir capacity) is not nearly as important as the air pressure, since it is the air pressure that creates the initial brake force. The reservoir capacity ensures that the pressure drop after a brake application is minimal, and therefore several brake applications can be made before the pressure drops to the cut-in pressure. As a result there is a longer compressor rest period, which increases its service life.

The application valve is positioned between the reservoir and the relay valve. It provides the driver or operator with a controlling device which meters the air (pressure) to the relay valve and gives the feel of the brake force as the driver or operator reduces or increases the air pressure.

The relay valve, as the name indicates, is a valve which relays the brake application from the application valve.

The air chamber converts the air pressure into linear force which is directed either onto a conventional master cylinder or onto a power pack unit. It is then called an air-over-hydraulic brake system.

On straight air brake systems the linear force is applied to the actuating mechanism. The actuating mechanism can be of a wedge brake design or of a cam brake design. When it is the former, the wedge increases the pushrod force. On the cam brake design, the slack adjuster converts the linear force into rotary motion (torque), and the cam converts the torque into force.

Slack Adjuster and Air Chamber As you know, different vehicles require different braking force,

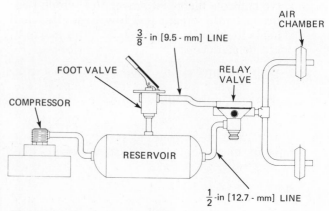

Fig. 18-1 Components of a basic air brake system.

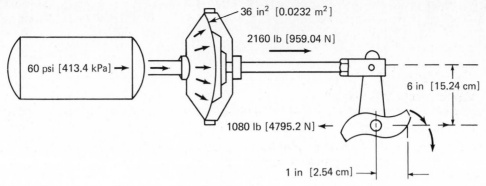

Fig. 18-2 Principle of converting air pressure into braking force.

and the foundation brakes must be made to these minimum and maximum requirements. This can be achieved by increasing the brake drum diameter and/or the lining area and/or the coefficiency of the lining. However, the simplest way of achieving this objective is to vary the air chamber area and/or the lever arm of the slack adjuster (see Fig. 18-2).

For example, if the chamber area is 36 in² [0.0232 m²], and the slack adjuster arm is 6 in [15.24 cm], and the applied air pressure is 60 psi [413.4 kPa], then the S cam torque would be 60 × 36 × 6/12 = 1080 lb · ft [1463.4 N · m], which, assuming that the radius of the S cam is 1 in [2.54 cm], would be the torque applied to each brake shoe. However, if the brake chamber area is increased by 10 in² [0.0064 m²], then the torque will increase by 300 lb · ft [406.5 N · m] (60 × 46 × 6/12 = 1380 lb · ft). Or,

if the slack adjuster arm is lengthened to 7 in [17.5 cm], the torque will increase by 180 lb · ft [243.9 N · m] (60 × 36 × 7/12 = 1260 lb · ft). Conversely, if the chamber area is reduced or the lever arm is shortened, the brake force will be reduced.

Before proceeding further, let us see how the components that make up a simple air brake system are designed, how they operate or function, what could cause them to fail or to operate inefficiently, and how to test and service them.

Compressors The air pumps used on on- and off-highway equipment are single-action (two strokes) reciprocating piston compressors (see Figs. 18-3 and 18-4). They are classified by their piston displacement in cubic feet [cubic meters] per rpm, ranging from 7.5 to 42 ft² [0.212 to 1.189 m³].

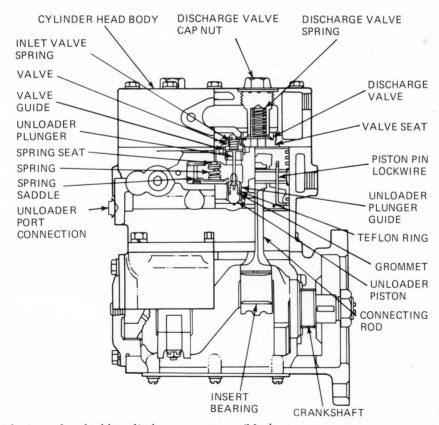

Fig. 18-3 Sectional view of a double-cylinder compressor. (*Mack Canada Inc.*)

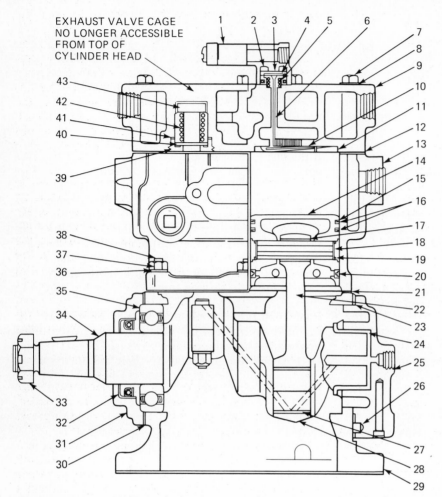

1. Unloader valve assembly
2. Spring cup expanders
3. Rubber diaphragm
4. Valve disk
5. Return spring
6. Inlet valve pin
7. Cap screw
8. Lock washer
9. Cylinder head
10. Inlet valve
11. Inlet valve guard
12. Gasket
13. Cylinder block
14. Piston
15. Expanders
16. Compression ring
17. Bushing
18. Piston pin
19. Snap ring
20. Oil ring
21. Gasket
22. Connecting rod
23. Gasket
24. Rear sleeve type bearing
25. Rear end bearing cap
27. Half bearing
28. Bearing cap
29. Crankcase
30. Gasket
31. Front end bearing cap
32. Oil Seal
33. Shaft end nut
34. Crankshaft
35. Front bearing
36. Lock washer
37. Nuts
38. Studs
39. Valve seat
40. Exhaust valve
41. Gasket
42. Exhaust spring
43. Exhaust valve cage

EXHAUST VALVE CAGE NO LONGER ACCESSIBLE FROM TOP OF CYLINDER HEAD

Fig. 18-4 Sectional view of a piston type air compressor. (*International Harvester Company*)

DESIGN All compressors—single, double, or V-4 piston—are designed similar to an internal combustion engine. The crankshaft is supported in the crankcase by roller bearings, ball bearings, tapered roller bearings, or insert bearings. The engine lubrication system supplies oil to the crankshaft and through internal passages supplies oil to the connecting rod bearings and piston pin. The connecting rod bearings are insert bearings. The cylinder block, which is bolted to the crankcase, is either air-cooled or cooled by the engine's cooling system. The right-hand side of the cylinder block is machined to accommodate the unloader mechanism, which consists of the unloader piston, the guide, the spring, spring seat, and saddle. The inlet valve, which is pressed into the cylinder block, is located above the unloader piston inlet valve seat. A valve guide holds the inlet valve with a light spring force against the valve seat. The inlet opening is covered with an intake filter (strainer) or with an intake adapter so that the compressor inlet can be connected with a hose to the engine's air intake system. **NOTE** The com-

ponents, as well as the shape of the unloader mechanism, vary to some extent between compressor types.

The pistons have two or three compression rings located in the ring grooves above the piston pin and one or two oil rings located in the ring groove below the piston pin. The piston pin is retained to the piston with two snap rings located in the piston pin bore. The major difference between an engine and a compressor is that the compressor has no camshaft, and the valves used are simple flapper valves. The cylinder head, bolted to the cylinder block, is cooled by the engine's cooling system. Coolant from the engine enters the cylinder block, flows around the water jackets, into the cylinder head, around its cooling jacket, and back into the engine's cooling system. **NOTE** The proper cooling is very important in order to maintain the discharge air temperature below 300°F [149°C]. The head is machined to accommodate the discharge valve, which is held against its seat by a light spring. The discharge stop is press-fitted into the head.

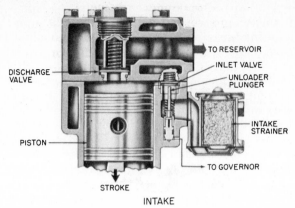

Fig. 18-5 View of compressor on the intake stroke. (*Mack Canada Inc.*)

OPERATION When the engine is operating, the compressor crankshaft rotates, and on the downstroke of the piston a low pressure is created within the cylinder (see Fig. 18-5). The higher atmospheric pressure enters the compressor intake adapter or strainer and fills the cavity between the inlet valve and unloader plunger guide. The higher atmospheric pressure lifts the inlet valve off its seat and fills the space vacated by the piston. After the piston passes BDC and begins its compression stroke (Fig. 18-6), the pressure within the cylinder and the atmospheric pressure are equal, and the inlet spring then closes the valve, trapping the air within the cylinder. As the piston continues to rise, it compresses the air, and the pressure holds the inlet valve firmly against its seat. However, as soon as the pressure within the cylinder is higher than the reservoir pressure, the discharge valve is forced off its seat, allowing the compressed air to pass by the open valve into the head cavity and onto the reservoir. As soon as the discharge line pressure is higher than the compressor pressure, the discharge valve spring, along with the higher pressure, closes the discharge valve, preventing the reservoir pressure from draining into the compressor. This cycle is repeated by all cylinders until the reservoir pressure reaches the set cutout pressure of the governor. When this is the case, the governor directs air from the reservoir to the inlet port of the unloader mechanism, and the pressure

acting on the unloader piston lifts the piston, the piston guide, and the unloader plunger, forcing the inlet valve off its seat. With the inlet valve open the piston cannot create a pressure within the cylinder, because air can pass freely into the adjacent cylinder and/or into the intake cavity (see Fig. 18-7). The compressor now rotates with reduced effort, minimizing wear and increasing engine power. As the reservoir pressure drops to the cut-in pressure, the governor responds and exhausts the air pressure from below the unloader piston. The unloader spring now forces the saddle, as well as the unloader guide, the piston, and the pin, downward, allowing the inlet valve spring to seat the valve, and the compressor then resumes its pumping cycle.

TROUBLESHOOTING The most common causes of the compressor's failing to maintain sufficient reservoir pressure, or not to achieve maximum pressure, are misalignment between the drive and driven pulley (causing belt slippage); loose or damaged drive belts; restricted air intake system; excessive leaks in the air brake system; improperly adjusted brakes; and excessive smallness of the compressor's displacement. **NOTE** The compressor must, within 25 s or less, be capable of increasing the air pressure within the reservoirs from 85 to 100 psi [586 to 689.5 kPa] when operated at the recommended rpm.

Less common, but equally unfavorable to compressor effectiveness, are piston rings and cylinder walls which are excessively worn, inlet or discharge valves which do not seat properly or are damaged, unloader mechanism which does not seal or operate properly, and a governor which is defective.

High reservoir pressure, though fortunately uncommon, can be caused by a defective or misadjusted governor, restricted air line from the governor to the unloader mechanism, and damaged unloader piston seals or binding unloader mechanism.

Another general complaint is that the compressor discharges excessive oil into the air system. In this case look for inlet air restriction due to dirty strainer or damaged air line, a damaged or kinked hose from the air intake system to the compressor, restricted oil return line's causing overfilling of the crankcase, high engine crankcase pressure, worn compression

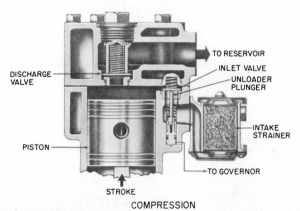

Fig. 18-6 View of compressor on the compression stroke. (*Mack Canada Inc.*)

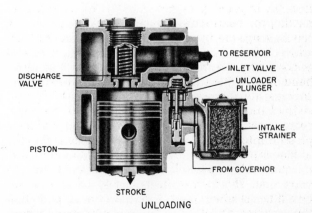

Fig. 18-7 View of compressor during unloading. (*Mack Canada Inc.*)

piston rings or cylinder walls, or high cooling (engine) temperature.

When the compressor is noisy, the defect is not necessarily easy to trace, but such system symptoms as (1) the compressor's discharging excessive oil into the system, (2) a wobbly pulley, (3) crankshaft seal leaking, or (4) the compressor's vibrating excessively indicate that the compressor is worn and should, therefore, be serviced.

TESTING   When a vehicle is in the shop for either preventive maintenance or for regular maintenance checkout, first inspect the air intake system and/or the strainer. Next, check drive belts and pulleys for wear and if necessary adjust the belt tension. Retorque all compressor mounting bolts. Check the cooling and lubrication inlet and outlet lines for leaks and for damaged hoses and connections. If the compressor is covered with oil and/or dirt, steam-clean the unit to ensure good cooling.

To check the general condition of the piston rings and cylinder walls, first disconnect the compressor discharge line and check for excessive oil or carbon deposit in the line. Bear in mind that a certain amount of oil which has passed the piston rings is carried through the air passage to the reservoirs. If the amount is excessive, the compressor must be removed for service.

To check the compressor performance, reduce the system pressure to 80 psi [551.2 kPa] and then operate the engine at high idle. Check the time it takes the system pressure to reach 100 psi [689 kPa]. The time span should not exceed 25 s. To check the seating ability of the inlet valve(s), the discharge valve(s), and the seals of the unloader piston(s), disconnect the compressor inlet adapter or remove the strainer and then bring the system up to maximum pressure. Stop the engine and listen for air leaks from the inlet port. If air escapes from the inlet port, the discharge valve(s) may be faulty or the seals on the unloader(s) may be damaged. To determine which valve is at fault, squirt a small amount of oil around the unloader piston(s). If this reduces the amount of leaking air, the piston seal is damaged.

To check the sealing capacity of the inlet valve(s), start the engine and listen at the inlet port for a sharp hissing sound. If hissing occurs, one or both inlet valves are leaking.

SERVICING   When the discharge valve, the unloader mechanism, the inlet valves, or the piston rings are worn or damaged, the compressor must be removed for servicing. (Only a few compressor designs allow you to service the unloader mechanism without removing the compressor from the engine.)

Because of the variance among drive arrangements, the procedure to remove a compressor from an engine varies accordingly. Nevertheless, the task is simple. Before removing the compressor, steam-clean the surrounding area, drive the vehicle to your work area, block the wheels, safely secure the hydraulic attachment, and then drain the air and cooling systems. Disconnect the coolant lines, lubrication lines, and air lines from the compressor and

cover all openings. Remove the mounting bolts and lift the compressor off its mounting. Examine the mounting surface, the pulleys, and the belt(s) for damage and wear or, when so equipped, examine the drive and driven gear or the drive and driven coupling for damage and wear. Before disassembling the compressor, clean it thoroughly and when necessary mark the components in relation to the crankcase and the cylinder block. Follow the service manual instruction in regard to the disassembly, checking, testing, and fitting. If you are in any way doubtful about reusing a part, don't take a chance—replace it, because the air compressor is the lifeline of the air brake system.

Practice good work habits. Do not drive old parts out or replacement parts into their respective positions—use a puller or press. Torque each bolt or nut precisely to the recommended torque. If you have to install a gear-driven or a coupling-driven compressor, first check the applicable service manual. When required, time the compressor to the engine to reduce engine vibration. Before installing a belt-driven compressor, check the belt and the pulley. When two belts are used but only one is damaged, replace both, because they are matched sets. When installing the belts, do not roll or pry them over the pulleys. Use the recommended bolts and washers and then loosely position the compressor. Align the pulleys within $\frac{1}{16}$ in [1.59 mm] for each $1\frac{3}{16}$ in [30.16 mm] between pulley centers and then tighten the bolts. Measure the belt tension by using a tension tool or with your index finger (in the middle of the belt span) push the belt straight downward; see Table 18-1.

NOTE   If the drive belts are new, check the tension 1 hour or so after operation because they tend to loosen (stretch) slightly and may need to be readjusted. Recheck them again after 8 hours of operation and thereafter at least every 5000 mi [8045 km]. If the drive belt(s) become dirty or greasy, remove the oil or grease as soon as it is detected so that it will not penetrate the belt. When removing the belts from the engine, clean both pulleys and belts with a nonflammable solvent or cleaner.

CAUTION   Never attempt to clean belt(s) when the engine is running and never use a flammable solvent.

Governors   Air compressor governors vary to some extent in design but not in performance. The governor can be mounted directly to the mounting surface of the compressor, or it may be remote mounted. When mounted to the compressor, one of the three

Table 18-1 CORRECT BELT TENSION

Belt width, in [mm]	Deflection per ft of span, in [mm]
$\frac{1}{2}$ [12.7]	$\frac{13}{32}$ [10.3]
$\frac{11}{16}$ [17.5]	$\frac{13}{32}$ [10.3]
$\frac{3}{4}$ [19.05]	$\frac{7}{16}$ [11.1]
$\frac{7}{8}$ [22.22]	$\frac{1}{2}$ [12.7]
1 [25.4]	$\frac{9}{16}$ [14.3]

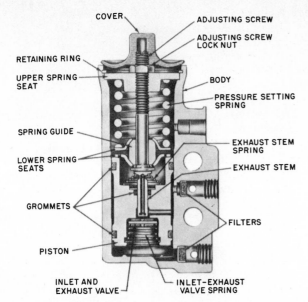

COVER — ADJUSTING SCREW

ADJUSTING SCREW LOCK NUT

RETAINING RING

UPPER SPRING SEAT

BODY

PRESSURE SETTING SPRING

SPRING GUIDE

EXHAUST STEM SPRING

LOWER SPRING SEATS

EXHAUST STEM

GROMMETS

FILTERS

PISTON

INLET AND EXHAUST VALVE

INLET-EXHAUST VALVE SPRING

Fig. 18-8 Sectional view of a D-2 governor. (*Mack Canada Inc.*)

governor unloading ports align with the compressor unloading port. When remote mounted, an air line (minimum of $\frac{3}{16}$-in ID) is used to connect the unloader ports with each other. The same size air line is used to connect the supply reservoir (wet tank) to the reservoir port of the governor.

The components of a common governor are shown in Fig. 18-8. **NOTE** Not all types of governors use identical components.

The governor body has four openings. The large center opening accommodates the upper spring seat, which is held to the body with a retainer ring. A rubber cover is screwed onto the adjusting screw to seal the opening and to prevent contaminants from entering the bore. The upper right opening is the exhaust port opening. The middle opening is the unloader port, and the lower one is the reservoir port connection. Inside the honed body bore is the piston which is center-drilled and cross-drilled and sealed at the lower and upper ends with a grommet (O ring). The larger lower center bore of the piston is machined to an inlet seat. A rubber-coated, one-piece exhaust inlet valve is held onto the inlet seat by the exhaust inlet spring. The exhaust stem is hollow and cross-drilled near the upper end and passes through the center bore of the piston. It is sealed to the piston bore with a grommet. A washer is positioned against the exhaust stem head, and a cone-type spring is situated between the washer on the exhaust stem and the piston. The lower half of the lower spring seat rests on the adjusting screw head. The spring guide rests against the seat, and the upper half of the lower spring seat rests against the spring guide. The pressure-adjusting spring is located between the spring guide and the upper spring seat. The upper end of the threaded adjusting screw is screwed into the upper spring seat.

OPERATION As the reservoir pressure is exhausted, the pressure-setting spring forces the lower spring seat downward, and with it, the piston. The exhaust

stem spring holds the exhaust stem (upward) against the adjusting screw head. The downward movement of the piston moves the exhaust stem seat away from the exhaust valve and allows the inlet and exhaust valve spring to seat the inlet valve against the inlet valve seat on the piston. As air under pressure enters the reservoir port, it passes through the bronze air filter, into the lower piston area, and onto the area of the inlet exhaust valve. As the air pressure increases, the force on the piston and the inlet exhaust valve increases. The piston is then pressured upward against the force of the pressure-setting spring. The lower spring seat and the spring guide slide upward on the adjusting screw.

Let us assume that the pressure-setting spring is adjusted to a cutout pressure of 120 psi [826.8 kPa]. When the reservoir pressure reaches about 100 psi [689 kPa], the piston has moved upward sufficiently to cause the exhaust valve stem end (exhaust valve seat) to rest against the exhaust valve. As the pressure reaches about 120 psi [826.8 kPa], the piston moves away from the inlet valve. The reservoir air can now pass by the open inlet valve, flow around the lower part of the exhaust valve stem, through the cross-drilled piston passage, through the bronze air filter, and into the unloading mechanism. This action causes the compressor to stop pumping.

As the inlet valve opens, it momentarily creates a slight pressure drop in the area below the piston. However, the pressure now acting on the additional piston area increases the upward force and thereby counteracts the pressure drop and ensures a positive inlet valve opening.

As the compressor's unloading action is completed, the air pressure above and below the inlet valve is equal, and the valve spring offsets the balance sealing the inlet valve and trapping the air pressure to the unloader mechanism.

As the reservoir pressure gradually drops (owing to brake application) to approximately 100 psi [689 kPa], it moves the piston partially downward, causing the exhaust valve to move away from the end of the exhaust valve stem. The trapped air in the unloading line and unloader piston then escapes through the cross-drilled passage in the piston, through the hollow exhaust stem and cross-drilled passage, into the area of the pressure-setting spring cavity, and out of the exhaust port.

TESTING To check the operation of the governor, install a master air gauge at any convenient place. Do not rely on the dashboard air gauge—it can vary up to 7 percent. Start the engine and note the cutout pressure. It should coincide with the pressure setting recommended in the service manual. Apply the brakes several times and note the cut-in pressure. If it is within 25 psi [172.25 kPa] of the cutout pressure, the governor operates satisfactorily. If the cut-in pressure exceeds 25 psi, the governor must be serviced.

If for some reason you must modify the cutout pressure, first unscrew the rubber cover and loosen the adjusting screw lock nut. To raise the cutout pressure (with a screwdriver), turn the adjusting

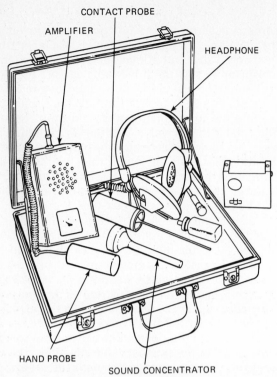

Fig. 18-9 Leak detector tester. (*International Harvestor Company*)

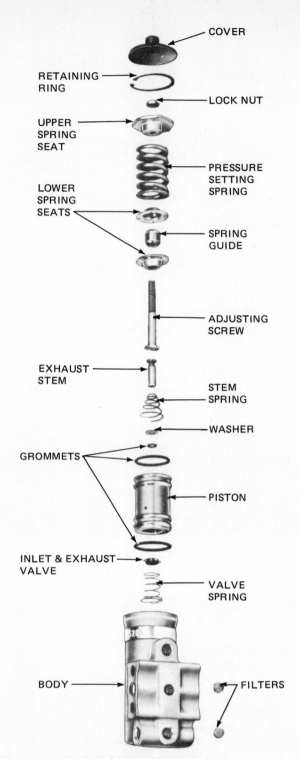

Fig. 18-10 Exploded view of D-2 type governor components. (*Mack Canada Inc.*)

screw counterclockwise, and to lower the pressure, turn the screw clockwise. One complete turn of the adjusting screw achieves a pressure change of about 10 psi [68.9 kPa]. Once made, lock the adjustment in and replace the rubber cover.

To check (for leakage) the inlet or exhaust valve or the O rings on the piston and exhaust stem, first operate the engine to achieve cutout pressure. Next, apply a soapy solution to the exhaust port. If more than three air bubbles are formed in less than 1 s, the governor must be serviced because the exhaust valve, the exhaust stem O ring, or the upper piston O ring is allowing air to pass by. Depedal the air pressure to cut-in pressure and again apply the soapy solution to the exhaust port. If more than three air bubbles are formed in less than 1 s, it is the lower piston ring or the inlet valve that is allowing air to pass by.

A better method of determining an air leak is with the use of an air leakage tester because this unit can detect very small air leaks, even those in confined areas where it is difficult to use the brush and soap solution method.

To test for air leaks, using the air leakage tester, bring the system to cutout pressure and then stop the engine. Put on the headphones, select the suitable sound concentrator, connect the amplifier, and then guide the probe around the fittings, connections, and ports. If there is an air leak, the sound will be audible on the headphones (see Fig. 18-9).

SERVICING Prepare the vehicle as outlined for servicing the compressor in this unit. Next, remove the reservoir air line from the governor, remove the governor mounting bolts, and lift the governor from the

compressor. If the governor is remote-mounted, disconnect the unloading line and the reservoir line from the governor before removing the mounting bolts. Clean the governor thoroughly before removing the rubber cover, and with a retainer or ring pliers, remove the retainer and lift the spring assembly from the body bore. Lift the exhaust stem, with washer and spring, from the piston. Tap the body on a piece of wood to remove the piston. (When using compressed air to remove the piston, hold the body about 1 in [25.4 mm] above a piece of wood and

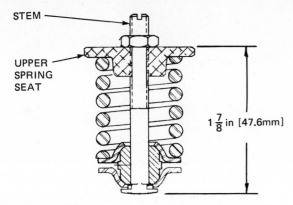

Fig. 18-11 Adjusting screw measurement.

then apply a short blast of air to the reservoir port.) Remove (if they have not already fallen out) the one-piece inlet exhaust valve and the valve spring. Remove both bronze filters and remove the O rings from the piston and the exhaust stem. Discard all seals and rubber parts.

Clean the disassembled parts. Inspect the body for cracks and damaged threads. If the body bore is grooved or scored, the body must be replaced. If the irregularities are small, the bore can be restored by honing it with a fine grit wheel cylinder hone.

If it is necessary to disassemble the spring assembly, loosen the lock nut and turn the adjusting screw to remove the nut from the upper spring seat. If the spring, the spring seats, or the screw is damaged, worn, or corroded, a replacement is necessary. If the piston is scored, the inlet seat is damaged, or the exhaust stem bore is rough or scored, the piston must be replaced (see Fig. 18-10).

REASSEMBLY Clean all parts again and lubricate all parts (including the spring guide and adjusting screw) with NLGI N² multipurpose lithium grease, silicone grease, or molybdenum disulfide lubricant. Reassemble the spring assembly as follows: Adjust the pressure-setting spring tension by turning the adjusting screw until the distance from the top of the upper spring seat to the head of the adjusting screw is 1.875 in [4.22 cm] (see Fig. 18-11). With

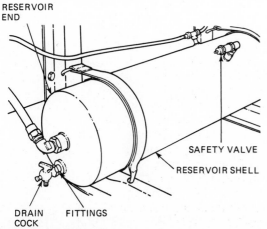

Fig. 18-12 Typical reservoir mounting. (*International Harvester Company*)

the lock nut, lock the adjustment. Install the O rings to the piston and place the one-unit intake exhaust valve onto the piston seat. Place the small coil end of the spring onto the valve and force the spring downward until the other end of the spring locks into the groove of the piston. Place the washer on the exhaust stem, the O ring in the stem groove, and the small spring opening onto the exhaust stem. Place this assembly into the piston and then place the piston assembly into the housing bore. Now slide the spring assembly into the bore, taking care not to dislodge the exhaust valve stem. Install the retainer ring. Check and adjust the governor by using shop air and a pressure regulator.

Reinstall the governor when you are assured that the mounting surfaces are clean, a new gasket was used, and the air lines were blown clean.

Reservoirs The reservoirs used for air brake systems are made from sheet steel. The ends are stamped, the shell is rolled to a cylinder, and it is electrically welded to a unit. The steel fittings are standard SAE dryseal pipe threads and are electrically welded to the shell and/or ends. The internal/external surfaces are coated as protection against corrosion. They are then tested for 10 min, at a hydrostatic pressure of 500 psi [3445 kPa]. A typical reservoir mounting is shown in Fig. 18-12.

To test the reservoir, the air line connections, and the drain valve for leakage, bring the reservoir pressure up to cutout pressure and then stop the engine. With an air leakage tester or a solution of soap and water, check for air leaks.

Application Valve The application, or brake, valve is a mechanical device with which the driver or operator can meter the air (pressure) into the application line, hold the applied air pressure, and reduce or fully release the applied air pressure. All application valves operate on the same principle and consist of the components shown in Fig. 18-13. Nevertheless, there are some differences among application valves, which, in the main, are the capacity of the valve which governs the size of the internal parts, the portings within the valve, and the port openings; the means used to control the application plunger, which may be a treadle, or a conventional brake pedal, or a hand lever; the pressure-graduating spring, which may be a coil spring or a rubber spring (coned rubber disk); or the application valve itself, which could have two independent application valves in one body (dual application valves).

OPERATION When the application valve is in the release position the force from the application plunger is removed, the pressure-graduating spring forces the application plunger upward. The upward movement is stopped by the treadle roller. The treadle roller travel is limited through the adjusting stop. The piston return spring has forced the application piston upward, lifting the exhaust valve from its seat. The inlet valve spring has seated the inlet valve (valve poppet) against its seat.

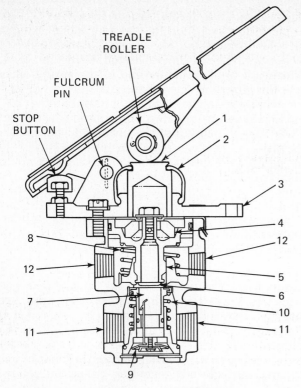

1. Application plunger
2. Boot
3. Mounting plate
4. Pressure graduating spring (rubber)
5. Application piston
6. Inlet valve and seat
7. Exhaust valve
8. Piston balance spring
9. Exhaust diaphragm
10. Inlet/exhaust valve balance spring
11. Reservoir ports
12. Service line ports.

Fig. 18-13 Sectional view of a treadle valve. (*Mack Canada Inc.*)

NOTE The poppet is composed of the exhaust valve, which is the inner circle, and the inlet valve, which is the outer circle.

To apply the brakes the driver moves the treadle (or pedal). This action exerts a force on the application plunger, and this force is transmitted onto the pressure-graduating spring. The spring force then moves the application piston downward, seating the exhaust valve against the exhaust valve seat. If the application (treadle) force does not exceed the force

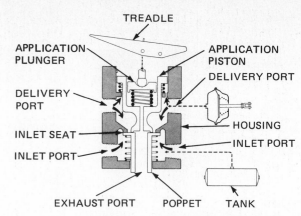

Fig. 18-15 Schematic view of the application valve in the holding position. (*Wagner Electric Sales Corporation*)

created by the reservoir pressure acting on the area below the inlet exhaust valve and piston return spring, no further action takes place. However, if the treadle force is higher, the inlet valve is lifted off its seat. This allows reservoir pressure to pass by the open inlet valve, around the lower part of the application piston, out of the delivery port, and into the brake chamber (see Fig. 18-14). As the application pressure builds up, so does the pressure in the area below the application piston, and the piston moves upward. **NOTE** The inlet and exhaust valve spring and air pressure keep the exhaust valve seated. When both forces are equal, the inlet and exhaust valve spring and the reservoir pressure upset the balance, close the inlet valve, and trap the delivery pressure. This is the hold or balance position (see Fig. 18-15). Any additional force on the application plunger moves the application piston; opens the inlet valve, allowing more air to enter the delivery line; and thereby increases the air pressure. Any reduction in force on the application plunger reduces the force on the graduation spring. As a result the air pressure acting on the lower area of the application piston is now greater in force and moves the application piston upward. The exhaust valve then opens, allowing the air from the delivery line to escape past the open exhaust valve, through the center bore of the poppet valve, into the atmosphere. This is the exhaust position (see Fig. 18-16).

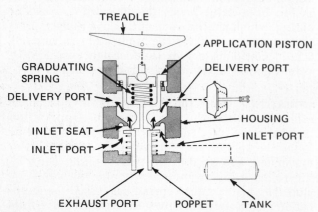

Fig. 18-14 Schematic view of application valve in the applying position. (*Wagner Electric Sales Corporation*)

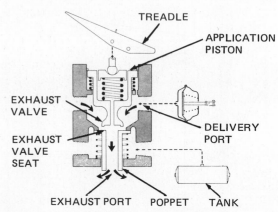

Fig. 18-16 Schematic view of the application valve in the exhaust position (*Wagner Electric Sales Corporation*)

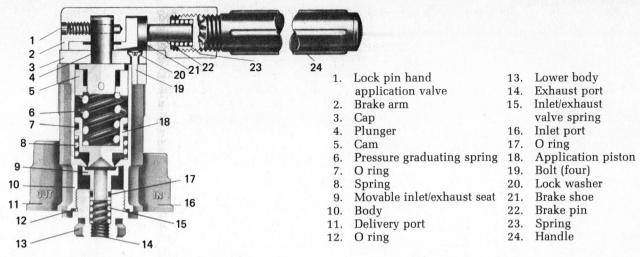

Fig. 18-17 Sectional view of a hand application valve. (*Sealco Air Controls Inc.*)

1. Lock pin hand application valve
2. Brake arm
3. Cap
4. Plunger
5. Cam
6. Pressure graduating spring
7. O ring
8. Spring
9. Movable inlet/exhaust seat
10. Body
11. Delivery port
12. O ring
13. Lower body
14. Exhaust port
15. Inlet/exhaust valve spring
16. Inlet port
17. O ring
18. Application piston
19. Bolt (four)
20. Lock washer
21. Brake shoe
22. Brake pin
23. Spring
24. Handle

As soon as the air pressure acting on the lower area of the application piston equalizes with the force of the graduating spring, the valve comes to a hold position. If the force from the application plunger is fully released, the exhaust valve remains open. All the air from the delivery line is then exhausted, and this releases the brakes.

Hand Application Valve Hand and foot application valves differ in that the hand valve is smaller, it has smaller portings, and the application plunger actuation is achieved through a handle and a ramp built onto the application plunger and cam. The hand valve handle is held (in any position) by a friction clutch or as shown (see Fig. 18-17) by use of a mechanical locking device.

OPERATION When the handle is partly turned in a counterclockwise direction, some of the spring force is removed from the brake pin, and the brake shoe loses friction. Under this condition the brake arm and application plunger are moved in a clockwise rotation, and as a result the ramp (incline) forces the cam downward. This increases the force on the graduating spring and moves the application piston downward, closing the exhaust valve and opening the inlet valve. **NOTE** The poppet valve is sealed and guided in the lower body. The reservoir air passes by the open inlet valve, below the application piston, and out of the delivery port.

The hold or balance position is achieved by the same means as by a foot-operated application valve.

If it is desirable to hold the particular brake application, the driver or operator must turn the handle about one-half turn (clockwise). This increases the spring force, which, in turn, increases the friction on the brake shoe, holding the handle in a fixed position.

To release the locked-handle position, rotate it counterclockwise. This reduces the brake shoe friction. The energy of the graduation spring acting on the cam forces the application plunger cam to slide into its lowest point. The brake arm then rotates

counterclockwise, removing the force from the graduating spring. The air pressure acting on the lower area of the application piston now exceeds the pressure-graduating spring force and moves the application piston upward. This opens the exhaust valve, allowing the delivery air to pass by the open exhaust valve, through the center of the poppet valve, and into the atmosphere.

Dual Application Valve The dual application valve has two independent application valves in one body. One is called the "primary circuit valve," which consists of components identical to those of a single foot valve. The application plunger is guided within the mounting plate bore; one end of the plunger rests against the spring seat and the other end rests against the treadle roller. A boot placed in the groove of the plunger's mounting bracket prevents contaminants from entering the valve. A rubber graduating spring located between the spring seat and application piston is used instead of a coil spring. The application piston is held upward by its piston return spring and thereby has moved the exhaust valve from its seat. The primary poppet valve assembly (inlet/exhaust) is guided in the extension of the relay piston and body. The inlet exhaust valve spring holds the inlet valve upward against the primary inlet valve seat.

The secondary circuit valve has the same components as a relay valve. The secondary poppet assembly (inlet/exhaust) is guided within the lower body, and the inlet and exhaust valve spring holds the inlet valve against its seat. The relay piston is located above the poppet valve. The piston extension is hollow and passes through the primary inlet and exhaust valve, and when the dual application valve is in the release position, its end rests against the primary application piston. The upper end of the extension has large right-angle openings which allow the delivery air from the primary circuit to enter and to escape through the hollow extension, out through the rubber exhaust diaphragm, into the atmosphere. The stem passes through the end of the

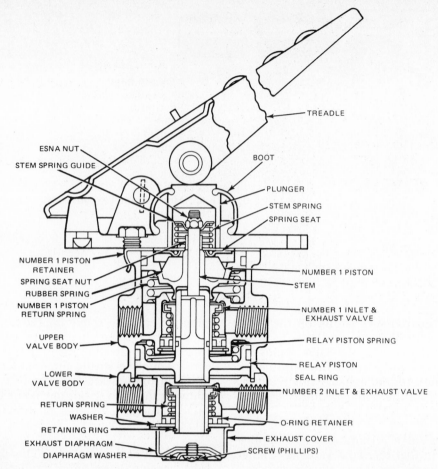

Fig. 18-18 Sectional view of a dual application valve in the release position. (*Ford Motor Company*)

extension and through the primary application piston. The stem spring rests between the spring guide (screwed to the extension of the primary piston) and the spring seat. In the release position, the spring and guide rests against the graduating spring seat and thereby holds the relay piston upward against the spring force (see Fig. 18-18).

OPERATION—BOTH RESERVOIRS CHARGED When the treadle is pivoted, the motion and force are transmitted to the application plunger. From there they are transmitted onto the spring seat, the rubber graduating spring, and the primary application piston. This action moves the primary piston and relay piston downward; however the relay piston does not, at this time, close the secondary exhaust valve. The primary circuit exhaust valve is closed and the inlet valve is open. Reservoir air passes by the primary inlet valve and out of one or both of the delivery ports. At the same time the delivery air passes through the (two) bleed passages and enters in the area above the relay piston (relay cavity). The delivery pressure forces the relay piston further downward, closes the exhaust valve, and opens the secondary inlet valve. The air from the secondary circuit reservoir can then pass by the open inlet valve and out through the secondary delivery ports. This entire sequence, that is, the closing of the primary exhaust valve and opening of the primary inlet valve, as well as the closing of the secondary exhaust and opening of the secondary inlet valve, is almost simultaneous (see Fig. 18-19).

BALANCE POSITION When the delivery pressure acting on the area below the primary application piston equals the mechanical force of the rubber graduating spring, the inlet-exhaust valve spring closes the inlet valve and holds the delivery pressure. At the same time the primary delivery pressure (from above) on the area of the relay piston and the secondary delivery pressure from below are equal in force. The secondary inlet-exhaust valve spring closes the secondary inlet valve, holding the secondary delivery pressure (see Fig. 18-20).

RELEASE POSITION When the treadle force is removed, the force from the primary application piston and relay piston is also eliminated. The primary and secondary delivery pressure and the primary piston spring force are now greater in force, moving the primary application piston upward. This action opens the primary exhaust valve, allowing the air to pass by the exhaust valve, through the large opening in the relay piston extension, through the hollow secondary inlet-exhaust valve, and out through the exhaust port. At the same time, the air pressure from above the relay piston is reduced, because the air passes through the two bleed passages into the area

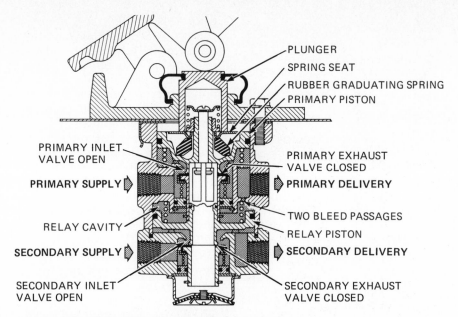

Fig. 18-19 Sectional view of the dual application valve in the applied position. (*International Harvester Company*)

below the primary application piston and exhausts with the primary delivery air. The upward movement of the relay piston opens the secondary exhaust port, and the secondary delivery air escapes past the open exhaust valve, through the hollow inlet-exhaust valve, into the atmosphere.

PRIMARY CIRCUIT OPERATION When there is no air pressure in the secondary reservoir, the primary circuit is actuated and functions as previously outlined in the section, "Operation—Both Reservoirs Charged." However, the secondary circuit cannot apply the brake, because of the lack of air pressure (see Fig. 18-21).

SECONDARY CIRCUIT OPERATION When there is no air pressure in the primary reservoir, the primary circuit cannot apply the brakes. When under this condition the treadle is moved, the application plunger force is exerted onto the primary piston, which mechanically moves the relay piston, closes

the secondary exhaust valve, and opens the inlet valve. The secondary air passes by the open inlet valve and out of the delivery port. As the secondary delivery pressure increases in force, the relay piston is moved upward, transmitting its force to the application piston and graduation spring. When both forces are equal, the secondary inlet valve closes, holding the delivery pressure. When the treadle force is removed, the higher delivery pressure forces the relay piston and application piston upward, opens the exhaust valve, and allows the secondary delivery air to escape (see Fig. 18-22).

MAINTENANCE AND TROUBLESHOOTING To maintain a foot application valve in good operating condition and extend its service life, a number of checks should be made with every engine oil change. Make

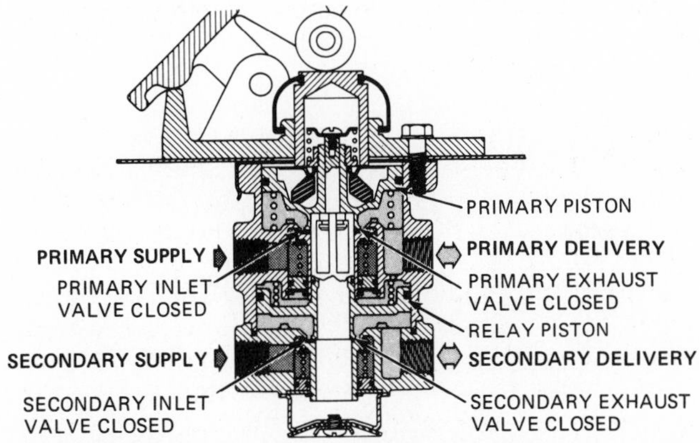

Fig. 18-20 Sectional view of the dual application valve in the balance position. (*International Harvester Company*)

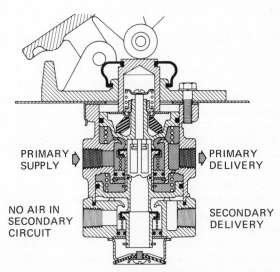

Fig. 18-21 Sectional view of the dual application valve in the applied position with loss of air in the secondary circuit. (*International Harvester Company*)

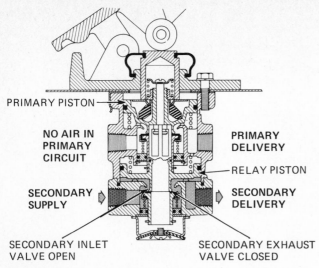

Fig. 18-22 Sectional view of the dual application valve in the applied position with loss of air in the primary circuit. (*International Harvester Company*)

certain that the movement of the treadle is not restricted owing to dirt, gravel, etc., below the treadle; the boot is undamaged and seats firmly in its grooves; the exhaust port is clean and the diaphragm is undamaged; the treadle pivot bores, hinge pin, roller, and roller pin are not damaged or worn, and the application plunger is not worn to the extent that it is loose in its bore; the free play of the treadle is adjusted properly.

To check the free play, gently lift the treadle against its stop and then place a 0.002 in [0.05 mm] feeler gauge between the application plunger and roller. If the clearance is greater, loosen the lock nut and turn the stop bottom screw to bring the roller in contact with the application plunger and then lock the adjustment. If the application plunger, roller, roller pin, or hinge pin is dirty or lacks lubrication, use compressed air to remove the dirt and then relubricate the components.

The most common cause of application valve failure is improper seating of the exhaust and/or inlet valve due to damage or dirt on the valve(s) or seat(s).

To determine if the exhaust valve is leaking, apply a high delivery pressure. If the valve is not seating properly, air passes by the exhaust valve seat and out of the exhaust port or past the O ring seals.

To check if the inlet valve is leaking, bring the reservoir pressure up to cutout pressure. Stop the engine, and if air leaks from the exhaust port, the valve(s) and/or O rings are damaged.

The second common cause of valve failure is contamination, which causes reduced valve action or valve and/or piston hangup.

Although it is somewhat rare, the graduating spring occasionally loses some of its energy and thereby reduces the maximum delivery pressure. To check the energy of the graduating spring and at the same time the operation of the valve, install master gauges into the primary and secondary delivery circuits (see Fig. 18-23). Bring the brake system to cutout pressure and depress the treadle to several different positions and note the response on the air

gauges. Normally, the primary pressure is about 2 psi [13.78 kPa] higher than the secondary delivery pressure. If the pressure differential is higher, the relay piston is hanging up or the piston, seal is leaking. If the primary piston seal is leaking you will notice that air escapes from around the mounting bracket or application plunger. When the treadle force is being reduced, the response on both air gauges should occur quickly and equally. Before depressing the treadle fully, make certain that the reservoirs are at the maximum pressure. When the treadle is fully depressed, the readings of the pressure gauges should equal those of the reservoir pressures. If this is not so, the energy of the graduating spring has lessened, causing the inlet valve to close earlier and reducing the service line pressure.

If the dual application valve has one or more of the malfunctions just mentioned, it must be serviced.

SERVICING The service procedure for all application valves is closely related. After the vehicle is prepared as outlined for servicing the compressor, identify the air lines in regard to their port connections. Remove them, cap the port openings, remove the three outer circle cap screws, and then lift the valve from its vehicle mounting. Thoroughly clean the assembly and dry it with compressed air, remove the three inner circle cap screws, and lift the treadle assembly from the valve body. When starting the disassembly from the bottom, remove, in sequence, the exhaust diaphragm screw, washer, diaphragm, exhaust cover screws, exhaust cover, and secondary poppet assembly consisting of retainer ring, exhaust inlet valve retainer O rings, washer, and inlet exhaust spring.

Next, remove the four lower body cap screws, the lower body from the top body, and the O ring from its groove. Using two screwdrivers, one placed in the slot of the stem guide screw and one in the slot of the stem, loosen and remove the stem guide screw. **CAUTION** The total spring force is about 50 lb [222 N].

NOTE Some dual application valves are equipped with a self-locking nut rather than a stem guide screw.

Once the spring guide screw or nut is removed,

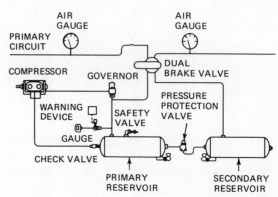

Fig. 18-23 Schematic view of a dual brake system. (*Ford Motor Company*)

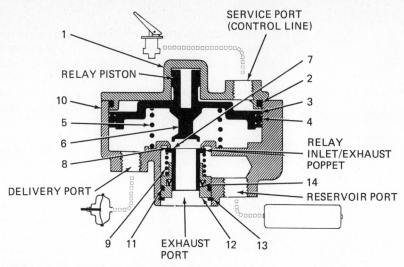

Fig. 18-24 Sectional view of a relay valve in the release position. (*Wagner Electric Sales Corporation*)

1. Valve cover
2. Cover to body seal
3. Relay piston
4. Relay piston seal
5. Relay piston return spring
6. Exhaust valve
7. Exhaust valve seat
8. Inlet valve and seat
9. Inlet/exhaust valve spring
10. Valve body
11. Valve guide seal
12. Valve guide
13. Snap ring
14. Tetraseal

remove the spring guide and the stem spring and let the stem fall through the hollow relay piston extension. Next, remove the relay piston and the relay piston spring and remove the O ring from the piston. Lift out the primary poppet retainer ring and the poppet assembly. If necessary, apply thumb force from below, onto the primary piston, to force the assembly from its bore.

To disassemble the primary piston assembly, turn the spring seat nut from the primary piston extension, remove the graduating spring seat and the graduating spring, and remove the O ring from the piston. Clean all parts in solvent and dry them with compressed air or, better yet, clean them in a hot tank. **CAUTION** The hot tank solution must be suitable for aluminum.

Discard all rubber parts and both inlet-exhaust valves, since they are included in the service kit.

Inspect all sliding surfaces and seats for wear, nicks, and scoring, or general distortion. Give special attention to the relay piston as it extends to the bores of the primary and relay piston surfaces; make sure that the threaded bores are not cracked or the threads damaged. Remove nicks and burrs or rough spots with fine emery cloth.

Reassemble the valve in precisely the reverse order of which it was disassembled but first make certain that all parts are clean, that the O rings are not twisted, that the parts are well lubricated, and that the screws and cap screws are torqued to specification.

Test the valve before reinstalling it to the vehicle. To make this test, connect an air gauge to the primary and secondary delivery ports. Connect a shop air line to the primary and secondary reservoir ports. Test the valve as outlined previously.

Relay Valve   The relay valve is a remote control application valve. It reduces the time lag of brake application and release. The relay valve may be located anywhere on (or near) the front or rear axles but always as close as possible to the brake chambers. The closer the relay valve is to the brake cham-

ber, the lower the air volume required to apply the brakes. When long air lines are used, obviously more air is needed (to fill the line) before the air enters the brake chamber. **NOTE** The sizes of the air lines used to connect the components are given in the service manual.

DESIGN   The greatest difference among the various relay valves lies in the reaction member. Some use a diaphragm, whereas others use a piston. The piston relay valve is very similar in design and operation to the secondary circuit valve of a dual application valve. However, in the former, the extended reaction piston is guided in the bore of the cover. The poppet assembly (inlet/exhaust) is likewise similar in design, and the inlet-exhaust valve is also guided by a guide. The relay valve has one control port (service line), two delivery ports, and one reservoir port. Each one is threaded to accommodate the respective hose fitting.

OPERATION   With no air pressure in the area above the relay (reaction) piston, the piston return spring forces the piston upward into the release position (see Fig. 18-24) and thereby creates a gap between the exhaust valve and valve seat and allows atmospheric air to enter or leave the exhaust port. The upward movement is stopped by the extended piston and body bore. The inlet-exhaust valve spring holds the inlet valve on its seat, and when the reservoir contains pressure, an additional force holds the valve on its seat. A tetraseal is positioned between the inlet and exhaust guide and the retainer, and an O ring is positioned between the guide retainer and the exhaust valve stem, effectively sealing the poppet assembly.

APPLICATION   When air under pressure is directed into the control port (service line), the service line pressure exerts a down force on the relay piston. The exhaust valve seat contacts and closes the exhaust valve and at the same time opens the inlet valve. The reservoir air (under high pressure) flows into

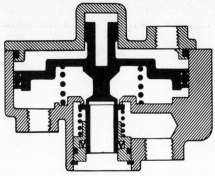

Fig. 18-25 Sectional view of a relay valve in the balance (hold) position. (*Wagner Electric Sales Corporation*)

the area below the relay piston and out of the delivery port. This is the application position. As the pressure rises in the delivery lines, so does the pressure below the relay piston. The pressure forces the piston upward and allows the inlet-exhaust valve to move upward. When the delivery pressure acting on the area (from below) and the service line pressure acting on the area of the relay piston (from above) are equal, the inlet-exhaust spring causes the inlet valve to seat and thereby traps the delivery pressure. This is the balance position (see Fig. 18-25).

Any increase in the service line pressure increases the down force on the relay piston, opening the inlet valve and increasing the delivery pressure. The inlet valve remains open until both forces are again equal.

If the service line pressure is reduced, the delivery pressure force is higher than the service line pressure. This forces the relay piston upward, opening the exhaust valve, and the air escapes through the center opening of the exhaust port into the atmosphere. Again, when both forces are equal, the relay piston is moved downward and thus achieves balance and causes the exhaust seat to rest against the exhaust valve.

TROUBLESHOOTING When there is an external leak while the relay valve is in the release position, either the O ring and/or the tetraseal is damaged, or the inlet valve does not seat properly. When there is an air leak while the relay valve is in the application position or the hold position, the exhaust valve does not seat properly. If the relay valve is slow to reset or hesitates to respond to the service line pressure variation, the piston seal is worn or damaged, the piston is hanging up owing to sludge within the piston bore, or the piston and bore are grooved or scored.

If any one of these malfunctions exists, the relay valve must be serviced.

SERVICING Prepare the vehicle as outlined for servicing the compressor. Next, mark the air lines in relation to their port connections and then remove them. Cover all openings; remove the mounting bolts and then the relay valve from the vehicle. Clean the exterior of the valve and remove the cover bolts and the cover. Remove the tetraseal from the cover; remove the reaction piston, the O ring seal, and the piston return spring.

To remove the poppet assembly, first remove the retainer ring, the exhaust shield, and the retainer. Remove the O ring from the retainer, remove the tetraseal, the inlet-exhaust guide, valve return spring, and inlet-exhaust valve. Discard all seals and O rings and the inlet-exhaust valve, since these parts are supplied in the service kit. Clean the remaining parts in solvent or a hot tank.

CAUTION When using the hot tank method, make certain all cleaning solution is rinsed out thoroughly before blowing the parts dry with compressed air.

Examine all sliding surfaces, as well as the bore surfaces for wear, damage, and/or score marks. Check the threaded bores for damaged threads and make certain the cover and body surfaces are free of nicks and burrs. If the inlet valve seat is damaged in any way, or if there are other parts which are not serviceable, a replacement is necessary.

Clean the parts again before lubricating the seals, O rings, body bores, reaction piston, and poppet valve assembly and do not forget to lubricate the piston extension and cover bore. You can then place the seals and O rings into position and reassemble the relay valve.

When placing the poppet valve assembly in the body, use your thumb to check the freeness of the valve before placing the spring and the relay piston into the body bore. Use a torque wrench to tighten the cover cap screw to the specified torque. Using your testing equipment, test the performance of the relay valve and check for air leaks. If no testing equipment is available, install the relay valve and then test the valve for its performance.

Quick-Release Valve All quick-release valves are common in design and operating principle. They are used when the air line distance from the application valve to the brake chamber is relatively short and therefore the time lag when applying the brakes is not increased. A quick-release valve has the capacity to release the air from the brake chambers as soon as the service line pressure is reduced by the application valve.

DESIGN The valve is composed of a body having one service line port (on the top) and two delivery ports. An inlet valve seat is formed to the inner body. The center bore of the cap serves as the exhaust port and has an exhaust seat. The diaphragm's upper, outer circle is the inlet valve, and the lower, smaller circle is the exhaust valve. The valve spring seat rests on the outer circle of the diaphragm, and the valve spring is positioned between the spring seat and cap.

OPERATION When the quick-release valve is in the release position, the diaphragm (owing to its cup tension) is flat, holding the exhaust valve off its seat. The spring holds the outer circumference of the diaphragm against the inlet valve seat. When air under pressure is directed from the application valve into the service line port, the air pressure forces the center of the diaphragm down, seating the exhaust

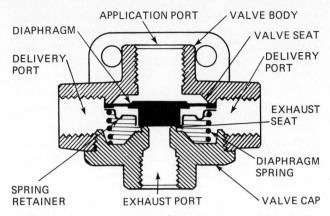

DIAPHRAGM
DELIVERY PORT
SPRING RETAINER
APPLICATION PORT — VALVE BODY
VALVE SEAT
DELIVERY PORT
EXHAUST SEAT
DIAPHRAGM SPRING
EXHAUST PORT — VALVE CAP

Fig. 18-26 Sectional view of a quick-release valve in the balance position. (*Wagner Electric Sales Corporation*)

valve. When the air pressure overcomes the diaphragm cup tension and light spring force, the outer edges bend downward, opening the inlet valve. The air passes by the open valve and flows out of the delivery ports to the brake chambers.

When the brake valve is in balance, that is, when a fixed delivery line pressure is achieved, the valve spring closes the inlet valve. If the service line pressure is partly reduced by the application valve, some force is removed from the top area of the diaphragm and the delivery pressure from the brake chambers is now higher. The center of the diaphragm is forced upward, lifting the exhaust valve from its seat and reducing the pressure in the brake chambers. When the application valve regains balance, the exhaust valve is forced back on its seat. If the delivery pressure is fully released, all delivery air is exhausted and the exhaust valve remains open. (See Fig. 18-26.)

TESTING AND SERVICING To test the quick-release valve for external air leaks, first make a normal brake application, and if air leaks from the exhaust port or around the cap flange, the valve must be serviced.

NOTE Although there is no method by which you can check for a leaking inlet valve, there is no need to check, because the valve becomes noisy or erratic in operation if it is leaking.

Since the quick-release valve is so simple in design, it is also simple to service. First, clean the valve. Clamp it by its mounting flange in a vise which has protected jaws and then place a socket wrench onto the nut formed on the cap. Loosen and remove the cap, spring, spring seat, and diaphragm. Check the inlet and exhaust seat for damage, nicks, burrs, and grooves, and the threaded bores for cracks and damaged threads. Remove nicks and burrs from the cap and body flanges. Before reassembling the valve, clean the cap and body once more and then reinstall the parts in an order precisely the reverse of that in which they were removed from the body. Reinstall the valve and retest it.

Brake Chambers The purpose of the brake chamber(s) is to convert delivery air pressure into linear force to actuate the brakes.

Three types of brake chambers are used on on- and off-highway vehicles. Where the stroke (pushrod travel) requires more than 2.5 in [6.35 cm], either rotary brake chambers or piston air cylinders are used (see discussion of air over hydraulics in Unit 17). Where the maximum stroke requirement is less than 2.5 in, the clamp ring brake chamber is used. The clamp ring, the piston, and the rotary brake chamber types vary in size to suit the particular brake force requirements. The brake chambers are classified by the effective area of the chamber diaphragm and stroke. The diaphragm area of the clamp ring chamber varies from 6 to 36 in² [38.7 to 232.2 cm²] and varies in maximum stroke length from $1\frac{5}{8}$ to 3 in [4.12 to 7.62 cm].

DESIGN AND OPERATION A clamp ring brake chamber consists of the parts shown in Fig. 18-27. Note the four vent holes which are equally spaced around the circumference of the nonpressure plate to allow the air to escape from the nonpressure chamber when the diaphragm is forced to the right. Also note that the pressure plate has two inlet ports. This design allows the outer delivery port to be positioned so that the air line does not require an elbow.

When the application valve directs air to the brake chambers, the pressure acts on the diaphragm area and forces the diaphragm and pushrod assembly to the right, actuating the brakes. When the air pressure is released from the pressure chamber, the diaphragm return spring and brake shoe return springs force the assembly to the left until it rests against the inner side of the pressure plate.

FAILURE AND TESTING The clamp ring brake chamber, when used on on-highway equipment, is nearly

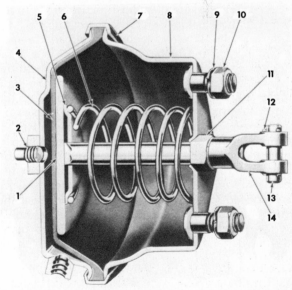

1. Push rod
2. Plug
3. Diaphragm
4. Pressure plate
5. Spring retainer
6. Spring
7. Clamp
8. Nonpressure plate
9. Lock washer
10. Nut
11. Lock nut
12. Cotter pin
13. Clevis pin
14. Clevis yoke

Fig. 18-27 Brake chamber (cross-sectional view). (*International Harvester Company*)

trouble free. However, when it is used on off-high-way vehicles, many difficulties may arise, such as external damage, which may deform the clamp ring and cause the diaphragm to leak; broken nonpressure plate mounting studs; misalignment between the pushrod assembly and slack adjuster, which would cause restricted pushrod movement and/or excessive wear on the diaphragm and pushrod; or a breaking loose of the pushrod from the pushrod plate.

When adjusting brakes, you should therefore check that the pushrod is not bent, the alignment is correct, and the chamber is mounted securely (see discussion of slack adjuster service and adjustment in Unit 16).

To test for air leaks on the brake chamber, first apply the maximum delivery pressure and then check for leaks. If air leaks from the clamp ring, you might try to tighten the clamp bolt to stop the leak. It is safer, however, to service the brake chamber when you do not know what caused the leak, for the clamp ring or flange may be corroded or bent, or the diaphragm may be cut at the lower end of the V.

SERVICING   First remove the air line and the yoke pin. Loosen and remove the mounting nuts from the stud bolts and lift the chamber from its mounting. With a wire brush clean the chamber exterior, particularly around the clamp ring and the clamp ring bolts. Apply penetrating oil to the bolts and pushrod threads. Pull the pushrod out and clamp it in a vise having protected jaws. Otherwise, use a pair of vise grip pliers to hold the pushrod. **NOTE** Use protection tape to prevent the pushrod from becoming scored when loosening the yoke locknut or when removing the yoke.

If the air line is connected to the outer inlet port, first mark the pressure plate position in regard to the mounting studs before removing the clamp ring. By using two deep socket wrenches, loosen and remove the clamp nuts and bolts; then use a soft-face hammer and tap on the clamp ring to loosen it from the flanges. Lift one end of the clamp ring over the plate flanges, pull sideways, and at the same roll the clamp ring from the flanges. **CAUTION** Take care not to permanently bend or twist the clamp ring. If the pressure plate sticks to the diaphragm, tap it lightly to loosen it, and then loosen and remove the diaphragm from the nonpressure plate flange. While holding the pushrod assembly and the nonpressure plate, loosen the vise grip and slowly release the spring force. Next, remove the pushrod assembly and the return spring from the nonpressure plate. Clean all parts, except the diaphragm, in solvent or with a glass blaster or a hot tank. Clean the diaphragm with a rubber-cleaning solvent or wood alcohol. Inspect the diaphragm for kinks, deterioration, or cuts. If the flanges are corroded, internally or externally, or if they are bent or twisted, the plates must be replaced. Also, if the stud bolts are loose or the threads damaged, the plates must be replaced.

NOTE If it is necessary to replace the spring, make sure it is replaced with the same type; otherwise

balanced braking would not occur. When checking the pushrod assembly, make certain that the rod is not bent, that it is not loose in the diaphragm plate, and that the plate is not damaged or bent. If necessary, paint the applicable parts with rust preventive fast-drying paint.

Lubricate the flanges and the V of the diaphragm and pushrod plate, using the recommended lubricant. Next, stand the pushrod assembly on a flat surface. Position the spring onto the pushrod plate, along with the nonpressure plate, and force the nonpressure plate downward, until it bottoms against the flat surface. Hold the assembly compressed by using a pair of vise grips. Next, clamp one stud bolt into the protected-jaw vise in such a way that the pushrod plate lies in a horizontal position. Place the diaphragm onto the nonpressure plate flange, place the pressure plate onto the diaphragm, and align the inlet port with your previous marking. Spread the clamp ring; position one end over the flanges and roll the ring in place. Assemble the bolts and nuts to the clamp ring lugs and tighten them (somewhat loosely).

NOTE When the brake chamber is installed, the clamp ring lugs should not face downward. Check that the clamp ring is correctly seated. After tightening the nuts to the recommended torque, tap on the outside of the clamp ring with a soft-face hammer to further ensure correct seating and then retorque the clamp ring nuts. Screw the lock nut and then the yoke onto the pushrod. If a dust boot is used, install it before screwing the locknut and yoke onto the pushrod.

If you have available a dummy brake assembly, install the brake chamber to it. Adjust the pushrod travel. Connect the inlet port to the shop application valve and test the chamber for air leaks; also test the pushrod action. If a dummy brake assembly is not available to you, install the brake chambers to the vehicle, connect the air line, adjust the pushrod travel, check the chamber for leaks, and check the action of the pushrod.

MODERN AIR BRAKE SYSTEM

The basic air brake system discussed so far in this unit would function, perhaps even trouble-free, over a long period of time. However, it has no safety features and no protection devices. In the interest of safety, and to increase its performance and the service life of the components, several components and valves would have to be added to the brake system (see Fig. 18-28).

A component which complements each of these, that is, performance and component service life, is the reservoir. Some requirements of our transport laws are that a truck, tractor, or any other air brake system must have at least three reservoirs; each reservoir must have a drain valve; and the total reservoir capacity must equal at least 12 times the total volume of all service brake chambers at maximum

compressed air and thereby condense the oil and water vapor.

Where does oil and water vapor (contamination) originate? The oil comes from the compressor itself. The compressor is like an engine; the piston rings and cylinder walls require lubrication, and a certain amount of oil therefore passes on with the compressed air. The water vapor is humidity from the inhaled atmospheric air. The inhaled (moist) air, when compressed to nearly nine times atmospheric pressure, heats to about 300°F [149°C], and as it passes onto the supply reservoir, it starts to cool. Because of the pressure, moisture drops out as it cools, and mixes with the oil vapor, to form a soupy, light-colored slush. This contaminant must be removed before it can infiltrate the air line and pass into the air system to cause control valve malfunction. Therefore, in order to maintain an air system free from contamination, each reservoir must have a drain valve.

Drain Valve The drain valve is a simple cock valve (see discussion of hydraulics), and when rotated from the closed position (horizontal) to the open (vertical) position, the air from the reservoir can escape. **NOTE** When you first open the drain valve and there is contamination in the tank, air and contaminants blow from the valve, for a few seconds only, after which, only air is released. This happens because the air pressure blows a hole through the contaminants, allowing the residual contaminants to resist the air stream, and this remains in the tank. It is therefore sound practice to open all drain valves after the vehicle is shut down and keep them open until the vehicle is to be brought back into service (see Fig. 18-29).

To automatically remove the contaminants, some reservoirs have automatic reservoir drain valves (sludge removers) connected to the supply reservoirs or have an air drier connected in the air line between the compressor and supply reservoir.

Automatic Drain Valve There are several types of automatic reservoir drain valves, or sludge removers, one of which is shown in Fig. 18-30.

NOTE Valves with a heater are available for vehicles which operate in areas where the temperature falls below the freezing point. The heater prevents the sludge from freezing and clogging the valve.

DESIGN The upper port is connected to the supply reservoir or special reservoir. The lower port is con-

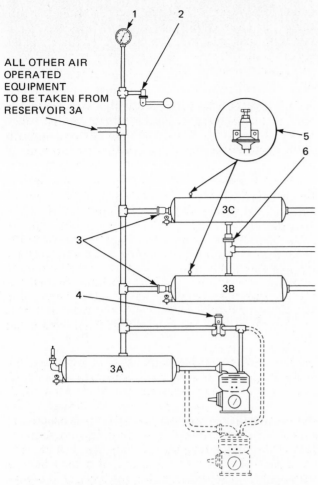

1. Air pressure gauge
2. Wig-wag
3. One-way check valves
3a. Supply reservoir
3b. Primary reservoir
3c. Secondary reservoir
4. Governor
5. Low-pressure indicator
6. Two-way check valve

Fig. 18-28 Schematic view of an improved air brake system.

travel of the diaphragms or pistons. Our laws also require that the trailer reservoir capacity must equal at least eight times the total volume of all service chambers at maximum travel of the diaphragms or pistons. Consequently, the diameter and length of reservoirs differ among vehicles, and some vehicles have more than three reservoirs.

The first reservoir is called the supply reservoir, or wet tank. The other two are called the primary or secondary reservoirs, or service tanks. The main purpose of the supply reservoir, in addition to increasing reservoir volume to the system, is to cool the

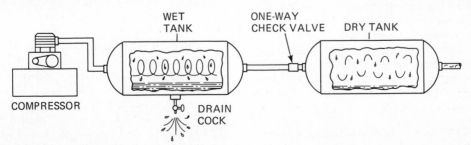

Fig. 18-29 Schematic view of effects of draining the reservoir.

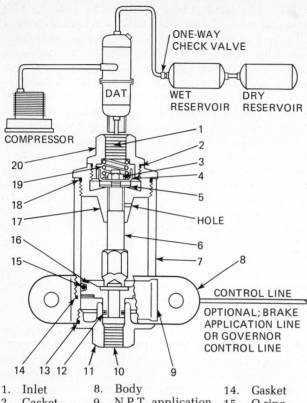

ONE-WAY
CHECK VALVE

DAT

WET
RESERVOIR

DRY
RESERVOIR

COMPRESSOR

1
2
3
4
5
HOLE
6
7   8

CONTROL LINE

OPTIONAL; BRAKE
APPLICATION LINE
OR GOVERNOR
CONTROL LINE

20
19
18
17
16
15

14 13 12   11   10   9

1. Inlet	8. Body	14. Gasket
2. Gasket	9. N.P.T. application	15. O ring
3. Lock nut	line (both sides)	16. Actuator
4. Spacer	10. N.P.T. exhaust	17. Guide post
5. Inlet seat	11. Lower body	18. Gasket
6. Plunger	12. O ring	19. Spring
7. Column	13. Gasket	20. Upper cap

Fig. 18-30 Sectional view of an automatic drain valve, or sludge remover, and connection. (*Sealco Air Controls Inc.*)

nected either to the service line of an application valve or to the unloader line of the compressor. When the reservoirs are not under pressure, the inlet valve spring holds the inlet valve against its seat on the guide post, and the actuator is forced downward. This action opens to the atmosphere the exhaust valve and the cavity above the actuator.

OPERATION—SERVICE LINE CONNECTED TO APPLICATION PORT As the reservoir pressure builds up, pressure is exerted onto the inlet valve. If sludge is in the reservoir, it gathers in the air line leading from the supply reservoir to the valve and accumulates above the inlet valve. When the operator applies the brakes, the same air pressure that applies the brakes is exerted on the area below the actuator, forcing the actuator upward. This causes the exhaust valve to contact the end of the plunger, closing the exhaust valve and forcing the plunger upward. The upward movement of the plunger lifts the inlet valve off its seat, and the reservoir pressure forces the sludge past the open inlet valve, around the upper part of the plunger, through the holes in the guide post, and into the area above the actuator. As long as there is air pressure below the actuator, the inlet valve remains open, and the pressure within the area above the actuator remains the same as the reservoir pressure.

When the service line pressure is removed, the pressure from below the actuator is also removed. The higher reservoir pressure forces the actuator down, closing the inlet valve and opening the exhaust valve. The compressed (contaminated) air is forced out through the open exhaust valve. The exhaust valve remains open until the next brake application is made, and the time between the brake application allows the remaining contaminants to drain by gravity, from the valve.

OPERATION—COMPRESSOR UNLOADER LINE CONNECTED TO APPLICATION PORT When the unloader line is not under pressure, the exhaust valve is open and the inlet valve is closed. When the unloader line is under pressure; that is, when the compressor is in the cutout position, the inlet valve is open and the exhaust valve is closed.

TESTING To test the drain valve, or sludge remover, for leakage, bring the system pressure to cutout pressure and stop the engine. If air exhausts from the exhaust port, it is evident that the inlet valve is leaking and the valve, therefore, requires servicing. To check the operation of the valve (unloader hookup), depedal the air pressure and then start the engine. When the cutout pressure is reached, a rush of air should exhaust at the exhaust port. If the valve is connected to the service line, apply the brakes and listen for a rush of air from the exhaust port. To test the heater (if applicable), measure the resistance of the heater coil with an ohmmeter. To test the wire connection and components for resistance, measure the voltage drop at the ignition switch, the heater fuse, and the fire wall terminal connection with a voltmeter. The voltage drop at each component should not be more than 0.1 volt.

SERVICING Prepare the vehicle as outlined for servicing the compressor; however, you may not have to remove the valve from the vehicle. Next, remove the reservoir line and service line from the drain valve. Check the lines for cleanliness and, if required, clean them thoroughly. Unscrew the lower body and remove it and the actuator. Loosen and remove the upper cap and spring. The next task is to unscrew the upper body from the column.

To remove the plunger from the plunger post, use a screwdriver and remove the screw, the lockwasher, and the inlet valve seat. Slide the plunger out from the plunger post.

Discard the adapter, the inlet valve, and all rubber parts since they are supplied with the service kit. Clean the remaining parts thoroughly and then check for nicks and burrs and damaged threads. If the inlet seat or guide post bore is worn or damaged, or the plunger worn, or the exhaust seat damaged, the entire valve must be replaced. If the column bore is scored or grooved, the column must be replaced. Before reassembling, clean all parts again and lubricate them with the recommended lubricant. Reassemble components in precisely the reverse order of disassembly.

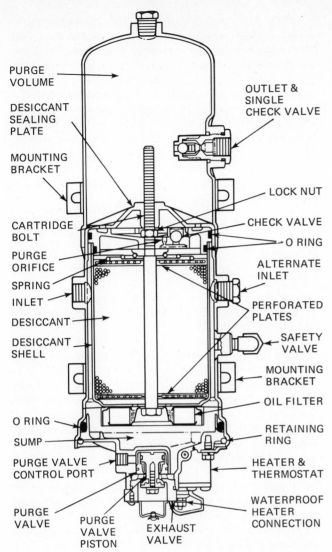

PURGE VOLUME

DESICCANT SEALING PLATE

MOUNTING BRACKET

CARTRIDGE BOLT

PURGE ORIFICE

SPRING

INLET

DESICCANT

DESICCANT SHELL

O RING

SUMP

PURGE VALVE CONTROL PORT

PURGE VALVE

PURGE VALVE PISTON

EXHAUST VALVE

OUTLET & SINGLE CHECK VALVE

LOCK NUT

CHECK VALVE

O RING

ALTERNATE INLET

PERFORATED PLATES

SAFETY VALVE

MOUNTING BRACKET

OIL FILTER

RETAINING RING

HEATER & THERMOSTAT

WATERPROOF HEATER CONNECTION

Fig. 18-31 Sectional view of an air dryer. (*International Harvester Company*)

Air Dryer As mentioned previously, the air dryer automatically removes contaminants. Its superiority over the automatic reservoir drain valve is that it collects the contaminants and then removes them before the air enters the supply reservoir.

The air dryer is vertically mounted to the frame, close to the compressor. A single or double wire braid hose 24 ($\frac{3}{4}$ in [19.05 mm] ID) connects the compressor with the inlet port of the air dryer. A 4 hose ($\frac{3}{16}$ in [4.77 mm] ID) is used to connect the governor (unloader port) with the purge control port.

DESIGN The air dryer is a cylindrical shell made of two halves welded to a unit (see Fig. 18-31). The top of the lower half has several large openings and the center bore is threaded to accommodate the cartridge bolt. The lower part of the lower half is enlarged to facilitate mounting of the end cover. An outlet fitting is welded to the upper half shell and the check valve is screwed into it. An inlet fitting and a safety valve fitting are welded into the lower half shell to which the respective components are fastened. The desiccant cartridge is sealed at the top by the desiccant sealing plate, which has a check valve and a purge

orifice. The O rings seal the desiccant sealing plate to the dryer shell and to the desiccant cartridge shell. The desiccant cartridge shell is closed at the bottom, but it has openings to the oil filters. One perforated plate rests on the lower shoulder of the desiccant shell, and desiccant beads are positioned between the upper perforated plate. The desiccants are small porous particles which have a very high water absorption capacity. A spring located between the desiccant sealing plate and the top perforated plate holds the desiccant compressed. The end cover is retained to the lower dryer shell by a retainer ring and four screws. The purge valve and the heater assembly are located within the end cover. The heater has a 60-watt heating element, and the thermostat maintains an operating range between 50 and 90°F [10 and 32°C]. The heater assembly is connected with a single 16 wire, leading from the ignition switch over a circuit breaker—6 amperes for 12 volts and 12 amperes for 24 volts—to the single terminal connection on the heater.

AIR FLOW When the compressor is pumping, the purge valve spring forces the purge valve upward, closing the exhaust valve. The compressor air enters the air dryer at the inlet port and flows around the desiccant cartridge shell toward the (low-pressure area) bottom of the dryer. Here it changes direction and flows upward through the oil filters, through the desiccant, through the ball check valve and purge orifice, into the upper dryer half (purge volume), out through the outlet fitting, and into the supply reservoir.

The water and oil molecules initially separate from the air when the air (which has a high velocity) hits the dryer wall and the desiccant cartridge shell. This occurs because the velocity head becomes a pressure head causing the molecules to form into droplets and cling to the walls and then gradually settle to the bottom of the dryer. Most of the oil molecules are removed from the air as the air passes through the oil filters. As the hot, moist air penetrates and passes through the desiccant, the water is absorbed, and dry air enters the purged volume area. **NOTE** The same air pressure that exists within the motor vehicle is equal to the pressure within the dryer (see Fig. 18-32).

PURGE CYCLE When the cutout pressure is reached, air under pressure is directed to the compressor's unloading piston and onto the purge valve piston (see Fig. 18-33). As the purge valve piston is forced downward, the purge exhaust valve opens. Because of the large valve opening, the pressure in the lower dryer half drops very quickly, and the air escapes and draws with it the contaminants in the oil filters and dryer sump. The dry compressed air from the upper dryer half (purge volume) can pass only through the purge orifice into the lower half because the air pressure has seated the check valve. Consequently the air pressure in the upper half drops to atmospheric pressure within 15 s. The dry air from the purge volume now penetrates in the reverse direction through the desiccant, absorbs the moisture,

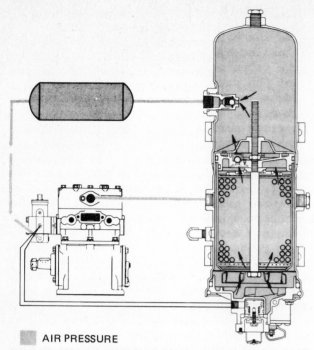

AIR PRESSURE

Fig. 18-32 Schematic view of air flow when the compressor is pumping. (*International Harvester Company*)

and sweeps the water molecules from the desiccant surfaces out through the purge exhaust valve and thereby makes the desiccant absorbent once more. The purge valve remains open until the governor exhausts the unloader line. The purge spring then closes the purge valve, and the cycle is repeated.

TESTING THE DRYER To determine if the heater assembly is operating properly, first turn off the ignition switch and blow compressed air onto the heater

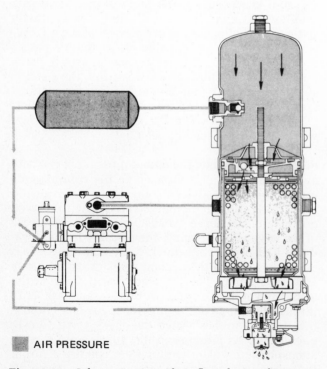

AIR PRESSURE

Fig. 18-33 Schematic view of air flow during the purge cycle. (*International Harvester Company*)

assembly to reduce its temperature to below 50°F [10°C]. Next, turn on the ignition switch and feel the end cover—it should, after a few seconds, increase in temperature. If the cover temperature does not increase, check the existing voltage (with a voltmeter) at the heater terminal—it should not be more than 0.3 volt lower than the open voltage of the battery. If the voltage is correct, switch off the ignition and measure the resistance of the heater coil with an ohmmeter.

To check the operation of the purge valve, or to check the purge valve for air leaks, or to check the safety valve, bring the system pressure to near cutout pressure and then stop the engine. Check at the various ports, the port openings, and the connections for air leaks, using the soap solution method or an air leakage tester. If there are any air leaks from or around the purge valve, the valve must be serviced.

To check the operation of the safety valve, first pull on the exposed stem. Air should exhaust from the valve, and when the stem is released, the valve should seat promptly.

If the air pressure drops rapidly but there are no air leaks on the entire brake system, the outlet check valve may be faulty.

To determine if the desiccant has lost its water absorption capacity, open the supply reservoir and check for the presence of water. However, note that water can also be present under the following circumstances: if the air brake system has excessive leaks, if the reservoir pressure rarely comes to the cutout pressure, if the compressor capacity is too small for the system, or if the vehicle operates at abnormal operating conditions. Each of these set of circumstances could create excessive water in the supply reservoir because each extends the operating cycle of the dryer.

Under normal operating conditions the desiccant functions satisfactorily for at least 1 year, after which time the air dryer should be completely serviced.

SERVICING THE AIR DRYER Prepare the vehicle as outlined for servicing the compressor. Remove the compressor and the air line connected to the purge valve. Disconnect the heater wire and remove the dryer mounting bolts. Clean the exterior of the dryer and then thoroughly blow it dry with air. Loosen the end cover cap screws and swing the clamps inward so that you can push the end cover inward into the lower dryer shell to remove the retainer ring. When the retainer ring is removed, pull the end cover from the shell.

To disassemble the purge valve, remove the screw that holds the exhaust diaphragm to the cover and the screws that hold the exhaust cover to the cap nut. By using a $\frac{7}{16}$-in socket wrench, loosen and remove the cap screw that holds the purge valve assembly as a unit. Remove all O rings from the disassembled parts and lift the exhaust diaphragm from the exhaust cover (see Fig. 18-34). **NOTE** If the heater assembly does not function adequately, the end cover must be replaced, since the assembly is not a separate replacement part. With a socket wrench, loosen and turn the cartridge bolt out of the

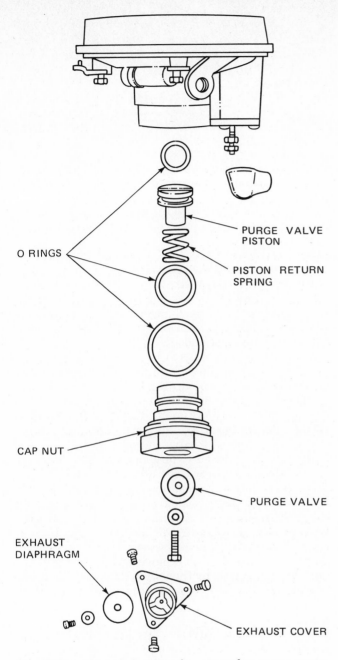

O RINGS

PURGE VALVE
PISTON

PISTON RETURN
SPRING

CAP NUT

PURGE VALVE

EXHAUST
DIAPHRAGM

EXHAUST COVER

Fig. 18-34 Exploded view of purge valve components. (*International Harvester Company*)

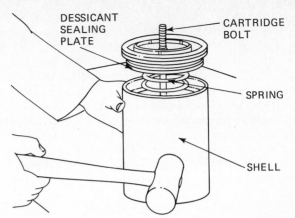

DESSICANT
SEALING
PLATE

CARTRIDGE
BOLT

SPRING

SHELL

Fig. 18-35 View of dessicant cartridge. (*International Harvester Company*)

liness and the seat of the check valve for damage. If any one of these parts is damaged, replace it.

REASSEMBLY Commence reassembly of the dryer by placing the well-lubricated O rings into their respective grooves. Straighten out any twisted O rings. Place a new rubber check ball onto its seat and position the ball retainer. Place one perforated plate into the cartridge shell so that it rests firmly on the shell shoulder (felt surface facing upward) (see Fig. 18-36). Place the oil filter (with the gasket surface facing against the cartridge shell) and then slide the cartridge bolt through the shell center bore and through the bore of the perforated plate so that the cartridge bolt head rests against the oil filter and the filter rests against the shell. Stand the assembly upright. Hold the cartridge bolt in the center while pouring the entire package of desiccant into the shell. Slightly tap on the shell to settle and level the desiccant and then place the upper perforated plate (felt facing downward) over the cartridge bolt and

center plate. This forces the cartridge and the desiccant sealing plate from the center section of the dryer. Loosen and remove the locknut from the cartridge bolt and from it lift the desiccant sealing plate, the spring, and the spring seat. Then pull the cartridge bolt and the oil filter from the cartridge shell (see Fig. 18-35).

Remove and discard the O rings, the ball check retainer ring, the rubber check ball, the oil filter, the desiccant, and the two perforated plates. Clean all remaining parts thoroughly and dry them with compressed air.

CAUTION When cleaning the end cover, do not immerse it in solvent, for solvent could penetrate the heater assembly. Check the purge orifice for clean-

Fig. 18-36 Reassembling dessicant cartridge. (*International Harvester Company*)

into the shell onto the desiccant. Place the cone spring with the large coil end onto the perforated plate. Position the spring retainer onto the spring and the desiccant sealing plate (with ball check valve facing upward) onto the cartridge bolt. Turn the locknut onto the cartridge bolt by using an $\frac{11}{16}$-in deep-socket wrench, and at the same time, with a soft-face hammer, tap on the shell to settle the desiccant. Tighten the lock nut until the desiccant sealing plate rests firmly against the cartridge shell. Take care not to cut the O ring, for the sealing plate slides into the cartridge shell. Lubricate the upper desiccant sealing plate O ring and the shell O ring sealing area and then carefully push the assembly into the dryer shell. When the cartridge bolt contacts the center plate, turn the assembly clockwise to start the bolt in the center plate threaded bore. Once the bolt is started, use a $\frac{3}{4}$-in socket wrench and turn the assembly until the upper side of the desiccant sealing plate seats firmly against the center plate. Reassemble the purge valve, install the cover to the dryer shell, and install the new check valve.

Safety Valve   To protect the entire air system from becoming overpressurized in the event of governor malfunction, a simple pressure relief valve (safety valve) is screwed into one of the fittings of the supply reservoir. The safety valve is commonly a spring-loaded ball check valve. When the air pressure acting on the lower ball face surface exceeds the spring force acting on the ball from above, the ball is lifted off its seat and air is allowed to exhaust into the atmosphere. As the air pressure in the supply reservoir is reduced, the spring force reseats the ball, holding the reduced air pressure in the supply reservoir (see Fig. 18-37).

The safety valve is commonly adjusted to open at 150 psi [1033.5 kPa]. To check the valve for leakage, bring the reservoir pressure up to the cutout pressure and, with an air leakage tester, check the seat.

To check the valve's performance, pull on the exposed stem to allow the air pressure to lift the ball off its seat. If no air exhausts, then the valve must be removed for service.

To check the spring adjustment, connect a shop air line and a master gauge to the system. When the system pressure is at or near 150 psi, loosen the locknut and turn the adjusting screw slowly, counterclockwise, until you notice that air passes by the

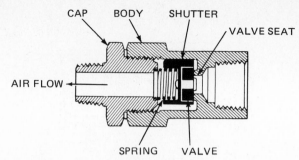

Fig. 18-38   Sectional view of a one-way check valve. (*Wagner Electric Sales Corporation*)

valve and seat. Next, turn the adjusting screw about 10° in clockwise rotation and lock the adjustment.

One-Way Check Valves   To protect the reservoir air pressure against a reverse air flow, one-way check valves are used which screw into the reservoir inlet fitting. Without these valves, a reverse air flow from the reservoirs could occur when the connecting air lines are leaking or broken or when the governor line is leaking or broken.

One of several one-way check valves is shown in Fig. 18-38. The air flow (from the right to the left) is indicated by an arrow on the body. The major differences between one-way check valves lies in the type of valve used. Although the shuttle valve design is considered to be more durable and reliable that the disk or ball valve design, the function of each is to allow the air to flow in only one direction. Some valves use a very light spring to hold the valve on its seat. The valve seat is part of the body or cap nut, the latter being sealed to the body with an O ring. When the valve is connected into the air system, and the air pressure on the valve is higher at the right side than the air pressure and spring force on the left side, the valve moves off its seat and allows the air to pass by the valve. When the air pressure on the left and right sides is equal, the spring force seats the valve.

Two-Way Check Valves   Two-way check valves are used as safety valves and also as directional valves, depending on where they are located within the system. Their purpose is to direct air from either of the two air sources (supply ports) to the common outlet port and automatically seal the supply port having the lower pressure.

DESIGN AND OPERATION   The housing or body of a two-way check valve has a cap which is sealed to the body with an O ring (see Fig. 18-39). The shuttle guide guides the shuttle, which has a seal bonded to each side. Two independent air supply lines are threaded into the right and left sides of the valve. The outlet air line leads to an air valve. **NOTE** Some valves also have a small upper port into which the stoplight switch is screwed.

When the air pressure at the right port is higher than that at the left port, the valve is forced against its left seat, sealing the left port, and the air from the right side leaves the upper center port. If the air pressure is higher at the left port, the valve shifts to the

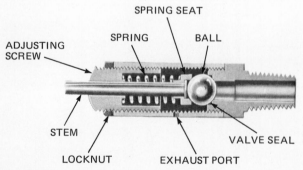

Fig. 18-37   Sectional view of a safety valve. (*Mack Canada Inc.*)

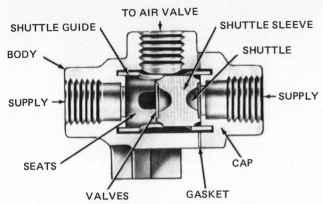

Fig. 18-39 Sectional view of a two-way check valve. (*Terex Division of General Motors Corporation*)

lower pressure side (the right), sealing the port, and the air from the left side is directed out of the upper port.

TROUBLESHOOTING AND TESTING As a general rule, one-way and two-way check valves operate trouble free if the system is kept free of contaminants. However, the one-way check valve on the supply reservoir could fail prematurely because of the pulsation pumping action of the compressor (which could damage the valve or seat).

When checking a one-way or a two-way check valve for external leakage, use an air leakage tester or the soap solution method.

To check if the valve is leaking internally, you might remove the inlet line at the one-way check valve and check for a reverse air leak. However, it is faster to remove the valve, disassemble it, clean each component, and then reassemble it.

To check the two-way check valve for leakage, you must remove first one side and then apply air pressure to the other port; then remove the other side and apply air pressure to the alternate port.

Pressure Gauge To keep the driver or operator constantly aware of the pressure existing within the primary or secondary reservoirs, dual pressure gauges are readily visible to the driver. **NOTE** On some types of air brake piping, the air gauge is connected between the supply and service reservoirs.

To give the driver a visual form of the application brake force, a pressure gauge is connected into each service line. These gauges must also be readily visible to the driver or operator. Furthermore, they must have an accuracy rating within 7 percent. To check the accuracy of the gauge, install a master gauge parallel to it and compare the two. Replace the vehicle's gauge if its readings are more than 7 percent different from the master gauge.

Low-Pressure Indicator To visually and audibly indicate to the driver or operator that the reservoir pressure has reached or dipped below 60 psi [413.4 kPa], two independent devices are used—a warning light and a buzzer (or a wig-wag and a buzzer). The low-pressure indicators are on/off switches which close or open the electric circuit to the warning light and buzzer. They are connected in parallel with the primary and secondary reservoir. The low-pressure indicator valve could be of the diaphragm or the piston design.

A diaphragm low-pressure indicator consists of the components shown in Fig. 18-40. The diaphragm

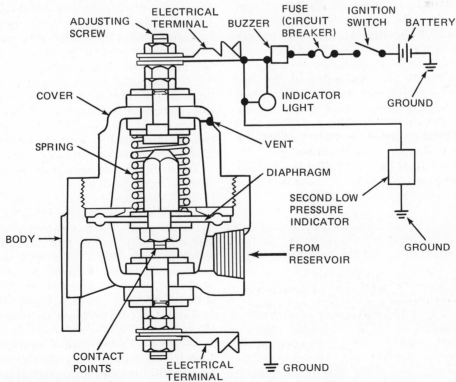

Fig. 18-40 Sectional view of a low-pressure indicator. (*International Harvester Company*)

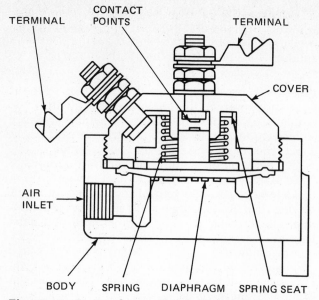

TERMINAL   CONTACT POINTS   TERMINAL
COVER
AIR INLET
BODY   SPRING   DIAPHRAGM   SPRING SEAT

Fig. 18-41 Sectional view of a stoplight switch.

(with disk) is located between the body and the cover. One insulated terminal screw is located in the body; the spring, the spring seat, and the insulated adjusting screw are located in the cover. The low-pressure indicators are connected electrically as shown in Fig. 18-40; that is, from the battery, ignition switch, over a circuit breaker, to the buzzer; from the buzzer to one low-pressure indicator, and then to ground. The other low-pressure indicator is connected in parallel with the first one.

OPERATION   When the ignition switch is turned on and no pressure exists in the primary or secondary reservoir, the spring forces the diaphragm downward and the diaphragm contact touches the lower contact, closing the electrical circuit. The buzzer sounds and/or the light glows. As the air pressure builds up and reaches the pressure setting, about 60 psi [413.4 kPa], the air pressure acting on the diaphragm area forces the diaphragm upward against the spring force, separating the contacts and thereby opening the electric circuit. The sound of the buzzer ceases and the light goes out. If either the primary or the secondary reservoir loses pressure and falls below 60 psi, the buzzer then sounds and the light glows. Nevertheless, this does not tell the driver or operator which circuit has the low air pressure.

Stoplight Switch   All vehicles, with the exception of track equipment, must have a warning device (stoplight) to signal others that the operator has applied the brakes. The stoplight switch must close the electrical circuit when the service line pressure is at or below 6 psi [41.34 kPa].

DESIGN AND OPERATION   The stoplight switch shown in Fig. 18-41 consists, in part, of a cast metal lower body and the plastic cover. The diaphragm lies between the body and cover. The lower contact is fastened to the diaphragm and the left terminal screw is electrically connected to it through the

spring and spring seat. The center (upper) terminal screw is the second contact. Electrically the switch is connected from the ignition switch over a circuit breaker to one terminal of the stoplight switch, and from the other terminal to the brake light and then to ground.

When the driver or operator applies the brakes, the air pressure acting on the diaphragm forces it upward, and the two contacts butt against each other, closing the electrical circuit. The stoplight then glows. If the brakes are released, the spring forces the diaphragm down, separating the contact and thereby opening the electric circuit.

Troubleshooting Low-Pressure Indicator and Stoplight Switch   The most common problem of either the low-pressure indicator or the stoplight switch is electrical, caused by a loose connection, a broken wire, or burned contacts. To check for burned contacts, open circuit, or high resistance, use an ohmmeter or a voltmeter. To check the low-pressure indicator, first drain all reservoir air and then switch on the ignition switch. When all components are in good working order and the electrical system does not have an open circuit or high resistance, the buzzer should sound, and the light should glow. If these warnings do not occur, measure the voltage at the buzzer and light. If the voltage at these points is 0.3 volt less than the open battery voltage, check the voltage drop at the circuit breaker, and the ignition switch at the ammeter terminal, buzzer, and low-pressure indicator.

To check the internal resistance of the switch, hold the two ohmmeter prongs to the terminals. If the contacts are good, the ohmmeter should show no resistance. If more than 2 ohms are shown on the ohmmeter, the switch should be serviced.

To check the pressure at which the low-pressure indicator closes the electrical circuit, first install a master gauge into the air system. Start the engine and note the pressure at the moment when the buzzing ceases and the light goes out. To adjust the low-pressure indicator to the recommended pressure setting, loosen the locknut and turn the adjusting screw clockwise to increase the spring force, which increases the pressure setting, or counterclockwise to reduce the pressure setting.

To check the stoplight switch, reduce the air pressure in both service reservoirs to about 15 psi [103.35 kPa] and hold the ohmmeter prongs to the stoplight switch terminals. With the ignition switch in the off position, have someone apply the brakes. The ohmmeter should read no more than 2 ohms resistance; otherwise the switch must be serviced. You may also use a voltmeter to measure the voltage drop across the terminals. As you check the switch electrically, you should pay attention to the speed at which the switch closes and opens.

Servicing the Low-Pressure Indicator and Stoplight Switch   Because of high labor costs, these switches are usually replaced if they cease to function. However, if it is possible to salvage 15 or more components, it is worthwhile to perform the service. The

Fig. 18-42 View of a wig-wag.

service of either component is a matter of cleaning the contacts and/or disk.

Wig-Wag The wig-wag is an air-pressure-controlled warning device which is connected into the air system, parallel to the supply reservoir. It has a lower body, an upper cap, and a lever arm (wig-wag) pivot mounted to the valve. The piston is positioned in the lower body and is sealed by an O ring to the body bore. A spring is located below the piston; its energy is equal to an air pressure of 60 psi [413.4 kPa] ± 5 psi [34.45 kPa]. The air line is connected to the cap, and air pressure acts from above, onto the piston (see Fig. 18-42).

When the lever arm is brought manually into the horizontal position and the reservoir pressure is below 60 psi, the piston is forced upward by its spring, and the lever arm therefore cannot be held in the horizontal position. When the air pressure reaches 60 psi, the piston moves downward. When the arm is now brought to the horizontal position the piston holds it up. In the event the supply reservoir loses its pressure and drops below 60 psi, the spring moves the piston upward, freeing the locked arm, which then falls and pendles on its hinge pin, visually warning the driver or operator. At the same time the buzzer should give the audible warning.

The wig-wag operates trouble-free as long as its components are not contaminated; nevertheless the pressure at which the wig-wag arm releases should be checked. To make this check, install a master gauge into the system. Bring the pressure above 60 psi and place the arm of the wig-wag into the horizontal position. Next, depedal the air from the system and note when the arm is released. To increase

the release pressure point, either replace the spring or install a shim above the spring to increase its energy.

DUAL AIR BRAKE SYSTEMS

To increase the air brake system's dependability, to make it safer, and to improve its performance, several different valves and components have been added which fulfill not only these but also other law-enforced objectives. Because certain motortrucks, truck-tractors, and other air brake vehicles are built for specific functions or operating conditions, their brake system designs vary accordingly. Some modifications made were to comply with individual state's or province's safety regulations.

Dual Application Valve Piping All new buses, motortrucks, truck-tractors, and related equipment use a dual application valve, and this split or dual system lends to many varying combinations. The most common combination includes the FMVSS 121, in which the primary reservoir supplies air to the primary section of the dual application valve, which services the rear brakes. The secondary reservoir supplies air to the secondary section of the dual application valve, which services the front brakes (see Fig. 18-43). If there is a loss of air pressure in either the primary or secondary circuit, the circuit having reservoir pressure becomes the emergency braking circuit. A dual brake system piping could be one wherein the primary section of the dual application valve services the front brakes and the front axle of the tandem rear axle, and the secondary section services only the rear axle of the tandem rear axle. Here again, if either circuit loses the air supply, the other one becomes the emergency braking circuit. Note, however, that, when the primary circuit remains under pressure, the front axle, as well as the front axle of the tandem rear axle, has brakes, whereas when only the secondary circuit is under pressure, only the rear axle of the tandem rear axle has brakes.

Another dual application valve piping design is one in which the primary section of the dual application valve services the front axle, as well as the rear axle of the tandem rear axle; the secondary section of the dual application valve services the front axle and the front axle of the tandem rear axle.

NOTE A two-way check valve is installed between the primary and secondary service lines connected to the front axle relay valve, and the relay valve is connected to a third reservoir. If either circuit loses its reservoir pressure, say for instance, the primary circuit, the secondary circuit service line pressure then actuates the front axle relay valve of the tandem rear axle and the secondary reservoir pressure applies the brakes. At the same time the secondary service line pressure is directed to the two-way check valve, the valve shifts, the air pressure actuates the front axle relay valve, and the reservoir pressure from the third reservoir then applies the brakes.

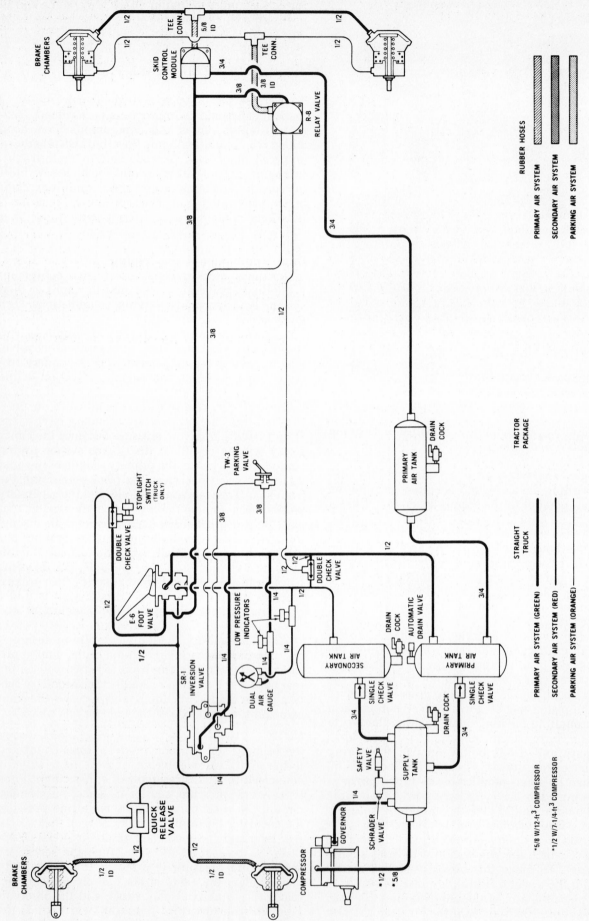

Fig. 18-43 Schematic view of a dual air brake system. (*Ford Motor Company*)

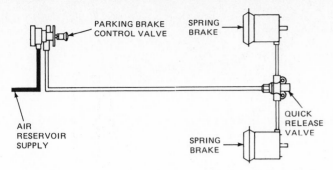

Fig. 18-44 Schematic view of a simplified parking brake control system.

If the secondary reservoir has lost its pressure and the brakes are applied, the primary circuit actuates the relay valve of the rear axle of the tandem rear axle, and the primary reservoir pressure then applies the brakes. At the same time the primary service line pressure moves the two-way check valve so that the pressure actuates the front axle relay valve, and the third reservoir pressure then applies the front brakes. **NOTE** If the third reservoir loses its pressure, no brake application is possible to the front axle.

Parking Brakes All buses, motortrucks, truck-tractors, and other air brake vehicles must have a parking brake that acts on one or both rear axles, which is capable, on its own, of holding the loaded vehicle stationary while it is parked on a specified grade. For instance, the grade requirement specified for an FMVSS 121 vehicle is 20 percent. In addition the parking brakes must automatically apply when the reservoir pressure drops to 40 psi [275.6 kPa] but not lower than 20 psi [137.8 kPa]. (This given pressure may vary between geographical areas and equipment design); also be effective if applied, regardless of any failure in the emergency system or service system; have a separate control; and meet standard emergency stopping distance requirements (see Fig. 18-44).

To comply with the FMVSS 121 regulations, the parking brakes of a bus, motortruck or truck-tractor must also have the ability to release at least once if they are the type that automatically reapplies. Furthermore, all parking brake piping must have the capacity to prevent compounding of the brake force. This means that, when the (parking) brake is applied, and in addition the service brake is applied, the parking brake force must reduce in proportion to the service line pressure and thereby prevent damage to the actuator mechanism.

Parking Brake Control Valve Although there are several different models of park control valves, each must perform the same function, which is to supply or exhaust the parking brakes' control pressure when actuated manually, or to automatically exhaust the control pressure when the service or supply reservoir pressure drops to a specified pressure. One type of parking brake control valve is shown in Fig. 18-45.

DESIGN AND OPERATION The parking brake control valve consists of an aluminum body having three ports. The first two are the inlet port (reservoir port) and the outlet port (control port). These two have threaded bores to which the respective ($\frac{5}{16}$-in ID) air lines are connected. The third port is the exhaust port.

The exhaust valve seat is located inside the body at the end of the smaller shuttle bore. The cap is screwed to the body and sealed with an O ring. The inlet valve seat is formed on the inner surface of the cap.

The shuttle piston has two different diameters and is cross- and center-drilled. The cross-drilled passage is open to the inlet port. The outlet port is connected through a passage with the exhaust valve. The O rings seal the inlet pressure toward the top and bottom of the shuttle. The large seal area (bottom) is the inlet valve, and the smaller one (the top) is the exhaust valve. The shaft is screwed into the threaded center bore of the shuttle. The spring is located over the shaft between the shoulders in the body and shuttle.

When there is no pressure in the reservoirs, the

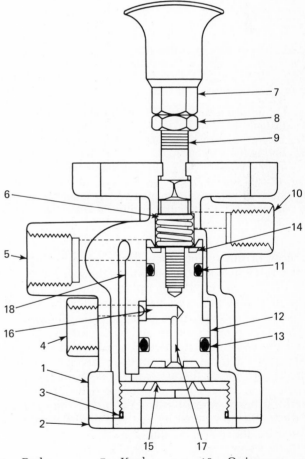

1. Body	7. Knob	13. O ring
2. Cap	8. Lock nut	14. Exhaust valve
3. Gasket	9. Shaft	15. Inlet valve
4. Inlet port	10. Exhaust port	16. Cross passage
5. Outlet port	11. O ring	17. Center passage
6. Spring	12. Shuttle	18. Outlet passage

Fig. 18-45 Sectional view of a parking brake control valve in the release position. (*Sealco Air Controls Inc.*)

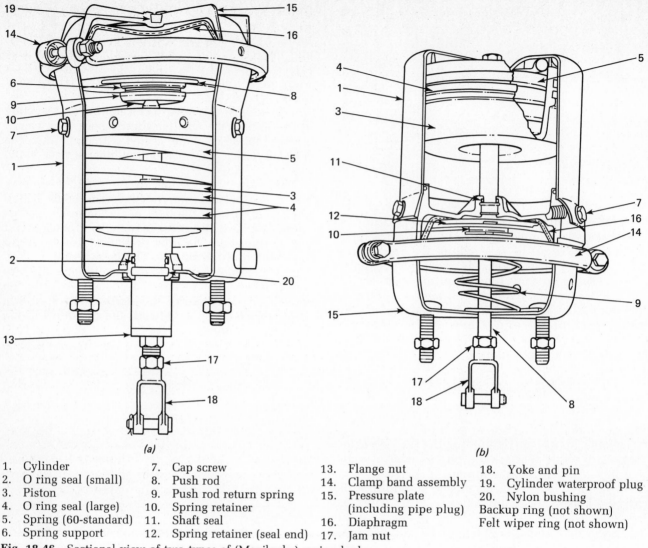

(a)   *(b)*

1.	Cylinder	7.	Cap screw	13.	Flange nut	18.	Yoke and pin
2.	O ring seal (small)	8.	Push rod	14.	Clamp band assembly	19.	Cylinder waterproof plug
3.	Piston	9.	Push rod return spring	15.	Pressure plate	20.	Nylon bushing
4.	O ring seal (large)	10.	Spring retainer		(including pipe plug)		Backup ring (not shown)
5.	Spring (60-standard)	11.	Shaft seal	16.	Diaphragm		Felt wiper ring (not shown)
6.	Spring support	12.	Spring retainer (seal end)	17.	Jam nut		

Fig. 18-46 Sectional view of two types of (Maxibrake) spring brake actuators. (*a*) Forward mounted spring chamber. (*b*) Top mounted spring chamber (*Maxibrake Spring Brakes—Aeroquip Corporation, Gustin-Bacon Division*)

energy of the spring forces the shuttle against the inlet valve seat and thereby opens the exhaust valve. As the air pressure builds up, reservoir pressure enters the inlet port and passes through the shuttle cross- and center-drilled passage. The air pressure acts on the inner circle formed by the inlet valve seat and the shuttle inlet valve. Regardless of reservoir pressure, the force on the shuttle is always less than the spring force; therefore it remains on the inlet valve seat. When the operator or driver pulls the parking brake control valve knob out, the exhaust valve is forced against its seat and the inlet valve is lifted off its seat, exposing the larger shuttle area. The reservoir pressure now creates a greater force on the shuttle and thereby holds the shuttle against the exhaust valve seat. The reservoir air then passes through the horizontal and center passages, by the open inlet valve into the outlet passage, through the outlet port, and into the control line, actuating the relay valve (park). On other brake designs the reservoir pressure is directed to the quick-release valve and from there to the parking brake air chambers, releasing the parking brake. If the operator or

driver pushes the control knob inward, the shuttle moves against its inlet seat, and the exhaust valve opens, exhausting the air from the control line through the exhaust passage, through the exhaust valve, and out of the exhaust port.

As an example, when the reservoir pressure drops to 60 psi [413.4 kPa] but not lower than 50 psi [344.5 kPa], the spring force of the park control valve is then higher than the force of the air pressure acting on the large shuttle area. This causes the shuttle to move against the inlet valve seat and to open the exhaust valve. As a result the air exhausts from the parking brake air chambers via the quick-release valve or relay valve.

TESTING Because of its simple design, the control valve of all parking brakes operates relatively trouble-free. However, if the air system is contaminated, it causes the shuttle valve to hang up and may delay the parking brake application, or, when the inlet valve is damaged, worn, or dirty, air is allowed to pass the inlet valve, and this could lead to the release of the parking brakes. If the exhaust valve were to leak, it would waste reservoir air. A broken spring or one which has lost some of its energy also causes valve failure.

To check the parking control valve for leaks and/or its general operation, first install a master gauge to the system and then start the engine. When the air pressure approaches 50 psi, pull the control knob out and then release it. Repeat this until the shuttle remains against the exhaust seat. At this point note the air pressure gauge. Say it was 55 psi [378.95 kPa]. Raise the air pressure another 10 psi [68.9 kPa] and then stop the engine. Now slowly reduce the air pressure and take note when the knob snaps inward and an exhaust of air occurs. This would (if the valve is operating properly) be about 5 psi [34.45 kPa] lower than the holdout pressure. If either the release pressure or the holdout pressure is not within the specified range, the valve must be serviced.

TESTING FOR EXTERNAL LEAKS The procedure for testing the valve for external leaks is the same as for any leakage test. To test the exhaust valve for leakage, raise the air system to cutout pressure and pull the valve out to release the parking brakes. If air leaks from the exhaust port, the exhaust seat or valve is damaged, dirty, or worn.

To check for a leaking inlet valve, push the shuttle inward (to apply the parking brake), and if air leaks past the valve, it gradually raises the shuttle and applys the parking brakes.

The steps to service the valve are simple, consisting of cleaning the valve assembly and replacing the shuttle and springs with those supplied in the service kit. However, if either the exhaust valve seat or the inner bores are damaged or worn, or the inlet valve seat is damaged, replace the entire valve.

After the valve is reassembled and the locknut and knob are screwed onto the shaft, you must adjust the knob to ensure that the inlet valve can seat fully. With the shuttle seated on the inlet valve, turn the locknut so that there is a space of about 0.625 in [15.87 mm] between the locknut and mounting flange, and in this position lock the nut against the locknut.

Parking Brake Design All parking brakes (spring brakes) are similar in design, all depending on the energy of a spring to apply the brakes once the air that has compressed the spring is exhausted from the chamber. All spring brakes have two independent air chambers—the service brake chamber and the parking brake chamber. However, some minor differences exist among the four major makes, and even among makes by the same company (see Figs. 18-46 to 18-49), such as the following: (1) The parking brake chamber may be clamped to the front or behind the service brake chamber. (2) A piston or a diaphragm parking brake chamber may be used to compress the spring. (3) A pushrod seal and guide may be used to support the pushrod and to seal the pressure side of the service brake chamber toward the pressure side of the parking brake chamber, or the parking brake piston extension may be supported with a nylon bushing, and a lip-type seal or

an O ring seals the pressure side of the parking brake air chamber.

All designs use the nonpressure plate part of a clamp brake chamber, the diaphragm, and pushrod assembly.

NOTE If the parking brake chamber is clamped in front of the service brake chamber, the parking brake chamber is provided with a mounting stud.

OPERATION Regardless of the spring brake type or model, when the air is exhausted from the service and parking brake chambers (see Fig. 18-50), the spring expands and the spring brake piston moves and forces the pushrod outward. The slack adjuster and cam shaft rotate, applying the brakes.

When air under pressure is directed into the parking brake air chamber, the air pressure acts on the piston or diaphragm. As the air pressure increases, so does the force, and at about 60 psi [413.4 kPa], the force on the piston or diaphragm starts its upward movement and comes to rest against its stop in the head assembly, or the piston (is) forced against the spring support. At the same time the brake shoe return springs have rotated the cam and slack adjuster, and the service brake pushrod return spring moves the pushrod assembly and the service brake diaphragm against the inner surface of the nonpressure plate (see Fig. 18-51).

When air under pressure is directed into the service brake chamber, the air pressure acting on the service brake diaphragm moves the pushrod assembly outward, rotating the slack adjuster and cam and thereby applying the brakes (see Fig. 18-52).

TESTING To determine if the service brake chamber or the rear diaphragm parking brake chamber is leaking, first bring the reservoir pressure to cutout pressure and then apply (exhaust) the parking brakes. Next, stop the engine. Apply maximum service line pressure and, with an air leakage tester, test for air leaks. If air leaks from the pushrod, the seal is dam-

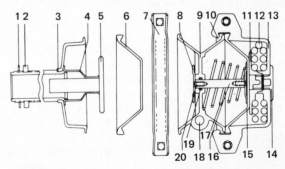

1.	Washer	11.	Pressure plate
2.	Nut	12.	Compression spring
3.	Housing assembly	13.	Chamber
4.	Rubber boot	14.	Plug
5.	Push rod assembly	15.	Diaphragm
6.	Diaphragm	16.	Adapter push rod
7.	Clamp assembly	17.	Return spring
8.	Plate	18.	Release stud assembly
9.	Adapter	19.	O ring
10.	Clamp assembly	20.	Nylok screw

Fig. 18-47 Exploded view of a wedge-type spring brake. (*Anchorlok*)

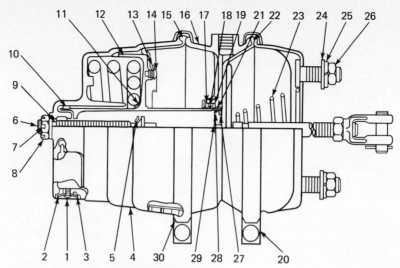

1. Screw
2. Exhaust diaphragm retainer
3. Exhaust diaphragm
4. Body
5. Thrust washer
6. Release bolt
7. Spirol pin
8. Hex nut
9. Sealing ring
10. Emergency piston bearing

11. Spring seat
12. Emergency piston
13. Emergency diaphragm retainer ring
14. Screw
15. Emergency diaphragm
16. Pressure plate
17. Retainer washer
18. O ring
19. Backup ring
20. Service cl. ring assembly

21. Emergency piston bearing
22. Service diaphragm
23. Push rod return spring
24. Washer
25. Lock washer
26. Nut
27. Retaining ring
28. O ring
29. Piston plug
30. Emergency cl. ring assembly

Fig. 18-48 Sectional view of a spring brake actuator. (*Bendix Heavy Vehicle Systems Group*)

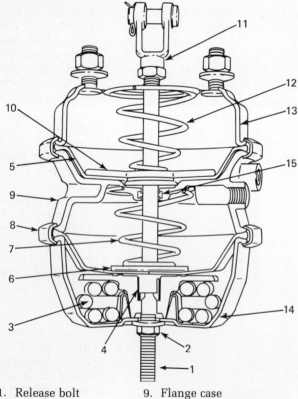

1. Release bolt
2. Release nut
3. Spring
4. Spring brake piston
5. Diaphragm
6. Push plate
7. Return spring
8. Clamp ring assembly

9. Flange case
10. Push plate service side
11. Push rod assembly
12. Return spring
13. Nonpressure plate
14. Head assembly
15. Seal
16. Thrust washer (not visible)

Fig. 18-49 Sectional view of a spring brake actuator. (*Anchorlok*)

aged or worn, and the assembly must be removed for service.

If the pushrod-to-slack adjuster is misaligned, or the pushrod is damaged or bent, the assembly must be removed for service.

Release the service brakes and, with an air leakage tester, check for air leaks. If air leaks from the head assembly, the parking brake, piston seal, or diaphragm is damaged. If the service brake gradually applies, the pushrod seal in the flange case is leaking, or the pushrod is bent, allowing parking brake air to enter the service brake chamber.

To check a piston-type front-mounted parking brake assembly, first release the parking brake, and

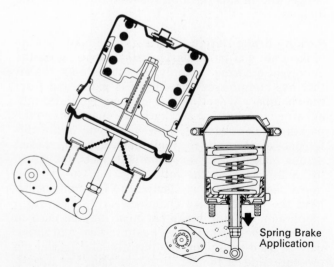

Spring Brake Application

Fig. 18-50 Schematic view of spring brake—applied position. (*Maxibrake Spring Brakes—Aeroquip Corporation, Gustin-Bacon Division*)

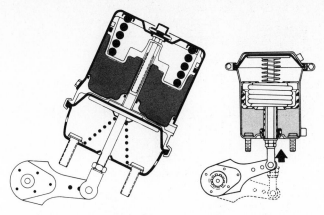

Fig. 18-51 Schematic view of spring brake—release position. (*Maxibrake Spring Brakes—Aeroquip Corporation, Gustin-Bacon Division*)

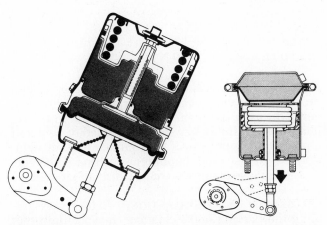

Fig. 18-52 Schematic view of spring brake—release and service brake applied. (*Maxibrake Spring Brakes—Aeroquip Corporation, Gustin-Bacon Division*)

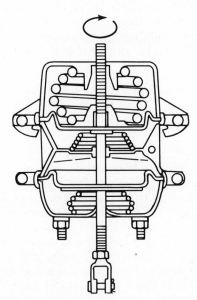

Fig. 18-53 Schematic view of manually releasing the spring brake. Turn release stud one-quarter turn clockwise in pressure plate to secure cross pin into cross pin area of pressure plate and lock into manual release position. (*GMC Truck and Coach Division of General Motors Corporation*)

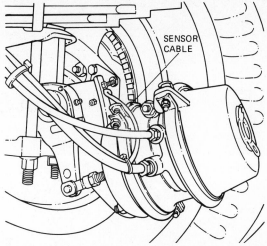

Fig. 18-54 View of parking brake installed. (*GMC Truck and Coach Division of General Motors Corporation*)

if air leaks from around the extension of the parking brake piston, either the seal or the extension piston surface is damaged. This could occur from misalignment of the slack adjuster to pushrod, or from excessive pushrod travel, or from damage to the extension surface.

SERVICING After the vehicle is placed in position and safely blocked, actuate the spring brake control valve to release the parking brakes. Remove the rubber cap from the end of the parking brake chamber and the stop bolt from the flange case. Clean and then lubricate the stud bolt threads before guiding the bolt, pin end first, through the center opening, into the slot opening of the spring piston. Rotate the stud bolt one quarter turn to engage the pin with the piston.

Next, finger-turn the stud nut until its shoulder rests against the chamber end and then use a wrench to tighten the nut until the spring is fully compressed, to about 40 lb · ft [54.24 N · m]. If the spring section is damaged to such an extent that you cannot use this method, then turn the stud nut (with a wrench) about 30 to 35 turns until the spring is fully compressed (see Fig. 18-53). If the spring is broken, you will not be able to engage the stud bolt pin with the piston lock. In this case, turn the slack adjuster nut to release the brakes sufficiently to remove the clevice yoke pin. **NOTE** You may have to loosen the mounting stud nuts to prevent damaging the actuator.

Next, disconnect the service and the parking brake air lines from the brake actuator. Remove the cotter pin and the clevice yoke pin, the locknuts, and the lock washers from the mounting studs and then lift the assembly off its mounting (see Fig. 18-54). Thoroughly clean the assembly and, using a stud bolt, clamp the assembly in a horizontal position, in a vise having protected jaws. Remove, in the following order: the parking brake chamber, to adapter clamp ring nuts and bolts, and the clamp ring. Lift the parking brake chamber, spring, and pressure plate (piston) as a unit from the adapter. Remove the parking brake diaphragm from the adapter.

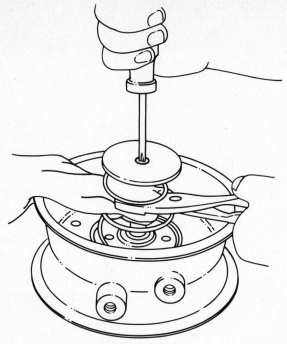

Fig. 18-55 Removing Nylock screw to remove return spring guide, ring, and seal. (*GMC Truck and Coach Division of General Motors Corporation*)

To remove the adapter, remove the adapter-to-service brake chamber clamp ring, nuts and bolts and roll the clamp ring from the adapter and service brake housing.

NOTE While performing this disassembly, hold the pushrod to keep the service brake pushrod's return spring compressed (see Fig. 18-47).

To replace the adapter pushrod O ring, hold the parking brakes' diaphragm return spring compressed while removing the Nylok screw from the adapter pushrod. Remove the plate, slide the adapter pushrod from the adapter, and lift the diaphragm return spring from the adapter (see Fig. 18-55).

To service the parking brake, you require two 4-in [10.16-cm] diameter tubes. One of the tubes must have a fairly large cutout so as not to impede turning the wrench to loosen the stud nut. The other end must be closed off. If your shop does not have these tubes, make them! Place the parking chamber onto the press bed and place the tube having the cutout onto the parking brake chamber (see Fig. 18-56). Adjust the press bed height so that you have at least an 8-in [20.32-cm] ram stroke and bring the ram in contact with the tube. After checking the alignment, exert a light force on the assembly but sufficient to loosen the stud nut and to unlock the stud bolt from the pressure plate. Remove the bolt and then slowly remove the force from the ram until the parking spring is fully expanded. If you suspect that the spring is broken, wrap a rag around the assembly to protect yourself and others, for part of the spring could fly from the assembly as the force is released.

NOTE Do not use any other method to remove the spring. The spring force at the beginning of release is about 2100 lb [9324 N], and after the adapter has

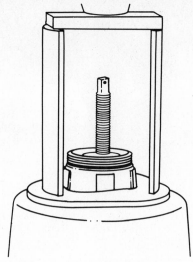

Fig. 18-56 Split tube in position to release spring tension.

moved out about 2 in [5.08 cm], the spring force is still about 1000 lb [4440 N].

INSPECTION After all metal parts have been cleaned (in solvent, or with a glass blaster, or by the hot tank method), examine them for damage and wear. Replace the parking spring if it is corroded or bent and replace the diaphragm if it is kinked, cut, or deteriorated. Replace the diaphragm pushrod if the surface is damaged, for this could cause an air leak.

REASSEMBLY AND INSTALLATION Before reassembling the parking brake chamber, make certain that all parts are clean, that the new O ring is positioned into the adapter, and that all parts are generously lubricated with the recommended grease. Install the spring to the parking brake chamber. Make certain that all parts are perfectly aligned before compressing the spring, that the release stud bolt is positively locked into the adapter plate, and that the stud nut is tightened to about 40 lb · ft [54.24 N · m].

NOTE Do not overtorque the clamp ring nuts to stop an air leak. The average torque is about 25 to 35 lb · ft [33.9 to 47.46 N · m]. If air leaks past the diaphragm, loosen the clamp ring nuts, tap on the clamp ring with a soft-face hammer, and retorque the nuts.

After the parking brake is assembled, install it to a dummy brake assembly and check the service brake chamber and the parking brake chamber for air leaks. If you do not have a dummy, reinstall the assembly to the vehicle, connect the air lines, and release the parking brake. Check the alignment between the slack adjuster and pushrod clevice yoke. Connect the pushrod with the slack adjuster, adjust the brakes, and check the pushrod travel and the angle between the pushrod and slack adjuster. If either the pushrod travel or the angle is not within specification, the service brake and parking brake spring force will be lessened and may not hold the vehicle, or the stopping distances will be increased.

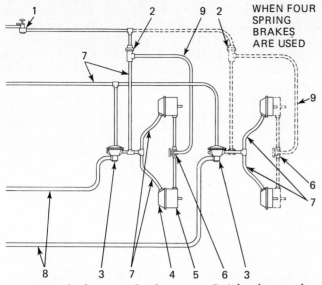

1. Spring brake control valve
2. Two-way check valve
3. Relay valve
4. Service brake chamber
5. Spring brake chamber
6. Quick release valve
7. Service line hose
8. Reservoir hose
9. Parking brake supply hose

Fig. 18-57 Schematic view of parking brake piping, using a quick release valve.

Parking Brake Piping   To be able to apply and release the parking brake manually (by actuating the parking valve), to apply the parking brake automatically, and to prevent compounding the brake application, several different types of piping are used.

NOTE   In all parking brake piping the air supply to the parking brake control valve comes from the service reservoir(s). Apart from this, the piping is dissimilar. In one system (see Fig. 18-57) the air supply from the parking brake control valve is directed to a two-way check valve. From there it is directed to a quick-release valve and to the parking brake air chambers. The service line is connected to the other supply port of the two-way check valve.

Some long-wheel-base vehicles or newer trucks and tractors use a relay valve instead of a quick-release valve. A relay valve ensures faster parking brake application and faster release. When a relay valve is used, the air supply that releases the parking brakes comes from the service reservoir, and the air that actuates the relay valve (control pressure) is directed from the parking brake control valve to the two-way check valve and from there to the control port of the relay valve. The service line connecting the relay (service) valve with the service brake chamber is also directed to the two-way check valve.

OPERATION   To release the parking brake, the parking brake control knob is pulled outward, and air from the service reservoir passes by the open inlet valve onto the two-way check valve. The check valve shifts, sealing the service line port. Air is then directed to the quick-release valve and into the parking brake air chamber, compressing the parking brake spring.

When the service brake is applied, the air that is directed from the service brake relay valve to apply the service brakes is also directed to the two-way check valve. However, the parking brake pressure is higher than the service line pressure, and therefore the valve does not move off its seat.

To apply the parking brakes manually, the control knob is pushed in (see Fig. 18-45). This closes the inlet valve and opens the exhaust valve. Air then exhausts from the parking control valve, releasing the pressure from the quick-release valve. This action opens the exhaust valve of the quick-release valve, and the air from the parking brake air chambers escapes out of the exhaust port of the quick-release valve. The parking brake spring applies the brakes.

If the service brake is applied under this condition, air from the service line which is applying the service brake is also directed to the two-way check valve. The valve shifts (sealing the parking brake supply port), and air at service line pressure is directed into the parking brake air chamber, compressing the parking spring. The spring force reduces in proportion to the applied force of the service brake chamber. When the service brake air pressure is released (through the dual application valve), the service relay valve responds and exhausts air from the service brake chamber. At the same time the air from the parking brake chamber exhausts, and full spring force again applies the brakes.

When a relay valve is used instead of a quick-release valve, the air from the two-way check valve is directed into the control port of the relay valve (park). The relay valve responds, and service reservoir pressure is directed into the parking brake air chambers, releasing the brakes. When the control knob is pushed in, the inlet valve closes and the exhaust valve opens. As a result the control pressure exhausts from the exhaust port and removes the force from the relay valve diaphragm. The relay valve responds and the parking brake air exhausts from the exhaust port of the relay valve (see Fig. 18-58).

AUTOMATIC APPLICATION   Assume that, owing to some unfortunate circumstance, both service reservoirs lose air, or the pressure suddenly is reduced. As the air pressure reaches or dips below 60 psi [413.4 kPa] but does not go below 50 psi [344.5 kPa], the parking brake control-valve's shuttle piston is forced down by its spring. This closes the inlet valve and opens the exhaust valve, and the air from the quick-release valve or relay valve (park) diaphragm is removed. The quick-release valve or the relay valve exhausts the air from the parking brake chamber, and the parking brake spring applies the brakes.

Spring Brake Valve   Instead of a two-way check valve, a spring brake valve is used to supply a specified limited holdoff pressure to the parking brake air chambers. In the event that the primary reservoir pressure is lost, the spring brake valve modulates the parking brake force by means of the application valve.

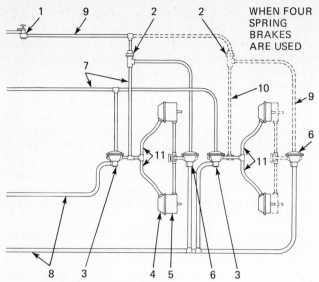

1. Spring brake control valve
2. Two-way check valve
3. Service line relay valve
4. Service brake chamber
5. Spring brake chamber
6. Parking brake relay valve
7. Service line hose
8. Reservoir hoses
9. Parking brake application hose
10. Brake application hose to two-way check valve
11. Service line application hose

Fig. 18-58 Schematic view of a parking brake pipe, using a relay valve.

The spring brake valve is connected into the spring brake and service line (secondary) air circuit, as shown in Fig. 18-59. This valve consists of the components also shown in Fig. 18-60, the main parts of which are the body in which the large piston B and the small piston A are located. Both pistons have two diameters and an exhaust valve seat. The larger piston has two springs whereas piston A has only one spring. The inlet exhaust valve poppet, located below pistons A and B, is similar in design to that of a relay (inlet exhaust) valve poppet. A check valve is positioned between the parking brake service port and supply port. The check valve prevents the control pressure from entering the piston cavity but allows air to flow in the reverse direction.

OPERATION With no air pressure in the reservoirs, the parking brakes are in the applied position because the exhaust valve of the parking brake control valve is open. As a result, the air pressure that was acting on the one-way check valve is removed and thereby allows the control pressure from the relay valve to exhaust. The relay valve opens its exhaust valve, exhausting the air from the parking brake air chambers. The two springs of piston B have forced the piston downward against the body shoulder. This action closes the exhaust valve B and opens inlet valve B. Meanwhile, the same action has occurred with piston A (see Fig. 18-59).

As the reservoir pressure is building up, air flows into the reservoir port of the spring brake valve and

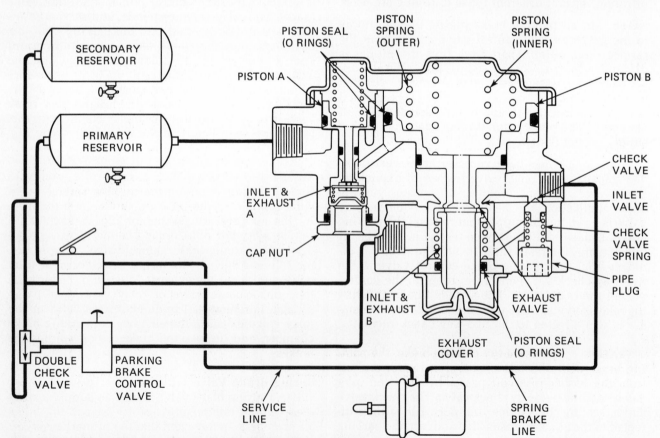

Fig. 18-59 Schematic view of spring brake valve and connections as the compressor starts pumping (below 55 psi) [378.95 kPa]). (*International Harvester Company*)

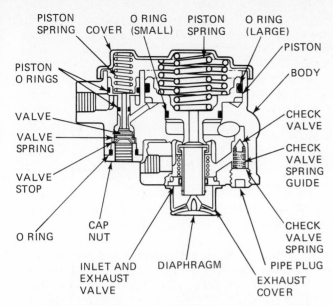

Fig. 18-60 Sectional view of the spring brake valve. (*International Harvester Company*)

acts on the larger area of piston A. But the pressure at this time is not high enough to overcome piston A's spring force, and the piston remains against its body shoulder, holding inlet valve A open. As the reservoir pressure approaches 50 psi [344.5 kPa] or near this pressure, piston A is forced upward, opening the exhaust valve. At the same time the valve spring closes inlet valve A. When the parking brake

control valve is actuated at a pressure of 50 psi [344.5 kPa] or higher (to release the parking brakes), the shaft of the parking brake control valve is held out by the air pressure which acts on the large area of the shuttle. Reservoir air passes by the open inlet valve and flows into the supply port of the spring brake valve, past open inlet valve B, out of the parking brake delivery port, and into the control port of the relay valve (park). At the same time the pressure is also acting on the check valve, holding the valve closed. The relay valve responds by directing reservoir air into the parking brake air chamber, releasing the parking brakes. When the reservoir pressure approaches the holdoff pressure, say, it is 100 psi [689 kPa], the pressure acting on small piston area B forces the piston B sufficiently upward to close inlet valve B without opening the exhaust valve (see Fig. 18-61).

Service Brake Application   When a service brake is applied, no action takes place within the spring brake valve, because the secondary service brake pressure cannot enter the valve, since inlet valve A is closed. The secondary reservoir pressure holds piston A upward.

APPLICATION WITH SECONDARY PRESSURE LOST   In the event that the secondary pressure is lost, the two-way check valve shifts over, maintaining primary reservoir pressure on the parking brake control valve. However, the pressure loss removes the air

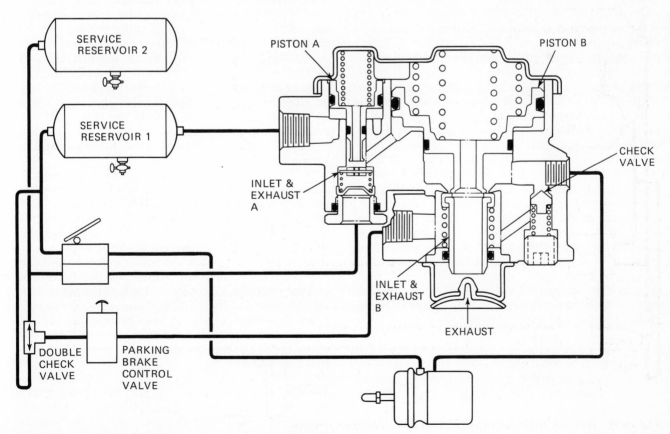

Fig. 18-61 Position of parking brake valve components when reservoir is fully charged. (*International Harvester Company*)

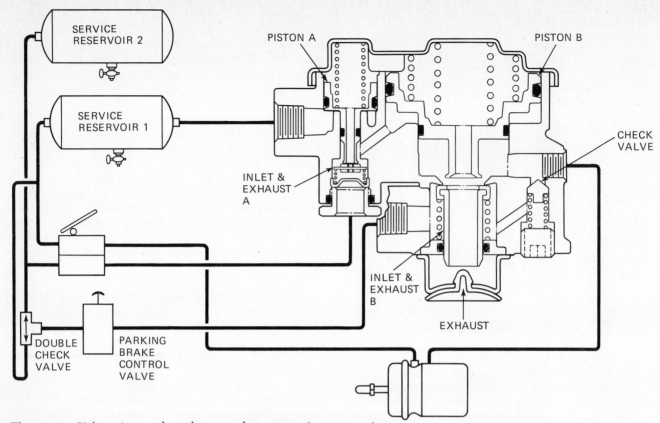

Fig. 18-62 Valve piston when the secondary reservoir pressure is lost and with a service brake application. (*International Harvester Company*)

pressure from below piston A, and as the pressure approaches about 50 psi [344.5 kPa], piston spring A forces piston A downward, closing exhaust valve A and opening inlet valve A. This action connects the primary service line (from the dual application valve) with the large cavity of piston B. If under these circumstances a brake application is made, it is the primary service line pressure which actuates the spring brake application. **NOTE** Which service brake axle is affected depends on the piping layout of the dual application valve. The service line air enters the control port, flows past open inlet valve A and through the passage leading into large cavity piston B, acts on the large piston area, forces piston B upward, and opens the exhaust valve. The air from the spring brake then passes by the open exhaust valve, through the hollow center of the poppet valve, and into the atmosphere (reducing the pressure from above the relay valve park), and the relay valve responds by opening its exhaust valve. The air pressure in the parking brake air chambers lessens, and the spring force applies the brakes. The pressure reduction within the air chamber of the parking brake is proportionate to the primary service line pressure. When the primary service line pressure is reduced (brakes released), the added pressure from below large piston B is removed, causing exhaust valve B to seat, and inlet valve B to open (see Fig. 18-62).

When the air pressure below the small area of piston B reaches the holdoff pressure, the piston moves upward, closing inlet valve B.

APPLICATION WITH PRIMARY PRESSURE LOST If primary pressure is lost, the secondary reservoir pressure shifts the two-way check valve to maintain the pressure on the parking brake control valve. Piston A maintains its position; that is, exhaust valve A remains open, and inlet valve A remains closed. If a brake application is now made, it is the secondary service line pressure that applies the relay valve (service brake). The relay valve responds and the secondary reservoir pressure applies the service brakes. No action whatsoever takes place within the spring brake valve.

Automatic Parking Brake Application If the air pressure in the primary and secondary air reservoirs drops to, say, 50 psi [344.5 kPa], the parking control valve's spring force is now higher than the force of the air pressure and closes the inlet valve and opens the exhaust valve. This removes the force from the one-way check valve and allows the parking brake control pressure to force the check valve open. The air exhausts via the parking brake control exhaust valve. The relay valve responds by opening the exhaust valve and closing the inlet valve and thereby releases the air from the parking brake air chambers (see Fig. 18-63).

TESTING AND SERVICING To test the spring brake valve for leakage and at the same time check its operation, first install a master gauge, block the vehicle securely, bring the air system to cutout pressure, and release the parking brakes. Watch the release re-

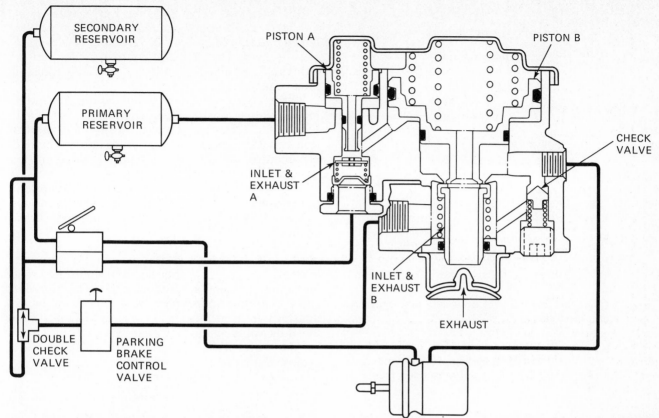

Fig. 18-63 Valve position when in parking brake application. (*International Harvester Company*)

sponse, note the holdoff pressure on the gauge, and check if the parking brake actuator fully releases the brakes. If the holdoff pressure is below the specified pressure, the parking brake may not fully release the foundation brake. A reduced holdoff pressure could be caused by weakness of piston B springs or leakage of the lower O ring of piston A or B, thereby allowing air pressure to act on large piston area B. This would lift it slightly and cause the exhaust valve to open and partly apply the brake.

If air leaks from the exhaust port, the inlet seat may be worn or damaged. However, it could be that the (poppet) valve, the guide, or the O rings are worn or damaged.

If air leaks from around the cover, the upper O ring on piston A is damaged or worn. If air leaks from the exhaust port of the dual application valve, the lower O ring on piston A is allowing air to pass by open inlet valve A. The air therefore passes by the open exhaust valve of the application valve.

To check the parking brake control valve, first activate it so that it applies the parking brake. The holdoff pressure gauge should quickly drop to zero. If it does not, the check valve is not operating properly, or the control air line is restricted, or the parking brake control valve is defective. To determine if the emergency brake functions as specified, first release the parking brake and note the holdoff pressure and the reservoir pressure. Next, drain the secondary reservoir. If the primary reservoir pressure drops, even though there are no other air leaks in the brake system, then the two-way check valve is not sealing properly and is allowing air from the primary res-

ervoir to pass into the secondary reservoir. When the secondary reservoir is drained, apply the brake and note the service line and the holdoff pressure gauge reading. (The holdoff pressure should be the same as the reservoir pressure.)

NOTE If the primary reservoir pressure drops to about 60 psi [413.4 kPa], the parking brake remains fully applied because the reservoir pressure is not high enough to raise large piston B against the spring force.

If the parking brake control valve is in any way defective, it must be serviced.

Since this valve design so closely resembles a relay valve, the service procedure need not be outlined. As an additional reminder, however, make certain that all parts are perfectly clean before lubricating the O rings, piston, and piston bores with the grease supplied in the service kit. Also check the freeness of the pistons, the poppet, and the check valve during the reassembly.

Front Axle Brake Piping Governmental controls and regulations detail the brake requirements for the front axle(s). It is true that some logging tractors do not require a front axle foundation brake; nevertheless, if required, any one of three different types of piping may be specified. For example, the piping would not correspond in each of the following circumstances: where the dual application valve services the rear axle of the tractor and a hand valve services the front axle of the truck tractor (see Fig. 18-64), where a limiting quick-release valve in con-

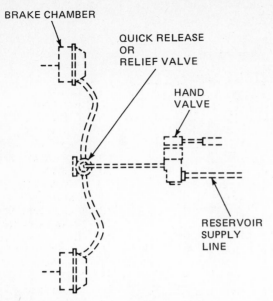

Fig. 18-64 Schematic view of front axle piping using a hand application valve.

junction with a two-way control valve is used to apply the front axle brakes (see Fig. 18-65), or where an automatic limiting (ratio) valve is used (see Fig. 18-67).

Limiting Quick-Release and Two-way Control Valves The purpose of the limiting quick-release and two-way control valves is to gain steering control during braking by limiting (reducing by 50 percent) the application pressure to the front axle in ratio to the application pressure directed to the rear axle(s). It is the prerogative of the driver to select equal or reduced air pressure to the front axle air chambers in comparison to that of the rear brake chambers.

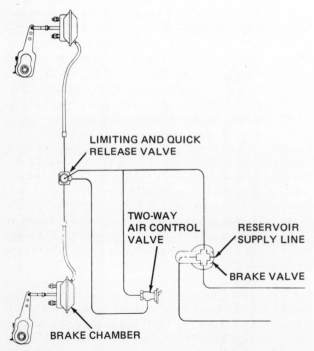

Fig. 18-65 Schematic view of front axle piping using a limiting quick-release valve.

The selection valve is a two-way control valve mounted within easy reach on the dashboard. Written on one side of the control valve dial is "dry road" and on the other side "slippery road." The limiting quick-release valve is mounted close to the front axle brake chambers.

The two-way control valve and the limiting quick-release valve consist of the components shown in Fig. 18-66. The service line from the dual application valve is connected to the inlet port of the two-way control valve and inlet port of the limiting quick-release valve. The limiting quick-release valve inlet port is connected to one of the control ports in the two-way control valve. The delivery ports are connected, with air lines, to the front axle brake chambers.

OPERATION—SLIPPERY ROAD When the two-way control valve lever is placed in the slippery-road position, the piston spring forces the piston upward and moves the exhaust valve seat away from the exhaust valve. The inlet valve spring then positions the inlet valve against its seat. The limiting quick-release valve spring moves the piston upward against the valve body shoulder and thereby closes the inlet valve and opens the exhaust valve.

NOTE The piston has two different diameters.

When the brakes are applied under this condition, service line pressure is exerted onto the inlet valve of the two-way control valve, but it can go no further, because the valve is closed. The pressure is therefore exerted onto the top area of the limiting quick-release valve piston. This forces the piston downward, closing the exhaust valve port and opening the inlet valve. Service line pressure passes by the open inlet valve into the spring cavity, out of the delivery port, and into the brake chambers. As the applied pressure increases, so does the force from below, and the piston is moved upward. Because the lower piston area is twice as large as the upper piston area, the lower area requires only half as much air pressure in relation to the service line pressure to equal the force on the piston. When both forces are relatively equal, the inlet valve closes, and consequently the delivery pressure is half that of the service line pressure.

When the application valve reduces the service line pressure, the delivery pressure acting on the lower piston area is then higher. This forces the piston upward, opens the exhaust valve, and reduces the delivery pressure. As the forces acting on the piston equalize, the piston again moves downward, closing the exhaust valve. If the service line pressure is fully released, the piston is forced against the body shoulder, and the exhaust valve remains open.

OPERATION—DRY ROAD When the two-way control valve is placed in the dry-road position, the lever forces the piston downward, seating the exhaust valve and opening the inlet valve. When the brakes are applied under this circumstance, the service line pressure passes by the two-way control valve's open inlet valve and enters the control port of the limiting quick-release valve, forcing the piston down against

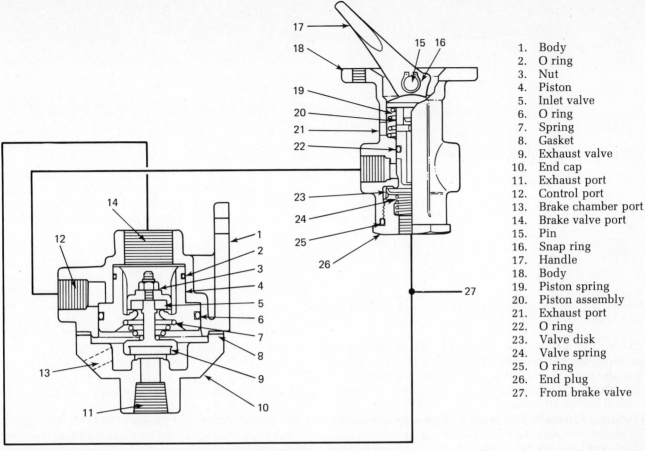

1.	Body
2.	O ring
3.	Nut
4.	Piston
5.	Inlet valve
6.	O ring
7.	Spring
8.	Gasket
9.	Exhaust valve
10.	End cap
11.	Exhaust port
12.	Control port
13.	Brake chamber port
14.	Brake valve port
15.	Pin
16.	Snap ring
17.	Handle
18.	Body
19.	Piston spring
20.	Piston assembly
21.	Exhaust port
22.	O ring
23.	Valve disk
24.	Valve spring
25.	O ring
26.	End plug
27.	From brake valve

Fig. 18-66 Sectional view of a two-way air control valve and limiting and quick release valve. (*International Harvester Company*)

the cover shoulder. In this position the piston areas are equal. The spring forces the exhaust valve onto its seat and opens the inlet valve. At the same time the service line air enters the service line port, passes by the open inlet valve, and flows out of the delivery ports and into the air brake chambers. When the delivery and service line pressures are equal, the forces on the pistons are equal. The spring offsets the balance, lifting it slightly and thereby closing the inlet valve. If the service line pressure is fully removed, the delivery pressure forces the piston upward, opening the exhaust valve and allowing the air from the brake chamber to exhaust past the open valve into the atmosphere.

TESTING To test the limiting quick-release valve and two-way valve, first install a master gauge into the delivery and service lines, bring the air system to cutout pressure, and place the two-way control valve in the dry-road position. Have your assistant apply and hold the brakes. Take readings of both gauges—they should show the same pressure.

If the delivery pressure is lower, the piston may hang up, or if the piston or piston ring is damaged, it will allow the piston to move upward. If air leaks from the two-way control valve exhaust port, the inlet valve seat or the valve is damaged, worn, or dirty. In any of these events the valve must be serviced. If these problems do not exist, the next procedure would be to release the brakes and note the response

on the pressure gauges. If the application pressure does not drop quickly, the piston is hanging up, or the spring is broken. Service accordingly. Next, place the two-way control valve in the slippery-road position and then let your assistant hold the brakes applied. Take note of the gauge readings. The delivery line pressure should be about half that of the service line pressure. If, under this condition, air leaks from the exhaust port of the two-way control valve, the inlet valve is allowing air to pass by. If air leaks from the exhaust port of the limiting quick-release valve, the exhaust valve is allowing air to pass by. Valve service is then necessary.

Automatic Ratio and Limiting Valve All vehicles which are governed by FMVSS 121 regulations require a ratio-limiting valve which operates automatically and controls the service line pressure to the front axle. The use of this brake valve improves the brake performance, reduces braking effort, achieves better braking balance, and improves steering control. Off-highway tractors and trucks therefore also employ this valve.

DESIGN The automatic ratio and limiting valve is placed either in the delivery line or in the service line. When placed in the service line, the service line from the application valve is connected to the supply port, and the delivery port is connected with the control port of a relay valve or quick-release

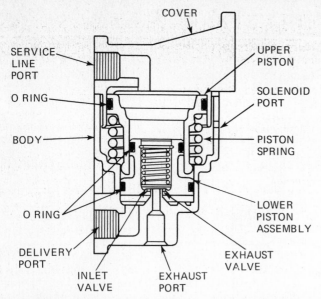

Fig. 18-67 Sectional view of a ratio and limiting valve. (*International Harvester Company*)

inner bore of the lower piston. The exhaust valve seat forms part of the center-drilled body which leads to the exhaust port. The upper piston (which has a diameter larger than the lower piston) is guided and sealed to the inner bore of the cover. The smaller portion of the upper piston is guided within and sealed to the lower body bore. The piston spring positioned between the body and piston holds the piston against the cover shoulder.

OPERATION When a brake application is made, the service air enters the supply port of the ratio and limiting valve and acts on the outer and inner piston areas. If the air pressure is at 40 psi [275.6 kPa] or lower, only the inner piston is forced downward because of the spring's superior force, which holds the outer piston against the cover. As the inner piston is forced downward, it closes the exhaust valve, causing the inlet valve to lift off its seat. Air from the service line is then allowed to pass by the open inlet valve, out of the delivery port, and into the control port of the front axle relay valve or quick release valve. The valve responds by effecting application of the brakes (see Fig. 18-68).

As the delivery pressure builds up in the brake chambers and reaches about half of the service line pressure, the inner piston is forced upward. The inlet valve then closes and the reduced pressure is held in the brake chambers. **NOTE** The brake chamber pressure is about 50 percent of that entering the supply port of the ratio and limiting valve.

When the service line pressure is released into the atmosphere, the inner piston is forced upward, the exhaust valve opens, and the air exhausts through the center passage, out through the exhaust port, and into the atmosphere. The relay or quick-release valve responds by releasing the brakes.

valve. The automatic ratio and limiting valve consists of the components shown in Fig. 18-67. The body has three ports: the solenoid, delivery, and exhaust port. The cover has the supply port. The lower piston is located inside the body. **NOTE** The lower piston has two different diameters, and its lower area is approximately twice that of the upper piston area. The smaller diameter of the piston is guided in the inner bore of the upper piston; O ring seals are used to seal the piston with the body and inner surface of the upper piston. The valve poppet is located inside the lower piston bore. The outer circle of the inlet exhaust valve is held through the poppet spring against the inlet seat. The latter forms part of the

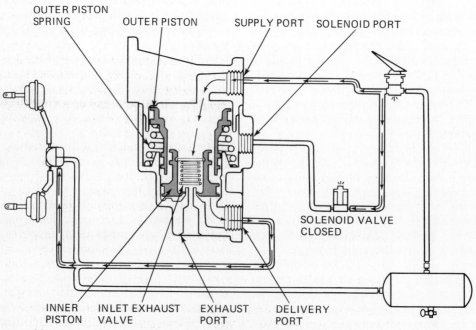

Fig. 18-68 Ratio and limiting valve action when the service line pressure is less than 40 psi [275.6 kPa]. (*International Harvester Company*)

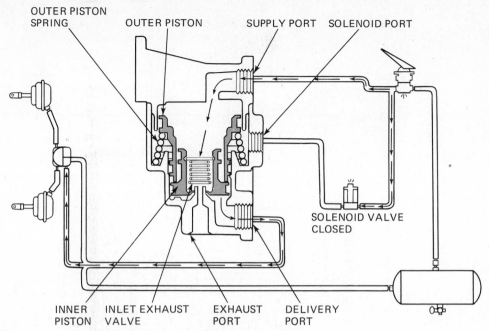

OUTER PISTON SPRING   OUTER PISTON   SUPPLY PORT   SOLENOID PORT

SOLENOID VALVE CLOSED

INNER PISTON   INLET EXHAUST VALVE   EXHAUST PORT   DELIVERY PORT

Fig. 18-69 Ratio and limiting valve action when the service line pressure is more than 40 psi [275.6 kPa]. (*International Harvester Company*)

When the service line pressure exceeds 40 psi [275.6 kPa] but does not exceed 60 psi [413.4 kPa], the inner piston is forced down. It first closes the exhaust valve and then opens the inlet valve. As the air pressure in the valve increases above 40 psi, the outer piston moves down against its spring force and comes to rest against the inner piston. The air pressure now acting on the outer and inner piston areas, has a greater force; therefore a higher delivery pressure is needed to close the inlet valve; for example, when the delivery pressure is about 50 psi [344.5 kPa], the pressure in the air brake chambers is only 40 psi [275.6 kPa]. When a service line pressure is above 60 psi [413.4 kPa], the air pressure acting on the outer and inner pistons has such a strong (downward) force that the delivery pressure acting on the inner piston cannot raise the inner and outer pistons and therefore cannot close the inlet valve. From this point on, the application valve controls the brake delivery pressure (see Fig. 18-69).

TESTING AND SERVICING   To test the automatic ratio and limiting valve, first install a master gauge to the brake chamber and another one into the service line. Bring the air system to cutout pressure and then stop the engine. Next, have your helper gradually apply the brakes while you watch the pressure gauges. The air brake chamber pressure should be 50 percent less than service line pressure. As the service line pressure increases above 40 psi, the air brake chamber pressure ratio should reduce, and after about 60 psi, both pressure gauge readings should be the same.

NOTE   If, during the testing, air leaks from the exhaust port, then the exhaust valve or seat is damaged, worn, or dirty. When testing the ratio and limiting valve, refer to your service manual for the specific pressure, since there are some slight variations.

If the automatic valve does not respond (as just outlined), the piston spring is weak or broken, the piston is hanging up, or the piston seal is damaged or worn, the valve must be serviced. NOTE   If, for some reason, an electric failure of the front axle antilock system occurs, the solenoid valve is automatically actuated (opened). When a brake application is made under such circumstance, air is directed into the solenoid port and thereby holds up the outer piston. This action places the ratio and limiting valves in the limiting position.

Tractor to Trailer Brake Piping   To supply the trailer reservoirs with air, to protect the tractor or truck air supply system, and to provide safety for the air brake system, the vehicle must be equipped with a tractor protection control valve (also called an emergency valve or trailer supply valve), as well as a tractor protection valve (see Fig. 18-70).

To direct the service line air to the trailer, the secondary circuit of the dual application valve is connected to a two-way check valve and from there to a tractor protection valve. To override the secondary-circuit service line pressure, that is, to increase the service line pressure to the trailer brakes, a hand application valve is piped into the system. The air supply to the hand valve can come from either the primary or secondary reservoir. The service line from the hand application valve is connected over the two-way valve to the tractor protection valve. The air supply to the tractor protection control valve also comes from the tractor service reservoirs and is directed from this valve to the tractor protection valve. From there it is directed to the glad hands onto the relay emergency valve. This air line is called the emergency line. The service line is the air line that leads from the dual application valve and the hand application valve to the tractor protection

346

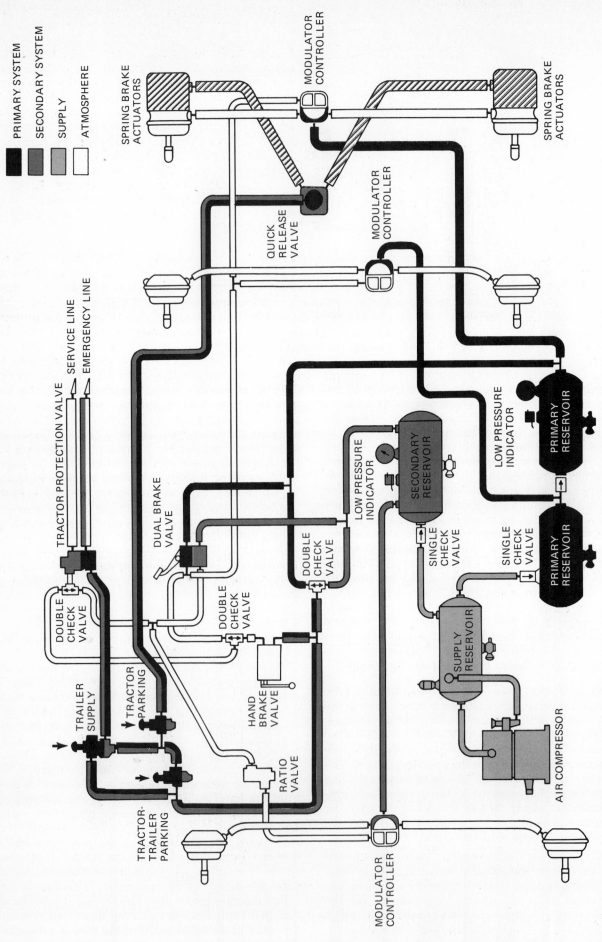

PRIMARY SYSTEM
SECONDARY SYSTEM
SUPPLY
ATMOSPHERE

SPRING BRAKE ACTUATORS

MODULATOR CONTROLLER

SPRING BRAKE ACTUATORS

QUICK RELEASE VALVE

MODULATOR CONTROLLER

SERVICE LINE
EMERGENCY LINE

TRACTOR PROTECTION VALVE

DUAL BRAKE VALVE

LOW PRESSURE INDICATOR

SECONDARY RESERVOIR

LOW PRESSURE INDICATOR

PRIMARY RESERVOIR

DOUBLE CHECK VALVE

DOUBLE CHECK VALVE

DOUBLE CHECK VALVE

SINGLE CHECK VALVE

SINGLE CHECK VALVE

PRIMARY RESERVOIR

TRAILER SUPPLY

TRACTOR PARKING

HAND BRAKE VALVE

SUPPLY RESERVOIR

TRACTOR-TRAILER PARKING

RATIO VALVE

AIR COMPRESSOR

MODULATOR CONTROLLER

Fig. 18-70 Schematic view of a motor truck dual air brake system when fully charged. (Freightliner Corporation)

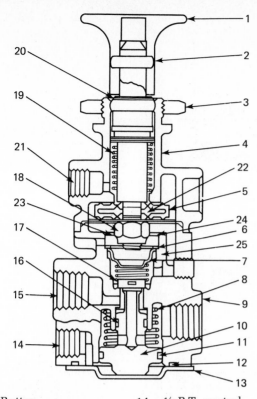

1. Button
2. Spirol pin
3. Thin nut
4. Body
5. Inlet and exhaust valve
6. Retaining ring
7. Inlet and exhaust valve spring
8. Spring
9. Lower body
10. Piston
11,12. O rings
13. End plate
14. 1/8 P.T. control
15. 1/4 P.T. delivery
16. O ring
17. Inlet and exhaust valve
18. Nut
19. Plunger return spring
20. Plunger
21. Supply port
22. Inlet valve and seal
23. Exhaust valve seat
24. Exhaust valve
25. Air passage

Fig. 18-71 Sectional view of trailer supply valve components.

valve. From here it leads to the glad hands and then to the relay emergency valve control port.

Tractor Protection Control Valve The tractor protection control valve must have the ability, when manually actuated, to direct air into the emergency line and to exhaust the air from the line. In addition it must automatically exhaust the emergency line when the tractor reservoir or emergency line pressure drops (for any reason) below the pressure specified for this valve. **NOTE** The automatic exhaust pressure ranges from 40 to 60 psi [275.6 to 413.4 kPa], depending on the type of control valve and brake system used. A parking brake control valve (see Fig. 18-45) or a trailer supply valve (see Fig. 18-71) could be used.

DESIGN The trailer supply valve consists of the upper body, the middle body, and the cap. They are held together by two screws and sealed by O rings. The plunger is located in the upper body bore. The control knob is fastened to one end of the plunger, and the inlet exhaust valve to the other end. The plunger return spring is positioned between the body and plunger shoulder, and the (trigger) piston and spring are positioned in the cap. The control inlet/exhaust valve is located between the piston and spring.

OPERATION When the reservoir pressure is about 55 psi [378.95 kPa] and the driver or operator pushes the plunger inward, the top inlet valve is moved away from its seat, and the exhaust valve comes to rest against its seat (see Fig. 18-72). This exposes the entire top inlet exhaust valve area to the reservoir pressure. An air pressure of about 50 psi [344.5 kPa] is needed to hold the exhaust valve seated against the force of the plunger spring. Air now passes through passage 25, onto the lower spring area, and onto the inlet valve. When the tractor-trailer park

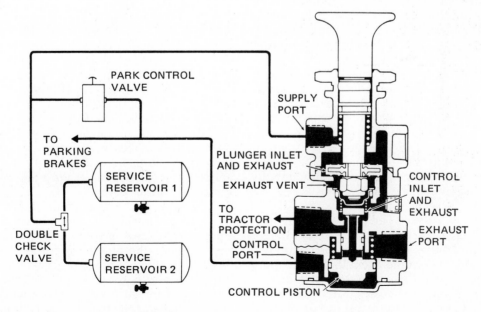

Fig. 18-72 Schematic view of valve position when the brake system is fully charged. (*International Harvester Company*)

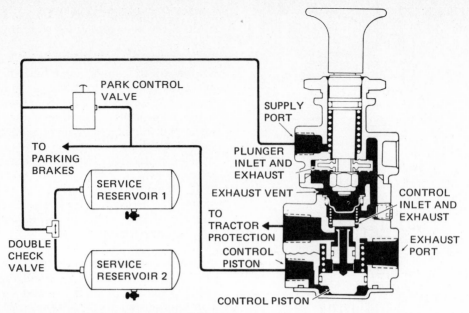

Fig. 18-73 Schematic view of valve position when the brake system is below 50 psi [344.5 kPa]. (*International Harvester Company*)

control valve is now actuated, air is directed into the control port and thereby forces the piston upward. This action closes the lower exhaust valve and opens the inlet valve. Air now can pass from the top of the inlet valve through passage 25, around the lower open inlet valve, and out of the delivery port. The air leaving the delivery port flows to the tractor protection valve. If the air pressure in the emergency line or supply line drops to approximately 40 psi [275.6 kPa], the force of the plunger spring becomes higher than the force of the air pressure acting on the inlet exhaust valve. The valve then snaps onto the inlet valve seat and opens the exhaust valve. The closed inlet valve protects the tractor reservoirs, and the open exhaust valve vents the emergency line. If the valve plunger hangs up, or if the plunger spring is broken and holding the plunger, or if the driver holds the plunger inward, the emergency line exhausts. The reason for this is that the tractor-trailer park valve control pressure has also exhausted, removing the control pressure acting on the (trigger) piston. This removes the force from the piston, and consequently the inlet closes and the exhaust valve opens, allowing the emergency air to escape (see Fig. 18-73).

The test procedures and leakage test procedures are much the same as those outlined in the discussion of the parking brake control valve, although the pressure specifications may vary.

Tractor Protection Valve   The purpose of the tractor protection valve, in conjunction with the tractor protection control valve, is to protect the tractor reservoirs against air loss in the event that the (supply line) emergency line develops an excessive leak or rupture or the (supply) emergency line glad hand disconnects. However, some tractor protection valves serve an additional function; that is, they are able to accelerate the trailer brake application, as well as the brake release.

The simplest but most efficient tractor protection valve is a relay valve. When a relay valve is used, the air from the tractor protection control valve flows unrestricted into the emergency line and to the relay valve (see Fig. 18-74). The air flows to the glad hands, into the emergency port of the relay emergency valve, or to the reservoir port of the trailer modulator controller. The service line from the application valve is connected to the control port of the relay valve. The relay valve service port is connected to the trailer emergency valve control port.

NOTE   All types of trailers, including trailer-converter dollies which are *not* governed by the FMVSS 121 regulation, use a relay emergency valve. Vehicles governed by this regulation must use a modulator controller (relay valve with a skid controller).

TESTING   To test the relay valve for an internal leak, actuate the tractor protection control valve (to charge the trailer with air). If air leaks from the exhaust port, the inlet valve is leaking, or the poppet O rings are worn or damaged and are allowing air to pass by. If air leaks out of the exhaust port when the trailer brakes are applied, the exhaust valve is leaking.

Another type of tractor protection valve is shown in Fig. 18-75. This valve body has four ports. The two upper ports are emergency line ports (inlet and outlet), and the two lower ports are the service lines (inlet and outlet ports).

The plunger, positioned inside the body, is guided and is sealed to the body and seat with an O ring, and the seat is secured by a retainer ring. The spring holds the plunger and the valve against the body seat. When the tractor protection control valve directs air into the (supply) emergency line, the plunger is forced down and the valve opens. This action connects the tractor service line port with the trailer service port. When the supply line is vented, the spring forces the valve onto its seat and thereby closes off the service line to the trailer.

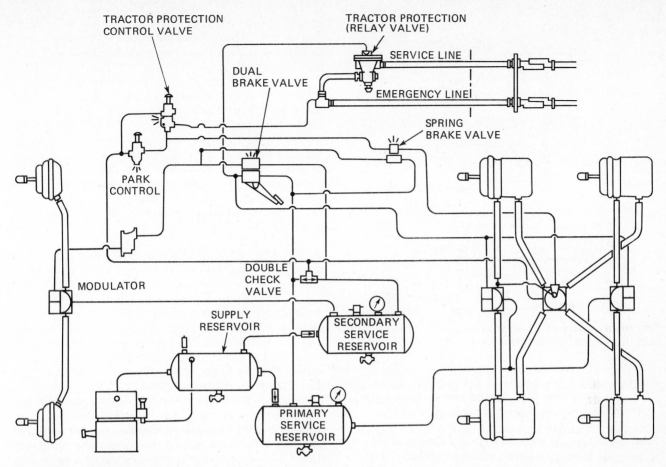

Fig. 18-74 Schematic view of a dual air brake system using a relay valve as tractor protection valve.

CAUSES OF FAILURE The valve operates relatively trouble-free because of its minimal movement, but if failure occurs, it is usually caused by a leaking O ring.

To test the valve for an internal leak, first bring the tractor reservoir pressure to cutout pressure. Stop the engine, uncouple the service line glad hand, and check for air leaks with a leakage tester. If air leaks from the tractor glad hand, the upper O ring is allowing air from the supply line to pass into the service line. If air leaks from around the diaphragm or retainer ring, the lower plunger O ring or the seat is damaged or worn.

Glad Hands The purpose of the glad hands (the hose couplers) is to make a leak-free connection between the tractor and trailer when a pair of glad hands are coupled together. The glad hands are made from cast iron, or forged steel, or cast aluminum. When made from aluminum, a steel strip is locked to the body to reduce wear between the mating surfaces.

Each glad hand is cast with a ramp and guide. One of the pair is equipped with a locking detent, whereas the other has a locking arm, a locking pin, and a limiting pin. The packing ring is positioned in a groove of the body coupling (see Fig. 18-76).

Before coupling the two glad hands together, make certain the ramps, the packing ring, and the detents are clean and that the packing ring is not damaged, deteriorated, or lacking in resilience. To

couple the two glad hands together, hold them about 25° opposite each other while starting both guides into the locking arm. Next, rotate them until they come to rest against the limiting pin. The spring-

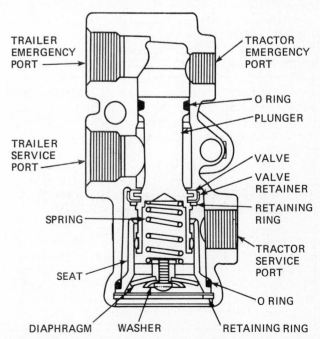

Fig. 18-75 Sectional view of a tractor protection valve. (*GMC Truck and Coach Division of General Motors Corporation*)

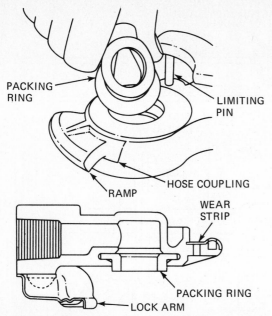

Fig. 18-76 View of a hose coupling. (*International Harvester Company*)

loaded lockpin then rests in the locking detent. As the glad hands are rotated, the ramps slide against each other and compress the packing rings.

TESTING Couple both service and emergency lines (or supply line) glad hands and then actuate (charge) the trailer supply valve in order to direct air to the trailer. Next, apply maximum service brake, using the dual application valve. Now, using an air leakage tester, check for air leaks around the couplings and hose fittings.

Relay Emergency Valve All types of trailers, including trailer converter dollies which are *not* gov-

erned by the FMVSS 121 regulation, use a relay emergency valve. Those governed by the aforementioned regulation must use a skid controller (modulator controller).

The relay emergency valve has many functions, such as to act as a relay valve and thereby reduce the time lapse of trailer brake application and release, to protect the trailer reservoirs from an air loss in the event the emergency line develops a leak or breaks away from the trailer, and to apply the trailer brakes automatically when the tractor reservoir's emergency line pressure, or the trailer reservoir's pressure falls within 60 to 40 psi [413.4 to 275.6 kPa]. The variance is dictated by (geographic) legal limits.

DESIGN AND PIPING The relay emergency valve is mounted to the trailer reservoir or close to it. Each trailer axle usually has its own emergency relay valve. The emergency air line which extends from the tractor protection valve is connected to the emergency port of the relay emergency valve. The service line extending from the tractor protection valve is connected to the control port of the relay emergency valve. The air brake chambers are connected with the delivery port (see Fig. 18-77).

Although there are several different types of relay emergency valves, they all serve the same purpose. This type of valve is distinguishable by two sections: the relay valve section, and the emergency valve section. One type of relay emergency valve is shown in Fig. 18-78. Notice that its relay valve section is very similar to the relay valve previously covered. The emergency section is located in the cover, and a passage leads from the trailer reservoir port to the spring cavity of the check valve, which extends into the area between the check valve and piston plug. The check valve is held on its seat with a light spring. Its purpose is to prevent a reverse air flow. The inlet/

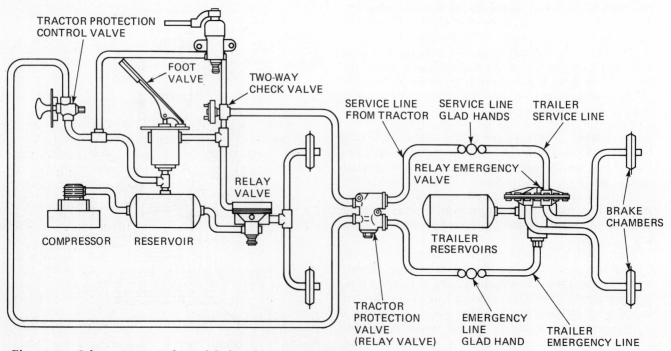

Fig. 18-77 Schematic view of simplified trailer air brake piping.

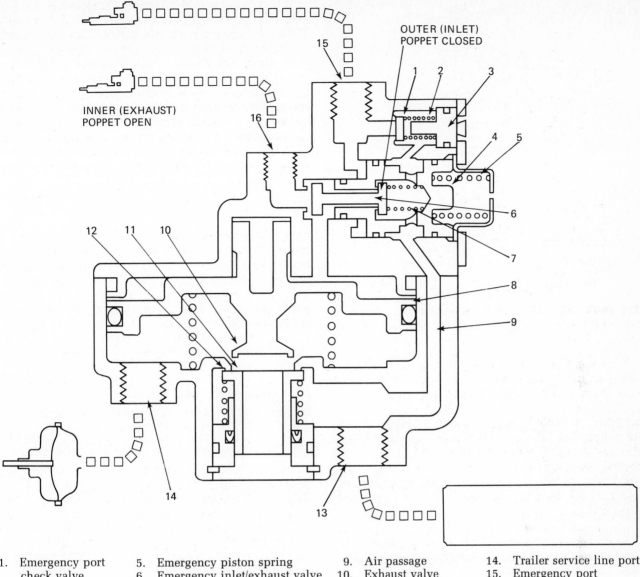

OUTER (INLET)
POPPET CLOSED

INNER (EXHAUST)
POPPET OPEN

1.	Emergency port check valve	5.	Emergency piston spring
2.	Spring	6.	Emergency inlet/exhaust valve
3.	Plug	7.	Emergency inlet/exhaust valve spring
4.	Emergency piston	8.	Relay piston

9.	Air passage
10.	Exhaust valve
11.	Exhaust valve seat
12.	Inlet seat and valve
13.	Trailer reservoir port

14.	Trailer service line port
15.	Emergency port
16.	Tractor service line port

Fig. 18-78 Sectional view of a relay emergency valve when the trailer reservoir is charged and the brake released. (*Wagner Electric Sales Corporation*)

exhaust (poppet) valve fits loosely in the emergency piston, and the poppet valve spring holds the inlet valve on its seat. **NOTE** It is physically impossible for both valves (exhaust and inlet) to seat simultaneously.

The emergency piston is forced through the emergency piston spring and against the shoulder in the cover bore, exerting an additional force on the poppet valve spring.

Air Flow to Charge the Trailer When the tractor protection control valve is pulled out (or pushed in, depending on the valve design), air passes by the open inlet valve and enters the service port of the tractor protection (relay) valve. It then passes into the emergency line and enters the emergency port of the relay emergency valve. The air pressure lifts

the check valve off its seat and the air flows through passages A and B (see Fig. 18-79) into the trailer reservoir. At the same time the air passes by the open inlet valve, in the space between the poppet stem and the emergency piston bore, onto the top surface of the relay (application) piston. The piston is then forced down, closing the exhaust valve but opening the inlet valve. The trailer reservoir air can now flow past the open inlet valve, out of the delivery port, and into the air brake chambers to apply the brakes. When emergency line pressure is approximately 50 psi [344.5 kPa], the air pressure acting on the large area of the emergency piston moves the piston to the right against the spring force, and the inlet seat contacts and closes the inlet valve. This action has opened the exhaust valve, exhausting the air from above the relay piston, and the air flows out through

352

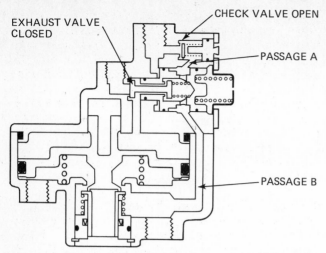

Fig. 18-79 Sectional view of valve position during the charging of the trailer reservoir. (*Wagner Electric Sales Corporation*)

EXHAUST VALVE CLOSED

CHECK VALVE OPEN

PASSAGE A

PASSAGE B

the application valve exhaust port. The piston is forced upward and thereby closes the inlet valve, opens the exhaust valve, and releases the trailer brakes. When the entire air system is at cutout pressure, or when the tractor reservoir pressure is less than trailer reservoir pressure, the check valve closes by the combined spring force and reservoir pressure.

Service Brake Application When either application valve is actuated, air is directed to the tractor protection (relay) valve, and the valve responds by closing the exhaust valve and opening the inlet valve. Air from the emergency line then enters the service line and is directed to the service port of the relay emergency valve. The relay valve responds by closing the exhaust valve and opening the inlet valve. As a result, air from the trailer reservoir passes by the open valve, out of the delivery port, and into the air brake chambers to apply the brakes. When the service line pressure and the delivery pressure are equal, the application piston of the relay emergency valve raises and thereby closes the inlet valve. Almost simultaneously the tractor protection valve closes its inlet valve, and at the same time (or a fraction of a second later) the application valve closes its inlet valve. There is always this chain reaction that uses reservoir pressure to apply the brakes, and it is a chain reaction in the reverse direction that achieves balance on all three valves.

If, on a downhill grade, the trailer starts pushing the tractor and causing difficulty in steering, the driver has the prerogative of placing a greater braking force onto the trailer brakes by rotating the hand application valve. When the hand application valve's service-line pressure exceeds the secondary-circuit's service line pressure, the two-way check valve shifts; this movement closes the secondary supply port and allows the higher air pressure to pass onto the tractor protection valve. The tractor protection valve, as well as the relay emergency valve, responds to the higher service line pressure. As a result, the relay emergency valve increases the delivery pressure into the air brake chambers.

When the hand application valve is released, it exhausts the service line pressure to the two-way valve. Subsequently, the following mechanical actions instantly take place: (1) the two-way check valve shifts and the previous secondary service line pressure is again exerted onto the tractor protection valve; (2) the tractor protection valve's exhaust valve opens, reducing the pressure in the service line; and (3) the relay emergency valve's exhaust valve opens, reducing the delivered pressure in the air chamber.

These actions take place within a fraction of a second, and therefore you may notice only that the service line pressure has dropped to the previous pressure of the secondary circuit's service line pressure.

BRAKE RELEASE When the brake application is released, the secondary circuit's service line pressure is removed from the tractor protection valve because the air is exhausted at the application valve. This action allows the service line pressure from the emergency relay valve to be exhausted at the tractor protection valve. The relay piston is then allowed to move upward, opening the exhaust valve and exhausting the delivery pressure from the air brake chambers.

Emergency Braking—Trailer Air Loss Under normal operating conditions the tractor and trailer reservoirs have equal pressures; however there is a variance between compressor cutout and cut-in pressures. If for any reason the trailer reservoir loses air, say, owing to a broken drain cock, a damaged trailer reservoir, or a ruptured service line, the trailer reservoir's pressure would reduce. The reduction may be quick or gradual, depending on the cause of the air loss. When the pressure drops gradually, the check valve opens and tractor air equalizes the pressure between the tractor and trailer reservoirs. If the leak is so great that the compressor cannot keep up with it, the pressure drops steadily. **NOTE** The driver is alerted by the warning light and/or buzzer and should, at this point, stop the vehicle and check for the cause of leakage.

The reduction in air pressure reduces the force on the emergency piston, and when the air pressure approaches approximately 60 psi [413.4 kPa], the emergency piston's spring forces the emergency piston to the left. This action closes the exhaust valve, opens the inlet valve, and allows the trailer reservoir air to flow into the top of the relay piston. The exhaust valve of the relay valve then closes, the inlet valve opens, and the trailer reservoir air then flows to the brake chambers and applies the brakes. Meanwhile the air pressure is continuously dropping in the emergency line. When the pressure approaches 50 psi [344.5 kPa] (varies with application), the tractor protection control valve responds to the low pressure by exhausting the emergency line. Now the air pressure is quickly exhausted, and consequently the emergency section's inlet valve opens fully and full reservoir pressure applies the trailer brakes.

NOTE As the trailer reservoir pressure gradually reduces to zero pressure, the trailer brakes gradually

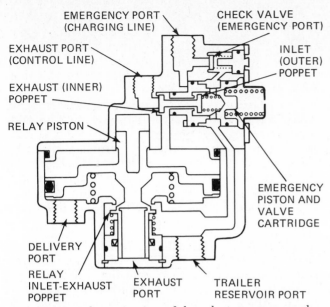

EMERGENCY PORT (CHARGING LINE)

CHECK VALVE (EMERGENCY PORT)

EXHAUST PORT (CONTROL LINE)

INLET (OUTER) POPPET

EXHAUST (INNER) POPPET

RELAY PISTON

EMERGENCY PISTON AND VALVE CARTRIDGE

DELIVERY PORT

RELAY INLET-EXHAUST POPPET

EXHAUST PORT

TRAILER RESERVOIR PORT

Fig. 18-80 Schematic view of the relay emergency valve in an emergency braking action. (*Wagner Electric Sales Corporation*)

release. However, as the trailer pressure deflates, the parking brake air chamber also deflates, and the spring force applies the trailer brakes.

Emergency Braking—Tractor Air Loss In the event that the tractor service reservoirs lose pressure owing to a ruptured compressor air line or a broken-off drain cock (see Fig. 18-80), the trailer air cannot flow in reverse to the tractor reservoirs, because of the check valves in the relay emergency valve.

As the tractor air drops to 60 psi [413.4 kPa], the warning light glows, the buzzer sounds, or the wig-wag is released. At about 50 psi [344.5 kPa] the tractor protection control valve responds by closing the inlet valve and opening the exhaust valve and thus vents the emergency line. This action removes the force from the left side of the emergency piston. The emergency spring then forces the emergency piston to the left, closing the exhaust valve and opening the inlet valve. This causes the existing trailer reservoir pressure to force the relay piston down, closing the exhaust valve and opening the inlet valve. Reservoir air at reservoir pressure applies the trailer brakes.

As the tractor air deflates and reaches the parking brake's control valve setting, its inlet valve closes and opens the exhaust valve. The air from the parking air chamber exhausts past the open exhaust valve into the atmosphere. The spring force now applies the tractor brakes. If this action actually occurred when the vehicle were traveling at a speed of 60 mph [96.5 km/h], the tractor-trailer could be completely destroyed. Make certain, therefore, that the rig is checked out properly and the driver is aware that he should stop the rig before the air pressure drops to the emergency level.

Emergency Braking—Service Line Rupture The driver may not be aware, nor will he be warned, when the service line to the trailer is ruptured or the

glad hands are uncoupled. However, as soon as the brakes are applied, the relay piston (tractor protection valve) is forced down, closing the exhaust valve and opening the inlet valve. This action allows the air from the emergency line to pass into the service line and out of the ruptured service line. As the emergency line pressure drops to 50 psi [344.5 kPa], the tractor protection control valve responds by closing the inlet valve and opening the exhaust valve and thereby protects the tractor reservoir air. The relay emergency valve responds by applying the trailer brakes.

Testing the Tractor and Trailer After the engine compressor is checked and the trailer is coupled to the tractor, bring the tractor air system to cutout pressure and note the pressure. Also note when the low-pressure warning device shuts off. (It should occur between 60 to 65 psi [413.4 to 447.85 kPa].) Apply the brakes several times and observe the compressor cut-in point. (It should be about 20 psi [137.8 kPa] below the cutout pressure.) Again raise the pressure to cutout pressure. Stop the engine and observe the reservoir gauges. A pressure drop of 20 psi [137.8 kPa] in 10 minutes is the maximum allowable air leak on a tractor. If air leaks occur, use an air leakage tester to locate the leaks and make the necessary repair before proceeding further with the tractor-trailer checkout. Again bring the pressure to cutout pressure and then actuate the tractor protection control valve to charge the trailer reservoir. At about 50 psi [344.5 kPa] the valve should remain open, and the low-pressure indicator should have actuated the warning device. Again bring the air system to cutout pressure and observe the pressure drop. The total pressure drop in 10 minutes should not exceed 30 psi [206.7 kPa]. With maximum pressure in the tractor and trailer reservoirs, apply maximum brakes by using the dual application valve. Hold the brake application and check the reservoir pressure drop. At the same time measure the pushrod travel and check the angle between the pushrod and slack adjustor. If the reservoir pressure has dropped more than 10 psi [68.9 kPa], locate (by using an air leakage tester) the air leak(s) and make the necessary repair before continuing the testing.

To check the operation of the automatic or limiting quick-release valve, follow the procedure outlined earlier in this unit in the discussion about limiting quick-release and two-way control valves.

Actuate the tractor protection control valve to exhaust the emergency line. The trailer brakes should apply instantly. With the trailer brakes applied, drain one reservoir at a time and note when the service brake application starts to release the brakes and when the parking brakes start to apply the (trailer) brakes. This should be an interaction. When the parking brakes are applied, actuate the trailer's parking brake control valve to release the brakes. There should be enough pressure in the parking brake reservoir to release the brakes at least once.

Actuate the tractor protection control valve to charge the trailer reservoir and then uncouple the emergency glad hands. The trailer brakes should ap-

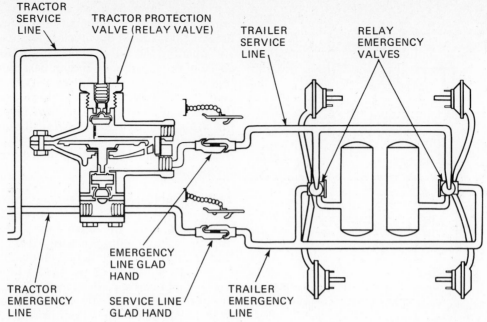

TRACTOR SERVICE LINE — TRACTOR PROTECTION VALVE (RELAY VALVE) — TRAILER SERVICE LINE — RELAY EMERGENCY VALVES

EMERGENCY LINE GLAD HAND

TRACTOR EMERGENCY LINE — SERVICE LINE GLAD HAND — TRAILER EMERGENCY LINE

Fig. 18-81 Emergency line rupture of glad hand uncoupled.

ply instantly (see Fig. 18-81). No air should leak from the tractor glad hand, but if it does so, the inlet valve of the tractor protection control valve is leaking. When air leaks from the trailer glad hand, the check valve in the relay emergency valve is leaking.

Recouple the emergency glad hands, recharge the trailer reservoir, and then uncouple the service line glad hands. Now apply the brakes; the trailer brakes should apply instantly. At this point you may have to restart the engine to bring the reservoir pressure above 80 psi [551.2 kPa], after which you should stop the engine and then apply the brakes several times to reduce the reservoir pressure. At about 60 psi [413.4 kPa] the warning device should actuate, and at about 50 psi [344.5 kPa] the tractor protection control valve should exhaust the emergency line and the trailer brakes should instantly apply.

Uncouple the trailer and drain the primary tractor reservoir. This also drains the supply reservoir.

NOTE After the low-pressure warning devices have actuated, apply the service brakes. The pressure gauge should indicate that the secondary system applies the brakes of the front axle and the front axle brakes of the tandem rear axle. Again bring the air system to cutout pressure and then drain the secondary reservoir. This also drains the supply reservoir and actuates the low-pressure warning devices. Now apply the brakes. The pressure gauge should indicate that the primary reservoir pressure is applying the brakes of the front axle and the rear axle brakes of the tandem rear axle (see Fig. 18-82).

When all the checks indicate that the brake system performs as specified, turn the vehicle over to the driver for a road test or personally road test the vehicle.

Emergency Dump Valve To ensure, in the event of failure of the tractor protection control valve, that the emergency line is exhausted when the pressure

drops to 45 psi [310.05 kPa], a second safety system is connected in parallel with the emergency line. The two components used are the low-pressure governor and the dump valve. The low-pressure governor inlet port is connected to the supply side of the reservoir, and the outlet port is connected to the dump valve. The opposite inlet side of the dump valve is connected to the emergency line. The governor used for this application is the same as a compressor governor except that its spring has less energy. The dump valve is a modified check valve (see Fig. 18-83).

OPERATION When the tractor pressure has reached about 55 psi [378.95 kPa], the governor allows air to pass into the dump valve and onto the top of the shuttle piston. The force on the shuttle closes the exhaust valve, closing off the emergency line. If the tractor protection control valve is then actuated, emergency line pressure is exerted from below onto the exhaust valve. When the air in the emergency line pressure drops to 50 psi [344.5 kPa], the tractor protection control valve should respond and exhaust the air in the emergency line. However, if the tractor protection control valve should fail owing to a sticking plunger or broken spring, even though the pressure drops to the low-pressure governor setting of 40 psi [275.6 kPa], the governor exhaust valve then opens, exhausting the air from above the shuttle piston. The emergency line pressure then opens the exhaust valve and the air is vented into the atmosphere. If the governor also fails to function and the emergency pressure drops to about 28 psi [192.92 kPa], the shuttle spring force increases over that of the air pressure in the emergency line, opens the exhaust port, and vents the emergency line, and the trailer brakes apply.

Water-Cooled Brake Drums In the logging industry of the Pacific Northwest the logging roads have

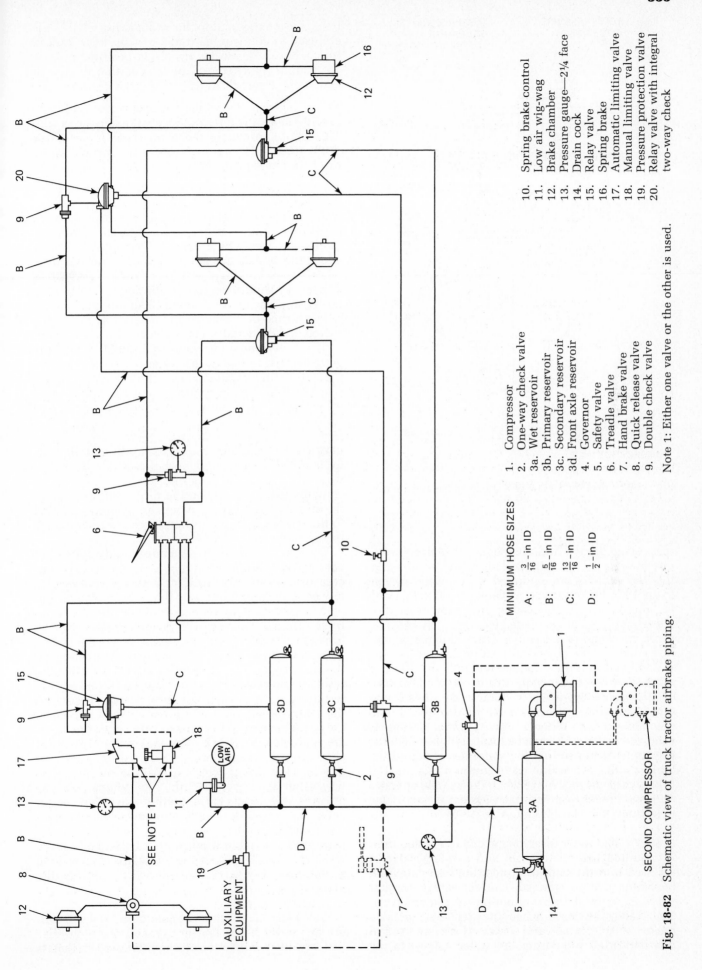

Fig. 18-82 Schematic view of truck tractor airbrake piping.

MINIMUM HOSE SIZES

A: $\frac{3}{16}$-in ID
B: $\frac{5}{16}$-in ID
C: $\frac{13}{16}$-in ID
D: $\frac{1}{2}$-in ID

1. Compressor
2. One-way check valve
3a. Wet reservoir
3b. Primary reservoir
3c. Secondary reservoir
3d. Front axle reservoir
4. Governor
5. Safety valve
6. Treadle valve
7. Hand brake valve
8. Quick release valve
9. Double check valve
10. Spring brake control
11. Low air wig-wag
12. Brake chamber
13. Pressure gauge—2¼ face
14. Drain cock
15. Relay valve
16. Spring brake
17. Automatic limiting valve
18. Manual limiting valve
19. Pressure protection valve
20. Relay valve with integral two-way check

Note 1: Either one valve or the other is used.

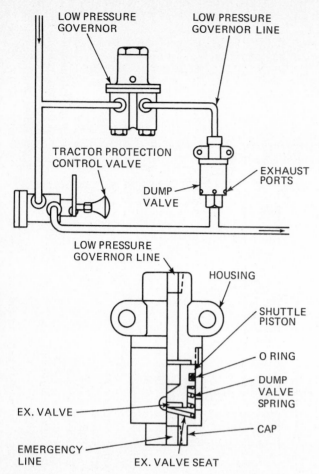

Fig. 18-83 Sectional view of a dump valve and its connections. (*Sealco Air Controls Inc.*)

long, steep grades, and the logging vehicles operate under overload conditions. It is therefore essential that the vehicles are equipped with a water system to cool the brake drums. Advantages of water cooling the drums are less lining and drum wear, less adjustment, no brake fade, less heat checks and drum breakage or excessive drum expansion, and increased tire life since less heat penetrates the tire.

Although several different methods are used to bring the water to the brake drum, common features of all systems are a water storage tank, hoses and pipes, and a nozzle that is correctly positioned onto the brake drum. When a gravity water system is used, the water tank must be located higher than the last trailer drum so that the water can reach all the brake drums. Since this water-to-drum relationship is very difficult to achieve when the vehicle operates on steep grades, a pressurized system is used. One of such systems is shown in Fig. 18-84.

DESIGN The water reservoir, which is a sealed unit, is mounted behind the cab, and a safety valve is screwed into the tank to protect the reservoir from becoming overpressurized. One air-actuated water valve is screwed into the bottom of the reservoir. Two valves are used when the tractor's rear axle brakes must also be water cooled. Hoses are used to distribute the water from the water valves, to the

tractor rear axles, and to the trailer axles. Glad hands are used to connect the trailer's water hose with its trailer hose. The water nozzle is positioned about 15° behind the center of the axle so that the nozzle end is about one-third from the brake drum rim.

NOTE When the vehicle speed exceeds 15 mph [24.13 km/h], the nozzle is located inside the drums. This action prevents the centrifugal force of the drum from spinning away the water which would result in inadequate cooling.

Actuation of the water valve can be achieved by two methods: connecting the air control port of the water valve to the service line or the driver's operating the manual control valve. The automatic actuation device (which permits water to flow only when the brakes are applied) should not be used when severe braking conditions exist. **CAUTION** The water should be turned on before the tractor-trailer approaches the downhill grade and should not be turned off until approximately 1 min after the severe braking conditions ceased.

The water panel (air control) includes a pressure gauge which indicates the water reservoir pressure, a combination regulator and shutoff valve, and a four-position three-way directional valve indicating off position, trailer only, tractor only, or tractor and trailer.

OPERATION Air from the accessory line of the tractor is piped to the supply port, directed to the three-way valve, and then goes into the inlet valve of the combination valve. When the three-way valve is in the off position, the rotor blocks air openings leading to the tractor or trailer outlet; therefore no air is directed to the water valve.

The combination valve is a mini-hand application valve. When the lever is moved to the right, it increases the spring force, and the diaphragm is moved downward, closing the exhaust valve and opening the inlet valve, and air flows into the water reservoir. As the reservoir pressure increases, the force on the diaphragm increases; when the spring force equals the force of the air pressure acting on the diaphragm, the inlet valve closes. To raise the reservoir pressure, the lever must be turned further to the right, increasing the spring force. To reduce the reservoir pressure, the lever must be turned to the left. This opens the exhaust valve until the forces are again equal. **NOTE** The maximum pressure is about 60 psi [413.6 kPa].

When the driver selects a position on the three-way valve (see Fig. 18-85), the rotor aligns with one opening and directs air into either one or both water valve control ports. The diaphragm is forced downward and opens the water valve, and water under pressure is forced into the supply hose(s) out of the water nozzles. The water valve remains open as long as the three-way valve is directing air onto the diaphragm.

SYSTEM FAILURE The most common causes of failure are water hoses that are broken off or nozzles that are bent out of position, inlet screen that is

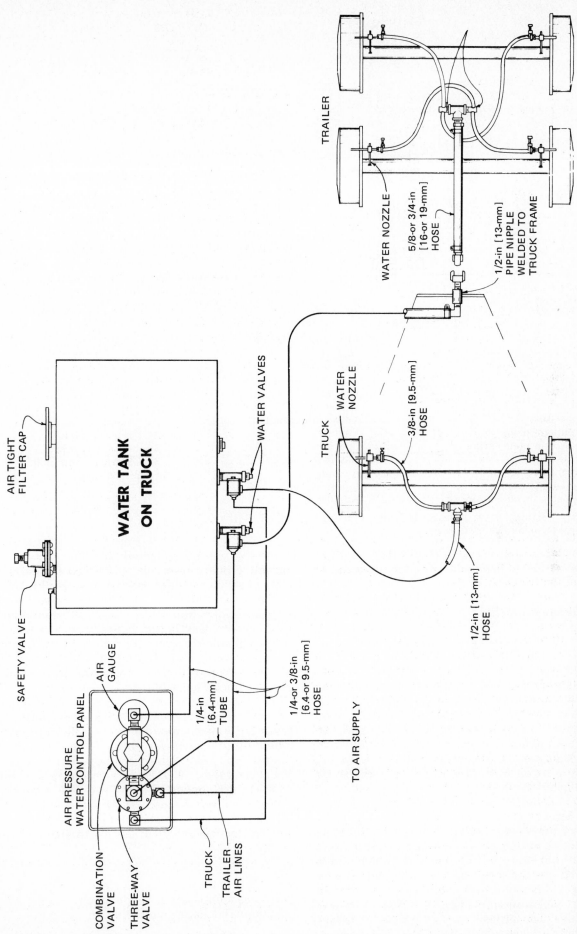

Fig. 18-84 Schematic view of components and piping of a water-cooled brake drum system.

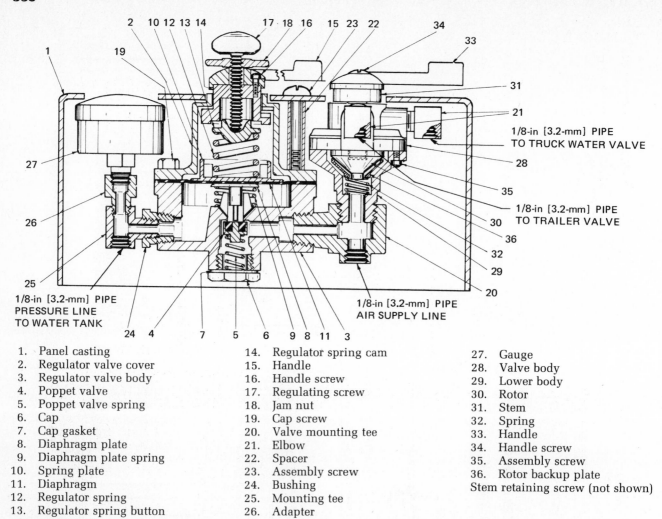

1. Panel casting
2. Regulator valve cover
3. Regulator valve body
4. Poppet valve
5. Poppet valve spring
6. Cap
7. Cap gasket
8. Diaphragm plate
9. Diaphragm plate spring
10. Spring plate
11. Diaphragm
12. Regulator spring
13. Regulator spring button

14. Regulator spring cam
15. Handle
16. Handle screw
17. Regulating screw
18. Jam nut
19. Cap screw
20. Valve mounting tee
21. Elbow
22. Spacer
23. Assembly screw
24. Bushing
25. Mounting tee
26. Adapter

27. Gauge
28. Valve body
29. Lower body
30. Rotor
31. Stem
32. Spring
33. Handle
34. Handle screw
35. Assembly screw
36. Rotor backup plate
Stem retaining screw (not shown)

Fig. 18-85 Sectional view of the air pressure water control panel. (*Williams Air Control Division Omark Industries*)

plugged owing to dirty water, or dirt that is lodged between the valve disk and seat, allowing water to leak from the water tank.

The combination valve or the three-way valve is never the cause of failure.

FMVSS 121 TRACTOR-TRAILER BRAKE SYSTEM

Various air brake piping systems are used on truck-tractors and trailers so that they will halt within the legally defined stopping distance and so that the vehicle stays within a roadway boundary of 12 ft [3.66 m] during braking. The piping for each individual brake system cannot be covered in this text. In any event, they are all very similar, except, perhaps, for the skid control units.

Typical System 121 Design A typical 121 tractor-trailer brake system is shown in Fig. 18-86. Let us compare this system with the one previously covered. Air from the supply reservoir of the 121 system is directed into the secondary reservoir and primary reservoir and is then directed to the second primary reservoir. Each reservoir is protected with a one-way check valve. The air from the first primary reservoir is directed to the reservoir port of the front rear-axle modulator controller (relay valve). (The modulator

controller will be explained later.) The air from the second primary reservoir is directed to the modulator controller of the rear-rear axle (of the tandem rear axle) and also to the primary reservoir port of the dual application valve. The air is further directed to the two 2-way check valves, onto the reservoir port of the hand application valve, onto the tractor-trailer's parking brake control valve, and finally onto the tractor protection control valve (trailer supply) and the tractor's parking brake control valve.

The secondary reservoir is connected to the two-way check valve, and a second air line connects the reservoir with the modulator controller of the front axle. From the two-way check valve it can flow to the reservoir port of the secondary-circuit's dual application valve. **NOTE** The second primary reservoir is also connected to the two-way check valve.

Consider for a moment how the three valves (tractor-trailer parking, tractor parking, and tractor protection control valve) direct air to the respective circuits.

NOTE The tractor protection control valve has a red eight-corner knob, the tractor-trailer parking valve has a four-corner yellow knob, and the tractor parking valve has a round blue knob.

When the tractor-trailer parking control valve is pulled out, or the force of the spring has moved the

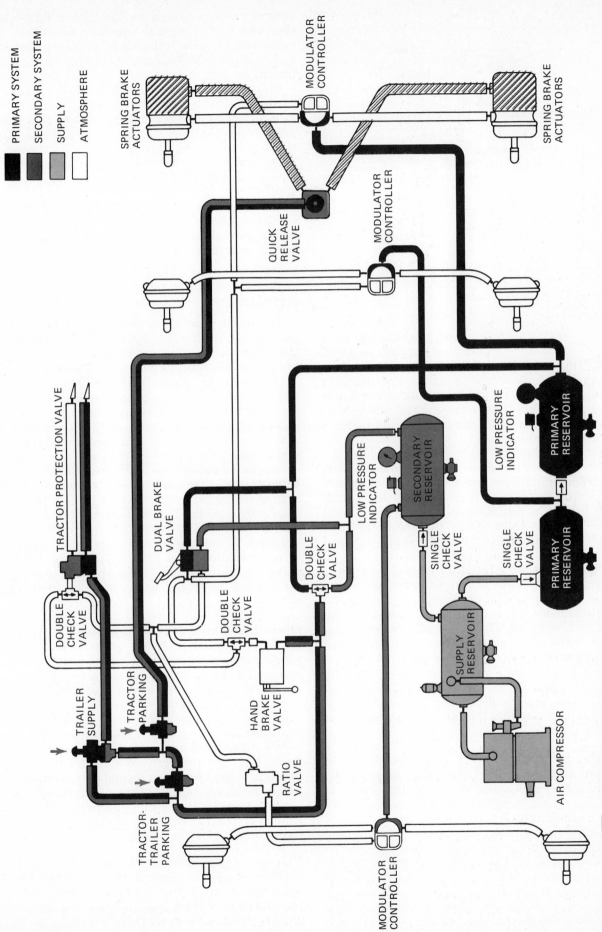

Fig. 18-86 A typical 121 tractor-trailer brake system. (*Freightliner Corporation*)

PRIMARY SYSTEM
SECONDARY SYSTEM
SUPPLY
ATMOSPHERE

SPRING BRAKE ACTUATORS
MODULATOR CONTROLLER
SPRING BRAKE ACTUATORS
QUICK RELEASE VALVE
MODULATOR CONTROLLER
TRACTOR PROTECTION VALVE
DUAL BRAKE VALVE
LOW PRESSURE INDICATOR
SECONDARY RESERVOIR
LOW PRESSURE INDICATOR
PRIMARY RESERVOIR
DOUBLE CHECK VALVE
DOUBLE CHECK VALVE
SINGLE CHECK VALVE
PRIMARY RESERVOIR
SINGLE CHECK VALVE
DOUBLE CHECK VALVE
HAND BRAKE VALVE
SUPPLY RESERVOIR
TRAILER SUPPLY
TRACTOR PARKING
RATIO VALVE
AIR COMPRESSOR
TRACTOR-TRAILER PARKING
MODULATOR CONTROLLER

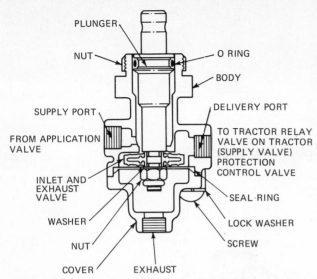

Fig. 18-87 Sectional view of a tractor and trailer parking control valve.

valve out owing to lack of air pressure, the inlet valve closes and the exhaust valve opens (see Fig. 18-87). This has exhausted the air (from the tractor's parking brake control valve) which was exerted onto the inlet exhaust valve, and the spring's force closes the inlet valve and opens the exhaust valve. This action removes the air pressure from the tractor's parking quick-release valve diaphragm, exhausts the air from the parking brake air chambers, and thereby applies the tractor brakes. At the same time the force from below the trigger piston of the tractor protection control valve was removed, and the piston spring forced the piston down, opening the exhaust valve. The inlet valve spring then seats the inlet valve. This exhausts the air from the supply line and thereby applies the trailer service brakes.

When the tractor protection control valve was pulled out, or the force of the spring has moved the plunger out owing to lack of tractor air pressure (on the inlet exhaust valve), the inlet valve seats and the exhaust valve opens. This action allows the supply air to be exhausted past the open exhaust valve and also removes the air pressure from the tractor-trailer's and tractor's parking brake valves. The valves respond by exhausting the air from the trailer's and tractor's parking brake air chambers. The spring force applies the tractor and trailer brakes (see Fig. 18-88).

Charging the Trailer Assume that the air system pressure exceeds 50 psi [344.5 kPa] and that the tractor-trailer's parking brake control valve is pushed in. The inlet valve is open, the exhaust valve is closed, and the air is then directed into the control port of the tractor protection control valve, forcing the trigger piston upward, closing the exhaust valve, and opening the inlet port. When the tractor protection control valve is now pushed inward, the inlet valve opens, the exhaust valve closes, and air flows into the supply line, through the tractor protection valve, into the spring brake trailer reservoir, and from there to the trailer parking brake valve, releasing the parking brake. When the tractor's parking

control valve is pushed in, the air is directed past the open inlet valve to the quick-release valve. The quick-release valve responds by directing air to the spring brake chamber, releasing the tractor's parking brakes.

The primary service line of the dual application valve is connected to the front-rear and rear-rear axles of the tandem rear axle modulator controllers. This service line also directs air over the two 2-way check valves, to and through the tractor protection valve, and to the control port of the trailer's modulator controller when the dual application valve is applied.

The secondary service line of the dual application valve is connected over the two 2-way check valves, to and through the tractor protection valve, into the control port of the trailer's modulator controllers.

NOTE The same air line is T'd off to supply service air to the ratio valve and from there to the control port of the front axle modulator controller.

The service port of the hand application valve is connected over the two 2-way check valves to the tractor protection valve and from there onto the control port of the trailer's modulator controllers.

Obviously the major difference between the two tractor brake systems' piping lies in the facts that (1) the primary reservoirs are connected in series, and the secondary reservoir supplies air to the front axle of the tractor as well as to the trailer; (2) a modulator controller is used on the front axle (to speed up the brake application and release) after the ratio valve instead of a quick-release valve; (3) another type of tractor protection valve is used in place of a relay valve; (4) the tractor protection control valve differs slightly; (5) two parking brake control valves are used; (6) modulator controllers are used in place of a conventional relay valve; (7) a quick-release valve is used in place of a tractor parking brake valve (or a relay valve and anticompounding two-way valve).

Operation—Service Brake Application When the tractor and trailer reservoirs are fully charged, the parking brakes release and a brake application is made with the dual application valve. The secondary circuit supplies service air to the trailer and to the front axle air chambers. The primary circuit supplies service air also to the trailer and to the tractor front-rear and rear-rear axle brake chambers.

When the hand application valve is rotated and its service line pressure exceeds the service line pressure of the primary or secondary circuit, the two 2-way check valves shift over and increase the service line pressure to the trailer. The modulator controllers respond, increasing the brake force on the trailer brakes (see Fig. 18-89).

Tractor Primary System Failure If the primary reservoir pressure were lost, the warning devices would be actuated, and (only) the service brakes to the rear axles of the tractor would be lost. However, when a tractor parking brake valve is used, the parking brake would act as a service brake in proportion to the service line pressure (see Fig. 18-90).

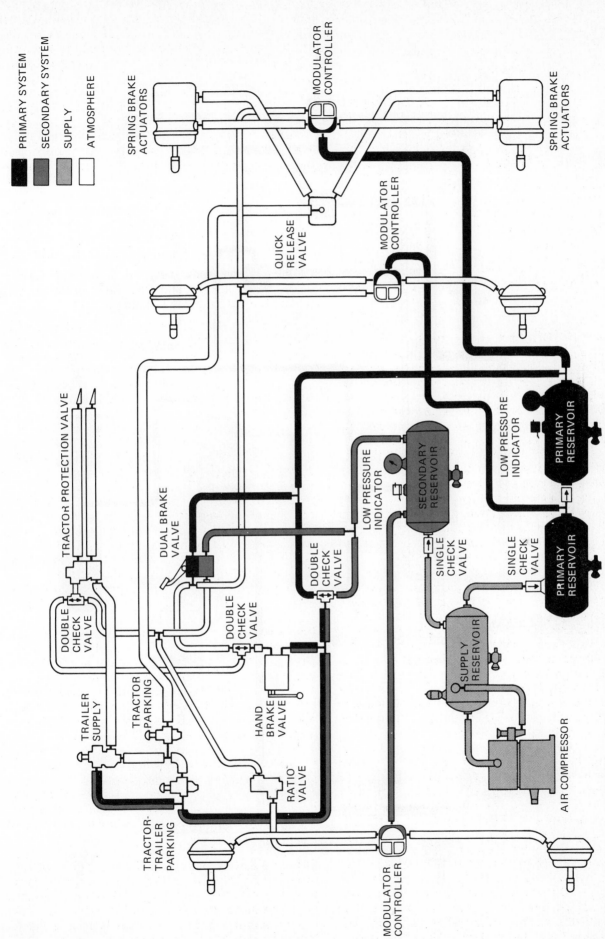

Fig. 18-88 Dual air brake system—tractor-trailer parking brake application. (*Freightliner Corporation*)

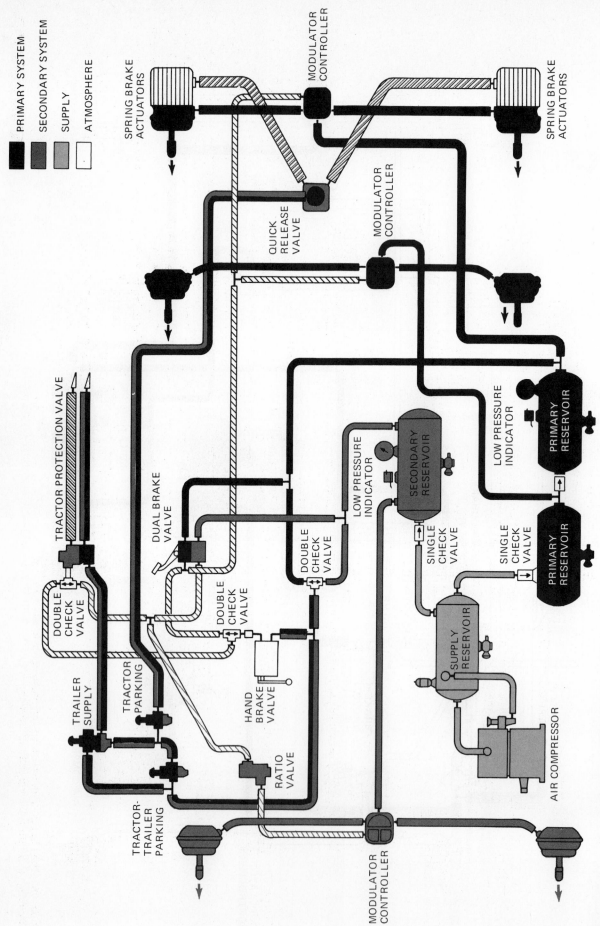

PRIMARY SYSTEM
SECONDARY SYSTEM
SUPPLY
ATMOSPHERE

SPRING BRAKE ACTUATORS

MODULATOR CONTROLLER

SPRING BRAKE ACTUATORS

MODULATOR CONTROLLER

QUICK RELEASE VALVE

LOW PRESSURE INDICATOR

PRIMARY RESERVOIR

TRACTOR PROTECTION VALVE

DUAL BRAKE VALVE

LOW PRESSURE INDICATOR

SECONDARY RESERVOIR

DOUBLE CHECK VALVE

SINGLE CHECK VALVE

SINGLE CHECK VALVE

PRIMARY RESERVOIR

DOUBLE CHECK VALVE

DOUBLE CHECK VALVE

HAND BRAKE VALVE

SUPPLY RESERVOIR

TRAILER SUPPLY

TRACTOR PARKING

RATIO VALVE

AIR COMPRESSOR

TRACTOR-TRAILER PARKING

MODULATOR CONTROLLER

Fig. 18-89 Dual air brake system—tractor service application. (*Freightliner Corporation*)

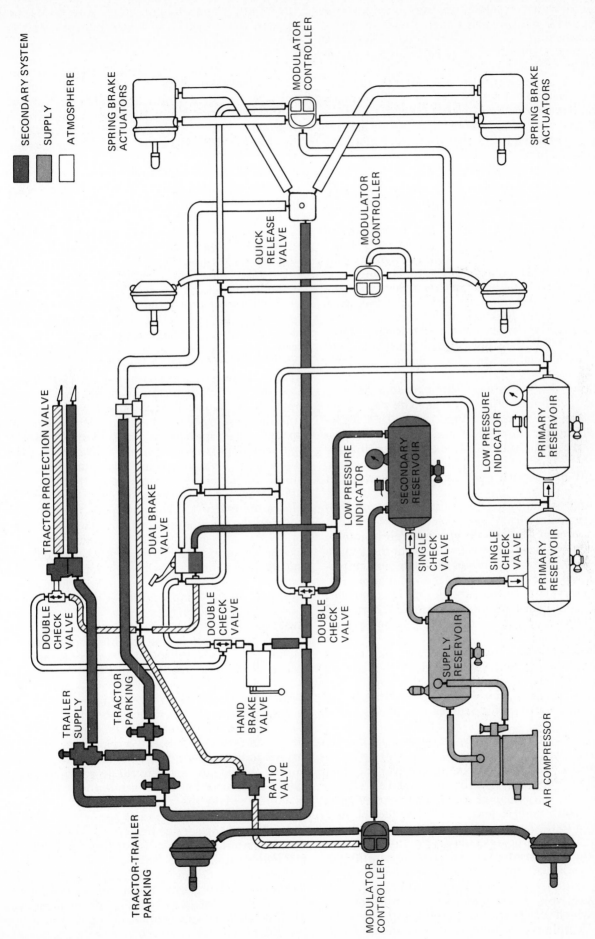

SECONDARY SYSTEM

SUPPLY

ATMOSPHERE

SPRING BRAKE ACTUATORS

MODULATOR CONTROLLER

SPRING BRAKE ACTUATORS

QUICK RELEASE VALVE

MODULATOR CONTROLLER

TRACTOR PROTECTION VALVE

DUAL BRAKE VALVE

LOW PRESSURE INDICATOR

SECONDARY RESERVOIR

LOW PRESSURE INDICATOR

PRIMARY RESERVOIR

DOUBLE CHECK VALVE

DOUBLE CHECK VALVE

DOUBLE CHECK VALVE

SINGLE CHECK VALVE

SINGLE CHECK VALVE

PRIMARY RESERVOIR

TRAILER SUPPLY

TRACTOR PARKING

HAND BRAKE VALVE

SUPPLY RESERVOIR

TRACTOR-TRAILER PARKING

RATIO VALVE

MODULATOR CONTROLLER

AIR COMPRESSOR

Fig. 18-90 Dual brake system with spring brake control valve (tractor primary system failure). (Freightliner Corporation)

If the secondary reservoir pressure were lost, the warning devices would be actuated and (only) the front axle would lose its service brake. **NOTE** If the primary reservoir or the secondary reservoir were to lose all its pressure, the hand application valve could, depending on which reservoir pressure was lost, override the service pressure of the primary or secondary service line (see Fig. 18-91).

If all reservoirs were gradually losing air and the pressure approached about 60 psi [413.4 kPa], the low-pressure indicator would actuate the warning devices. As the pressure reached 40 psi [275.6 kPa] or lower, the tractor protection control valve would snap out and thereby vent the supply line to the trailer, causing the parking brakes on the trailer to apply. The inlet of the tractor protection control valve would seat and protect the tractor reservoir air. However, the pressure would exhaust from the tractor's parking brake control valve and thus exhaust the tractor's parking brake air chambers, and the spring force would apply the brakes. Furthermore, the tractor-trailer's parking control valve air is also exhausted, which in turn, forces the trigger piston downward and thereby opens the exhaust valve and causes the inlet valve spring to close the inlet valve.

121 Trailer Brake Piping There are four or more different 121 trailer brake pipings. The most common is the one shown in Fig. 18-92. This trailer brake piping has three reservoirs; one service reservoir serves each trailer axle, and one (the third) is used for the parking brake. Some trailers, however, have only one service reservoir which serves both axles.

Air from the supply line is directed (paralleled) into each reservoir. A one-way check valve (not shown) on each service reservoir inlet port protects them from a reverse air flow in the event the supply line is disconnected or ruptured. Each service reservoir is directly connected to the modulator controller reservoir port; the service line is connected to each modulator controller service line port, and the delivery ports are connected to the service brake's air chambers.

Some trailer brake systems use only one modulator controller on the front-rear axle of the tandem trailer axle, since, during braking, the front trailer axle tends to skid earlier than the rear axle, owing to the weight transfer of the suspension during braking.

The parking brake valve in this case is an amplifying relay valve (see Fig. 18-93). Its inlet port is connected to the parking brake reservoir, the delivery port is connected to the spring brake air chamber, the air supply (emergency) line is connected to the emergency control port, and the service line is connected to the service control port.

The delivery ports are connected to the air chambers of the two parking brake units. The amplifying relay valve has an anticompounding two-way valve located in the upper valve body. The reaction (relay) piston has two different diameters. The area ratio is 1.75:1, which allows the parking brakes to be fully released with a controlling pressure of about 50 psi

[344.5 kPa]. The valve poppet is very similar in design to the valve poppet of a conventional relay valve or dual application valve.

OPERATION When the tractor protection control valve is pushed in, the supply air enters over the one-way check valve into the parking brake reservoir and is also directed onto the anticompounding two-way valve. The air pressure shifts the valve to the left, closing the service line port, and air pressure is exerted onto the reaction piston. This action forces the piston down, closing the exhaust valve and opening the inlet valve. Parking brake reservoir pressure is now allowed to flow past the open inlet valve, into the parking brake air chambers, to release the parking brakes (see Fig. 18-93b) when the two pressures acting on the reaction piston (from above and below) become equal in force (not pressure), the inlet valve closes and thereby holds the parking brake in the release position.

If the tractor protection control valve is actuated to exhaust the supply line (emergency) air, or if the supply air line glad hand is disconnected, the force from above the reaction piston is quickly reduced. As the pressure approaches about 50 psi [344.5 kPa], the trailer reservoir pressure acting (from below) on the reaction piston forces the piston upward, opens the exhaust valve, and thereby releases the air from the parking brake chambers. The parking brake spring's force applies the brakes (see Fig. 18-93c).

If, under this condition, the service brake is applied (and the parking brake reservoir still has pressure), the service line pressure shifts the two-way valve and forces the reaction piston down. This closes the exhaust valve and opens the inlet valve, causing the parking brakes to be released at a ratio of 1.75:1. This means that 75 percent pressure in excess of service line pressure is directed to the spring brake air chambers, to release the parking brakes in proportion to the service line pressure and thereby prevent compounding of brake application.

TESTING, SERVICING, AND CAUSES OF FAILURE Since routine procedures for the amplifying relay valve so closely resemble those for a conventional relay valve, they are omitted from this text.

Trailer Parking Brake Valve Design Another type of trailer parking brake valve is shown in Fig. 18-94. The parking brake reservoir is connected to the lower left reservoir port, the service reservoir is connected to the upper left service port, and the trailer supply line is connected to the lower right (supply port). The lower left port, beside the exhaust port, is connected to the air chambers of the parking brake, and the exhaust port is connected to the delivery line of the service brake.

The control piston is cross-drilled and partly center-drilled. It has two different diameters and is sealed with an O ring to the body bore. The spring holds the control piston to the right and holds the exhaust valve seat away from the inlet exhaust valve. The inlet exhaust spring holds the inlet valve against the inlet seat. The service reservoir check valve

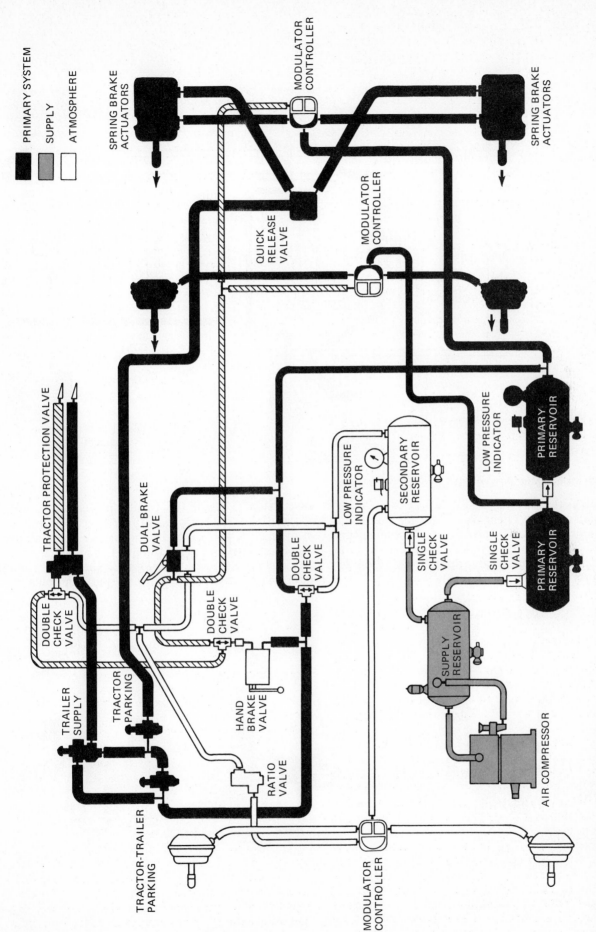

Fig. 18-91 Dual air brake system without spring brake control valve (tractor secondary system failure). *(Freightliner Corporation)*

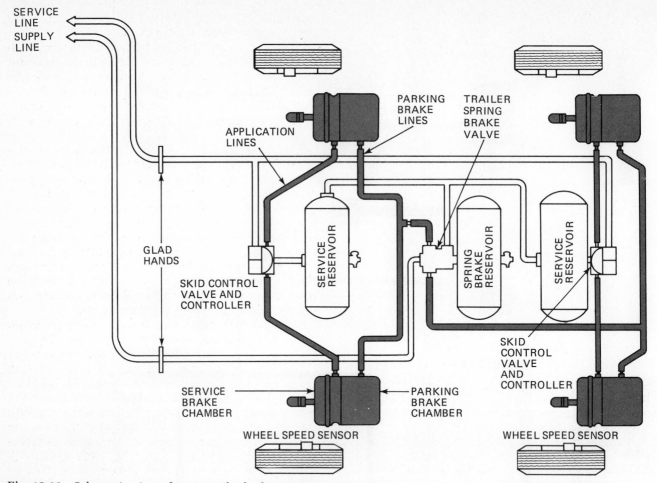

Fig. 18-92 Schematic view of a 121 trailer brake piping.

spring forces the valve against its seat, and the parking brake reservoir check valve spring holds the valve against its seat. The pressure protection spring holds the piston against the body shoulder, and the pressure protection inlet valve spring holds the inlet valve on its seat.

OPERATION When the tractor protection control valve directs air into the supply line, it enters the supply port, and several actions take place almost simultaneously (see Fig. 18-95): (1) it moves the control piston to the left, closing the exhaust valve and opening the inlet valve; (2) if the parking brake res-

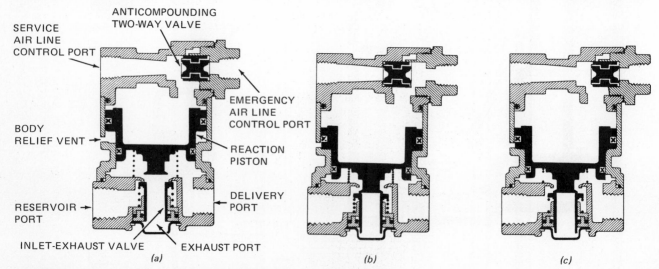

Fig. 18-93 Sectional view of an amplifying relay valve. (a) In the spring brake applied position. (b) When the emergency line pressure actuated the reaction piston and the parking brake reservoir pressure has released the parking brake. (c) In the parking brake release position but emergency air pressure lost. (*Wagner Electric Sales Corporation*)

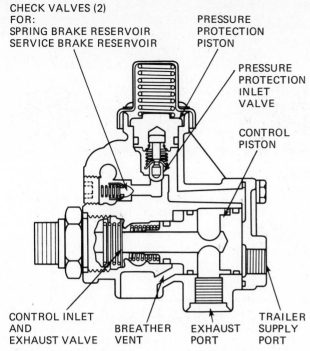

CHECK VALVES (2)
FOR:
SPRING BRAKE RESERVOIR
SERVICE BRAKE RESERVOIR

PRESSURE
PROTECTION
PISTON

PRESSURE
PROTECTION
INLET
VALVE

CONTROL
PISTON

CONTROL INLET
AND
EXHAUST VALVE

BREATHER
VENT

EXHAUST
PORT

TRAILER
SUPPLY
PORT

Fig. 18-94 Sectional view of a trailer parking brake valve. (*International Harvester Company*)

ervoir is charged, the air from it flows past the open inlet valve into the parking brake air chambers, releasing the brakes; (3) at about 55 psi [378.95 kPa] it moves the pressure protection piston upward, opening the inlet valve, and this action allows the supply air to flow over the check valve into the service reservoirs; (4) the air pressure also opens the parking brake reservoir check valve, and the air

flows into the reservoir and into the parking brake air chambers, releasing the brake.

When the tractor and trailer reservoirs are at cut-out pressure, the service and spring brake reservoir check valves are closed by their springs. The service reservoir check valve prevents a reverse air flow to the tractor reservoir, and the parking brake reservoir check valve prevents an air flow to the service brake reservoir.

When the tractor protection control valve or tractor-trailer parking brake control valve is pushed inward, or the supply line glad hands are uncoupled, the supply line is vented. The control piston instantly moves to the right, closing the inlet valve and opening the exhaust valve. The air from the parking brake air chambers passes by the open exhaust valve, travels through the center- and cross-drilled passages (in the control piston), out through the exhaust port, into the delivery line, through the open exhaust valve of the modulator controller, and out into the atmosphere (see Fig. 18-96).

When the trailer service reservoir loses pressure, a pressure loss also occurs in the supply line and the tractor reservoirs. When the air leak exceeds the amount of air that the compressor can supply, the pressure descends, and at about 60 psi [413.4 kPa] the low-pressure warning device is actuated, and the pressure protection valve spring forces the pressure protection valve on its seat. The supply line pressure and the tractor reservoir pressure are therefore maintained at about 50 psi [344.5 kPa]. This pressure is sufficient to hold the control piston to the left (see Fig. 18-97). If for some reason the supply line pressure drops even further, then the tractor protection control valve responds to the lower pressure and ex-

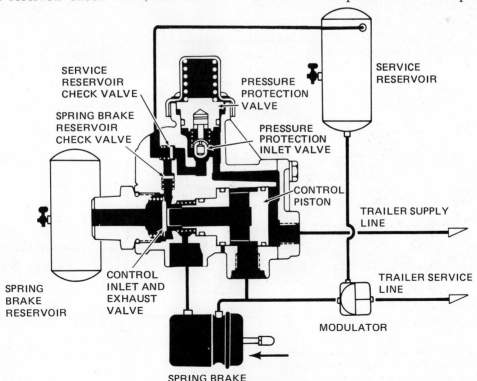

SERVICE
RESERVOIR
CHECK VALVE

SPRING BRAKE
RESERVOIR
CHECK VALVE

PRESSURE
PROTECTION
VALVE

SERVICE
RESERVOIR

PRESSURE
PROTECTION
INLET VALVE

CONTROL
PISTON

TRAILER SUPPLY
LINE

TRAILER SERVICE
LINE

MODULATOR

SPRING
BRAKE
RESERVOIR

CONTROL
INLET AND
EXHAUST
VALVE

SPRING BRAKE

Fig. 18-95 Schematic view of the trailer spring brake valve during charging of the service and parking brake reservoirs. (*International Harvester Company*)

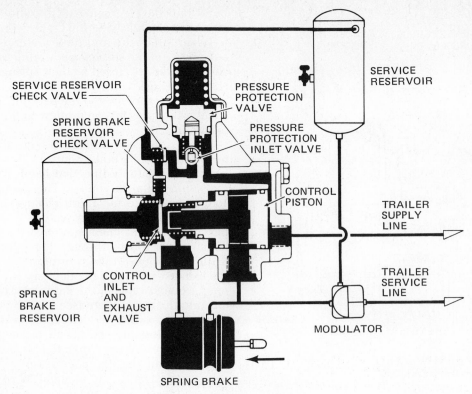

Fig. 18-96 Schematic view of the valve position when the supply pressure is lost.

hausts the supply line. This action removes the force from the control piston, opens the exhaust valve, closes the inlet valve, and the parking brake is applied.

TESTING Install to the trailer service and parking brake reservoirs air master gauges, and install a master gauge to the tractor reservoir. Start the engine, push the tractor protection valve in, and note the

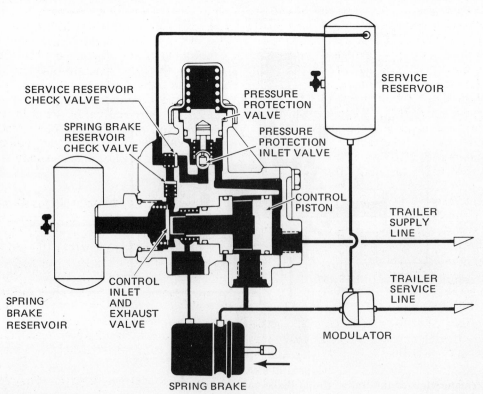

Fig. 18-97 Schematic view of the valve position when the service reservoir has lost pressure.

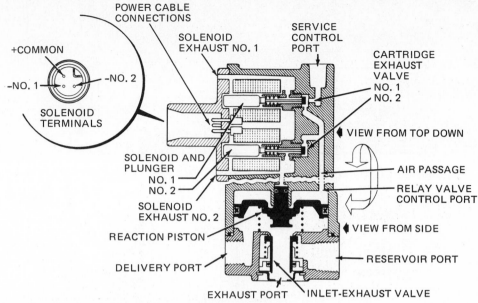

Fig. 18-98 Sectional view of a skid control, or modulator controller, valve. (*Wagner Electric Sales Corporation*)

tractor reservoir pressure. When the test gauge reads about 55 psi [378.95 kPa], it should reflect in the two trailer air gauges because the pressure protection piston will have lifted and opened the inlet valve. When the trailer pressure reaches this pressure, the parking brakes should begin to release. When the tractor reservoir pressure reaches cutoff pressure, you will note that the trailer reservoir pressure is slightly lower. At this point, stop the engine. If air leaks from the modulator controller exhaust port, supply air is leaking past the O ring on the control piston in the spring-brake valve, allowing air to enter the delivery line.

If air leaks from around the cap of the pressure control piston, its O ring is defective.

Next, uncouple the supply line glad hands—the trailer brakes should instantly apply, and no air should leak from the tractor glad hand. If air does leak, the inlet valve of the tractor protection control valve is not sealing properly. If air leaks from the trailer glad hand, the service reservoir check valve and the pressure protection inlet valve are leaking.

Recouple the supply line and actuate the tractor protection control valve to charge the trailer. The parking brakes should quickly release. Stop the engine and drain the trailer service reservoirs; the parking brake should remain released. Now actuate the tractor protection control valve to exhaust the supply line. The parking brake should apply quickly. Next, push the tractor protection control valve and the tractor-trailer parking control valve inward and hold them in this position. The parking brake should fully release.

NOTE The service procedure for the trailer parking brake valve is very similar to a relay valve and therefore need not be covered.

Modulator Controller The modulator controller (commonly called a *skid control valve*) is similar in design to a relay valve and performs the following

functions: it is instrumental in applying and releasing the service brake, and it responds to computer signal by reducing the service brake force, allowing the tires to roll, and thus prevents lockup.

DESIGN The valve body (which contains two solenoids and two exhaust cartridges) is fastened to a conventional relay valve. A passage runs from the service control port, past the exhaust valve 1, and to the control port of the relay valve, and another passage leads to the exhaust valve 2. The solenoid plunger is loosely fitted within the solenoid iron core. The exhaust valve cartridge is screwed into the housing, and the spring holds the exhaust valve closed. Each exhaust valve cartridge has its own exhaust valve passage leading out into the atmosphere. A three-wire pin connector is fastened to the cover and electrically connects the solenoid coils with the computer logic module. One pin is either positive or negative, depending on the polarity of the vehicle, and the other two are connected to the solenoid coil ends—one to the first solenoid coil end, and the other to the second solenoid coil end (see Fig. 18-98).

ELECTRICAL CONNECTIONS The modulator controller of a Wagner truck/tractor skid control system is connected, electrically, as shown in Fig. 18-99. From the tractor ignition switch or the trailer's seven-pin electrical connector, it is connected to the fault indicator terminal box (which also provides the connection for the tractor or trailer warning indicator). From the fuse box the wires are connected to the solid-stage computer modules. The wheel speed sensors from each wheel and the modulator valve are connected to the computer.

WHEEL SPEED SENSOR DESIGN There are two basic types of wheel speed sensors: the point type and the annular type (see Figs. 18-100 and 18-101). On both

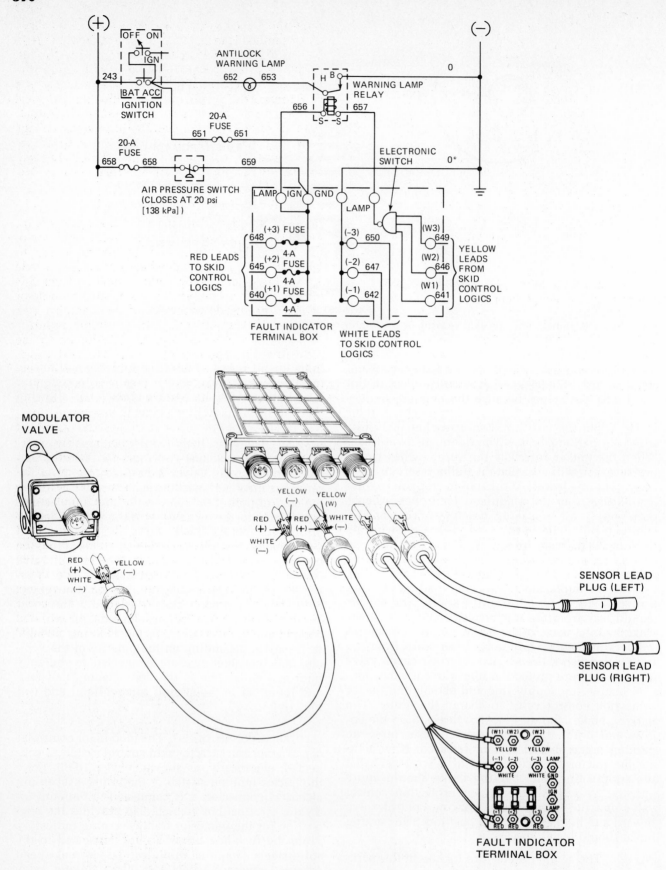

Fig. 18-99 Schematic of diagram of skid control system wiring. (*Wagner Electric Sales Corporation*)

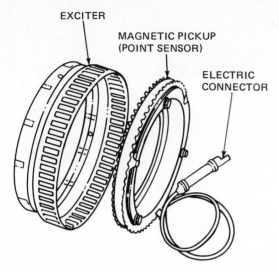

Fig. 18-100 View of an annular wheel speed sensor. (*Wagner Electric Sales Corporation*)

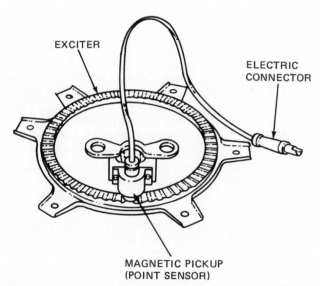

Fig. 18-101 View of a point wheel speed sensor. (*Wagner Electric Sales Corporation*)

types the exciter (which may have teeth or round or oblong holes) is fastened to the drum or wheel hub. The exciter diameter and the number of teeth (120 or 60) vary according to the wheel hub and/or the brake drum combination. The point or stator sensor is a permanent magnet variable reluctance device, and when the wheel turns, it generates an alternating-current frequency signal. The alternating voltage generated is in proportion to the wheel speed. At high speed the voltage and the frequency are high, and at low speed the voltage and frequency are low (see Fig. 18-102).

OPERATION Under normal conditions and appropriate brake application the relay valve responds to the service line pressure and applies the brakes. If, however, any individual wheel on the same axle slows down, the voltage and frequency from this wheel sensor decreases. The computer modulator receives the signal, responds to it, and energizes and deenergizes the solenoid with electronic rapidity. The solenoid plunger (armature) is forced to the right (through the magnetic action within the solenoid), into contact with the exhaust stem, opens exhaust valve 1, and closes the service air supply passage (see Fig. 18-103). Air from above the reaction piston slowly exhausts past the open exhaust valve, through the cartridge-valve stem, past the outside of the solenoid coil, into the atmosphere. The relay valve responds, reduces the delivery pressure, and thereby reduces the braking force. As the coil is deenergized, the service line pressure and cartridge spring close the exhaust valve and open the service line passage, and service line pressure is again directed onto the reaction piston. **NOTE** The rapid closure of the service line passage and the opening of the exhaust valve through exhaust valve 1 bring the relay valve into balance position. If the speed of one wheel is still lessening, the sensor voltage and frequency reduce further, and the computer modulator actuates solenoid 2 (rapidly cycled) and thereby opens and closes its exhaust valve. Exhaust

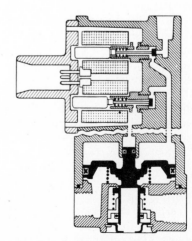

Fig. 18-103 Sectional view of modulator valve in the balance position (exhaust valve 1 open). (*Wagner Electric Sales Corporation*)

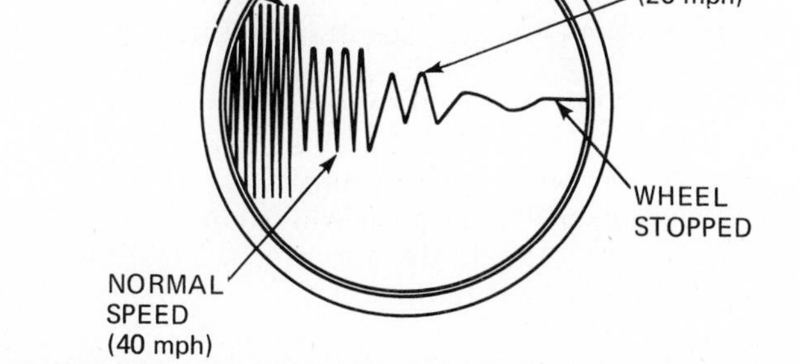

Fig. 18-102 View of an oscilloscope showing voltage and frequency at various wheel speeds. (*Wagner Electric Sales Corporation*)

372

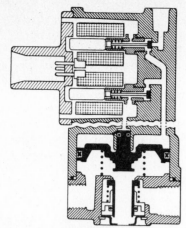

Fig. 18-104 Sectional view of modulator valve in the quick-exhausting position (exhaust valves 1 and 2 open). (*Wagner Electric Sales Corporation*)

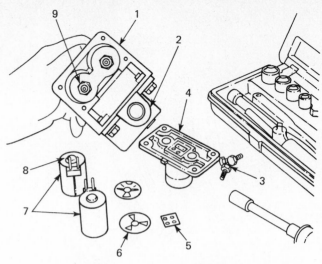

1. Upper valve body	6. Solenoid cover plate
2. Lower valve body	7. Solenoid coils
3. Cover screws	8. Solenoid coil cover
4. Cover	9. Exhaust valve cartridges
5. Insulator gasket	

Fig. 18-105 Exploded view of upper valve components. (*Wagner Electric Sales Corporation*)

air from above the reaction piston is speeded up and thus reduces delivery pressure and prevents a wheel lockup (see Fig. 18-104).

TESTING AND SERVICING To check for an internal air leak, bring the air system to cutout pressure and gradually apply the brakes. If air leaks from exhaust port 1, exhaust valve 1 fails to seat. If air leaks from exhaust port 2, exhaust valve 2 fails to seat.

To check the solenoid coil for open, short, and ground, connect one lead of the ohmmeter to the common ground (or positive terminal) and the other lead first to solenoid 1 and then to the solenoid 2 connection. Compare the ohmmeter reading with the resistance specified in the service manual.

To check that exhaust valve 1 closes the service line passage, connect a 12-volt battery to the common terminal and the other battery lead to solenoid 1. (Be sure to check the polarity.) This action opens the exhaust valve and closes the service line passage. Now apply the brakes, and if air leaks from the exhaust port, the exhaust valve is not closing the service line passage.

To service the modulator controller, prepare the vehicle as outlined for servicing the compressor. Next, remove the service line, the reservoir line, and the delivery line and then unscrew and remove the cable connector. After the valve is removed and cleaned, remove the upper valve body and service the relay valve as previously outlined.

To replace the exhaust valve cartridge, remove parts as follows: the cover screws, the cover, the two plungers, the solenoid cover plate, the insulator gasket, the two solenoid coils (with covers), and the spring washer and then unscrew the two exhaust valve cartridges (see Fig. 18-105).

Discard all parts which are supplied in the service kit.

After cleaning the upper valve body, check the surface for warpage, the service line passage seat for damage, and the threaded bores for damaged threads. If everything proves satisfactory, reassemble the valve parts precisely in the reverse order of that in which they were disassembled.

CHECKING AND TESTING THE SENSOR Any correctly mounted point sensor automatically adjusts to the correct distance from the exciter. However, when the wheel bearings are too loosely adjusted, damaged, or worn, they cause excessive exciter runout. Reduced sensor voltage out-put will result and the warning light will react as soon as the vehicle moves. **NOTE** If the point sensor is accidentally forced back while the wheel hub is being installed, it must be readjusted to the minimum distance from the exciter (see Fig. 18-106). The annular wheel speed sensor does not require adjustment; however, loose wheel bearings create the same problems as those encountered on the point-type sensor.

To remove the point-type sensor (in order to check for excessive point wear), you may have to cut the tie strap which holds the sensor cable to the delivery line, remove the sensor computer cable, and then remove the sensor mounting bolts. **NOTE** The mounting and the self-adjusting device vary in accordance with the type of point center.

CAUTION When the gauge blocks are worn, they must be replaced, and when the point face shows excessive bare metal, the sensor must be replaced. After removing the sensor, check it with an ohmmeter for an open, short, or ground circuit.

To check the exciter for wear and damage, rotate the wheel slowly as you examine the exciter. (Some slight wear is always noticeable.)

When reinstalling a sensor which checked out satisfactorily, always refer to, and precisely follow, the service manual instructions.

TESTING THE COMPONENTS Defective electric wiring is usually the cause of skid control malfunction. Electrical defects are reflected in the antiskid warn-

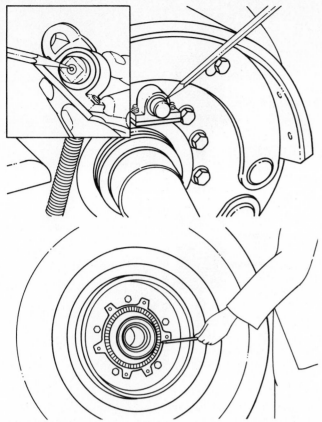

Fig. 18-106 View of point sensor and exciter. (*Wagner Electric Sales Corporation*)

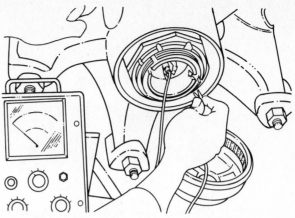

Fig. 18-107 Measuring sensor or cable for resistance. (*Wagner Electric Sales Corporation*)

ing light or otherwise indicated by uncontrolled wheel lockup. In order to successfully check out the skid control electrical system, you must be completely conversant with the entire circuit system. You will also require such aids as the pertinent service manual and an ohmmeter and a voltmeter. In view of variations among the numerous skid control systems, only a general testing procedure can be outlined.

Normally, the first step is to check all fuses and to visually inspect the cables and wires for damage to determine if the connections are resistance-free. Next, determine if the point sensors are properly adjusted. Check the power supply (correct voltage) at the power terminal. Voltage below specification indicates high resistance occurring at a point prior to the power terminal of the skid control.

Next, measure the voltage leading to each axle and determine if power is available to each axle system. This decision can be reached by following the procedures outlined in the service manual. If you find a faulty axle, remove the connection between this axle and the computer module and then measure the voltage. If it does not come within manual specification, there is high resistance in the power cable, the fuse, or the connection.

Next, use an ohmmeter and check the sensor wire for continuity and the coil for open, short, or ground (see Fig. 18-107). Check both solenoid coils of the modulator controller for an open, short, or ground circuit. Your service manual will give you the correct coil resistance.

To check if the sensor is adjusted and operating properly, raise the axle to lift the wheels off the ground. Connect a voltmeter to the sensor connectors, switch the voltmeter to ac voltage, and then rotate the wheel (by hand) about one to two revolutions per second (see Fig. 18-108). Note the voltage. Repeat the procedure for the other wheel of the same axle. The voltmeter reading from both sensors should be about the same (around 0.02 to 0.05 volt). If the adjustment is correct, there will be very little or no voltage difference.

If, after all tests are made, the electrical components check out satisfactorily but the skid control still does not operate properly, exchange the computer module and recheck the skid control system.

NOTE Where a truck, bus, or tractor air brake system is not designed to accommodate air brakes to the trailer (see Fig. 18-109), the following components would not be present: hand valve, tractor-trailer parking control valve, tractor protection control valve, tractor protection valve and glad hands, and the two 2-way valves.

Pressure Protection Valve Nearly all air brake vehicles use accessories that are air actuated. A pressure protection valve is therefore used to protect the air brake system and to maintain emergency pressure in the event that the accessory devices develop

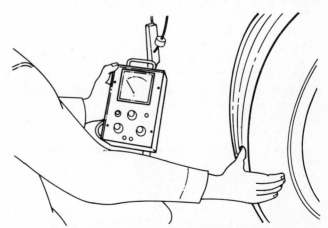

Fig. 18-108 Measuring wheel sensor voltage. (*Wagner Electric Sales Corporation*)

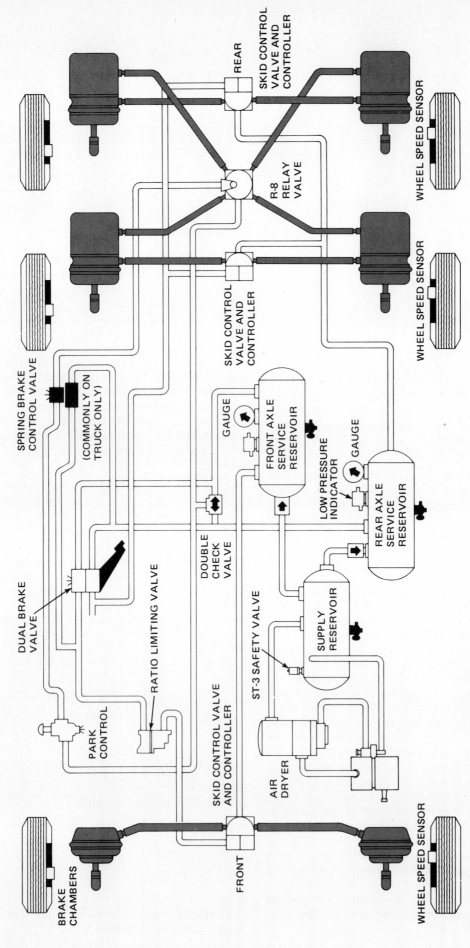

Fig. 18-109 Schematic view of a motor truck 121 piping. (*International Harvester Company*)

375

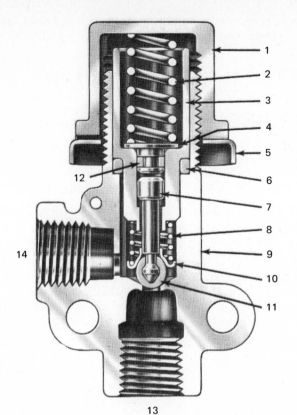

1. Adjusting cap
2. Piston return spring
3. Piston
4. Piston ring
5. Nut
6. O ring
7. Valve stem
8. Valve return spring
9. Body
10. Valve guide
11. Valve
12. Seal ring
13. Outlet port
14. Inlet port

Fig. 18-110 Sectional view of pressure protection valve. (Terex Division of General Motors Corporation)

an excessive air leak. It is placed into the air line leading from the supply reservoir to the accessories (air horn, transmission, etc., control valves).

DESIGN AND OPERATION The valve body has a threaded inlet and outlet port. Inside the body is the piston, which contains the valve stem and the valve. When no air pressure is being exerted onto the piston, the piston spring forces the piston against its stop, and the valve spring forces the valve against its seat. As the reservoir pressure builds to the adjusted pressure, approximately 60 psi [413.6 kPa], the piston is forced upward and lifts the valve off its seat, allowing air to flow to the accessory control valves. As soon as the pressure is equal (inlet and outlet), the check valve spring closes the inlet valve, preventing a reverse flow from the accessories to the tractor (see Fig. 18-110).

TESTING With the reservoirs void of air, start the engine and actuate the air horn control valve. Using an air leakage tester, hold the detector near the check valve to determine if the check valve is seating properly. Take note when the air horn is first audible.

When using an air leakage detector, note when the air flow first occurs. The air should flow at a reservoir pressure of about 60 psi [413.6 kPa].

Review Questions

1. What advantages has an air brake system over other types of brake systems?

2. (a) List the components of a basic air-brake system. (b) State the purpose of each air brake system component. (c) Outline the test or service procedure for each component.

3. Explain why nearly all air brake valves are similar in design and operating principle.

4. Explain the operation of the foot application valve (brake valve) (Fig. 18-13): (a) in the release position, (b) in the applied position, (c) in the hold position, (d) during releasing of the application pressure.

5. For what purpose are dual-brake valves used (on-highway motor trucks and truck tractors)?

6. (a) Service the following: a relay valve, a brake chamber, and a dual-brake valve. (b) List, for each valve, the components which you would replace to prevent valve malfunction.

7. Select a training motor vehicle having a dual-brake valve. (a) Sketch its air-brake system on a sheet of paper. (b) List the components which are additional to a basic air brake system. (c) Record the sizes and types of air brake hoses used to connect the components.

8. Referring to question 7, explain the use of: (a) three reservoirs, (b) an air dryer or sludge remover, (c) a safety valve, (d) in several places, single- and/or double-check valves.

9. What is the purpose of: (a) a low pressure indicator, (b) a stoplight switch?

10. (a) What is the purpose of the parking brake? (b) What are the performance requirements of the parking brake?

11. (a) What are the functions of a parking brake control valve? (b) Explain the mechanical action and air flow within the parking brake, after the reservoir pressure has dropped to about 50 psi [344.5 kPa].

12. (a) In what way are all parking brakes similar? (b) What are the main differences?

13. Using a training motor vehicle, list the relative recommended steps and safety precautions when: (a) removing a parking brake chamber from the selected motor vehicle, (b) when disassembling the brake chamber, (c) when reassembling the parking brake chamber.

14. Explain the mechanical action and air flow of the spring brake valve when: (a) the reservoirs are being charged, (b) the service brake is applied and the secondary system has lost its pressure, (c) the service brake is applied and the primary system has lost its pressure, (d) the secondary pressure and primary pressure drop below 50 psi [344.5 kPa].

15. (a) What are the two functions of the two air valves (that is, the limiting quick-release valve and the two-way control valve)? (b) Which valve is used to replace the limiting quick-release valve and the two-way control valve?

16. (a) Name the air valves that are located on a truck-tractor to supply the full or semitrailer with supply air or emergency air and service air? (b) What is the purpose of each of these valves?

17. Which two types of air valves could be used to prevent an air loss of the motortruck or truck-tractor in the event the full or semitrailer is not connected, or it accidentally breaks away?

18. (a) List the three functions of a relay emergency valve. (b) Explain the mechanical action and air flow when the trailer reservoir pressures drop to, say, 40 psi [275.6 kPa].

19. Assume you have a truck-tractor with a dual air brake system, and the semitrailer uses emergency valves. List all the air brake checks and tests you would make when servicing such equipment, before turning it back to the operator.

20. List five reasons why some motor vehicles and pole trailers have water-cooled brake drums.

21. What is the primary function of an FMVSS 121 truck-tractor trailer's air brake system?

22. (a) What additional or alternate air brake valve components complement the truck-tractor trailer's FMVSS 121 air brake system? (b) State the purpose of each of these components.

23. Explain the current flow, the electrical action, the mechanical action, and the air flow when the brakes are applied, but the tires of one axle start to skid.

24. List the steps and tests you must make when servicing the brakes, to ensure that the three electrical or electronic brake components are functioning correctly or are adjusted correctly.

Unit 19
Engine Brakes

Engine Brakes, Exhaust Brakes, and Hydraulic Retarders The purpose of an engine brake is to increase the retarding force of an engine. This improves braking control and extends the service life of the vehicle's brake drums, brake linings, and tires. Exhaust brakes and hydraulic retarders are devices of different design that may be fitted to diesel engines to perform the same function.

Two types of engine brake are manufactured by the Jacobs Manufacturing Company, both called the Jacobs engine brake, and one is designed and manufactured by Mack Truck, Inc., and is called the Mack Dynatard. The Jacobs engine brakes can be installed on all Cummins and Detroit engines and on the six-cylinder Maxidyne and 711 Series Mack diesel engines.

Both Mack Dynatard and Jacobs engine brake designs convert a power-producing diesel engine into a power-absorbing air compressor, a conversion made possible by the interaction of electrical components, hydraulic valves, and pistons, and the engine itself. It is achieved by using the engine compression stroke to gain mechanical friction. As the piston nears top dead center (TDC), the exhaust valve allows the compressed cylinder air to expand into the exhaust manifold and then into the atmosphere. Therefore there is no power stroke. In other words, the retarding power is realized during the compression stroke, and no force is exerted on the piston on the following power stroke, resulting in an increased energy loss.

JACOBS ENGINE BRAKE

The type of engine and the engine model onto which the brake housing will be installed govern the housing design and size (see Fig. 19-1). For instance, the K-model engine brake unit serves only one cylinder, and the master cylinder is actuated by the lug formed on the rocker arm. The brake unit used for other Cummins engines serves two cylinders, and the master cylinder is actuated by the rocker arm adjusting screw.

Design The engine brake unit for the Detroit diesel engine serves only one cylinder, and the brake housing design varies according to the engine model. The engine brake unit used on Mack engines serves three cylinders.

Notwithstanding the foregoing inconsistencies, all these engine brake units use the same components within or fastened to the brake housing. Both the Detroit diesel and Cummins engine designs use the combined effort of the camshaft, follower, pushrod, and rocker arm to accomplish injection. Furthermore, the beginning of injection is about 17° before TDC.

The illustrations, (see Figs. 19-2 to 19-4) show the design of the components, the electrical circuit, the switches, the solenoid, the oil flow, and the mechanical components.

You will note from the cutaway view (Figs. 19-1 to 19-4) that the solenoid housing is screwed into the brake housing and the O rings are used to seal the oil passages. A three-way valve (spool) is located inside the solenoid valve. One end of the solenoid coil is internally grounded; the other end of the coil is connected in series with the throttle switch (Cummins) or the buffer switch (Detroit), and to the clutch switch, the dashboard switch, the fuse or the circuit breaker, and then to the ignition switch. When the electrical circuit is deenergized, the spool is forced upward by the valve spool spring, and the oil supply port is thereby closed.

Mechanical Notes

- With the engine clutch pedal fully released the clutch is engaged, the clutch switch is closed, and as soon as the clutch pedal is forced down (commencement of clutch release), the clutch switch opens.
- The fuel pump switch is open when the throttle lever is above the low idle fuel position, and it is closed when the throttle lever is at idle position.
- The buffer switch is open when the differential lever contacts the buffer switch pin (Detroit).
- The dashboard switch is an on, off switch.
- A diode is placed in parallel with the fuel switch to protect the switch contacts against transit voltage.

The control valve piston with ball check valve is fitted within its bore. The piston is center- and cross-drilled, and the center-drilled passage is held closed by the check ball. The control valve spring holds the control valve piston down and thereby opens the oil passage from the slave and master pistons, allowing the oil to leave the control valve. The slave piston spring is fitted within the bore of the slave piston, and the U-shaped end of the piston straddles the valve bridge but allows the rocker arm unrestricted movement. The slave piston spring forces the piston upward against the adjusting screw. The master piston is held within the master piston bore with a forklike spring. The injector pushrod rocker arm adjusting screw rests against the lower circle of the master piston.

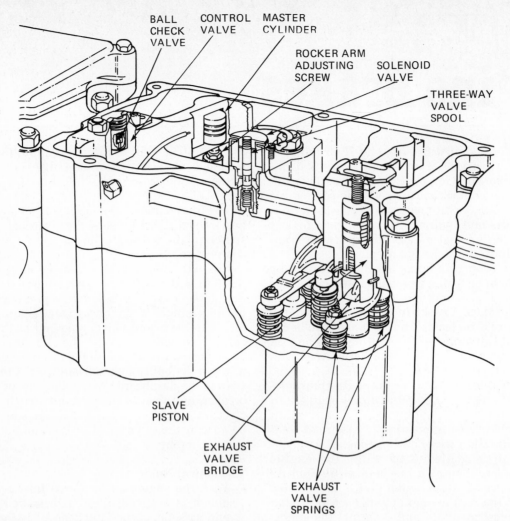

BALL CHECK VALVE
CONTROL VALVE
MASTER CYLINDER
ROCKER ARM ADJUSTING SCREW
SOLENOID VALVE
THREE-WAY VALVE SPOOL
SLAVE PISTON
EXHAUST VALVE BRIDGE
EXHAUST VALVE SPRINGS

Fig. 19-1 Cutaway view of a Jacobs brake used on a Cummins engine. (*The Jacobs Manufacturing Company*)

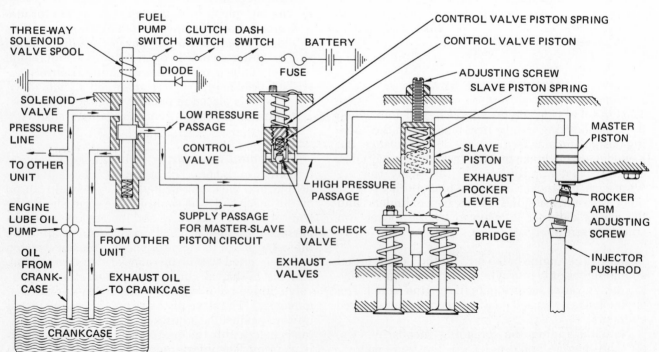

THREE-WAY SOLENOID VALVE SPOOL
FUEL PUMP SWITCH
CLUTCH SWITCH
DASH SWITCH
BATTERY
DIODE
FUSE
CONTROL VALVE PISTON SPRING
CONTROL VALVE PISTON
ADJUSTING SCREW
SLAVE PISTON SPRING
SOLENOID VALVE
PRESSURE LINE
TO OTHER UNIT
LOW PRESSURE PASSAGE
CONTROL VALVE
SLAVE PISTON
EXHAUST ROCKER LEVER
MASTER PISTON
ENGINE LUBE OIL PUMP
FROM OTHER UNIT
HIGH PRESSURE PASSAGE
ROCKER ARM ADJUSTING SCREW
OIL FROM CRANKCASE
SUPPLY PASSAGE FOR MASTER-SLAVE PISTON CIRCUIT
BALL CHECK VALVE
VALVE BRIDGE
INJECTOR PUSHROD
EXHAUST OIL TO CRANKCASE
EXHAUST VALVES
CRANKCASE

Fig. 19-2 Schematic illustration of Jacobs engine brake components (Cummins). (*The Jacobs Manufacturing Company*)

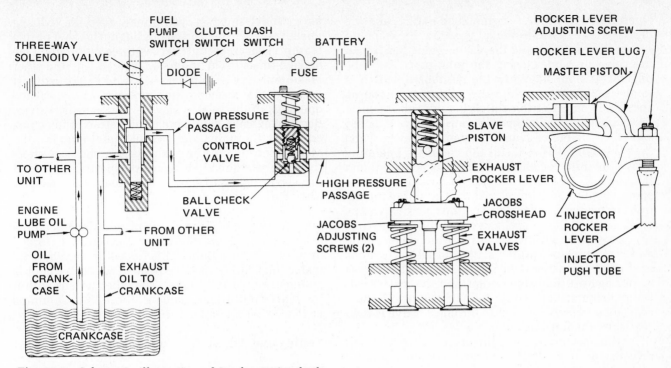

Fig. 19-3 Schematic illustration of Jacobs engine brake components (Cummins K model). (*The Jacobs Manufacturing Company*)

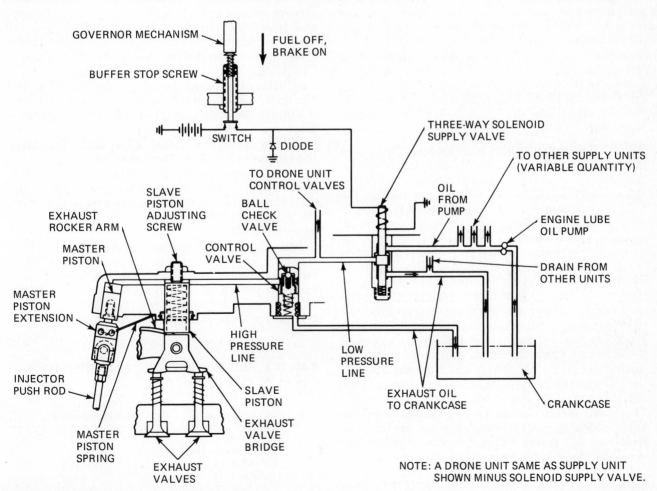

Fig. 19-4 Schematic illustration of one of the diesel brake units. (*The Jacobs Manufacturing Company*)

Operation   When the engine is operating, and the dashboard switch is in the off position, the solenoid coil is deenergized, and the valve spring has forced the valve upward, closing the inlet port. The lube oil flow is stopped. When the dashboard switch is in the on position, while the engine is operating above idle speed or the clutch is released, the electrical circuit remains open because the fuel pump switch or the buffer switch is open. However, when the throttle is released, and the engine is operating above low idle speed, the solenoid is actuated, and the valve spool allows lube oil to flow through the spool valve to the control piston. The following actions immediately take place: (1) the check valve lifts off its seat; (2) the control valve piston lifts, and lube oil passes through the valve onto the slave piston and master piston; (3) the slave and master pistons are forced down, the U-end of the slave piston comes to rest against the valve bridge, and the master cylinder piston comes to rest against the injector rocker arm adjusting screws; and (4) the check valve is then seated by the force of its spring.

As the injector cam lobe lifts its follower, it moves the injector pushrod upward, pivots the rocker arm, and moves the injector plunger downward. At the same time the following actions occur: (1) the push rod forces the master piston upward; (2) this increases the oil pressure within the passage, between the master piston, and the check valve; (3) the engine piston is now on compression stroke and has reached a position of about 20° BTDC; (4) the master piston continues to move upward; and (5) the increased oil pressure exerted on the slave piston now forces the piston down, and the valve bridge is moved onto the exhaust valve stem ends, opening the exhaust valves. This action releases the compressed air within the cylinder into the exhaust manifold.

NOTE   The exhaust valve remains open during the power stroke, the exhaust stroke, and part of the intake stroke (Cummins). On the Detroit diesel engine, at about 120° BTDC, the injector cam lobe allows the follower to come onto the base circle of the cam. If no change occurs electrically, the same cycle is repeated until the throttle lever moves away from the fuel switch or the differential lever moves away from the buffer switch (see discussion of adjustment), or the solenoid is deenergized, or the clutch pedal is depressed. Under any of these conditions, the solenoid is deenergized, and the valve spring moves the valve spool upward, closing the inlet port. The control valve piston comes to rest against the bottom of the bore and opens the return port (not shown), allowing the oil in the passage and from the bores of the slave piston and master piston to drain onto the top of the cylinder head, reducing the oil pressure. The slave piston spring moves the slave piston against its stop (away from the valve bridge), the master piston spring forces the master piston upward, and the engine returns to normal operation.

Mack Jacobs Engine Brake   Mack diesel engines use a Bosch fuel injection system; therefore, the mas-

ter cylinder must be positioned over the exhaust pushrods to actuate the Jacobs engine brake. For this reason each brake unit serves three cylinders. One brake unit serves cylinders 1, 2, and 3, and the other brake unit serves cylinders 4, 5, and 6. The exhaust valves of the master piston are used to control the openings of the related slave piston exhaust valves. Because exhaust valves are used instead of injectors, as on the Cummins and Detroit diesel engines, the Mack Jacobs engine brakes are somewhat less effective. The relationship between the master piston and the slave piston is shown in Table 19-1. **NOTE** The firing order is 1–5–3–6–2–4.

OPERATION   When the piston of cylinder 1 is on the exhaust stroke, and the exhaust pushrod is forced upward, master cylinder 1 is forced upward and actuates the cylinder 3 slave piston (which cylinder is on the compression stroke). The other actions within the brake unit are the same as those of a Cummins or Detroit diesel brake unit.

Testing and Adjusting—Cummins

CAUTION   When the engine is operating above low idle, do not manually depress the solenoid plunger, because a higher fuel flow is present at this time, and more fuel is injected into the cylinders.

When engine brake failure occurs, visually check all connections and check the adjustment of the fuel and clutch switches (see Fig. 19-5). To check the clutch switch adjustment, depress the clutch pedal 2 in [5.08 cm] and then slowly release the pedal. You should hear the switch click about $\frac{1}{2}$ in [12.7 cm] before the clutch pedal is fully released. You can then be sure that the switch is open shortly after the clutch pedal is moved but before the free play is taken up.

To check the fuel switch adjustment, first bring the engine to idle speed and then stop it. Move the throttle lever to the off idle position and then slowly move it to the idle position. Immediately before the throttle reaches the idle position, you should hear the switch click (see Fig. 19-6). If this occurs, the adjustment is correct.

Next check the electrical system. With the engine stopped and with the ignition and dashboard switches at the on position, measure (with a voltmeter) the voltage at each solenoid. It should not read less than 0.4 volt of the open battery voltage. If it is less, then measure the voltage drop at each

Table 19-1 RELATIONSHIP BETWEEN MASTER PISTON AND SLAVE PISTON

Master piston exhaust valve	Slave piston exhaust valve
Cylinder 1	Cylinder 3
Cylinder 5	Cylinder 6
Cylinder 3	Cylinder 2
Cylinder 6	Cylinder 4
Cylinder 2	Cylinder 1
Cylinder 4	Cylinder 5

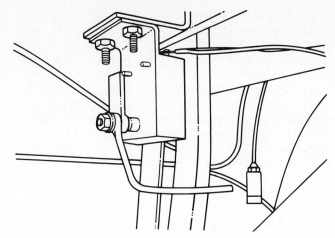

Fig. 19-5 View of clutch switch installation. (*Cummins Engine Company, Inc.*)

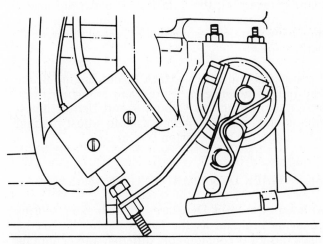

Fig. 19-6 View of fuel switch installation.

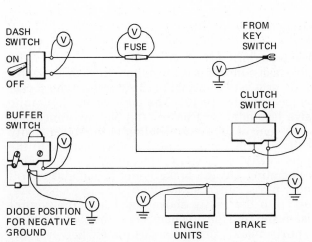

Fig. 19-7 Schematic view of voltmeter connections to check the electrical circuit. (*The Jacobs Manufacturing Company*)

Fig. 19-8 Measuring and adjusting slave piston clearance on a Cummins K model. (*The Jacobs Manufacturing Company*)

switch or (with an ohmmeter) measure the resistance of each switch to determine which of the components has the high resistance (see Fig. 19-7).

CAUTION Do not forget to turn off the ignition switch before using the ohmmeter; otherwise you will ruin the meter.

To check the solenoid coil for an open, short, or grounded circuit, measure each coil's resistance with an ohmmeter and compare it with the specification in the service manual. If the solenoid coil is open, short, or grounded, remove the valve cover, disconnect the solenoid wire, and loosen and remove the solenoid with a solenoid wrench. Clean the bore making certain that no rubber particles remain in the bore. Place well-lubricated O rings in the upper and center O ring grooves of the new solenoid, and one O ring into the bottom of the solenoid bore. Guide the solenoid into its bore and tighten it to the specified torque. Connect the wire and recheck its operation. If other mechanical failures are suspected, replace the brake unit.

After the new brake unit is installed, torque it to specification. Position the locking taps and recheck the rocker arm for clearance. You must then adjust the slave piston clearance. To do this, first turn the crankshaft until the VS mark of the cylinder requiring adjustment lines up with the timing mark. At this position, the exhaust and intake valves should be closed. If they are not closed, then you are on the wrong stroke and you will therefore have to turn the crankshaft an additional 360°. After turning the crankshaft, insert the specified feeler stock gauge between the slave piston and cross-head (valve bridge). Turn the adjusting screw with an Allen wrench until a slight drag is felt as the gauge is moved in and out. When the adjustment is made, hold the wrench while tightening the locknut to lock in the adjustment. Refer to service manual when adjusting the slave piston clearance on Cummins K model (see Fig. 19-8).

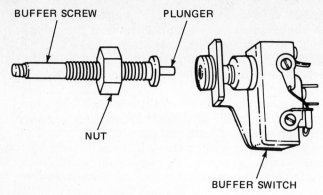

Fig. 19-9 Buffer switch and buffer screw. (*The Jacobs Manufacturing Company*)

Testing and Adjusting—Detroit Diesel The Cummins procedure covered in the previous paragraphs also applies to the following Detroit diesel tests and adjustments: the electrical test, clutch switch adjustment, replacement of the solenoid, and adjustment of the slave piston, except that the slave piston clearance differs between the Detroit and Cummins engines and that the Detroit engines have no VS timing marks. Refer to the appropriate service manual for the specified clearance with regard to model and engine timing.

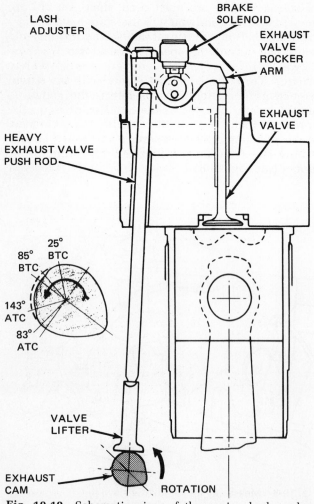

Fig. 19-10 Schematic view of the engine brake valve train. (*Mack Canada Inc.*)

The adjustment of the buffer switch is not necessarily the same. Furthermore, before checking the switch adjustment, the buffer screw adjustment should be checked. To check the buffer switch, first loosen the nut to separate the buffer switch from the buffer screw (see Fig. 19-9). **CAUTION** Do not loosen the switch-mounting screws, because the switch is preadjusted by the manufacturer. Next, start the engine and adjust the buffer screw in accordance with the service manual instructions. Insert the buffer switch plunger and reattach the switch to the buffer screw. To check your adjustment, start the engine, switch on the dashboard switch, fully open the throttle (manually), and then release it quickly. The governor should respond by forcing the differential lever to contact the buffer screw spring, moving the buffer switch plunger against the buffer switch, closing the switch, and actuating the brakes. When the engine speed is reduced to about 900 rpm, the force on the differential lever is reduced, and the buffer switch opens. If the switch opens too early or too late, check the service manual regarding the adjustment, make the necessary adjustment, and then reattach the switch to the mounting part of the governor and retest the switch's performance.

Testing and Adjusting—Mack Jacobs Engine Brake The only difference in testing and adjusting these brakes as opposed to Cummins and Detroit diesel engine brakes is the method used to adjust the fuel switch and the slave piston clearance.

MACK DYNATARD ENGINE BRAKE

Although the Mack Dynatard engine brake performs the same function as the Jacobs engine brake, the Mack design is considerably different and cannot be transferred from one engine to another, because each exhaust camshaft lobe base circle is specially contoured with a small lift profile. The contour is ground (timed) so as to open the exhaust valve near TDC when the piston is on compression stroke and the engine brake is actuated.

Design To control the exhaust valve clearance for normal exhaust valve action, and to close up the clearance during the Dynatard braking, a hydraulic valve lash adjuster is screwed into the exhaust valve rocker arm, and a special pushrod rests in the socket piston (see Fig. 19-10). The body of the hydraulic valve lash adjuster (rocker arm) has two inner passages—one at the center leading to the lower cavity of the control piston, and the other leading to the upper cavity of the control piston. When the engine is operating but the brake is not actuated, lube oil under pressure flows into the two passages (see Fig. 19-11), to the cavity above and below the control piston and into the oil chambers of the socket piston. A fairly heavy spring is positioned between the spring retainer (sealed to the body) and the control piston, upsetting the equal force of the oil pressure that is exerted on the control piston and thereby

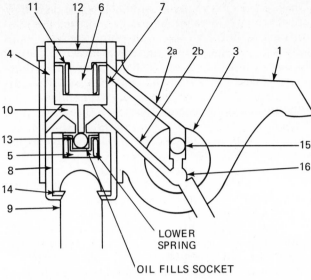

LOWER
SPRING

OIL FILLS SOCKET

1. Rocker arm	9. Push rod
2a. Top passage	10. Reservoir
2b. Center passage	11. Spring
3. Rocker arm shaft	12. Spring retainer
4. Valve lash adjuster	13. Ball valve
5. Lower oil cavity	14. Retainer ring
6. Upper oil cavity	15. Rocker arm shaft oil
7. Control piston	passage control gallery
8. Socket piston	16. Constant supply gallery

Fig. 19-11 Sectional view of the rocker arm, rocker shaft, and valve lash adjuster. (*Mack Canada Inc.*)

holding it downward against the body bore. The extended tip of the control piston forces the ball check valve off its seat.

The socket piston fits in the lower body bore, and a spring located between the spring seat cage and socket piston holds the piston against the pushrod. The piston's downward movement is restricted by a retainer ring.

The rocker arm shaft has two rifle-drilled passages—one called the *constant supply gallery* and the other known as the *on-off control gallery*. A solenoid, having a free-floating ball check valve, is screwed into the rocker arm shaft. **NOTE** Two solenoids are used for a six-cylinder engine, and four solenoids, for an eight-cylinder engine. (Each eight-cylinder head has its own solenoid.) The lower O ring seals off the constant supply gallery from the on-off control gallery, and the other O ring is used as a seal between the solenoid and the rocker arm shaft (see Fig. 19-12). The cross-drilled passage connects the on-off control gallery oil with the cavity below the ball check valve, and the center passage is open to the constant supply gallery oil. When the solenoid is deenergized, the armature extension allows the ball check valve to float upward but without closing the control passage leading to the upper inlet port in the hydraulic lash adjuster.

Electric Circuit and Components The electric system (see Fig. 19-13) consists of the engine brake's on-off switch, mounted to the dashboard; the fuel injection pump switch, mounted to the fuel injection pump governor housing, which closes the switch

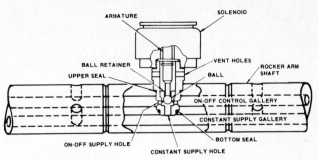

Fig. 19-12 Sectional view of rocker arm shaft and solenoid. (*Mack Canada Inc.*)

when the fuel rack is in the no fuel position and opens the switch when the fuel rack is above low idle fuel position; the control relay, which reduces the current flow over the fuel injection pump switch to protect against transit voltage; and the solenoids, which control the direction of oil flow.

Operation When the ignition switch is on, current flows from the ignition switch over a circuit breaker (not shown) to the heater relay terminal 1. From terminal 2 the current flows to the dashboard engine brake switch, from there to the control relay, and then to the fuel rack switch. **NOTE** A diode is connected to the engine terminal to protect the fuel microswitch against transit voltage (not shown).

If the fuel rack is in the no fuel position, the switch is closed, and current flows in parallel to the two or four solenoids. The solenoid coils are then energized, the armature is forced down, and the valve stem forces the ball check valve onto its seat. This stops the oil flow into the on-off control gallery, into the controlled oil supply passage, and into the upper control piston cavity. The oil pressure in the cavity is reduced as the oil flows in the reverse direction into the solenoid, around the valve stem, and out of the vent hole. The control piston spring is

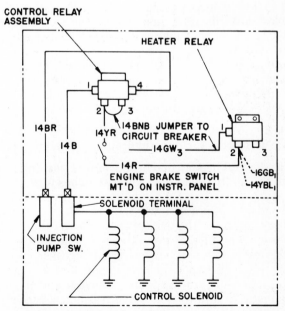

Fig. 19-13 Schematic view of the electrical components and circuits. (*Mack Canada Inc.*)

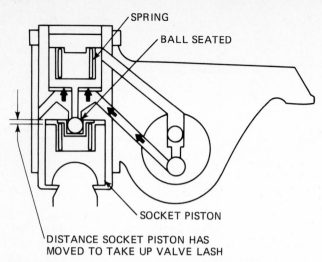

SPRING

BALL SEATED

SOCKET PISTON

DISTANCE SOCKET PISTON HAS
MOVED TO TAKE UP VALVE LASH

Fig. 19-14 Sectional view of valve adjuster when the constant supply oil is blocked. (*Mack Canada Inc.*)

now weaker than the oil pressure acting from below. This lifts the piston and seats the ball check valve. Immediately before the ball check valve seats, the socket piston spring forces its piston down, and oil enters the enlarged oil chamber, causing the ball check valve to seat and trap the oil in the chamber. This action reduces the valve lash until the brake is deenergized (see Fig. 19-14). As the engine piston approaches TDC, the follower is forced upward (by the specially grounded contour on the base circle of the exhaust cam) and opens the exhaust valve. When the solenoids are deenergized, the valve stem allows the ball check valve to float, and consequently the oil from the constant supply oil gallery flows into the on-off control gallery, then into the rocker arm, and onto the top of the control piston. With equal oil pressure on both sides of the control piston, the control piston spring forces the piston down, which, in turn, moves the ball check valve off its seat and allows the oil from the oil chamber in the socket piston to escape. The socket piston then moves upward and achieves the specified exhaust valve lash clearance for normal exhaust valve action.

Testing When brake failure is reported, first visually check all electric wires, all connections, and the circuit breaker. Next, start the engine and then check the low idle speed and the engine oil pressure.

NOTE An oil pressure lower than 30 psi [206.7 kPa] will not actuate the hydraulic lash adjuster.

With the fuel rack switch in the no-fuel position and with the ignition and dashboard switches turned on, measure the voltage at the solenoid terminals. The voltage should not be lower than .4 volt of the open battery voltage. If the voltage drop is lower than this, measure the voltage drop at each of the following locations: the ignition switch, circuit breaker, heater relay, engine brake switch, and control rack switch. Otherwise, turn off the ignition switch and use an ohmmeter to find the excessive resistance. Measure the resistance of the solenoid coils and compare your measurement with the service manual specification.

If any of the components listed above are defective, replace them. However, before you discard the control rack switch (the injection pump switch), manually actuate the switch and then measure the resistance across the switch with an ohmmeter. If there is any resistance, the switch must be replaced. Always refer to the applicable service manual when adjusting switches since there are three alternate designs—one when an aneroid is used, another when a puff limiter is used, and a third for a specific fuel injection pump.

If the electric system checks out satisfactorily, the cause of brake failure may be in the hydraulic lash adjuster, or it may be that the engine exhaust valve adjustment is too high.

To determine which set of cylinders brought about the engine brake failure, remove the valve covers, turn the ignition switch and dashboard switches to the on position, and move the fuel shutoff lever to the off position. The moment the fuel rack hits the fuel rack switch, the solenoid should actuate. Another method is to operate the engine at low idle speed and manually actuate the solenoids one at a time. The engine will run rough if some pistons are operating without a power stroke.

When the solenoids are manually actuated and the set of cylinders does not respond, do not replace the hydraulic lash adjuster until you have checked the valve lash. Too much exhaust valve lash can bring the socket piston against its retainer ring without the follower's contacting the special contour on the cam lobe, and the exhaust valve therefore cannot be opened.

When the engine starts and then fades out or runs rough, and yet the mechanical condition of the engine is good, and there is nothing wrong with the fuel injection system, you might consider the following possibilities: that the ball check valve in the solenoid is jammed to its seat, preventing oil from flowing to the cavity above the control piston; or that the hydraulic adjuster is defective and is holding the socket piston down.

When the dashboard switch is turned to the on position but the engine throttle is above low idle position, and the engine stops or runs rough, the fuel rack switch is damaged, permanently closing the electric circuit to the solenoid.

EXHAUST SYSTEM COMPRESSION BRAKE

The exhaust system compression brake serves the same purpose as the engine brake, and it also converts the engine into a compressor (see Fig. 19-15). However, the conversion is to a low-pressure air compressor, and therefore this brake does not have the high engine-retarding power of the Jacobs or Mack Dynatard engine brake. Nevertheless it has good retarding power, it is quieter during braking, it gives the engine a uniform temperature, and it places a uniform load on the engine during braking. Unfortunately it can be used only on a four-cycle engine.

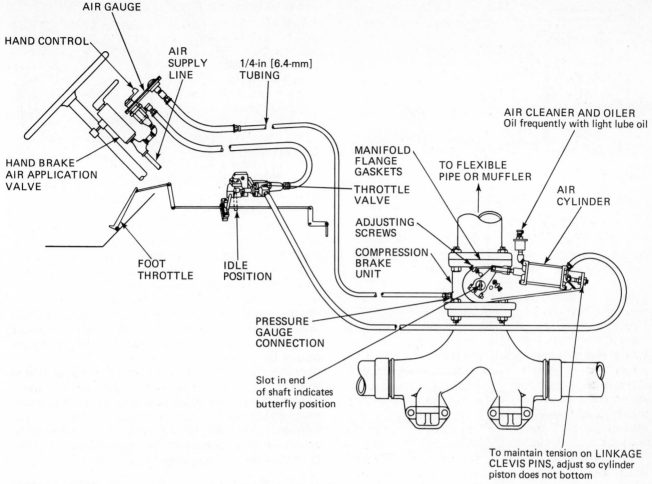

Fig. 19-15 Schematic view of engine compression brake components and piping. (*Williams Air Control Division Omark Industries*)

Design This brake can be controlled by air or electricity. When the brake is controlled by air, it consists of the following four major components (excluding the power source and the air reservoir): the hand control and air gauge, the throttle valve, the air cylinder, and the compression brake unit.

The dash control valve is a mini-hand application valve. It can be fitted with a four-position locking device which allows the driver to manually select the amount of exhaust restriction he needs to assist him in braking. The driver can select from the off position $\frac{1}{3}$, $\frac{2}{3}$, or full exhaust restriction. Because of the similarity between the dash control and a hand application valve, the design, operation, and service procedure need not be covered.

THROTTLE VALVE The throttle valve is a simple air valve (see Fig. 19-16). It is mounted to the fuel injection pump or fuel pump (Cummins) in such a way that, when the throttle lever reaches the low idle fuel position, the lever has pivoted the lever assembly and has moved the stem cap, stem, and inlet poppet downward, opening the inlet valve and allowing air from the dash control valve to flow into the air cylinder. When the throttle moves away from the lever assembly, the stem spring forces the stem upward, allowing the air in the cylinder to exhaust into the

atmosphere and at the same time allowing the inlet valve poppet spring to seat the poppet.

NOTE The throttle valve may be positioned in some other place as long as the fuel pump or injection pump throttle is linked with the lever assembly.

AIR CYLINDER The air cylinder is a one-way, air-applied, spring release, short-stroke cylinder. It is pivot-mounted to the cylinder bracket, and its piston rod is pivot-mounted to the lever arm of the brake unit. The combination air cleaner and oiler is connected to the front end cap.

BRAKE UNIT The brake unit is a simple butterfly valve, mounted in the valve body which is placed into the exhaust system, onto the exhaust manifold, or between the exhaust pipes, or directly onto the turbocharger (if used) (see Fig. 19-17). It is so placed that the butterfly valve closes against the exhaust gas flow. An air hose fitting screwed into the valve body preceding the butterfly valve is connected to the pressure gauge. The gauge indicates to the driver the extent of the exhaust back pressure.

Operation When the hand control is rotated, it closes its exhaust valve and opens the inlet valve.

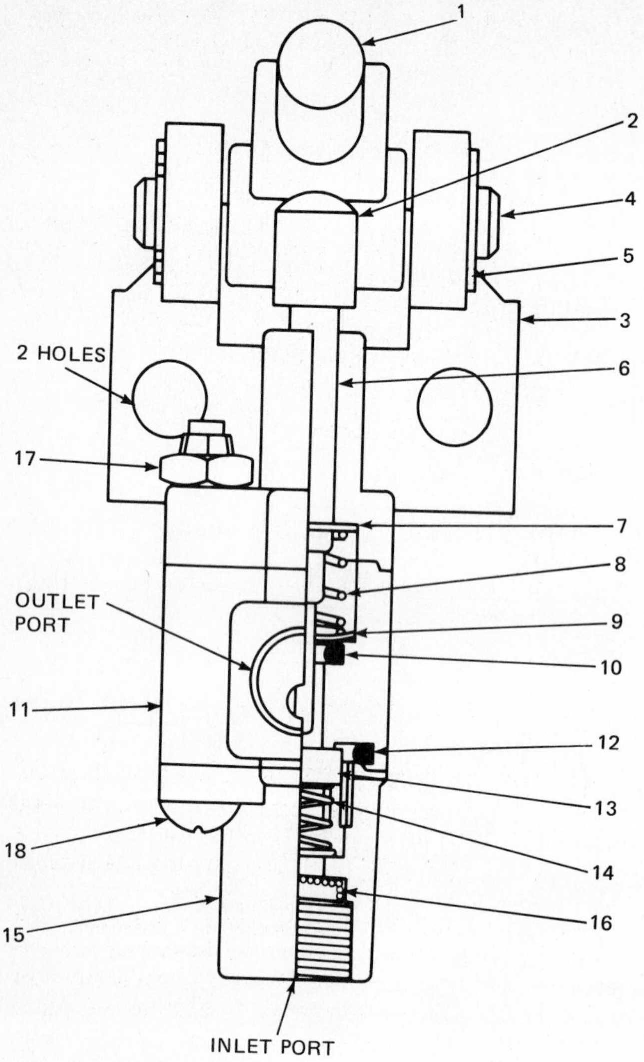
1
2
4
5
3
6
2 HOLES
17
7
8
OUTLET PORT
9
10
11
12
13
18
14
15
16
INLET PORT

1. Lever assembly
2. Stem cap
3. Bracket body
4. Lever pin
5. Retainer ring
6. Stem
7. Retainer ring
8. Stem spring
9. Seal retainer ring
10. O ring
11. Body
12. O ring
13. Inlet poppet
14. Poppet spring
15. Inlet body
16. Inlet screen
17. Lock nut
18. Screw

Fig. 19-16 Sectional view of the throttle valve. (*Williams Air Controls Division Omark Industries*)

The reservoir air can now pass by the open inlet valve and onto the throttle inlet valve, where it is stopped. As soon as the fuel pump or injection pump throttle reaches low idle position, the throttle valve lever assembly moves the stem, the stem moves the inlet valve off its seat, and air is then directed into the air cylinder. The piston rod is forced out, pivoting the butterfly shaft and closing the butterfly. This action restricts the exhaust gas flow that escapes into the atmosphere. With each additional exhaust stroke, the exhaust pressure rises, causing a buildup of pressure 30 to 40 psi [206.7 to 275.6 kPa] between the piston, which is on the exhaust stroke, and the butterfly. This back pressure is exerted on the engine piston(s), adding to the mechanical friction of the

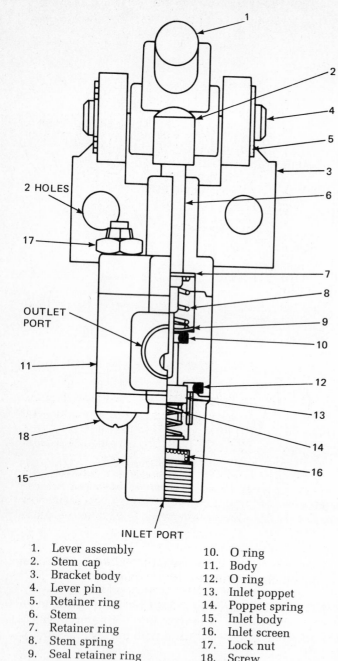

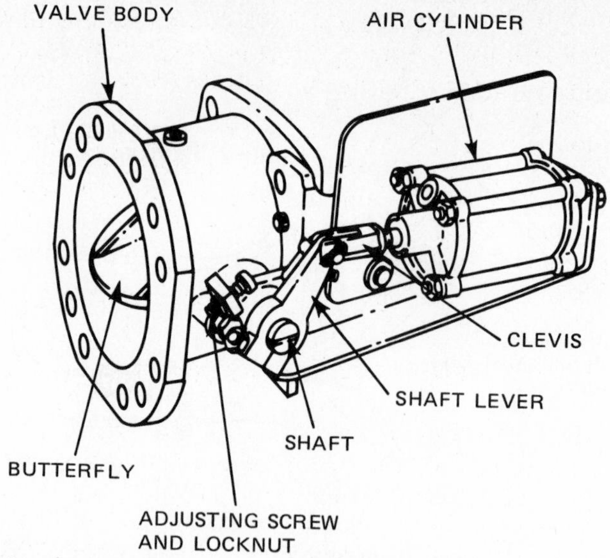
VALVE BODY
AIR CYLINDER
CLEVIS
SHAFT LEVER
SHAFT
BUTTERFLY
ADJUSTING SCREW
AND LOCKNUT

Fig. 19-17 View of brake unit and air cylinder.

engine, and this increases the engine retardation. When the driver moves the throttle from the idle fuel position to any other position, the throttle valve stem allows the poppet to seat, closing the air supply and opening the exhaust port. The air cylinder piston rod return spring now retracts the piston. This pivots the butterfly, allowing the exhaust gases to flow unrestricted through the valve. If you are curious about why only 30 to 40 psi exhaust back pressure can be achieved, it is because of the valve overlap and the energy of the valve spring.

Testing The exhaust compression brake is subjected to excessive vibration, and it is therefore expedient to check the entire exhaust system regularly for cracks, leaks, and loose fasteners, since any exhaust leak (before the butterfly) reduces the brake's effectiveness. The air cylinder should be lubricated at regular intervals to extend the packing and seal life and to prevent corrosion. Also lubricate the throttle valve regularly; otherwise the stem hangs up and therefore does not release the brake quickly enough, or else the fuel pump or the injection pump may not come to the low idle fuel position.

To check the action of the brakes, first start the engine. When it reaches operating temperature, check the low idle speed. Check the freeness and the adjustment of the throttle valve. Make certain that the fuel pump throttle has a few hundredths of a millimeter of motion still available when the lever assembly is in the fully open position and then apply the brakes and recheck the low idle speed. If the lever stop screw is correctly adjusted, the engine low speed will not have dropped more than 50 rpm, and the engine labors slightly. If the speed drop is more than 50 rpm, loosen the stop screw locknut and turn the stop screw until the restriction is reduced sufficiently to bring the low idle speed within 50 rpm. If it will not come within 50 rpm, stop the engine and check the pushrod-to-butterfly adjustment. To make this adjustment, remove the cotter pin and the clevis pin and manually move the butterfly to fully open position, that is, with the slot in the shaft parallel with the valve body. If the butterfly will not come into fully horizontal position, adjust the stop screw until the valve comes into position.

When the adjustments are completed, lift the cylinder to align the clevis hole with the lever hole. The clevis hole must be $\frac{1}{16}$ in [1.58 mm] away from the lever hole to prevent the air piston from bottoming before the butterfly valve comes against the adjusting stop screw.

HYDRAULIC RETARDERS

Hydraulic retarders serve the same function as engine brakes. They use the mechanical friction of the engine to its fullest advantage to achieve maximum retardation. As indicated by the name, hydraulic retarders use fluid to create the retarding power and carry away developed heat by the fluid circulating in the retarder system. A retarder is a mechanical device which, in conjunction with the fluid, converts the kinetic energy of a moving vehicle into heat energy.

Design No matter what the retarder design may be, or how the rotor may vary in diameter and width, or what method is used to control and direct the oil flow, or where the retarder is mounted, the retarder itself consists of only three components: two stationary housings and a rotating member—the rotor.

The retarder may be mounted in any one of the following ways: directly to the engine (between the flywheel and flywheel housing), between the torque converter housing and the power shift transmission housing, to the torque converter, or to the forward and reverse shaft of a power shift transmission. Reference to the stationary housing is made according to its mounting; that is, the front one is named retarder, converter, or flywheel housing, and the rear one is named stator or transmission housing (see Fig. 19-18). The housings are cast from iron or aluminum alloy with integrally curved vanes or odd-shaped pockets. The number, width, depth, or length of the vanes or pockets vary, depending on the retarding power, which also governs the diameter and width of the rotor. The rotor, too, is cast from iron or aluminum alloy and could have curved vanes or odd-shaped pockets on both sides. On some designs the pockets extend through the rotor. The shaft (turbine) to which the rotor is fastened is so supported that the rotor rotates within a fixed clearance between the two stationary housings. The clearance between the rotor and housings is held to a minimum to increase the efficiency of the retarder. The retarding efficiency of some retarders is as high as 115 percent of engine power, while others have only an 80 percent efficiency, paralleling that of the engine brakes.

Hydraulic Piping A pump is used to commence oil flow; a pressure control valve, to control the oil pressure; a closed center spool valve, to direct the flow of oil from the pump to the retarder; and an oil cooler, to cool the engine or transmission oil.

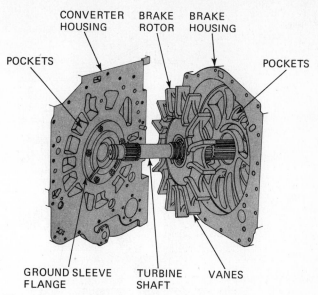

Fig. 19-18 A hydraulic retarder. (*Terex Division of General Motors Corporation*)

NOTE Each of these components is covered in the discussion of hydraulics.

To indicate to and thereby warn the operator when the oil temperature exceeds the safe operating temperature, a temperature gauge is connected to the system. Some retarder installations also use a pressure gauge to indicate the retarder pressure.

Depending on the location of the retarder, the control valves and pump could form part of the power shift transmission or torque converter or could be mounted at any suitably convenient place according to the design of the vehicle. One common piping arrangement is shown in Fig. 19-19. The hydraulic pump is driven by a gear on the flywheel or by the gear on the torque converter impeller. The transmission's oil sump serves as the oil reservoir. From the oil pump the oil is channeled to the pressure regulator, where the pressure is reduced.

NOTE The maximum retarder pressure varies among designs from 40 to 120 psi [275.6 to 826.8 kPa] when the engine operates at high idle.

From the pressure control valve the oil is directed to the closed center retarder valve. When the valve is in the on position, oil flows through the passage into the retarder, close to the center of the rotor. The return oil passage, at the outer circumference of the housing, directs oil back to the retarder valve, then to the oil cooler, and back to the oil sump. **NOTE** By moving the retarder valve partly open, it can be used as a flow control valve and thereby reduce the oil flow and likewise the pressure within the retarder. A check valve is used to prevent the hot retarder oil from entering the torque converter. This retarder valve is so designed that it restricts the outlet flow and thereby controls the retarder pressure.

Operation When the retarder valve is moved into the off position, it prevents the oil from flowing into the retarder, but the pressure control valve maintains

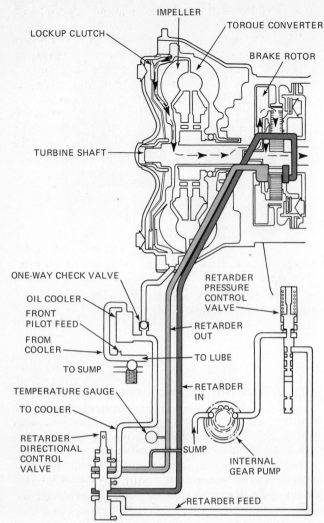

Fig. 19-19 Schematic view of a hydraulic retarder, its components, and piping.

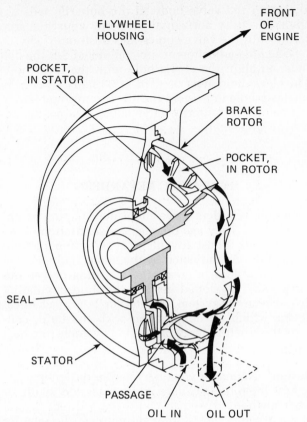

Fig. 19-20 Schematic view of a typical in-and-out oil flow within the retarder. (*Caterpillar Tractor Co.*)

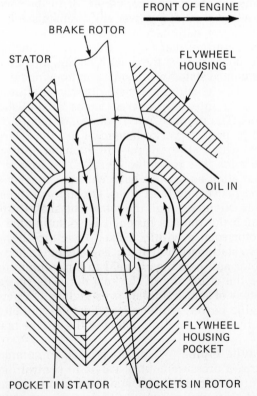

Fig. 19-21 Schematic view of oil flow within the retarder during retarder operation. (*Caterpillar Tractor Co.*)

the line pressure (see Fig. 19-20). Under this condition the retarder (turbine) shaft bearings and the retarder inner housing are lubricated by the oil that passes into the retarder from the torque converter and from the transmission (lubricating passages). When the retarder valve is moved toward the on position, oil flows into the retarder, and the pressure within it varies according to the amount of oil flow.

On the assumption that maximum oil is flowing into the retarder, maximum pressure would occur within the retarder housing. If the rotor is not moving, the oil within the retarder would accumulate in each little space and would solidify between the transmission housing, the brake rotor, and the torque converter housing. Consequently a lot of power would be required to rotate the turbine shaft.

Suppose the vehicle is forced downhill by its gross weight, the operator has released the throttle, the retarder valve is fully open, and maximum pressure is achieved within. Under this circumstance the brake rotor is rotating at engine speed and must cut through the coagulated oil (see Fig. 19-21). As a result, a great amount of power is converted into heat, but in order to rotate, the vanes and/or pockets must be so designed that the rotor pumps and controls the

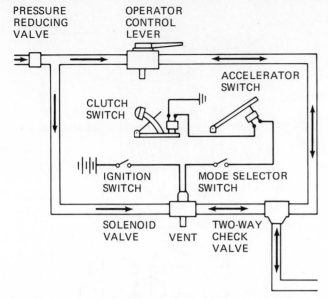

Fig. 19-22 Schematic view of brake-saver (automatic and manual) components and piping.

oil flow within the retarder, so as to pump the oil out of the retarder to remove the developed heat.

To operate efficiently and to use the mechanical friction of the engine, the rotor shaft (or in this case, the turbine shaft) must be connected to the engine crankshaft. This is accomplished by connecting (using a lockup clutch) the impeller to the turbine (see the discussion of power shift transmission). **NOTE** Some hydraulic designs direct the retarder outlet oil (pressure) to the main pressure control valve in order to increase the clutch pressure and to prevent clutch slippage.

As the engine speed is reduced, the mechanical friction of the engine is reduced, as is the rotor

speed. These factors adversely affect retarder efficiency.

When the retarder valve spool reduces the oil flow to (and in some cases from) the retarder, the pressure within the retarder is lessened, minimizing the amount of power required to cut through the oil; consequently less retarding effort is achieved.

The length of time a retarder can be operated is relevant to the cooling capacity of the system, but in any event, the retarder valve should always be placed in the off position when the oil temperature approaches 350°F [177°C].

BRAKE-SAVER

A different method of directing and controlling the oil flow to and from the retarder is shown in Figs. 19-22 and 19-23. Two independent control circuits are used—one is mechanical, while the other is controlled automatically (electrically). **NOTE** Do not operate both control circuits at the same time, for this causes the oil temperature to rise rapidly.

Design and Operation The truck air reservoir pressure is reduced by a pressure-reducing valve, which maintains a maximum pressure of 40 psi [275.6 kPa]. From there the air is directed to the hand control valve and to the solenoid valve. When both valves are closed, no air can flow to the two-way valve. If the hand control valve is partly rotated toward, or fully rotated to, the open position, air flows to the two-way valve and onto the control valve spool, shifting the spool to allow engine oil to flow into the retarder. The automatic control circuit consists of the ignition switch, mode selector switch, clutch switch, accelerator switch, and the solenoid

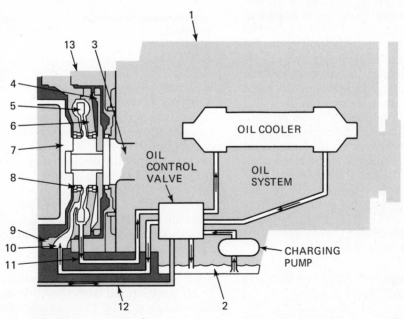

| 1. Engine | 3. Crankshaft | 5. Brake rotor | 7. Flywheel | 9. Housing | 11. Oil out | 13. Flywheel housing |
| 2. Oil pan | 4. Ring gear plate | 6. Stator | 8. Seals | 10. Oil in | 12. Air line | |

Fig. 19-23 Schematic view of brake-saver components and oil flow. (*Caterpillar Tractor Co.*)

with the air valve. When the mode selector switch is placed in the manual position, the electric circuit is open, and when it is placed in the automatic position, the electric circuit is closed. The clutch switch and the accelerator switch used are nearly the same in design as those used with a Jacobs engine brake. When the clutch is released, the clutch switch is closed, and it opens just before the clutch pedal takes up the free play. The accelerator switch is fastened to the governor, and when the fuel rack is in the low idle position, the switch is closed; when it is in the off idle position, the switch is open.

Automatic Control   When the mode selector is placed in the automatic position, the clutch is released, and the throttle is forced down, away from low idle speed position. Under this condition the current flow is stopped at the accelerator switch because the switch is open. As soon as the accelerator pedal is released, the fuel rack, owing to the governor action, is brought to the low idle fuel position, closing the switch. Current now flows to (and through) the solenoid coil to the accelerator, and then to the clutch switch, to ground, energizing the solenoid coil, whereupon the armature opens the air valve. Air under maximum pressure 40 psi [275.6 kPa] actuates the control valve spool. **NOTE** In the automatic position, the oil flow into the retarder is always at its maximum because the air pressure is not controlled. If the clutch pedal is depressed, or the fuel rack moves away from its low idle position, the solenoid is deenergized, and the spring force closes the air valve.

Retarder and Control Valve Design   As illustrated (see Fig. 19-24), the retarder (brake-saver) is located between the flywheel housing and the engine flywheel. The brake rotor, the engine flywheel, and ring gear plate are bolted with the same bolts, to the engine crankshaft. The flywheel housing is bolted to the cylinder block, the brake housing is bolted to the flywheel housing, and the stator is bolted to the brake-saver housing. Bronze piston seals, which rest against wear sleeves, are used to seal between the rotor and flywheel housing, and between the rotor and stator. Lip-type seals are positioned in the stator and brake-saver housing to prevent oil from seeping into the flywheel or brake-saver housing. Trapped oil can escape through passages in the stator and flywheel housing and reroute back to the crankcase.

The control valve is bolted to the flywheel housing. The oil outlet port of the control valve is connected through a passage with the rotor. It directs the oil near to the center of the rotor. A passage from the outer circle of the brake-saver housing directs oil back to the return port of the control valve.

The air line is connected to the left valve cap, and the oil coming from the engine lubrication pump is directed into the center port. The left upper (return) port leads to the oil filter and then back to the crankcase. The upper right port leads to the inlet port of the oil cooler, and the adjacent port is the oil cooler return port. The lower left port connects the inlet passage with the retarder, and the lower right port

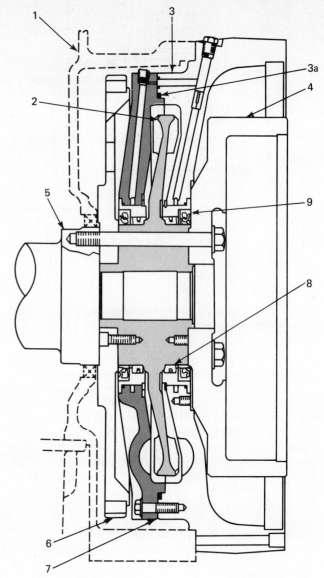

1.	Flywheel housing	5.	Crankshaft flange
2.	Brake rotor	6.	Ring gear plate
3.	Brakesaver housing	7.	Stator
3a.	O ring seal	8.	Piston-type seals
4.	Flywheel	9.	Bearing

Fig. 19-24 Sectional view of brake-saver components. (*Caterpillar Tractor Co.*)

connects the return passage with the retarder. The check (poppet) valve is placed in such a position that the engine oil pressure can lift the check valve off its seat when the valve spool is in the off position and allow the oil to flow through a small passage into the retarder. The restricted passage allows about 1 gal/min [3.8 l/min] of oil to flow into the retarder to lubricate the bronze seals. When the valve spool is in the on position, the retarder oil pressure and the spring force closes the check valve. (The valve spool is of the closed center design.) When it is in the off position, oil from the oil pump is directed as follows: around the valve spool, into the oil cooler, back into the valve around the valve spool, out of the return port to the filter, and then to the crankcase. The valve spool lands have closed the outlet and inlet ports leading to the retarder. Located in-

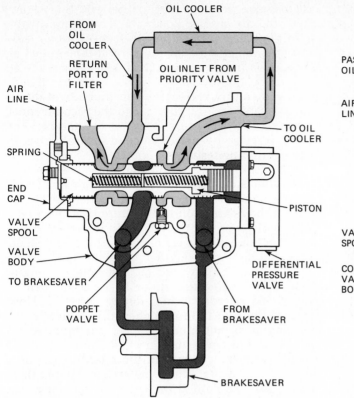

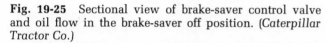

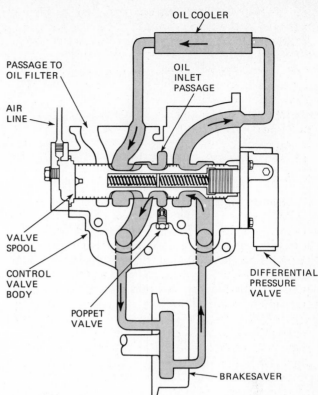

Fig. 19-25 Sectional view of brake-saver control valve and oil flow in the brake-saver off position. (*Caterpillar Tractor Co.*)

Fig. 19-26 Schematic view of brake-saver control valve in brake-saver on position. (*Caterpillar Tractor Co.*)

side the hollow valve spool is a spring and a piston (see Fig. 19-25).

The differential-pressure valve is bolted to the right side of the oil control valve and is connected thereto by three passages. The engine oil passage leads onto the top of the differential piston; the center passage connects the valve spool with the piston; and the third passage connects the retarder return oil pressure onto the bottom of the valve spool.

Oil Flow and Control Valve Action When the engine is operating and the oil pressure is higher than 35 psi [241.15 kPa], it passes through the priority valve, enters the valve spool, and from there flows to the oil cooler, back to the control valve, and then back to the crankcase. When the automatic- or manual-control circuit is actuated, air is directed onto the left valve spool area, causing it to shift to the right. This action stops the oil flow to the filter. The valve spool connects the brake-saver in/out with the oil cooler in/out making it a closed hydraulic circuit to ensure quick pressurization within the retarder.

Oil is directed to the inlet passage leading to the retarder. It is then pumped from the brake-saver by the rotor and further directed by the valve spool to the oil cooler, and from the oil cooler again through the valve spool back to the brake-saver. This causes an oil flow of 42 gal/min [158.97 l/min] within the brake-saver when the engine operates at high idle (see Fig. 19-26). While the brake-saver is filling with oil (which takes about 2 s), the priority valve, owing to the drop in pressure, reduces the oil flow to the

brake-saver to maintain the same oil flow to the engine lubricating system. Also, as the retarder is filling, engine oil pressure acts on the differential piston and moves it downward. The piston closes the center passage that leads to the spring bore within the valve spool. When the retarder is filled, the outlet pressure increases to about 42 to 62 psi [289.3 to 427.1 kPa] above the engine oil pressure, which is about 70 psi [482.3 kPa] because of the pumping action of the rotor. **NOTE** The pressures and flow quotations given here should not be used as test specifications. Test specifications should be obtained from the service manual.

The higher brake-saver outlet pressure forces the differential piston upward, and this allows the outlet oil to pass into the center passage and into the spring area of the valve spool. The additional force of the oil pressure moves the valve spool to the left against the force of the air pressure, and the spool land opens the passage to the oil filter port (see Fig. 19-27). This action reduces the outlet pressure, as well as the inlet pressure. At the same time, however, owing to the lower outlet pressure, the differential piston moves, reducing the pressure in the spring area. The force of the air pressure is now higher, moving the valve spool to the right, which in turn reduces the oil flow to the oil filter port and increases the retarder inlet pressure, as well as the retarder outlet pressure. The valve spool is now an automatic flow control valve and maintains a constant retarding power.

If the hand control valve reduces the air pressure from its maximum, say, to 30 psi [206.7 kPa], the

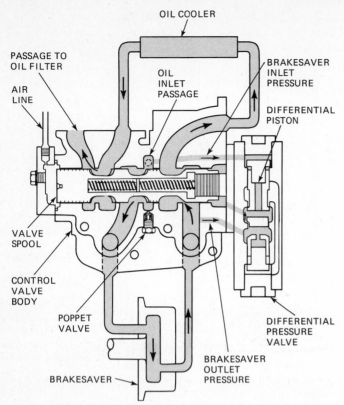

OIL COOLER

PASSAGE TO OIL FILTER

AIR LINE

OIL INLET PASSAGE

BRAKESAVER INLET PRESSURE

DIFFERENTIAL PISTON

VALVE SPOOL

CONTROL VALVE BODY

POPPET VALVE

DIFFERENTIAL PRESSURE VALVE

BRAKESAVER

BRAKESAVER OUTLET PRESSURE

Fig. 19-27 Schematic view of brake-saver control valve in flow control position. (*Caterpillar Tractor Co.*)

valve spool in conjunction with the differential valve maintains a fixed, reduced pressure within the brake-saver and also reduces the retarding power.

NOTE Retarders operate at peak efficiency when the engine is operating at high idle, the fuel rack is in the low idle position, and there is maximum oil pressure within the retarder. Any reduction in engine speed or in oil pressure reduces the retarding power.

Testing If the operator complains of little or no retarder power, visually check as follows: (1) for fly-wheel- and brake-saver housing oil leaks, which indicate that the seals are damaged or the O ring between the stator and ring gear plate, or the O ring between the brake-saver housing and flywheel, is damaged or worn; (2) for damaged, bent, or twisted air hoses or hydraulic hoses; (3) the engine cooling system and the engine oil level; (4) the wire, terminals, connections, and the circuit breaker.

If (1) to (4) check out satisfactorily, then start the engine and bring it to operating temperature. Next, check the engine oil pressure (it should be at least 30 psi [206.7 kPa]) when operating at high idle. If the oil pressure is lower, check the priority valve; it may be sticking or the spring may be broken, allowing more oil to flow to the retarder than to the engine; (2) the high idle (and at the same time note the engine performance); (3) the truck air pressure.

After completing these checks, install pressure gauges to the air-control valve (to check the air pressure), to the engine oil pressure port, and to the retarder outlet pressure port. Start the engine, bring

the reservoir pressure above 70 psi [482.3 kPa], and then stop the engine. Rotate the hand control valve to full retarder on position. Next, check for air leaks and note the applied air pressure. If the applied air pressure is below 40 psi [275.6 kPa], check the air pressure at the pressure-reducing valve and then at the hand control valve. If the air pressure at the reducing valve is low, adjust it to the recommended pressure. If the pressure is low at the hand control valve, service or replace the hand control valve before continuing testing.

If air leaks from the solenoid air valve, the two-way valve is damaged. Service it. An air leak in the retarder control valve is not easily detected; however, if the retarder oil temperature rises quickly, it is an indication that there is air in the retarder oil.

When these checks are made, start the engine, operate it at high idle, and then move the hand control valve to the full on position and note the engine rpm. If the engine rpm drops to the recommended speed, the retarder is functioning correctly. However, if the rpm drop is higher, this indicates that the engine is not producing its maximum horsepower. A tuneup is then needed. And if the rpm drop is less than specified, the retarding performance is inadequate. When you are conducting these tests, also take note of the engine oil pressure and the retarder outlet oil pressure.

If the brake saver outlet pressure is less than specified, say, about 130 psi [895.7 kPa] when the engine oil pressure is 70 psi [482.3 kPa], check the operation of the brake-saver control valve. To do this, stop the engine, reduce the truck air reservoir pressure to below 70 psi [482.3 kPa], and then restart the engine. Have someone actuate the hand control valve to the full on position while you stand close to the brake-saver control valve. As the hand control valve is placed in the off position, you should hear the valve spool hit the end cap. If this sound is audible, the valve spool is operating properly. If it is not audible, check for the following: a damaged valve spool or bore, a broken or damaged spring, restricted passages leading to the differential valve, or worn or damaged differential piston or bore. If the brake-saver control valve is operating correctly and the pressures are as specified, the cause of reduced brake-saver power must lie within the brake-saver itself.

AUTOMATIC CONTROL CIRCUIT If you suspect that the automatic control circuit is causing reduced retarder power or eliminating retarder power, disconnect the battery, turn on the ignition switch, and move the mode selector switch to automatic position. Next, using an ohmmeter, measure the resistance across the ignition switch, clutch, accelerator, and mode selector switch. If the accelerator or the clutch switch shows high resistance, check the switch adjustment. To determine if the solenoid coil has an open, ground, or short circuit, measure the resistance and compare your readings with the service manual specifications. After completing the necessary checks and tests, reconnect the battery and then start the engine and operate it at high idle with the mode selector switch in the automatic position. Next, remove your foot from the accelerator pedal and compare the air pressure, engine oil pressure, and brake-saver outlet pressure readings with service manual specifications.

If the accelerator switch functions adequately, place a jumper wire across the accelerator switch, operate the engine at high idle, and actuate the clutch pedal. Immediately before the pedal end play is taken up, the pressure gauges should show the specified pressures. During this test NO air should leak from the hand control valve exhaust port or from the solenoid air valve.

Review Questions

1. What principle permits an engine brake to use the engine to achieve retardation?

2. The "Jacobs engine brake" relys on three individual systems to achieve engine retardation. Name these three systems and list the component for each system.

3. Describe the (a) electrical action, (b) hydraulic action, and (c) mechanical action which takes place when the engine operates above low idle speed, and the throttle is in the release position, and the dashboard switch is at the on position.

4. Why should you never manually actuate the solenoid when the engine is operating at low idle speed?

5. Explain how to check and adjust (a) the clutch switch, (b) a Cummins fuel pump switch, (c) a GM buffer switch, (d) the electrical circuit.

6. List the variances between the Jacobs engine brake and the Mack Dynatard engine brake.

7. Which components control the actuation of the Dynatard engine brake, and which components actuate the brake?

8. What are the most apparent dissimilarities between an engine brake and an exhaust system compression brake?

9. Name the components which make up an exhaust compression brake and state the purpose of each.

10. (a) Define "hydraulic retarder"; (b) list its main components; (c) list the main hydraulic components.

11. Identify the two factors which determine the maximum retarding power of an individual hydraulic retarder.

12. Explain the design change through which the retarding power of an individual retarder can be increased.

Conversion Tables

Well over 95% of the world's population already uses metric units of measurement or is converting to them. The tremendous advantage of the metric system is its simplicity and its universality: All relationships between the various units of the metric system work in powers of 10, and unified symbols are used for each unit instead of many different abbreviations.

However, North America still relies primarily on the United States Customary system of measurement, and it is the primary system used in this textbook. To assist you when you must work with both systems, these conversion charts are supplied. They will provide you with a fast and simple means of converting USCS to metric units, and vice versa.

For example, if you want to know the displacement in liters or cubic centimeters of a diesel engine having a displacement of 600 in^3 (cubic inches), select the capacity and volume conversion table. Refer to the in^3 entry in the left-hand column. The comparable amount in liters (l) and in cubic centimeters (cm^3) is shown to the right. Since 1 in^3 equals 16.39 cm^3, 600 in^3 equals 600 × 16.39, or 9834 cm^3. Since 1 in^3 is also equal to 0.0164 l, 600 in^3 equals 600 × 0.0164, or 9.84 l.

Area The metric units of area are based on the square meter (m^2). Other units are created by multiplying or dividing by a factor of 10.

AREA

	in^2	ft^2	yd^2	mm^2	cm^2	dm^2	m^2
1 in^2 =	—	0.0069		645.2	6.452	0.06452	0.00064
1 ft^2 =	144	—	0.1111	92,903	929	9.29	0.0929
1 yd^2 =	1296	9	—	836,100	8361	83.61	0.8361
1 mi^2 =		27,878,400					2,589,998
1 mm^2 =	0.0015			—	0.01	0.0001	0.000001
1 cm^2 =	0.155	0.0017		100	—	0.01	0.0001
1 dm^2 =	15.5	0.1076	0.01196	10,000	100	—	0.01
1 m^2 =	1550	10.76	1.196	1,000,000	10,000	100	—

Capacity The metric units of capacity are based on the liter (l). Other units are created by multiplying or dividing by a factor of 10.

Volume The metric units of volume are based on the cubic meter (m^3). Other units are created by multiplying or dividing by a factor of 10.

CAPACITY AND VOLUME

	in^3	ft^3	U.S. qt	U.S. gal	Imp. qt	Imp. gal	cm^3	dm^3	m^3	l
1 in^3 =	—		0.01732		0.01442		16.39	0.01639		0.0164
1 ft^3 =	1728	—	29.92	7.481	24.92	6.229		28.32	0.02832	28.32
1 yd^3 =	46,656	27	807.9	202	672.8	168.2		764.6	0.7646	764.6
1 U.S. qt =	57.75	0.03342	—	0.25	0.8327	0.2082	946.4	0.9464		0.946
1 U.S. gal =	231	0.1337	4	—	3.331	0.8327	3785	3.785	0.003785	3.785
1 Imp. qt. =	69.36	0.04014	1.201	0.3002	—	0.25	1136	1.136		1.136
1 Imp. gal =	277.4	0.1605	4.804	1.201	4	—	4546	4.546	0.004546	4.546
1 cm^3 =	0.06102	0.003	0.105	0.0264	0.088	0.022	—	0.001	0.000001	0.001
1 dm^3 =	61.02	0.03531	1.057	0.2642	0.88	0.22	1000	—	0.001	1
1 m^3 =	61,023	35.31	1057	264.2	880	220		1000	—	1000
1 l =	61.02	0.03531	1.057	0.2642	0.88	0.22	1000	1.0	0.001	—

Energy The metric unit of energy is the newton-meter (N·m) or joule (J). One joule is the amount of work done when a force of one newton moves an object a distance of one meter (or 1 J = 1 N·m).

ENERGY

	J	N·m	Btu	ft·lb
1 J =	—	1.0	0.00094	0.7376
1 N·m =	1.0	—	0.00094	0.7376
1 Btu =	1055.01	1055.01	—	778.3

FORCE   The metric unit of force is the newton (N). It is defined as the force needed to move a mass of one kilogram a distance of one meter. It also can be defined as the force which, when applied to an object with a mass of one kilogram, accelerates it at a rate of one meter per second per second (1 m/s^2). The force of the earth's gravity acting on a mass of one kilogram = 9.81 N, so 1 kg = 9.81 N.

$$1 \text{ kg} = 9.81 \text{ N}$$
$$1 \text{ lb} = 4.448 \text{ N}$$
$$1 \text{ oz} = 0.278 \text{ N}$$
$$1 \text{ N} = 0.101 \text{ kg} = 0.224 \text{ lb} = 0.138 \text{ oz}$$

Length   The metric units of length are based on the meter (m). Other units are created by multiplying or dividing by a factor of 10.

LENGTH

	in	ft	yd	mi (statute)	nmi	mm	cm	m	km	μm
1 in =	—	0.08333	0.02778			25.4	2.54	0.0254		25,400
1 ft =	12	—	0.3333	0.00019	0.00016	304.8	30.48	0.30488		
1 yd =	36	3	—	0.00057	0.00048	914.4	91.44	0.9144		
1 mi (statute)	63,360	5280	1760	—	0.8684			1609.3	1.609	
1 nmi =	72,960	6080	2027	1.152	—			1853.3	1.853	
1 mm =	0.03937	0.003281				—	0.1	0.001		1000
1 cm =	0.3937	0.03281	0.01094			10	—	100		10,000
1 m =	39.37	3.281	1.094	0.00062	0.00053	1000	100	—	0.001	
1 km =	39,370	3281	1093.6	0.6214	0.5396	10^6	100,000	1000	—	
1 μm =	0.000039					0.01	0.0001	0.000001		—

Mass   The metric units of mass are based on the kilogram (kg), which is defined as the mass of one liter of water at 4°C [39° F]. Other units are created by multiplying or dividing by a factor of 10.

MASS

	oz	lb	g	kg
1 oz =	—	0.0625	28.35	0.02835
1 lb =	16	—	453.59	0.45359
1 g =	0.03527		—	0.001
1 kg =	35.27	2.2046	1000	—

Power   The metric unit of power is the watt (W). This is the power required to move a weight of one newton a distance of one meter in a time of one second (1 W = 1 N·m/s).

POWER

	hp	hp (metric)	ft · lb/ s	kg · m/ s	kW	W	Btu/ min
1 hp =	—	1.014	550	76.04	0.746	746	42.4
1 hp (metric) =	0.986	—	542.5	75.00	0.736	736	41.8
1 ft · lb/s =			—	0.30488		0.0226	0.001285
1 kg · m/s =			3.281	—		0.0741	0.0042
1 kW =	1.341	1.360	737.28	102.00	—	1000	56.8
1 W =	0.00134	0.00136	0.737	0.102	0.001	—	
1 Btu/min =	0.0236	0.0239	12.96	3.939	0.0176	17.6	—

Pressure   The metric unit of pressure is the pascal (Pa). One pascal is produced when a force of one newton is applied to an area of one square meter.

Pressure (Pa) = force/area = N/m^2

PRESSURE

	inH$_2$O	cmH$_2$O	inHg	cmHg	psi	kg/cm^2	atm	kPa
1 inH$_2$O =	—	2.54	0.0735	1.866	0.0361	0.0025	0.0024	0.248
1 inHg =	13.6	34.544	—	2.54	0.491	0.0345	0.0334	3.386
1 psi =	27.7	70.104	2.036	5.171	—	0.0703	0.068	6.89
1 kg/cm^2 =	393.73	1000.0	28.96	73.55	14.22	—	0.9678	37.97
1 atm =	407.19	1033.0	29.92	75.96	14.70	1.033	—	101.28
1 kPa =	4.01	10.18	0.295	0.750	0.145	0.026	0.0098	—

The boiling point of water varies with atmospheric pressure, which varies with altitude as follows:

ATMOSPHERIC PRESSURE AT VARIOUS ALTITUDES VERSUS THE BOILING POINT OF WATER

Altitude		Atmospheric pressure			Boiling point of water	
ft	m	psi	inHg	kPa	°F	°C
Sea level		14.69	29.92	101.28	212	100
1000	304.8	14.16	28.86	97.56	210.1	99
2000	609.6	13.66	27.82	94.11	208.3	98
3000	914.4	13.16	26.81	90.67	206.5	97
4000	1219.4	12.68	25.84	87.36	204.6	95.9
5000	1524.0	12.22	24.89	84.19	202.8	94.9
6000	1828.8	11.77	23.98	81.09	201.0	94.1
7000	2133.6	11.33	23.09	78.06	199.3	93.0
8000	2438.4	10.91	22.22	75.16	197.4	91.9
9000	2743.2	10.50	21.38	72.34	195.7	91
10,000	3048.0	10.10	20.58	69.58	194.0	90

Temperature   The metric unit of temperature is the degree Celsius. Use the following formulas to convert from degrees Celsius to degrees Fahrenheit, and vice versa:

$$°F = 1.8C + 32$$
$$°C = (F - 32) \div 1.8$$

Example 1   Convert 0 and 100°C to degrees Fahrenheit.

$$1.8 \ (0°) + 32 = 32°F$$
$$1.8 \ (100°) + 32 = 212°F$$

Example 2   Convert 32 and 212°F to degrees Celsius.

$$(32° - 32) \div 1.8 = 0°C$$
$$(212° - 32) \div 1.8 = 100°C$$

In most cases, however, you will find it simpler to refer to a conversion chart, such as the one on the following page, for your answer.

398

TEMPERATURE CONVERSION

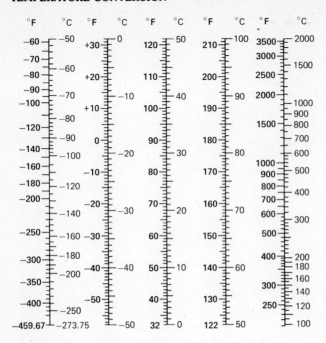

| | °F | °C | °F | °C | °F | °C | °F | °C | °F | °C |

Torque The metric unit of torque is the newton-meter (N·m). This measurement is replacing the kilogram-meter (kg·m), which you may still encounter in your work.

TORQUE

	lb·ft	kg·m	N·m
1 lb·ft =	—	0.1383	1.355
1 kg·m =	7.233	—	9.80
1 N·m =	0.738	7.233	—

Work Work is related to energy and is measured in the same unit, the newton meter (N·m).

Glossary

ABDC Abbreviation for *after bottom dead center.*

Abrasion A wearing away caused by rubbing.

Absolute pressure Gauge pressure plus atmospheric pressure.

Absolute temperature Temperature measured using absolute zero as a reference. Absolute zero is −459.69°F [−273.16°C]. See *Kelvin scale.*

Acceleration The rate of increase of velocity per time unit, measured in feet per second per second or meters per second per second.

Accumulator A device used for storing liquid under pressure (sometimes used to smooth out pressure surges in an hydraulic system).

Accumulator, diaphragm type An accumulator in which the liquid and gas are separated by a flexible diaphragm.

Accumulator, piston type An accumulator in which the liquid and gas are separated by a floating piston.

Accumulator, spring An accumulator having a spring or a group of springs as the opposing force.

Ackerman principle A slight inward bending of the outer ends of the steering arms so that the inside wheel will turn more sharply than the outer wheel when the vehicle is making a turn. This principle produces toe-out on turns.

Actuator A device which uses fluid power to produce mechanical force and motion.

Additive A substance which is added to improve the performance of a fuel or lubricating oil.

Advance To adjust the fuel injection so that fuel enters the engine a greater number of degrees before top dead center.

After-cooler A device used on turbocharged engines to cool air which has undergone compression.

Air bind The presence of air in a pump or pipes which prevents the delivery of liquid through the system.

Air bleeder A device used to remove air from a hydraulic system. Types include a needle valve, capillary tubing to the reservoir, and a bleed plug.

Air cleaner A filter for removing unwanted solid impurities from the air before it enters the intake manifold.

Air cleaner, dry A filter made from dry material (i.e., paper, fabric, or metal).

Air cleaner, wet Method of cleaning of air through an oil bath filter.

Air compressor A device used to increase air pressure.

Air/fuel ratio The ratio (by weight or by volume) between air and fuel.

Air gap The distance between two components.

Air pollution Contamination of the earth's atmosphere by pollutants such as smoke, harmful gases, etc.

Air resistance A measure of the "drag" or retarding effect on a vehicle's motion due to the air turbulence produced by its movement.

Air starting valve A valve which admits compressed air to the air starter for starting purposes.

Align To bring two or more components of a unit into the correct position with respect to one another.

Allowance The difference between the minimum and the maximum dimensions of proper functioning.

Alloy A mixture of two or more different metals, usually produced to improve physical characteristics of the metals involved.

Alloy steel A steel to which any alloying element (other than carbon) is added to improve physical properties.

Alnico magnet A magnet composed of aluminum (Al), nickel (Ni), and cobalt (Co).

Alternating current (ac) An electric current that continuously changes polarity.

Alternator An electromechanical device which produces alternating current.

Ambient temperature Surrounding air temperature.

Ammeter An instrument used to measure the rate of current flow in amperes.

Ampere (A) A unit of measurement defined as the current that 1 V can send through 1 Ω of resistance. See *Volt* and *Ohm.*

Ampere-hour (Ah) capacity A measurement of the battery capacity to deliver a specified current over a specified length of time.

Aneroid A pressure-measuring device containing no liquid.

Angle Inclination of two lines to each other.

Angle-dozer A tractor with a front pusher blade that can be set at an angle.

Angularity Having or being at an angle.

Anneal To toughen metals by heating and then cooling them.

Annular In the form of an annulus; ring-shaped.

Annular groove The smaller-diameter grove of a spool valve. When the annular groove is aligned with an oil passage, fluid flows through that groove.

Annulus A figure bounded by concentric circles or cylinders (e.g., a washer, ring, sleeve, etc.).

API Abbreviation for *American Petroleum Institute.*

API gravity Gravity expressed in units of standard API (hydrometer).

Apron (scraper) The front enclosure of the scraper bowl.

Arc Portion of a curved line or of the circumference of a circle.

Arcing Electrons leaping the gap between the negative and positive poles.

Armature The movable part of a relay, regulator, or horn or the rotating part of a generator or starter.

Asbestos A heat-resistant and nonburning inorganic mineral.

Aspirate To breathe (to draw out gas by suction).

ATDC Abbreviation for *after top dead center.*

Atmosphere The mass or blanket of gases surrounding the earth.

Atmospheric pressure (barometric pressure) The pressure exerted by the atmosphere, averaging 14.7 psi [123.3 kPa] at sea level with a decrease of approximately 0.5 lb per 1000 ft of altitude gained.

Atom The smallest particle of an element.

Atomizer A device which disperses liquid (e.g., fuel) into fine particles (pulverized spray).

Attrition Wearing down by rubbing or by friction; abrasion.

Automatic valve A valve assisted by a spring, which is opened by a difference of pressure acting in one direction and closed by a difference in pressure acting in the opposite direction.

Auxiliary An aid to the main device which may only be used occasionally.

Axis A centerline.

Axle A crossbar which supports a vehicle and with which, or on which, its wheels turn.

Axle, elliot Front axle having forged yokes within which the steering knuckles rotate.

Axle end (side) gear A bevel gear that is splined to the inner end of the drive axle.

Axle, full floating An axle used to drive the wheels. It does not hold them on or support them.

Axle, live Driven axle.

Axle, pusher Nonpowered rear axle, located in front of the drive axle.

Axle, reverse elliot A front axle having forged ends that are inserted between the bosses of the yoked steering knuckles.

Axle, semifloating An axle whose outer wheel bearings are carried directly on the axle shaft. The axle shafts and wheel bearings not only support the weight but also transmit driving and braking torque to the wheels.

Axle windup Oscillatory motion of an axle about the horizontal transverse axis through the axle's center of gravity.

Axle yaw Oscillatory motion of an axle around the vertical axis through the axle's center of gravity.

Babbit An antifriction metal used to line bearings, thereby reducing the friction of the moving components.

Backhoe A hydraulically operated digging-scooping device attached to a (separate) frame.

Backlash The distance (play) between two movable components.

Backpressure A pressure exerted contrary to the pressure producing the main flow; pressure encountered on the return side of a system.

Baffle A device which slows down or diverts the flow of gases, liquids, sound, etc.

Balanced valve A valve in which the fluid pressure is equal on both sides (i.e., the opening and closing directions).

Ball bearing A bearing using steel balls as its rolling element between the inner and outer ring (race).

Ball check valve A valve consisting of a ball held against a ground seat by a spring. It is used to check the flow or to limit the pressure.

Ball joint A flexible socket joint which permits relative angular movement.

Barometer An instrument which measures atmospheric pressure.

Basic size The theoretical or nominal standard size from which all variations are derived.

Battery An electrochemical device that produces electric current.

Battery charging See *Charge (battery)*.

BBDC Abbreviation for *before bottom dead center*.

BDC Abbreviation for *bottom dead center*.

Bearing The contacting surface on which a revolving part rests.

Bearing clearance The distance between the shaft and the bearing surface.

Bell housing (clutch housing) The metal covering around the clutch or torque converter assembly.

Bending movement The product of force and distance from the support point to the point where force is applied, causing bending or distortion.

Bendix starter drive (inertia starter drive) A type of starter drive that causes the gear to engage when the armature starts rotating and to automatically disengage when it stops.

Bernoulli's principle Given a fluid flowing through a tube, any constriction or narrowing of the tube will create an increase in that fluid's velocity and a decrease in its pressure.

Bevel gear A gear used to transmit power at an angle.

BHP Abbreviation for *brake horsepower* (which see).

Bleeding the brakes Refers to the removal of air from the hydraulic system.

Blowby Exhaust gases which escape past the piston rings.

Blower A low-pressure air pump, usually of the rotary blade or centrifugal type.

BMEP Abbreviation for *brake mean effective pressure* (which see).

Body A structure for cargo or passengers, mounted on the chassis.

Bogie A combination of two axles, usually pivoting, about a common trunnion.

Bond The holding together of different parts.

Bonded brake lining Brake lining that is attached to the brake shoes, band, and disk by an adhesive.

Boom A steel structure to which the dipper, stick, and handle are attached, hinged to the tractor frame or revolving machine deck.

Bore A cylinder or hole, or the inside diameter of the cylinder or hole.

Bore diameter The diameter of a hole or cylinder.

Boring Enlarging cylinders by cutting or honing them to a specified size.

Boring bar (cylinder) A tool used to machine cylinders to a specific size.

Bosch metering system A metering system with a helical groove in the plunger which covers or uncovers ports in the pump barrel.

Bound electrons The inner-orbit electrons surrounding the nucleus of the atom.

Bowl scraper A steel boxlike structure attached to a scraper to load, transport, and discharge the load.

Boyle's law The absolute pressure which a given quantity of gas at constant temperature exerts against the walls of the containing vessel is inversely proportional to the volume occupied.

Brake The mechanism used to retard or stop the movement of a vehicle.

Brake anchor A steel stud upon which one end of the brake shoes is attached, or against which it rests.

Brake backing plate A rigid steel plate upon which the brake shoes are mounted.

Brake band A flexible steel band, internally or externally faced with brake lining, which encircles a brake drum.

Brake booster A device for increasing brake application pressure.

Brake burnish The conditioning of a brake's friction surfaces by wear and temperature, either by a test procedure or by in-service operation.

Brake chamber A unit in which a diaphragm converts pressure to mechanical force to actuate the brake.

Brake diaphragm The synthetic rubber which divides a brake chamber.

Brake, disk-type On this kind of brake, steel disks are used as the reaction surface (instead of drums). Lining pads (one on each side of the rotating disk) are forced against the disk, which causes the breaking force.

Brake drum A steel, cast iron, or aluminum machined housing, bolted to the wheel, that rotates with the wheel around the brake shoes.

Brake drum lathe A machine used to refinish the inside of a brake drum or the surface of a disk.

Brake effectiveness The ratio of input force to output torque in a brake.

Brake, emergency A secondary brake system whose application is independent of the service brake. It is used when the vehicle is parked and for controlling the vehicle's motion if the service brake fails.

Brake, engine A device using engine compression pressure as the retarding medium.

Brake, exhaust A device using engine exhaust backpressure as the retarding medium.

Brake fade The loss of braking torque as a result of overheating in the brake lining.

Brake feel Driver sensitivity to the amount of brake pedal pressure and the actual braking force being exerted.

Brake fluid A special fluid used in hydraulic brake system.

Brake horsepower (bhp) The usable power delivered by the engine.

Brake limiting valve A valve in the brake application system which limits the maximum permissible pressure passed on to the front axle brakes.

Brake mean effective pressure (bmep) Mean effective pressure acting on the piston which would result in the given brake horsepower output, if there were not losses due to friction, cooling, and exhaustion. Equal to mean indicated pressure times mechanical efficiency.

Brake power (bp) The amount of net available power produced by an engine as measured at the crankshaft.

Brake rating Tested performance. In terms of horsepower, it is the maximum power that the brakes will absorb or dissipate as heat in a specified period of time.

Brake release The opposite of brake actuation.

Brake shoe(s) Part of the foundation brake located within the brake drum upon which the brake lining is mounted.

Brake shoe heel The trailing end of the brake shoe.

Brake shoe toe The leading end of the brake shoe.

Brake system A brake or combination of brakes and the hydraulic cylinders, lines, and other components which provide the means of operation and control.

Brake system application time or distance The elapsed time or travel distance from the moment or point at which the driver starts to move the braking controls until the moment or point when the brakes first retard the vehicle's motion.

Brake thermal efficiency Ratio of power output in the form of brake horsepower to equivalent power input in the form of heat from fuel.

Brazing Method of fastening one piece of metal to another by heating the edges of both, placing the heated edges together, and then melting brass or bronze onto the parts to be joined.

Breakaway (tractor protection) valve The valve added to a tractor brake system which safeguards the air supply on the tractor and automatically applies the brakes on any trailing units which inadvertently become separated.

Breaker arm The movable arm to which one of the breaker points is attached.

Breather pipe A pipe opening into the crankcase to assist ventilation.

Bridge formula A formula used to determine the maximum gross weight permissible on any group of axles.

Brinnell hardness The surface hardness of a metal, alloy, or similar material according to J. A. Brinnell's method of measurement. A metal's surface is struck with a given force by a rigid steel ball of given diameter and the indentation is measured.

British (imperial) gallon A gallon measurement equal to 277.4 in^3.

British thermal unit (Btu) A U.S. Customary System unit of measure. Approximate definition: the amount of heat required to raise 1 lb of water 1°F. Exact definition: One-eighteenth of the amount of heat required to raise 1 lb of water from freezing to boiling at a standard atmospheric pressure.

Brush The pieces of carbon or copper that make a sliding contact with the commutator or slip rings.

BTDC Abbreviation for *before top dead center.*

Bunk log The structural crossmembers which form a bed for logs on a logging truck.

Buoyancy The upward or lifting force exerted on a body by a fluid.

Burnish To polish or shine a surface with a hard, smooth object.

Bushing A metallic or synthetic lining for a hole which reduces or prevents abrasion between components.

Butane A hydrocarbon gas. This gas becomes a liquid when under pressure.

Butterfly valve A valve in the venturi used to control the air flow.

Bypass filter An oil filter that only filters a portion of the oil flowing through the engine lubrication system.

Bypass valve A valve that opens when a set pressure is exceeded. This allows the fluid to pass through an alternative channel.

Cable (wire rope) A rope made up of individual wires twisted together.

Cage A housing in which a valve operates and is seated.

Calibrate To make an adjustment to a meter or other instrument so that it will indicate accurately its input.

Calipers A tool for measuring diameter, usually having curved legs and resembling a pair of compasses.

Calorie The amount of heat required to raise 1 g of water from 17 to 18°C.

Calorific value The amount of heat produced by burning 1 lb of fuel. (See *Heating value.*)

Cam A rotating component of irregular shape. It is used to change one type of motion to another, e.g., a rotating cam will impart reciprocating or variable motion to a part held against it.

Camber The amount, in millimeters or degrees, that the front wheels of a motor vehicle or vehicle are tilted outwards at the top from a true vertical. Outward tilting of the wheels at the top produces "positive" camber and inward tilting produces "negative" camber.

Cam follower (valve lifter) A part which is held in contact with the cam and to which the cam motion is imparted and further transmitted on to the pushrod.

Cam-ground A piston that is ground slightly oval but becomes round when heated.

Cam nose That portion of the cam that holds the valve wide open. It is the high point of the cam.

Camshaft A shaft with cam lobes.

Camshaft gear A gear fastened to the camshaft.

Capacitor An arrangement of insulated conductors and dielectrics for the accumulation of an electric charge with small voltage output.

Carbon A nonmetallic element that can be used both as a fuel and a lubricant.

Carbon dioxide (CO_2) A colorless, odorless gas which results when hydrocarbon fuels are burned completely.

Carbon monoxide (CO) A colorless, odorless, *poisonous* gas which results from the incomplete burning of hydrocarbon fuels.

Carbon pile Carbon disks or plates capable of carrying high current.

Carbon tetrachloride A colorless liquid, the fumes of which are toxic. Used in fire extinguishers and as a cleaning agent.

Carburizing To combine or add carbon to a metal for hardening purposes.

Case-harden To harden the outer surface of metal to a given case or shell depth, while leaving the inner portion soft to absorb shocks and allow bending. (See *Carburizing*.)

Caster The amount the centerline of the kingpin or ball joints tilt forward or backward from their true vertical.

Cavitation The formation of cavities in a pump fluid due to excessive speed of the activator; results in the loss of efficiency in the pump.

Cell connectors The lead straps connecting the cell groups.

Cells (battery) The individual (separate) compartments in the battery which contain positive and negative plates suspended in electrolyte.

Celsius (centigrade) Thermometer scale in which the freezing temperature of water is 0°C and boiling temperature of water at atmospheric pressure is 100°C.

Center of gravity That point in a body at which all its mass can be concentrated so that if supported at this point the body would remain motionless regardless of its position.

Center point steering See *Steering, center point.*

Center steering linkage A steering linkage utilizing two tie rods and an idler arm.

Celsius thermometer A thermometer with a Celsius (centigrade) scale.

Centrifugal force A force exerted on a rotating object in a direction outward from the center of rotation.

Centrifugal governor A governor which uses flyweight force to sense speed in order to control the amount of fuel supplied to the combustion chambers.

Centrifugal pump A pump using the centrifugal force produced by a rapidly rotating impeller to displace liquid.

Centrifuge A device with a rapidly rotating bowl which separates the impurities of a fluid by intense centrifugal force. It is one of the most efficient means known for purifying fuel and lubricating oils.

Chamfer (taper lead) The taper at the thread end of a tap or the throat of a die, made by cutting away the crests of the first few threads. This distributes the work of cutting over several threads and acts as a guide in starting the tap or die. The chamfer is relieved to facilitate cutting. The tap is classed as taper, second, or bottoming according to the length of chamfer, as approximately given here:
- Taper tap : 4° per side
- Second tap: 8° per side
- Bottoming tap: 23° per side
- Nut tap: approximately 75 percent of the thread length

Charge (battery) To force current (electrons) into a battery to restore it to a full state of electric charge.

Charles' law The physical law which states that the rise of temperature in all gases produces the same increase in volume if the pressure remains constant.

Chassis The framework of a motor vehicle including the power plant (engine), power transmission units, axles, and wheels. (Cab and body are excluded.)

Check valve A valve which permits only one direction of flow.

Chemical change A change which alters the composition of the molecules of a substance, producing new substances with new properties.

Choker A round-shaped hook attached to a wire rope.

Clamshell A dredging box or bucket shaped and hinged like the shell of a clam.

Circuit (electric) A source of power. A path for current flow with one or more resistant units.

Circuitbreaker (lighting system) A device that opens the circuit when the current draw becomes excessive and closes the circuit when the current flow is reduced.

Circulating pump The term applied to cooling-oil pumps which provide circulation of the fluid.

Circumference The distance around, or perimeter of, a circle. Equal to π times the diameter of the circle.

Clearance The space between two components.

Clearance volume The volume remaining above the piston when it is at TDC.

Clevis A U-shaped or stirrup-shaped piece of iron used as a connecting device.

Closed cooling system A cooling system which is not exposed to the atmosphere.

Closed nozzle A fuel nozzle having a valve between the combustion chamber and the fuel chamber.

Clutch A device used to connect or disconnect the power input to the power output.

Clutch diaphragm spring A circular, dish-shaped, flat, steel spring.

Clutch disk A part of a clutch assembly which is splined to the clutch or input shaft, and which is faced with friction material.

Clutch, friction A coupling device that provides a means of smooth and positive engagement and disengagement of engine torque to the vehicle power train. Transmission of power through the clutch is accomplished by bringing one or more rotating driving members into contact with the complimentary driven members.

Clutch housing or bell housing The cast-iron or aluminum housing surrounding the flywheel and clutch assembly.

Clutch pedal "free travel" The distance the clutch pedal travels before the clutch release mechanism starts to disengage the clutch.

Clutch pilot bearing A small bushing or ball bearing positioned in the crankshaft or flywheel.

Clutch pressure plate That part of a clutch assembly which, through spring force, squeezes the clutch disk against the flywheel, thereby transmitting a driving torque to the clutch shaft.

Clutch release assembly A device that straddles the clutch release bearing assembly.

Coefficient of friction The horizontal force required to move a body on a relatively smooth, level surface divided by the weight of that body. The coefficient of rolling friction is the maximum retarding force that can be applied to a rolling body on a relatively smooth, level surface without causing a cessation of rolling divided by the weight at the contact surface.

Coil spring A spring steel wire wound in a spiral pattern.

Color code Colored markings or wires to identify the different circuits.

Combination A motortruck or tractor coupled to one or more trailers.

Combustion The act or process of burning.

Combustion chamber The chamber in which combustion mainly occurs.

Combustion chamber volume The volume of the combustion chamber [when the piston is at TDC] measured in cubic inches [cubic centimeters].

Combustion cycle A series of thermodynamic processes through which the working gas passes to produce one power stroke. The full cycle involves intake, compression, power, and exhaust.

Commutator In an electric motor or generator, a number of copper bars connected to the armature windings but insulated from each other and from the armature.

Companion flange A circular flanged plate which connects the drive shaft to the transmission or axle.

Compound A combination of two or more elements that are mixed together.

Compressed air Air confined within a given space whose density is greater than that normally produced by atmospheric pressure.

Compressibility The property of a substance (e.g., air) confined within a given space by virtue of which its density increases and its volume decreases through the application of pressure.

Compression The process by which a confined gas is reduced in volume through the application of pressure.

Compression check A measurement of the compression of each cylinder at cranking speed or under the conditions recommended by the manufacturer.

Compression gauge A test instrument used to test cylinder compression.

Compression ignition The ignition of fuel through the heat of compression.

Compression pressure Pressure in the combustion chamber at the end of the compression stroke, but without any of the fuel being burned.

Compression ratio The ratio between the total volume in the cylinder when the piston is at BDC and the volume remaining when it is at TDC.

Compression release A device to prevent the intake or exhaust valves from closing completely, thereby permitting the engine to be turned over without compression.

Compression ring The piston rings used to reduce combustion leakage to a minimum.

Compression stroke That stroke of the operating cycle during which air is compressed into a smaller space, creating heat by molecular action.

Compressor A mechanical device that increases pressure within a container by pumping air into it.

Concentric Having the same center.

Condensation The reduction of a vapor or gas to a liquid state.

Condense To reduce from a gas or vapor to a liquid.

Condenser An arrangement of insulated conductors and dielectrics for the accumulation of an electric charge.

Conduction The transmission of heat through matter without motion of the conducting body.

Conductor Any material or device forming a path for the flow of electrons.

Connecting rod The rod joining the piston with the crankshaft.

Connecting rod bearing The bearing used in the connecting rod bore.

Constant-pressure combustion Combustion which occurs without a change in pressure. In an engine, this is achieved by a slower rate of burning than with constant-volume combustion.

Contamination The presence of harmful foreign matter in a fluid or in air.

Contour Outline.

Contract To reduce; to make smaller.

Control To regulate or govern the function of a unit.

Controlled port scavenging Scavenging method using ports which are controlled by valves in addition to the power piston.

Controlled stop The ability to slow a vehicle down to a complete stop from any speed without wheel hop, chatter, or lockup.

Control valve A device used to regulate the functions of a machine.

Control valve body A complex, multiple valve assembly for controlling the shifts and shift quality in automatic transmissions.

Convection The transfer of heat through a liquid by motion of its parts.

Converge To incline to or approach a certain point; to come together.

Converter A hydraulic clutch which multiplies the torque of the engine.

Coolant A liquid used as a cooling medium.

Cooling system The complete system for circulating coolant.

Core The central or innermost part of an object.

Corrode To eat or wear away gradually by chemical action.

Corrosion The slow destruction of material by chemical agents and electromechanical reactions.

Corrosive Having the ability to corrode.

Counterbalance A weight, usually attached to a moving component, that balances another weight.

Counterweight A counterbalancing weight used to offset the weight of the tractor or machine attachments.

Coupling A device used to connect two components.

Coupling point The point when the impeller and turbine in a torque converter travels at the same speed.

Crankcase The casing which surrounds the crankshaft.

Crankcase scavenging Scavenging method using the pumping action of the power piston in the crankcase to pump scavenging air.

Crankpin The portion of the crank throw (defined below) attached to the connecting rod.

Crankshaft A rotating shaft for converting rotary motion into reciprocating motion.

Crankshaft gear The gear that is mounted to the crankshaft.

Crank throw One crankpin with its two webs (the amount of offset of the rod journal).

Crank web The portion of the crank throw between the crankpin and main journal. This makes up the offset.

Crest The top surface joining the two sides of a thread.

Crest clearance For a screw form, the space between the top of a thread and the root of its mating thread.

Critical speeds Speeds at which the frequency of the power strokes synchronize with the crankshaft's natural frequency or that of torsional damper. If the engine is operated at one of its critical speeds for any length of time, a broken crankshaft may result.

Crocus cloth A very fine abrasive polishing cloth.

Crossmember A metal structural shape which connects the frame side rails.

Crowned A very slight curve in a surface (e.g., on a roller or raceway).

Crude oil Petroleum as it comes from the well (unrefined).

Crush A deliberate distortion of an engine's bearing shell so that it will be held solidly in place during operation.

Curb (vehicle) weight The weight of the empty vehicle, without load or driver but including fuel, coolant, oil, and all items of standard equipment.

Current The flow of electrons passing through a conductor. Measured in amperes.

Cycle A series that repeats itself in the same sequence.

Cylinder The piston chamber of an engine.

Cylinder, double-acting A cylinder in which fluid force can be applied in either direction.

Cylinder, double end rod A cylinder with two rods, one extending from each end.

Cylinder head The replaceable portion of the engine that seals the cylinder at the top. It often contains the valves, and in some cases it is part of the combustion chamber.

Cylinder hone A tool used to bring the diameter of a cylinder to specification and at the same time smooth its surface.

Cylinder liner A sleeve which is inserted in the bores of the engine block which make up the cylinder wall.

Cylinder, single-acting A cylinder in which the fluid force can be aplied in one direction only.

Dead axle A nondrive axle.

Dead center Either of the two positions when the crank and connecting rod are in a straight line at the end of the stroke.

Deceleration Opposite of acceleration—that is, implying a slowing down instead of a speeding up. Also called *negative acceleration.*

Deflection Bending or movement away from the normal position, due to loading.

Deflection rate Term used in regard to springs: the number of pounds required to compress or deflect a spring a distance of 1 in. For torsion springs, this distance is measured at the end of the control arm attached to the springs.

Deglazer A tool used to remove the glaze from cylinder walls.

Degree (circle) 1/360 of the circumference of a circle.

Degree wheel A wheel marked in degrees to set the lifter height.

Density The weight per unit volume of a substance.

Depth of engagement The depth of a thread in contact with two mating parts measured radially. It is the radial distance by which their thread forms overlap each other.

Detent A spring-loaded plunger, pin, ball, or pawl used as a stop or checking device on a rachet wheel or shaft.

Detergent A chemical with cleansing qualities that is added to the engine oil.

Detonation Burning of a portion of the fuel in the combustion chamber at a rate faster than desired. (See *Knocking.*)

Dial indicator (dial gauge) A precision measuring instrument.

Diaphragm Any flexible dividing partition separating two compartments.

Die Mating metal part containing a desired form impression.

Die casting Forcing molten metal into a steel die to form a casting.

Die thread A thread-cutting tool.

Differential A set of gears in a carrier that will drive both axle shafts at the same time, while allowing them to turn at different speeds when making turns.

Differential area When opposing faces of a valve spool or piston are acted upon by the same pressure but their areas differ in size, the ratio of their surface area will determine the strength of the relative force.

Differential case That part of the carrier to which the ring gear is attached.

Differential pressure fuel valve A closed fuel valve with a needle or spindle valve which is seated on the inner side of the orifices. The valve is lifted by fuel pressure.

Dilution Thinning, e.g., as when fuel mixes with the lubricant.

Diode A device which allows current to pass in one direction only.

Dipper A steel structure hinged to the boom.

Dipstick A device to measure the quantity of oil in the reservoir.

Direct-cooled piston A piston which is cooled by the internal circulation of a liquid.

Direct current (dc) Current that flows in one direction only.

Directional control valve A valve which selectively directs or prevents flow to or from specific channels. Also referred to as a *selector valve, control valve,* or *transfer valve.*

Directional stability (steering) The ability of a vehicle to move straight ahead and to remain relatively unaffected by road surface irregularities.

Discharge A draw of current from the battery.

Displacement In a single-acting engine, the volume swept by all pistons in making one stroke each. The displacement of one cylinder in cubic inches [cubic centimeters] is the circular area in square inches [square centimeters] times the stroke in inches [centimeters].

Distillation Heating a liquid and then condensing the vapors given off by the heating process.

Division plate A diaphragm surrounding the piston rod of a crosshead engine, usually having a wiper ring to remove excess oil from the piston rods as it slides through. It separates the crankcase from the lower end of the cylinder.

Dolly A two-wheel trailer equipped with a drawbar, the lower portion of a fifth wheel, and other components necessary to convert a semitrailer to a full trailer.

Dolly hitch A coupling device between the leading trailer and the dolly, consisting of a pintle hook and drawbar connection.

Double-acting Producing work or movement in both directions.

Double clutching Disengagement of the clutch twice prior to completing the shift in transmission.

Double flare Flared end of a tubing having two wall thicknesses; (v) the forming of the end of a tubing so that two wall thicknesses are used.

Double reduction Two reduction gear sets.

Doubles Semitrailer and full trailer combination.

Dowel A pin, usually of circular shape like a cylinder, used to pin or fasten something in position temporarily or permanently.

Downshift Shifting to a lower gear.

Dribbling Unatomized fuel running from the fuel nozzle.

Drill A tool used to bore holes.

Drill press A stationary machine to drive a tool in rotary motion.

Drive fit A fit between two components whose tolerance is so small that the two parts must be pressed or driven together.

Drive line The drive connection between the transmission and the carrier, or between two carriers.

Drive shaft The shaft (tubing) to which the universal and/or slip joint carrier are (is) connected.

Drop center rim Referring to tires—the two outer edges of the rim lying above its center.

Drop-forged Formed by hammering or forcing into shape by heat.

Dry cell (dry battery) A battery that uses no liquid electrolyte.

Dry-charged battery A battery in a precharged state but without electrolyte. The electrolyte is added when the battery is to be placed in service.

Dry sleeve A cylinder sleeve (liner) where the sleeve is supported over its entire length. The coolant does not touch the sleeve itself.

Dual axle A tandem axle or two axles in combination.

Dual valves Refers to cylinders having two valves performing one function, e.g., two intake valves, two exhaust valves.

Dump body A metal body generally hinged at the rear and raised by hydraulic means.

Dynamic balance Condition when the weight mass of a revolving object is in the same plane as the centerline of the object.

Dynamic pressure The pressure of a fluid resulting from its motion, equal to one-half the fluid density times the fluid velocity squared. In incompressible flow, dynamic pressure is the difference between total pressure and static pressure.

Dynamometer A device for absorbing the power output of an engine and measuring torque or horsepower so that it can be computed into brake horsepower (or watts).

Eccentric Circles which do not have the same center.

Edge filter A filter which passes liquid between narrowly separated disks or wires.

Efficiency In general, the proportion of energy going into a machine which comes out in the desired form, or the proportion of the ideal which is realized.

Electrolyte A solution of sulfuric acid and water.

Electromotive force (emf) Forces that move or tend to move electricity.

Element (battery) A group of plates—negative and positive.

Elliot axle A solid bar front axle on which the ends span the steering kunckle.

Emergency stop A term used when a stop is made by using the emergency brake system alone.

Emulsify To suspend oil in water in a mixture where the two do not easily separate.

End play The amount of axial movement in a shaft that is due to clearance in the bearings or bushings.

End yoke A yoke-shaped forging forming part of the universal joint connecting the drive shaft to the transmission or pinion.

Energize To make active.

Energy Capacity for doing work.

Engine displacement The volume each piston displaces when it moves from BDC to TDC times the number of cylinders.

EP lubricant See *Fluid, extreme pressure lubricants.*

Erode To wear away.

Ethylene glycol A compound added to the cooling system to reduce the freezing point.

Evaporative cooling system A cooling system in which the heat finally passes to the atmosphere by evaporation. This system may be either open or closed.

Excavator An hydraulically operated digging-scooping device attached to the superstructure of a vehicle.

Excess air Air present in the cylinder over and above that which is theoretically necessary to burn the fuel.

Excite To pass current through a coil or starter.

Exhaust manifold A device which connects all the exhaust ports (see below) to one outlet.

Exhaust port The opening through which exhaust gas passes from the cylinder to the manifold.

Exhaust valve The valve which, when opened, allows the exhaust gas to leave the cylinder.

Expansion ratio Ratio of the total volume when the piston is at BDC to the clearance volume when the piston is at TDC (nominally equal to compression ratio).

Eye bolt A bolt threaded at one end and bent into a loop at the other.

Fahrenheit Temperature scale in which the freezing temperature of water is 32°F and boiling point 212°F.

Fair lead A device to guide the wire rope onto the winch drive and prevent it from chafing or fouling.

Fatigue Deterioration of a material caused by constant use.

Feeler gauge A strip of steel ground to a precise thickness and used to check clearance.

Field The area affected by magnetic lines of force.

Field coil An insulated wire wound around an iron pole.

Fifth wheel A coupling device mounted on a truck, tractor, or dolly and used to connect a semitrailer. It acts as a hinge point to allow changes in direction of travel between the tractor and semitrailer.

Fillet A curved joint between two straight surfaces.

Filter A device for cleaning or purifying fluid or air.

Final drive The last reduction gear set of a motortruck, truck-tractor, tractor, or machine.

Finishing stone (hone) A honing stone with a fine grid.

Fire point Lowest temperature at which an oil heated in a standard apparatus will ignite and continue to burn.

Firing order The order in which the cylinders deliver their power stroke.

Firing pressure The highest pressure reached in the cylinder during combustion.

Fish plate A reinforcement plate attached to the web of the frame running along the frame length.

Fit The closeness of contact between machined components. Applied to service, it may be considered as "drive-," "press-," "force-," or "hand-fit" where external force may be used.

Fixed displacement pump A type of pump in which the volume of fluid per cycle cannot be varied.

Flange A metal part which is spread out like a rim; the action of working a piece or part spread out.

Flange yoke A yoke with a circular flange matching end yoke on the drive shaft to make a universal joint.

Flank (side or thread) The straight part of the thread which connects the crest with the root.

Flank angles The angle between a specified flank of a thread and the plane perpendicular to the axis (measured in an axial plane).

Flare To open or spread outwardly.

Flaring tool A tool used to form a flare on tubing.

Flash point The temperature at which a substance, usually a fluid, will give off a vapor that will flash or burn momentarily when ignited.

Flat crank A crankshaft in which one of the bearing journals is not round.

Flotation The ability to float generally when referring to large, low-pressure tires.

Flow control valve A valve which is used to control the flow rate of fluid in a fluid power system.

Flowmeter An instrument used to measure the quantity or flow rate of a fluid in motion.

Fluctuating Wavering, unsteady, not constant.

Fluid A liquid or gas, or a mixture thereof.

Fluid coupling. The simplest form of hydrodynamic clutch. It does not have the ability to multiply torque.

Fluid drive Either a fluid coupling or a torque converter.

Fluid, extreme pressure lubricants Fluids compounded with certain additives which increase their load-carrying ability.

Fluid, flash point The temperature at which a fluid first gives off sufficient flammable vapor to ignite when approached by a small flame or spark.

Fluid flow The stream or movement of a fluid; the rate of a fluid's movement.

Fluid, hydraulic A fluid suitable for use in hydraulic systems.

Fluid, pour point The lowest temperature of a fluid at which it will flow or can be poured.

Fluid power Power transmitted and controlled through the use of fluids, either liquids or gases, under pressure.

Fluid, specific gravity The ratio of the weight of a given volume of fluid to the weight of an equal volume of water.

Flute The grooves of a tap that provide the cutting rake and chip clearance.

Flux (magnetic) Magnetic force.

Flyball governor Conventional type of centrifugal governor, commonly called a *mechanical governor*.

Flywheel A device for storing energy in order to carry the piston over a compression and to minimize cyclical speed variations.

Flywheel ring gear A circular steel ring having gear teeth on the outer circumference.

Foot brake valve A foot-actuated valve which controls the air pressure delivered to or released from the air chambers.

Foot-pound (ft·lb) In the U.S. Customary System, the amount of work accomplished when a force of 1 lb produces a displacement of 1 ft. (See *Newton-meter.*)

Force The action of one body on another tending to change the state of motion of the body acted upon. Force is usually measured in pounds [kilograms].

Force-feed lubrication A lubricating system in which oil is pumped to the desired points at a controlled rate by means of positive displacement pumps.

Forged Shaped with a hammer or machine.

Foundation The structure on which an engine is mounted. It performs one or more of the following functions: holds the engine in alignment with the driven machine, adds enough weight to the engine to minimize vibration, adds to rigidity of the bed plate.

Four-in-one bucket A multipurpose bucket.

Four-stroke cycle Cycle of events which is completed in four strokes of the piston, or in two crankshaft revolutions.

Frame The main structural member of an engine.

Free electrons Outer-orbit electrons surrounding the atom's nucleus.

Free flow Flow which encounters negligible resistance.

Free wheel The action of a motor vehicle when the power is disconnected or the clutch is slipping with a resultant loss of engine braking.

Frequency Vibration periods occurring in unit time.

Friction The resistance to motion due to the contact of two surfaces moving against each other.

Fuel filter A filtering or screening device for cleaning the engine fuel.

Fuel mixture A ratio of fuel and air.

Fuel transfer pump A mechanical device used to transfer fuel from the tank to the injection pump.

Fuel valve A valve admitting fuel to the combustion chamber. In a more general sense, this term may also apply to any manual or automatic valve controlling flow of fuel.

Fulcrum The pivot point of a lever.

Full-floating Refers to a type of axle in which the axle housing supports all the weight.

Full-floating piston pin A piston pin free to turn in the piston boss of the connecting rod eye.

Full-flow oil filter All engine oil passes through this filter before entering the lubrication channels.

Gallery Passageway inside a wall or casting.

Galvanic action When two dissimilar metals are immersed in certain solutions, particularly acid, electric current will flow from one to the other.

Gas Matter that has no definite form or volume, but instead tends to expand indefinitely when not confined.

Gasket A layer of material used between machined surfaces in order to seal them against leakage.

Gassing Hydrogen bubbles rising from the electrolyte when the battery is being charged.

Gate valve A common type of manually operated valve in which a sliding gate is used to obstruct the flow of fluid.

Gauge pressure Pressure above atmospheric pressure.

Gauge snubber A device installed in the fuel line to the pressure gauge used to dampen pressure surges and thus provide a steady reading. This helps protect the gauge.

GCW Abbreviation for *gross combination weight*. The total weight of a fully equipped vehicle [truck-tractor, tractor, or motortruck, along with attached semitrailer and/or full trailer(s)], including payload, fuel, driver, etc.

Gear A toothed mechanical device that acts as a rotating lever to transmit torque from one shaft to another.

Gear pump A pump which uses the spaces between the adjacent teeth of gears for moving the liquid.

Gear ratio The number of revolutions a driving gear requires to turn a driven gear through one complete revolution. For a pair of gears the ratio is found by dividing the number of teeth on the driven gear by the number of teeth on the driving gear.

Gear ratio, axle Ratio of the speed of the drive shaft to the speed of the axle shafts.

Gear ratio, fast Low numerical ratio, as 3.00:1.00 (high speed).

Gear ratio, slow High numerical ratio, as 9.00:1.00 (low speed).

Gear ratio, transmission Ratio of the transmission input shaft speed to the speed of the output shaft.

Gear reduction Torque is multiplied and speed decreased by the factor of the gear ratio.

Gear train A group of intermeshing gears that form an assembly and provide for one or more torque changes as the power input is transmitted to the power output.

Generator An electromagnetic device used to produce electricity.

Glad hand A mechanical device (coupling) used to join air line hoses.

Gland A device to prevent the leakage of gas or liquid past a joint.

Glaze A smooth, glassy surface finish.

Glow plug A heater plug for the combustion chamber of diesel engines. It has a coil of resistance wire heated by a low-voltage current.

Governor, air A device for controlling air pressure.

Governor, engine A device to automatically control maximum rpm.

Grab hook A hook so designed that a chain link can be placed into the hook to hold it.

Grader A self-propelled machine designed to spread and level road material.

Grappel skidder A mechanical device (clamp) for grasping logs.

Gravity The force which tends to draw all bodies toward the center of the earth. The weight of any given body is the result of the gravitational forces exerted upon that body.

Grid (battery) The lead frame to which the active battery material is affixed.

Grille The screen or protective structure located in front of the radiator.

Grinding Removing metal from an object by means of a revolving abrasive wheel, disk, or belt.

Grinding compound Abrasive for resurfacing valves and other components.

Ground (battery) The battery terminal that is connected to the engine or the framework.

Grouser A steel or cast-steel structure bolted to the track chain, or to form a track chain.

Growler A test instrument used for testing the armature of a starter or generator for open, short, and grounded circuits.

Gussett The flat steel or aluminum plates which tie in crossmembers to the frame side rails.

GVW Abbreviation for *gross vehicle weight*. The total weight of a fully equipped vehicle and its payload.

Half-cab One-person cab usually located beside the engine.

Half-moon key A fastening device shaped roughly like a semicircle. (See *Key*.)

Heat A form of energy.

Heat exchanger A device used to cool by transferring heat.

Heat treatment The process of heating and cooling a metal throughout a temperature range for the purpose of obtaining certain desired mechanical or physical properties.

Heating value Amount of heat produced by burning 1 lb of fuel.

Helical gear A gear wheel shaped like a spiral. (The teeth are cut across the face at an angle with the axis.)

Helix A line shaped to form a screw thread.

Helper spring An additional spring device, which permits greater load on an axle.

Herringbone gears "Double-helical" gears in which the angle of the teeth form a V.

Hone A tool with an abrasive stone used for removing metal.

Horsepower (hp) A unit of power equivalent to 33,000 ft·lb of work per minute (U.S. Customary System) or 75 kg·m/s (metric). (See *Brake horsepower* and *Indicated horsepower*.)

Horsepower, gross The brake horsepower of an engine without allowing for the power absorbed by the engine's accessory system or components.

Horsepower-hour (hp·h) A unit of energy; 1 hp·h is equal to approximately 2545 Btu (U.S. Customary System).

Horsepower, net The brake horsepower remaining at the flywheel of the engine to do useful work after the power required by the engine accessories (fan, water pump, generator, etc.) has been provided.

Hub That part of the wheel assembly to which the rim is fastened.

Hunting Alternate overspeeding and underspeeding of the engine caused by governor instability.

Hydrair See *Hydrospring (Hydrair)*.

Hydraulic The movement of liquids, or the force exerted by the movement of water, oil, or other liquids.

Hydraulic brakes Brakes that are actuated by an hydraulic system.

Hydraulic governor A governor using fluid to operate the fuel control.

Hydraulics That branch of mechanics or engineering which deals with the action or use of liquids forced through tubes and orifices under pressure to operate various mechanisms.

Hydrocarbon (HC) A compound of hydrogen and carbon. Petroleum and its derivatives are mixtures of various hydrocarbons.

Hydroflotation A tire filled with a solution of water and calcium chloride.

Hydrogen One of the elements; used as a fuel and a lubricant.

Hydrometer A test instrument for determining the specific gravities of liquids.

Hydrospring (Hydrair) A suspension spring using nitrogen gas and oil.

Hypoid gear Gear with diagonally positioned teeth.

Hypoid gearing A reduction gear in which the pinion gear centerline is below the centerline of the ring gear.

Idling An engine running without load.

Ignition The start of combustion.

Ignition lag The time between start of injection and ignition.

Immersed To be completely under the surface of a fluid.

Impact wrench An air wrench or an electrically driven wrench.

Impeller A wheel or disk with fins.

Independent suspension Attaching parts (including spring) in which the wheels are not connected by an axle beam but are mounted separately on the chassis and are capable of independent vertical movement.

Indicated horsepower (ihp) The power transmitted to the pistons by the gas in the cylinders.

Indicated thermal efficiency The ratio of indicated horsepower to equivalent power input in the form of heat from fuel.

Indicator An instrument for recording the variation of cylinder pressure during the cycle.

Indicator card A graphical record of the cylinder pressures made by an indicator.

Indirect-cooled piston A piston cooled mainly by the conduction of heat through the cylinder walls.

Induction, electromagnetic Using a magnetic field to produce electricity.

Inertia That property of matter which causes it to tend to remain at rest if already motionless or to continue in the same straight line of motion if already moving.

Inhibitor Any substance which retards or prevents chemical reactions such as corrosion or oxidation.

Injection pump A high-variable pressure pump delivering fuel into the combustion chamber.

Injection system The components necessary for delivering fuel to the combustion chamber in the correct quantity, at the correct time, and in a condition satisfactory for efficient burning.

Injector A device used to bring fuel into the combustion chamber.

In-line engine An engine in which all the cylinders are in a straight line.

Input The amount of energy delivered to a machine (by a battery or other energy source).

Insert A reinforcing alloy pressed within a bore.

Insert bearing A removable, precision-made bearing.

Insulator (electrical) A material that, under normal conditions, will not conduct electricity.

Intake manifold A connecting casting between the air filter or turbocharger and the port openings to the intake valves.

Intake valve The valve which, when open, allows air to enter into the cylinder.

Integral Combined to act as a single unit.

Interaxle differential A gear set or device that divides the torque equally between two carriers.

Intercooler Heat exchanger for cooling the air between stages of compression.

Intermediate gear The gear ratio in the transmission between low and high.

Internal combustion engine An engine that burns fuel within itself as a means of producing power.

Internal gear A ringlike gear with the gear teeth cut on the inside of the ring.

Isochronous governor A governor having zero-speed droop.

Jack Mechanical or hydraulic lifting device.

Jackknife Skidding of a tractor-trailer, causing the units to close like a jackknife.

Jack shaft An intermediate driven shaft.

Jet A small hole in a carburetor passage to measure the flow of gasoline.

Jet cooling A method of passing cooling oil below the piston by means of a jet or nozzle.

Joule (J) The unit of work in the International System of metric units. It is equal to the amount of work done when a force of 1 N is applied through a distance of 1 m, measured in the direction in which the force acts.

Journal The portion of a shaft, crank, etc., which turns in a bearing.

Kelvin scale A temperature scale having the same size degree divisions as the Celsius scale, but whose zero point, known as *absolute zero*, is equal to $-273.1°C$.

Key A fastening device wherein two components each have a partially cut groove, and a single square is inserted in both to fasten them together.

Keyway The groove cut in a component to hold the key.

Kickdown switch An electric switch that will cause an automatic winch transmission or overdrive unit to shift down to a lower gear.

Kilometer (km) A metric measurement of length equal to 0.6214 mile (U.S. Customary System).

Kilowatt (kW) A metric unit of power equal to 1000 W.

Kilowatthour (kWh) A metric unit of electric energy.

Kinetic energy The energy which an object has while in motion. See *Potential energy*.

Kingpin For a front axle, a hardened steel pin which connects the front axle and steering knuckles and about which the knuckles pivot; for a semitrailer, a hardened steel pin which is locked into the fifth wheel on a truck-tractor to effect coupling of the trailer with the tractor.

Kingpin inclination The inward tilt of the tops of the kingpins which results in the centerline of the steering axis coming nearer the centerline of the tire where it contacts the road.

Km/h Abbreviation for velocity in *kilometers per hour* (metric).

Knocking A sharp pounding sound occurring periodically in an engine.

Knurling A method of placing ridges in a surface, thereby forcing the areas between those ridges to rise.

Laden or Lading That which constitutes a full load; the maximum freight load of a vehicle.

Lag To slow down or get behind; time interval, as in *ignition lag*.

Laminar A layer of fluid.

Laminar flow A smooth flow in which no crossflow of fluid particles occurs.

Land The projecting part of a grooved surface; for example, that part of a piston on which the rings rest.

Landing gear Retractable supports for a semitrailer to to keep the trailer level when the truck-tractor is detached from it.

Lap (lapping) A method of refinishing (grinding and polishing) the surface of a component.

Law of direct drive Direct drive is obtained by locking any two planetary members together, or by driving any two members at the same rpm and in the same direction.

Law of neutral When there is an input, but no reaction member, the condition is neutral.

Law of reduction When there is a reaction member and the planet carrier is the output, the condition is gear reduction. The two possible combinations are sun gear driving with the internal gear as the reaction member, or internal gear driving with the sun gear as the reaction member.

Law of reverse When the planet carrier is held, reverse is obtained by having either the sun gear or the internal gear act as the input.

Letter drills Drills on which the size is designated by a letter.

Leverage The mechanical advantage obtained by use of a lever or combination of levers.

Limited-slip differential A differential unit which gives superior traction by transferring driving torque, when one wheel is spinning, to the wheel that is not slipping.

Line A tube, pipe, or hose which is used as a conductor of fluid.

Liner The sleeve forming the cylinder bore in which the piston reciprocates.

Linkage A movable connection between two units.

Liquid Matter which has a definite volume but takes the shape of any container into which it is placed.

Liter A metric measurement of volume equal to 0.2642 gal (U.S.).

Live axle A revolving axle shaft (drive axle) to which the road wheels are rigidly attached.

Live wire A conductor which is carrying current.

Load The power that is being delivered by any power-producing device. The equipment that uses the power from the power-producing device.

Load distribution Distribution of the load on a truck, trailer chassis, or semitrailer.

Load factor The mean load carried by an engine, expressed in percent of its capacity.

Load line A centerline indicating the points of contact where the load passes within the bearing.

Load-line angle The angle of a load line with respect to the shaft center or bearing radial centerline.

Load torque The torque which the vehicle load presents to the output shaft of a transmission.

Lobe The projecting part, usually rounded, on a rotating shaft.

Lockup clutch A clutch used to achieve direct drive.

Log book The driver's book record of hours, routes, etc.

Louver The ventilation opening in cab, hood, radiator grille, or compartment.

Low-pressure indicator A unit or

a combination of units which provides a visible or audible warning signal whenever the system pressure is below a predetermined value.

LPG Abbreviation for *Liquified petroleum gas;* used as an engine fuel.

Lubricant A substance used to decrease the effects of friction, commonly a petroleum product (grease, oil, etc.)

Lubricator A mechanical oiler which feeds oil at a controlled rate.

Lug (engine) Condition when the engine is operating at or below its maximum torque speed.

Magnaflux A method used to check components for cracks.

Magnetic field An area affected by magnetic lines of force.

Magnetorque An electromagnetic clutch.

Main bearing A bearing supporting the crankshaft on its axis.

Mandrel A mounting device for a stone, cutter, saw, etc.

Manual linkage Mechanical connection to achieve actuation.

Manual valve A valve which is opened, closed, or adjusted by hand.

Master cylinder That part of the hydraulic brake system which develops pressure.

Matter Any substance which occupies space and has weight. The three forms of matter are solids, liquids, and gases.

Mean effective pressure (mep) The calculated combustion in pounds per square inch [kPa] (average) during the power stroke, minus the pounds per square inch [kPa] (average) of the remaining three strokes.

Mean indicated pressure (mip) Net mean gas pressure acting on the piston to produce work.

Mechanical advantage The ratio of the resisting weight to the acting force. The distance through which the force is exerted divided by the distance the weight is raised.

Mechanical brakes Foundation brakes that are actuated by a mechanical linkage.

Mechanical efficiency (1) The ratio of brake horsepower to indicated horsepower, or the ratio of brake mean effective pressure to mean indicated pressure. (2) An engine's rating which indicates how much of the potential horsepower is wasted through friction within the moving parts of the engine.

Mechanical injection Mechanical

force pressurizing the metered fuel and causing injection.

Mechanically operated valve A valve which is opened and closed at regular points in a cycle of events by mechanical means.

Metal fatigue Condition where metal crystallizes and is in jeopardy of breaking due to vibration, twisting, bending, etc.

Metering fuel pump A fuel pump delivering a controlled amount of fuel per cycle.

Metric size Size of a component, part, etc., in metric units of measurement (e.g., meters, centimeters, milliliters, and so forth).

Micrometer (mike) A precision measuring tool that is accurate to within one/one-thousandth of an inch or one/one-hundredth of a millimeter.

Micron (micrometer, un) One/one-millionth of a meter, or 0.000039 in.

Millimeter (mm) One/one-thousandth of a meter, or 0.039370 in.

Milling machine A machine used to remove metal or cut splices, gears, etc., by the rotation of its cutter or abrasive wheel.

Misfiring Condition where the ignition timing in the cylinders of an engine is not synchronized correctly because the pressure of combustion in one or more cylinders is lower than that in the remaining cylinders.

Mixed cycle Condition where fuel burns partly at constant volume and partly at constant pressure. Sometimes applied to the actual combustion cycle in most high-speed internal combustion engines.

Molecule The smallest portion to which a substance may be reduced by subdivision and still retain its chemical identity.

Motor An actuator which converts fluid power or electric energy to rotary mechanical force and motion.

MPH Abbreviation for velocity in *miles per hour* (U.S. Customary System).

Muffler The expansion chamber used to muffle the noise of combustion.

Multiviscosity oil An oil meeting SAE requirements.

Needle bearing A roller bearing in which the rollers are smaller in diameter than in length proportionally to the race.

Negative terminal The terminal from which the current flows back to its source; has an excess of electrons.

410

Neoprene A synthetic rubber highly resistant to oil, light, heat, and oxidation.

Neutron A neutrally charged particle in the nucleus of an atom.

Newton (N) The unit of force in the International System of metric units. A force of 1 N accelerates a mass of 1 kg at a rate of 1 m/s².

Newton-meter (N·m) The metric unit of torque. A torque of 1 N·m is applied when a force of 1 N is exerted at a radius of 1 m from the center of rotation of an object, for example, a tension wrench.

Newton's third law For every action there is an equal and opposite reaction.

Nitrogen (N) An odorless, colorless, gaseous element.

Nitrogen oxide (NO$_x$) The combination of nitrogen and oxygen that occurs during the combustion process.

Nonferrous metals Any metal not containing iron.

North pole (magnet) The pole from which the lines of force emanate (thereafter entering the south pole).

Nozzle The component containing the fuel valve and having one or more orifices through which fuel is injected.

Number drills Drills on which the size is designated by a number.

Odometer Mileage recording instrument.

Offset To balance; to cancel. Anything regarded or advanced as a counterbalance or equivalent setoff.

Offtracking The difference in radiuses from the turning center to the vehicle centerline at the foremost and rearmost axles of a vehicle, or combination, and represents the increase beyond the tangent track caused by a turn.

Ohm (Ω) The metric unit of electric resistance.

Ohmmeter An instrument for measuring the resistance in a circuit or unit in ohms.

Ohm's Law The number of amperes flowing in a circuit is equal to the number of volts divided by the number of ohms.

Oil bath air cleaner An air filter that utilizes a reservoir of oil to remove the impurities from the air before it enters the intake manifold or the compressor of the turbine.

Oil cooler A heat exchanger for lowering the temperature of oil.

Oil filter A device for removing impurities from oil.

Oil gallery A pipe-drilled or cast passage in the cylinder head block and crankcase that is used to carry oil from the supply to an area requiring lubrication or cooling.

Oil pump A mechanical device to pump oil (under pressure) into the various oil galleries.

Oil pumping An engine condition wherein excessive oil passes by the piston rings and is burned during combustion.

Oil seal A mechanical device used to prevent oil leakage, usually past a shaft.

Oil slinger A special frame disk fastened to a revolving shaft. When the shaft rotates and oil contacts the disk, it is thrown outward away from the seal, and thus reduces the force on the seal lip.

Oil splash system An engine oiling system that utilizes the connecting rods to dip into oil troughs and "splash" oil onto the moving parts.

Open circuit A circuit in which a wire is broken or disconnected.

Opposed piston engine An engine having two pistons operating in opposite ends of the same cylinder, compressing air between them.

Orderly turbulence Air motion which is controlled as to direction or velocity.

Orifice An aperture or opening.

Oscillate To swing back and forth like a pendulum; to vibrate.

Oscillating action A swinging, shaking action.

Oscillograph A recording instrument electronically operated to make visible representation of the oscillations of an alternating current.

Oscilloscope A device for recording waveforms proportional to the input voltage (on a fluorescent screen).

Output The actual torque or energy delivered by a machine.

Output shaft The shaft which delivers the power.

Overdrive A gear set (ratio) used to decrease the output in relation to engine speed.

Overhead camshaft A camshaft which is mounted above the cylinder head.

Overrunning clutch A clutch mechanism that transmits power in one direction only.

Overrunning clutch starter drive A mechanical device that locks in one direction but turns freely in the opposite direction.

Overspeed governor A governor that shuts off the fuel or stops the engine only when excessive speed is reached.

Oversquare engine An engine that has a larger bore diameter than the length of its stroke.

Oversteer The tendency for a vehicle, when negotiating a turn, to turn more sharply than the driver intends.

Oxidation That process by which oxygen unites with some other substance, causing rust or corrosion.

Packing A seal made of flexible material used to seal two parts which move in relation to each other.

Paper air cleaner An air filter with a special paper element through which the air is drawn.

Parallel circuit An electric circuit with two or more branch circuits. It is wired so as to allow current to flow through all branches at the same time.

Pascal (Pa) The unit of pressure (that is, force per unit area) in the International System of metric units. A pressure of 1 Pa applies when a force of 1 N is exerted on an area of 1 m². 6895 Pa = 6.895 kPa = 1 lb/in² (U.S. Customary System).

Pascal's law Pressure applied anywhere to a body of confined fluid is transmitted undiminished to every portion of the surface of the containing vessel.

Pawl A stud or pin that can be moved or pivoted into engagement with a hole or teeth cut on another part to lock the parts.

Payload The weight of the cargo carried by a truck, not including the weight of the body.

Peen The thin end of a hammer head (opposite to the face).

Peening Flattening the end of a rivet, etc., using the force of a hammer.

Penetrating oil A special oil that aids in the removal of rusted parts.

Perforate To make full of holes.

Periphery The external boundary or circumference.

Petroleum An oil liquid mixture made up of numerous hydrocarbons chiefly of the paraffin series.

Phosphor-bronze A bearing material composed of tin, lead, and copper.

Physical change A change which

does not alter the composition of the molecules of a substance.

Pilot shaft A shaft position in or through a hole of a component used as a means of aligning the components.

Pilot valve A valve used to control the operation of another valve.

Pintle hook A hook mounted on a truck or semitrailer used to couple on a full traaler.

Pintle nozzle A closed nozzle having a projection on the end of the fuel valve which extends into the orifice when the valve is closed.

Pipe In diesel applications, that type of fluid line the dimensions of which are designated by nominal (approximate) inside diameter.

Piston A cylindrical plug which slides up and down in the cylinder and which is connected to the connecting rod.

Piston boss The reinforced area around the piston pin bore.

Piston displacement The volume of air moved or displaced by a piston when moved from BDC to TDC.

Piston head The portion of the piston above the top ring.

Piston lands That space of the piston between the ring grooves.

Piston pin (wrist pin) A cylindrical alloy pin that passes through the piston bore and is used to connect the connecting rod to the piston.

Piston ring A split ring of the expansion type placed in a groove of the piston to seal the space between the piston and the wall.

Piston ring end cap The clearance between the ends of the ring (when installed in the cylinder).

Piston ring groove The grooves cut in the piston into which the piston rings are fitted.

Piston ring side clearance The clearance between the sides of the ring and the ring lands.

Piston skirt The portion of the piston which is below the piston bore.

Piston speed The total distance traveled by each piston in 1 min. The formula is as follows: piston stroke (ft) [m] × rpm × 2 or stroke (in) [cm] × rpm/6.

Pitch The distance between two corresponding points on a sprocket wheel or on a chain.

Pitman arm A lever arm splined to the steering gear cross shaft.

Pivot The pin or shaft on which a component moves.

Planetary carrier The member of a planetary gear to which the planetary gears are attached.

Planetary drive A planetary gear reduction set where the sun gear is the drive and the planetary carrier is the output.

Planetary gear set A constant-mesh gear set consisting of the ring gear, the sun gear, three or four planetary carrier gears, and the planetary carrier.

Plate (battery) A flat, square, rigid body of lead peroxide or porous lead.

Play The movement between two parts.

Plunger pump A pump which displaces fluid by means of a plunger.

Ply rating (PR) A measure of the strength of tires based on the strength of a single ply of designated construction. An eight-ply rating does not necessarily mean that eight plies are used in building the tire, but simply that the tire has the strength of eight standard plies.

Pneumatics That branch of physics pertaining to the pressure and flow of gases.

Pneumatic timing The time required for transmission of air to or from the brake chambers upon brake actuation or release.

Polarity Can refer to which (positive or negative) is the grounded battery terminal, an electric circuit, or the north and south poles of a magnet.

Polarizing To develop polarization of the pole shoes in respect to battery polarity.

Polar timing diagram A graphic method of illustrating the events of an engine cycle with respect to crankshaft rotation.

Pole (magnet) Either end of a magnet.

Pole shoe A soft piece of iron over which a field coil is placed.

Port bridge The portion of a cylinder or liner between two exhaust or scavenging ports.

Ports Openings in the cylinder block and cylinder head for the passage of oil and coolant. (Also exhaust-intake connection and valve openings.)

Port scavenging Introducing scavenging air through ports in the cylinder wall when they are uncovered by the power piston near the end of the power stroke.

Positive terminal The terminal toward which current flows; has a deficiency of electrons.

Potential energy The energy possessed by a substance because of its position, its condition, or its chemical composition. See *Kinetic energy*.

Pour point The lowest temperature at which an oil will flow.

Power Rate of performance of work.

Power flow The flow of power from the input shaft through one or more sets of gears, or through an automatic transmission to the output shaft.

Power steering A steering system utilizing hydraulic pressure to reduce the turning effort required of the operator.

Power take off (PTO) A device usually mounted on the side of the transmission or transfer case, and used to transmit engine power to auxiliary equipment such as pumps, winches, etc.

Power train A name applied to the group of components used to transmit engine power to the wheels. The power train includes the clutch, transmission, universal joints, drive shafts, carrier(s) and final drives.

Precision insert bearing A precision type of bearing consisting of an upper and lower shell.

Precombustion chamber A portion of the combustion chamber connected to the cylinder through a narrow throat. Fuel is injected into and partly burned in the precombustion chamber. Heat released by this partial burning causes the contents of the precombustion chamber to be ejected into the cylinder with considerable turbulence.

Preloading Adjusting tapered roller bearings so that the rollers are under mild pressure.

Press fit See *Drive fit*.

Pressure Force exerted per unit of area.

Pressure, back See *Backpressure*.

Pressure bleeder A device to force brake fluid (under pressure) into the cylinder so that one person can remove existing air from the brake system.

Pressure cap A special radiator cap with a pressure relief and vacuum valve.

Pressure differential The difference in pressure between any two points of a system or a component.

Pressure gauge An instrument used for measuring the existing air or fluid pressure in a circuit system or chamber.

Pressure, head The force due to the height of a columnar body of fluid, expressed in feet [meters].

Pressure lubrication A lubricating system in which oil at a controlled pressure is brought to the desired location.

Pressure, operating The pressure at which the system is operated.

Pressure (regulator) relief valve A valve that limits the maximum system pressure.

Printed circuit An electric circuit where the conductor is pressed or printed into or on an insulating material (panel) and at the same time is connected to the resistors, diodes, etc.

Prony brake A friction brake used for engine testing.

Proton The positively charged particle in the nucleus of an atom.

Prussian blue A blue pigment, obtainable in tubes, which is used to find high spots in a bearing.

Pulley A wheel grooved to receive a rope or wire rope.

Pulsate To move with rhythmical impulse.

Pulverize To reduce to powder or dust.

Pump A device for moving fluids.

Pump, axial piston fixed delivery A power-driven pump having multiple pistons disposed with their axes parallel to the drive shaft and actuated by a member having fixed angularity to these axes.

Pump, axial piston variable delivery A power-driven pump with an adjustable, controlled volumetric output, having multiple pistons disposed with their axes parallel to the drive shaft and actuated by a member having variable angularity to these axes and suitable means of changing stroke.

Pump, centrifugal A power-driven device for converting mechanical energy into fluid energy; has an impeller rotating in a volute housing with liquid carried around the periphery of the housing and discharged by means of centrifugal force.

Pump, gear A power-driven pump having two or more intermeshing gears or lobed members enclosed in a suitably shaped housing.

Pump, hand A hand-operated pump.

Pumping loss The power consumed by replacing exhaust gas in the cylinder with fresh air.

Pump, power A power-driven mechanical device of rotary design that creates fluid flow.

Pump, radial piston rotary fixed delivery A power-driven pump with a controlled volumetric output, having multiple pistons disposed radially and actuated by a member having a fixed eccentricity.

Pump, radial piston variable delivery A power-driven pump with an adjustable, controlled volumetric output, having multiple pistons disposed radially and actuated by a member having variable eccentricity and suitable means of changing stroke.

Pump, reciprocating single-plunger A power-driven pump in which a single piston reciprocates.

Pump scavenging Using a piston pump to pump scavenging air.

Pump, torque converter Same as *Impeller,* which see.

Pump, vane fixed-delivery A power-driven pump having constant volume, with multiple vanes within a supporting rotor, encased in a cam ring.

Pump, vane variable-delivery A power-driven pump having multiple vanes within a supporting rotor, and suitable means of changing the volume.

Push fit The part of the bearing that can be slid into place by hand if it is square with its mounting.

Pushrod A rod used for transmitting cam motion to a rocker arm.

Pyrometer A temperature indicator used for comparing exhaust temperatures of the various cylinders.

Quench To cool heated steel or iron by thrusting it into water.

Quick-release valve A valve used to accelerate the release of air pressure from the brake chambers.

Quicksilver Metallic mercury.

Race (bearing) The inner or outer groove or channel bearing ring.

Raceway The surface of the groove or path which supports the balls or rollers of a bearing roll.

Radial Perpendicular to the shaft or bearing bore.

Radial clearance (radial displacement) The clearance within the bearing and between the balls and races, perpendicular to the shaft.

Radial load A "round-the-shaft" load—that is, one that is perpendicular to the shaft through the bearing.

Radiator A heat exchanger in which cooling water gives up heat to the air without coming into direct contact with it.

Radius The distance from the center of a circle to its outer edge or the straight line extending from the center to the edge of a circle.

Ratio The numerical relationship between objects.

Reaction member The member opposing the applied force or flow.

Reaction pressure A fluid pressure that opposes a spring pressure or combination of spring pressure and fluid pressure on the opposite end of a spool valve.

Rebore To bore out a cylinder to a size slightly larger than the original.

Reciprocating action A back-and-forth (alternating) movement.

Rectifier A device used to convert alternating current into direct current.

Reefer A truck with a heavily insulated body and having a refrigerating unit.

Regulator (electrical) An electromagnetic or electronic device used to control generator voltage.

Relay An electromagnetic switch which utilizes variation in the strength of an electric circuit to effect the operation of another circuit.

Relay valve, air A valve used to accelerate the air flow to and from the air brake chambers.

Relay valve, hydraulic A directional valve of spool design which directs fluid flow and pressure in hydraulic circuitry.

Relief valve An automatic valve which is held shut by a spring of correct strength. Excess pressure opens the valve and releases some of the gas or liquid. This valve is used to protect filters, air tanks, etc., from dangerous pressures.

Reservoir A chamber used to store hydraulic fluid or air under pressure.

Resistance (electric) The opposition offered by a body when current passes through it.

Resisting bending moment Section modulus x yield strength. This is used when comparing the strength of two frames made of different materials.

Resistor A device placed in a circuit to lower the voltage, reduce the current, or stabilize the voltage.

Retard (injection timing) To set the timing so that injection occurs later than TDC or fewer degrees before TDC.

Retarder An auxiliary speed-reducing device to retard movement of the vehicle.

Reverse elliot axle A solid-beam front axle on which the steering knuckles span the axle ends.

Reverse flush To pump water or a cleaning agent through the cooling system in the direction opposite to normal flow.

Reverse idler gear The transmission gear which effects reverse rotation of the transmission output shaft.

Rheostat A device to regulate current flow by varying the resistance in the circuit.

Riding the clutch Slang for undue resting of the driver's foot on the clutch pedal when driving.

Rig Slang for truck or truck-trailer combination.

Rim pull Actual amount of force in pounds [kilograms] available at point of contact of tire and road surface.

Ring expander A type of spring which is placed between the ring and ring groove to hold the ring with fixed force against the cylinder wall.

Ring groove A groove machined in the piston to receive the piston ring.

Ring job Service work on the piston and cylinder, including the installation of new piston rings.

Ripper A mechanical device attached to a tractor or other machine to break up the ground.

Rivet A soft-metal pin having a head at one end.

Road rolling resistance Rolling resistance is a measure of the retarding effect of the road surface to forward movement of the vehicle. It varies with the type and condition of the road.

Rocker arm A first-class lever used to transmit the motion of the pushrod to the valve stem.

Rocker arm shaft The shaft on which the rocker arms pivot.

Rockwell hardness A measurement of the degree of surface hardness of a given object.

Rod Refers to a connecting rod.

Roller bearing An antifriction bearing using straight (cupped or tapered) rollers spaced in inner and outer rings.

Roller tappets (roller lifters) Refers to valve lifters having a roller at one end which is in contact with the camshaft; used to reduce friction.

Rolling radius The distance in inches [centimeters] from the center of the tire to the ground with the tire at its rated capacity.

Roots blower An air pump or blower similar in principle to a gear pump.

Rope brake A friction brake used for engine testing.

Rotary blower Any blower in which the pumping element has rotary motion, with the exception of centrifugal blowers.

Roughing stone (hone) A coarse honing stone.

RPM drop Drop in rpm between shifts in transmission.

Running fit A machine fit with sufficient clearance to provide for expansion and lubrication.

SAE Abbreviation for *Society of Automotive Engineers*.

SAE horsepower (rated horsepower) Formula to determine power: bore diameter^2 × number of cylinders/2.5 = hp.

SAE viscosity numbers Simplified viscosity ratings of oil based on Saybolt viscosity (defined below).

Safety factor Providing strength beyond that needed as an extra margin of insurance against parts failure.

Safety valve See *Relief valve*.

Sand blasting (glass blasting) A cleaning method using an air gun to force the sand at pressure (about 150 psi [1030.5 kPa]) against the surface to be cleaned.

Sander Device for supplying sand to drive wheels in order to increase traction.

Saybolt viscosimeter A container with a calibrated outlet tube for determining the viscosity of liquids. (This method is now obsolete.)

Saybolt viscosity The number of seconds necessary for 60 ml of liquid to pass through the outlet tube of a Saybolt viscosimeter under standardized test conditions.

Scale Precipitated hardness (salts) from water.

Scavenging The displacement of exhaust gas from the cylinder by fresh air.

Scavenging air The air which is pumped into a cylinder to displace exhaust gas.

Scavenging blower A device for pumping scavenging air.

Scavenging pump A piston pump delivering scavenging air to an engine.

Scoring Marks on a surface from cuts, etc.

Scraper Any instrument used for scraping; a self-propelled machine having a large metal box for scraping up, transporting, and dumping dirt.

Scraper ring An oil control ring.

Screw extractor A device used to remove broken bolts, screws, etc., from holes.

Scuffing Wearing rough on the surface.

Sealed bearing A bearing which is lubricated and sealed at the factory and thus cannot be further lubricated thereafter.

Sealing, positive A fluid sealing method which completely prevents any leakage of fluid.

Seat (rings) Rings fitted or seated properly against the cylinder wall.

Section modulus A measure of the strength of frame side rails (between two crossmembers) determined by the cross-sectional area and shape of the side rails.

Sediment Solid impurities in a liquid.

Self-energizing (servo) A foundation brake that wedges one or both brake shoes against the brake drum when the brakes are applied, assisting or boosting the braking force which is applied to the wheel cylinder.

Semiconductor A material which, because of its composition, can be used both as a conductor and an insulator.

Semifloating piston pin A piston pin which is clamped either in the connecting rod or in the piston bosses.

Semitrailer A trailer used in connection with a truck or truck-tractor.

Separator (battery) A porous insulating material placed between the positive and negative plates.

Sequence In order of succession; a number of things following one another.

Series circuit An electric circuit wired so that the current must pass through one unit before it can pass through the other.

Series-parallel circuit A circuit with three or more resistance units in combination with a series circuit and a parallel circuit.

Servo A piston in a cylinder assembly which converts hydraulic pressure into mechanical force and movement.

Shackle A pivoting link between the spring eye and frame bracket used to attach the ends of a leaf spring to the frame.

Shaft horsepower Power delivered at the engine crankshaft. This term is commonly used instead of brake horsepower to express output of large marine engines.

Sheave A grooved pulley wheel. (See *Pulley.*)

Shift fork A device that straddles the slots machined in a sliding gear or sliding clutch.

Shift point The engine rpm at which the transmission should be shifted to the next gear.

Shift rail A sliding rod to which the shift fork(s) is (are) attached.

Shift valve A valve that responds to mechanical action or to the governor and throttle pressure by directing fluid to the appropriate clutch to cause an upshift or downshift.

Shim Thin, flat pieces of brass or steel used to increase the distance between two components.

Shimmy Vibration causing front wheels to wobble (move in a side-to-side direction).

Shock absorber A vibration-dampening device used with chassis springs to lessen road bounce.

Short circuit A circuit whose resistance is reduced in power owing to one or more coil layers contacting one another.

Shovel A self-propelled machine used for digging, lifting earth, etc.

Shrink-fit To fit two components together by heating the outer one so that it will expand and fit over the inner one. As the outer component cools, it shrinks and thereby fits tightly over the inner component.

Shroud The enclosure around the fan, engine, etc., which guides the air flow.

Shunt A parallel circuit where one resistance unit has its own ground.

Shunt winding A resistance coil with its own ground.

Shutoff valve A valve which opens and thereby stops the flow of a liquid, air, or gas.

Silencer A device for reducing the noise of intake or exhaust.

Single-acting cylinder An actuating cylinder in which one stroke is produced by pressurized fluid and the other by some other force such as gravity or spring tension.

Slack adjuster An adjustable brake lever.

Sliding gear A transmission gear that is loosely splined to the main shaft.

Slip angle The difference in the radius taken by a motor vehicle when making a turn and the radius it would have taken if it had followed as the front wheels were pointed.

Slip joint A connection of two shafts that transfers driving torque while allowing longitudinal movement between the two shafts.

Sludge Deposits inside the engine caused by dust, oil, and water being mixed together by the moving components.

Snap ring A fastening device in the form of a split ring that is snapped into a groove in a shaft or a groove in a bore.

Sodium valve A valve designed to allow the stem and head to be partially filled with metallic sodium.

Solenoid An electromagnetic device used to do work.

Specific gravity The ratio of the weight of a given volume of any substance to the weight of the same volume of water.

Speed ratio Expressed as a percentage, it reflects the efficiency of a fluid drive, or impeller speed versus turbine speed. Speed ratio = turbine speed/impeller speed.

Spider A spiderlike casting or forging which contains axle differential or brake parts.

Spider (pinion) gears Small bevel gears mounted on a shaft or spider which is pinned to the differential case.

Spindle (wheel) A machined shaft or part of the spindle upon which the bearing races of the wheel hub rest.

Spiral bevel gear A gear set where the teeth of both the ring and the pinion gear are cut in a spiral so that the centerline of the pinion passes through the center of the ring gear.

Spline The land between two grooves.

Splined joint A coupling between two parts in which one part has external splines and the other internal splines.

Spongy pedal A brake pedal which, due to air in the system, has a springy or spongy feel when the brakes are applied.

Spool valve An hydraulic directional control valve in which the direction of the fluid is controlled by means of a grooved cylindrical shaft (spool).

Sprag clutch A one-way clutch that will transmit torque in one direction but will lock up in the opposite direction.

Spring A flexible or elastic member which supports the sprung weight of a vehicle and which can return to its original shape when released after being distorted.

Spring brake An emergency or auxiliary brake system utilizing a spring force to apply the service brake.

Spring capacity at ground The total weight (both sprung and unsprung) which will deflect the spring its maximum normal amount.

Spring capacity at pad The amount of sprung weight which will bend a leaf spring its maximum normal amount.

Spring clip U bolts which anchor a spring to the axle.

Spring force The tension in a spring when it is compressed or stretched.

Spring seat The seat or support on which the spring is anchored.

Sprocket A wheel with a projection on the periphery for engaging with the links of a chain.

Sprung weight The weight of all the parts of the vehicle that are supported by the springs, such as the frame, engine, body, payload.

Spur gear A toothed wheel having external radial teeth.

Squish area The area confined by the cylinder head and flat surface of the piston during the compression stroke.

Stability The resistance of a fluid to permanent change such as that caused by chemical reaction, temperature changes, etc.

Stabilizer A device used to stabilize a vehicle during turns, sometimes referred to as a *sway bar.*

Stabilizer bar A transverse-mounted spring steel bar that controls and minimizes body lean on corners.

Stall Engine rpm with the transmission engaged and the vehicle stationary; the throttle can be in any position between low and high idle.

Stall speed The measured engine rpm with the transmission engaged, the vehicle stationary, and the throttle at maximum open position.

Stall torque The maximum designed torque ratio of a torque converter under stall speed conditions.

Starter An electric motor used for cranking an engine.

Starting air Compressed air used for starting an engine.

Starting air valve A valve which

admits compressed starting air to the cylinder.

Static balance Refers to a wheel and tire assembly, flywheel, and crankshaft, in which the weight is uniformly distributed around the axle of rotation.

Static electricity Electricity at rest or not in the form of current; pertaining to stationary charges.

Static pressure The amount of pressure that is maintained in an hydraulic system or circuit by a valve when the system is in neutral.

Static pressure (brakes) The amount of pressure that always exists in the brake lines—even with the brake pedal released.

Stator The stationary part of a machine or device in relation to the rotating components.

Stator (torque converter) The reaction member that changes the direction of the fluid.

Staybolt A stress bolt running diagonally upward from the bedplate to the opposite side of the frame.

Steady flow A flow in which the velocity components at any point in the fluid do not vary with time.

Steering arm An arm, either bolted to, or forged as an integral part of, the steering knuckle.

Steering, center point A front axle having the kingpin perpendicular to the ground line and its intersecting centerline.

Steering gear A gear set mounted in a housing that is fastened to the lower end of the steering column. It is used to multiply driver turning force and change rotary motion into longitudinal motion.

Steering geometry A term used to describe functions of the steering system such as toe-out on turns, camber, caster, and toe-in.

Steering knuckle The part of the spindle that is affixed to and pivots on either a kingpin or upper and lower ball joints.

Stethoscope A device for conveying the sound of a body (engine noise) to the mechanic.

Stick shift A transmission that is shifted manually through the use of various forms of linkage.

Strain To effect a change in size or form by application of external force.

Streamline flow Nonturbulent flow, essentially fixed in pattern.

Stresses The forces to which parts are subjected.

Stress relief A process involving heat treatment for the purpose of reducing internal residual stresses in a metal.

Stroboscope (timing light) An instrument used to observe the periodic motion of injection visible only at certain points of its path.

Stroke One of a series of recurring movements of a piston or the distance of such a movement.

Stroke-to-bore ratio The length of stroke divided by the diameter of bore.

Stud A rod having threads on both ends.

Stud puller A device used to remove or to install stud bolts.

Stuffing box A chamber having a manual adjustment device for sealing.

Suction The process of producing a pressure differential (partial vacuum).

Suction valve Often used interchangeably with intake valve.

Sulfur An element which is found in petroleum in amounts varying from a slight trace to 4 or 5 percent.

Sump A receptacle into which liquid drains.

Sump pump A pump which removes liquid from the sump.

Sun gear The center gear of a planetary gear set.

Supercharger An air pump driven by the engine which fills the cylinders with a higher pressure than atmospheric pressure.

Supply line A line that conveys fluid from the reservoir to the pump.

Surge A momentary rise and fall of pressure or speed in a system or engine.

Suspension Attaching parts including springs for securing axle or axles to the frame.

Swivel A pivoting coupling device that permits either half of a mechanism to rotate independently.

Synchromesh A mechanism that equalizes the speed of the gears that are clutched together.

Synchronize To make two or more events or operations occur at the proper time with respect to each other.

Synchronous Happening at the same time.

Synchrotransmission A transmission with mechanisms for synchronizing the gear speeds so that the gears can be shifted without clashing, thus eliminating the need for double clutching.

Synthetic material A complex chemical compound which is artificially formed by the combining of two or more compounds or elements.

Tachometer An instrument indicating rotating speeds. Tachometers are sometimes used to indicate crankshaft rpm.

Tandem drive A two-axle drive combination.

Tap A cutting tool used to cut threads in a bore. (See *Chamfer.*)

Tap and die set A set of cutting tools used to cut internal and external threads.

Taper A cone-shaped object or form.

Tapered roller bearing See *Roller bearing.*

Tappet The rocker arm.

Tappet noise The noise caused by excessive clearance between the valve stem and the rocker arm.

TDC Abbreviation for *top dead center.*

Temper The condition of a metal with regard to hardness achieved through heating and then suddenly cooling.

Temperature The intensity (or degree) of heat.

Temperature of compression The temperature of the compressed air charge in a power cylinder at the end of the compression stroke before combustion begins.

Temporary hardness Dissolved substances which precipitate out when water is heated.

Tension Stress applied on a material or body.

Terminal The connecting point (post) of a conductor.

Theory A scientific explanation that must be tested by observations and experiments to be proven true.

Thermal efficiency See *Brake thermal efficiency* and *Indicated thermal efficiency.*

Thermal expansion The increase in volume of a substance caused by temperature change.

Thermocouple The part of a pyrometer which consists of two dissimilar metal wires welded together at the inner end and held in a protective housing.

Thermometer An instrument for measuring temperature.

Thermostat A temperature-responsive mechanism used for controlling heating systems, cooling system, etc., usually with the purpose of maintaining certain temperatures without further personal attention.

Throttle linkage Additional linkages connectd to the transmission to operate a throttle valve.

Throttle valve, automatic transmission A valve that is controlled mechanically by throttle linkage and that sends a pressure signal to the shift valve spool to control shifting in relation to engine speed.

Throttling Reducing the engine speed by reducing the flow of fuel.

Throughbolt Term usually applied to the stress rod passing through the engine frame that carries combustion stresses.

Throw The part of a crankshaft to which the connecting rod is fastened.

Thrust A force exerted endwise, usually through a shaft.

Thrust bearing (washer) A bearing or washer of bronze or steel which restrains endwise motion of a turning shaft, or withstands axial loads instead of radial loads as in common bearings.

Thrust load A load which pushes or reacts through the bearing in a direction parallel to the shaft.

Tie-rod A connecting rod between the steering arms.

Tilt cab A C.O.E. (cab-over-engine) which can tilt forward for accessibility.

Time lag of ignition See *Ignition lag.*

Timing gears Gears attached to the crankshaft, camshaft, idler shaft, or injection pump to provide a means to drive the camshaft and injection pump and to regulate their speed and performance.

Timing marks (injection) The marks located on the vibration damper or flywheel, used to check injection timing.

Tire bead That part of the tire resting against the rim flange.

Tire casing The main body of the tire excluding the tread.

Tire plies The layers of cloth, nylon, and/or rayon that are used to form the tire casing.

Tire rotation Interchanging of the tires to equalize wear.

Tire sidewall That part of the tire between the tread and the bead.

Tire tread That part of the tire which contacts the road surface.

Toe-in The degree (usually expressed in inches [millimeters]) to which the forward part of the wheels are closer together than the rear part, measured at hub height.

Toe-out on turns The degree that the inside wheel has turned more sharply than the outside

wheel when the vehicle is negotiating a turn.

Toggle switch A switch that is actuated by flipping a small handle (switch).

Tolerance A fractional allowance for variations from specification.

Tooth "heel" (carrier) The wider outside end of the ring gear tooth.

Tooth "toe" (carrier) The narrower inside end of the ring gear tooth.

Torque A force or combination of forces that produces a twisting or rotary motion.

Torque converter A device (similar to a fluid coupling) that transfers engine torque to the transmission input shaft and can multiply engine torque by having one or more stators between the torus members.

Torque, engine The amount of twisting effort exerted at the crankshaft by an engine.

Torque, ratio An expression of the gear ratio factor on torque effect.

Torque rods See *Stabilizer.*

Torque wrench A wrench used to measure the turning force being applied.

Torsional vibration The vibration caused by twisting and untwisting a shaft.

Torsion bar A springing system, used on some suspension designs, in which straight bars, anchored at one end, are subjected to torsion by the weight of the vehicle, thereby acting as springs.

Torsion spring A spring effect developed through torsional stress in steel rods.

Tow bar A bar or V-shaped device attached to the chassis of a trailer dolly or front axle.

Tractor A motor vehicle (without a body) which has a fifth wheel and is used for pulling a semitrailer.

Track, axle The distance between the centerlines of the tire treads at ground on the front or rear axles.

Track (crawler) A set of rails having connecting links and track shoes.

Tractive effort The amount of power required to move a vehicle.

Trailer A platform or container on wheels pulled by a truck or tractor.

Trailer, full A trailer where the chassis is so constructed that all its own weight and that of its load rests upon its own wheels.

Trailer, semi See *Semitrailer.*

Tramp The act of wheels hopping or bouncing heavily on the road surface at regular intervals.

Transfer case A gear box which transmits torque to the front and rear carriers.

Transfer pump A mechanical device for moving fuel from one tank to another or bringing fuel from the tank to the injection pump.

Transmission A device used to transmit torque at various ratios and which can usually also change the direction of the force of rotation.

Transmission (auxiliary) An additional transmission used to increase the gear ratio.

Transmission (main) A selective gear box which provides various combinations of gear ratios.

Treadle valve A foot-operated, air service, brake actuation valve.

Troubleshooting The analyzing, testing, and measuring of an engine or other vehicle component to remedy any problems it may have in performing its function(s).

Trunnion Journals which allow pivoting or turning such as a tandem axle spring or a walking beam assembly.

Tube cutter A tube-cutting tool having a sharp disk which is rotated around the tube.

Tubing That type of fluid line whose dimensions are designated by actual measured outside diameter.

Tuneup The checking, testing, measuring, repairing, and adjusting of engine components in order to bring the engine to peak efficiency.

Turbine A series of curved vanes mounted on a shaft and actuated by the action of a fluid or gas under pressure.

Turbocharger An exhaust-gas-driven turbine directly coupled with a compressor wheel.

Turbulence The swirling charge of fuel and air in the combustion chamber.

Turbulence chamber A combustion chamber connected to the cylinder through a throat. Fuel is injected across the chamber and turbulence is produced in the chamber by the air entering during compression.

Turning radius Radius of the minimum turning circle.

Turnpike Expressway or freeway.

Two-speed axle A carrier having

two selective gear ratios using a planetary gear set.

Two-stage combustion Combustion occurring in two distinct steps such as in a precombustion chamber engine.

Two-stroke cycle Cycle of events which is complete in two strokes of the piston or one crankshaft revolution.

Underdrive The lowest ratio in an auxiliary transmission or multispeed transmission.

Understeer The tendency of a motor vehicle, when in a turn, to turn less sharply than the driver intends.

Uniflow scavenging Scavenging method in which air enters one end of the cylinder and exhaust leaves the opposite end.

Unit injector A combined fuel injection pump and fuel nozzle.

Universal joint A coupling providing transmission of torque through an angle.

Unsprung weight The weight of a vehicle not supported by springs such as tires, wheels, and the axle assembly.

Upshift Shifting to a higher gear.

U.S. gallon A gallon measurement equal to 231 in³.

Vacuum A pressure less than atmospheric pressure.

Vacuum gauge A gauge used to measure the amount of vacuum existing in a chamber or line.

Vacuum pump A pump of any type that produces (vacuum) low pressure.

Vacuum tank A reservoir in which a low pressure (vacuum) exists.

Valve Any device or arrangement used to open or close an opening to permit or restrict the flow of a liquid, gas, or vapor.

Valve, check A valve which permits flow of fluid or air in one direction only.

Valve, detent-positioned A valve which has a device to hold the valve spool in position until actuated by an external force.

Valve, directional A valve which selectively directs or prevents fluid flow through desired channels.

Valve duration The time (measured in degrees of engine crankshaft rotation) that a valve remains open.

Valve float A condition where the valves are forced open due to valve spring vibration or vibration speed.

Valve, flow-dividing A valve which divides the flow from a single source into two separate branches of a circuit at a constant ratio regardless of the difference in pressure between the two branches.

Valve grinding Resurfacing the valve face with a special grinding machine.

Valve guide A shaft pressed into the cylinder head to keep the valve in proper alignment.

Valve keeper (valve retainer) A device designed to lock the valve spring retainer to the valve stem.

Valve lift The distance a valve moves from the fully closed to the fully open position.

Valve margin The distance between the edge of the valve and the edge of the face.

Valve, needle A valve used to start, stop, or limit flow of fluid or air.

Valve oil seal A sealing device to prevent excess oil from entering the area between the stem and the valve guide.

Valve overlap The period of crankshaft rotation during which both the intake and exhaust valves are open. It is measured in degrees.

Valve, pilot A small directional control valve used for actuating other valves.

Valve, pilot-operated A valve, the valve spool of which is positioned by pilot pressure.

Valve rotator A mechanical device locked to the end of the valve stem which forces the valve to rotate about 5° with each rocker arm action.

Valve seat The surface on which the valve face rests when closed.

Valve seat insert A hardened steel ring inserted into the cylinder head to increase the wear resistance of the valve seat.

Valve, spring-centered A valve, the valve spool of which is held in the center position by means of a spring (or springs) until moved by some external force.

Valve timing The positioning of the camshaft (gear) to the crankshaft (gear) to ensure proper valve opening and closing.

Vaporization The process of converting a liquid into a gas.

Variable-pitch stator A stator wherein the vane angles can be changed through an external force.

Varirate spring A spring providing variable effective length through cam action to suit load.

Velocity Rate of motion.

Venturi A specially shaped tube with a small or constricted area used to increase velocity and reduce pressure.

Vibrate To move back and forth continuously over the same path.

Vibration damper A specially designed device mounted to the front of the crankshaft to reduce torsional vibration.

Viscosity The property of an oil by virtue of which it offers resistance to flow.

Viscosity index (VI) Oil decreases in viscosity as its temperature is raised. The measure of this rate of change of viscosity with respect to temperature is called the *viscosity index* of the oil.

Volatile Evaporating readily at average temperature on exposure with air.

Volatility A measurement of the ease with which a liquid may be vaporized at relatively low temperature.

Volt (V) A unit of electromotive force that will move a current of 1 A through a resistance of 1 Ω. See *Ampere* and *Ohm*.

Voltage Electric potential expressed in volts.

Voltage drop Voltage loss due to added resistance caused by undersized wire, poor connections, etc.

Voltmeter A test instrument for measuring the voltage or voltage drop in an electric circuit.

Volume The amount of space within a given confined area.

Volumetric efficiency The difference between the volume of air drawn in on the intake stroke and the air mechanically entering the cylinder.

Vortex flow The fluid flow from member to member generated by the impeller and moving through the turbine, and stator back to the impeller.

Walking beam A horizontal beam, pivot-attached to a frame. Each end of the beam is fastened to the axle housing.

Wander Refers to steering, where a vehicle moves or drifts from a fixed direction without control.

Water brake A device for engine testing in which the power is dissipated by churning water.

Water jacket The enclosure directing the flow of cooling water around the parts to be cooled.

Watt (W) The metric measurement of power, equal to 0.00134 hp (U.S. Customary System).

Weight distribution The distribution of body and payload weight on a truck-trailer.

Wet sleeve A cylinder sleeve which is about 70 percent exposed to the coolant.

Wheel alignment The mechanics of keeping all the parts of the steering system in the specified relation to each other.

Wheel alignment tools Devices used to check camber, caster, toe-in, etc.

Wheelbase The distance between the center of the front wheels and the center of the back wheels.

Wheel cylinder A cylinder which converts pressure from the master cylinder into force to apply the brakes.

Wheel hop The tendency of tires and wheels to hop during braking or acceleration of the vehicle.

Winch A manual or powered device, employing a drum with cable or rope, for pulling objects where added power is required.

Wire rope A rope made up of wires firmly wound together.

Worm and roller A steering gear which utilizes a worm gear on the steering shaft, whereby a roller on one end of the cross shaft engages the worm.

Worm and sector A steering gear using a worm gear sector which is a two- or three-toothed portion of a gear fastened to the cross shaft.

Worm and taper pin A steering gear using a worm gear on the steering shaft. The end of the cross shaft engages the worm by a taper pin.

Yield strength The maximum amount of stress in pounds per square inch [kilopascals] to which material (such as in a frame) may be subjected through loading and return to its original shape after the stress is removed.

Yoke A link which connects two points.

Zener diode A diode that allows current to flow in reverse bias at a designated voltage.

Zerk Lubrication fitting.

Index